# JERSEY BLUE

# JERSEY BLUE

## Civil War Politics
## —in New Jersey—
## 1854–1865

## WILLIAM GILLETTE

## RUTGERS UNIVERSITY PRESS
### NEW BRUNSWICK, NEW JERSEY

Library of Congress Cataloging-in-Publication Data

Gillette, William.
    Jersey blue : Civil War politics in New Jersey, 1854–1865 / by
William Gillette.
        p.  cm.
    ISBN 0–8135–2120–3
        1.  New Jersey—Politics and government—1861–1865.   2.  New Jersey—
Politics and government—1775–1865.   I.  Title.
    F138.G55   1994
    974.9'03—dc20                                                     94–10143
                                                                          CIP

British Cataloging-in-Publication information available


Publication of this book was supported, in part, by a grant from the Tomlinson
Family Foundation, Inc.

*To Three New Jerseyans Who Earned Degrees at Rutgers:*
*Elisa Gillette, M.L.S., 1978; Scott Gillette, B.A., 1993;*
*and Wendy Gillette, B.A., 1994*

# Contents

# Preface and Acknowledgments

The purpose of this book is to explain the political role of New Jersey before, during, and just after the Civil War. The response of New Jerseyans to various challenges during this period can provide insight into the state's political history, its wartime activity, its local identity, and its regional ties, as well as cast light on this pivotal period of American history in general.

The book's title refers to the name commonly attributed to New Jersey's troops, who fought in blue uniforms in the French and Indian War. In the American Revolution, George Washington, designating New Jersey's troops as Jersey Blues, authorized blue uniforms for Jersey units. During the Civil War, state regiments as well as New Jerseyans as a group continued to bear the name. The term often carried a patriotic overtone, frequently conveyed strong support for the war, and expressed pride in the fighting ability of state units. The motto "Jersey Blue" epitomizes the thesis of this book.

In so titling the book, however, it is not my purpose to brush away old legends merely to replace them with new myths. I want to avoid gratuitous debunking and iconoclasm, on the one hand, and provincialism and sentimentalism, on the other. Rather, I attempt to square the state's reputation with its actual record in the hope of reaching a deeper, fuller understanding of New Jersey's wartime experience.

I have owed much to many during the decade of my research. The Research Council of Rutgers University, the faculty leave program of Rutgers, the New Jersey Historical Commission, and the American Philosophical Society furnished research grants and time. I thank the staffs of the History Department and the Rutgers University Library as well as many university colleagues. In Special Collections in Alexander Library, crackerjack librarian Bonita Grant and master sleuth Ed Skipworth provided vital help, as did the staffs of the New Jersey Historical Society, the New Jersey State Archives—especially resourceful Dan Jones—as well as the New Jersey Historical Commission, the Princeton University Library, the Library of Congress, the National Archives, and many other libraries throughout the nation. In addition, I thank Rutgers, the State Archives, the New Jersey Historical Society, and all those persons who aided in arranging the microfilming of the Society's collection of New Jersey Civil War newspapers. The year in Austria at the University of Salzburg while serving as a Fulbright lecturer provided me with time to do some general reading. For a publication subvention, immense thanks go to the Tomlinson Family Foundation, specifically to Norman B. Tomlinson, Jr.

Special thanks go to Stuart Alterman, Tyler Anbinder, Brandon Atkinson, Jacques Barzun, John Beardsley, Ron Becker, Rudy Bell, Ira Berlin, Ken Betza, Marilyn Campbell, Tom Clark, Dan Crofts, Charles Cummings, Phil Curtin, Linden DeBie, Jeff Dorwart, Henk Edelman, Sharla Fett, Mary Fetzer, Eric Foner, George Frederickson, Greg Gill, Brandy Gillette, John Gillis, Michael Gordon, Chet Gotarz, Howard Green, Jeff Green, Gerald Grob, Michael Hembree, Mike Holt, Renee House, Ferne Hyman, Reese Jenkins, Robert Johannsen, Dick Kearney, Frank Kelly, Cynthia Kierner, Everett Landers, Russell Leaf, Maurice Lee, Leo Lemay, Mark Lender, Bruce Levine, David Lewis, Jim Livingston, Bob Lunde, Jon Lurie, Peggy McPherson, Fred Main, Jim Martin, Mike Meier, Jane Mihalick, Paul Mott, Mary Murrin, Walt Myers, Mark Neely, Bill O'Neill, Oliver Orr, David Oshinsky, Robin Postorio-Newman, Phil Pauly, Karen Poling, Clem Price, Ernest Reock, Blackwell Robinson, Michael Rockland, John Rodrigue, Andy Rudczynski, Gordon Schocket, John Sellers, Alan Siegel, Joel Silbey, Don Sinclair, Raymond Smock, Mark Snell, John Synder, Dick Sommers, Charles Stansfield, Paul Stellhorn, Helen Silvester, Bob Szuter, Ryoko Toyama, Hans Trefousse, Rod Troch, Peter Wacker, Dick Waldron, Bennett Wall, Charles Webster, Carl West, Jack Wood, Bill Wright, Esmond Wright, Ginny Yans, and Enid Yourstone.

David Herbert Donald permitted me to use his index to find the letters of New Jerseyans who wrote to Charles Sumner. Margaret Douglas sent copies of letters by New Jerseyans from her collection of Stephen A. Douglas papers. Maurice Tandler lent notes and photocopies of sources, the fruit of his research done thirty years ago. In this way copies of a few letters, the originals of which had been missing at the New Jersey Historical Society, were rediscovered.

My students at Rutgers—Mike Berg, Terry Brown, Scott Burd, Ghis Butrica, Buddy Carrea, Tony Christopher, Peter DeBrul, Paul Donlon, Felicia Fell, Chris Fischer, Paul Fisher, Jennifer Fowler, John Friel, Matt Gordon, Brian Kahn, Andy Kearns, John Kosinski, Eric Kressman, Jon Lehner, Gordon Long, Pete Luscko, Lou Melograna, Steve Paglione, Luke Rooney, John Sutor, Andy Talkov, Bill Throne, Deidre Tompson, Jason Topolsky, Reginald West, and Dave Zimmerman—did research on New Jersey's servicemen. Phil Blair, Joe Chouinard, Jim Cowan, Terence Dalton, Andre Meade, Randy Rauscher, Drew Stauffer, and Joe Stefani explored topics in the political and economic history of wartime New Jersey. Jill Bernstein and Graham Peabody searched for iconography. I extend special thanks to two unpaid researchers who helped with manuscript research: Glenn Gilmore, now an attorney, and Louis Moore, now a Ridgewood High School teacher and Rutgers graduate student who is currently writing his doctoral dissertation on New Jersey's politics during Reconstruction. John Kruszewski searched daily newspapers. Elisa Gillette helped locate articles in New York City's newspapers and did research in the Military History Institute.

I give immense thanks to those who made time in their busy schedules to read the manuscript. Bill Jackson, Ed Longacre, Dave Martin, and Randy Rauscher vetted the military account. John Chambers, Scott Gillette, Richard P. McCormick, Bill McFeely, Don Skemer, Dave Steltenkamp, and Marlie Wasserman read parts of the manuscript. Those who read the entire manuscript in various drafts and made helpful suggestions are Fitz Brundage, Alice Calaprice, Dick Current, Karen Feinberg, Elisa Gillette, Jim Halsey, Maxine Lurie, Bob Morris, Hermann Platt, Willa Speiser, Murray Tandler, and Eleanor Wyckoff. Professor Lex Renda of the University of Wisconsin vetted the political history and completed the ecological regression analysis of voting. I greatly appreciate all the help I received, but I remain of course responsible for all faults of organization, selection, and interpretation as well as errors in research, typing, and proofreading.

I welcome suggestions for subsidizing a paperback edition of this book in order to make it more widely available for a larger readership.

W.G.
East Brunswick, N.J.

# JERSEY BLUE

# Introduction

Several historians have characterized New Jersey as politically reactionary before the Civil War and disloyal during the war. According to this interpretation, New Jersey in the antebellum period fit the mold of either a border slave state or a "doughface" state, that is, a northern state with southern sympathies. Historians further contended that in the wartime years New Jersey was controlled by the "copperheads," that is, persons who steadfastly opposed and obstructed the war.

In 1905 journalist Lincoln Steffens popularized the notion of New Jersey as a stronghold of privilege, a state with plutocratic politics in which robber barons held sway. The Progressive muckraker saw a historical continuity between an antebellum New Jersey controlled by the Camden and Amboy Railroad and the New Jersey of the 1890s, when giant corporations received convenient charters of incorporation from the state government and in turn controlled the state's economy and politics. In a sweeping indictment of New Jersey, one subtitle in his article read, "Disloyalty an Old Charge Against Jersey."[1]

The first historian to suggest that New Jersey resembled a border slave state was Francis B. Lee. His brief account of the period formed part of his general history of the state, which was published in 1902. In 1924 Charles M. Knapp fleshed out this view in his survey of the state's politics during the Civil War. Knapp likened New Jersey to the border states in its conservatism during the 1850s. According to Knapp, New Jerseyans in the secession crisis expressed ambivalence about unionism. Knapp found that during the Civil War copperhead proclivities dominated by 1863.[2]

Subsequent writers on wartime New Jersey accepted Knapp's views and made them more explicit. William S. Myers, in a work published in 1945, entitled chapter 15 "The Civil War—New Jersey as a Border State." William C. Wright, in his 1965 sketch of copperheads, entitled his first chapter "New Jersey a Border State." This view was elaborated in two surveys of the state designed for a popular audience. John T. Cunningham's *New Jersey: America's Main Road* (1964) depicted antebellum New Jersey as the "Northernmost of the Border States." So, too, did Thomas Fleming's *New Jersey* (1977). Fleming characterized the state thus: "In heart and mind, in politics and economics, New Jersey was a border state, separated only by an accident of geography from the rebellious South."[3]

Over the years such characterizations of New Jersey have become clichés by sheer repetition and unquestioning acceptance in monographs, textbooks, and newspaper articles. Reflecting this prevailing view, a colleague once asked me jokingly whether a petition of New Jerseyans requesting admission of their state to the Confederacy had yet been discovered.

The view of New Jersey as a border state grew out of misinterpretation. When New Jerseyans in the Civil War era used the term "border," they usually did so in a geographical sense. To them it simply meant that New Jersey formed part of the lower North, which bounded the upper South. Free-labor New Jersey faced slave-labor Delaware across the Delaware River and Bay. The notion was so strong and so pervasive that it was taken for granted; the term was shorthand for something that was clarified only occasionally.

Editorials expressing all political persuasions—nativist, Republican, and Democratic—on occasion referred explicitly to New Jersey as one of the "border Northern States." An 1860 editorial in the *Jersey City Standard* referred to the "border free States—to Pennsylvania, New York, and New Jersey." Sometimes an editorial used a different and more specific meaning for comparative purposes. Thus in 1862 the *Newark Advertiser* commented about "states like New Jersey, which lie contiguous to the Border States."[4]

New Jerseyans, then, did not mean or imply that New Jersey had important elements in common with border slave states or thought like southerners. Yet historians in the twentieth century have assumed mistakenly that "border" meant "border slave state."

When New Jerseyans used "border" in a political sense, its meaning varied according to time, circumstance, party, and faction. Frequently, especially before the outbreak of the Civil War, inhabitants maintained that the state stood on the middle ground, "geographically and politically, between all extremes," in the words of one Republican congressman. New Jerseyans preferred moderate positions; they wanted the state to play a balancing role to preserve the nation from the noisy ideologues on the fringes, both the extremists of the South and the abolitionists of the North. The *Camden Democrat* pointed to the "Central States" that served as a "breakwater against which the waves of disunion from either section will vainly spend their force." Similarly the Democratic *Newark Journal* declared, "New Jersey has now thrown herself into the breach between the North and the South." The Republican *Newark Advertiser* asserted that New Jersey occupied a "middle ground between the fanaticism of the North and the fanaticism of the South."[5]

While New Jersey's moderates within each party denounced the excesses of both northerners and southerners, a sectionalist double standard crept into the thinking of the extreme Democratic and Republican factions. Doughfaces and copperheads in the state's Democratic party denounced northern Republican abolitionist troublemakers but ignored the southern secessionist militant variety. Radical Republicans in the state did the opposite. Yet the majority of New Jerseyans, Democratic and Republican alike, remained cautious, prudent, and centrist. According to the *Freehold Democrat*, New Jerseyans observed "that golden mean between radicalism and old fogyism."[6]

These historians, following the conventional view of New Jersey as conservative and borderlike, claimed that New Jersey diverged from other northern states by tilting in a southern direction. New Jersey, they wrote, marched to a different tune, out of step with the rest of the North. Proponents of this view supported it with five arguments. The first concerned race relations: although New Jersey had free labor, it also was the last state north of the Mason-Dixon line to abolish slavery in the antebellum years. Indeed, in 1860 a few slaves remained, working mainly as house servants; they were legally lifetime apprentices who could not be sold without their permission. Second, although New Jersey is attached geographically to the North, the extreme southern part of the state is well below the Mason-Dixon line. Third, New Jersey's people and its politicians were sensitive, even sympathetic, toward the plight of the South because of their vital trade connections with the region. New Jersey's factories manufactured many products specifically for the southern trade. Thus New Jerseyans became heavily dependent on southerners for continued prosperity. Fourth, New Jersey had a social connection with the South; many students at the College of New Jersey (Princeton) were southerners, and numerous influential southerners vacationed on the Jersey shore in the summer. Fifth, New Jerseyans shared with southerners a firm belief in state rights. New Jerseyans believed in the right of secession; at least, from 1861 on, they were skeptical about the constitutionality and expediency of coercing the South to return to the Union. In the 1860 presidential election, New Jersey was the only free state in the North not to award every electoral vote to Abraham Lincoln. It gave strong support to the southern Democratic candidate, John C. Breckinridge. In 1864 New Jersey was the only free state in the North to reject Lincoln.

Granted, some of these general points contain elements of truth, but they tell us little about an entire state's people, society, economy, and politics. Noting a few of New Jersey's imports and exports yields no relevant clues to the state's nature and character. The roll call of southerners at a single college in the state and the guest list of southerners visiting shore resorts tell us little about New Jerseyans themselves. Today many Canadians vacation on the Jersey shore, yet no one assumes that this amounts to a vital Canadian connection that influences the political behavior of New Jerseyans. As to the southern connection at Princeton, students from the South constituted a minority of the undergraduates, and a declining one at that. Moreover, they neither voted nor stayed in the state to influence its politics, but returned to their homes after graduation. In fact, most Princetonians, both faculty and students, demonstrated strong unionist, prowar sympathies during the Civil War. If one still entertains the dubious notion that colleges imprint their character on a state, then surely a more representative pattern is provided by Rutgers College, with its New Jerseyan composition and its unionist influence.

It is equally misleading to assume that New Jersey was the only northern state to enjoy an extensive trade with the South. Most northern states did so. In fact, eight states exceeded New Jersey in the total liabilities of firms that failed during 1861 and 1862 because of the loss of southern business and the general economic uncertainty. Likewise, even though New Jersey manufactured carriages, hats, boots, clothes, and jewelry for export to the South, this fact in itself does not tell us how New Jerseyans thought and reacted during the burgeoning sectional crisis. To be preoccupied with the southern trade is to disregard the importance of New Jersey's commercial relations with the rest of the North, especially with New York City and Philadelphia, only ninety miles apart. New Jerseyans profited greatly by providing manufactured goods and agricultural products to both of these nearby cities. As one observer put it, the improvement in and the prosperity of the state's agriculture—a situation equally applicable to manufacturing—was "chiefly due to our location near New York and Philadelphia, the best markets on our continent."[7]

Moreover, it is only assumed, not proved, that trade patterns determined New Jerseyans' political positions on the great issues at that time. That customers in the South dictated how New Jerseyans cast ballots in Newark is not substantiated by close examination of election returns in either Newark or Essex County. The *Newark Mercury* questioned the necessity of political agreement with the South as the price for continued trade with that region. "A more ridiculous idea of the relations between the producer and the consumer could not be conceived. On the same principle the Chinese ought to force us to embrace the doctrines of Confucius with their teas." The *Mercury* advised: "Sell our Goods, but Not our Principles."[8]

To be sure, businessmen and conservatives in New Jersey and elsewhere in the antebellum years were loath to offend southerners with strident talk. When the crisis of the Union came, however, this reluctance did not control how they thought, voted, or fought. In 1861 one Newarker responded as follows to the loss of the southern trade and the economic depression that gripped much of the North and his city: "Such privation is a capital test of patriotism. Newark has toed the mark manfully, and proved to the world that she values this unequaled Union at a higher figure than ten times the money she ever made out of the South."[9]

Other points in this interpretation of New Jersey as a border state also need examination. In regard to race relations, it is misleading to concentrate on the infinitesimal minority of 18 quasi-slaves in 1860 rather than on the state's 25,318 free African Americans. Moreover, slaves lived in other free states as recently as 1840, when the federal census reported 331 slaves in Illinois, 64 in Pennsylvania, 17 in Connecticut, and 4 in New York. One of the characteristic features of a border slave state was a relatively high proportion of blacks in its population, yet the percentage of blacks in New Jersey's population was strikingly below the border average. In 1860, blacks made up 4 percent of New Jersey's population and more than 18 percent of the population of the four border slave states; in 1870, that had decreased to a little over 3 percent for New Jersey and almost 14 percent for the borderland. The fact that part of South Jersey lies below the Mason-Dixon line has no historical or political meaning. The southern part of New Jersey was consistently the most politically progressive region of the state and a stronghold of the Republican party.[10]

To be sure, abolitionism was weak in New Jersey at midcentury. Few religious leaders or newspaper editors championed the abolitionist cause. Newark businessman, philanthropist, and Republican Marcus L. Ward confessed that he did not know a single abolitionist in his city. According to another observer, "Anti-slavery sentiment in New Jersey is not a moving power among the people." The Democratic *Trenton American* conceded, "We do not know that as yet there are a great many out and out abolitionists in New Jersey." Only 829 New Jerseyans backed the Liberty or Free-soil party in 1848. Between 1840 and 1852, the percentage of support for such parties in the state was consistently less than the national average.[11]

Opposition to abolitionism, however, did not mean sympathy or support of slavery. One Belleville resident, who advocated containing the expansion of slavery, explained his position: "We are no Abolitionists. We go for no reckless following out of abstract doctrines on human rights, regardless of consequences—which we take to be the essence of Abolitionism." This commentator regarded slavery as a practical rather than a theoretical matter, and so believed in gradual emancipation. Immediate emancipation, he predicted, would be a "curse to the South and no mercy to the slaves." Moreover, he disagreed with the abolitionists' "damnation of every individual at the South who happens to be a slaveholder." The abolitionist approach, he maintained, infuriated southerners and jeopardized northern moderates' opposition to the extension of slavery.[12]

The great majority of New Jerseyans disliked slavery and distrusted the political power of the slave owners. As the *Newark Advertiser* observed in 1854, "New Jersey has no love for slavery." Most New Jerseyans opposed pro-slavery fanatics and disapproved of their efforts to use the federal government to force the territorial expansion of slavery and secure the political supremacy for the South. Several prominent Jersey Whigs, notably two federal senators, William L. Dayton and Jacob W. Miller, opposed the extension of slavery into the western territories.[13]

Regardless of their dislike of slavery, however, most New Jerseyans upheld the Constitution and the rule of law. They did not enact personal liberty acts to nullify federal fugitive slave laws. Speaking for his party, Samuel J. Bayard declared in 1865 that the "Democratic party defended the constitutional rights of the states," and thus opposed interference with slavery in the states where it existed. "But," Bayard added, "we never defended slavery."

Clearly, narrowly sectionalist politics should not be confused with the broad-gauged nationalist variety. During the 1860s most New Jerseyans did not blindly worship tradition, but moved with the times and supported constructive change. They tended to be pragmatic and moderate, not dogmatic and rigid. New Jersey's reputation for crusty conservatism and border-slave-state political proclivities in the mid-nineteenth century was largely undeserved.[14]

As for the treatment of blacks, the record was mixed. New Jersey authorities, unlike those in the border states, followed the other northern states in espousing voluntary, gradual emancipation (in 1804) and legally abolishing slavery (in 1846). An underground railroad, operated mainly by Quakers and Negroes, did function in the state, but the number of runaway slaves transported was negligible. Racist beliefs and practices prevailed in New Jersey, as in the rest of the antebellum North. Many people doubted that blacks could hold their own in the white world of America. Black Jerseymen, mainly farmers and unskilled laborers, were treated as second-class citizens and were barred from voting. Yet Afro-Americans lobbied for egalitarian reform. With only a few exceptions, however, the state evidently was troubled little by racial strife in the first sixty years of the nineteenth century, despite the fact that New Jersey had the highest proportion of blacks in any free state in 1860.[15]

During this time some prominent white and black New Jerseyans, as well as the state government, favored colonization of Negroes to Africa as the best solution to racial problems. Nobody, however, made any substantial effort to achieve it. Between 1817 and 1866 New York sent 295 blacks to Africa, while Pennsylvania dispatched 337. These figures represented less than half of one percent of each state's black population. New Jersey dispatched 77 persons, or half the rate of New York and Pennsylvania. Despite the burden of racial discrimination, black New Jerseyans for the most part preferred to remain in their state. New Jersey was hardly a racial paradise; yet by no stretch of the imagination did New Jersey resemble South Carolina or even Delaware, as a few partisan editors contended in the 1860s.[16]

Equally misleading is the emphasis placed by Knapp on New Jersey's adherence to state rights. When virtually unrestricted state rights prevailed in fact under the Articles of Confederation during the 1780s, New Jersey was at the mercy of its bigger, more populous, and more powerful neighbors, New York and Pennsylvania, which refused to accept New Jersey's currency for payment of goods, imposed two separate taxes on foreign imports to New Jerseyans, and set port fees on Jersey vessels. Such actions added insult to the injury of higher costs and led to economic and political impotence.[17]

Resenting control of their trade by outsiders, New Jerseyans believed this intolerable situation could be ended only by replacing the defective Confederation with a stronger central authority. The new government could regulate interstate and international commerce, set a tariff on imports, and sell western lands; thus it could put the finances of the new government on a firm footing without requiring New Jerseyans to pay higher taxes. New Jerseyans wanted a national government worthy of the name to allow both the new nation and their state to prosper. They hoped, too, that the new federal capital, with the financial benefits it would bring, would be located near Trenton.

At the Constitutional Convention in 1787, two New Jersey delegates advocated strong powers and supreme authority for a national government. In advocating such positions, they implicitly rejected state-rightist assumptions. During the struggle over ratification of the federal Constitution, opposition within the state was virtually nonexistent. No New Jerseyan wrote any tracts attacking the Constitution. When the state convention considered ratification for only one week, the convention approved it unanimously, less than three months after submission. New Jersey was the third state to ratify the Constitution and the second to do so by a unanimous vote. In the nineteenth century, moreover, few devotees of John C. Calhoun could be found in the state. New Jerseyans most decidedly were not addicted to state rights. They easily circumvented them when it served their interests and strongly defended them when it did.[18]

The significance of the 1860 election outcome in New Jersey also requires examination. Because Lincoln did not receive the state's entire electoral vote, some observers believe that New Jersey's support for the Union was weak. This fact, however, obscures the unionist strength reflected in the combined electoral vote for the two northern candidates, Lincoln and Stephen A. Douglas. Moreover, support for slave-state candidate Breckinridge was much stronger in other northern states than in New Jersey. Thus New Jersey was hardly a backwater of southern reaction or a breeding ground of state rightists or secessionists. New Jersey's political position was not ultraconservative or pro-southern at all, as demonstrated conclusively by the state's prewar election returns of 1854, 1858, 1859, and 1860. In 1864 Jerseymen voted for the unionist Democratic candidate George B. McClellan partly because he was regarded as a home favorite by many residents. Throughout the period New Jerseyans exhibited no sympathy toward the South and its views. New Jersey did not resemble a southern slave state in any significant way.

New Jersey also did not fit the mold of a border slave state, with its mix of southern and northern influences and loyalties. The state continued in the mainstream of northern developments and experienced an industrial revolution, increasing immigration, and rapid growth. Politically New Jersey did not evince the typical border-state pattern of electoral support for John Bell in the presidential election of 1860. Unlike border-state residents during the Civil War, New Jerseyans did not wrestle with divided loyalties while brother fought brother, did not endure anguish as a battleground, did not experience guerrilla warfare. Their vital interest did not differ fundamentally from the national interest. They never had to agonize over possessing economic ties with the North and a social system rooted in the South. Unlike Kentuckians, whose state government espoused a policy of official or de facto neutrality during the early years of the war, New Jerseyans and their state government supported the war from beginning to the end. Moreover, wartime elections in New Jersey, unlike those in the border states, were not characterized by instability, cheating, violence, or army intervention.

After the war New Jersey did not revert to monolithic Democratic control, as the border states did. For three decades in the postwar period, New Jersey's Democrats usually carried presidential elections and regularly captured the governorship, but Republicans won control of the legislature twelve times between 1866 and 1894. The two parties tied several times as well. Republicans and Democrats competed on equal terms for seats in Congress, and Republicans often dominated the state's delegation on Capitol Hill. Moreover, once the Fifteenth Amendment became part of the federal Constitution, New Jerseyans (with a single isolated exception) did not try to nullify or neutralize black suffrage by force or fraud, nor did the state government attempt disfranchisement. Unlike blacks in the borderland, New Jersey's blacks continued to vote. Indeed, New Jersey in 1871 ratified the Fifteenth Amendment, in 1875 affirmed the right of blacks to vote, and in 1881 enacted a measure to guarantee their civil rights. In addition, blacks were not lynched in New Jersey, as they were in the border states. Between 1882 and 1930 Kentucky witnessed 151 lynchings; Missouri, 63; West Virginia, 35; and Maryland, 27. In contrast, only one lynching occurred in New Jersey during those years. New Jersey thus bore no resemblance to a border slave state before, during, or after the war.[19]

New Jersey had a Mid-Atlantic political orientation. The state's politics closely resembled those of its Mid-Atlantic neighbors, New York and Pennsylvania. Bounded for 272 miles by the free states of New York and Pennsylvania (78 percent), and for 78 miles by the slave state of Delaware (22 percent), New Jersey was not the northernmost of the border states but the southernmost of the Mid-Atlantic states. Unlike its midwestern counterparts in the lower North—Ohio, Indiana, and Illinois—New Jersey had very few residents who had been born in slave states. According to the 1860 census, New Jersey residents born in the free states numbered 543,139, or 98.8 percent of the native population. Only 6,008 New Jerseyans, a mere one percent, hailed from the slave states. New Jersey also lacked the configuration of those three western states, with their geographical division between a conservative, pro-southern, downstate region and a progressive, pro-northern upstate section. Because of the state's interdependence with New York City and Philadelphia, New Jerseyans regarded their interests as similar, if not always identical, to those of New York and Pennsylvania. Like their neighbors, New Jerseyans wished to preserve the peace and to maintain the Union. They might disagree about how best to accomplish this goal—and their elected representatives reflected this disagreement—but they shared a broad consensus.[20]

When war came, New Jersey ignited with patriotic fire, along with the rest of the North. New Jerseyans strongly supported the suppression of the rebellion and a vigorous prosecution of the war. Residents flocked to volunteer in the Union army. There was no strong sympathy for the South. Although opinion shifted according to the outcome of a military campaign, support for the war and its purposes did not change fundamentally in New Jersey. The political tide turned, however, in November 1862, when the Democrats swept the gubernatorial, legislative, and congressional elections. Such sweeps also occurred in the other lower northern states—New York, Pennsylvania, Ohio, Indiana, and Illinois—which together formed the region where most northerners lived. Nevertheless, the minority of Democrats who opposed the war must not be confused with the majority of Democrats who supported it, for the reactionary fringe never captured control of the State House. War supporters outwitted and outmaneuvered those in the peace camp. Our attention must shift from the noisy copperheads to the real leaders of the state Democratic party.

As elsewhere in the North, New Jersey's copperheads tried to take advantage of military setbacks and unpopular policies to break the will of the people and of their government to wage war and to win. They attracted attention but did not succeed in sabotaging the state's war effort and military recruitment. They failed in their 1863 attempt to pass a legislative resolution calling for a unilateral armistice championed by Daniel Holsman. The election of the antiwar James W. Wall to the United States Senate to fill six weeks of an unexpired term was a fluke; he failed to win reelection to a full term. Furthermore, no murders of federal recruitment officers took place in New Jersey, and no draft disturbances were as serious as those in New York City and elsewhere in the North. The copperheads never represented a majority of New Jerseyans or even a majority of the state's Democrats. New Jersey all along remained one of the "free and loyal states," in the words of Democratic war supporter Jacob Vanatta.[21]

In general, then, observers' remarks about New Jersey contrast sharply with the complex realities. Conservatives lauded New Jersey for southern sympathies and secessionist convictions that in fact few persons in the state harbored. Progressives outside and sometimes inside the state incorrectly branded New Jersey as reactionary and even disloyal. The state's reputation in the Civil War era had no relation to its record. Yet a legend about New Jersey began and has flourished ever since. The myths of difference fed on themselves and prevailed both in popular thinking and in academic circles.

It is time now to replace the state's outdated reputation as a southern state, a border state, a doughface state, or a copperhead state with a fresh reappraisal rooted firmly in the facts.

K nowing what New Jersey was *not* is a beginning. Recognizing what New Jersey had become by the middle of the nineteenth century requires an understanding of the circumstances that molded the state.

Lying on the Atlantic seaboard in the Mid-Atlantic region of the United States, New Jersey is a peninsula bound by ocean and two major rivers, the Hudson and the Delaware. It extends 166 miles at its greatest length; its average width is 50 miles. Despite a land surface of less than 5 million acres, the state's physical features vary dramatically. Mountains rise in the northwest, with foothills to the east. Across the narrow waist of the peninsula between New Brunswick on the Raritan River and Trenton on the Delaware, where rapids mark the end of the highland and the beginning of the lowland, a gently rolling but increasingly flat coastal plain slopes southward to surrounding waters, bordered by pine forests, marshes, and sand barrier islands. Diverse environments create marked differences within short distances.[22]

New Jersey was both cursed and blessed by geography. Inhibited by dependency, New Jersey nevertheless benefited by interdependence. The earliest settlements clustered on the eastern and western peripheries of the peninsula on the Hudson and Delaware rivers, which served as natural trade channels with the people across the river in New York City or Philadelphia. Because of the nearness, accessibility, and size of these cities and because they offered better prices, longer credit, and a larger choice of products, eighteenth- and nineteenth-century inhabitants of eastern Jersey continued to look to New York City, while those in western Jersey set their sights on Philadelphia. Both cities, with their extensive hinterlands, became great commercial hubs; they developed into manufacturing centers, and their gigantic seaports dominated foreign trade.

Like mighty city-states, these metropolises overshadowed New Jersey economically and culturally, hindered the state's internal development, and retarded the formation of a state character. One observer likened colonial New Jersey to "a cider barrel, tapped at both ends," with all the cider running into New York City and Philadelphia. In 1846 the Episcopal bishop of New Jersey, George Washington Doane, agreed: "It has been too literally true. We have been too well content to lose ourselves in the broad shadows of the two great states, which stretch on either side of us. We have been too willing to become but little more than an appendage to the two chief cities, which lie upon us on the right, and on the left." He pointed to New Jersey's lack of state identity, great cities, and a vital core. He characterized the development of the state as marked by localism, dissension, and disunity.[23]

During the first half of the nineteenth century, New Jersey did benefit from its strategic location between New York City and Philadelphia. Energetic New Jersey entrepreneurs helped to revolutionize travel, especially in the state's central corridor. They upgraded existing roads, bridged rivers, and started regular stagecoach service. They developed steamboat ferries on the Hudson and Delaware rivers and Raritan Bay. During the 1830s they built canals and railroads. To haul hard coal from Pennsylvania to the iron forges and factory furnaces of North Jersey and to the Atlantic seaports, entrepreneurs began construction of the Morris Canal in the hilly area between Jersey City and Phillipsburg. In the same decade a wider, deeper, more efficient canal, the Delaware and Raritan, was constructed on almost level ground. It crossed the narrow waist of the peninsula, connecting Bordentown on the lower Delaware with tidewater at New Brunswick on the Raritan. Vessels avoided the rough ocean voyage around the Cape by using this much shorter route between New York and Philadelphia. The canal generated heavy traffic and made money.

New Jersey's railroads provided the vital link between New York and Philadelphia, the nation's two largest cities. The Camden and Amboy Railroad laid track during the 1830s between Camden on the Delaware and South Amboy on the Raritan. Soon rail lines connected with Jersey City. The legislature encouraged the effort by granting the railroad a lucrative, long-term monopoly of metropolitan rail traffic. In return, the legislature expected the state treasury to receive a guaranteed annual income without risking cash or credit for new transportation and without having to tax residents for it. Its expectations were fulfilled: income from railroads and canals, 70 percent of which came from the Camden and Amboy Railroad and the Delaware and Raritan Canal, paid the expenses of the state government.

To prevent the financial collapse of the canal and to avoid ruinous competition between the canal and the railroad, the state also approved the merger of the Delaware and Raritan Canal and the Camden and Amboy Railroad into the Joint Companies, which would share the profits. The canal hauled bulk freight, mainly coal; the railroad carried passengers and light freight. Other railroad lines later crossed the state, and railroad mileage more than doubled in each decade between 1850 and 1870. By 1860 every major city in New Jersey had a rail link with other parts of the state. Railroad construction, however, was concentrated in the main corridor, which already enjoyed extensive population, capital, technology, and opportunity.[24]

Railroads shaped and spurred growth in the state and the region by modernizing the economy. By building up the population of major cities, connecting them with satellite towns and outlying suburbs, and harnessing seaports, railroads created jobs by supplying raw materials to manufacturers, who in turn found larger markets by shipping their finished products. The Mid-Atlantic region became the core of the emerging northeastern megalopolis, whose cities were tied together by railroad tracks. New Jersey at one key crossroad commanded the main line and exploited its advantage as a major transportation hub.

The Camden and Amboy Railroad helped shape economic growth while it played an important but changing role in state politics. After 1844, the railroad formed a political alliance, ironically, with the Democrats, who in principle distrusted monopolies but in practice aided the C & A's monopoly. Democrats pointed out the advantages of internal improvements and ample state revenues, compared to the fearful public debt and high individual taxes prevalent in other states. The railroad monopoly charged the highest rates for interstate travelers and shippers in the Northeast and the lowest rates for intrastate patrons. By this arrangement, people from other states paid the expenses of New Jersey's government. The Whigs, who in principle favored monopolies, in practice tended to oppose this particular monopoly because of its alliance with the Democrats.

Railroad lobbyists supported friendly Democratic governors and legislators. The lobbyists also courted partisans of all persuasions and worked assiduously for gubernatorial appointments of judges who would decide cases in favor of the railroad. Using the ample funds at their disposal, emissaries for the railroad furnished politicians, judges, lawyers, and editors with dinners, railroad passes, jobs, advertisements, subsidies, and campaign contributions. This symbiotic alliance between the railroad and many Democratic politicians allowed the railroad to keep its monopoly intact and to undercut competitors while maximizing profits.[25]

Antimonopolists concocted all sorts of conspiracy theories and blamed the demon railroad for every wrong. Journalist William Sackett expressed a widely held view of the monopoly that bound New Jerseyans as its slaves: "There never was a more complete master anywhere of the destinies of a State than was this monster monopoly of the affairs of New Jersey."[26]

The railroad lobby's reputation for omnipotence exceeded its grasp. The lobby never held absolute sway over the state, and it was not always victorious in party conventions, in races for Congress, in the legislature, or in the courts. New Jersey was not a sparsely settled western state in which a single railroad operated and acquired everything worth owning. The universal corruptibility of legislators in Trenton was exaggerated. Not all Democratic politicians were the railroad's vassals.

In 1855, after the election of an antimonopoly Opposition speaker of the assembly, the lobby's influence gradually began to decline. By the late 1860s even the lobby could not prevent the demise of the railroad's monopoly. Antimonopolists, moreover, have ignored the political disunity within the railroad's inner circle. The power of the monopoly's lobby should not be overestimated. In addition, other pressing concerns displaced railroad issues.[27]

Aided by faster, easier transportation and cheaper sources of energy, materials, and labor, factories in New Jersey sprouted and diversified. In 1860 about 4,200 manufacturing plants, mainly small enterprises, existed in the state. As the number of self-employed artisans diminished, the numbers of unskilled and semiskilled wage laborers increased.[28]

Leading industries in antebellum New Jersey engaged in the kinds of manufacturing characteristic of the Northeast. Major products included ironware, food and beer, clothing, and leather products. A few industries, notably ironmaking in North Jersey and glass production in South Jersey, stayed in the countryside because of the availability of raw materials. By 1860 New Jersey was an industrial powerhouse; Newark, the state's chief manufacturing center, ranked as the fifth most important industrial producer in the Northeast.[29]

Farm production increased to supply the expanding urban market inside and outside New Jersey. Farmers, most of whom owned their farms, raised specialized crops, particularly grains, potatoes, peas, and beans. They began to use the latest methods of fertilizing crops and breeding livestock as well as improved plows and harvesters to increase output and cut labor costs.[30]

As higher-paying jobs lured farm hands to factories, the percentage of the state's workers engaged in agriculture gradually declined. In 1840 almost 90 percent of New Jerseyans worked in the countryside; by 1880 fewer than half did so. In these forty years, however, several counties in the state became a highly productive and profitable truck garden supplying New York City and Philadelphia. Bergen, Hudson, and Essex as well as Burlington and Camden counties enjoyed the largest share of the metropolitan produce market. By 1860 the net worth of New Jersey's farms amounted to 186 million dollars, as compared with 82 million for industry.[31]

As manufacturing grew, people flocked to jobs in factory towns along the central corridor. In Jersey City, Trenton, Paterson, Camden, Elizabeth, New Brunswick, and Hoboken the combined population mushroomed from about 51,000 in 1850 to almost 320,000 by 1880. Newark dwarfed all of them and by 1860 was the nation's twelfth-largest city. Population was concentrated in the northeastern counties closest to New York City; these counties grew during the 1850s at a rate almost double that for the state as a whole. Essex and Hudson, the state's two most populous counties, together accounted for more than half the statewide increase. Meanwhile, the state's population tripled.

The rate of urbanization at midcentury became striking. The urban share of the state's population catapulted by 118 percent in 1850 and by 155 percent in 1860. Although most New Jerseyans still lived in rural areas at midcentury, the urban percentage increased to 18 percent in 1850, to 33 percent in 1860, to 44 percent in 1870, and to 54 percent in 1880. Fueled by this urban growth, the state's total population rose by 31 percent in 1850 to almost 490,000; in 1860 it jumped by 37 percent to 672,000. During the Civil War the number of people increased by only 15 percent, reaching almost

774,000 by 1865. After the war, the population rose sharply; by 1875 the number of New Jerseyans exceeded one million. Thus a state small in size rapidly became highly urban and densely populated.[32]

Immigration accompanied improving transportation, intensifying industrialization, and expanding urbanization. First Britons, then Irish, and later Germans came to New Jersey to build railroads, dig canals, mine minerals, man dockyards, and work as factory hands. The stream of immigrants reached a flood by the 1850s; the number of foreign-born persons in the state doubled between 1850 and 1860 from 60,000 (12 percent) to 123,000 (18 percent). Most of the foreigners, many of them Catholic, settled in corridor cities extending from Paterson to Camden along the major railroad lines. By 1860 the foreign-born constituted 42 percent of the population of Hudson County, 34 percent in Essex County, and 29 percent in Passaic County. Recent immigrants formed a powerful potential voting bloc, especially in Jersey City, Hoboken, and Newark.[33]

Most New Jerseyans, however, were not immigrants. In 1860 almost 82 percent of the state's residents were native-born. Coming from diverse ethnic backgrounds, by midcentury they nevertheless had much in common. The whites shared a western European, mainly British, origin. Except for the most recent immigrants, New Jerseyans without a British background had frequently Anglicized their names and spoke only English. Ethnic influences had declined gradually through intermarriage and Americanization. Most New Jerseyans attended Protestant churches. Moreover, New Jerseyans shared a common nationality and a state experience. They took pride in their personal independence and egalitarian society. Middle-class New Jerseyans had common materialistic values. Class mattered, of course, but observers pointed out that the range of extremes between wealth and poverty among native New Jerseyans was not as great as among the inhabitants of many other states.[34]

Geography, much more than class, divided New Jerseyans, at midcentury. Since its settlement Jersey had been divided between East Jersey and West Jersey, a division that generated internal conflict in the colony and the state. During the nineteenth century the regional rivalry continued, but the balance of power began to shift eastward. The northeastern counties increasingly became tied to materialistic, enterprising New York City, while the southeastern counties reinforced their links with more sedate, slower-moving Philadelphia. The economic boom, however, which started during the 1830s and gained momentum during the 1840s and 1850s, mainly benefited North Jersey. South Jersey fell behind in railroad construction, economic development, and population growth. Investment capital virtually dried up in that section during the 1850s, and the rate of conversion from water power to steam power lagged behind that of North Jersey. By 1860 the only county seats still lacking rail service—Toms River, Salem, and Cape May Court

House—were located in South Jersey, whose inhabitants bitterly resented the relative loss of their economic influence to the North Jerseyans.[35]

To harness political power, New Jerseyans had a rich tradition of political organization and popular participation. North Jerseyans especially prized town government while South Jerseyans relied more on county governance. Parties took root early in New Jersey, thrived immediately, and became tightly organized and highly competitive. New Jerseyans used party conventions, both state and county, to nominate candidates and forge party unity. They also established legislative party caucuses and state central committees. Between the 1790s and the 1850s New Jersey's parties were strong and largely nonideological. Party coalitions attempted to bridge internal differences in order to win elections and dispense patronage; on the state level, in adherence to the laissez-faire tradition, they tended to minimize public services and to keep taxes low.[36]

On the national level at midcentury, two political parties competed for power. The Democratic party was the majority party. The Whig party, formed in opposition to President Andrew Jackson's policies and his rejection of rechartering the Second Bank of the United States, had enjoyed only rare success in Washington. Both parties, rooted in the political-economic conflicts of the 1830s, failed to respond to the changes of the 1850s. A generation of party leaders had died, fierce party loyalties were fading, and traditional party positions became increasingly blurred, even irrelevant.

New parties developed in answer to new concerns. The massive immigration of Irish and Germans had caused great tensions between native-born residents and foreigners. Nativists demanded that alcohol consumption be prohibited and that the immigrants be restricted in voting and office holding. Promoting anti-Catholic, anti-foreign causes, the nativists formed the American party, which flourished briefly in the middle of the 1850s.

More important, a series of sectional disputes convulsed national politics. When southern leaders demanded that slavery be allowed to expand in the West, northerners formed the Republican party, which grew rapidly by championing anti-expansionist issues and northern interests. Meanwhile, the Whig party and the American party, each torn apart by disunity between the southern wing and the northern wing, became demoralized by defeat and disintegrated. The Democratic party became increasingly debilitated by internal dissension and division between pro-slavery forces and northern opponents of slavery.

New Jersey's politics mirrored national developments in various ways. Frequently the two major parties were evenly matched, and one observer concluded that since the 1830s New Jersey had been a "doubtful state as to politics." The keen competition for office and patronage resulted in bitter, sometimes corrupt contests. Exciting campaigns roused the interest and enthusiasm of voters, who turned out in large numbers. Although statewide majorities usually were slim, the Federalists dominated during the 1790s, the Democrats until 1837, and the Whigs until 1850. The Whigs petered out by the early 1850s, and the nativists and the Republicans filled the void. The latter two groups formed a loose coalition, known as the Opposition, against the Jersey Democrats, who experienced disaffection and defection when some Democrats joined the Opposition.[37]

Historians, as noted previously, have contended that New Jerseyans were conservative. Yet they actively participated in the reformist movements that swept the antebellum North; they established public schools, a state teachers' college, a mental institution, and a penitentiary. Jerseyans even joined the Fourierist movement and founded a few utopian communities such as the North American Phalanx and the Raritan Bay Union. Unlike other northern inhabitants, New Jerseyans, however, did not extend their reformist zeal to their prized applejack and beer. Prohibition of alcoholic beverages found little favor and provoked intense opposition.

Progressive currents were responsible for political reform as well. Under the Democrats' leadership, the state's antiquated constitution was replaced in 1844 by a more progressive one, which contained a bill of rights for the first time. A property requirement for voting was ended; voters, instead of the legislature, now elected the governor for a single three-year term. The governmental structure was streamlined, and some gubernatorial powers were strengthened. Representation based on population began in the assembly, the lower legislative chamber; assemblymen were elected annually in sixty districts. The upper chamber was the senate, to which one member from each county was elected for a term of three years. As democratic politics expanded, the wealthy, prominent families, which earlier had governed the state, were displaced gradually by prosperous businessmen, professional politicians, and war heroes.[38]

As internal development and material progress occurred in the nineteenth century, identity and confidence in New Jersey at midcentury grew, despite the still-overshadowing influence of New York City and Philadelphia. When outsiders said that New Jersey was a backward, undesirable place to live, New Jerseyans refuted the charges that Jersey consisted merely of rocky hills in the north, mosquito-infested swamps in the center, and barren sand in the south. Surprised by the dismissal of New Jersey as a nonentity by New Yorkers, the British traveler Charles Mackay countered: "But New Jersey can afford to despise the joke—if joke it be; for, although one of the smallest, it is one of the most prosperous states of the Republic." Jacob Miller remarked in 1854 that New Jersey's two metropolitan neighbors "cannot deprive us of our locality. And New York City and Philadelphia, although outside of our boundaries, afford to us the two best markets in the country. The barrel may be tapped at both ends, but *the barrel* is still *our own*, to be filled or emptied at our pleasure, according to the demand and the supply." Similarly, the

*Belvidere Intelligencer* pragmatically observed in 1861 that New Jerseyans "have just as much interest in the growth and prosperity of these cities as if they were within the limits of this State, for with their growth and prosperity, will every material interest of New Jersey grow."[39]

New Jerseyans' pride of place in their "little, but much beloved state" had many sources. They were inspired by the physical beauty of their state: the jagged Delaware Water Gap, pristine lakes, forested hills, sheltered valleys, the spectacular Palisades of the Hudson, the towering Highlands of the Navesink, the breezy back bays, the sparkling beaches on the Jersey shore pounded by the waves of the Atlantic.[40]

New Jerseyans relished their fruits from the land and the sea. Residents celebrated their towns and two colonial colleges. New Jerseyans pointed to their state's strategic position as the cockpit of the American Revolution and to their part in winning independence and establishing the new nation. The boast of Trentonians in 1911 with their electric sign on the bridge across the Delaware River proclaiming "Trenton Makes, The World Takes" carried a message expressed by earlier New Jerseyans. They extolled the quality, variety, and prices of their manufactured products. Residents of Jersey agreed with Mackay that their state, although small, was one of the most prosperous. For this and many other reasons, they radiated justifiable pride as New Jerseyans.[41]

# Chronology

| | National Events | New Jersey |
|---|---|---|
| **1854** | *May 30:* Kansas-Nebraska Act | |
| | *Nov. 7:* Anti-Nebraska forces won U.S. House of Representatives | *Nov. 7:* Opposition won 4 congressmen, legislature |
| **1856** | *Feb. 25:* American party picked Millard Fillmore for president | |
| | *June 6:* Democrats chose James Buchanan<br>*June 18:* Republicans picked John Fremont | *June 4:* Republicans picked William Newell for governor<br><br>*Aug. 6:* Democrats selected William Alexander |
| | *Nov. 4:* Buchanan elected; Democrats narrowly won House of Representatives | *Nov. 4:* Buchanan won; Democrats won legislature, U.S. senator, 3 congressmen; Opposition, governor |
| **1857** | *March 6:* Dred Scott decision | |
| | *Dec. 3–9:* Stephen Douglas fought pro-slavery Lecompton constitution for Kansas backed by Buchanan | |
| **1858** | *April 30:* House defeated Lecompton plan | |
| | *Nov. 2:* Opposition regained House of Representatives | *Nov. 2:* Opposition won legislature, all congressional seats |
| **1859** | | *March 17:* Legislature elected Republican senator John Ten Eyck |
| | | *Aug. 24:* Democrats picked Edwin Wright for governor |
| | | *Sept. 7:* Opposition chose Charles Olden |
| | *Oct. 16–18:* John Brown's raid. | |
| | | *Nov. 8:* Olden elected governor |

| | National Events | New Jersey |
|---|---|---|
| **1860** | *April 23–May 2:* Democratic split at Charleston | |
| | *May 9:* Unionists chose John Bell for president<br>*May 18:* Republicans selected Abraham Lincoln | |
| | *June 23:* Democrats backed Douglas; Southern Democrats nominated John Breckinridge | |
| | *Nov. 6:* Lincoln elected | *Nov. 6:* Lincoln won 4 electoral votes, Douglas 3; Democrats gained 1 congressman |
| | *Dec. 20–Feb. 1:* Lower South seceded | |

| | National/N.J. Unit Combat | State Developments |
|---|---|---|
| **1861** | *Jan. 16–Mar. 2:* Senate defeated John Crittenden's plan | *Jan. 24–25:* Democrats for Crittenden's plan<br>*Jan. 29:* Republicans opposed |
| | *Feb. 4–20:* Confederacy created<br>*Feb. 4–27:* Washington peace conference failed<br>*Feb. 27:* House of Representatives rejected Crittenden's plan | *Feb. 21:* Lincoln visited state |
| | *March 4:* Lincoln inaugurated<br>*March 29:* Lincoln ordered Fort Sumter reinforced | |
| | *April 10–12:* Confederates demanded the fort<br>*April 12–13:* Bombardment of fort; war began<br>*April 17–20:* Upper South seceded | *April 17, 24:* Governor Olden supported war, summoned legislature, April 20 |
| | | *May 7–10:* Legislature backed, funded war |
| | *July 21:* First Bull Run: major Union defeat | |
| | | *Oct. 8:* Democrats won Newark election |
| | | *Nov. 5:* Legislative standoff |
| **1862** | *Feb. 8, March 14:* North Carolina Coast campaign: 9th N.J. fought at Roanoke Island, New Bern | *March 27:* Legislature backed war |
| | *May 5:* 2d N.J. Brigade took heavy casualties at battle of Williamsburg<br>*May 31–June 1:* 2d Brigade in battle of Fair Oaks | |
| | *June 27:* Outnumbered 1st N.J. Brigade defeated in battle of Gaines' Mill; suffered heavy casualties | |

| National/N.J. Unit Combat | State Developments |
|---|---|
| *July 2:* General George B. McClellan's Peninsula campaign failed | |
| *Aug. 29–30:* 2d Bull Run: Union defeat | *Aug. 21:* Republicans picked Marcus Ward for governor |
| *Sept. 14–17:* Antietam: Union army stopped rebel invasion but failed to capture rebel army; 1st N.J. Brigade seized Crampton's Gap<br>*Sept. 22:* Lincoln issued Preliminary Emancipation Proclamation to free slaves in Confederacy | *Sept. 4:* Democrats chose Joel Parker |
| *Oct. 14:* Democrats won Pa., Ohio, Ind. | |
| *Nov. 4:* Democrats won in lower North, gained seats in Republican Congress | *Nov. 4:* Democrats gained governor, legislature, 1 congressional seat |
| *Dec. 13:* Union defeat at Fredericksburg | *Dec. 1:* Republican Richard Field appointed interim senator |
| **1863**    *Jan. 1:* Emancipation Proclamation took effect | *Jan. 14:* Copperhead Democrat James Wall elected senator for 42 days in 37th Congress |
| | *Feb. 26:* Hard-line Democrat William Wright elected senator for full term in 38th Congress |
| *Mar. 3:* First Conscription Act | *Mar. 17:* Legislature protested Lincoln's policies<br>*Mar. 24:* New war loan<br>*Mar. 25:* Unionist resolutions |
| *May 1–4:* Union defeat at Chancellorsburg<br>*May 5:* Clement Vallandigham of Ohio arrested | |
| *July 1–3:* Union victory at Gettysburg | |

| National/N.J. Unit Combat | State Developments |
|---|---|
| *July 4:* Vicksburg captured<br>*July 13–15:* Draft riots in<br>New York City | |
| *Nov. 23–25:* Battles around<br>Chattanooga, Union victory | *Nov. 3:* Minor Republican<br>gains in legislature |

**1864**

*May 5–6:* Battle of the Wilderness:
N.J. Brigades battered
*May 8–21:* Battle of Spotsylvania

*June 1–3:* Battle of Cold Harbor
*June 8:* Republicans renominated
Lincoln

*July 9:* Battle of Monocacy:
14th N.J. participated

*Aug. 31:* Democrats nominated
McClellan

*Sept. 2:* Atlanta captured by
Union army, including several
N.J. units
*Sept. 19–Oct. 19:* Rebels
defeated in Shenandoah
Valley; N.J. 3rd Cavalry,
1st Brigade participated

| *Nov. 8:* Lincoln won reelection | *Nov. 8:* McClellan won;<br>Republicans picked up one<br>congressional seat, tied in<br>assembly |

**1865**

*Jan. 31:* Congress proposes
Thirteenth Amendment

> *March 1, 16:* Legislature
> rejected Thirteenth
> Amendment
> *March 15:* Legislature chose
> Democrat John P. Stockton
> as U.S. senator

*April 2:* Petersburg, Richmond
abandoned
*April 9:* Lee surrendered at
Appomattox
*April 14:* Lincoln assassinated

| National/N.J. Unit Combat | State Developments |
| --- | --- |
| | *July 20:* Republicans picked Ward for governor |
| | *Aug. 30:* Democrats selected Theodore Runyon |
| | *Nov. 7:* Ward elected governor; Republicans captured legislature |

# 1 Change and Continuity, 1854–1856

In early January 1854, New Jerseyans digging out of heavy snows learned of two schooners shipwrecked off Cape May Point during gales. Theater-going New Yorkers saw the anti-slavery play *Uncle Tom's Cabin*. Selected Washingtonians attended a magnificent reception at the executive mansion. Throughout the nation, Americans relished the prevailing peace and prosperity; they reveled in the progress of their robust republic. Only a prophet of doom would have predicted that in just over seven years American citizens would be shooting at one another.

Sectional tensions, which led ultimately to war, escalated sharply following January 4, 1854, when Senator Stephen Douglas of Illinois proposed a bill authorizing settlers of the Nebraska country to decide by popular vote whether to allow slavery there. Since 1820 the Missouri Compromise had excluded slavery from this region. Douglas's bill challenged the prohibition and reopened the controversy over the expansion of slavery. That expansion threatened to upset the delicate balance between the free North and the slave South.[1]

Assessing the bill and considering the fall congressional election, Representative George H. Vail of Morristown complained to a fellow New Jersey Democrat, Governor Rodman M. Price: "The Nebraska question has been sprung upon us much against the wishes of the North, and a very impolitic measure at this time." Vail viewed the bill as a device that would allow the leading Democrats to jockey for the presidential nomination in 1856 by picking up southern support. By championing the bill, Democratic president Franklin Pierce sought to "secure the majority of the Southern vote" for a second term, which, Vail wrote, "I very much question and which will injure the Democratic party at the North very materially." If Pierce failed, Vail predicted, Douglas would be the likely nominee; he had proposed the bill for that reason.

Vail also worried about his constituents, who bombarded him with advice about how to vote on the bill, mixed with threats if he failed to follow their advice. "I am receiving letters that if I do not wish to be a yearling, I must vote against it. Also on the other side I am told it will kill me if I do not go for it. . . . Under these circumstances I am silent." Despite deep misgivings, Vail came down on his party's side: "I do not see how I can honestly vote against it. It is upholding the right of people to self-government. How can a Democrat go against it?"[2]

The bill sparked a fierce debate in Congress and in the country at large.

Proponents of the measure believed that imminent settlement in the northern Plains necessitated immediate organization of the federal territory. Instead of Congress dictating matters, the people most directly affected and most knowledgeable about local conditions would decide. Although in theory the residents of the territories could accept slavery, backers of the measure predicted that slavery would never take root on the Plains because northern settlers there would not allow it. With no need to fear the expansion of slavery, popular sovereignty would end the wrangling between pro-slavery and anti-slavery forces. Slavery, promised the supporters of Douglas's bill, would disappear from politics with this measure.[3]

Opponents were unconvinced by these facile arguments and condemned the legislation as mischievous. Members of New Jersey's legislature proclaimed that this unnecessary measure would reopen the sectional struggle. Newark's German Protestants denounced the aggressive designs of the slaveholders against liberty. Most clergymen avoided such controversial issues in sermons, but a few attacked the bill from the pulpit as unjust. During the debate no prominent New Jerseyan championed ending slavery without compensation to slaveowners, but many people believed that slavery retarded economic progress and morally tarnished society. They sought to curtail slavery in the West and to contain pro-slavery power in Washington. Opponents of the bill argued that it made a mockery of Douglas's pledge of direct democracy, because the president, not the inhabitants, would select the governor and other territorial officials, who would do the president's bidding.[4]

Skeptics doubted the Democratic contention that the inhabitants of the territories would bar slavery. Southerners, after all, had created the territory of Kansas, lying just west of the slaveholding state of Missouri, for the express purpose of making it a slave state. Northerners would counter by pouring men and money into Kansas to create a free state.[5]

New Jerseyans also expressed shock that the Compromise of 1850, regarded as a permanent bulwark against sectional quarrels, appeared to be ephemeral after only four years. Their disillusionment turned to anger when they recognized that the durable Missouri Compromise of 1820 also would be repudiated. Anti-Nebraska Democratic congressman Charles Skelton of Trenton observed, "We of New Jersey require peace; we demand peace; we desire to foment no sectional feelings . . . in a word, to do nothing that shall in any way disturb the harmony and prosperity of our common country." He feared for the stability of the nation if Congress passed the Kansas-Nebraska bill. The *Trenton Gazette* remarked, "For once Mr. Douglas has gone too far." The newspaper expressed a widely held view: "The people of the North are willing always to give up much for the sake of peace and harmony. They are willing, in good faith, to adhere to the compromises of the constitution and to carry them into effect, but when they are asked to surrender to slavery territory which has been solemnly set apart to freedom, they will be found to refuse their consent. . . . Let the South be protected in all her rights but let the rights of the North also be respected."[6]

Opponents of the Kansas-Nebraska bill pointed out that the Missouri Compromise had long secured peace by establishing a line between slave and free states. They denounced the lopsided new arrangement, which would obliterate the line that stabilized the situation. The *Newark Mercury* declared that northern "interests, principles, rights, and conscience must all give way before the demands of Slavery. We are not to be regarded—our existence is not to be recognized." The newspaper charged that the "South wants the empire of Slavery extended, and as it cannot be acquired elsewhere, she demands and will take it from the North. Nothing but the utter obliteration of Freedom in all the territory north of 36 deg. 30 min. will appease the ravenous appetite she has engendered for conquest and power." The *Newark Advertiser* contended that the Kansas-Nebraska bill "does not settle slave agitation; but inflames its rage, and gives it venom."[7]

New Jerseyans feared that the mistrust between North and South would break the bonds holding the Union together. If the South repudiated the Missouri Compromise, Skelton observed, "what confidence can we have in each other in the future? No more compromises can ever be made. No more concessions on either side—conciliation and harmony are at an end." Sharing this sentiment, the dissident Democratic *Newton Herald* stated that if nobody trusts anybody, no one will compromise, and so "our faith in compromise will be gone. In fact, we fear that the country will be beyond the reach of compromise."[8]

As the *Woodbury Constitution* pointed out, when the people of one section observe a national compromise only so long as it proves beneficial to them, the inhabitants of the other region will quickly start to distrust them and will repudiate all compromises. A North Jerseyan observed: "Old party lines will be wiped out, and instead of them we shall have sectional parties—the North against the South, and the flood-tide of Northern indignation will sweep every thing before it" with the future election of a northern sectional president. The *Newton Register* feared that sectional antagonism soon would lead to national disruption: "Under such a state of affairs, the Union could not endure more than ten years."[9]

The Kansas-Nebraska bill not only troubled Vail and many New Jerseyans but also split the state's delegation in Congress. Democratic senators John R. Thomson of Princeton and William Wright of Newark supported the administration's measure, as did Democratic representatives Vail and Samuel Lilly of northern Jersey. Democratic representatives Nathan T. Stratton and Skelton of southern and central Jersey defected, however. Both joined the opposition to the bill, as did Whig representative Alexander C. M. Pennington of North Jersey. Thus, the delegation was narrowly divided, four in favor and three opposed.

The Democratic Senate, the bastion of southern power, approved the bill on March 3, 1854. When the House of Representatives, which reflected greater northern influence, voted on the bill on May 22, not a single northern Whig supported the bill. Democrats and Whigs of the South supported the measure, but half the northern Democrats rejected it. Pierce's assurances of patronage pressured the remaining northern Democrats to support the bill as a test of party loyalty, and thus secured passage. The *Newton Register* echoed the alarm of many northerners upon enactment: "From henceforth the great issue is joined, and either Slavery or Freedom must go to the wall. The era of compromises is past."[10]

The controversy came to a head in early June, when Douglas arrived in Trenton for a brief stopover. The reception turned into a heckling demonstration against him and the other "Nebrascals." The local crowd cheered Skelton, who was described at the rally as "the Anti-Nebraska member of Congress from this district" and "the true exponent of New Jersey Democracy" (Democratic party). The Democratic *Trenton American* dismissed the incident as the work of a few rioters. Defending the state Democracy, Price apologized to Douglas. The incident, he reported, repelled the great majority of state Democrats and would work only to reinvigorate support for both Douglas and his position.[11]

In the fall campaign for Congress, opponents of the Kansas-Nebraska Act still strongly opposed the new legislation, but they were flexible in selecting candidates and building coalitions with an eye to local conditions. In the first district (Atlantic, Camden, Cape May, Cumberland, Gloucester, and Salem), rumors suggested the possibility of an anti-Nebraska coalition between the Whigs and the nativists. The nativist convention met first, however, and nominated Isaiah D. Clawson, a firm anti-Nebraska man. Although outmaneuvered and infuriated, the Whigs recognized that the nativists held the balance of power in the district. Therefore they must not throw away their chances of victory by dividing this potential coalition with two candidates, as had occurred before. They grudgingly accepted the nativist Clawson as their nominee and, striking a nativist chord, criticized the appointment of foreigners to public office. Their platform condemned the Kansas-Nebraska Act.

In the second district (Burlington, Mercer, Monmouth, and Ocean), the Whig convention adopted a forthright anti-Nebraska platform and nominated George R. Robbins, a straightforward anti-Nebraska Whig and future Republican. The third district (Hunterdon, Middlesex, Somerset, and Warren) witnessed the most momentous development. The Whig convention and the newly formed anti-Nebraska convention met separately but simultaneously in the same courthouse; then they combined and nominated a coalition candidate, nativist James Bishop, who firmly opposed the Nebraska policy, as did the platform of the convention.

In the strongly Democratic fourth district (Bergen, Morris, Passaic, and

Sussex), residents followed still another tack in rallying the various forces of the opposition. The Whig party convention attacked the Nebraska Act but did not nominate a candidate; instead it threw its support to the independent, anti-Nebraska candidate, Democrat Peter C. Osborne. In the fifth district (Essex, Hudson, and Union created in 1857), the Whig convention renominated Pennington, the anti-Nebraska Whig (who later became a Republican) and repudiated repeal of the Missouri Compromise. Except for the first district, the Whig and coalition conventions avoided nativist issues in their platforms.

New Jersey Whigs kept their party organization intact, but they did not conduct politics as usual. Whigs made concerted efforts everywhere to organize wide-ranging opposition to the Kansas-Nebraska Act. The Whigs' search for power made use of complete coalition, virtual alliance, active conciliation, and informal cooperation. Yet conservative Whiggish habits persisted: in contrast to the accelerating pace of political reorganization carried out by Whigs outside the state, the more cautious Jersey Whigs did not create a new party outright, and so they rarely used the term "Republican."

New Jersey Democrats grasped the importance of the Nebraska issue as well. Although downstate Democrats refused out of party loyalty to renominate their anti-Nebraska rebels in the first and second districts, they still approached the election with caution. At their convention in the first district, Democrats evaded the unpopular issue of the Kansas-Nebraska Act. Because nativism was strong locally, they rejected a motion denouncing nativism. Then they selected a party regular as their congressional candidate. Democrats in the second district nominated an apolitical nobody who avoided the Kansas-Nebraska issue during the campaign. In a similar spirit, the party convention failed, on the flimsy pretext that they had no time because of the rush to catch trains home, to adopt any resolutions.

In stronger Democratic districts the party sometimes acted more confidently and took firmer positions. In the third and fourth districts, Democratic delegates renominated pro-Nebraska incumbents Lilly and Vail. Although both platforms supported direct rule by the people, they did not expressly support the Kansas-Nebraska Act. Only in the fifth district did the delegates accept an explicit pro-Nebraska platform, while selecting a regular Democrat who enjoyed great local popularity.

In general, pro-Nebraska incumbents attempted to downplay the troublesome issue by emphasizing state matters. No Democratic platform attacked nativism, and only in the fourth district did Democrats champion the rights of Catholic Americans by denouncing any religious test as a requirement for public office. Democrats added strident racist appeals by accusing their opponents of favoring "negro freedom." Only Democrats, the *Trenton American* claimed, championed the "freedom of white men."[12]

Although the expansion of slavery played a central role, it did not

monopolize the campaign. Immigrants resented attempts to restrict or eliminate alcohol consumption. The progressive group of German Protestants in
particular had difficulty reconciling their desire to drink beer unrestricted
with their opposition to the Nebraska measure. The *Newarker Zeitung* resolved
the dilemma neatly by pointing out that the liquor issue was involved only in
state and local contests, not in congressional elections. Germans could oppose local prohibitionist candidates with a clear conscience and still vote for
the anti-Nebraska nominee for Congress.[13]

Another issue in the campaign concerned the Camden and Amboy Railroad. Anger against it intensified after March 16, 1854, when the Democratic
legislature approved the extension until 1869 of the railroad's monopoly.
Whigs generally opposed this extension. Democrats, with some exceptions,
supported it. Many, particularly in South Jersey, wanted rail connections for
their localities and blamed the C & A for blocking rail construction there.[14]

In the November 1854 elections New Jerseyans rejected most of the pro-
Nebraska Democrats. The state's previous delegation in Congress had consisted of four Democrats and one Whig, but the ratio was reversed in 1854,
when voters chose four anti-Nebraska men and a single Democrat. The opposition also gained control of the legislature. Some Democrats and most
Whigs in the state supported the newly emerging coalition. Specifically, about
one-quarter of the Democratic voters in the presidential election of 1852
and roughly 80 percent of the Whigs supported the anti-Nebraska coalition
in 1854. Many Democrats stayed away from the polls in protest against the
Kansas-Nebraska Act.[15]

Democrats attributed their remarkable reversal to the array of issues against
them: anti-Nebraska sentiment, Whigism, temperance, antimonopolism, and
nativism. Nativism as well as temperance and opposition to the Camden and
Amboy Railroad figured importantly in certain places. Yet dissatisfaction with
the administration's Nebraska policy influenced most voters. As the *Newark
Mercury* put it, "never perhaps did a public measure fall with a more stunning effect upon the mind of the North, than this repeal of a sacred Compromise." Newspapers throughout the state echoed the editorial observation
of the *Trenton Gazette*: "Before the magnitude of this question all other subjects dwindle into insignificance."[16]

The moderate majority in New Jersey cast a vote of no confidence in Pierce
and his pro-southern policy. New Jerseyans repudiated the Kansas-Nebraska
Act as an extremist measure inaugurated by the "aggressive and sectional
designs of the South." In the words of the *Hightstown Record*, the act was advanced with "reckless disregard" of public opinion in the North. Even the
*New York Tribune*, a steadfast critic of New Jersey's politics, tardily congratulated New Jerseyans for the election results, as "emphatic as they were for
Freedom."[17]

During 1854, then, New Jersey formed part of an anti-Nebraska coalition that swept to victory in the North and caused the Democrats to lose their majority in the House of Representatives. The Kansas-Nebraska Act proved a colossal miscalculation in public policy and a political disaster for the Democrats.

Shrewd observers recognized that the political landscape had been redrawn. "We are in the midst of a political revolution," exclaimed the *Camden Jerseyman.* The *Salem Standard* observed, "Old party lines in a great measure were disregarded and the People independently arrayed themselves upon new issues." Voters were tired of traditional politics and professional politicians; the desire for fresh new faces and new leaders produced a "mighty political slaughter among the 'old line' politicians." They rejected both Democratic doughfaces and "Old Fogey Cotton-Headed Whiggery," according to the *Hightstown Record*.[18]

Although the *Newark Advertiser* dubbed the emerging movement "New Whigs," the new coalition was not the old Whig party in a new guise. The old-line Whig press might claim to view anti-Nebraska triumphs or partial nativist successes as Whig victories, but many people knew better. The opposition victory resulted neither from traditional Whig issues nor from the customary strength of the Whig party organization. The state Whig party could no longer compete for power by relying on its old independent identity, its distinctive appeal, and its separate support. In fact, support for the Whigs declined sharply during the early 1850s, both statewide and nationally. Necessity forced the state Whig organization to form a grand anti-Democratic coalition with other groups.[19]

In the minds of many people, a new political era had dawned. Both parties had outlived their day. Old issues had become defunct, and previous partisan loyalties had weakened.[20]

While the old parties crumbled in the North between 1854 and 1856, political leaders struggled to build new ones. Nativists made an issue of the recent immigrants, mainly Catholic, who were pouring into the country and the state. As a result of this influx, the proportion of foreign-born white males in the potential electorate increased dramatically. Resentment against these newcomers and their different ways spread among native-born New Jerseyans.

Nativist leaders fed the fear of foreigners by denouncing what they called "the Catholic menace." The so-called Irish heathen and German infidels refused to observe the Sabbath. They preferred to send their children to Catholic schools. Nativist speakers blamed all problems on these immigrants, who allegedly corrupted elections, broke strikes, took away native workers' jobs by accepting lower wages, and increased pauperism, alcoholism, and crime. To combat the newcomers, nativists began to form secret societies. Because the members claimed they knew nothing of such groups, people dubbed the nativists Know-Nothings. The Know-Nothings organized a new political party, the American party, which championed religious bigotry and proscription of aliens.

By 1856 the American party's national platform demanded a political curb on immigrants. Nativists called for an extension of the residence period required for naturalization from five to twenty-one years to prevent voting by the newcomers, who were just starting to participate in politics. Nativists also lobbied to restrict office holding and public employment to the native-born.

People joined the nativist movement for many reasons. Some, especially in the early 1850s, were attracted by the clever propaganda, which catered to the audience's fascination with Catholic misconduct. Know-Nothings titillated the gullible with wild tales of church conspiracies and sexual escapades in convents. Nativists also contended that Protestantism promoted American democracy by fostering individualism and equality, whereas the Catholic Church's authoritarianism, censorship, and demands for public funds to operate parochial schools undermined democracy and public education. In addition to this blatant anti-Catholicism, the secrecy and the rituals of nativist fraternal orders attracted recruits. Other native-born xenophobes simply wished to prevent control of their communities from passing into the hands of their immigrant neighbors. Many blamed the severe economic recession on foreigners; natives wished to protect American labor against cheaper foreign labor. Still others backed the nativists not out of bigotry or fear but simply because they, unlike the Democrats, strongly favored a limit on the consumption of alcohol.

With the breakdown of the older political parties, some joined the nativist movement in 1854 by default; others championed a populist, antiestablishment third-party movement. For still others, especially in 1855 and 1856, the American party offered a safe haven from extremism because they, as patriots and moderates, sought a political center that could save the Union. Repelled both by northern abolitionism and by southern sectionalism, such nationalists sought to sidestep the slavery controversy altogether.

The nascent American party attracted politicians who regarded it as the wave of the future and wished to use it to further their own purposes. This movement, then, had many followers, from high-minded individualists to prejudiced hooligans. Experienced politicians as well as apolitical amateurs jockeyed for leadership. The nativists rose quickly to national prominence in the mid-1850s, when they scored stunning electoral triumphs.[21]

As early as 1853, nativists formed a political movement in New Jersey. From the start, the American party appealed to some elements in South Jersey, a rural region with a homogeneous British Protestant population. Living relatively close to Philadelphia and its growing immigrant population, some South Jerseyans feared that the immigrant tide might inundate them and threaten their way of life. Politicians could exploit such fears without worry of retaliation from foreign-born voters.

Nativism emerged in other parts of the state as well. In 1854 and 1855, chapters of the national secret order were organized in northeastern New Jersey in response to resentments against the new immigrants there. In 1855 the nativists elected the mayor of Trenton and for the first time sent party members to the legislature from North Jersey. Other political forces in the state, ambivalent about the American party, mixed denunciation of nativism with astonishment or acquiescence. Politicians in several sensitive districts achieved accommodation or forged alliances with nativist forces. The remnants of the Whigs frequently curried nativist favor because the two parties had a common enemy in the Democrats and in the immigrants who flocked to the Democracy. The Democrats alternated between opposition to nativism and evasion of the issue, evidently hoping the movement would disappear as quickly as it had emerged.[22]

Meanwhile, antagonism occurred wherever natives and foreigners rubbed shoulders. New Jersey natives assaulted Irish Catholics and damaged or burned some of their churches. On September 5, 1854, nativist rowdies marched through the streets of Newark, spoiling for a fight. They illegally carried revolvers, which they fired into the air to the cheers of friendly bystanders. When the men entered an immigrant neighborhood and marched past a large crowd of Irishmen standing in front of a German Catholic church, however, one of the Irishmen tossed a rock at the taunting paraders. In the ensuing riot both sides wildly fired pistols and threw stones. Dashing for cover, the Irish ran into the church, barricaded the doors, and continued to fire from the windows. Infuriated, many of the paraders rushed toward the church, battered down the doors, and drove the men outside. Then the nativists broke the church windows, tore up benches and pictures, and smashed the organ and the altar. Some shouted orders to set the church on fire, but police arrived in time to prevent it. In the melee someone shot an Irishman twice in the stomach, and he died soon afterward. Another Irishman received a flesh wound from a sword. A number of marchers also were injured slightly. As a result of this and other, similar experiences, immigrants formed armed units to defend themselves against nativist troublemakers.[23]

The American party held its national convention in Philadelphia in February 1856. The upstart party needed a credible candidate to win supporters nationwide and turned to a respectable mediocrity, Millard Fillmore of New York, the recent president and an old-line Whig conservative. In the balloting for the presidential nominee, New Jersey's delegates first had favored Robert F. Stockton, part owner of the Joint Companies and leader of one nativist faction. On the final ballot, however, Jersey's delegates switched to Fillmore.

Fillmore was nominated by the Know-Nothings even though many delegates knew little or nothing of his views on nativism. Although it was not widely known, he belonged to the secret order. Calling himself a "National American," Fillmore emphasized unionism instead of nativism in his campaign.

Fillmore and the Americans in New Jersey tried to capture the political center. They denounced the Democrats for supporting a pro-southern policy and decried the anti-southern appeal of the emerging Republican party. If the Democracy won the election, the South would triumph over the North. If the Republicans succeeded, the North would prevail over the South. Only Fillmore, they argued, could settle national problems. Fillmore received additional backing when a remnant of the national Whig party, meeting in September, also nominated him, widening support for his candidacy and further deemphasizing its nativist character.[24]

Southern Americans also played a pivotal role in the new American party. They, after all, had insisted on Fillmore as the nominee because they regarded him as a reliable friend. As president he had supported their interests by signing and enforcing the new fugitive slave law. This faction also received a pro-southern platform.

The actions of the so-called South Americans outraged many North Americans: roughly one-quarter of the delegates walked out of the convention in protest against the price of southern support. New Jersey's delegates did not join the bolters because most of them supported Fillmore in the hope that he would maintain both national unity and party harmony.

In mid-June the bolters held a rump convention in New York City. At this gathering a new group from New Jersey, which had spurned Fillmore, backed Stockton. The convention, however, nominated Massachusetts congressman Nathaniel P. Banks. Banks, a stalking-horse for the Republicans, then refused to run. This step left the defecting Americans with no one to turn to but the Republican nominee.

Meanwhile, the true believers, led by the New Jersey delegation, persuaded a small number of the bolters to bolt again. They resented Republican maneuvers and regarded Fillmore as too weak a Know-Nothing and too old-fashioned to head the nativist movement. These seceding North Americans, who called themselves Open Americans and who convened while the North American convention continued, nominated Stockton, who tentatively accepted. A Philadelphia correspondent termed Stockton "doubly bolted": "Political flour of his degree of fineness will never be made into Presidential bread." Sensing this reaction, Stockton later declined the nomination, backed Fillmore, and lamely tried to reassure him by writing: "New Jersey is coming to the rescue." Such endemic factionalism, in which National Americans, South Americans, North Americans, and Open Americans jockeyed for position, suggested serious problems in maintaining any national nativist party and in mounting a viable presidential campaign.[25]

Both the national and the state American parties suffered from defections, miscues, and misunderstandings during the campaign. Some New Jersey voters, still considering Fillmore too strongly tainted by his southern support and previous pro-southern inclinations, attacked him as the nominee of the South Americans. One Camden County nativist requested assurances from Fillmore: "There are doubts in the minds of some in reference to your position upon the Slavery question because the nomination was made by a majority of Southern men." A Monmouth County resident, seeking from Fillmore a denial of his alliance with the South, observed more bluntly, "They say that you are a northern man, with southern principles, that you advocate slavery as much or more than [Democrat James] Buchanan."[26]

In a speech at Albany on June 26, Fillmore exploded a bombshell. He was understood to say that the South would be justified in seceding from the Union if the Republicans won the presidency. This speech was widely misinterpreted; in fact, Fillmore simply regarded southern secession as inevitable if such an event occurred. He caused an outcry, however, by raising the question publicly in the first place.

Many New Jersey nativists denounced this speech. A Burlington County resident who had leaned toward Fillmore changed his mind after the speech, finding its message repugnant to the principle that "the majority shall rule. And as the Constitutional opportunities for changing our rulers are abundant and frequent, any resistance, by the North, or the South, or any other section, to the properly elected officers of the Country, would be treason of the deepest dye." Theologian and Princeton Republican Charles Hodge contrasted Fillmore to Andrew Jackson, who opposed South Carolina's nullification of federal law. "Fillmore has committed himself to worse nullification than South Carolina ever dreamt of. He has drawn a broader line beneath the North and South."[27]

An Elizabeth nativist joined party leaders in pressuring Fillmore to clarify his Albany speech and counter the prevailing impression so damaging to his campaign. "The most unwarrantable use has been made of this sentiment and in the state of New Jersey it has cost your cause many votes," he warned. Fillmore, however, made no move to end the controversy. As for Kansas, where in 1855 and 1856 guerrilla warfare broke out between pro-slavery and anti-slavery forces, he failed to criticize the terrorist tactics of the pro-slavery forces but did criticize northerners who cried out against such tactics. This pro-southern approach contrasted sharply with the American party's platform in New Jersey, which condemned the Democrats for the bloodshed in Kansas.[28]

Defections also occurred on the conservative side. Some old-line New

Jersey Whigs, wary of Republicans and increasingly pessimistic about Fillmore's electoral chances, turned in desperation to the Democratic ticket. Fillmore himself became extremely cautious. Virtually silent on leading questions after late June, he remained an inattentive, inactive candidate. All in all, Fillmore's reputed political sense seemed to have deserted him altogether in 1856.[29]

Meanwhile, on the state level, the coalition of Opposition forces, which controlled the legislature in 1855, failed to enact any important legislation, such as nativist and temperance measures or an anti-Nebraska resolution. This lack of achievement was inauspicious for the Opposition's campaign for the legislature in the fall of 1855. Democrats clearly benefited from this disorganization, especially when Opposition candidates ran against each other in the same districts. Because of these factional divisions between nativists and nonnativists in the Opposition, Democratic candidates in the election of 1855 received a majority of the votes cast in 45 percent of assembly districts yet won 52 percent of assembly seats. For the session beginning in 1856 the Opposition lost control of the assembly because of a major reaction to the extreme temperance advocates and a minor reaction to the nativists. The stalemate between the parties continued.[30]

The Republican party in New Jersey began with a meeting in New Brunswick in the spring of 1855. A dozen prominent people from all parts of the state gathered in response to an invitation by Horace N. Congar, editor of the *Newark Mercury*. After agreeing on a policy of free soil for the West, the group decided to contact influential supporters in every county. Thirty of these individuals met a month later in Newark to organize the new party.

Organization bore fruit in 1856. The first statewide Republican convention met in April; at that time the delegates pledged to oppose the encroachment of slavery into the territories. The delegates specifically condemned the use of force and fraud in Kansas by pro-slavery outlaws who connived with the "weak and wicked" Pierce administration. The Republicans demanded that Kansas be admitted as a free state. Joseph C. Hornblower had a few months earlier expressed the general spirit of the delegates when he declared that the "cruel and accursed sin of human slavery shall never pollute another square foot of American soil." In late May, at another statewide meeting, the delegates decided to postpone nominating a gubernatorial candidate and naming presidential electors until they had united all factions of the Opposition.[31]

The Republican national convention met in Philadelphia in June. The new party, unfettered by tradition, could afford to take risks: in a combination of evident desperation and supposed inspiration, the party gambled on John C. Fremont, the legendary explorer of the West. An impulsive loner and political novice, Fremont appeared unqualified. Nevertheless, his dashing personality and his reputation as a national hero captivated the delegates.

In selecting their candidate for vice-president, the Republicans made a concerted appeal to voters in the closely balanced, critically important Mid-Atlantic states. The delegates chose New Jerseyan William Dayton in order to translate state pride into Republican votes. Dayton also could appeal to Pennsylvanians as a respectable moderate and a prominent Whig from a neighboring state. His candidacy appeared to make sense because the warring nativist factions in Pennsylvania could not agree on a native-son candidate, while Republicans and nativists on the national level failed to agree on a compromise candidate.[32]

Although the choice of Dayton seemed shrewd, his selection immediately became a problem. Pivotal Pennsylvania possessed twenty-seven electoral votes, the second largest number in the nation; New Jersey had only seven. In addition, Pennsylvania was the home of the Democratic presidential candidate. An available New Jerseyan was no substitute for a needed Pennsylvanian. Moreover, Dayton, who was not a nativist, had no special appeal to American party supporters, who craved a fellow party member for the vice-presidency.[33]

Later Fremont, trying to win the indispensable support of the North Americans, purportedly promised that their candidate for vice-president, a former Pennsylvania governor, would replace Dayton on the Republican ticket. Unfortunately, however, Fremont failed to ask Dayton to withdraw. When Dayton learned about this arrangement, he furiously refused to step down. In the end, neither the North Americans, the Pennsylvanians, nor even the Republicans selected the right running mate, because the Americans held the balance of power in both Pennsylvania and New Jersey in 1856.[34]

The Republican national platform concentrated on the prohibition of slavery in the federal territories, especially in Kansas. The strident tone of other planks, which attacked slavery and southern power, repelled moderate voters in the North. Such high-flown, heedless statements contrasted sharply with the deftness of those Republicans who outmaneuvered the die-hard nativists at their North American convention.[35]

Fremont's suitability for the presidency became a major campaign issue in New Jersey. Republicans tried hard to turn his inexperience to advantage. Unlike the other candidates, Republicans asserted, Fremont had not prostituted himself in the gutter of politics. Instead, he had been educated in the practical school of life; he knew the people and the country firsthand. Capitalizing on the popular fascination with a romanticized version of the West, Republicans emphasized Fremont's well-known exploits. Party journals portrayed him chasing buffalo, grappling with grizzlies, climbing mountains, crossing deserts, always pressing onward. Republicans portrayed Fremont as another heroic western president following in the footsteps of Jackson. Fremont would as president have the courage, will, and independence to stamp out corruption and aristocracy in Washington.[36]

Democrats dismissed Fremont on the grounds of his political inexperience; he had served only twenty-one days in Congress. Several Democratic critics regarded Dayton as the best lawyer in the state, a more experienced politician, and infinitely more qualified for the presidency than Fremont. The *Flemington Democrat* attacked Fremont's nomination as an attempt to make the issue "more personal than political. Principle will be abandoned for the sake of popularity." Democrats conceded that Fremont performed well as an intrepid explorer who gloried in eating mule steaks and grasshopper pies, but they joked about his most notable accomplishment—catching a bumblebee on the highest peak of the Rocky Mountains. In a more serious vein, they pointed out that on his western adventures, this soldier of fortune had revealed an impulsiveness that proved him unsuited for the presidency. A New Brunswicker summed up the Democratic case: "Fremont is nothing but a cow boy at most; and what he does know about politics is nothing." Fremont intended, he added with a racist twist, "to abolish slavery and have a horde of black rascals let loose upon us and have every negro equal to us."[37]

In June the Democrats held their national convention in Cincinnati. The Democracy needed solid support from the South as well as electoral votes from the southernmost states of the North if it was to retain the presidency. Clearly, too, Pierce, sponsor of the Kansas-Nebraska Act, had become a liability and a likely loser.

James Buchanan, from powerful Pennsylvania, appealed to the entire Mid-Atlantic region—the strategic battleground of the campaign. Not only did he come from the right place, he also fit the bill for the presidency. As an experienced bureaucrat, party war horse, and elder statesman, Buchanan, with his taciturn personality and his legalistic cast of mind, emanated respectability and soothing conservatism. Absent for years when he was ambassador to Britain, he had no involvement with the slavery controversy in Kansas. New Jersey's delegates backed him unanimously and enthusiastically. The Democrats nominated him at their national convention. In their platform they reaffirmed their policy of popular sovereignty in the territories. In an earlier speech, Buchanan had declared the Missouri Compromise "gone, and gone forever."[38]

The New Jersey Democrats praised their nominee. A Westfield man asserted that Buchanan "is the best man for the whole country." In the words of ex-governor Peter D. Vroom, "Mr. Buchanan is a tried man—a safe man. He has longer experience, and is fitted for the exigency of the times." As the *Trenton American* remarked, people regarded Buchanan as a "prudent, capable, and sagacious statesman, who will do nothing rashly." In such perilous times only he could save the Union from dissolution, settle the Kansas question, end sectional agitation.[39]

Republicans viewed Buchanan as the most formidable opponent the Democrats could have fielded, but still found him unfit for the presidency.

Although Buchanan had considerable public experience, he had no great achievement in statesmanship. Moreover, he had demonstrated unsound judgment in his reckless attempt to obtain Cuba in 1854 by drafting the Ostend Manifesto in order to create future slave states.

Throughout his career Buchanan always did his party's bidding. "Proverbially weak-backed," quipped the *Morristown Jerseyman,* this cold, calculating partisan sought only personal advancement. Also, he had become a tired, worn-out old man. Furthermore, in depending on the South for the bulk of his electoral votes, he would become its obliging servant. After all, he had pledged publicly to continue the discredited policy that Pierce pursued in Kansas. Buchanan, predicted the *Newark Advertiser,* "will be another Pierce, only worse—Pierce with compound interest added." Observers asked how Buchanan could succeed as president with that policy when Pierce had failed so miserably.[40]

Aside from the candidates and the platforms, several issues figured in the 1856 campaign in New Jersey. On May 22 a South Carolina congressman attacked anti-slavery senator Charles Sumner of Massachusetts with a cane and injured him severely. Republicans condemned the assault in the name of decency and free speech. One outraged New Jerseyan found "very little sympathy with demonstrations of Southern chivalry by revolver, bowie knife, or bludgeon." A Republican campaign motto at a Newark rally read: "We strike for Freedom—but not with a Cane." State Democrats played down the incident; they condemned it but criticized the speech of abrasive Sumner as provocative. They dismissed the affair as a purely personal quarrel, conveniently ignoring the fact that the attacker received support from southerners and had become a symbol of the militant South. For many Jersey Republicans, the assault unmistakably expressed slaveholders' aggressiveness.[41]

Meanwhile, the crisis in Kansas continued. Republican speakers and newspapermen throughout New Jersey hammered away at the theme of bleeding Kansas. Jersey Republicans pointed to the infringement of the rights of the free-state settlers in Kansas, summed up in the Republican campaign motto, "Free Soil, Free Labor, Free Speech, and Fremont." Tapping a rising current of anti-southern feeling, they pointed to an aggressive slaveholders' power as the source of the virtual reign of terror in Kansas against the Free-Soilers.[42]

Republicans not only denounced the atrocities of the pro-slavery forces, but sometimes also condemned southerners in general. Yet they said nothing about the cold-blooded, senseless slaughters committed by John Brown and his followers in Kansas. In a typical display of the emotions aroused by the plight of the Free-Soilers, Newark Baptist minister Henry C. Fish attacked those "infuriated fiends," who with "hands and lips red with blood" seized a "preacher of the gospel, and tie him to a log and throw him into the river; now they shoot a man at work in his field; now they break open the doors of quiet habitations, commit barbarities upon the women and children."[43]

Republicans lauded free labor for its benefits to whites. Countering Democratic claims that Republicans cared more about helping blacks than whites, the *Newton Register* asserted, "Republicans are called 'negro-worshipers'—a phrase entirely inappropriate. The Republican party is emphatically the white man's party. We want to have our territories filled up by white men—we prefer free labor to slave labor—we desire to dignify and exalt honest toil." The newspaper contended that whites should not be degraded morally or contaminated physically by association with lowly, malodorous blacks. Instead of "blackening our new territories with plantations of slaves," declared the editorial, Republicans "aim to brighten them with the homesteads of white freemen forever."[44]

Democrats responded defensively. At the outset, many Democratic journalists and politicians dismissed as exaggerations the reports of violence by pro-slavery ruffians in Kansas. They claimed that Republican propagandists were making Kansas bleed for political purposes. If abolitionists stopped their incessant agitation about the slavery question, the fuss over Kansas would end immediately. Although some Democrats admitted the occurrence of terroristic incidents, they claimed that these took place only because armed Yankee fanatics goaded pro-slavery men into action.

A few Democratic newspapers, however, confessed dismay at the continuing lawlessness in Kansas. Even while they criticized the Republicans for their lurid propaganda and condemned the reckless methods of the free staters, the *Belvidere Journal* and the *New Brunswick News*, for example, conceded that the pro-slavery side in Kansas had enacted outrageously unfair laws to rig elections. Indeed, the editor of the *News* admitted, "We hate slavery," and pledged to use all constitutional means to block its extension. Many Democratic papers claimed, in the words of the *Trenton American*, that Democrats were "the only true and reliable friends of freedom in Kansas, in Massachusetts, or anywhere else."[45]

Democrats claimed sectionalism to be the very life's blood of the Republicans. They denounced Republicans as disunionists because Republicans elevated the slavery question above all others in order to arouse northern animosity toward southerners, so as to gain power with exclusively northern votes. The Republican *Newark Mercury* observed: "One great objection to the Republican Party, which, in the minds of the Buchaniers, seems to over top all others, is that it is a sectional organization" which pursues an "aggressive and oppressive policy against the South." If the narrowly sectional Republicans won, Democrats warned, they would inaugurate policies that would exacerbate sectional disputes and soon would cause civil war. Only the broadly national Democratic party could keep the Union intact, because it bridged competing views and promoted fraternal feeling between the North and the South.[46]

Candidate Dayton countered that the repeal of the Missouri Compromise and, "as a consequence, the extension of Slavery, are not issues raised by us; they are issues forced upon us, and we act but in self-defense when we repel them. That section of the country which presents these issues is responsible for them; and it is this sectionalism which has subverted past compromises, and now seeks to force Slavery into Kansas." Congressman Pennington argued that southern Democrats had only themselves to blame when northerners worried about the "bad faith of the South. It is an issue in which the South, with the Democratic party as its ally, are united on one side, and the opposition in the North must be united on the other."[47]

To the Democratic claim that Fremont was "a sectional candidate," Ephraim Marsh, a prominent convert to the Republican cause from nativist ranks, responded, "This is neither his fault nor the fault of those who support him." After all, he maintained, the extension of slavery beyond its previous boundary figured as a national question. "If, as in the repeal of that compromise, national compacts were violated, may not the people seek national redress?"[48]

Responding to the negative appeal of the campaign, a Woodbury resident suggested that the "feeling is so strong against the doings of the present administration and the Cincinnati platform that the opposition is strengthening more from hatred of them both than for love to the principles of either the Republican or American Parties." Republicans reminded anti-southern New Jerseyans that for too long the ruling circles of the South in Washington had held the upper hand over the North, although the South constituted a minority in the nation's population. Republicans rallied an increasingly solid North in opposition to pro-southern Democratic policies and the slaveholding oligarchy's power.[49]

Thus, each side castigated the other as the party of sectionalism. In truth, however, both represented sectional approaches to a national problem. New Jersey Republicans correctly characterized the Democracy as sectional because since 1854 the Democrats had advanced solely southern interests by repealing the Missouri Compromise and doing nothing to stop the disorder in Kansas. The *Mercury* pointed out that it "was the South that nominated James Buchanan, and it is in the lap of the South that he has placed himself, with pledges of eternal constancy, and promises of unswerving loyalty. Where is the Buchanier in New Jersey or elsewhere, who will deny that Buchanan relies for his election upon Southern votes, or that his party does not sympathize in the contest now upon us, with Southern policy?"[50]

New Jersey Democrats, however, also demonstrated correctly that Republicans championed only northern interests and had exclusively Yankee supporters. The Republican party appealed to no voters in the slave states. Both political organizations represented sectional parties; both promoted sectional issues.

Because of the "imminent danger" that Kansas would be "made a slave

State" if Democrats regained control of Congress, New Jersey Republicans regarded the races for the House of Representatives as vitally important. In addition, the next legislature would elect a federal senator. To maintain its majority in the House, the Opposition in the state needed to summon all its strength and unity. Yet because each wing of the Opposition was conducting a rival presidential campaign and sniping at the other, trouble loomed as the presidential campaign came to overshadow the congressional races.[51]

Despite such divisions, the combined Opposition in southern and central New Jersey mounted unified campaigns as the "friends of freedom" by nominating the same candidate in each congressional district. Each party, Republican and American, held a separate convention and unanimously renominated the incumbent Opposition congressman, who would "uphold the banner of Free Kansas in the great struggle now upon us."[52]

Unity remained elusive in North Jersey, however. In the fourth district, the Gibraltar of the Democracy, the Opposition bungled the contest. The Republicans nominated their own candidate and declined to agree on a candidate in combination with the Americans. Then the nativists, in a huff, also put their own nominee in the field. By failing to unite behind a common candidate, the two groups handed the seat to the Democrats. Similarly, in the fifth district, Republicans renominated incumbent Pennington. He refused to run, partly because the nativists, acting out of pique, did not back him. Instead they nominated their own candidate, thus virtually assuring defeat. The Democrats, for their part, clung to the national party line and hoped Buchanan's coattails would carry their congressional nominees to victory. Although the best potential Democratic candidates declined the nomination in the stoutly anti-Democratic first district, the Democrats elsewhere fielded strong candidates, who tried to stem what they considered the fierce tide of fanaticism and sectionalism.[53]

The Opposition fared better in the gubernatorial nomination. In a shrewd maneuver, the leaders of the Opposition convened on June 4, before the Republican and the North American national conventions met to choose their presidential nominees in mid-June. The timing represented a concerted effort by the Opposition to forge a unified state campaign before rival national campaigns could jeopardize chances of success in other contests. The members of the convention agreed to oppose both state and national Democratic policies. Steering clear of all divisive questions, the delegates prepared a short but emphatic platform. They promised to replace Democratic waste, mismanagement, and corruption with economy and honesty in state government. They denounced the violation of rights in Kansas and backed a change of leadership in both Washington and Trenton.

The convention chose the man who could best unite the two wings of the Opposition in the state: William A. Newell, an Allentown physician. Newell commanded the support of the Americans as one of their number. He also won Republican support as a former Whig; earlier as a congressman and now as gubernatorial candidate, he strongly opposed the expansion of slavery in the West. Newell's political moderation and his suave, friendly personality made him an ideal candidate to lead the disparate coalition, which he dubbed the " 'Opposition party' of New Jersey." Also, as a former congressman, Newell had helped establish the federal lifesaving service, so vital to the people on the Jersey shore, and this achievement enhanced his candidacy.[54]

Newell's nomination drew praise even from some Democratic newspapers. The *Flemington Democrat* conceded that the various factions of the combined Opposition had united on Newell "even beyond their own expectations." The neutral *Hightstown Record* suggested that the Opposition "could not have selected a stronger man, and it will take a fleet nag to beat him." The *Trenton American*, however, scoffed at the whole movement: "Never before has there been a political party organized as a mere opposition party, without any principle but 'opposition,' and with no other name than 'opposition.'"[55]

Just as many Democrats respected Newell, so did the Opposition think well of William C. Alexander, whom the Democrats selected on August 6 as their gubernatorial candidate. Although Alexander was a staunch Democrat and their strongest possible adversary, the Opposition regarded him as an able lawyer and an experienced legislator. Democrats praised the choice; one enthusiastic journal nicknamed him "Alexander the Great." Democrats emphasized Alexander's record in helping people qualify more easily to vote and to receive public education. This populist stance made Alexander, who lived in Princeton and had an aristocratic air, more appealing to the common folk.[56]

The New Jersey Democrats in their platform lauded popular sovereignty yet did not endorse explicitly the Kansas-Nebraska Act, as the national platform had. Jersey Democrats even proclaimed that they personally did not espouse "slavery in any form."[57]

The outcome of the presidential campaign depended on whether the anti-Democratic forces could forge an alliance to win the state's electoral vote, but making common cause proved difficult. After the presidential race became a triangular contest between Buchanan, Fremont, and Fillmore, each branch of the Opposition felt obliged to support its own candidate.

Members of the Opposition offered various proposals to present a common slate of presidential electors. Leaders in both wings engaged in serious negotiations during September, but stubborn partisans on both sides insisted on separate electoral tickets. In October negotiators again tried unsuccessfully to devise a single electoral ticket. Some enthusiasts in each camp greatly overestimated their own side's ability to win on its own. Moreover, ideological purists in both parties, equating compromise with corruption of their ideals and finding any alliance an entangling one, disdained horse-trading for mere political expediency. Mutual distrust, recriminations, and personal quarrels also undermined negotiations. A Salem County man observed the irony in the squabbling "of two parties which (without much apparent cause) were so embittered against each other."[58]

To some overzealous Republicans, the effort to neutralize Fillmore became more important than stopping Buchanan. Yet they still considered that federal policy in Kansas represented the supreme calamity for the country and the North. If elected, Buchanan assuredly would have much greater potential, with congressional party allies, to persist with this catastrophic policy. Some overwrought Americans could not abide Fremont's alleged Catholicism and his supposed disunionism, which made him more dangerous than Buchanan in their minds. American leader and editor Charles D. Deshler epitomized the reluctance to join forces when he wrote to Fillmore of "our determination to stand by our colors" regardless of the consequences. From the beginning Deshler described himself as "bitterly opposed to any agreement" with the Republicans to form a common electoral ticket. Even though he believed that a coalition ticket "would give us the electoral vote of the State," he feared that such a ticket might damage Fillmore's prospects elsewhere.[59]

Yet at one point in the feverish negotiations, Opposition leaders in fact had reached an agreement on a combined electoral ticket. Deshler deliberately sabotaged it, however, when he insisted that he had to consult first with local Americans to ascertain their wishes. Having gained time, Deshler behind the scenes "sounded the alarm throughout our entire State." At the very last minute the Americans rejected the compromise package, exactly as Deshler had intended all along. Camden lawyer and Republican leader Thomas H. Dudley stated that Deshler and his cronies had decided "to rule or ruin." In the end, fusion was scuttled by their evident political immaturity and their power to veto any agreement as an independent party. They showed themselves to be genuine Know-Nothings. Thus New Jersey's Opposition continued to field two different electoral tickets, one for Fremont and the other for Fillmore.[60]

The nature of each party's coalition also had worked against fusion. Republicans desperately needed immigrant recruits in the northeastern part of the state, but nativists maligned them. Thus the sharpest disagreements between the Americans and the Republicans occurred where the greatest tensions between the native-born and the foreign-born existed. Immigrants naturally regarded American partisans as their enemies and warned Republicans not to negotiate with them. Some Germans, who had championed the Republican cause in the late spring, named their own candidate for governor in the middle of October to protest the coalition's nomination of nativist Newell. As the campaign built to a frenzied pitch, Republicans became incensed when nativist rowdies disrupted Republican rallies and American editorials crudely attacked Fremont. American partisans simultaneously were infuriated by Republican denunciations of Fillmore as a doughface, and of nativists as bigots.[61]

Rival presidential and congressional campaigns undercut the Opposition's campaign for other offices. The disarray almost jeopardized the gubernatorial campaign in North Jersey and assumed statewide proportions when many legislative contests pitted Americans against both Republicans and Democrats. Many Republicans complained that the expected deal, whereby Republican votes would be secured for nativist Newell in return for American votes for Fremont's electors, was backfiring. Dayton accused the nativists of promising coalition but then breaking bargains. As retribution, some Republicans vowed not to vote for Newell, but the Republicans had no time to launch a separate gubernatorial campaign. The opportunistic nativists stayed behind Newell and united with the Republicans in the lesser but more compelling goal of winning state power for the sake of patronage. Moreover, the October elections in neighboring Pennsylvania had gone badly for the Republicans. Dispirited, the New Jersey Republicans gave up the fight, knowing Fremont had no chance. As the Fremont campaign steadily lost ground in the last weeks, Dayton knew he would lose, and he complained bitterly about his inability to swing his own state into the Republican column.[62]

"Great strife but good humor" prevailed on Election Day in New Jersey. The fierce contest brought a huge turnout of voters: 77.5 percent, the highest proportion in the decade before 1860. Buchanan won New Jersey's electoral vote, but received only 47 percent of the popular vote. He carried the entire state except for Camden, Gloucester, and Cape May, which went for Fillmore, and Ocean, which Fremont won. Buchanan succeeded because the larger ranks of the Opposition remained divided; they were split almost evenly between support for Fremont, with 29 percent, and Fillmore, with 24 percent. The Opposition had defeated itself.[63]

In the nation at large, Buchanan became a minority president, winning only 45 percent of the popular vote but 59 percent of the electoral college because of the divided opposition. Ominously, every slave state except Maryland, which supported Fillmore, backed Buchanan. Every state in the upper North supported Fremont. In the lower North, however, five states, including New Jersey, supported Buchanan by extremely narrow margins of the popular vote. Among those states, New Jersey showed the second smallest (behind Illinois) percentage of support for Buchanan. Pierce, by contrast, had won New Jersey by almost 53 percent in 1852.[64]

In congressional contests the Democrats regained two seats by taking the third and fifth districts. The Opposition scored a notable victory in winning the governorship. Newell won narrowly by 2,557 votes (51 percent) out of a total 99,049 cast, faring proportionally much better than the previous Whig candidate. The Democrats, however, retained control of the legislature, in part because Americans and Republicans ran against each other in many assembly districts. Thus Democratic candidates received most of the votes cast in only twenty-five districts. Yet they won thirty-eight districts.[65]

The Republicans suffered not merely defeat but demoralization. The *Newark Mercury* regarded the debacle as a "blow to freedom of the direst portent," and Republicans blamed the result on a few die-hard nativist leaders. Overall the divided Opposition lost the presidential race, two congressional seats, the legislature, and the federal senatorship. United, the Opposition elected Newell governor and held on to two congressional seats. The *Newton Register* declared that if the forces of the Opposition failed to unite, "the ultraists, honest and dishonest, who have already had too much to do with shaping the course of both branches of the Opposition, shall continue to exert a disastrous influence upon our counsels. It is high time for the moderate, practical men in the ranks of the Opposition to take the lead, and bring 'order out of the confusion' which has too long reigned supreme." Yet the election results suggested that many matters still divided the Opposition.[66]

Republicans, too, shared blame for the outcome. Their choice of the underqualified Fremont caused insuperable problems. Looking back, one Newarker regarded Fremont "as a boy on a man's errand." At the very least, Republicans should have chosen a Pennsylvania American for vice-president. Moreover, the Republicans' single-minded concentration on narrowly sectionalist themes diminished an already narrow base of support. To moderates, this rhetoric made credible the Democrats' charges of Republican sectionalism, disunionism, and abolitionism. Finally, Republican organization in many counties remained inefficient or nonexistent. The *New York Tribune* summed up as "disastrous" the conduct and the outcome of the national election in New Jersey.[67]

New Jersey and the other states of the lower North did not experience the complete realignment of the parties that occurred in the upper North. The furor over Sumner's caning, and bleeding Kansas, did not drum up additional recruits in moderate ranks. Nativists voted mostly for American candidate Fillmore; Democrats backed Old Buck. In the 1856 congressional elections, only 4 percent of the Democrats of 1854 crossed party lines to join the Opposition. This changing by Democrats to the Republican side was only one-fourth as great as the crossover of the Opposition to the Democrats. Some defectors of 1854 returned to the Democracy in 1856, evidently because they regarded the Republicans as too radical or the Americans as too Whiggish. In the first three congressional districts, where the Whig-nativist coalition had existed in 1854, the voters returned to the Democratic fold. Only in the fourth and fifth districts did Democrats cross over, perhaps either in a belated completion of the first phase of the realignment that had occurred elsewhere in 1854 or possibly because of the distinctly Republican congressional campaigns in those districts in 1856.[68]

In the nation at large, the precipitous fall of nativism mocked its rapid rise. Originally it succeeded because of its ability to exploit local discontent and dissension while remaining neutral on the broader issue of slavery. Yet when its leaders tried to operate a national political party and to take national stands, internal division destroyed the movement. Without the earlier secrecy and flexibility, and above all without the freedom to remain neutral on national slavery issues, the American party was mortally weakened as southern and northern Americans attacked each other.

In New Jersey, contradictory developments buffeted the American movement. The 1856 election returns showed strong voter support for the American party. New Jersey registered the highest percentage, except for California, of popular support for Fillmore in the North. The party received strong backing in the first and fifth districts, and also in Middlesex and Monmouth, as the Americans successfully exploited the continuing tension between immigrants and natives. Thus, after the election, the state American party did not decline immediately, as the national American party did. Because relatively few votes separated the Democrats and the two branches of the Opposition, both in statewide races and in control of the legislature, American voters still controlled the balance of power in New Jersey.

The strength of the American party in the state was more apparent than real, however. The lack of party unity, strong leadership, and tangible achievement in the legislature undercut the state party's appeal, and scattered hoodlum tactics further discredited the movement. In addition, New Jerseyans had not all voted for Fillmore for the same reasons. Fillmore had appealed not only to nativists but also to nonnativists who feared sectionalism. Hard-core nativists still led the state party but failed to convert the mass of Fillmore's supporters to their views. The latter voters counted themselves as nationalists and moderates rather than as nativists and extremists. If faced with alternatives, they would abandon the American party or favor coalition with the Republicans.[69]

State Democrats greeted Buchanan's election with relief. The *Belvidere Journal* exclaimed: "We feel as if a heavy load were lifted from us—a dread of great but unknown danger brushed away." The widespread fear of political extremism, sectional strife, and national suicide disappeared. Many Democrats believed that Buchanan's elevation to the presidency assured the stability of the Union and the supremacy of the Constitution. The *Flemington Democrat* added a racial dimension by declaring in a headline, "The People Have Spoken And white man decided good as nigger!" According to the Democrats, Buchanan's victory assured a bright future for the territories. The *Somerville Messenger* expected Buchanan quickly to settle the question of slavery in the territories ("we believe all will be free"), thus ending the mission and the existence of the sectionally divisive Republican party.[70]

Republicans and a few Democrats, however, worried about the future. The

Republican *Newark Advertiser* remained skeptical of Buchanan's intentions. "Will he, can he make Kansas a slave State? Will he dare to do it? This remains to be seen." Trenton Democrat Stacy G. Potts similarly predicted that the next few years would provide only a temporary respite: "The termination of our great political struggle has given a new lease of four years at least to the Union. Whether 'true sober second thought' will, at the end of that time, rescue us from the vortex into which we are rushing is yet to be seen." James Wall of Burlington, the unsuccessful Democratic congressional candidate, observed even more pessimistically that all the "elements of fanaticism are still grumbling like the pent up fires of the volcano. They will burst forth in the next presidential struggle and carry devastation in their pathway."[71]

# 2 Precarious Balance, 1857–1859

After the setbacks of 1856, the Republicans and the Americans began painstakingly to rebuild their coalition. The Opposition benefited from the evenhanded patronage of Governor Newell. The Democrats interfered when they could; because they held a majority in the legislature, they blocked some appointments. Newell, however, succeeded in appointing Republican William Dayton as attorney general and American Charles Perrin Smith to the lucrative clerkship of the state supreme court. Nevertheless, division in Opposition ranks persisted.[1]

Events outside New Jersey started to arouse Republicans within the state. The issue of slavery in the federal territories assumed greater urgency in March of 1857, when the United States Supreme Court handed down the Dred Scott decision. The court ruled that Congress lacked the constitutional authority to exclude slavery from the territories. Thus, without political prudence or institutional self-restraint, the nation's highest court, under southern control, brought federal governance to a bizarre juncture. The justices denied Congress, no longer under southern sway, the traditional right to govern the federal territories and to regulate slavery there.

Reaction to the decision was intensely partisan. The supremely confident Democratic *Trenton American* immediately wrote the obituary of the Opposition: "This puts a quietus on black republicanism." Because the court supposedly had disposed permanently of the slavery question, agitation by northerners would serve no purpose. The Republican *Newark Advertiser* disputed this prediction and condemned the political coup. The justices deliberately had handed down a sweepingly pro-southern opinion to "strike the thorn of slavery deeper and deeper into the loins of the people of the North."[2]

Meanwhile a sharp, if short-lived, depression occurred in 1857. With the Democrats controlling the federal government, bad economic times probably would favor the Opposition. Nevertheless, Democrats won the legislative elections in 1857. Despite losing a few seats, they increased their share of the popular vote. Their continued strength and the local character of the campaign made the Dred Scott decision seem unimportant to those not already in the Republican camp. In contrast to the Democrats, the Opposition ran a lackluster campaign. The various branches of the Opposition nominated either rival tickets or no candidates. In Middlesex County, for instance, the two wings of the Opposition formed a union, but the "putty wouldn't stick." Turnout plummeted, especially for the Americans.[3]

The thorn of slavery penetrated still deeper into northern flesh in December 1857, when Buchanan surrendered to the South by sacrificing Kansas. Hoping to end chaos and escape political embarrassment, he requested Congress to admit Kansas to the Union as a slave state. In effect he accepted the pro-slavery constitution—the product of unrepresentative voter registration, a fraudulent election, and a packed convention held in Lecompton, Kansas. In his disturbing message on Kansas in February 1858, Buchanan hid behind the letter of the law and its technical forms, deliberately ignoring the Lecompton swindle as he glossed over or falsified the facts. Buchanan had broken his promise to the people of Kansas that they would have an opportunity to vote on the entire constitution; the Lecompton convention refused to submit the full document to the voters. The *Advertiser* denounced as infamous the "attempt in this free country to force down the throats of the people a government and a constitution, which most of them detested."

As soon as Buchanan endorsed the Lecompton constitution, Douglas opposed this violation of majority rule. Douglas, up for reelection in Illinois, organized a coalition in Congress to reject the constitution. Thus, Douglas, previously cursed by New Jersey's Republicans as a traitorous devil for promoting the Kansas-Nebraska Act, became a patriotic hero virtually overnight for opposing the Lecompton constitution. Not only Republicans but also Americans and anti-Lecompton Democrats joined the indignation against Buchanan's action. Their unity spurred greater organization and coordination among Opposition forces in New Jersey.

Buchanan persisted, bringing to bear party pressure, federal patronage, and presidential power on recalcitrant members of Congress. As with the Kansas-Nebraska Act, conservative Democratic senators John Thomson and William Wright consistently supported Buchanan's policy. On March 23, 1858, the Democratic, pro-southern Senate approved the Lecompton constitution.

In the northern-oriented House of Representatives a bipartisan bloc of Republicans and some northern anti-Buchanan Democrats rejected Buchanan's proposal in early April. In the voting, two New Jersey Democrats, John Huyler and Jacob R. Wortendycke of the fourth and fifth districts, respectively, supported Buchanan at every stage. Democrat Garnett B. Adrain of the third district did not, however, thus becoming the only Douglas Democrat in the state's delegation. Opposition members Isaiah Clawson and George Robbins consistently opposed Buchanan's position.

On April 30 the deadlock in Congress finally was broken by a compromise measure calling for settlers in Kansas to vote on the Lecompton constitution as a whole. If it was rejected, statehood would be delayed. This measure, face-saving for Buchanan and the southerners, could not disguise the fact that their attempt to make Kansas a slave state had failed.[4]

While Congress argued about the Lecompton constitution, the legislature in Trenton also grappled with the issue. In mid-January 1858 two downstate

Democrats, Charles Mickle and John L. Sharp, stunned party conservatives by introducing resolutions denouncing the Lecompton constitution and requesting that the state's congressional delegation reject admission of Kansas until Kansans had the opportunity to review the constitution. These resolutions transformed the private restiveness of many state Democrats into open rebellion. Pro-Buchanan newspapers immediately denounced the dissident Democrats for challenging the prerogatives of Congress and meddling in federal affairs. Legislators, they declared, should concern themselves strictly with state matters. Buchanan's forces counterattacked, pressuring state Democrats to toe the party line.

The Douglas Democrats refused to back down, and on February 4 the assembly weakened the resolutions only cosmetically. Instead of instructing the state's delegation, the legislature merely recommended it to oppose statehood for Kansas under the Lecompton constitution. The resolutions expressed confidence in Buchanan's patriotism and statesmanship, but in effect cast a vote of no confidence in his Kansas policy. As the Republican *Newark Mercury* described the double-faced maneuver, it seemed "proper to smile, when putting a dagger under the fifth rib."[5]

The key resolution denounced the Lecompton constitution as contrary to the principles of self-government and urged its rejection. The assembly approved this resolution by a bipartisan vote of 41 to 17. On this important vote the Democrats were divided evenly; Buchanan's supporters were recruited almost exclusively from North Jersey, especially from Monmouth, Essex, Hunterdon, and Bergen. The Douglas Democrats received support from South Jersey, but hailed mainly from North Jersey, particularly from the fourth and fifth congressional districts. Reflecting the strong current of public opinion, one Sussex politician informed Douglas: "Three quarters of the Democrats of our County are anti-Lecompton." On February 9 the more conservative senate, in which few members were up for reelection in the fall, tried to strangle the anti-Lecompton resolutions by referring them to a committee. In the closing hours of the session the senate considered the resolutions and killed them.[6]

Nevertheless, the assembly had voiced its opinion and supported censure. Buchanan in 1858, like Douglas in 1854, received a rebuke from some New Jerseyans. As the *Mercury* observed, "New Jersey is thus placed on the record as repudiating and condemning the Lecompton fraud. We are glad that the democrats of New Jersey cannot be dragooned."[7]

While the debate over the Lecompton constitution raged in both Washington and Trenton, New Jerseyans expressed strong opinions about the momentous issues at stake. Maverick Adrain observed, "It is clear beyond all dispute that the Lecompton constitution does not employ the will of the people of Kansas, but is against that will." Adrain went on to reflect that "no constitution which does not express or reflect the will of the people is really republican in its true sense and meaning. . . . All written constitutions are supposed to express their will, and if they do not, they are a cheat and fraud upon the rights of the people."

In a second argument, Adrain countered Buchanan's advice to fellow Democrats to lie low; in the words of an editorial in the anti-Buchanan *Newton Herald*, "We are now told we 'must hold still'—to prevent a rupture in the party. . . . we must pretend that 'all is right'—when we know it is 'all wrong.'" As Adrain pointed out, "I am not in favor of agitation. We have had enough of it, but in my opinion agitation can never be put down by any attempt to stifle the people's voice, and override the great principle of popular sovereignty. This would only have the effect to increase that agitation and render it more universal and dangerous."[8]

New Jerseyans also worried that if southern forces could resort to force and fraud in Kansas, and thus repudiate free elections, the same thing could happen elsewhere in the territories. New Jerseyans wished for a fair and lasting settlement of the Kansas question before it was too late. Otherwise the repeal of the Missouri Compromise would become, according to the *Advertiser*, the "real Pandora's Box from which has sprung and will spring on the admission of every new State, a desperate battle on the question of slavery."[9]

During the spring of 1858, when elections for Congress began in earnest, prospects for New Jersey's Opposition brightened. Having learned that self-imposed divisions brought defeat, leading Americans and Republicans began to reach a consensus and strengthen their coalition. The Americans, worried about illegal voting, especially by immigrants, were pleased by the proposal to enact more effective laws qualifying people to vote and mandating that ballots be counted properly. At a time of a severe depression, the call for a tariff to protect home industry increased support. The strongest point of the Opposition's message declared opposition to Buchanan's Kansas policy and upheld the principle that the will of the people must prevail in forming a constitution for a new state. Thus both the proscriptive themes of nativists and the harsh anti-slavery demands of radical Republicans became muted. This broad platform appealed to anti-Lecompton Democrats, to Americans, and to Republicans. It endorsed, as they termed it, a union formed for the sake of the Union.[10]

The Opposition's planning and organization also improved. The energetic Republican state executive committee, in an early effort in May, canvassed county leaders about local prospects and requested suggestions for a statewide strategy. Creation of a state executive committee for the entire Opposition also led to greater cohesion. To advertise the movement, anti-Buchanan publications received subsidies. Politicians also suggested new names for the Opposition, such as Union party, Union Opposition party, National party, and People's party. Most important, the Americans and the Republicans generally agreed to unite behind common candidates. The Opposition selected strong contenders and mounted harmonious, enthusiastic, skillfully managed campaigns.[11]

As before, the Democrats tried to exploit divisions within the Opposition. The search for trouble elsewhere, however, could not conceal the disharmony within Democratic ranks. Discord prevailed not only among the politicians but also among some of the molders of public opinion, specifically the editors of several influential county weeklies. For varying lengths of time such important journals as Morris R. Hamilton's *Newton Herald*, Louis C. Vogt's *Morristown Banner*, Augustus Green's *Trenton Democrat*, and Isaac W. Mickle's *Camden Democrat* joined in an open revolt against Buchanan's Lecompton policy, as did the *Hackettstown Gazette*, the *Salem Sunbeam*, and the *Bordentown Register*. At first, pro-Buchanan newspapers, such as the *Trenton American* and the *Newark Journal*, denied the existence of any differences over Kansas. Then they conceded disagreements but declared that such disputes would not divide the party, because they related merely to means rather than to ends. After Congress adjourned and the campaign began in earnest, these Democrats asserted that such differences no longer mattered.

As elections neared, the *American* predicted hollowly that the "Democracy of New Jersey will be a unit at the coming election, and stronger than ever before." The nation, declared Democrats, required Buchanan's steady hand, because if the Republicans won control of Congress the South would secede from the Union. The Democrats added an economic threat, predicting that if Republicans seized control, southerners would stop purchasing New Jersey's manufactures. Unemployment and hardship would follow.[12]

Rounding out their arguments with the usual racist appeal, the Democrats accused Republicans of elevating blacks over whites. According to an editorial in the *Journal*, "We scotched the nigger in 1856, let us smoke him out in 1858, so that he may not again appear in this vicinity." At the same time Democrats once again condemned the Opposition for talking about change but opposing every measure of genuine reform in the legislature.[13]

Throughout the campaign the Opposition outpaced the Democrats. The contest in the first district illustrated the reduction in the role of the hardcore nativists. The anti-Democratic coalition required a moderate American candidate in a constituency with nativist strength, but such a man had to be acceptable to Republicans. This requirement marked a sea change from the 1854 campaign, when the nativists presented the Opposition with a fait accompli. The Opposition first shrewdly selected John T. Nixon, a Bridgeton lawyer and a former legislator. Then Nixon's supporters and opponents attempted to pack the American convention. When Nixon's opponents, nativist dissidents, failed to block his endorsement, they defected and nominated Camden nativist journalist John H. Jones. Jones, the leader of the so-called

Stockton Americans, pleased neither Republicans nor many Americans. Such a separate nomination by dissident nativists probably would once have proved fatal to the Opposition, but this was no longer the case.

Single Opposition conventions in other districts nominated popular candidates, such as Mount Holly lawyer John L. N. Stratton in the second district and William Pennington of Newark, a lawyer and the former governor, in the fifth district. These two candidates, former Whigs, now espoused Republicanism. Opposition declarations emphasized Kansas and reiterated the state platform.

In return for American support of Republican nominees in these constituencies, Americans received plums in the form of local nominations. The coalition did not always enjoy smooth sailing, however, although it remained intact. One American denounced Republican tactics in Burlington County's convention. "The 'Republicans' take the meat," he declared, "and leave the bone for the 'Americans.' I tell you the 'Americans' are very sore at the way they have been used."[14]

As the campaign progressed, some Democrats tried to dodge the Kansas issue. Several Democrats, hoping to divert attention from it, blamed Republicans for exacerbating sectional strife. The Democratic congressional candidates generally avoided the Lecompton dispute in major speeches. Even the second district's conservative candidate, James Wall, did not mention the matter of Kansas in his acceptance letter. Democrats frequently defended the right of dissent but urged unified support for the party's nominees. Unlike Democratic candidates downstate, the nominee in the third district approved Buchanan's course in Kansas. Democrats renominated Lecomptonite incumbent Huyler. Similarly, in the fifth district, Democrats again chose Wortendycke. Wortendycke pronounced Buchanan's Kansas policy a success, prompting the *Advertiser* to ask, if rejection of every Kansas measure proposed by Buchanan added up to a success, what in the name of heaven constituted a failure?[15]

Evasion characterized the platform planks on Kansas in most district conventions. Democrats called for a lawful constitution in Kansas but avoided discussion of how to accomplish this—the heart of the dispute. In the strongly anti-administration first district, for example, the Democratic platform made no reference to Kansas. The relevant plank for the second district, for instance, endorsed any constitution Kansans formed "in their own way," a statement that naturally invited contradictory interpretations. The platform of the third district convention likewise brushed aside all minor differences on Kansas, as it termed them, and supported regular admission of the territory, whatever that meant. The fourth district's platform echoed that of the third, but in a less partisan and less argumentative fashion. In a unique departure, the platform in the fifth district both explicitly endorsed the administration's handling of Kansas and ambiguously championed the will of the majority in Kansas.

Democratic infighting grew especially fierce in the heavily Democratic third and fourth districts. When anti-Lecompton Democrats drummed up support, Buchanan's supporters at first dismissed them as an inconsequential band of disappointed office seekers and spoilers. "There was a good deal of smoke for so little fire," remarked the *Somerville Messenger*. Buchanan's men, however, began to take the defections more seriously when Douglas Democrats bolted both regular Democratic conventions. The bolters then organized separate conventions; they nominated Jetur R. Riggs, a Paterson doctor, in the fourth district and anti-Lecompton Democratic incumbent Adrain in the third district. These nominees received the support of Opposition forces in both districts.

By fall the weighty political dispute among Democrats had become a bitter family feud. Faced with a rebellion, Buchanan's forces tried to whip dissidents into line by firing anti-Lecompton postmasters and replacing unfriendly newspaper editors. Douglas's men resisted such pressure, denouncing Buchanan as a puppet to his southern masters and a traitor to the party's platform of popular sovereignty. Throwing down the gauntlet, they declared their independence of presidential policy and party edicts.[16]

Regular Democrats upbraided these dissidents and read them out of the party. One Warren County man frowned on "those of the party, who for selfish purposes, turned traitors . . . by the 'aid and comfort' they gave to the enemy." The *New Brunswick News* lashed out at the duplicity of the anti-Lecompton forces, who continued to consider themselves Democrats while aligning with the Opposition. Buchanan's loyalists viewed the congressional campaign as a struggle for the very existence of the Union, which only the Democratic party could keep intact. Such defection depressed some moderate leaders of the state party. Peter Vroom lamented that Democratic division was "as unnecessary as it is unnatural and virulent."[17]

A visitor in Sussex County found the campaign "beats anything they ever had there." The contest in this Democratic bastion took an unsettling turn when some of the most prominent Democrats in the county defected. Martin Ryerson, dubbed "the Douglas of New Jersey," became the leader of the state's dissidents; his name and judgment commanded attention and respect in all political circles throughout the state. An able Newton lawyer and state supreme court judge until he resigned to participate in the campaign, Ryerson had grown disenchanted with southern demands.[18]

The platform of the anti-Lecompton convention repudiated "as anti-republican and monarchical" the notion that Democrats must give up the right of judging for themselves whether the measures of a particular administration agreed with true Democratic principles. The defectors refused to "blindly acquiesce in all its measures, or be denounced as traitors to the party." In another plank they pledged to "resist the arrogance of Southern dictators."[19]

Ryerson and others stumped the county almost daily, mobilizing support for Riggs. One incident revealed the raw feeling in the campaign. While addressing a public meeting, Ryerson saw a skunk thrown at his feet. He remarked that it was the strongest argument the Democrats had advanced in the entire campaign! Meanwhile the Republican *Trenton Gazette* declared that defeat of pro-Lecompton candidates would "be a warning to the tribe of doughfaces in this State."[20]

Sowing the wind, Buchanan reaped the whirlwind. On November 2, 1858, northern voters cast a vote of no confidence in both Buchanan's presidency and his policy. His forces lost control of the House of Representatives. In New Jersey, Democratic, American, and Republican voters supported anti-Lecompton candidates. As Ryerson observed, "We have succeeded beyond our most sanguine expectations." The Opposition in the state fared even better than in 1854; it defeated every pro-Lecompton candidate for Congress. New Jerseyans sent three Republicans and two anti-Lecompton Democrats to Washington. Jersey's Opposition apparently had secured enough votes in the legislature to elect the next United States senator as well. New Jersey now stood in the front ranks of the reformists.[21]

The newspapers were quick to respond to the change. The *Advertiser* announced a revolution in state politics. "The State of New Jersey is essentially an Opposition State," declared the *Mercury*. The *Morristown Jerseyman* stated that Lecomptonism now was "crushed out!!" The headlines of the *Flemington Republican* summarized the meaning of the election returns: "*The Administration Rebuked! New Jersey Redeemed.*" An editorial in the *New York Herald* observed, "Lecompton, it appears, has settled the business for New Jersey, the opposition, upon that hue-and-cry, having made a pretty clean sweep of the State." In the words of the *Mercury*, "*Subserviency to the South is political death.*" Ryerson expressed the view that Buchanan had received his comeuppance: "If Mr. Buchanan's attempt to destroy the independence of the Representative Branches, as well as to coerce the opinions of private members of the party, was not signally rebuked, our Government would soon, with its immense patronage and expenditure, become virtually a despotism. These questions appeared to me of infinitely more moment than that of freedom or slavery in the territories."[22]

An editorial in the *New York Times* entitled "A Tribute to New Jersey" observed that if any of the actors in the electioneering drama just closed came for curtain calls, let it be New Jersey; none had fulfilled its duty so well; none had more pointedly thrown off the arbitrary control of party. New Jersey beyond doubt had joined the "opposition to a Southern slave-driving faction usurping the much abused name of Democracy." The *St. Louis Democrat* similarly congratulated the state: "Well done for New Jersey. The contest there . . . has been fought with a zeal and pluck surpassed nowhere in the Union."[23]

Buchanan's supporters regarded the election in New Jersey as a catastrophe but found excuses for it. Douglas Democrats, however, ascribed defeat to Buchanan's Kansas policy; most state Democrats believed in popular sovereignty, but Buchanan had violated it and then tried to punish all Democrats who disagreed. The question of slavery once again caused a party to founder in defection and disarray. As the *Mercury* predicted, the "Democratic party is about to be shattered on the same rock which has already destroyed all the old party organizations."[24]

The legislature, which convened in early 1859, faced the task of electing a senator. Forty-one votes constituted a majority in joint session; the Opposition numbered forty-four members and the Democrats thirty-seven. If the Democrats voted as a unit and if four Americans defected to their side, the Democrats could gain a majority. The Democrats, however, remained uncertain whom to back. Buchanan's loyal supporter, incumbent senator Wright, was a liability. Indeed, some Democratic legislators had pledged during their election campaigns to oppose his reelection.

In the meantime the restive ranks of the Opposition had not yet reached consensus on a candidate. This unstable situation moved opportunist Robert Stockton to seek the seat or select an ally by forming a bipartisan coalition of Democrats and wavering members of the Opposition. Despite frantic maneuvers, he failed; the defeat underscored the decline of his political influence. In the end the Democratic caucus rejected both Wright and Stockton and backed the compromise candidacy of popular Vroom.

Meanwhile, the Opposition caucus rejected various candidates who were identified too closely with either the Americans or the Republicans. Juggling geographical and factional interests, the caucus of Americans and Republicans finally selected John C. Ten Eyck, a relatively obscure Mount Holly lawyer and former Whig. Because Ten Eyck had no strong ties to either wing of the Opposition, both wings viewed him as an available candidate, even though he had strongly supported Fremont in 1856. He was elected senator in a joint meeting of the legislature. In his victory speech, the reserved Ten Eyck positioned himself as a centrist on the major issues.

Despite harmony on the surface, the outcome bitterly disappointed leaders of the American wing. The Republicans had outmaneuvered the Americans by securing an ostensible but not a true compromise candidate. American candidate Joseph Fitz Randolph considered that the "Americans in New Jersey lost their candidate and elected a Republican senator, in consequence of divisions" among themselves. The Americans felt tricked and resented it. They correctly charged the Republicans with deliberately nominating several Republicans solely because they attracted the support of American legislators for personal or local reasons. Having succeeded in dividing the Americans, the Republicans then obtained enough American votes to elect Ten Eyck, their real choice, when the caucus finally decided on him on the ninth ballot. The divided Americans voted for Ten Eyck in the joint meeting for the sake of appearing to compromise. Thus they "swallowed the bitterest pill of their lives."[25]

The 1859 gubernatorial election again challenged Democrats to recover and rally their forces. In confidential letters, regular Democrats sounded pessimistic about their prospects. Opposition leaders regarded the election as a referendum on their executive leadership of the state and on the viability and durability of their coalition. Many state government appointments hinged on the outcome.

At the Democratic convention, held on August 24, delegates speculated about general amnesty for Douglas's followers. As a peace offering to them, the regulars, with ostensible neutrality, refused to allow rival Sussex delegations, one pro-Buchanan and the other anti-administration, to vote. Many observers expected a platform fight to erupt over the Lecompton dispute, but this did not occur. The Democrats knew they must regain previous substantial majorities in their traditional strongholds, particularly Sussex, in order to carry the state. To that end the state party broke loose from Buchanan's administration and let the anti-Lecompton men write the controversial sections of the platform dealing with slavery in the West.

Ryerson drafted resolutions emphatically embracing popular sovereignty. With a touch of irony he referred to the solemn pledge made by Buchanan in his 1856 acceptance letter to abide by the will of the majority in a territory. Ryerson opposed both the Republicans' 1856 call for Congress to exclude slavery from the free territories and the current southern demand that Congress protect slavery there.

Despite Buchanan's demand to have his administration endorsed by the convention, the state party refused. The *Philadelphia Press* found this rebuke "withering." Conceding the platform to the anti-Lecompton forces did not extend to relinquishing the nomination to them, however.[26]

Several candidates vied for the nomination. Observers predicted that without a clear-cut front-runner the delegates would settle on a moderate who could receive the full Democratic vote throughout the state and also could attract independents from the Opposition. Speculation again centered on Vroom.

The stalemate on the convention floor provided the friends of Edwin R. V. Wright of Jersey City with an opportunity to find an opening. Still smarting from the state party's failure to support his reelection bid, former senator William Wright (unrelated to Edwin Wright) reportedly bribed delegates to nominate Edwin Wright, his favorite. After a protracted, angry struggle the two Wrights pulled a coup; the pair secured Edwin Wright's nomination on the sixth ballot. Wright was a printer by trade, a lawyer by profession, a prosecutor by appointment, and a legislator by election. A talented, bold, and resourceful man, he had unsuccessfully sought the gubernatorial nomination many times. Tired of waiting his turn, he seized the opportunity.

Edwin Wright was a colorful, if controversial, candidate. The Democrats touted him as a man of the people. The Opposition conceded that Wright was a genial companion, a fluent speaker, and a fine ballad singer. They suggested that he was much more—a drunkard, a whoremaster, a promoter of racehorses and prizefights. Critics especially condemned Wright's role seventeen years before in persuading a fledgling Irish amateur boxer to fight a professional. The young fighter received 128 blows, which blinded him before he fell dead in the ring.

In addition to attacking his unsavory personal reputation, Wright's opponents characterized him as a machine politician. The *Paterson Guardian* regarded Wright's private life as simply unsuitable for a governor, a "stench in the nostrils of the community." The *Jersey City Standard* remarked that if New Jersey's voters elected Wright, the "whole State was drunk *clear through.*" Democrats in public dismissed Wright's alleged activities as mere youthful indiscretions. Some prominent Democrats, however, regarded Wright in their private letters as a disgrace to the party. During the campaign, many embarrassed Democratic leaders did not stump for him.[27]

Many New Jerseyans also objected to Edwin Wright's political views. Wright had strongly supported Buchanan's Lecompton policy and his attempted purge of the party, as well as William Wright's bid for reelection. Ryerson, characterizing Edwin Wright as a thorough Lecomptonite, vowed publicly not to vote for him. So did Adrain and Riggs. Wright nevertheless remained a formidable adversary, immensely popular with his party's rank and file, particularly the workers and immigrants in the northern cities of the state. He conducted an aggressive campaign and tried to seize the initiative by charging Newell with making excessively partisan judicial nominations. This claim boomeranged, however: the Democrats had rejected Newell's nominations for chancellor in their own partisan interest.[28]

Meanwhile, the Opposition, buoyed by recent triumphs but unable to boast any great legislative accomplishments, entered the gubernatorial race hopeful but cautious. Because the constitutional mandate did not allow the governor to succeed himself, Newell did not figure in the calculations. Many Americans expected an American to be the gubernatorial nominee because Senator Ten Eyck hailed from Republican ranks. The Republicans, however, remained quietly uncommitted. Then the Democratic convention galvanized the Opposition. The prospect of Wright sitting in the governor's chair surrounded by his cronies upset both Americans and Republicans. The Democrats could not have selected a better candidate to unite the Opposition. On the third ballot, the Opposition turned to Charles S. Olden to lead the coalition.

Olden, then sixty, was a physically robust man with one prominent physical feature—his small, piercing blue eyes. Simple yet urbane, unassuming, and amiable, he carried himself with poise and an unaffected dignity. Olden's voice was soft and musical. He preferred to make few speeches, and those were brief and direct. Businessman, banker, gentleman farmer, and an old-line supporter of Whig presidential candidate Henry Clay, Olden had served two terms as a state senator, remaining in that office until 1851.

The Republicans selected Olden for several compelling reasons. First, he was the complete opposite of Wright. Olden's candidacy raised no question of character or reputation; everyone regarded him as honorable. In contrast to Wright's unabashed scrambling for the nomination, Olden left retirement only reluctantly, though graciously, to accept the nomination out of a sense of civic duty. Olden also provided a geographical compromise: attracting support in western Jersey, he could gain votes there to counter Wright's popularity in parts of eastern Jersey. Furthermore, on political grounds, he appealed to both wings of the Opposition. His support of Fillmore in 1856 pleased the Americans, yet he was no nativist and remained a Whig, which pleased the Republicans. Olden adroitly explained that he had voted for Fillmore because as a Whig he could not vote for Fremont, a former Democrat.

Nothing in Olden's mercifully obscure record made him objectionable to either branch. He proclaimed himself neither an American nor a Republican but the leader of the united Opposition. Such a neutral, centrist posture enabled Opposition politicians and editors to represent him as an American to Americans and as a Republican to Republicans. Above all, Olden's supporters took pride in his personal qualities; they described him as sagacious, capable, and firm. He also inspired respect and goodwill even from political adversaries.

Olden's moderate views made him an eminently suitable candidate to the many New Jerseyans who shared such views. He did not desire radical change, yet he willingly accepted constructive change to ensure order. He believed that northerners and southerners shared common interests. For the sake of national unity, he advocated the coexistence of the slaveholding South and the free North. Accordingly, he opposed both expansion of slavery on free soil in the West and abolition of slavery in the South.

In his acceptance letter and in various campaign speeches, Olden deliberately did not specify what role Congress should play in containing slavery. He personally regarded slavery as "odious" and looked forward to the day when it would end by legal means, yet he insisted on the enforcement of the current fugitive slave law. National unity, Olden thought, required sectional compromise. He stated that "nothing is ominous [or] of greater danger to the welfare of the country than the hostility which has been engendered between different sections by the subject of slavery." Above all, he believed both regions must stand by the Constitution. As Olden declared in January 1860, just as New Jersey was among the first of the states to "ratify the Constitution, so will she be among the last to violate any of its provisions." New Jersey, he said, "has always been true to her federal engagements, and has fallen behind none of her sister States in fidelity to the Union"; she "sympathizes with no party which seeks its dissolution." Such political views made Olden every inch a Jerseyman.

His nomination, clearly a masterstroke, outshone even the sensible selection of Newell in 1856. Even as fears mounted about the likelihood of a divisive presidential election in 1860, many New Jerseyans believed the state safe under Olden's leadership.[29]

Caution also characterized the Opposition convention's platform, which condemned Buchanan's record and praised Newell's. The convention opposed revival of the African slave trade, as did the Democrats. Unlike the Democrats, however, the Opposition strongly endorsed a protective tariff. Olden and other spokesmen maintained that it would promote industrial growth and fuller employment. In contrast to the Democrats, the Republicans avoided divisive questions such as the possibility of the encroachment of slavery on free soil or the power of Congress to exclude slavery. Such omissions seemed so glaring to an embarrassed *New York Tribune* editor that he incorrectly assumed an error had been made in a brief news summary. In fact, however, Opposition managers deliberately omitted certain matters in order to avoid alienating moderate voters in the state, especially American party supporters and anti-Lecompton Democrats. When a delegate proposed a resolution recommending a potential presidential candidate, delegates cut him off with cries of "Don't destroy the harmony" and "You will cause a split."[30]

The Democrats accused their opponents of trying to emphasize the New Jersey Democrats' internal differences while ignoring their own. Many Democrats renewed the criticism that the bipartisan coalition amounted to opposition for its own sake. Charging that the Opposition lacked an alternative policy, the *New Brunswick Times* referred to the opposition as "the little end of nothing whittled down to a point."

Democrats found Olden a more elusive target than Wright, but they did their best. One reporter, noting the shantylike "Olden Farm House" built in Trenton for the campaign, mocked the plebeian pretensions of plain farmer Olden. The correspondent told readers that the candidate in fact "lives in a princely mansion [Drumthwacket], within the atmosphere of the aristocratic village of Princeton, surrounded by exotic plants in hothouse preservation." The Democrats dismissed Olden as an aloof aristocrat and a heartless reactionary, completely out of touch with the common people. Infuriated, they inveighed against his sphinxlike ability to avoid contentious issues. The *Belvidere Journal* found it a deliberate strategy of the Opposition leaders to play the "game of representing him as all things to all men."

The Democrats also charged Olden with timidity. They called him "as tight as an oyster," and found him "as silent as the grave." Democrats also derided the platform's noncommittal stand on sectional issues. Some Democrats even suggested that such evasive tactics camouflaged something sinister. The *Flemington Democrat* exhorted New Jersey voters to repel sectional fanaticism and to make "deadly war upon negro worship."[31]

Whether the Opposition alliance of 1858 could hold together became the overriding question in the 1859 campaign. Everyone knew that without the united support of the Americans, the Democrats might succeed. Yet in the spring and summer of 1859, after the session of the legislature and the election of a Republican senator, it became increasingly evident that many Americans in the state had become restive. They lacked a viable national party to provide support and direction. Their state organization lost influence and adherents because of the diminishing appeal of nativist causes. Many Americans complained that they had not received their fair share of nominations and appointments. The Americans suspected that the Republicans now took them for granted. As the state American party began to degenerate into a collection of splinter groups, some of the more talented individuals turned to the larger, more successful Opposition organization as the best way to advance their careers.

The small but mischievous faction of the Jones-Stockton Americans began again to stir up trouble. Opposition politicians worried that they intended to run their gubernatorial candidate. By siphoning off roughly four thousand votes, they might well throw the election to the Democrats, who would reward them for their efforts.

Disaffected Americans scheduled a meeting at New Brunswick in June. They wished to increase their bargaining power with the Republicans in securing nominations, or even to consider scrapping the coalition outright. Opposition leaders anticipated the meeting with dread, remembering what had resulted from separate organizations, nominations, and campaigns in 1856.

To the rescue came activist Smith, who stormed the American garrison with his supporters, including former Americans who now were allied firmly with the Opposition. The outcome was a draw. On one hand, the meeting endorsed the notion of resuming a more independent position, maintaining an autonomous party organization, and holding a separate state convention—all setbacks to the Opposition. On the other hand, however, the meeting agreed by a single vote to schedule the American convention on the same day and in the same city as the Opposition's—a major victory for the Opposition because it kept open the possibility of joint action and a common nomination.

To sabotage the likelihood of coalition, the Jones-Stockton faction nominated Flemington lawyer Peter I. Clark for governor just before the state American convention met. Opposition party members implored the Americans to exercise caution, and talked of harmony. So matters stood on September 7, when both the Opposition and the American conventions convened in Trenton.[32]

Because of the influence of the Jones-Stockton faction, the American managers scheduled their convention to start at 11 A.M. Their opponents, coming by train from the north, could not reach Trenton until an hour later. Thus the group headed by Jones had a chance to capture control of the convention and to make nominations before noon, when the Opposition convention began. The plan backfired, however: a reinforced contingent of moderate Americans from South Jersey under Smith's leadership arrived just in time and ready for action.

When the meeting convened, bedlam ensued. Delegates and outsiders alike shouted, hooted, cursed, cheered, hissed, and stomped, trying to disrupt the proceedings and seize control of the convention. The faction led by Jones and the Democrats played tug-of-war with the Fillmore Americans and the Republicans. The American conclave reached a farcical nadir, falling into the hands of whichever group demonstrated the most nerve in taking charge.

Thanks to Smith, the moderate forces captured control of the convention by electing their man presiding officer. His group then delayed the proceedings by all kinds of devices until the Opposition convention selected its candidate, rammed Olden's nomination through the American convention, and adjourned immediately without even adopting a platform.[33]

Such strong-arm tactics naturally infuriated many Americans, who charged collusion and trickery. This indignation, however, appeared to be directed toward the way Olden's supporters in the American convention had ratified his nomination rather than toward the nominee himself. To the dismay of the Democrats, various Americans in the state began to jump on Olden's bandwagon. Olden, after all, had supported Fillmore, whereas Wright offended them by his personality, his positions, and his allies. James Bishop, a leading dissident American, considered Olden so far superior to Wright that the Americans had no choice but to work for Olden. The editorials of the *Jersey City Standard* suggested the changes in Americans' attitudes, from anger at the outset to fatalistic acquiescence to enthusiastic acceptance of Olden. When Clark later turned down the nomination of the Stockton Americans and endorsed Olden, other rebellious Americans followed his lead and aligned with Olden.[34]

The state American party committee endorsed Olden. During the campaign, Republicans opened up more local nominations to the Americans; members of both sides attended meetings and served as campaign speakers. Thus, the relationship between the two wings of the Opposition changed from profound disaffection to effective cooperation. The Jones-Stockton Americans, however, refused to budge and in effect worked for Wright. Their defection remained a serious matter.

In mid-October 1859, in the midst of the campaign, New Jerseyans learned that fanatical abolitionist John Brown and a score of supporters in the night had briefly seized the undefended federal arsenal at Harper's Ferry, Virginia. During the raid not a single slave volunteered to join the insurrection. Then marines counterattacked, killing or capturing the raiders. By the end of October authorities had convicted Brown and his accomplices of treason and sentenced them to death.

People were jolted by the news of the incident. New Jerseyans wondered what it portended for the nation. The Democrats pounced on Brown's raid to boost their flagging effort in the final three weeks of the campaign. With Olden so unassailable and Wright so vulnerable in certain circles, Brown might serve as the perfect scapegoat. By associating Brown with the abolitionists and in turn identifying the abolitionists with the Republicans, the Democrats denounced the treasonable doctrines that nurtured Brown's fanaticism. They pointed out that the abolitionists had furnished the money, the guns, the moral support, and the undisguised sympathy that had spurred Brown to action.[35]

The Democrats singled out Senator William H. Seward of New York, the front-runner for the Republican presidential nomination, for his prediction in 1858 of an "irrepressible conflict" between slavery and freedom. The *Newark Journal* announced: "At Harper's Ferry Seward's 'irrepressible conflict,' which the *Mercury* so warmly advocates, has had its first legitimate expression." Unless voters rejected Republicanism, declared the *Journal*, the South would suffer from future slave insurrections with inevitable pillage and massacres. Worse, the *Paterson Register* predicted, the policy of the Republican party would cause the nation to drift into civil war. According to the Democrats, every patriot now knew that John Brown's raid demonstrated the danger of disunion as advocated by the party of disunion, the Republicans. If things continued on their present course, Americans would "reap the fruits in a bloody and desperate sectional war, where brother will be arrayed against brother, and father against son." If Harper's Ferry failed to open the people's eyes to the subversive, dangerous ideas of the Republican leaders, contended the *New Brunswick Times*, little hope remained of saving the Union. The *Times* urged New Jersey voters to defeat the fanatical Republicans, who espoused sectionalism, abolitionism, and Sewardism.

Some Democrats did distinguish between the generally moderate New Jersey Republicans and the more radical Republicans in some other states. For example, when Democratic politician Joel Parker referred to the dangers of Republican sectionalism that resulted in bloodshed and riot, he admitted that these dangers were "not probably of the Republicans of New Jersey, but from the incendiary speeches of such men as Seward."

Other Democrats regretted that the Harper's Ferry incident had not occurred earlier in the campaign, so the full meaning of the raid would have been able to sink in by Election Day. Thomson reported that "if we had a month more, before Election, we would show a very heavy vote on our side." The *Trenton American*, working the issue up to the final hour, sent the final Democratic message to the voters the day before the election: "Every man who votes for Olden votes to encourage rebellion and treason."[36]

Thrown on the defensive by Brown's raid, Republicans responded in various ways. Many repudiated the "horrible insurrection." Four days after the incident, the moderate *Newark Advertiser*'s position became still stronger: "We condemn, denounce, and abhor all such atrocities." The newspaper disavowed the madcap schemes of a madman. Even the usually radical *Newark Mercury* conceded that "the direst curse that could befall our country would be an unchecked slave insurrection." Republicans also dissociated themselves from both the Brown party and the abolitionists; neither, they said, had any connection with the Republican party.

Turning its attention to motives, the *Flemington Republican* charged that the town's *Democrat* had the impudence to assert that "'the Republican party is stained with the blood of insurrection, that they are responsible before God for the victims at Harper's Ferry!'" The *Republican* blamed Democrats "for the blood spilled at Harper's Ferry, over which the *Democrat* is shedding so many 'crocodile' tears." Hoping to frighten timid voters, declared the *Republican*, Democrats tried to "magnify the affair—to make a mountain out of a mole-hill—for political effect." In the past, the *Advertiser* noted, insurrections had "found the country less excited, less divided, than it is now, and therefore not so susceptible of panic."

In their strongest counterattack, Republicans asserted that the explosion at Harper's Ferry followed directly from the repeal of the Missouri Compromise. Democrats invited strife by removing this effective buffer between free and slave land. When the expansion of slavery became too difficult and too dangerous for congressmen to handle, they irresponsibly left the task to the divided, inflamed people of Kansas. Popular sovereignty rooted in misplaced populism and mindless optimism could offer no satisfactory or permanent solution. As a result, the policy pleased neither northerners nor southerners, and produced only violence and anarchy. Without the Kansas-Nebraska Act and with the support of the peace-preserving Missouri Compromise,

Congress in due course would have admitted Kansas in a regular, undisputed way as a free state. Then Brown would have minded his own business and stayed at home, away from trouble both in Kansas and at Harper's Ferry.

Despite these disturbing developments, the Republicans emphasized the ludicrous aspects of the raid, especially the southern overreaction after Brown's gang had surrendered. Poking fun at the unfounded fears of many southerners, the *Mercury* scoffed, "We have never believed that twenty men could march into the Southern country, imprison all the inhabitants, and run off with the niggers." Newarker John P. Jackson made a Republican audience roar with laughter when he pointed out that Brown's small force was no match for the entire United States Army. He and others derided southern governors' absurd offers of military assistance "to still the mighty tempest that has been gotten up in a tea-pot!" Jackson contrasted the uproar over Brown's raid with the earlier lack of concern when pro-slavery ruffian forces molested free-staters in Kansas with Buchanan's knowledge, and yet escaped prosecution. But, said Jackson, "if a crazy lunatic with fifteen white men and five negroes stop the [railroad] cars at Harper's Ferry and surround three thousand inhabitants, upsetting the President and all his cabinet, and turning topsy-turvy two states and all the military, what a fuss is made about old John Brown."[37]

On November 8, 1859, Olden won the governorship by a mere 1,601 votes (51 percent), or slightly less than half of Newell's majority. The Opposition lost seats in the assembly. This tenuous margin of victory in the gubernatorial election indicated the need for a heavier dose of radicalism, suggested the *Mercury*. The newspaper deplored the Opposition's practice of subordinating principle to expediency. It criticized the Opposition's platform for failing to take bold positions on the issues growing from the unacceptable sectional demands of the South. Yet the *Mercury*'s views remained outside the political mainstream. Such stands surely would have backfired by frightening away moderate American and Democratic voters as well as some conservative Republicans; three times as many anti-Lecomptonites voted Democratic as abstained. The Opposition lost as many voters to the Democrats or to abstention as they gained from both.[38]

Clearly, Olden won because of Wright's liabilities, which Democrats readily conceded. Thomson attributed defeat to the "reputed bad character of our candidate—which drove from him the support of every clergyman in New Jersey." The editor of the *New Brunswick Times* remarked that the "personal popularity of our candidate in some quarters was counterbalanced by the effect of charges against him in other quarters." An estimated 10 percent of Democrats who voted for William Alexander in 1856 voted for Olden in 1859; this group constituted only half of the percentage that changed between 1856 and 1858. As the Republican *Advertiser* observed, "it was *character* that elected"

Olden, while Wright was "conquered by his character." Thus, although the number of votes was greater in 1859, Wright actually received fewer votes and a lower percentage of the vote than did Alexander in 1856 in six counties (Sussex, Middlesex, Bergen, Burlington, and Somerset).

Sound organization and hard work surely helped Olden. Not a single commentator, in analyzing the election, mentioned John Brown's raid as even a minor influence on the election result. Yet the raid probably scared some voters, thus offsetting Wright's liabilities and making the election closer.[39]

**B**rown's raid continued to hold New Jerseyans' attention after the election. Brown's abortive action polarized public opinion, assuming a historic importance and a symbolic significance out of all proportion to the event itself.

Extreme radical Republicans in the North, including the few who lived in New Jersey, began to empathize with Brown. They admired his stoic, dignified behavior during his trial and imprisonment. When Brown received the death sentence, the *Mercury* opposed it. This newspaper, previously unsympathetic to Brown, pronounced him insane and thus not responsible for his self-deluded actions. When Brown was hanged, some mourned him as a fallen hero. Admirers forgot those who had died at Harper's Ferry.

In such circles criticism of Brown had shifted to sympathy, then to maudlin sentimentalizing and blatant mythologizing. Brown's supporters exaggerated some of his personal qualities and ignored others. Concerned only with the anti-slavery cause, they rationalized his actions as a desire to avenge the deaths of his sons, who had been murdered in Kansas by pro-slavery cutthroats. They overlooked Brown's cold-blooded murders of unarmed people in Kansas.

The *Mercury*, ignoring Brown's apocalyptic belief that the sin of slavery must be atoned in blood, characterized him as a "man crazed by misfortune and wrong." ("Poor John," replied the Democratic *Newark Journal* sarcastically.) Other commentators regarded Brown's raid as misguided and his method as wrong, but considered his zeal and bravery laudable. Regarding him as a martyr to the noble cause of abolition, they contended that no one could doubt his sincerity or convictions, but at the same time they ignored his fanaticism of conscience that made his act no less fanatical.

Even if Brown deserved martyrdom, as some opponents of slavery contended, the *Mercury* remained unpersuaded. Referring to persons mainly outside New Jersey, this newspaper observed, "We will not dignify John Brown with the title of martyr, but there are tens of thousands who will." Other Republicans, too, refused to eulogize Brown. The Republican *Newton Register* declared that the "proceedings of Old Brown at Harper's Ferry—whether the result of insanity, fanaticism, or demonism—have our heartiest abhorrence and detestation." The *Advertiser*, although it praised Brown's personal traits, commented that his "heroic daring," characteristic of a true monomaniac, was "worthy of a better cause."[40]

Democrats continued to use the controversy to embarrass Republicans. Reacting to the plea by the *Mercury*'s editor not to judge Brown harshly, the *Journal* retorted, "Of course not. Nobody expects you to. Your business is to laud the old murderer, and stimulate other fanatics to follow his example." The *Camden Democrat* described a scene of a seething cauldron surrounded by the witches of disunion, who tossed into it the liver of blaspheming demagogues, the sprigs of sectionalism, the idiot's brain, and the traitor's spleen, all the while chanting a blasphemous hymn in praise of dissolution and inhaling the poisonous stench arising from their evil concoction. After describing this gruesome scene, the editorial cautioned that the nation had fallen on strange times indeed: "When Southern Sovereign States talk of dissolution, when Northern fanatics bid them God-speed, when it is necessary to hold 'Union Meetings' to *convince* the nation that we *are* loyal to the American Union, as though *that* fact was not apparent without reaffirming it." Only the moderate national forces in the Mid-Atlantic states, Democrats contended, could save the nation by repudiating both extremes, the fanatics of the North and the fire-eaters (secessionist militants) of the South.[41]

The abolitionists at Perth Amboy's Eagleswood School reacted differently. When they received word of Brown's raid, Rebecca B. Spring went to Charlestown, Virginia, to see Brown. He told her he had made great mistakes and deserved execution. She replied that it was better to die for a great cause than of a mere disease. Brown and his accomplices were hanged on December 2, 1859. Two other men who were involved lost their appeals later and were executed on March 16, 1860. The Eagleswood abolitionists arranged to have the bodies of the two latter martyrs buried, according to their wishes, in the free soil of the North. When rumors spread that troublemakers intended to throw the bodies into Raritan Bay when they arrived in Perth Amboy, the abolitionists arranged to have the corpses shipped to Rahway instead and hidden until nightfall. Under cover of darkness a sympathizer brought the bodies by wagon to Eagleswood. After a simple but moving funeral service, the abolitionists buried the bodies in unmarked plots in the cemetery at Eagleswood beside the graves of several illustrious abolitionist leaders.

One abolitionist at Eagleswood described her reaction: "It seemed terrible then, as I walked home thinking about it, that we should have allowed it to be done—that we could take them then calmly and bury them instead of leaving all to rush desperately against those who cut short for them the joys of life and robbed the world of the bravery it could not spare." Viewing the situation in apocalyptic terms, this frustrated revolutionary longed to avenge the executions and, if all else failed, to "fling ourselves, a living protest, to be crushed at least against the solid walls we could not break down or scale."[42]

Brown's raid raised the specter of a northern-led revolution in the South. People wondered whether southerners would opt for independence to prevent future raids. Many northerners, including New Jerseyans, thought the South had received the false impression that the North overwhelmingly supported Brown's raid or felt personal sympathy for him. Therefore many people throughout the North, including New Jersey, held meetings to demonstrate their loyal support of the Union and to reassure southerners.

Congressman Pennington remained unimpressed. He criticized his constituents and local businessmen who called for "every condescension and submission from their representatives," commenting they had become "unnecessarily alarmed." Republican newspapers agreed, and pointed to some curious developments. The *Mercury* described northerners' efforts to conciliate southerners "who denounce the Union, while doubting our fidelity to it." Similarly, the *Trenton Gazette* characterized several southern politicians as "so exceedingly anxious to save the Union that they threaten its dissolution every day."[43]

At the Union meetings, Republicans soon detected Democratic preelection maneuvering for 1860. The Democrats used these meetings to reiterate their claim as the only party that could enforce the law, maintain the Constitution, eliminate southern disaffection, and thus preserve the Union. Despite misgivings, some Republicans took part as speakers in such meetings.[44]

Early in 1860 the legislature and Newell mulled over the raid. In an effort to counter the Democratic offensive, Opposition senators denounced both Brown's insurrection and southern disunionism. The Democrats controlled the senate, however; thus a two-man senate committee had the last word in a one-sided campaign document in which the Democrats blamed the North entirely for the sectional problems besetting the nation.[45]

As southern demands grew bolder, however, Republicans adamantly refused to be intimidated by southern threats to dissolve the Union if a Republican became president. A Morristown man who signed his impassioned letter "Jersey Blue" stated that patriotic Americans must reject disunionist "attempts to excuse Democratic treason at the South by Abolition treason at the North." Fearful of losing the next presidential election, southern fire-eaters resorted to blackmail; they tried to subvert the popular will of the American people by preventing the election of a Republican president. Patriotic Americans, he declared, must not allow the Union to be "broken by the force of arrogant treason."[46]

The *Princeton Standard* argued along the same lines: "If our slave holding brethren must either be our master or withdraw from the Union, the responsibility of disunion will be upon them, not upon us." Similarly, in a measured editorial the *Newark American* regarded the "threat of dissolving the Union because of sectional issues comes with a bad grace from a people who are using all their efforts to extend slavery into free territory, contrary to the Constitution, the whole genius and spirit of our Government, their own agreements, and the wishes of the actual settlers themselves. To us Southern sectionalism is as odious as Northern sectionalism; both are wrong. When the South clears her skirts of this charge she may then complain, but not till then." In the meantime, the *American* continued, the North must grant and respect all the constitutional rights belonging to the South. If these rights are in question, the North should give the South the benefit of the doubt. Having done so, the North also must claim and exercise all its own rights. In particular, northerners have a right to nominate for president anyone they please, and to elect him if they can. By doing so, "we would disregard this threat of Disunion as we would the braying of an ass."[47]

The Democrats publicly pledged to preserve the Union at all hazards, but in private they alluded to a most ominous change, a loss of faith and a new sense of insecurity. Staring into the abyss and unnerved by what he saw, Wall remarked, it seemed incredible that the future of the Union, which once had been assumed, appeared to be in question after Brown's raid. Similarly, Vroom observed, "One thing is certain, that until the present time I have never entertained any serious doubt as to the safety of the Union. I think now it is in great danger."[48]

Since 1854, New Jersey's Whig party had disintegrated, then disappeared. The Democrats in the meantime became divided and decimated, yet survived as a weakened but still competitive party. The Americans and the Republicans had emerged to recruit the disaffected and had formed the two branches of the Opposition. In the polarized politics following the passage of the Kansas-Nebraska Act, the Opposition achieved success in 1854, in its first contests for Congress. In the next three years, however, the coalition almost destroyed itself by endemic division and constant bickering. In 1856, because of its divisions, the Opposition lost the presidential and senatorial races as well as some congressional seats, although the coalition in the state maintained enough unity to elect a governor.

In 1858, in another polarizing election, the Americans, the Republicans, and the anti-Lecompton Democrats regrouped their Opposition coalition against Buchanan's supporters, who controlled the Democratic party. The Opposition elected every New Jersey congressman, increased the number of its legislators, and in early 1859 chose a Republican as federal senator. Although internal problems still plagued the Opposition in 1859, the group overcame its differences and again elected its gubernatorial candidate. Such victories marked the high tide for the Opposition in the decade.

Similarly, by the late 1850s, the Opposition was making progress toward internal consolidation. The Republicans, working behind the scenes, began to gain the upper hand within the coalition. They did so by absorbing nativist voters at the expense of the Americans. Then, too, prominent Americans, such as Newell and Nixon, became full-fledged Republicans and party leaders. Political managers Smith and Thomas Dudley, as well as several influential newspaper editors, also enlisted in the Republican party. Many American sympathizers no longer identified with the American party, but instead regarded themselves as loyal members of the Opposition. Thus the Opposition gradually evolved from a loose organization representing two disparate branches and became identified increasingly with the state Republican party. At least on the surface, the future looked promising.

Those leaders who continued to consider themselves Americans pretended to play the role of party managers, when in fact their rump party now amounted to a handful of contentious factions that exerted only limited influence as pressure groups. By 1860 only a handful of legislators identified themselves as American separatists. They belonged to the Jones-Stockton faction, which in effect had allied with the Democrats.[49]

New Jersey's politics in the decade did not follow the conservative pattern of a border slave state. As the *Mercury* remarked, "In 1854 and 1858 New Jersey showed the same popular feeling in relation to the repeal of the Missouri Compromise and the Lecompton measure as other northern States, and the consequence was the enormous majorities of those years."[50]

Although the Republicans became dominant in the coalition, they did not fully consolidate their position. Narrow victories, sharp reversals, and negligible accomplishments marked their tenuous status. They were still plagued with the problems and perils inherent in coalition politics. Interparty differences still jeopardized success. The Opposition included cranky, die-hard Americans and impatient, idealistic Republicans, all clinging stubbornly to their own hobbyhorses. When such leaders, followers, and other independently inclined individuals walked out and joined other caucuses, parties, and coalitions, it became difficult to achieve durable consensus and concerted action in the legislature. Intraparty differences represented another obstacle, for within Republican ranks doctrinaires and pragmatists disagreed on numerous national and state issues.

The problems of fostering unity and strength in a fledgling party troubled the young Republican party in other northern states as well. In New Jersey, however, the work of constructing a new party for the most part progressed unsteadily. When Republicans did take command of the executive branch, Democrats usually retained control of the legislative. Divided government produced a stalemate, as reflected in the infinitesimal statewide majorities.

The power and influence retained by New Jersey's Democrats indicated their skill in surviving the blunders of Democratic administrations in Washington. Resourceful state Democrats tried to deflect damaging national issues by equating the Opposition with extremism and by exploiting the divisions within the Opposition, especially when rival Opposition candidates vied for seats in the legislature and in Congress. Except for the sessions of

1855 and 1859, the Democrats between 1855 and 1861 secured a majority of the legislature on a joint ballot of both chambers. In the same period Democrats retained control of both chambers of the legislature four times and shared control with the Opposition three times. When the Opposition achieved congressional victories, often it did so only by slight majorities. The Opposition frequently succeeded in a Democratic district when former Democrats, not American or Republican candidates, ran as Opposition nominees.

Similarly, the Opposition won the gubernatorial races by the thinnest of margins. In both 1856 and 1859, the Opposition chose strong candidates more often by luck than by planning. In 1859, even after six years of experience and some success, the leaders and editors of the Opposition revealed insecurity and instability during the gubernatorial contest. The Opposition achieved victory in state contests by ignoring the national problem of a truculent South bent on spreading slavery. This issue, the raison d'etre of national Republicans, was a lasting source of annoyance for the Americans. Thus the Opposition remained the opposition in more than name.

In 1859 the nativist *Jersey City Standard* observed: "There must be harmony and union, and that harmony and union can only be attained by the prevalence of moderate counsels, especially on the topic of slavery," where the "line is most definitively drawn" between Americans and Republicans. Republicans wished to assert the right and duty of Congress to exclude slavery from the territories, but Americans refused. Referring to the victory of the coalition in 1859, the *Standard* drew the lesson that by a "cordial union of all the elements constituting the OPPOSITION, New Jersey can be carried against the Democracy, *and that it cannot be carried in any other way.*" The *Standard* pointed to the size of the majority, "sufficient though it be with union, [it] is yet far too small to render either of the branches of the Opposition independent of the other, or competent to a single-handed contest with the Democracy." Only the branches in combination could defeat the Democrats.[51]

Thus, despite its victories, the state's Opposition remained an uneasy alliance, a creature of caution by necessity. The Opposition relied upon the blunders of the Democrats in Washington to see it through. The coalition was no substitute for a fully developed Republican party able to command a reliable majority of the state's voters and to win responsible supporters in the legislature. Demographic conditions in New Jersey, however, precluded establishment of the Republicans as the majority party during the 1850s. Because many of the new inhabitants in the northeastern counties in that decade were males from outside the state, they accounted for a large share of persons eligible to vote there. The ranks of the Democrats were swelled by the steady growth of the state's cities: Newark's population, for example, nearly doubled from 38,904 in 1850 to 72,065 in 1860. The increase in the number of urban immigrant voters, mainly Irish and German Catholics who tended to vote Democratic, usually offset the gains made elsewhere by the Opposition during the decade.[52]

The political pendulum in New Jersey, which swung sharply to the Opposition in 1854, did not go as far in New Jersey as in many other northern states, especially in the upper North. The pendulum moved rightward in 1856; in 1858 it swung left again to just beyond its position in 1854. Parties developed in the process, but were not realigned completely. The characterization by the *Trenton Gazette* of the Opposition as "no mere alliance or coalition between different parties; but . . . a compact, organized, homogeneous party" simply did not correspond to reality. New Jersey's political development continued to be inconclusive, contradictory, and fragile. More than in any other northern state, uncertainty characterized New Jersey's politics, creating a precarious balance.[53]

# 3 Contests for the Presidential Nominations of 1860

**D**ivisions in the anti-Buchanan coalition made unity elusive on the national level, as in New Jersey. Although the combined opposition won a majority of the House of Representatives in the 1858 elections, the Republicans, Americans, and anti-Lecompton Democrats who opposed Buchanan's policies differed over strategy, tactics, and leadership. When the House convened in December 1859, opposition forces faced a crisis. Control hinged on selection of the speaker. He in turn named the members of the key committees, which set the agenda, decided on appropriations, and launched investigations.

The contest also loomed as a test of strength between southerners and northerners. Fear of slave rebellions, which increased after Brown's raid, touched the southerners' rawest nerve. Their representatives vowed to prevent election of an anti-southern speaker and to block any Yankee interference with slavery. One Jersey City Democrat became exasperated with them. "From the accounts we have of proceedings at Washington it would seem that old John Brown is not yet dead," he observed, "Southern members seem determined to make the most of him, and disunion is their favorite word when addressing the North."

The battle over the speakership lasted two months. The paralysis of Congress heightened fears that the Union might disintegrate. In late January 1860 the stalemate was broken by the withdrawal of one Republican candidate and changeovers by various independent-minded members. The struggle ended on February 1, when the opposition settled on a compromise candidate, William Pennington. A moderate Republican, Pennington became speaker on the forty-fourth ballot by a margin of one vote. Every New Jerseyan backed him but Jetur Riggs.

In his inaugural remarks Pennington vowed to serve the whole country. *The New York Times* breathed a sigh of relief: "If the Union had been cracked in the contest, the seams were again sealed." Many New Jerseyans hailed Pennington's election. Relieved that a moderate had won over more radical Republicans, even state Democrats praised him. Proud New Jerseyans celebrated the honor of his selection. Bonfires blazed in the streets of Newark, and cannons boomed. People felt reassured that good sense had triumphed. The choice of Pennington signaled a rebuke to extremist congressmen, both southern and northern, who had overplayed their hands by inflaming sectional animosity. The outcome convinced New Jerseyans that the Union remained indestructible.[1]

The presidential campaign began at the same time. The Opposition's executive committee organized and announced a state convention for early March to prepare for the Republican national convention in May. The call outraged American ranks because the announcement described this obviously Republican convention as an Opposition event and referred to the national conclave as "the Convention to meet at Chicago." The *Jersey City Standard* denounced the call as a trick to round up American recruits for the Republican campaign. The editorial pointed out that Republicans, by abandoning their party name during the campaign, confessed "their intrinsic weakness in the State." Anticipating a negative reaction by the Americans, the Republican *Newark Mercury* breezily commented that this call "conclusively puts an end to all quibbling," although plainly it did not. Later the *Mercury* perpetuated the fiction by using the labels "Republican" and "Opposition" interchangeably.[2]

The convention, held in Trenton on March 8, appeared to be something less than the usual statewide Opposition conclave and something more than a strictly Republican meeting. Republicans predominated, although some Americans and independents also attended. Three issues faced the members: hammering out a platform for the state campaign, choosing national delegates, and deciding whether to endorse a presidential candidate. Because of their strong disagreement on a candidate, the delegates decided not to commit themselves. The unpledged delegates thus were free to act as changing circumstances might dictate. Even so, the selection of delegates revealed early maneuvering for favorite sons, as supporters of various candidates lobbied hard to have their men named. Meanwhile the drafters of the platform reached a consensus without evading important issues.

The moderate state platform, which would closely resemble the Republican national platform later in 1860, condemned Buchanan's administration as corrupt and unpatriotic. It also called for a protective tariff. One plank evenhandedly opposed the invasions of both pro-slavery thugs into Kansas and of anti-slavery zealots into Virginia. Another plank denounced avowed disunionists in national Democratic ranks. Still another opposed the expansion of slavery into new territory by the "power and influence" of the federal government. Nevertheless, in a move to woo moderates in all camps, the delegates did not call for the outright abolition of slavery in the territories, a cornerstone of the national Republican platform in 1856. To attract German-Americans, the convention disregarded previous nativist demands and opposed adding two years to the current residence requirement for voting.

In assessing the convention, Democrats as usual dismissed the meeting as mere opposition to everything. A reporter relished the commotion on the floor when a dog repeatedly barked his displeasure at such a discordant convention. Nativists also condemned the convention for caving in to the Germans. The campaign had begun in earnest.[3]

Although Republicans disagreed about the best presidential nominee, they needed someone who could sweep New Jersey, carry the entire lower North, and thus expand beyond the Republican base of the upper North, which had been won in 1856. Democrat Buchanan had succeeded in 1856 only because he captured virtually all of the South and most of the lower North. The populous "Pivot States" of Illinois, Indiana, Pennsylvania, and New Jersey figured as the major battlegrounds in the presidential campaign of 1860. If Republicans failed to carry Pennsylvania, Buchanan's home state, New Jersey and the other states would become critically important. With Jersey Republicans scoring victories in local elections during the spring, confident party members believed the state to be within their grasp.

Winning the state entailed stopping the front-runner William Seward. Seward was regarded as unacceptable because he alienated the moderate majority and had other weaknesses as well. His past support of government aid to Catholic schools and his denunciation of nativism angered American voters. Seward also sounded extreme in his controversial, highly publicized speeches. Supposedly he had embraced a higher law than the Constitution, and he predicted an irrepressible conflict between slavery and freedom. Moderates were unsettled by his outspoken attacks on slavery and his opposition to the Compromise of 1850.

Seward's ostensible radicalism and sectionalism frightened people in the Mid-Atlantic states. Observing the mood of Seward's colleagues, Pennington found little support in Congress for his nomination; he was "too radical" to win the election and opposed him—"not personally but as to his availability." Most Republican politicians agreed with this assessment, for he "cannot carry the State of New Jersey as things now stand, that's certain." Leader James T. Sherman similarly predicted that his "nomination will revive the divisions of 1856 in Pennsylvania and New Jersey and will be fatal to us in these two states."

Yet Seward's backers persisted. Editor Horace Congar rallied supporters, who made up about one-third of the state's delegation and hailed mainly from North Jersey. Even Congar admitted that only a candidate with a "very moderate position" could win New Jersey, but he refused to support such a centrist because he might well forget he was a Republican. In his view, principle mattered more than expediency.[4]

Most state Republicans, however, preferred success to Seward. John Stratton counseled one convention delegate: "There will be an immense pressure for him at Chicago, and he will go there with a large number of delegates, anxious for his nomination. He must be headed off. With whom you can best do it, it seems difficult to say." Convinced that Seward's nomination represented the "certain forerunner of defeat," Stratton nevertheless found no obvious alternative. The delegates from the lower North opted for a holding action to stop Seward's bandwagon. They supported the candidacies of various favorite sons in order to deny Seward a majority on early ballots, and sought to have one of those candidates secure the first spot.

This tactic backfired for state Republicans when they backed rival favorite sons. South Jerseyans pushed for Attorney General William Dayton. Some North Jerseyans, especially from Hudson and Essex, proposed Pennington, who worked hard behind the scene to secure support. The protracted struggle between the two camps exacerbated existing rivalries within the ranks of the Opposition. Nativists suspected an ominous strategy to lure their moderates into the Republican tent. Dayton's camp feared that Pennington's supporters really intended to advance Seward.

Pennington's side, especially Pennington himself, also suspected assorted conspiracies, especially that of Dayton's false friends, who backed Dayton only to derail Pennington. Opponents of Dayton pointed to his singularly ineffective record as Fremont's running mate: four years before he had won only half of the state's Opposition voters; he had not even carried his own state. They doubted he could win over both Americans and Germans, not to mention the lower North. As the convention neared, Pennington's candidacy flagged. Dayton's did not flourish.

When New Jersey's delegates met in Chicago, they agreed to give all their votes to candidate Dayton on early ballots. At an important meeting early in the evening of May 17, the second day of the convention, the leaders from New Jersey and three other pivotal states of the lower North decided to combine their opposition to Seward. They planned to unite behind a less controversial candidate, who possibly could carry their states.

Dovetailing his strategy with that of Abraham Lincoln's managers, delegate Thomas Dudley recommended a way to break the deadlock created by the surfeit of favorite sons. He suggested selecting the strongest favorite son as the bloc's nominee after they had cast complimentary votes for their own favorite sons on early ballots. New Englanders also promised to back this candidate on the condition that the leaders of the lower North agreed on a single contender. They did, and selected Abraham Lincoln.

Lincoln, a highly successful Illinois lawyer, enjoyed the assets of availability and a reputation as a political moderate. The leaders returned to their hotels to persuade their delegations to ratify their choice. After midnight on May 18 Dudley held a caucus of the state's delegates. Possibly the promise of diplomatic appointments for both Dayton and Dudley could have sweetened matters, but probably it did not change the votes. It is likely that most delegates, convinced of the strategic wisdom of this choice, did not need the inducements of patronage. Also, they probably sensed by this time (as indicated by newspaper reports from Chicago) that Dayton lacked support outside the state delegation.

Many New Jersey delegates considered Seward a liability and decided to derail him. Thus the changeover to Lincoln as the compromise candidate was altogether in keeping with what most delegates desired from the outset—a Republican presidential candidate who had the best chance of carrying the state. This consideration appeared so compelling that the delegation endorsed Lincoln. In the morning, when the convention met to select its nominee, Lincoln, not Seward, had the inside track.

On the first ballot, New Jersey's delegation cast its entire fourteen votes for Dayton, the only delegation to support him. Seward received solid backing from the upper North and took a commanding lead, 173 over 102 for Lincoln. As previously arranged, delegates from many states of the lower North scattered their votes among numerous favorite sons. On the second ballot, New Jersey's delegation divided, casting ten votes for Dayton and four for Seward.

The break to Lincoln began when delegates from Ohio, Vermont, and New Hampshire swung over to him. After the second ballot most of Pennsylvania's delegates changed decisively from their favorite son to Lincoln. As more supporters of favorite sons switched, the contest narrowed to a horse race between Seward and Lincoln. Instead of the previous two-thirds margin for Seward, the race became a dead heat, with 184 for Seward to 181 for Lincoln. On the next ballot, the third, Maryland and then Massachusetts swung into Lincoln's column. New Jerseyans gave eight votes to Lincoln and five to Seward; only one delegate stayed with Dayton. When pivotal Ohio moved to back Lincoln, almost clinching his nomination, delegations stampeded to Lincoln. Seward, despite his early lead, lost, while Lincoln, despite his lack of immediate prominence, won.

Like Lincoln, the platform presented a blend of realism with a dash of idealism. With calculated economic appeals to all regions and interests in the North, the declaration particularly pleased New Jerseyans and Pennsylvanians by supporting a protective tariff. For naturalized voters, Republicans advocated immigrants' rights and avoided nativist posturing. Flexible yet firm, conciliatory on the central issues, the platform pleased many people, particularly moderates. The Republicans denounced extremists who made "threats of disunion" and "contemplated treason." Yet they shunted aside other controversial issues such as the fugitive slave law and its enforcement in the North, slavery in the District of Columbia, and the matter of future slave states. As in the state party's declaration, the national Republican platform rebuked "lawless invasion by armed force of the soil of any State or Territory," whether by supporters of slavery or by abolitionists. Republicans endorsed free soil in the territories, but in contrast to 1856, they did not demand a federal law to prohibit slavery in the territories and recognized the legality of slavery in the states where it already existed.

Unlike the Republicans of 1856, the party in 1860 spoke cautiously and made a broad-gauged appeal. Now that power was a possibility, Republican politicians no longer could afford idealistic amateurs as their platform makers and leaders. Political professionals, eager for results and hungry for power, prevailed.

After the convention three New Jersey delegates, along with their counterparts from other states, visited Lincoln at his home in Springfield, Illinois. Lincoln's frank, open manner and fluent conversation put everyone at ease. Railroad owner John I. Blair depicted the nominee as "quite a plain man. Very intelligent and cautious." The visitors described Lincoln as not handsome but tall, lean, and rugged. Lincoln served "cold water. Nothing else," so Blair viewed Lincoln as "very temperate." Evidently Lincoln was making a pitch for the temperance vote; his champagne, stored in the kitchen, awaited a more festive occasion.[5]

Lincoln's nomination naturally took most New Jerseyans by surprise. The *Mercury* admitted it had preferred Seward but considered Lincoln a fine candidate. Although Lincoln was the second choice of most delegates, those who knew him did not regard him as a second-rate man. Republicans contended that his judgment, together with his perseverance and resourcefulness, made him just the leader the country needed. At a time of corruption in Washington, "Honest old Abe" would set things straight. The *Flemington Republican* contrasted the two party leaders in the North: Republican Lincoln could split fence rails, while Democratic front-runner Douglas could split hairs. In addition, Lincoln, as a self-reliant son of the frontier and a self-made man who rose from the ranks, commanded the sympathy and support of the common people. The *Newton Register* remarked that there was "something, in the plain, old-fashioned, homespun manhood of Abe Lincoln that goes straight to the hearts of the masses and warms them up."[6]

Democrats and a sprinkling of die-hard nativists scoffed that the nomination put availability before fitness. Lincoln, they insisted, remained a political nonentity with neither Fremont's popularity nor Seward's ability. The *Jersey City Standard* dismissed him as a "fifth rate man, with no public experience, with coarse and uncouth manners, whose oratory is a vile compound of clumsy jests and clownish grimace." The newspaper criticized the gullibility of those who took a fancy to Lincoln's surface characteristics. His height could not compensate for his intellectual dwarfishness and lack of education. His prowess as a riverboatman and a rail splitter hardly substituted for the experience and expertise required of a statesman. Opponents painted Lincoln either as an extreme radical who would out-Seward Seward or as a fanatical abolitionist revolutionary who would relentlessly carry out the program of Brown.[7]

In response, the Republicans reiterated Lincoln's consummate moderation. He had never espoused radicalism. He had firmly pledged not to interfere with slavery where it then existed. Lincoln, moreover, did not believe in social and political equality for blacks. As to Lincoln's federal inexperience—he had served only a single term in the House of Representatives—the Republicans stated that Democrats overrated experience. Buchanan, after all, had had plenty of experience and had learned nothing.[8]

Some Democrats reacted more candidly. The *Freehold Democrat* regarded Lincoln's selection as the "stronger one than that of Mr. Seward" because Seward appeared "personally unpopular and Lincoln comparatively unknown" in the state. The *Camden Democrat*, still bolder, assessed Lincoln's nomination as the "very strongest the Republicans could have made, as to the individual, his locality, and his political sentiments." Even so, these qualities did not assure success in New Jersey. The *Paterson Register* considered New Jersey one of "the most *uncertain* of any of the doubtful States."[9]

On the national scene, some remnants of the American and the Whig parties, especially southern moderates, formed a new political movement called the National Union party, which was dedicated to restoring fraternal feeling and preserving the Union. They met early in May at Baltimore. Proponents dismissed the fact that the new party lacked a real platform: the simpler the platform and the stronger the keynote of patriotism, the better, they insisted.

As promised, the party's platform was simple indeed. It merely proposed to combat growing sectionalism, which if unchecked would tear the nation apart. It pledged tersely to uphold the Union, the Constitution, and the rule of law, but did not indicate how it would do so. Significantly, the declaration made no mention of any nativist issue. The party's presidential nominee, John Bell, the former Whig senator from Tennessee, championed moderation. Supporters expected to do especially well in the upper South.

In New Jersey, the leaders and followers of this movement came from American party ranks and thus threatened to undercut or possibly disrupt the Opposition coalition. During the campaign, die-hard nativists, notably Charles Deshler, became active again in building the party. Moderate Americans, including Joseph Fitz Randolph, James Bishop, and Peter Clark, joined them. In contrast to their support of Fillmore in 1856, however, few Jersey Americans supported Bell. Of the important newspapers in the state, only Deshler's *Jersey City Standard* backed him.[10]

Most state newspapers, both Republican and Democratic, took a dim view of this upstart group. Organizing a new party was a formidable task in itself; starting a third party struck them as Herculean. The Republicans, at only six years of age, had the most to lose by formation of this splinter party. The *Mercury* contended that Bell's followers were nothing more than opportunistic spoilers, bent on mischief. Bell's movement, moreover, represented a dangerous neutralism when the very existence of the nation was at stake. Indeed, this new party might give in both to slavery in the West and to secession of the South because it proposed no new policy. The Democratic *Paterson Register* dismissed the movement with the remark: "It won't do in these times for a party to hide itself behind a plausible claim of Union Savingism." Critics emphasized that merely to stand upon the Constitution begged every question. After all, as the *Register* pointed out, "Mr. Yancey says it is one thing, Mr. Seward another, Mr. Douglas still another," while Bell claimed to differ from all of them. Bell, moreover, gave the impression of an uninspiring has-been, leading a group of old gentlemen of a bygone age to nowhere in particular. Most commentators regarded the movement as irrelevant in New Jersey.[11]

As New Jersey's Democrats prepared for their state and national conventions, party members disagreed about platforms and candidates. Maneuvering to outwit Douglas's state forces, the anti-Douglas leaders suggested a southerner as the presidential nominee, instead of a northerner with a pro-South policy, as was done in the 1850s. The national ticket could achieve geographical balance by selecting the top of the ticket from a border slave state and the vice-presidential nominee from the lower North. Specifically, Kentucky could furnish the presidential nominee, either James Guthrie, the former secretary of the treasury, or the popular vice-president, John Breckinridge. New Jersey could provide a man for vice-president, possibly William Alexander. Such candidates, unconnected with the slavery controversy, would appeal to both the North and the South. A southerner in the presidential slot would eliminate Douglas. By exploiting Alexander's statewide popularity, New Jersey's anti-Douglas leaders could load their state's delegation to the national convention with anti-Douglas men.[12]

The Douglas forces, led by Martin Ryerson, were aware of this strategy. They calculated that "our greatest difficulty will arise from Colonel Alexander's popularity: Senator Thomson, and those who act with him, will no doubt avail themselves of that to secure a delegation ostensibly for Alexander for vice-president, but really for a Southern President."

Douglas's supporters, however, maintained that no pro-southern Democrat could carry the state. And to select a southern nominee for president, in the words of one Trenton man, would "brand the Democracy as upholding the ultra ideas of Southern secessionists, and the party has already load enough to carry in the North, without imposing upon them this additional burden." As he put it, "There is but one man now named by the democracy who can carry New Jersey, and that man is Stephen A. Douglas," especially because the anti-Lecompton men held "the balance of power in New Jersey."

Douglas received support from all parts of the state. Gritty ally Jacob Vanatta of Morristown assured Douglas that he enjoyed substantial support in both numbers and influence. At this early stage of the campaign the *Jersey City Standard* went so far as to estimate that three-fourths of the state's Democrats backed Douglas.

Douglas's forces were active and articulate, but questions remained about how effectively the Douglas men could secure delegates to the party conventions. In view of the strength of the popular movement for Alexander, Ryerson regarded the effort to oppose Alexander as futile. Instead he proposed to "fall in with it, taking care, however, to get such delegates as at the proper time would vote for you." The problem, however, was how to have enough reliable Douglas men selected as ostensible Alexander delegates. Although the Douglas men controlled some primary meetings, it remained unclear how many others the anti-Douglas men packed.[13]

On March 28 the state convention met in Trenton. In the battle to select delegates to the national convention, Buchanan's forces outmaneuvered Douglas's supporters, who obtained less than one-third of the delegation. Although formally unpledged, the convention requested the delegates to cast a united vote for Alexander for vice-president, and thus indirectly pressured them to support a southerner for president. Most of the delegates ranked among the state's Lecomptonites and included an unprecedented array of lame ducks recently rejected by the electorate. The delegates selected seemed to be out of touch with the rank and file of state Democrats, and thus gave the delegation an unrepresentative character.

Observers regarded the platform as unfocused, consisting largely of a hodgepodge of accusations against Republicans for their blatant disregard of the Constitution and federal laws protecting slavery. The convention professed its loyalty to popular sovereignty, but it failed to endorse its champion, Douglas, and praised its enemy, Buchanan. In a defensive move, the Democrats embraced a protective tariff.

As the delegates prepared for the national convention in Charleston, South Carolina, in late April, Pennington predicted they "will have a sweet time at the Charleston Convention, for a more discordant crew than the democratic at this day can hardly be conceived." Some friends of Douglas even hoped some southern disunionists might walk out of the convention. Such defections could enhance Douglas's prospects in the North and could convince the moderate southern delegates who remained in the convention that only the support of Douglas could prevent election of a Republican president.[14]

In Charleston, southerners lavished hospitality on their political friends but withheld it from Douglas's delegates. Within the state delegation the tug-of-war continued. While some of Douglas's supporters were absent, the state delegation decided in an important caucus to vote as a unit during the convention. Douglas's delegates, however, protested this arrangement, demanded individual voting, and appealed to the convention as a whole. After a stormy fight on the convention floor, where pro-Douglas forces seized control, the Douglas men in the state delegation won the right to vote individually.

In the ensuing struggle to write the party's platform, extremist southerners demanded a federal slave code that actively protected the institution in the territories. As northerners saw it, southerners demanded that the Democratic party support slavery not only where it existed, but wherever it chose to go; such support was tantamount to making slavery a national institution. Considering this demand unacceptable, even suicidal, supporters of Douglas rejected this unreasonable demand and backed popular sovereignty as the only palatable choice to northern voters. On such matters, in decisive votes, most of New Jersey's delegates supported the platform proposals of the Douglas men by a vote of five to two.

Members of the extreme southern wing, unable to get their way, walked out of the convention. As they left, some northern delegates on the floor jeered, while Charlestonians in the galleries cheered. Many of the bolters from the lower South hoped their tactic would force concessions from the delegates who remained. Instead, the Douglas managers concentrated on nominating their candidate and expected mistakenly that now they could do so easily. The pro-southern chairman of the convention, however, ruled that nomination required a two-thirds majority of the original number of delegates before the southern walkout. Many delegates, hoping for patronage or compromise, supported his position. On this critical vote the New Jersey delegation remained divided; five and one-half votes supported the two-thirds rule and one and one-half opposed it.

When the actual balloting began for the presidential nomination, the New Jerseyans unanimously supported Guthrie instead of Alexander. Evidently they did so to preserve the tenuous unity of the state delegation and to maximize its influence. On subsequent ballots, however, they split, with a vote of five for Guthrie to two for Douglas.

The voting dragged on for more than a week. One exhausted delegate, Benjamin Williamson of Elizabeth, decided to return home before it ended. In writing out instructions for casting his vote, he endorsed any reasonable effort to conciliate the South but refused to cave in to southern demands. He declared: "I am unwilling to yield one jot to any demand which in any manner compromises the self respect or integrity of a Northern man, no matter what consequences may follow such refusal."

On the tenth day of the convention, after fifty-seven ballots, it became clear to Douglas's managers that they lacked enough votes to reach the required two-thirds majority. In early May, acknowledging failure, the convention adjourned for a month and a half with the hope that the delegates would have sober second thoughts when the conclave resumed in Baltimore.[15]

Nothing had turned out as expected in Charleston. The city in the southern heartland, chosen as the site of the convention for the sake of harmony, became itself a source of disharmony. The *Mercury* considered it poetic justice to bury the "sham democracy in Charleston, the home of nullification. Calhoun inoculated the party with his pro-slavery doctrines; the virus has worked; let South Carolina bury the carcass." The national party convention, touted as the great unifier, instead made agreement unreachable. Compromise, the essential ingredient of American politics, fell victim to those Democrats, both proponents and opponents of Douglas, who insisted on their platform planks and nominees. Such delegates seemed more interested in having their own way than in having a Democratic party at all. The southern Democrats in particular had so lost faith in their fellow Democrats from the North that they mistrusted Douglas's supporters as deeply as they distrusted Republicans. The dismal proceedings at Charleston called into question the viability of the Democracy as a national party and its ability to hold the nation together.[16]

New Jersey's Democratic newspapers severely criticized the actions of the southern extremists. These editorials hardly sounded like opinion pieces from newspapers in the southern or border states. None defended the walkout outright. Although the *Newton Herald* condemned Douglas and his allies for not accepting the slave code plank and blamed them for causing the secessionist stampede, the journal denied any sympathy with the secessionists and denounced both sides as narrow-minded sectionalists. Implicitly, if not explicitly, the Democratic papers rebuked the destructive behavior of the southern seceders. Typifying the attitude of state Democrats, the *Paterson Register* pointed out the irony of the bolters' "handing the reins of government over to their implacable enemies—the Black Republicans."[17]

On the issue of sectionalism, even the ultraconservative *Newark Journal* confessed, "We can see no practical difference between a sectional Democratic and a sectional Republican party. One is as bad as the other." The still blunter *Belvidere Journal* stated, "To the extreme South we would say your ultra views are obnoxious to a large majority of the party, so let them rest, for they never can nor never will be adopted" by the Democracy or Congress. This editorial told disunionists to persist in their folly "if you wish to break up the Democratic party, and have no one left at the North to fight your battles and defend your rights." The pro-Douglas *Morristown Banner* denounced the motives of the bolters, for "what they really want is a quarrel with everybody and everything at the North" in order to cause southerners to be "'fired' with resentment against the people of the free States. . . . We have no hesitation in pronouncing Mr. Yancey's scheme bold, rank treason to the Union." The *Banner* further contended that "concessions to such men, with such objects, are not only degrading and useless, but dangerous. . . . Concessions to them at Baltimore will only strengthen and encourage them in their treasonable purposes."

State Democrats tempered criticism of the fire-eaters with the hope that they did not represent most southerners. Mutual interest in retaining the presidency might still prevail and create party harmony at the upcoming Baltimore convention. Yet if the New Jersey Democracy served as an indicator, the prospects looked bleak.

Upon their return from Charleston, the state delegates engaged in an unseemly public dispute about their roles in reaching decisions, handling divisions, and voting at the convention. There erupted a heated debate as to which delegates remained true to the spirit and meaning of the original instructions laid down by the state convention. This quarrel rekindled the dispute over the Lecompton constitution and further embittered Douglas's supporters against Buchanan's cronies.[18]

Republicans naturally applauded the impending divorce. "The Democracy are in a peck of trouble," gloated the *Flemington Republican.* The *Trenton Gazette* dubbed the Charleston convention the "*Great* Bustification." The *Princeton Standard* remarked that just as the controversy over slavery had divided the Whigs, it now was destroying the Democrats. The *Mercury* considered the slavery question the "pivot upon which all others turn" because it touched the core of national life, debased its politics, and shamed civilization. The newspaper predicted a repeat performance at Baltimore because both the southern and the northern wings of the Democracy had gone too far to yield. Even Democratic delegate James Wall observed pessimistically: "Tomorrow I leave for Baltimore to be *in at the death* of the Democratic party." Between what he regarded as the malevolent folly of Buchanan and the demagogic ambition of Douglas, Wall predicted that "we will be crushed as between the upper and the nether millstone." He saw no chance for compromise because "rule or ruin appears to be the motto of both."[19]

Reconvening on June 18 in Baltimore, the Democrats found their differences still irreconcilable. As the delegates grappled with the situation, New Jersey's delegates remained divided; a majority voted against the various positions of the pro-Douglas forces. The convention refused to readmit most of the bolters.

Realizing that they could not block the nomination of Douglas and recognizing that the South had lost control of the Democracy, the extremist southerners attending the convention bolted and formed their own party. On June 23 they nominated John Breckinridge as their presidential candidate. Breckinridge, a moderate who had just turned extremist, campaigned on a narrowly sectional platform endorsing federal protection of slave property in the territories.

Also on June 23, the Democrats at the reduced regular convention failed to reach the required two-thirds majority on the second ballot: Douglas remained twenty-one votes short. Therefore the delegates nominated Douglas by acclamation. In the balloting for the presidential nominee, Douglas

received two and one-half votes from New Jerseyans; the rest of the delegation abstained. Douglas stood on a platform endorsing popular sovereignty,
but it included a conciliatory plank relegating to the Supreme Court any
disputed question concerning the power of a territorial legislature to regulate slavery.[20]

Believing that no southern man could carry a single northern state and
no northerner could win any southern state, disunited Democrats made
double nominations and double platforms. The schism now was complete.
The delegates from the North refused to surrender to the South; the delegates from the South refused to capitulate to the North. Thus did the Democracy cease to exist as a national party. Republicans predicted victory by
their united party against a divided rival.

Only a month intervened between the national convention and New
Jersey's Democratic convention to choose its presidential electors. The Jersey Democracy was divided before and during both Democratic national conventions; thus it came as no surprise that Democratic lack of unity continued.
Having lost the presidential nomination, the disgruntled Breckinridgers denounced the nominating process as defective. They accused Douglas's forces
of sabotaging the conventions and violating both the two-thirds rule and the
usual procedure to admit delegates. Further, they charged that the Douglas
men's sharp convention tactics and their sham policy of popular sovereignty
had caused the split in party ranks. According to this view, advanced vigorously by Edward N. Fuller of the *Newark Journal* and James J. McNally of the
*Newton Herald*, only Breckinridge had been chosen legally and properly; therefore he was the legitimate national party's candidate. Editor Alexander E.
Donaldson of the *Somerville Messenger* also backed Breckinridge, but he candidly considered one nomination as regular as the other.

Supporters blamed Douglas and his New Jersey contingent of anti-
Lecompton Democrats for the humiliating defeats in 1858 and 1859, and
viewed them as partly to blame for the loss of the speakership in 1860. They
vowed to get even. The *Journal* dubbed Douglas the "squatter sovereign" and
reviled him as a demagogue, an egomaniac, and a traitor to the party. Moreover, if Douglas won the presidency, the anti-Douglas Democrats expected
no patronage from him. Without this compelling incentive, they saw no reason to back him.[21]

Douglas's supporters regarded their candidate as the regular nominee of
the party. His selection by the authorized convention at Baltimore conformed
to the party's established procedures at previous conventions. Before 1860 a
regular nomination usually required only a majority of two-thirds of the delegates present. Douglas had obtained 180 votes (93 percent) of the 194 cast,
or fifty more than two-thirds of the votes actually cast. (Yet because more
than one-third of the delegates refused to vote, Douglas did not have the
needed two-thirds of the accredited delegates, as required under the new

ruling adopted at Charleston. Supporters of Douglas considered this rule highly irregular and later irrelevant, when the motion to make his nomination unanimous by a voice vote received approval.)

The *Trenton American* observed that Douglas's nomination came the closest to regularity, "If the Convention which nominated Mr. Douglas was irregular, it certainly cannot be claimed that the one which nominated Mr. Breckinridge was regular." Vanatta dismissed Breckinridge's nomination "by a small knot of bolting secessionists," who rejected the will of the majority. Their convention represented a mere fragment of the original convention with less than one-third of the number of delegates who attended the Charleston convention. The losers, pointed out the *American*, rejected "submission which is the basis of all party organization." No party, concluded the *Morristown Banner*, can exist unless its members support party nominations.[22]

Douglas's supporters believed the Illinoisan was not only the regular nominee, but also the right one. Nationalistic Douglas made a stronger nominee than sectionalistic Breckinridge, who now was regarded as a mere figurehead of the southern disunionists. Douglas had formulated and championed Democratic principles that Breckinridge now opposed. The *Paterson Register* argued that Americans "stand on the brink of a volcano, and we know not the moment the grand explosion may take place." Only Douglas, with his Titan intellect and his Jacksonian nerve, could rescue the Republic from both abolitionist Republicans in the North and treasonable disunionists in the South. The *Camden Democrat* described this nomination as the best possible and condemned Breckinridge's adherents. It criticized the *Newark Journal's* disregard of both public opinion and party convention tradition, and accused the *Journal* of advocating the "cause of the disunion seceders with reckless effrontery."[23]

The Douglas men blamed Buchanan for disrupting the Democracy when he broke his word on the party's pledge of popular sovereignty. The *Camden Democrat* contended, "It is high time that the blame for any rupture in the party were placed where it belongs—upon the Executive, who deceived the party." For all these reasons, supporters of Douglas viewed fusion with Breckinridge's forces as unacceptable. The *Mount Holly Herald* advised New Jersey Democrats to "touch not, handle not, taste not the Yancey baked pot pie. It is sprinkled over with intrigue and hotly spiced with secession."[24]

In response to this barrage of criticism and in recognition of their weak position in the state, the increasingly desperate managers of Breckinridge resorted to all kinds of maneuvers and proposals. Sometimes bullying, sometimes cajoling, they tried to persuade the supporters of Douglas that only a coalition ticket could defeat Lincoln in New Jersey. The Democratic state central committee, dominated by Breckinridge supporters, proposed a presidential electoral ticket with four Douglas men and three backers of Breckinridge. Jersey voters could select a ballot marked either "Douglas" or

"Breckinridge." Whichever ballot obtained the greater vote would receive the total electoral vote of the state if the fusion ticket succeeded. With sarcasm the *Mercury* proposed an unlikely pair to head the electoral ticket—Buchananite William Wright and Douglasite Martin Ryerson—and suggested that the platform should contain "three-sevenths of Protection to Slavery in the Territories mixed with four-sevenths of Squatter Sovereignty."[25]

Ignoring this incompatibility, the *Newark Journal* and many other Democratic newspapers pressed hard for a common front. The *Journal* denied that New Jersey adherents of Breckinridge endorsed disunion and emphasized that they differed from his southern supporters. Breckinridgers contended that as long as the storm raged, the ship's crew must not quarrel about the validity of their officers' commissions but must follow their orders to save the ship. Only by preserving the Democracy could the party preserve the Union against "scoffs of disunion or the threats of Abolitionism."[26]

The Douglas men rejected these overtures and scorned any alliance with deserters. They pointed to the fundamental differences between Douglas and Breckinridge regarding defection from the party, expansion of slavery, and southern secession. These very differences, the *Morristown Banner* remarked, had prompted the Breckinridgers to secede from the Charleston and Baltimore conventions and to organize a new party with a pro-southern platform. At that time the Breckinridgers had pronounced such differences as unbridgeable; now the New Jersey allies of the defectors and disunionists had the effrontery to appeal to the backers of Douglas and the friends of the Union to form a coalition with them. The *Banner* responded, "How absurd! Make a union with the *disunionists* to support the Federal Union!!!" One might as well go into a blast furnace to freeze ice cream, the editorial added, or join an invading army to preserve peace. The *Banner* warned Jersey voters: "We say to democrats and all other friends of the Federal Union, Beware of *the disunionists—beware of their allies and camp-followers, and beware of their candidates!*"

If the dissident New Jersey Democrats really desired party harmony and success in the state, they had only to withdraw rump candidate Breckinridge and support regular candidate Douglas. They also had to repudiate the disunionist platform of Breckinridge and substitute Douglas's national platform, the party's only official position. Douglas supporter James M. Scovel of Camden asked, "How long has it been a doctrine of Democracy that they who abandon the regular nominee for President can dictate a ticket for the people? Where do they get the power?"[27]

Douglas himself, fighting for party control and his own political survival as well as for the very existence of both the northern Democracy and the nation, wanted nothing to do with Breckinridge and his allies. He declared he would not reward treachery by trading nominations with people who had stabbed him in the back. He would not bestow legitimacy on a bastard candidacy born of a movement of mutineers who broke up conventions. He had nothing to surrender, nothing to compromise, nothing to accept, nothing to offer.

In a meeting on July 10, Douglas instructed his New Jersey supporters to act alone. These Douglas men agreed wholeheartedly and promised to carry out his wishes. Beyond questions of party policy, many of them considered cooperation inexpedient in the state because Breckinridge enjoyed little popular support there.[28]

Breckinridge's forces represented many, but not all, of the older, established politicians, who were extreme conservatives and intensely loyal followers of Buchanan. They vowed to defeat Douglas and destroy his supporters' influence in the state party. Under orders from Buchanan, most federal employees in the state backed Breckinridge. Entrenched in power, Breckinridge's men controlled the state party organization and prepared to use it on behalf of their nominee to counter Douglas's numerical advantage. The *Trenton Gazette* regarded the Douglas men as "much stronger in this State" than the recruits in Breckinridge's camp.

Douglas attracted mostly younger recruits and mainly moderates. His ranks also included two former governors and other prominent state Democrats. The *Mercury* estimated that Douglas had about two-thirds of the state's Democrats on his side; other supporters optimistically claimed four-fifths. Disputing such estimates, overoptimistic Breckinridgers claimed half of the state's Democrats. By the middle of July, however, Douglas had obtained endorsements from more than three-fifths of the Democratic newspapers in the state.[29]

During July the struggle between the two sides for control of the party's electoral convention intensified as the party held primaries in towns and city wards. These contests sometimes ended in fistfights. A Camden man described the rival branches of the Democratic party as "waging war against each other with a great deal of bitterness."

Breckinridge's supporters scheduled the state convention earlier than usual, on July 25, to deny Douglas's forces time to organize and elect their delegates. To counteract this move, Douglas's adherents either resorted at the outset to separate primaries of their own or later left those controlled by Breckinridge's supporters and organized their own meetings. Contests over representation seemed likely at the state convention. One newspaper found that Douglas attracted the most support in larger towns while Breckinridge won favor in some rural districts. New Jerseyans had seldom witnessed such a fight in a primary.

On the eve of the convention, angry politicians descended on Trenton. Intense excitement sparked long caucuses, heated discussions, and dire predictions, with cursing and more drinking than usual. Fights broke out in bars. As dawn broke on July 25, the red-eyed delegates sobered up, faced the incontrovertible fact of Democratic disruption, and agreed to disagree. Because the two factions assembled in separate conventions, the simplified proceedings themselves ran smoothly. Douglas's supporters seized the initiative by renting the largest hall in the city, leaving their rivals to go elsewhere. In due course each Democratic convention formed a separate electoral ticket for president.

Breckinridge's convention, however, lacking confidence in its candidate's strength, decided not to act alone and thus fashioned a fusion ticket with electors chosen from every party opposed to Lincoln. It sought allies among alienated friends in the Douglas camp and former enemies in the Bell party. The die-hard nativists, also meeting in Trenton, rebuffed overtures from Breckinridge's emissaries. Significantly, the Breckinridge convention endorsed the Democratic national platform of 1856, which championed congressional nonintervention in the territories, contradicting its own nominee's extremist and sectionalist position.

Defiance marked the tone of Douglas's spirited supporters, who harshly denounced Buchanan and Breckinridge. Douglas's men objected to both sectional parties, the Lincoln party that desired to place the Union under northern control and the Breckinridge faction that sought either southern domination or separation. Douglas's delegates thus formed their own state committee.

The events of the day had ironic aspects. New Jersey's Douglas men championed the regular national nominee in the forum of a self-constituted convention because they did not wish their opponents to outvote them in a regularly constituted convention. Thus they placed themselves in the position of irregulars, even while they denounced the Breckinridgers as irregulars. Meanwhile the Jersey contingent of the Breckinridge faction, which refused to back the regular nominee, sanctimoniously acted under the official auspices of the state party's central committee. The members spoke soothingly of compromise and unity, at complete variance with their allies at Charleston and Baltimore. They proclaimed their fidelity to the Union by supporting southern disunionists; they declared their avowed opposition to Lincoln but refused to support his chief opponent and their own party's nominee. Meeting in the assembly chamber of the State House, they assumed the trappings of regularity and tried to legitimatize their defection. Divorce, then, was the ultimate price of the day's peace at Trenton.[30]

# 4 Party Paralysis and Unionist Consensus: The Election of 1860

In the presidential campaign, politicians discussed a wide range of issues. The proceedings at the state conventions contradict the view that either party focused narrowly on economic matters in order to avoid more controversial topics. Once again in the debate most New Jerseyans, regardless of party affiliation, disputed or simply ignored southern constitutional claims and the notion of slaves as movable property. Democrats, however, regarded the likelihood of slavery in the West as so remote that they saw no reason to jeopardize the Union for a mere abstraction.[1]

For Republicans the spread of slavery raised a question that could not be dismissed so readily. It was a real problem and would soon arise again for other territories. The *Princeton Standard* found no other issue "with such momentous moral, social and political consequences as this one."[2]

The Republicans contended once again that the status of slavery in the West must not depend on which party controlled the federal machinery and dictated appointments of territorial officials. To leave the decision on this question of slavery in the territories up to the people of the territories, as the Douglas Democrats advocated, evaded the issue and condoned slavery. Republicans urged restriction of the lands allowing slavery.

Above all, the Republicans wished to curb the power of slavery both in the West and in Washington. Disputing the Dred Scott decision, Republicans contended that Congress possessed ample authority to restrict the expansion of slavery and had done so many times in the past. Indeed, Congress always had settled such matters for the territories. Now only the Republican party could assure the future of freedom in the West. Only Lincoln could split rails to fence in slavery where it belonged—in the South. The *Princeton Press* summed up the dominant view of the party: "Vote for Lincoln, to secure the Free Territories for the Free White man" and "to settle this everlasting slavery question."[3]

Douglas naturally made the best case for popular sovereignty. Unlike the other candidates, he disregarded the campaign custom of remaining silent. Lacking contributions for speakers and a viable organization to mount a national campaign, he went directly to the voters throughout the nation.

Douglas addressed a large, enthusiastic audience of about five thousand people in Newark on August 22. Recalling George Washington's warning about the danger of sectional parties to the Union, he declared, "We are now threatened with that very danger." He criticized the Republican call for the federal government to prohibit slavery in places where the inhabitants wanted it, and likewise condemned the southern demand that Congress protect slavery in places where the people did not want it. He counted both sides guilty of the sins of sectionalism and interventionism in opposition to the expressed will of the people. Douglas reiterated his populist solution for the territories: "Let them make their own laws, establish their own institutions, regulate their own affairs, mind their own business."[4]

This stirring speech met with mixed reactions. On the right, the pro-Breckinridge *Newark Journal* quibbled over the regularity of his nomination and ignored the substance of the speech. In the center, pro-Douglas newspapers heaped praise on his speech and his policy. Echoing Douglas, the *Morristown Banner* contended that Republicans wished to force freedom down everybody's throats, while southerners wished to cram down slavery. On the left, Republican papers mixed praise with criticism. The *Newark Mercury* complimented Douglas for his gallant fight against unreasonable southern demands but then chastised him for ignoring the central matter, the evil of slavery, with his delusory populist formula that might sanction the expansion of slavery.[5]

New Jersey Democrats countered by again equating Republicanism with abolitionism. They accused Republicans of ignoring the constitutional guarantees to slaveholders, including the fugitive slave law. Although the Democrats conceded that few, if any, avowed abolitionists were active in public life in the state, they depicted Jersey Republican leaders as disguised revolutionaries who admired John Brown and his fanatical schemes. Someday these leaders would throw off their mask of moderation to beat the drums of revolution at the head of an abolitionist brigade. As soon as possible, a Republican administration in Washington would end slavery by bayonet.[6]

New Jersey Republicans, as before, moved quickly to dissociate themselves from the taint of abolitionism. They reiterated their opposition to abolishing slavery where it currently held sway but spoke out boldly against slavery expanding elsewhere. At a Republican rally in New Brunswick, Robert Voorhees described the change in the pro-slavery rationale. Southerners formerly had considered slavery a necessary evil, but now regarded it as an unmitigated blessing. Once southerners had denounced stealing slaves from Africa as an act of piracy; now some southerners wished to reopen the same trade as a mission of mercy. Once they condemned the sale of slaves within America and regarded it as a curse; now white southerners viewed it as a "black tie that binds States together in harmony." Breckinridge Democrats now proposed sending "their black tides through all territories." Once freedom had ruled the land, and slavery constituted the exception; now slaveocrats worked to reverse that situation. "Because we resent all this, we are called abolitionists," Voorhees remarked, but added, "How can we be abolitionists when there is nothing for us to abolish, except this miserable administration" of Buchanan? He predicted that "if slavery is to be an eternal fact, you may expect an eternal agitation." So, said Voorhees, Democrats "call us Black Republicans," and "we accept it because a rose by any other name will smell as sweet to us as a nigger will to them."[7]

Distancing themselves further from the abolitionists, the Republicans stressed that abolitionists denounced Lincoln for his moderation. They also pointed out that abolitionists in the North constituted only a fanatical fringe whose small numbers and negligible influence no sober person could take seriously. Far more numerous and more influential in the South were the fanatical disunionists who threatened national unity and peace. These demagogues, constituting a majority in some states of the lower South, posed the real danger and had to be defeated.[8]

Democrats used racist propaganda to scare voters. Once the Republicans freed the slaves, the savagelike blacks would "pour into New Jersey" and bring anarchy. The *Trenton American* sketched this apocalyptic scenario: "Men of the North, have you comprehended it? Have you thought of three million negroes . . . wild with their freedom, uneducated, unrestrained by any moral perceptions and ideas, led by their passions alone, lazy, vicious, and uncontrollable?—Have you thought of the horrors which this exodus from the South would entail upon you—of this mass of negroes perambulating your country, stealing and murdering as they go?"[9]

To further discredit Republicans, Democrats predicted that Republican regimes would force equality between the races and would desecrate the rights of whites on the "altar of negro worship." Democrats communicated this scenario in a large picture that they carried in their parade in Newark. Lincoln stood in the bow of a ship steered by Republican editor Horace Greeley. White women aboard sat on the laps of black men and embraced them, while Uncle Sam tried to prevent them from landing. The motto read, "No Negro Equality." A Somerset County man feared the "fatal black vomit of Republicanism." Just before Election Day, the *Freehold Democrat* made its final, calculated appeal: "Citizens of New Jersey, are you ready to admit the negro to political and social equality with you? If not, say so by your votes on Tuesday next."[10]

In response the Republicans assured white voters that Republican opposition to expansion of slavery did not elevate blacks' interests above those of whites. As the Republican *Trenton Gazette* put it, "We will not say that we love 'Sambo' more, and all the rest of the free white people of the country less." Slavery, after all, degraded not only blacks but also whites. It insulted free labor and created competition to white workers. Voorhees pointed out that slavery not only conflicted with the best interests of humanity, but also "puts poor whites below a nigger." Warning southern slaveholders, he declared, "Let them do what they will with the African but they must keep hands off of the Anglo Saxon." The *Gazette* said of the Republicans, "It is not for the slave that they are contending, but for freemen." The *Flemington Republican* reminded voters that Republicans did not intend to raise blacks to the same level with whites: "That such is not the case, but is only an election humbug got up by the Democratic press."[11]

Another campaign issue focused on the method of election. With four presidential candidates dividing the vote, it seemed possible that Congress might select the president if no candidate obtained a majority of the electoral college. Lincoln's supporters attacked selection by Congress as sneaky, arrogant, and undemocratic. Recalling that it had taken nine weeks to elect a speaker, Republicans predicted that election of a president by Congress would paralyze government for an extended time. A vote for Lincoln, however, would secure victory in the electoral college, preventing uncertainty and danger. The prospect of protracted discord frightened many voters and sowed distrust of anti-Lincoln stratagems to throw the election into the lap of Congress. With a populist appeal, Republicans had succeeded in placing their opponents in a bad light.[12]

Many state voters considered the possible breakup of the Union to be the most pressing matter. They feared that southerners might carry out their threat to secede if Lincoln won. The Democrats exploited these fears ruthlessly. The *Newark Democrat* sounded the alarm that the South would consider a Republican victory "won avowedly on the issue of hostility to her institutions, and of animosity to her on account of those institutions, as the success of her bitter enemy." The *Newton Herald* hoped that "no man will coolly and deliberately sanction the destruction of the American union by aiding either directly or indirectly the election of Abraham Lincoln." One new resident of the state, former Kansas governor Robert J. Walker, told fellow Democrats that the party must do everything to prevent the success of northern sectionalism, which Republican victory signified. He said, "I cannot so vote as to imperil the safety of the Union. I cannot vote for civil war."[13]

Although Democratic newspapers in the state acknowledged that the southern states probably would secede if Lincoln won, these journals did not justify secession. "We notice the matter," observed the *Freehold Democrat*, "not to justify the South in secession under any circumstances, but to warn every friend of the Union . . . that there is trouble ahead if the Republicans are allowed to succeed." The Democrats made disunion the paramount issue on which to defeat Lincoln and save the Union.[14]

Jersey Republican politicians often made light of southern threats of secession and northern fears of disunion. In their opinion the stronger bond of common interests between northerners and southerners would overcome the recent bad feelings. William Pennington advised New Jerseyans not to fear that southerners seriously entertained ideas of secession. The sensible, patriotic majority, he observed, would prevail over a hothead minority bent on destroying the Union. Republicans also pointed out that the upper South would never secede and so the lower South would not attempt secession on its own.[15]

The *Mercury* dismissed the whole secession scare as a hoax: "It is a mere electioneering dodge, and has so often succeeded before that it is brought forward through the force of habit." Denial of the possibility of secession not only soothed fears; it also neutralized the Democrats' strongest means of scaring northern voters away from a candidate unpalatable to the South. Even some Democrats ridiculed the secession scare. A Salem County man proposed an instant solution. "Disunion! Bah! I wish General Jackson, or one just like him, was President for six months or so, to string up a few of the Northern abolitionists and Southern fire eaters, and we should hear no more of this bluster for at least a generation." Regardless of the election outcome, the *Cape May Wave* contended, the "country is safe." Opponents nevertheless attacked the Republicans' misguided confidence that the "Union never has been or can be endangered, and further that it is absolutely indissoluble and indestructible."[16]

While Republicans and Democrats argued about the effect of a victory by Lincoln on southerners, Archibald A. Hodge, a New Jerseyan who had served for a decade as a minister in a church in Fredericksburg, Virginia, expressed pessimism about the future in letters to his father in Princeton. Although he sympathized with the Republican cause, he believed that most northerners simply did not understand the mood of many southerners. Writing in October 1860, he observed, all Virginians "judge that you in the North greatly underrate the danger of immediate dissolution of the Union and civil war upon the election of Lincoln." He predicted that Virginia would not take the initiative, but was equally certain that South Carolina would do so. Furthermore, it seemed only a matter of time before Virginia itself seceded: "Whigs and democrats, all here agree in judgment that there is little hope of preventing Virginia from being drawn into the vortex," because of the "excited passions of the people," and their intense state pride and deep-seated southern loyalty.

Hodge understood that northerners were sincere both in their assurances that Lincoln's election would change nothing in the South and in their warnings that dissolution would bring disaster. Yet these views fell on deaf ears because the "actions of Southern men and States can be determined rationally only by a reference to Southern fixed ideas, be they true or false." Southerners regarded slavery as the normal condition of society and intended to perpetuate and even extend it. "Here I think they are mad," he wrote, but nonetheless "they can afford to fight for it. Hence I am afraid they will."[17]

Democrats predicted that economic disaster would follow political chaos. Republican hostility toward the South would increase sectional conflict. The resulting dislocation of trade would trigger cancelations of orders, closing of factories, and loss of jobs. As Election Day neared, Democratic politicians in cities stressed this issue.[18]

Republicans scoffed at Democratic predictions that grass soon would grow in city streets. Lincoln would not take any action to upset southerners; business would continue as usual. In any case, the prosperity and trade of New Jersey ultimately depended not on political events but on the enterprise of its manufacturers and the skill of its workers to produce the best goods at the lowest prices. State workers, moreover, did not depend on the South for their existence. They had no reason to sacrifice their convictions to keep their jobs.[19]

Hoping to gain from economic appeals, Republicans had included in their national platform planks pledging governmental promotion of economic growth. The Republican House of Representatives had supported federal subsidies of internal improvements, a liberal homestead policy, and a higher tariff. Democrats in the Senate and in the executive branch, however, stymied such proposals. Moreover, few New Jerseyans took an intense interest in the first two federal projects.

The Republican proposal for a higher tariff did arouse interest. Platform committeeman Thomas Dudley had worked hard to wedge that plank into the national Republican platform. New Jerseyans considered higher tariffs vital to the prosperity of the state's manufacturing, especially its iron and glass furnaces. The legislature became involved in March 1860, when a bipartisan senate committee with a Democratic majority supported a protective tariff. With few exceptions, New Jerseyans representing all parties favored a higher tariff. Both state Republican and Democratic platforms endorsed such a tariff.

Economic recovery, with a return to full employment after the 1857–1858 depression, took the immediacy out of the tariff issue. Overwhelming bipartisan support of a protective tariff throughout the state also undercut the usefulness of the issue for Republicans. Democrats went out of their way in congressional platforms to endorse a protective tariff in the second and fourth districts. The tariff question, then, played only a minor role in the state campaign.[20]

Congressional races in the state reflected the usual sectional proclivities. Republicans enjoyed smooth sailing downstate. Following the custom of giving first-term congressmen automatic renomination and exploiting the advantage of incumbency, the Republicans selected personable moderates, John Nixon and John Stratton. Quarrels occurred among the disparate factions of the Opposition, however, when Nixon courted the Americans; some Republicans criticized him for this, while dissident nativists grumbled as usual. Radical Republicans attacked Stratton as too moderate.

To counter these formidable candidates, Democrats in the first district nominated Cape May lawyer Joseph F. Leaming as their reluctant candidate.

In the campaign Leaming played an inactive role; he even refused to disclose which presidential candidate he favored, although he supported any fusion effort to defeat Lincoln. In the second district journalist Augustus Green, a Ewing man and a staunch supporter of Douglas, ran as the Democratic nominee. He paid Republicans the supreme compliment of stealing many of their national platform planks, including support of a protective tariff. On the territorial question, however, Green retained his standard-bearer's formula of popular sovereignty.

Upstate, polarized politics produced sharper differences between the parties. The Republicans criticized Democratic attempts to form coalitions with footloose Americans on local fusion tickets. The Democrats courted the immigrant electorate by condemning both nativism and the Republicans' previous accommodation to it.

In the strongly Democratic third and fourth districts, both anti-Lecompton Democratic incumbents decided to retire. With potential Democratic support shaky without prospects of bipartisan Opposition coalitions to conduct campaigns, the Republicans decided to put up their own candidates. In the third district, Republicans nominated Alexander P. Berthoud of Warren County, a popular, prosperous engineer who would pay for his own campaign. Democrats in this district selected Somerville bank cashier William G. Steele, a strong Douglas man. Steele, evidently trying to ride both Douglas's and Breckinridge's horses at the same time, favored attempts to form an anti-Lincoln fusion ticket. He also received support from Bell's supporters.

Republicans in the fourth district nominated Benjamin B. Edsall, the able editor of the highly regarded *Newton Register* and a strong advocate of a higher tariff. Faced with deep-seated divisions between Douglasites and Breckinridgers, fourth district Democrats in a masterstroke chose a compromise candidate, George T. Cobb of Morristown. Cobb, a retired iron manufacturer and a staunch Douglas Democrat, supported fusion of the anti-Republican forces.

The fifth district contest figured as the most interesting and most important in the state. Much to their own surprise, Democrats in both the Douglas and the Breckinridge conventions in effect nominated a compromise candidate, Nehemiah Perry. Perry, chairman of the Democratic state central committee, was an active, busy person who previously had served as Newark alderman and member of the assembly. A wealthy businessman, he bankrolled his own campaign. Perry supported both Douglas's bid for president and any possible fusion effort. Like Cobb, Steele, and Green, he tried to build districtwide coalitions on behalf of both Douglas and himself. Democrats, contended the candidates, must control Congress so that they could block Lincoln's program if he became president.

The Republican incumbent in the fifth district, Pennington, reluctantly accepted renomination for the sake of party unity and the need to bolster the national Republican ticket. Democrats calculated that they held the advantage because they had carried the district by a narrow majority of just under three hundred in the gubernatorial election of 1859, thanks in part to the Democrats' resourcefulness in recruiting immigrants. Perry was far less experienced than Pennington, but by the middle of October he harbored hopes of winning because the anti-Pennington forces in the district had forged an effective coalition. By default Perry secured the support of the Bell followers, who had failed to persuade anyone to run as their candidate.[21]

The Democrats attacked Pennington as a radical sectionalist masquerading as a conservative nationalist. They criticized his aristocratic background and his narrow outlook as a lawyer. Perry, they claimed, with firsthand business experience as a self-made entrepreneur, could better represent the district's manufacturing and commercial interests, as well as its people. The Republicans dismissed Perry as a "gentleman who by selling coats and pantaloons to the South, and his principles with them, has received the nomination of that party of fusions and confusions."

Early in the campaign Pennington's return to Congress seemed assured. Yet as Election Day neared, "Knee-High-Miah" Perry's challenge grew more formidable. To make matters worse, the aristocratic Pennington regarded the business of seeking support as beneath him. He refused to canvass the district, remarking, "It might do for some men but it would appear like hugging for votes which is out of my line." In contrast, Perry worked energetically and spent heavily. In truth, the patrician Pennington did not have his heart in the campaign. The plutocrat Perry did.[22]

Although the presidential and congressional races overshadowed state contests, politicians maintained a keen interest in which party would gain control of the next legislature. Confirmation of gubernatorial appointments and the revamping of assembly and congressional districts hinged on this power. Thus, although state issues did not figure importantly in the campaign, legislative control was significant.

The exciting presidential campaign stirred New Jerseyans deeply. They interrupted their everyday routines to participate. The beginning of the campaign resembled the arrival of the circus. People lined the streets to admire the smart military outfits of the high-spirited Republican Wide Awakes or their opponents, the Minute Men. Young men dressed in brilliant martial uniforms and carrying torches of red, white, or blue marched in unison as they lustily sang campaign songs and cheered their candidates. With drums beating, trumpets blaring, flags flying, torches gleaming, candles flickering, and rockets soaring, spectators thrilled to such demonstrations. Mass rallies featured famous speakers, flaming bonfires, and spectacular fireworks. After one local demonstration, the *Paterson Guardian* exclaimed that virtually "every citizen of the place was for one night wide-awake."

Each town had its flag raisings, colorful bunting and banners, and public barbecues, where guests mingled with good humor and camaraderie. Participation and patriotism marched briskly to the tune of partisanship. An invitation to join the Trenton Wide Awakes worked nicely in the recent victories of the Republicans: "Our friends in Maine, led off the van; the Keystone followed—true; And now we'll try, with might and main; What 'Jersey Blues' can do." Sometimes, however, partisanship got out of hand. Hecklers disrupted meetings. Rowdies stole torches, tried to break up parades, or sawed down poles with flags bearing the names of rival candidates.

Canvassing efforts redoubled. Newspapers of both parties advised campaign workers to search out every voter in every election district and to compile voting lists by party. Workers also were advised to organize neighborhood clubs to discuss the issues, furnish the uninformed with pamphlets, arouse the indifferent, convert the undecided, and combat opponents. Special campaign newspapers, especially those of Douglas's supporters, began operations in major cities and some county seats. Both parties in North Jersey made frantic efforts to appeal to immigrant groups, particularly the Irish, as well as the Dutch in Bergen County and the Germans in Newark. Nativist remnants, however, denounced such appeals. While national Republicans distanced themselves from nativists, state Republicans in many parts of New Jersey still sought appealing speakers with American credentials who could recruit former American party supporters.

The Republicans rode a wave of optimism; they rejoiced over the disruption of the Democracy in the nation and the state. Even some Democrats privately predicted Lincoln's victory in New Jersey. Although respectful of Douglas's early strength, the Republicans became so confident about Lincoln's sweep of the state that their leaders periodically issued warnings against overconfidence.[23]

Only the possibility of a coalition of all the forces opposed to Lincoln disturbed Republicans. Although some observers regarded fusion as impossible, others expected to carry the state, fusion or no fusion. They predicted that Lincoln's margin of victory would be between five thousand and twenty-five thousand. Referring to its own side, the supremely optimistic *Trenton Gazette* asked, "Is there any 'Opposition' party now in New Jersey? We think not." The *Gazette* regarded its fellow partisans in New Jersey as "Republicans, and nothing else. . . . It was well enough, probably, to call the party 'Opposition' while in an infantile state, but now that it has reached full age and assumed all the duties and responsibilities of manhood, it shows a lack of moral courage and a mean subserviency to call it Opposition. There is not, and cannot be, any intermediate ground between Republicanism and Democracy, and those who are not of the one must be of the other party."

These were brave words, but the reluctance in many places to use the label "Republican" betrayed insecurity. Only the congressional conventions in

North Jersey's fourth and fifth districts used the name. Most Republicans continued to employ the usual party designation—Opposition—or some equivalent word. Opponents noted that Lincoln's supporters often chose not to use the national party's title.[24]

As Lincoln's prospects grew brighter, the struggle between the proponents and the opponents of fusion intensified. Opponents urged the managers of the Douglas forces to stand firm because striking the colors would prove demoralizing, even self-defeating. Proponents, especially Bell's supporter Joseph Randolph, insisted that the leaders of the three parties had to find a way to arrange an alliance to defeat Lincoln. Supporters of fusion scheduled meetings with the Douglas men in September and October and proposed new compromises to fashion a common electoral slate.

Meanwhile, Breckinridge's and Bell's state leaders reached agreement on a fusion ticket. They placed electors from each side on the ticket and even included a few of the most prominent Douglas leaders. Yet throughout most of the fall campaign the managers of the Douglas forces, sensing the disadvantages, rejected all such alliances. They also regarded it as unprincipled to ally with party defectors and Know-Nothings.

Although Douglas's side continued firm in negotiations, some members of that camp began to waver as they became convinced of the necessity of fusion. After Republican victories in mid-October in Pennsylvania, Ohio, and Indiana, most people expected Lincoln to sweep the North. This likelihood further eroded the resolve of the Douglas managers and candidates in the state. Wondering whether they would oversee the destruction of the state party and fearing for their individual survival, they felt compelled to join the coalition.

After numerous abortive efforts, representatives of the three groups opposing Lincoln hammered out a joint electoral ticket on October 27 at 4 A.M. A horrified Republican declared that fusion "is just what we have feared from the start as the only chance to beat us." The coalition also displeased many ardent Douglas followers, who rejected what they regarded as a hypocritical and cowardly arrangement. As James Scovel explained to Douglas, "We felt our cheeks tingle with shame when we heard that the Electoral ticket contained the names of two Breckinridge men and two Bell men opposed to yourself and having us in a *minority* of the Ticket." Some prominent Douglas leaders claimed that they had not been a party to the early morning negotiations and swiftly repudiated the agreement. They steadfastly continued to support the separate electoral ticket for Douglas.

For other Democrats, the last-minute changeover caused only confusion. The frantic maneuvers and countermaneuvers left them unsure about the legitimacy of substituting the fusion electoral ballot for the straight Douglas ticket. Confusion degenerated into chaos in some counties in South Jersey, where Douglas's managers had distributed Democratic ballots before the last-minute agreement on a fusion electoral ticket. Various groups in several counties rejected or substituted names on the electoral ticket. Leaders found their alliances repudiated by followers. Enemies thrown into unexpected alliance did not forget enmities. So-called union savers attacked doughfaces, infuriating the Breckinridgers. Douglas Democrats continued to condemn nativists, who became enraged. The party leaders had imposed a peace in the interest of victory, only to witness renewed conflict.

The continual shuffling of the electoral cards with changing players and new deals brought derision from both Douglas Democrats and Republicans. The pro-Douglas *Paterson Register* denounced the whole business of party leaders authorizing different official ballots as a "humbug, a sham and a cheat." In truth, stated the editorial, this hybrid ticket reflected merely fragments of tickets and parties. In any event, now that three of the same regular Douglas electors appeared on both the final fusion ticket and the straight Douglas ticket, a partial fusion was achieved at the eleventh hour.

Then, too, no one knew what the union electoral slate represented, except opposition to the Republicans. Hoping to discourage fusionist votes but raising honest questions, the *Mercury* found the alliance unnatural.

> But what is a man voting for who deposits a ballot for the Fusion ticket? Does it represent any principle? Does it represent any party? Does it decide any question? Does it determine any controversy? Do you vote for Slavery, or against Slavery, or for non-intervention? Do you vote for Squatter Sovereignty, or for Disunion, or for Know Nothingism? The ticket is made up of men who hold contradictory opinions, who represent antagonistic parties, and who are aiming at hostile ends. A part of the Electors are supposed to be for Bell and the Constitution; a part of them are known to be for Breckinridge and Secession, and all of them pledged for Douglas and the Union. What can a sensible man do with such a bundle of incongruities?[25]

With the election only days away, excitement mounted across the state. Last calls to the faithful stressed patriotic duty and state pride. Democrats spoke of the waves of spreading anti-slavery fanaticism, which only the state's unionist dike could withstand. Characterizing New Jersey as the battlefield of liberty in the Revolutionary War, Republicans declared that those Jersey troops who fought and won key battles "proved, in '76, that Jerseymen were a liberty-loving and a slavery-hating people." Republicans hoped the descendants of those patriots who had laid down their lives to establish the nation would rally behind Lincoln in 1860 to save the nation. The *Hightstown Record* described the campaign in its village as follows: "Never in our recollection have the citizens of this place become more excited at the approach of an election, than during the present campaign. All have caught the infection of political enthusiasm. Party spirit runs high among men; ladies heartily wish they could vote, and children are betting oyster stews and gingerbread on the success of their favorite candidates. From morn till eve party and politics are the only topics discussed."

On November 6, 1860, a pleasantly mild Election Day, spirited last-minute demonstrations took place. In Atlantic County local Wide Awakes, out in large numbers, marched behind a wagon on which stood a man splitting a cedar log into fence rails. One voter in Perth Amboy waited in a long line at the polls to cast his vote in what he described as this "unequalled contest." Despite crowding, veiled threats, even occasional brawling, voters experienced little disorder. Convinced that their votes mattered, New Jersey voters went to the polls in record numbers on Election Day and registered the highest turnout in sixteen years. Believing his party's campaign message, a Morristown man declared that the election "will determine whether the Union is to dissolve or not." If Lincoln won, he predicted "this union is done."[26]

New Jerseyans learned of Lincoln's national victory the next day. He amassed 180 electoral votes, or 59 percent of the total. This victory in the electoral college suggested a popular landslide, but in fact Lincoln polled only 40 percent of the popular vote. Douglas (29 percent), Breckinridge (18 percent), and Bell (13 percent) together garnered 60 percent. Lincoln received electoral votes solely from the more populous North, where he won 55 percent of the popular vote. The southern electoral votes went mainly to Breckinridge and to Bell; Breckinridge outpolled Bell.

The Republican *Paterson Guardian* saluted Lincoln's victory with an obituary notice for the Buchanan Democrats, outlined boldly in black: "Died at his residence, of internal Corruption, on the evening of November 6th, *Sham Democracy*, whose grandfather was Nullification, whose father was Disunion. He leaves an only son, Slavery Extension, in very feeble health. He cannot survive, and his funeral will be attended on the 4th of March next, at Washington. The services will be conducted by Abe Lincoln."[27]

In New Jersey, however, confusion reigned as canvassers slowly tallied the vote. The result remained unclear for some time because voters selected individual electors on a number of different ballots for the four presidential candidates in various counties and because the major parties appeared to be matched evenly. At first, as each county's canvassers reported their returns to officials in Trenton, many people believed that the fusion presidential ticket had carried the state by two to five thousand votes. Four days after the election, however, the *New York Tribune* predicted that Lincoln and Douglas would divide New Jersey's seven electoral votes, four to three.

As returns trickled in during the second week after the election, Republicans began to harbor hopes of winning certainly three electoral votes and probably four. For the first time the Democrats grudgingly conceded the possibility that Lincoln might have won some of the state's electoral votes.

The final tally showed the *Tribune* right all along: Lincoln won four of New Jersey's electoral votes, Douglas, three. Although Lincoln won only a minority of the popular vote, he capitalized on his opponents' factionalism to secure a majority of the electoral vote. A small but significant group of anti-Lincoln voters (6 percent), refusing to vote for the fusion slate, cast ballots either for straight Douglas tickets, especially in Sussex and Salem, or for straight Bell tickets, as in Camden and Cumberland. This group took enough votes from Breckinridge's and Bell's electors on the fusion electoral ticket to allow four Republican electors to win. Thus the four highest Lincoln electors won by slim pluralities that resulted from the division of the anti-Lincoln vote.

Slightly fewer than 4,500 votes separated the winning electors on the fusion and the Republican ballots. Had the Democrats and Bell's unionists joined forces completely on one electoral ticket and received united support, they would have won the state's entire electoral vote.

A comparison of voting patterns between 1856 and 1860 reveals significant shifts. Voters who did not or could not vote in 1856 and who subsequently cast ballots in 1860 went Democratic by more than a two-to-one margin. The proportion of new voters who voted Democratic was four times the proportion of Buchanan supporters who switched to Lincoln. Democrats succeeded especially among voters in cities, and notably among new immigrant voters such as Irish Catholics in Newark and Trenton. In 1860 the fusion ticket carried four of the state's largest cities (Newark, Jersey City, Trenton, and Camden); Lincoln won only Paterson. Thus, despite disastrous divisions, the Democracy remained a powerful force in the state.

Republicans, too, consolidated. An estimated 7 percent of the state's Democrats who supported Buchanan in 1856 voted for Lincoln in 1860, while about 80 percent of the Fillmore Americans moved into Republican ranks, thus marking the end of the Americans' statewide influence as a separate party. Republicans enormously increased their share of the vote in virtually every county between 1856 and 1860 (from 28.5 percent to 47.9 percent), even though they still did not become the dominant political force in the state. They acquired recruits while maintaining virtually all of their supporters from 1856.

This significant increase in Republican strength occurred statewide, with the notable exception of Sussex. Republicans there increased their share of the popular vote by a mere two percentage points. Sussex, home of Martin Ryerson, gave Douglas his strongest straight vote in the state, roughly 20 percent of the vote cast. The straight Douglas ticket received 19 percent in Salem and 13 percent in Cumberland.

Democrats swept seven of ten upstate counties. Lincoln managed to carry Passaic, Morris, and Mercer by only marginal votes. Except for Camden, which narrowly went for Douglas, Republicans swept South Jersey. The counties located between the Raritan and Passaic rivers experienced the most dramatic and most important shifts. Essex went Republican in 1858 by 57 percent and again in 1859, but by only 51 percent; yet in the 1860 presidential race the county went Democratic by 52 percent, even as it supported Republican Pennington for Congress by the same percentage.

The greatest surprise and disappointment to the Republicans occurred in Middlesex. Although Democrats had performed poorly there since the mid-1850s and polled only 41 percent of the vote in 1859, they achieved a startling 55 percent of the vote in both the 1860 presidential and congressional elections. The *Princeton Press* observed: "Middlesex county has astonished the State. It should have given 500 for Lincoln; it has given more than 600 against him." The alliance of Bell's, Breckinridge's, and Douglas's forces in arranging local nominations contributed to this result. So, too, did the campaign contributions made by the Camden and Amboy Railroad, which sought to block construction by a rival railroad in Middlesex and Somerset. As the *Press* contended, "In the Railroad question lies the secret of the result." The *New Brunswick Fredonian* agreed; it attributed Democratic victory to bribery. "In this section of the State immense sums of money were used at the polls in buying up the votes at prices varying *from one to seven dollars*—a kind of argument which the Republicans could not match." A key member of the Republican state central committee analyzed the returns and discovered that "if Monmouth, Middlesex, and Somerset had made even a decent approach to the calculating of our friends there, we should have carried the electoral vote and Assembly." The Democratic victory in Middlesex probably resulted from the combination of the fusionists and campaign contributions.[28]

As for the fusion vote, it remains difficult to determine the precise share of the three groups that combined. Previous estimates gave Bell roughly one of every twenty fusionist votes; this figure is probably correct. But to credit Douglas and Breckinridge with dividing the remaining fusionist vote equally, as historians have done, gives too much credence to the Breckinridgers' exaggerated claims. The evidence suggests strongly that Douglas enjoyed greater popular support than Breckinridge in New Jersey. In view of the various estimates of Douglas's strength in the state made during the campaign, the strong editorial support of Douglas in the state's newspapers, and the fact that Douglas had the most electors on the fusion ticket, it is incorrect to assume that supporters of Breckinridge and Douglas carried equal weight.

The evidence also suggests that Douglas held a commanding lead over Breckinridge and Bell. The *Philadelphia Press* may well have come close to the truth in estimating Breckinridge's New Jersey supporters as about one of every four fusionist voters and Douglas's voters as roughly seven of every ten fusionists. (Interestingly, in supposedly more strongly anti-slavery Connecticut, Breckinridge received 20 percent of the vote; he could not have done so in New Jersey unless he were credited with 41 percent of the fusion vote. He received 37 percent in Pennsylvania, 33 percent in Oregon, and 29 percent in California.)[29]

Postelection reaction to New Jersey's role in the presidential contest mirrored the topsy-turvy returns and then became overreaction. Rash judgments partly reflected blind partisanship and incorrect information, but nonetheless helped to form attitudes and to establish certain fixed ideas about the state and its politics.

Northern Democrats, including New Jerseyans, licked the wounds of a national defeat and found solace in assuming that the final count would bring a fusion triumph in New Jersey. Thus the state would stand alone in the North as the single bastion of unionist conservatism. In a self-congratulatory mood, the *Belvidere Journal*, for example, printed the headlines "One Bright Star in the North. All Hail New Jersey. The Jersey Blues True to the Constitution and the Union." The *New York Express* glorified New Jersey: "Of the whole North, she alone keeps step to the music of the Union"—that is, to a Democratic-fusionist tune. Exaggeration reached absurdity when the pro-slavery *New York Day Book* asserted that people in Bergen County "feel and think pretty much as they do down in South Carolina." This must have come as startling news to the 41 percent of Bergen County's voters who voted for Lincoln, or to those talented Democratic leaders in the county who steadfastly supported Douglas, or, for that matter, to supporters of Douglas who voted the fusion ticket.[30]

New Jersey Republicans, overreacting early to what they feared would prove a humiliating loss in the state's presidential election, went to the opposite extreme. Engaging in wholesale condemnation and bitter self-recrimination about the presumed statewide debacle, they denigrated New Jersey and demeaned its inhabitants. Mortified by their loss, Jersey Republicans, as the *Trenton Gazette* put it, went into mourning over their dishonored state. Jacob Miller lamented (inaccurately) that if only the Republicans had selected William Seward as the Republican nominee, "Jersey might have been saved from her present disgrace."[31]

Republicans outside the state gleefully joined in vilifying New Jersey's voters and the state itself. The headline in the *New York Times* read "New Jersey the Only Free State known to be Untrue to Freedom." Going further, the *Times* caricatured New Jersey as "the South Carolina of the North" and characterized its unique politics as monopolized by the concerns of its railroads, which overshadowed every other interest in the state, presumably just as the plantation oligarchy dominated the politics of South Carolina. A Philadelphian sarcastically offered a drastic solution to take New Jersey out of its misery: Pennsylvania and New York could carve up and devour New Jersey. Or instead, he asked, "Does the State of New Jersey perhaps propose to join her sister South Carolina in quitting the Union?"[32]

The tardy, unexpected final returns dividing the electoral vote between Lincoln and Douglas made the state Republicans' earlier agonizing and the Democrats' premature overpraising of the state look equally foolish. Yet over-reaction to the election results molded opinion about the state, especially among people outside the state. In various political circles and for different reasons, New Jersey acquired a reputation for being more southern than northern, a reputation that did not correspond to reality. A myth began, took hold, then assumed a life of its own.[33]

The final returns lifted the morale of Republicans, who considered the fusion cause discredited. The *Trenton Gazette* declared in relief that the "Re-publicans of New Jersey feel that a great stigma has been removed from the State. . . . Now, Jerseymen can meet their brethren of New York and Pennsyl-vania without a blush mantling their cheek, and when the election of *Abraham Lincoln* is spoken of they can say, we too helped to make him President." Thus total defeat was transformed into "our substantial triumph," as the *Pater-son Guardian* put it. The *Guardian* overlooked the flimsy nature of the Re-publican victory, which amounted to a draw of sorts. Lincoln's percentage of the popular vote, moreover, was less than the combined Opposition forces amassed in the 1856 presidential race, the 1858 congressional race, and the gubernatorial races in 1856 and 1859.[34]

Republicans maintained that the Breckinridge Democrats now had noth-ing to brag about. Noting the defeat of the fusionists, the *Guardian* pointed out that among the non-Republican victors, only the three straight Douglas electors had won. The winners included "the very men who confused the fusion by their obstinate opposition to any arrangement." Similarly, the *Mer-cury* observed that the fusionists, despite all their efforts, had failed to achieve their objectives. They had neither destroyed Douglas nor defeated Lincoln.[35]

With victory in the nation and partial victory in New Jersey, the *Gazette* displayed magnanimity toward the Douglas men: "We cannot say that we are very sorry that the three Douglas Electors in this State are elected." Imply-ing that the supporters of Lincoln and of Douglas agreed more than they disagreed on the vital questions, the newspaper invited Douglas men to join Republican ranks. After all, the paper reasoned prophetically, the "lines be-tween freedom and slavery—whether voluntary or involuntary—are now fairly drawn, and every day will but add to their distinctness." The paper reserved its scorn for the Breckinridge men, who disgraced themselves by selling out to their southern masters.[36]

The congressional contests registered an even higher turnout than the presidential election. The Democrats won almost 42 percent of the poten-tial electorate, and the Republicans gained almost 41 percent. Most winners won by a slim majority. Republicans retained their two seats; the Democrats retained their hold on two upstate districts. In the statewide congressional vote the Democrats won narrowly, only by 50.6 percent of the popular vote. In the struggle for control of the State House, the Democrats obtained a majority on the joint ballot.

The major change occurred in the fifth district. In a surprising upset, Democrat Perry edged out Pennington by 50.6 percent of the vote cast. Although Pennington succeeded in both the city of Newark and Essex County, he trailed in the district's other two counties. He narrowly lost Union, where anti-Newark feeling prevailed. In that county the Republican organization did not quite match its 1859 performance. Defeat came decisively in Hudson, which Olden had lost the year before by a somewhat smaller margin. Some Republicans complained of widespread fraud in Hudson, but fusionists also accused Republicans of irregularities. The Democrats evidently benefited by the immigrant voters there.

Despite his lackluster campaigning and his ambivalent attitude about re-election, Pennington ran well ahead of Lincoln, who lost all three counties. Pennington as a forthright Republican criticized southern extremists in his canvass. His win in both the city of Newark and the county of Essex belies the contention that voters there so feared the loss of southern business that a majority supposedly voted against him. His defeat in the congressional district remained no less bitter, however. The rejection of Pennington prompted the *Gazette* to observe that it brought discredit on the state. A Newarker termed the defeat a "State disgrace." A Trentonian remarked that "if we looked upon his elevation to the Speakership as the glory of New Jersey, so you may be sure we regard his defeat as our shame."[37]

In the state campaign as a whole, each side exploited certain issues while playing down other damaging issues. The Republicans of New Jersey did well with their powerful anti-Buchanan and anti-southern arguments. The Democrats struck a responsive chord with calls for peace in the Union and prosperity in the North. The clear menace of secession and the imminent danger that business in New Jersey would suffer as a result surely scared at least some voters away from Lincoln, but not from all Republican candidates. The Democrats' racist arguments probably were effective as well, although Republicans also made their own muted racist appeals. In addition, some Republican politicians in several counties sensed victory because of Democratic division and became overconfident. After doing less well than they expected, some Republicans lamely blamed pro-southern traders within the state and in New York City and Philadelphia for using their money to corrupt New Jersey politics. Republicans also found the similarly unpersuasive excuse that the anti-Lincoln fusion, emerging at the last minute, placed the Republicans at a great disadvantage.[38]

The split in the state's electoral vote resulted from the division in Democratic ranks. In a larger sense the electoral split reflected the political stalemate within New Jersey: Douglas carried eleven counties and Lincoln ten. The results of the congressional contests also indicated a deep-seated political division along regional lines, between marginal Republican down-state districts and generally marginal Democratic upstate districts. Political flux continued with the return of some previously disaffected anti-Lecompton Democrats to the Democracy. Such a development was especially marked in the third and fourth districts, where voters in 1858 had elected anti-Lecompton Democratic congressmen. The narrow margin of control of the legislature reflected the same pattern.[39]

Observers then and historians since have pointed to the anomaly that New Jersey in 1860 became the only state in the North not to give its entire electoral vote to Lincoln. Their emphasis on this outcome implied that New Jersey did not belong in the roll call of true northern states. In fact, the results in New Jersey duplicated the pattern throughout the lower North: Lincoln won by extremely narrow popular margins, ranging from 50 to 54 percent of the popular vote, in Illinois, Indiana, Ohio, Connecticut, and New York. He received only one-third of the popular vote in Oregon and California. In a close contest in New Jersey, fusion tickets won a popular majority by 52 percent; Lincoln trailed only slightly at 48 percent. Admittedly, unlike the other lower northern states, New Jersey gave Lincoln most rather than all of its electoral votes.

The further implication that voting for Lincoln was the only defensible position belies the circumstances in 1860. Many people agreed that Lincoln, lacking federal experience and political training, had fewer qualifications for the presidency than Douglas. Moreover, if Douglas had served as president he might, as a Democrat, have had a better chance to keep peace. Thus it hardly seems disgraceful that New Jersey failed to give all of its electoral votes to Lincoln. The state's division of electors between Lincoln and Douglas simply mirrored the choices of voters in the nation at large: roughly 1,865,000 Americans voted for Lincoln and 1,385,000 backed Douglas.[40]

As northerners, most of New Jersey's voters favored the northern candidates, Lincoln and Douglas. Although the two men differed significantly on such important matters as tactics and timing, they essentially agreed on a national strategy to forestall disunion. Also, like northerners in general, New Jerseyans did not agree fully about the necessity or desirability of containing the expansion of slavery in the West. They agreed with Lincoln and Douglas, however, that it had become necessary to limit southern power.

New Jerseyans between 1854 and 1860 acted directly or indirectly to curb southern power in Washington and to preserve the Union against southern subversion and secession. As a Somerville man declared, northerners must resist the "attempt of the South to govern the North." New Jersey's resolve to limit southern influence resulted in the decisive anti-Nebraska majority during 1854 and in the complete anti-Lecompton victory in the congressional elections of 1858. In 1860, with the stakes even higher, no Democratic congressional candidate backed Breckinridge; most Democrats in the state supported Douglas. Meanwhile, the state Republican party doubled its support between 1856 and 1860 and secured a majority of state electors to Lincoln.[41]

Significantly, Bell, whose unionism remained singularly inexplicit, did not provide a strong rallying point for New Jerseyans, in contrast to his appeal in the border slave states. Popular support for Breckinridge within New Jersey came not only from the few avowed secessionist or southern sympathizers, but also from conservative voters who sincerely desired bisectional compromise and considered him the candidate most likely to prevent secession.

New Jersey's voters, then, united firmly behind the Union and backed pro-Union candidates. In the words of the *Mercury*, the "conservatism of our people is that conservatism which looks to the preservation of the Union."[42]

State voters also rejected extremism and showed again their fear of sectionalism. Only a small minority accepted Breckinridge's view that the differences between the North and the South had become irreconcilable and that the North must submit to the South's terms to maintain the Union. Some voters also objected to Lincoln's support of outright exclusion of slavery in the federal territories because it polarized the parties, a position that they believed the Republican party represented. Thus, many New Jerseyans remained in the moderate majority of American voters who supported both Douglas and Bell (who together outpolled Lincoln in the national popular vote). Although some New Jerseyans feared the perils of change and the danger of disunion, others believed the time had come to end Democratic misrule. All of these considerations were reflected in the electoral deadlock. Thus, to regard New Jersey's electoral bottle as almost half empty for the Union rather than more than half full for Lincoln obscures the larger unionist meaning of the election in the state.

To be sure, New Jersey's deadlocked politics, like its divided electors in 1860, remained unique in the nation. Observers took notice and commented widely. As the *New York World* observed, "It cannot be denied that New Jersey maintains her 'difference discreet' with more independence than ever." Observers invented a fictitious image of New Jersey's politics and either commended or condemned it, depending on their own politics. Thus, to observers, that sense of difference that seemed for a time to set New Jersey apart began to loom larger than the limited difference itself. New Jersey began to be regarded as an anomaly.[43]

Difference, however, did not mean departure from the northern mainstream. New Jersey exhibited the characteristics of a typical state in the lower North. New Jersey in 1860 could not be characterized as a backwater of southern reaction or a breeding ground for secessionists or state righters. New Jersey did not receive the mixed southern and northern influences of a border slave state; it did not in 1860 exhibit the typical border slave state pattern of support for Bell or southern support for Breckinridge. Certainly New Jerseyans disagreed, as did the candidates, over how best to save the Union and contain the power of the South. New Jerseyans, however, like their final electoral choices, remained strongly nationalist. A Republican campaign banner in Somerville summed up the dominant sentiment of New Jerseyans toward southerners: "We are for Union. They are not."[44]

# 5 The Union in Peril: New Jerseyans React to Secession

After Election Day, New Jerseyans kept one eye on their state's electoral results and the other on developments in the lower South. The *Flemington Republican* overconfidently taunted secessionists: "Lincoln is elected! and now let us see if the fire-eaters, who have been threatening to dissolve the Union in case of this event will attempt to put their treasonable threat into execution."[1]

Such bravado faded when southern threats of disunion became more than their usual election-year bluff. The extremists seized the initiative in South Carolina, where secessionists tore down American flags, took over federal offices, manhandled northerners, and intimidated local opponents. America, predicted the *Trenton American*, appeared on the verge of "anarchy and ruin."[2]

On December 20, 1860, South Carolina withdrew from the Union. In January 1861, most of the Gulf states followed its example. On February 8, the seven states of the lower South formed the Confederate States of America. Ten days later the regime installed Jefferson Davis as its president. The upper South tentatively remained in the Union, anxiously awaiting some coercive act by the federal government. As each southern state departed, its congressmen and bureaucrats in Washington resigned en masse. Virtually every army fort and arsenal in the seceded states surrendered without resistance or rebuke, without cost or punishment.[3]

Political instability caused economic instability across the North. Southerners canceled orders and refused to pay bills. Some northern manufacturers cut or stopped production. Factories worked half-time and laid off workers. Panic in financial markets spread as banks suspended specie payments. By February a Morristown man found business "completely prostrate and has been for a long time, and failures are of daily occurrence." Newark, Rahway, and other towns with southern trade as one of their mainstays reeled from the crisis.[4]

In New Jersey, reaction to secession resembled the response to Brown's raid the year before. Republicans claimed that Democrats had abetted southern secessionists by equating Republicanism with abolitionism. Democrats, frustrated by their loss of power and appalled by secession, declared their worst predictions fulfilled by the Republican victory. Because Republicans had inflamed northern feelings against the South, Republicans must convince southerners to change course.[5]

Yet, reactions of New Jersey Republicans fluctuated. At the outset of the crisis, the *Cape May Wave* characterized conditions as "somewhat squally." Then, with an abrupt change of both mood and metaphor, it expressed the hope that the whole affair would become "more smoke than fire." As late as February a concerned Ocean County man still expected no dissolution of the Union. Marcus Ward similarly observed that although "matters look very badly, I still think we will come out all right. And when the trouble is over, we will have a stronger government than ever." Some observers even expressed relief at the departure of South Carolina, "our little spoiled and petted sister," as the *Wave* dubbed this perpetual malcontent.[6]

Republicans resolutely denied the right of secession. The people as a whole, not the individual states, formed the Union. The Union remained perpetual and permanently binding on every state. The crux of the matter was not favoring union, but maintaining *the Union*. States could leave the Union only as they had come in, by the consent of the people of the whole country. No state could simply dissolve its ties to the Union whenever it was annoyed by a law, a policy, or a president. No state could defy the supreme power of the federal government.[7]

Although New Jersey Democrats blamed Republicans for the crisis, they also regarded secession as both illegal and unnecessary. Even the *Newton Herald*, which had backed Breckinridge, remarked that New Jersey "will never consent to the mad and destructive scheme of a dissolution of the Union." The mainstream *Camden Democrat* contended that secession amounted to "treason to the nation, treason to mankind, treason to liberty." The ultra-conservative *Somerville Messenger* criticized South Carolina for having "acted foolishly, precipitately and ungratefully" toward its northern friends and its sister southern states. Now the state stood pathetically alone with nothing but a questionable divorce decree in hand. The *Jersey City Standard*, which had backed Bell, condemned South Carolina for being so "imperious and dictatorial, so fanatical and presumptuous." Such reactions were strikingly different from the positions advanced in editorials in the southern or border states.[8]

Garnett Adrain admonished southerners for misrepresenting their actions. "Secession—peaceable secession, as it is called," he declared, meant "in fact, rebellion." He maintained that "this whole theory of a peaceable secession is utterly fallacious, and was never dreamed of by the men who formed the Federal Constitution." Paraphrasing Daniel Webster, Adrain said that if a state could leave the Union on a mere whim, then the Union is "nothing but a rope of sand, of no strength whatever to hold the States together, and which may be broken at any moment."[9]

Most New Jerseyans looked beyond abstract questions about secession to the more pressing practical considerations of the two sections' well-being. A Presbyterian minister from Basking Ridge predicted dismemberment of the

Union: "Like the dead members of a lifeless body, one limb after another will slough off in its rottenness, leaving nothing behind but a stench." Without the cement of union and a strong national government that bound the parts together, fragmentation would follow inevitably and bring certain ruin in its wake.[10]

New Jerseyans also were disturbed by the secessionists' contempt for that cornerstone of democracy, majority rule. The *Morristown Jerseyman* pointed out that just four years previously Buchanan had received a minority of the popular vote while winning a majority of the electoral college. Yet his opponents, who carried most of the northern states, had quietly accepted the outcome of a fair election. Southerners, according to the *New Brunswick Fredonian*, accepted majority rule only as long as the South retained control of the federal government and ran the nation. The *Newark Mercury* remarked that southerners had become so accustomed to dominance in Washington that they could not tolerate their loss of power in the executive branch. If sore losers refused to abide by the verdict at the ballot box, predicted the *Mercury*, "elections would decide nothing, for everybody would wait to see what the defeated party would demand as the price of submission." Then recurrent crises of political confidence would paralyze politics, discredit democracy, and tear the nation apart, producing anarchy or a dictatorship. As the newspaper observed, "If this Government is not founded on the will of the majority, clearly expressed under the forms of the Constitution, then it is a miserable sham."[11]

The practical effect of secession also angered many Democrats in the state. They considered it foolish for the southern states to secede when the Democratic party had just regained control of the House of Representatives. Because the Democrats were dominant in both chambers of Congress, they could readily block any odious proposal made by Lincoln. The stampede of southern states to secede, however, and their congressmen's rush to resign left northern Democrats a hopeless minority in both chambers. When the southern Democrats surrendered congressional control to the Republicans, New Jersey Democrats felt betrayed.[12]

Discredited Buchanan vowed to preserve the Union and denied that any state had the option to secede from the nation. At the same time he denied that the federal government possessed the constitutional power to keep a state in the Union. To his credit, Buchanan prevented bloodshed; he avoided both giving the lower South any pretext for beginning war and giving the upper South any excuse for seceding. To his discredit, he pursued a bankrupt policy. In his view, the possible destruction of the Union resulting from the efforts of the national government to stop secession by force was a worse alternative than the certain destruction of the nation that would follow federal acquiescence to secession. Few New Jersey newspapers defended Buchanan's handling of the secession crisis. The *Somerville Messenger* did so, but weakly: "Instead of cracking the whip, he resorts to conciliation—instead of forcing the South to go out of the Union, he recommends them to stay in."[13]

Republican editorials roasted Buchanan for both mishandling the secession crisis and abdicating presidential responsibility. The *Trenton Gazette* called "simply preposterous" his position that although no state had the right to secede, federal power could not block the exercise of this nonexistent right. The *Newark Advertiser* found Buchanan's position "brave only in theory, but shirking responsible action." Charles Perrin Smith remarked that Buchanan acted as if the Constitution lacked a remedy to prohibit the nation from committing suicide. William Pennington stated in early December that the South had received exactly what it wanted from Buchanan—inaction. Thus Buchanan "put off any necessity for executive action until Lincoln comes in." In late December Pennington bitterly observed of Buchanan's pandering to the South, "You never hear one national sentiment emanating from the White House. All he can do is to abuse the North and apologize for the South. His conduct is truly pitiable." Pennington concluded, "He is a pusillanimous old buffoon without any nerve or patriotism." The *Morristown Jerseyman* similarly condemned Buchanan's "shilly shally, namby pamby, vacillating, weak minded and foolish course." Some newspapers even called for Buchanan's impeachment. The *Paterson Guardian* dismissed him as a "cringing coward" who "whimpers like a superannuated granny." In February the *Jerseyman* complained of "imbecile old Buchanan," who gave the secessionists time and freedom to build strength and prepare for war.[14]

During the secession crisis New Jerseyans living in the South reported their observations and expressed their forebodings to relatives at home. From Augusta, Georgia, Edward E. Ford told his brother in Morristown, Henry A. Ford, that northerners had "no idea of the wild excitement that prevails 'Down South'" against Republicans, Lincoln, Yankees, and the Union. Southerners, wrote Ford, widely regarded Lincoln's election as a declaration of war against the South and slavery. Georgians clamored for southern independence to protect themselves and their slaveholding from northern attack. After the election, Georgians "pulled down the Stars and Stripes" and raised rebel flags in their place with such mottos as "'Independence,' 'Out of the Union,' the 'Lone Star,' and the 'Red Flag.'" Southern upholders of the Constitution, stated Ford, "stem the torrents against them" to no avail, so "we are in the course of a *Revolution*—and most certain—a revolution I fear whose end is *Blood*." Ford adamantly opposed secession, but "I don't express any political sentiments, know I have to keep mum." Certain "it would be dangerous to say anything inimical to the powers that be," he feared Georgians would put "a halter round his neck." Feeling isolated, Ford concluded plaintively, "my heart is in New Jersey."[15]

From Fredericksburg, Virginia, Archibald Hodge informed his father, "If the Federal Government attempts *coercion*," civil war would follow—an "instant secession and appeal to arms upon the part of every Southern State. There is but one voice and opinion here upon that subject." Southerners would rush to fight, "risking everything upon the one issue of the Federal Government leaving every Southern State to act as she pleases." In Hodge's mind the greatest danger resulted from mutual ignorance between northerners and southerners and result in fatal miscalculation. He noted, "Even now the North appears to misapprehend the real state of feeling in Virginia and the other border Slave States," where disunionist feeling spreads "like an epidemic." Moreover, wrote Hodge, the secession of the lower South left the upper South in such a hopeless and ineffectual minority in Congress that the people of the upper South had no interest in staying in the Union if the lower South did not return. Hodge said he found that "my unchanged opinions on the subject of slavery are becoming heretical, and even dangerous in the tide of the incoming madness." Southerners dismissed as abolitionists anyone who did not embrace the extremist demands of the headlong secessionists. Hodge reluctantly made plans to leave his position and to bring his family north. Resigning his pastorship, he returned to Princeton with his family at the end of April.[16]

New Jerseyans at home also agonized over the proper course. They faced five choices in responding to secession: join it, accept it, appease it, circumvent it, or oppose it.

Only a handful of Democratic commentators advocated the secession of New Jersey from the Union, and they did so only as a last resort. The *Paterson Register* admonished that "if anything can be done to avert the catastrophe, we are in favor of doing it." The limited and reluctant secessionist sentiment depended on whether all or most of the slave states seceded. If secession became widespread, proponents argued, New Jersey should secede in its own interest. By casting its lot with the seceding southern states, New Jersey would safeguard the sale of its manufactured goods in the southern market. Similarly, membership in the Confederacy would guarantee an important role for Perth Amboy as a thriving port in the new nation because of its strategic northeastern location and its protected harbor. If all the Mid-Atlantic states joined the Confederacy, they could avoid becoming a battleground. The result of secession, assured Rodman Price, would be continuance of "our prosperity, progress and happiness uninterrupted, and . . . without any sacrifice of principle or honor, and without difficulty or danger."[17]

Most New Jerseyans viewed as quixotic the assumption that the state's secession would guarantee peace and prosperity without cost or adverse consequence. Small in territory and limited in resources, New Jersey was dwarfed by larger, more populous neighbors. If those states did not join the Confederacy, New Jersey could muster no force equal to their powerful militias and the overwhelming might of the federal army and the navy. The state could not count on reliable support from the southerners for its defense. More-over, given its exposed position at the northeastern extremity of an envisioned confederacy, New Jersey was likely to become an early battleground in a war between the South and the North. Invaders would occupy New Jersey's coasts and block entrance to its ports. The *Camden Democrat* soberly weighed New Jersey's chances: "Who can doubt our gallant little State would be crushed and trampled to death between the two contending forces?"[18]

Proponents of the madcap scheme of secession also ignored New Jersey's vital interest in free labor, industry, and a protective tariff, all of which con-flicted with the South's support of slave labor, agriculture, and free trade. As one New Jerseyan observed, the "prosperity of New Jersey is wrapped up in the stability and prosperity of New York City"—and, he could have added, that of the nation's second-largest city, Philadelphia. The state's outlooks, values, and institutions lacked congruence with those of the South. The no-tion that New Jersey as a free northern state could become a member of the Confederacy and yet have a separate life of its own, enjoying all the advan-tages but suffering none of the disadvantages of such an association with the slave states, bordered on fantasy. Besides, no great interest, strong organiza-tion, or influential leadership advanced a plan for New Jersey's secession. Most New Jerseyans never questioned that the state would stay in the Union. In fact, the great majority of New Jerseyans regarded even the suggestion of secession as ridiculous, even treasonable.[19]

As Olden stated in his annual message in January 1861, the "people of this State, beyond all question, stand as a unit in favor of the Union, and are prepared to defend it." The *Princeton Standard* asked, "Who would have thought that New Jersey had any adventuring politicians so ignorant of the temper of true Jerseymen as to even suggest that this true old State would now abandon the stars and stripes which have so long waved over her sacred soil?" Leaders of both parties in the legislature and in Congress voiced antisecessionist sentiment. So, too, did staunch Democratic newspapers, in-cluding the *Newark Journal* and the *Trenton American.* They regarded Price's statement about the advantages of secession as misguided and, more impor-tant, irrelevant. Responding to Price's proposal, the *Camden Democrat* de-clared, "No! Governor, let us drop the consideration of such a future for New Jersey. . . . Her people dearly love the old Union which our fathers es-tablished, and will submit to almost any sacrifice to maintain it."[20]

Other New Jerseyans disdained the notion of joining the southern repub-lic, but opted for coexistence with the new regime. Peace at any price was their paramount objective. At various junctures during the secession crisis, such dissimilar journals as the Republican *Newark Advertiser* and the Demo-cratic *Freehold Democrat* advocated letting the South go without a fight.

Although pacifists regarded secession as the supreme misfortune, they rec-

ognized that the antagonism between the North and the South now precluded reconciliation. For the *Freehold Democrat* the choice seemed obvious:
"If the Union must be dissolved with or without war, why not let the dissolution come peaceably?" The pacifists insisted that force could never unite a
nation founded on the consent of the governed. As John Thomson phrased
it, "If we cannot preserve them in the Union without force," then in the name
of liberty "let them go in peace." A Mercer County resident predicted that
by amputating the diseased southern parts of the country, the North could
pursue its own economic growth and industrial development unencumbered.
Such a course of action, however, meant permanent dismemberment of the
nation. The likelihood of stable, peaceful boundaries between the North and
the South struck many people as doubtful. Then, too, secession invited the
gradual dissolution of the rest of the United States. Only a small minority of
New Jerseyans supported acceptance of secession.[21]

The third alternative, appeasement through negotiation, attracted greater
support. Advocates sought to fashion a compromise to keep the upper South
in the Union and to induce the lower South to return. This tactic appealed
especially to supporters of Bell and Breckinridge, but also to many moderates, including some of Douglas's followers. Immediately after the election,
this loose coalition of disparate politicians and editors lobbied vigorously for
some sort of accommodation.

One advocate suggested a mass meeting in New Jersey to persuade
southerners not to secede. Yet in urging compromise, he did so in most uncompromising terms: the voice of the meeting must "be sent forth in thunder tones against the secession of a single State or the blotting out from our
national banner of a single star." The *Jersey City Standard* embraced appeasement, for the "fanatics and secessionists of the South" attempted to stampede southerners into leaving the Union. These secessionists "must not be
permitted to have things all their own way." To allay southern fears, only the
anti-Lincoln forces could take part in this proposed meeting: "No man having a spark of Black Republican blood in him will be permitted to participate." This combination of anti-Republicanism and anti-secessionism
appealed to New Jersey's conservatives, especially to the fusionists who had
taken part in the recent presidential campaign.[22]

The fusionists met on December 11 in Trenton. Trying to save the Union
by conceding what the South wanted, fusionist leaders opted for open-ended
appeasement instead of evenhanded negotiation. Fusionists also prejudged
the sectional controversy at the outset, heaping all the blame for the crisis
on the North in general and on the Republicans in particular. Accordingly
they urged the North to take the first steps toward conciliation by repealing
the personal liberty laws and ending all agitation against slavery.[23]

Republican journals condemned the appeasers' patent unreasonableness.

The *Paterson Guardian* considered it unseemly in the face of avowed rebellion to "beg and implore, importune and beseech, weep and lament that the South shall not commit perjury and treason." In the same vein the *Newark Mercury* objected to the sacrifices expected of the North: "All her convictions, no matter how dear, must be abandoned; all her rights, however precious, must be surrendered; all her principles . . . must be repudiated." Princeton Republican Richard S. Field observed: "Public sentiment in New Jersey has been shamefully misrepresented." Thus statewide efforts to advance compromise during the last two months of 1860 were hampered by the explicitly anti-northern and anti-Republican message of the appeasers, which only ensured adamant opposition from the Republicans. Local unionist meetings in Newark, Camden, and elsewhere, however, were more bipartisan in tone.[24]

One-sided pronouncements even provoked sharp disagreement in the original Trenton meeting of appeasers. One dissenter blamed the South, not the North, for all the trouble. During the debate over the resolutions, leader Robert Stockton emphasized the need to avoid any criticism of the South in the proposed resolutions. Yet despite his influence, the participants rejected the original pro-southern resolutions and added a declaration that blamed the North and the South equally for the crisis. Another adopted resolution declared that neither side had any grounds for conducting rebellion or subverting the Union. Furthermore, New Jerseyans would help preserve the federal government under the Constitution. The meeting then named a delegation, top-heavy with supporters of Bell and Breckinridge, to confer with representatives of the southern states and to offer to serve as mediators in the dispute. Yet the disagreement at the meeting strongly suggested that New Jersey's intermediaries had made an unpromising start toward averting a national divorce.[25]

Developments became more promising as 1861 began. Olden and a bipartisan delegation agreed to support the convening of a national peace conference. Olden devoted one quarter of his annual message to the crisis and considered it in his characteristically moderate way. As a nationalist he rejected secession outright. He did not believe that the South's security was in jeopardy. He pointed out that southerners who deemed a constitutional election of a president "sufficient cause for dissolving the Union . . . do not desire to remain in it." However much secessionists wished to secede, Olden (like most New Jerseyans) regarded division of the nation as the seed of interminable anarchy and wished to avoid it at all cost. The governor then offered an olive branch to southerners. Chastising extremists in both sections, he recommended mutual forbearance and concession, as well as strengthening common interests and bonds, "without which our Union is but a name."[26]

Such statements placed Olden at odds with many state Republicans, and a few took him to task for breaking rank. They feared that his conciliatory stance would play into the hands of southern extremists. Disregarding the context of the speech, the *Paterson Guardian* observed tartly that Olden's characterization of slavery as a burden to the South did not square with southerners' professions that slavery constituted a blessing whose value warranted secession. The *Guardian* found "this Governor of the *Olden* time" not quite up with the times; he showed himself too eager to grab any bargain, including an empty one. Most Republican papers remained silent, however. Democratic newspapers, pleased that Olden agreed with them on many points, applauded him for rising above partisanship.[27]

When the legislature convened, the organization of both chambers took an unexpected turn. Although the Republicans had a majority of one in the senate, Burlington County Republican senator Thomas L. Norcross of Pemberton defected, thus enabling the Democrats to organize the senate. Norcross purportedly received a large amount of money for his desertion, and the Democrats named one of his relatives senate secretary.

In the assembly, the Republicans and the Douglas Democrats combined forces to elect several Douglas Democrats as their officers, thus defeating Democratic caucus nominees. In the process they ignored the rump Americans in the assembly, who had long received patronage from the Democrats in return for their support in organizing the chamber. The Democratic *New Brunswick Times* sharply criticized the callous treatment accorded to these Americans by the Douglas Democrats and warned fellow Democrats not to ignore them: "When it is found necessary in Middlesex, Essex and Hudson to make a union to secure the Legislature, let us at least recognize the help we receive, and do justice to our allies." In addition, the Democrats in the legislature rushed through the redistricting of the assembly with an eye to increasing the number of Democratic seats.[28]

These developments amounted to minor diversions in comparison to the secession crisis. The time had arrived for the legislature to take a stand. Kentucky senator John J. Crittenden, a founder of Bell's party, provided the rallying point in his plan to restore and extend the Missouri Compromise line to the Rocky Mountains. Federal authority would ban slavery north of this line and would protect it permanently south of the line. The legislature referred the entire matter to a joint select committee, which in turn urged Congress to approve Crittenden's proposal or some equivalent plan. If Congress failed to act, the committee, along with Olden, supported a national convention of the states in Washington, D.C., during February to devise an acceptable compromise. The committee authorized a state delegation to attend and named delegates—mainly Democrats and Americans but also three Republicans, including Olden.[29]

Republican congressmen rejected Crittenden's proposal. Instead they favored the current Republican proposal to admit New Mexico Territory as a state and to leave the matter of slavery to the residents of the territory to decide. Republicans thus opposed the effort to make slavery permanent in the territories south of the Missouri Compromise line, as Crittenden proposed, but they did not ban slavery outright in New Mexico, as the strict free soilers desired. Both the majority and the minority denied the right of secession and supported preservation of the Union as well as maintenance of the Constitution.[30]

On January 24, 1861, the state senate approved the Democratic proposal by a strict party vote. The assembly accepted it the next day. In both chambers the Democrats toed the line, but the Republicans did not. A large percentage of Republicans did not vote at all (40 percent in the senate and 61 percent in the assembly, where arbitrary tactics on the part of Democrats caused angry Republicans to walk out of the chamber). Despite intense party pressure to vote against Crittenden's plan, many Republicans refused to take a stand, and abstained from voting. Not a single Republican voted for Crittenden's plan, however. The *Newark Mercury* declared that any person who favored Crittenden's scheme undermined both Republican principles and Lincoln's presidency, stating, "It is far more impossible for one who favors the Crittenden propositions to be a Republican than it is for a cable to go through the eye of a needle." Nevertheless, Olden signed the Democratic joint resolution. Evidently he favored some sort of sectional compromise, but not Crittenden's. Rumor had it that he had lobbied successfully behind the scenes to soften the wording of the resolutions. The Republicans, for the most part, did not criticize Olden's endorsement.[31]

The Republican leaders wanted to eliminate doubts about their position and to stiffen the backbone of New Jersey's Republican congressmen who might be seduced by other plans of conciliation. The Republican legislators met on January 29, 1861, and unanimously pledged to oppose Crittenden's proposal, just as they had done on December 20, 1860. Thomas Dudley evidently organized both meetings. In December he had declared that "if slavery is wrong, it ought not to be extended." To yield to the South, he contended, would destroy the Republican party without settling the slavery question, quieting sectional agitation, or solving the problem of state secessions.[32]

Many Republicans questioned the necessity of compromise. If the South desired assurance of protection for slavery, Lincoln would enforce existing legal guarantees. The Republicans, however, rejected the southern demand to open all federal territories to slavery. In addition, the *Mercury* found in Crittenden's so-called compromise only "unconditional surrender of Northern sentiments and rights," because "by this plan the North gets nothing that she has not already got, and the South gets all she asks for." Ward expressed the view of many party members when he asked of Crittenden's plan,

"Where is the *compromise?*" A Camden County man cautioned, "Let us beware that we do not obtain peace by a sacrifice of liberty." Republicans refused, as they put it, to confuse conciliation with capitulation.[33]

Crittenden's proposal exacerbated differences rather than solving them, Republican critics argued. His plan to make his unrepealable compromise a permanent part of the Constitution, the *Paterson Guardian* declared, would mean that every Republican must get down on his knees and confess that he had "sinned against the great god of Slavery which Mr. Crittenden's amendment is to deify and enthrone forever as a part of the National Constitution. It would place the Idol of Slavery so secure in that instrument that no future amendment of the Constitution could ever dethrone it."[34]

As a result of this reaction, the *Princeton Standard*, proposed to enact Crittenden's plan as an ordinary law, subject to future repeal. This tactic, which pointedly ignored the Dred Scott decision, might well secure additional support for Crittenden's compromise in the North but certainly would lose adherents in the South. The problem of future territorial expansion also loomed large. Charles Hodge observed that Crittenden's proposal skirted rather than solved this matter: "It settles nothing. Every proposed acquisition of new territory would be an occasion of new conflicts." Republicans worried that in the future the South would try to carve out new slave territory in Cuba and elsewhere in the Caribbean, thus extending conflict over slavery beyond the present borders of the nation. Republican opponents added a racial reason in demanding that the vast federal territory in the West remain free soil. As Camden Republicans declared, the region must "be kept for the white man and not be given up to the negro."[35]

Republicans, moreover, did not intend to surrender victory in an election won fairly. Southerners and northern Democrats now expected the triumphant Republicans and the majority North to make vital concessions, while the defeated Democrats and the minority South need give up absolutely nothing of importance. In support of this double standard, the Democratic *Trenton American* demanded that "either the Chicago platform, so far as it relates to slavery, must be relinquished or the Union will be dissolved." The newspaper warned that Republicans must embrace Crittenden's compromise; otherwise the upper South also would secede.[36]

The *Newark Mercury* considered such a proposal tantamount to "abandonment of the principles of the Republican party. We are asked virtually to adopt the platform of the Breckinridge wing of the Democracy." The *Paterson Guardian* agreed, contending that Democrats wished not so much to save the Union as the "hulk of the Lecompton-Breckinridge platform as embodied in the Crittenden surrender, which is whitewashed and rechristened '*a compromise.*'" Republican assemblyman Samuel A. Dobbins of Mount Holly similarly characterized Crittenden's proposal as an "attempt to reverse, by indirect means, the verdict of the people recorded at the ballot box in November last."[37]

In any case, New Jersey Republicans regarded it as unwise even to consider a compromise before the inauguration of their own administration. A binding agreement would restrict the negotiatory power of their president, cautioned the *Mercury*, and amounted to "surrendering that freedom of political action without which we are slaves indeed." Republicans tried to outflank both the disunionists and the compromisers by repudiating any agreement allowing slavery to expand in the territories. By standing firm on this issue they hoped to strengthen the position of unionist moderates in the South. The *Morristown Jerseyman* speculated that the Democrats wished to break down the Republican party by creating divisions in its ranks and undermining Lincoln's administration at the start. Also, the secessionists naturally hoped to capitalize on the political flux of the interregnum in order to bully the North into new terms of union.[38]

Spurning concession under duress, the *New Brunswick Fredonian* opposed any effort to appease those who had carried threats on their tongues and guns in their hands: "Now the disunion blunderbuss, loaded to the muzzle, is held to Mr. Lincoln's head by fanatical declaimers and demagogues at the South, and he is told that if he does not surrender, not his own opinions only, but such opinions as will pacify the South, that the weapon will be discharged."[39]

The secessionists, pointed out Dudley, act like spoiled children; the more they get, the more they want, with no end to it. The *Mercury* agreed: "Every time the United States Government takes one step backward, the traitors will take two steps forward." The *Princeton Press* observed that negotiation seemed pointless because "that mob means to have a revolution, and nothing short of that will suit them." The *Mercury* believed that no government worthy of the name should rely on the forbearance of rebels. The *Princeton Standard* advised "conciliation, but no sacrifice of righteous principle, no parleying with treason." The *Paterson Guardian* rejected any concession of "rights to wrongs, of liberty to slavery, of God to the devil." A Hunterdon man said in scorn that the "man who will sacrifice principle through fear of rebellion cannot be made loyal to his own convictions of right by remonstrances. Cowards will always run when danger appears."[40]

Pennington summed up the national Republican position: "The Party word here is—say little, be firm, avoid irritation in language or manner." He remained skeptical about reaching a compromise: "I doubt much whether any compromise is enough. The secessionists and extreme Republicans (the last grow daily) don't want any compromise and the moderate men have become disgusted with South Carolina and Southern movements generally and indeed cannot yield to their arrogant pretensions."[41]

New Jersey Democrats countered that compromise had made and saved the Union before, and only compromise could save it again. The *Freehold Democrat* denounced Republicans who dignified their rigidity as firmness. As for Crittenden's specific proposal to restore the Missouri Compromise line, the *Paterson Register* pointed to the inconsistency of Republicans who in 1854 had condemned the repeal of that line and now called for its immediate restoration. Yet, the *Register* asked, "If it were just and righteous to restore it, then, what event has occurred since to render it unrighteous? None." Republicans responded that times had changed since 1854, as had (necessarily) the Republican position.[42]

Pointing out Democratic inconsistency, the *Mercury* charged the Douglas Democrats with abandoning their great principle of popular sovereignty. They had accepted Crittenden's plan that slavery be decided in the territories by fiat of Congress rather than by popular referendum of the territorial inhabitants. The *Trenton American* remained adamant, however, that only Crittenden's compromise could "remove the bone of contention forever." If secessionists repudiated compromise, at least the blood would not be on northern shoulders. The *Morristown Banner* sternly warned both secessionists and compromisers of the limits to northern patience: "Woe to those who take this clinging to peace as acquiescence in treason. It will be the most fatal of all mistakes to confound forbearance with weakness, or the spirit of conciliation with either childishness or slavishness."[43]

Democrats also reinforced their attack on Republican resistance to compromise by introducing a racist appeal to whites. If spurning compromise triggered war, the *Paterson Register* again warned whites that a "swarm of runaway niggers would infest" New Jersey. "Are you prepared to spill your blood and the blood of your Southern brother in order to elevate the nigger to an equality with yourselves?"[44]

Rejecting secession, coexistence, or appeasement, most Republicans embraced a fourth choice, circumvention. They hoped inactivity and delay would carry the nation peacefully through the interregnum. The Republicans expected that their refusal to compromise would eventually undermine the secessionists. When Republicans took the reins of power in early March, their moderation would bring southerners back to their senses and to loyalty to the Union. The *Morristown Jerseyman* expected that the "difficulties now existing will soon pass away without serious damage, if we meet them in a kind and fraternal, but manly and decided spirit." In the same spirit an Ocean County man advised confidently, "Stand *firm* to our cause, and in a few months all will be well."[45]

Such optimism led a Jersey City Republican in December to characterize the secessionists as drowning men who "grasp at disunion as the raft of safety, because they think it is the only way to injure the free States," especially the commercial and manufacturing interests of the North. He predicted that the secessionists would injure only themselves and expected only South Carolina to take the "fearful leap" and leave the Union. He observed, "'Second sober thoughts' (and they had no first sober thoughts) are now at work."

The Republicans' optimism contrasted sharply with the Democrats' gloom. As the *Freehold Democrat* saw it, the latest reports from the South "give us not a gleam of hope. The secession feeling appears to be on the increase," even taking hold in previously moderate parts of the South.[46]

Not surprisingly, the major compromises failed. The New Jersey members of the lame-duck Congress split along party lines in the same pattern as had occurred in the legislature. Although the state's delegation unanimously supported a number of more moderate, largely peripheral proposals, no plan induced the secessionists to turn back. The editorials of the state's newspapers, Republican and Democratic, criticized the refusal of the lower South to enter discussions. Preferring confrontation to compromise, the secessionists believed that delay or negotiation only jeopardized their rush toward independence.[47]

A fifth option remained, more drastic than the others: coercing southerners back into the Union. Although some New Jersey Republicans wished to suppress the rebels, few at first favored pressing matters to the limit and advocated the use of force before other alternatives were explored and exhausted. Moreover, coercion would trigger a war that nobody in New Jersey wanted.

Later in the crisis, however, when negotiation failed and vehement southerners refused to delay secession and to try out a Republican administration, some New Jerseyans believed that the national government had to impose a settlement. John Ten Eyck likened the solemn duty of national self-preservation to an individual's sacred right of self-defense. One North Jerseyan maintained that "there can be no peaceable secession. There ought not to be. It is treason; it is rebellion . . . and it should be resisted and punished. . . . There is no escape from civil war. Nay, it now exists, though fortunately, so far bloodless." A Hunterdon man observed that with the South arming to destroy the Union, the time had arrived for the North to start arming to save the Union.[48]

More New Jerseyans suggested the use of federal force to crush resistance to federal authority. After all, remarked the *Princeton Standard*, "our government is certainly worth fighting for." "If the rebels of the South prefer civil war, they can have it," promised the *Newton Register*, but it opposed the North's declaring war on the South or provoking hostilities. Instead the *Register* preferred to keep the responsibility for starting a war with the secessionists. The *Trenton Gazette*, although it deprecated war, endorsed the power of the government to prevent disunion; otherwise the government could preserve neither itself nor the Union. The *Morristown Jerseyman* reasoned, "Coercion is the last resort, yet if the integrity of the government can be maintained in no other way, it must be maintained by force." Pennington advised Republicans to "go just as far as duty demands and no farther for peace." Pennington became pessimistic sooner than most people. In the middle of December he sensed "war a certainty in the plans of the South for secession," a development "that I never imagined down to Lincoln's election."[49]

Still, most New Jerseyans shied away from the use of force. Coercion could end only in "that worst of all wars, internecine or Civil War," warned the *Jersey City Standard*. The *Newton Herald* found it unjust, even inhumane, to make war on secessionists, who only acted in self-defense against "Northern aggression." "To scalp or tommy-hawk them into obedience" would stir the whole South to rise up in arms in its defense, and a "horrible and bloody civil war will ensue." But if bloodshed occurred, the *Herald* added, "let South Carolina strike the first blow, and be responsible for the consequences that follow."[50]

In early February a businessman in Morristown spoke for many when he predicted, "Everything looks like war." By that time many New Jerseyans wondered where and when the rebels would start the fire. They speculated about southerners' capture of a fort occupied by the army, seizure of Washington, or an invasion of the North. A North Jerseyan in the *Newark Advertiser* observed:

> *That* step will rouse the North. We are not yet aroused. We do not yet feel angry. We cannot understand why the South should. They puzzle us. We can hardly believe them in earnest or if we do, it is because we consider that they are either fools or lunatics. They have done everything to aggravate us. They have seized our forts, our ships of war, and other national property; fired at our vessels, insulted the flag so long their defender, maltreated our citizens. If a foreign government had done a tithe of all they have done—yea, a hundredth part—the whole nation would have been in arms—and yet we do not get enraged. They raise troops by thousands. We none. We hope against hope, and pray without faith that this madness may pass away. But when the Capital is seized, then the North *will* rise, and rise in her might![51]

The nation had reached an impasse. Secessionists demanded, and Republicans rejected, the protection of slavery in the territories. Many in the South refused to remain in the Union if the South did not get its own way in Washington; many in the North refused to allow this. Many people in the lower South, seized by fear and hysteria, reached impulsively for the narcotic of escapism—secession. Even the more thoughtful people in the upper South accepted the idea of secession if fighting broke out between the North and the South.

Meanwhile, partisans in New Jersey pursued different courses throughout the crisis. Republicans took their cue from Lincoln, who urged caution but insisted on the territorial containment of slavery. Democrats maneuvered to preserve the Union by compromise and placed their faith in Crittenden's plan. In the words of the *Camden Democrat*, "We look upon the Union as paramount to almost everything else, and like the seamen in a storm, we are willing to throw overboard everything to save the vessel and the crew."[52]

Most Republicans considered Crittenden's proposal unrealistic, even irrelevant. It did not meet the demands of the rabid secessionists who would settle for nothing less than political domination of the federal government and legalization of slavery in all federal territories, both present and future. Otherwise the secessionists demanded northern recognition of southern independence. Both demands were unacceptable to most northerners in 1861. The northern opponents of compromise were too numerous, and had the votes to defeat it. Meanwhile the secessionists had proceeded too far. In the panicky South much action but little thought took place. In the paralyzed North, much talk but no action was the rule.

Although New Jerseyans were divided over the causes of secession, they remained largely united in rejecting it. Many Democrats, however, read the depth of secessionist sentiment throughout the South more realistically than did most Republicans. Even when rebellion stared New Jerseyans in the face, many Republicans closed their eyes to the fact that the secessionists already had taken action to dissolve the Union and had prepared for war. Many Republicans preferred instead to believe that Confederates were only bluffing. Many Democrats overestimated the possibility of successful negotiation, despite repeated refusals of the secessionists to engage in serious negotiation. Thus both the Republicans and the Democrats indulged in their own forms of wishful thinking. Those who sensed danger ahead agonized over their inability to prevent or prepare for it.

D espite the severity of the crisis, the scramble for patronage proceeded as usual. A Republican administration assured New Jersey partisans federal appointments as attorneys, postmasters, marshals, and customs collectors. Selection of New Jerseyans for positions in Washington and abroad meant prestige for the state and recognition for the state party. Politicians bombarded Lincoln with requests to appoint William Dayton to the cabinet. As Dudley pointedly reminded Lincoln, state Republicans, including himself, had helped nominate Lincoln.

Lincoln had different priorities. Yet such a closely contested state as New Jersey needed special attention, and Lincoln recognized his campaign debts, so he rewarded three prominent Republicans with foreign appointments. The able but aging Dayton was named minister to France, instead of to Britain as Lincoln originally had proposed. Secretary of State William Seward wished to place a shrewder, more energetic man in the more demanding London post, and political considerations intruded as well. Seward declared bluntly, "Jersey gives us little, and that grudgingly." Lincoln posted Horace Congar, the able editor, to Hong Kong as consul, although Congar had preferred Glasgow. Later in the fall Lincoln chose reliable and resourceful Dudley as consul in Liverpool.[53]

Republicans in the state expressed pleasure with these appointments. Yet federal patronage had an ironic twist, because filling these positions deprived the state party of some of its foremost talent: its elder statesman, its chief propagandist, and its manager. In the years just ahead, when these three were needed most, they were unavailable.

As the inauguration approached, speculation about Lincoln's intentions increased. His trip from Springfield to Washington assumed the character of a whistle-stop campaign tour combined with the fanfare of a hero's triumphal procession. By this method Lincoln attempted to shape public opinion and increase popular support. His brief comments on this tour riveted attention; observers studied his remarks for indications of future policy in handling the secession crisis. Never before or afterward did Lincoln make so many speeches in so few days. Following the lead of other states, the New Jersey legislature extended Lincoln a bipartisan invitation to address it.

On Thursday, February 21, 1861, Lincoln stepped off a handsome new ferryboat at Jersey City to begin his seven-hour visit in the state. The twenty thousand people who jammed the mammoth railroad station at dockside burst into applause. In delivering the opening remarks, Dayton declared that New Jerseyans stood unwavering in their loyalty to the Constitution and the Union. (This theme was repeated throughout the day by those who welcomed Lincoln, both Republicans and Democrats.) Turning to the president-elect, Dayton continued that the people of New Jersey had faith in his ability to meet the present crisis.

Lincoln graciously complimented Dayton, his state, and the beautiful women in front of him, and stepped aboard his special railroad car. Flags and bunting festooned the presidential train. The smokestack of the magnificent locomotive was painted with bands of red, white, and blue. On the front of the smokestack appeared the date "1776." The word "Union" adorned each side.

Immense crowds gathered along the entire route. More than twenty-five thousand persons turned out in Newark. Women smiled, threw kisses, tossed flowers, waved handkerchiefs. Men yelled themselves hoarse. Newark never before had experienced such an outpouring of affection for a president-elect. The sincerity of Lincoln's brief, well-chosen remarks, coupled with the simplicity of his demeanor and clothes, inspired respect and confidence. Ordinary people instinctively liked and trusted him.

On its southward journey the train stopped briefly or slowed down at Elizabeth, Rahway, New Brunswick, and Princeton to acknowledge the spectators. By noon the presidential party arrived in Trenton. Twenty thousand people crowded along the route of the parade from the railroad station to the State House.

Democratic speaker Frederick H. Teese of Newark, a Douglas man, introduced Lincoln in the assembly chamber. Teese empathized with the weighty burden of disunion and wished the president-elect well in his efforts to bridge the widening chasm between the North and the South. In reply, Lincoln, speaking plainly and directly, made his clearest statement thus far on the secession question. Assemblymen, both Republican and Democratic, loudly cheered him on. Lincoln pledged to take the stand he found safest and fairest to the whole country, "and from which I may have no occasion to swerve." Next he promised to do everything in his power to promote a peaceful settlement between the sections. He assured his audience that he bore no malice toward any section. Then, in a striking turn of phrase, Lincoln declared, "The man does not live who is more devoted to peace than I am; none who would do more to preserve it; but it may be *necessary to put the foot down firmly*."

In addition, the president-elect pointedly observed that although most members of the legislature did not call themselves Republican, their warm reception conveyed their devotion to the integrity of the Union and the maintenance of the Constitution. Lincoln warned that the fate of the nation hung in the balance. As president he would pilot the "Ship of State through this voyage, surrounded by perils as it is, for if it should suffer wreck now, there will be no pilot needed for another voyage." He said he needed their support, and he received it in their roaring assent.

Northerners seeking a leader with a firm voice and the right tone had found their man. One Democratic observer in the assembly chamber considered Lincoln's delivery firm, his language good, his points well taken. Richard B. Duane, a Trenton minister who served as the chaplain that day and stood only six feet away from Lincoln, regarded his words as kind, conciliatory, even gentle, "but firm as adamant. He said the time might come when it will be 'necessary to put down the foot.' He accompanied this with a very decided and appropriate gesture, paused, and one cheer went up from the assembled hundreds there." Duane described Lincoln as a strong leader who promised decisive action.

The whirlwind visit to New Jersey stirred enthusiasm and created good will for the most part. As Duane put it, "Mr. Lincoln made a very favorable impression here." The *Morristown Jerseyman* and other Republican newspapers found Lincoln "the man for the times." This view, however, was not shared by editorials in most Democratic newspapers. The *Somerville Messenger* scoffed that "the *man* is not equal to the *occasion*." Lincoln himself, according to reports, was especially pleased by Jerseyan hospitality.[54]

In his inaugural address on March 4, 1861, Lincoln elaborated on the double-edged theme of firmness and flexibility. He promised to protect the Union, maintain national authority, and enforce federal law. His pledge not to interfere with slavery where it existed and his strong desire to avoid war reflected his conciliatory, forbearing spirit. Blood would be shed, he said, only if the rebels made war. They had no justification for attacking the government, but he, as president, had just sworn his solemn duty to defend the government. Terming secession "the essence of anarchy," Lincoln pledged to preserve the Union—peacefully if possible, forcibly if necessary.

New Jerseyans saluted the beginning of Lincoln's presidency. On Inauguration Day they raised flags, rang bells, fired cannons. By early evening people across the state had read Lincoln's words in the daily newspapers. Republican journals praised the address: Lincoln meant what he said and would do what was needed. The *Bordentown Register* found no words of ambiguity, but only the "honest sentiment of the honest heart of an honest American." The editor, present at the inaugural ceremonies, found conviction and an iron will in the tone of Lincoln's voice, the compression of his lips, the flashing of his eyes. He concluded that America now had a government in Washington and at long last "had a *President.*"

Democratic editorials in the state varied from condemnation to confusion and even to cautious hope. The *Newark Journal* denounced Lincoln's message as hypocritical. It was outwardly conciliatory but in fact recommended war. The *Paterson Register* regarded the inaugural address as vacillating, while Lincoln evidently marked time. The *Freehold Democrat* agreed and found his pronouncement full of honeyed phrases and double meanings. The country found itself no nearer a solution of this fearful crisis on Inauguration Day than after Election Day. The *Camden Democrat* contended that Lincoln sounded sufficiently warlike to inflame secessionists and insufficiently conciliatory to encourage unionists. As an intellectual effort, the *Jersey City Standard* considered the speech the worst ever given by a president. Yet as a clue to his future policy, the newspaper interpreted the speech to mean that Lincoln preferred peace to war and would not resort to extreme coercive measures.

Exactly how Lincoln would achieve his objectives remained unclear. In any event, the Republicans had gained control of the new Congress in both chambers. The prospects that Congress would fashion a compromise, always remote, now evaporated.

Meanwhile, as the Confederacy assumed the trappings of an independent nation, secessionists grew increasingly bellicose. Most people in the North grew weary of the interminable crisis, which had dragged on since Election Day. Northerners believed that Lincoln would not tolerate the shameful defeats and ignominious retreats allowed by Buchanan. Yet people remained torn between the "uncertainty of peace and the fear of war," as the *Trenton American* observed. Attention shifted from the possibilities of compromise to the probable need for coercion.[55]

The focus of the crisis became dangerously concentrated at a single point, Fort Sumter in Charleston's harbor. The South regarded this federal fort with the stars and stripes floating over it as a violation of Confederate sovereignty and an insult to southern pride. The North viewed the fort as one of the last footholds of federal authority and national honor in the seceded states. Supplies in the fort, already low, would run out by the middle of April.

Meanwhile, the Confederates reinforced their gun positions, which encircled the fort.

Lincoln could either evacuate the fort or reinforce it. He hesitated. Surrender of the fort meant political suicide for the North and for his party. Retreat surely would strengthen secessionist forces in the South and would demonstrate presidential and federal weakness, hardly the way to win over moderates in the upper South. Both symbolically and in fact, giving up the fort meant giving up the cause of the Union by virtually recognizing the Confederacy. Nevertheless, during March Lincoln still seriously considered abandoning the surrounded fort because it could not be defended indefinitely and soon would be starved out. He did not wish to force a showdown by mounting a rescue mission to reinforce the fort and thus to become responsible for starting a war. As a result of his inaction, rumors that the fort would be evacuated spread rapidly across the North during mid-March.

Republican newspapers in New Jersey, as elsewhere in the North, disagreed among themselves about Lincoln's caution. Some Republican editorials, willing to follow Lincoln regardless of events, defended the proposed withdrawal of the garrison from the fort. The staunchly Republican *Paterson Guardian* justified evacuation by dismissing the beleaguered fort as militarily worthless and administratively useless. Its guns could not reach Charleston, and, being stationary, it could not serve as a movable customhouse. Thus the vulnerable fort seemed a poor choice to symbolize federal authority; it was not worth the fuss or a fight. The journal preferred strategic withdrawal with honor to the humiliation of surrendering the fort to the attacking enemy. Other Republican papers, waiting for a definite signal from Lincoln, mirrored his indecision.[56]

Still a third group of Republicans challenged Lincoln to take a stronger stand. The *Newark Mercury* favored reinforcing and holding Fort Sumter. By March 25 the newspaper, almost desperate, feared that Lincoln would follow a pacifistic, temporizing policy that might grant de facto recognition of the Confederacy. On March 27, for the first time, various articles in the *Mercury* attacked the do-nothing drift of Lincoln's government. One critic condemned the disparity between Lincoln's previous promise of a vigorous, decisive policy to save the Union and his current inaction. Although Lincoln had pledged in his inaugural address to hold federal forts in the South, he now appeared ready to let them go. Abandoning Fort Sumter without lifting a finger would telegraph that "treason is stronger than the Government." A Newton man agreed, declaring that if the national government could not defend federal property on its own soil, it became "no government at all." Similarly, the *Camden Press*, which earlier had supported evacuation, reconsidered and attacked the prevailing double standard: the Confederates could engage in hostile actions without punishment or rebuke, but Democrats regarded any effort by the federal government to maintain itself and defend its authority as bellicose coercion. The time had arrived, declared the *Press*, to stand firm and uphold the Union, whatever the risk.[57]

The state's Democratic newspapers contemptuously dismissed Lincoln's temporizing course. The *Trenton American* characterized his first month in office as vacillating and incompetent. Democratic journals taunted the Republicans for changing positions to support Lincoln, just as the Republicans had taunted them for supporting Buchanan's policy. After the Republican editors' earlier condemnation of Buchanan for his handling of the defense of Fort Sumter, such acquiescence in retreat by the same editors struck Democrats as the height of hypocrisy. Democratic newspapers favored the proposal to remove federal troops from Fort Sumter as both a military and a political necessity.[58]

On March 29, 1861, against the advice of Democrats and conservative Republicans, Lincoln at long last "put the foot down firmly." Many persons in the cabinet, in Congress, and throughout the North had recommended that Lincoln act decisively to end the crisis. Both national self-respect and self-preservation required immediate, firm action.

Lincoln therefore decided to send a naval expedition to retain Fort Sumter. The order went out on April 4, and by April 10 every vessel in the operation had set sail. On April 8 the governor of South Carolina received word that an unarmed vessel would furnish supplies to Fort Sumter. If it was not permitted to land, the fleet would attempt to replenish and reinforce the fort, using force if required.

Confederate authorities, revealing their revolutionary fervor as well as their impatience and impetuosity, moved toward a showdown. The rebel government wanted to ensure control of its military forces in Charleston harbor before hotheaded Charlestonians, spoiling for a fight with the Yankees, took matters into their own hands. The Confederate government also wished to establish its political authority throughout the new nation. Confederate authorities declared they could no longer tolerate any foreign installation on their soil and ordered rebel forces in the harbor to attack the outpost before the federal expedition arrived. Confederates did not wish to fight the fort and the fleet simultaneously. In addition, Confederate authorities calculated that their bold stroke in resorting to arms would immediately bring the upper South into the Confederacy.[59]

While waiting for more news from Charleston, New Jerseyans had a taste of the prevailing southern hospitality. A Jerseyan schooner bound to Savannah with a load of ice put into Charleston harbor to escape a gale, only to have a Confederate shore battery fire a shot through its rigging.[60]

Newspapers prepared New Jerseyans for the worst. The *Freehold Herald* declared: "War Close At Hand!" The *Paterson Guardian* announced: "The Crisis

Approaching," adding, "A Policy Decided Upon by the Administration"; now Lincoln intended to treat secession as treason. A Morristown businessman regretted the likelihood of "civil war but the Union ought to be preserved," regardless of the price. Jacob Vanatta regarded "war as inevitable and *unavoidable.* That being the case the sooner it is commenced and the more vigorously it is prosecuted the better it will be. When it becomes apparent that the federal government has the inclination and power to maintain itself and is determined to do it, peace will dawn upon us and not before."[61]

The *Newark Mercury* similarly found the people unwilling "any longer to stand by in silence and see the government crumbling to pieces without an apparent effort to save it." The *Mercury* contended that "there never was but one really proper policy for the government, and that was to maintain its rights at whatever hazard." The *Princeton Standard* agreed; the North must meet the issue of rebellion head on. "It seems impossible to recognize the existence of an independent and hostile confederacy or government within our own nation, set up without the consent of the people of the United States." The *Trenton Gazette* welcomed the replacement of Lincoln's do-nothing policy with a long-awaited do-something policy. Meanwhile Republicans made gains in local elections on April 8 and 9, notably in Trenton, Paterson, and Elizabeth, in support of Lincoln's show of force.[62]

With both sides on a collision course, the *Gazette* reported that a clash seemed likely at any moment. On April 8 the Confederates readied their forces in Charleston harbor. On April 10 the Confederate secretary of war demanded the immediate surrender of Fort Sumter. On that day the *Mercury* contended that the time had arrived to "show secession that its days of insulting and trampling on the Government of the United States are coming to an end. . . . If war comes, it will be secession that will inaugurate it, and on the head of secession will be the responsibility." The government had to prevent the national flag from being dishonored, federal forts from being surrendered, treason from being allowed to destroy the nation. In a similar vein the *Camden Press* remarked that "if peace is to be secured only upon the terms, which are submitted by traitors and rebels, we are for war, and while we love peace and hate war, we prize too highly our National honor and the supremacy of the laws of our country to yield their defense to the arrogant demands of insolent and treasonable conspirators."[63]

Passionate opposition to Lincoln's decision also surfaced. Democratic newspapers variously described Lincoln's course as deceitful, cowardly, blind, reckless, ruthless, outrageous, insane, or wicked. The *Newark Journal* predicted that Lincoln's initiative would prove fatal because the people of the North would not support it and the people of the South would not abide it. The *Journal* declared that "with peace upon their tongues," Lincoln's cronies "let loose the dogs of war against a people which they may conquer, but can never subject to their rule." The *Jersey City Standard* considered Lincoln's plan a Machiavellian ruse; under the guise of humanity toward the beleaguered men in Fort Sumter, it actually was intended to bombard Charleston and subdue South Carolina. The *Standard* regarded the unarmed vessel as a "mere decoy to draw the first fire from the people of the South, which act by the predetermination of the government is to be the pretext for letting loose the horrors of war. It dare not itself fire the first shot or draw the first blood, and is now seeking by a mean artifice to transfer the odium of doing so to the Southern Confederacy."[64]

Despite such partisan criticism of Lincoln's actions, many other New Jerseyans expressed relief that at last a showdown was near. Certainly most Jerseyans did not care about the fate of the slaves themselves; white New Jerseyans on the whole were as prejudiced and as discriminatory as other white northerners. Certainly, too, Jerseyans did not agree as to the proper way to handle the secession crisis or the struggle for control of the fort in Charleston harbor. Still, most remembered the helpless exasperation and endless humiliation they had suffered when weak-kneed Pierce and Buchanan did the South's bidding. Above all, the people of New Jersey, especially the staunch Republicans, had lost patience with the intransigent Confederates, who had received every benefit of the doubt.[65]

The crisis, then, had reached the point of no return. Enough people on both sides had decided they must fight out their differences, and Fort Sumter became the test. If southerners now started a fight, northerners, including Jerseymen, would fight back. But, if fighting broke out, each side would fight for different reasons. Southerners defended the South; they wished to maintain liberty for whites and slavery for blacks. Northerners defended the flag; they wished to save the Union and democracy. They had no thought of destroying slavery.

Confederate guns opened fire in the early hours of April 12, 1861. By striking the first blow even before the federal expedition reached the approaches to Charleston harbor and well before the naval force could pose a threat, the southerners became the aggressors. They discarded any pretense of self-defense or humanitarian appeal by denying food and water to the men inside the fort. Instead, they demanded its immediate surrender.[66]

The Confederates overreacted to federal provocation. With one bold but foolhardy stroke, southerners succeeded in uniting previously divided northerners and in making the conflict a war for the Union. Looking back, William Smith, a New Brunswick minister, declared, "Our enemies fired on Sumter to fire the Southern heart; but I thank God that in so doing they fired the Northern brain and nerved the Northern arm."[67]

# 6 The Politics of Patriotism, 1861

The attack on Fort Sumter let loose a flood of patriotism across New Jersey. The bombardment "aroused the Union sentiment of our citizens to the highest pitch," reported a Democratic newspaper in Hackettstown. Olden praised the "spirit and enthusiasm of our people" in their determination to save the Union from destruction.[1]

The people's indignation, long pent up, burst forth. Expressing the prevailing view, Democrat Jacob Vanatta contended that without provocation or justification, southerners had declared war on the North. Northerners had no choice but to fight. George D. Bayard of Woodbury, who would become a general, remarked, "Southerners have made a great mistake in attacking" Fort Sumter. "All my sympathy with the South is now gone. It is now war to the knife." The *Egg Harbor Democrat* asserted that "if we don't whip the South," the "South will whip us." Republican editor Orestes A. Brownson of Elizabeth similarly argued that "either the government must crush the rebellion or the rebellion crush the government. . . . We must either put down or be put down."[2]

War fever swept the state. People crowded newspaper or telegraph offices and railroad depots to hear the latest news. In Newark, one observer described the scene: "Nothing is talked of but war, war." In Morristown, a farmer commented, "The people are crazy with excitement." He found everyone "all ready to fight."[3]

At war meetings across New Jersey, people raised huge liberty poles to the accompaniment of eloquent speeches and rousing songs. Jerseyans lighted bonfires, launched rockets, fired cannon, and marched in parades. Parishioners flocked to churches to hear stirring prowar sermons. People hung bunting and banners on buildings and donned patriotic ribbons and badges. Even dogs and horses sported small Union emblems. When citizens in Elizabeth saw a white flag atop one rooftop, they searched for rebel sympathizers, only to find the flag the innocent work of some children "whose little hearts beat for the Union." In separate incidents indignant patriots threatened to sink two vessels offshore unless they hauled down rebel flags and ran up the national colors.[4]

New Jerseyans displayed the American flag spontaneously, in contrast with New York City, where the flags were not put out immediately. Traveling southward, one man in late June observed: "The farm-houses in Jersey frequently show the flag. South of Philadelphia they do not."[5]

Although war united the great majority of New Jerseyans in the early months of the conflict, it divided others. In Godwinville (Ridgewood), Union men showed their support of the war by displaying an American flag on the steeple of the Reformed Church. Antiwar members of the congregation demanded its removal. Minister Edward T. Corwin, supported by prowar members, refused. Finally, in a showdown, armed supporters blocked the way to the steeple and threatened to shoot anyone who attempted to haul down the flag. The governing body of the church approved a motion to keep the flag flying. Yet despite the success of the prowar parishioners, discord within the church took its toll. As the minister reported in April 1863, the "political dissensions of the country have not failed to leave their mark upon the Church. Advantage has also been taken of a supposed limitation in the pastoral relation to the Church to create some disaffection. Hence coldness and apathy have seized upon us to a considerable degree." Corwin resigned.[6]

The outbreak of war divided some New Jersey families as well. The Wandling family of Warren County endured its own civil war when one brother joined Confederate forces and another joined the Union army. Jacob, the Yankee enlistee, conceded, "You are just as set in your belief as I am in mine." Jacob Wandling, however, criticized his brother for mistakenly assuming that southerners monopolized patriotism. After all, they had unnecessarily "rushed into an armed rebellion and plunged the Country into the worst of all possible evils, a civil war." A few persons born in New Jersey but living for a long time in the slave states enlisted in the Confederate army and became high-ranking rebel officers, including Samuel Cooper, the adjutant general. (More prominent Confederate generals, John Pemberton and Josiah Gorgas, hailed from Pennsylvania.) Other native New Jerseyans living in the South fled to avoid inhospitable, intolerant rebels or Confederate conscription.[7]

Patriotic fervor placed pressure on newspaper editors who had backed Breckinridge and Bell to demonstrate their loyalty by displaying the colors. Although at first these editors denounced such pressure as mob rule, they soon adjusted to wartime opinion, at least for the moment. David Naar of the *Trenton American* and Charles Deshler of the *Jersey City Standard* eventually decided not only to raise the national flag but also to pledge support for the government and the Union cause. Naar soon endorsed Lincoln's vigorous prosecution of the war. Convinced of the futility of negotiating with the South, he even defended Lincoln's handling of the Fort Sumter crisis. Deshler, previously an acerbic critic of Lincoln, went further. He condemned those who obstructed the war effort and adamantly rejected any negotiations with the rebels, stating, "No measure of compromise should be for a moment entertained which in the remotest degree admits the right of secession or a willingness for a peaceful dissolution of the union." Edward Fuller of the *Newark Journal* acceded to a mob's demands by displaying the flag, but defiantly attached to it the words "Free Speech, Free Press." Similar incidents occurred elsewhere.[8]

The attack on Fort Sumter made converts across the political spectrum. The moderate Republican *Newark Advertiser*, which for a time during the secession crisis had hedged, now vowed that the rebels must not smash the Union and the Constitution as they had the ramparts of Fort Sumter. Democratic senator John Thomson, previously a supporter of the South, denounced those supposed friends of the Union who had used him while plotting disunion. "I feel ashamed of my blindness and stupidity, and almost despise myself for being in any degree made the dupe of such selfish and unprincipled secessionists," he confessed. Once a staunch conservative, Thomson now looked forward to the day when "not a vestige of slavery should remain in our land."[9]

Supporters of Douglas, notably the editors of the *Camden Democrat* and the *Morristown Banner*, defended their efforts, which had ended in failure. Looking back over the last year, one Newarker observed, "As 'old line,' 'Henry Clay Whigs,' 'Union men,' and 'Douglas Democrats,' we stood up, true to the last." Although condemned by Republicans for supporting John Crittenden's compromise, "as 'old fogies,' 'conservatives,' 'concessionists,' 'Union Savers,' all but cowards, we have singly and together done everything to avert this dire calamity. At the proper time and place we were not met in the right spirit nor with a patriotic purpose, and failed, lamentably failed. It is too late for regrets, commiserations, or recriminations." The "rebels and traitors must be met at all points and *subdued*. There is no blinking the issue." But "if the Union must go down, let it be in blood enough to float the Capitol from its foundations." Edwin Wright, who had defended Buchanan, agreed. Even some ultraconservative newspaper editors believed the time had come to stop debating about whether Republican rigidity or southern stupidity had set the national house on fire and instead to start putting the fire out.[10]

New Jerseyans of various political persuasions supported the war effort. *Trenton Gazette* editor Jacob R. Freese, an ardent Republican, remarked, "Say to the President that the Republicans of New Jersey all stand by him now that he has 'put his foot down.'" The Democratic *Mount Holly Herald* declared that the "Democratic party of New Jersey is a unit for the Union and the Constitution." Southern aggression, observed Democrat Joseph Potts, forced New Jerseyans to recognize a situation worse than war: the specter of mob rule without national government. People feared the chaos of Mexico, where one revolution followed another, would spread to America unless the North put down the insurrection. The Democratic *Morristown Banner* judged war, bad as it was, to be not "so bad as national extinction—not so bad as no government—not so bad as mock governments." Brownson found a failure of the prewar government to govern: Americans "have overlooked the necessity and authority of government; we have forgotten that freedom is impossible without order, and order impossible without authority." Army officer James F. Rusling in 1864 contrasted what he believed were southerners' and northerners' reasons for waging war: "*They* fight for anarchy; *we* fight for government. *They* fight for lawlessness; *we* fight for law."[11]

Most New Jerseyans agreed that democracy was on trial. They considered secession a declaration of war against majority rule. Southern aristocracy attempted, according to the *Morristown Banner*, to "crush out the great right of universal suffrage." New Jerseyans rejected the southern repudiation of the decision of the ballot box. The *Jersey City Standard* saw "*The Sovereignty of the People*" trembling in the balance. Vanatta asserted in 1862 that the "supremacy of the majority and the acquiescence of the minority are the keystone of the arch" of the American form of government—"strike that out and the whole edifice crumbles." If the Union failed, the American experiment of free government failed. Faith would die for the downtrodden tens of millions overseas who looked to America as the last "great hope of oppressed humanity throughout the world," as the legislature declared in a joint resolution. After all, pointed out the *Newark Mercury*, the conflict represented a people's war to uphold the "*People's* Government."[12]

The enthusiasm of the people, their widespread support of the Union cause, both underscored the point made by the *Jersey City Standard:* "Truth is," it reported, "the war is *Popular*." The *Paterson Guardian* contended that the "people understand this war; it is their own." The *Newark Advertiser* observed that this "*people's war . . .* is waged for the preservation of *their* rights, *their* interests, *their* future." New Jerseyans rallied not only against a common danger, but also for a common ideal.[13]

During April and May, New Jerseyans, like other northerners, closed ranks and formed a common front against secession. Republican Richard Field noted that the "brutal and cowardly attack upon Fort Sumter" had the effect of "firing the North and fusing us together in one united mass." A Douglas Democrat announced: "We are no longer 'Republicans,' 'Democrats,' or 'Whigs;' *we are Union men*." A call for a Union meeting in Metuchen was headed: "*Not Partisans but Patriots*." Thomson declared proudly, "Our glorious little State comes up to the color beautifully and promptly."[14]

Unity in resolve did not represent unanimity in viewpoint, however. Under the political armistice, party loyalties and differences were only temporarily put aside; both could quickly reassert themselves. Some religious pacifists, the increasingly introspective Quakers who lived mainly in South Jersey, did not become politically active, although their anti-slavery beliefs remained strong and they petitioned for emancipation. Many but not all Quakers also applied for exemption from military duty. One observer characterized the passive political role of this religious denomination in the state during the war: "Quakerism seemed at a low ebb there." Moreover, the state still contained a few die-hard southern sympathizers. Certain factions within the Democratic party presented more formidable problems for the state's war effort.[15]

Most of Breckinridge's editorial supporters expressed ambivalence during the first months of the war. They regarded secession as political heresy and wanted to preserve the Union. Only reluctantly, however, did they support measures to wage war. They frequently criticized various emergency actions of Lincoln's administration and the army. Republicans, they claimed, waved the "bloody flag of Abolitionism," in the words of the *Flemington Democrat*. Conservatives criticized Lincoln for forcing a showdown in Charleston harbor.[16]

Speaking for many of Douglas's men, Morris Hamilton of the *Camden Democrat* made it clear that support for ending the rebellion did not imply unquestioning acceptance of Lincoln's policies. He pointedly reminded Republicans that worthwhile ends did not justify any means. In particular he objected to Republicans' attempts to discredit Democrats by insinuations of Democratic disloyalty. Hamilton warned that Republicans' attempts to reap partisan advantage under the cloak of patriotism would backfire: "Beware of the return tide—the day of reckoning. The people are patriotic, but they are not fools."[17]

Suggestive of the differences and difficulties ahead, New Jerseyans disagreed in their speculations about how long the war would last and what the cost of the war effort would be. Some Republican newspapers contended that the North's greater power and larger population would ensure an easy, quick victory. Other observers, both Democratic and Republican, feared a protracted struggle. The Democratic *Paterson Register* considered the South a formidable foe with "millions of brave and warlike people, fighting on their own territory, at their own homes, in defense of what they have been taught was right and just." As the Democratic *Newark Journal* cautioned, "We have men's work before us; let us not treat it as boy's play." The *Journal* questioned whether Republicans had the nerve to wage such a war or could ever win it. Republican Brownson predicted a "long, severe, and bloody struggle" against resolute, courageous southerners. The Republican *Paterson Guardian* feared that the South might achieve some startling military victory in the first major campaign. Only the shock of such a setback, it predicted, would awaken the North to the immensity of the task ahead.[18]

When war broke out, Olden took decisive action. On April 17 he requested volunteers in response to Lincoln's call for troops. His straightforward message made no mention of a rebellion and contained no patriotic flourishes. The tone of the proclamation sounded almost leaden, as if the governor remained stunned five days after the outbreak of war. The wording and the delay in issuing the proclamation prompted impatient Field to criticism: "What a *cold freezing* thing it was. Not one spirit stirring word, not one patriotic appeal. It looks very much as if his heart was not in it. . . . Oh! that we had a *man* in the Governor's chair and not an old woman!" Field's criticism was unwarranted and premature: Olden did not delay in complying with Lincoln's call or in organizing military units, and on April 24 he issued two additional and more strongly patriotic proclamations, now explicitly supportive of the war effort. In the two messages the governor warned citizens to guard against treason and called a special session of the legislature to enact necessary war measures.[19]

On April 30 the legislature convened and heard his message. In a stirring appeal Olden declared the unswerving loyalty of New Jerseyans to the Union, to the Constitution, and to the nation's laws. He stated that no allegiance to any state could conflict with higher loyalty to the nation. He considered secession to be without excuse or justification and regarded it as a synonym for treason. In this extraordinary emergency New Jerseyans must do everything in their power to defend the Union from attack.

Olden requested authorization of a loan of two million dollars to raise an army for the common defense and a property tax to pay off the loan. He outlined various measures to furnish the needed men as well as to arm and equip them. In concluding, the governor declared, "New Jersey will meet the crisis, and rise to the height of her great duty, ever standing firm by the Union." Legislators, editors, and citizens applauded the message.[20]

The Democratic legislature backed the war. Speaker Frederick Teese referred testily to rumors of pro-southern sentiment in the state. He responded: "How mistaken was the opinion that in this state any party or faction of a party could be found to give aid or comfort to treason. New Jersey is today, as she has always been, loyal to the Union." The presiding officer of the senate, Edmund Perry of Flemington, expressed the consensus in the state: "Our duty is clear. New Jersey has never failed or faltered in her constitutional obligations; she will not do so now." In a series of resolutions passed in May, both chambers of the legislature endorsed the efforts of Lincoln and Olden to maintain the Union. The legislature also declared that the surest, fastest way to peace lay in waging war to the fullest in order to stamp out the rebellion.[21]

The legislature put the state on a war footing: it accepted Olden's recommendations by financing mobilization and authorizing cities or counties to aid families of volunteers. Aware of what other state governments in the North were doing to support the war effort, members of the legislature as well as most New Jerseyans did "not mean to be behind any State," as Martin Ryerson confided. Thus, when the legislature considered whether to appropriate one or two million dollars for the war effort by issuing a state loan, some legislators probably were influenced to favor the higher amount by the fact that Connecticut, with a smaller population, had just approved that sum. Yet on May 7, most Democrats in the assembly balked at first at the Republican governor's recommendation of two million dollars and preferred one million instead. The Democratic-controlled assembly unanimously approved the lower amount.[22]

The next day in the senate, two Democrats—Joseph T. Crowell of Rahway and Edward C. Moore of Newton—joined the Republicans to support the higher figure, and the measure passed the upper chamber. On this vote all except one of the Democrats in opposition hailed from North Jersey. In the final vote on the bill as a whole, three Democratic senators—Ralph S. Demarest of Bergen, James K. Swayze of Warren, and Samuel Wescott of Hudson, along with Republican defector Thomas Norcross—continued their opposition to this major war measure.[23]

During the fight in the legislature Olden brought his influence to bear behind the scenes. He prevailed upon Democratic leader Edwin Wright to intervene personally. Wright forcefully told Democratic legislators that vacillation would prove disastrous. He lobbied for two million dollars and gave Olden his wholehearted support. Nevertheless, the fight over the senate bill in the assembly was close. In a test vote on May 9 the assembly gave only narrow support (52 percent) to the senate's proposal to fund the war effort with two million dollars. Two Democrats, John R. Graham of Camden and James E. Smith of West Orange, supported the full amount, as did all the Republicans.

Clearly the Democrats' distrust of the Republicans and the new Lincoln administration remained deep-seated. On May 10, however, when the war loan bill came up for a final vote in the assembly, many Democrats changed sides. In the end the assembly approved this key war measure overwhelmingly, by 87 percent. Seven Democrats, all from North Jersey, refused to support the bill.[24]

In another test vote, held earlier on May 8, one member had introduced an amendment to reduce the number of weapons purchased from ten thousand to five thousand. By a vote of 46 to 5, the assembly soundly defeated this proposal to cripple the defense of the state. The special session had done its work well and quickly, but the closeness of the vote in the assembly on May 9 recommended caution, not complacency.[25]

In this early phase of the war, observers surveyed with satisfaction what New Jerseyans had done to help save the country: the rapid rush of volunteers to enlist, the spontaneous offers of money to the families of volunteers, the vote of the legislature to fully fund the war effort by outfitting state regiments. Such actions, the *Trenton Gazette* declared, left no doubt where New Jersey stood. The contribution of two million dollars and four thousand soldiers, commented the *Jersey City Standard*, "will make their hearts thrill with patriotic emotion; and 'Jersey Blue' will ever remain a title of just pride as the cognomen for unswerving steadfastness as patriots."[26]

In the first twenty-one months of the war, Olden showed his mettle. Although he lacked military training and experience, he demonstrated his administrative skills in an unfamiliar field. The state was totally unprepared for a military emergency; he created an organization where none had existed and selected officials to take charge. Lavishing all his time and energy on the war effort, he and his able staff worked efficiently and unceasingly. He prevailed upon the banks and the Joint Companies to advance funds to outfit troops. He raised all the money required for war purposes at low interest and sold state bonds at a premium. During a time of severe shortages of military supplies, under his direction agents went to great lengths to secure the best available clothing, equipment, and arms for troops. He also tried to provide soldiers with decent accommodations and food. In addition, the governor attempted to bolster wartime morale by paying attention to unit spirit at the front and to state pride at home. Above all, he resourcefully met federal calls for troops.[27]

Despite these heroic efforts, bureaucratic bungling and foul-ups were inevitable in creating an army almost overnight. Local considerations intruded and prominent persons who organized regiments demanded to command them. Critics, both in and out of the army, found fault, especially with the quality of company-grade officers. One private in the Twenty-first Regiment remarked: "How in God's name they ever selected such officers is a mystery." Republicans resented Olden for appointing a great number of Democratic officers, especially regimental commanders. Yet Olden as well as Lincoln intended to broaden public support of the war effort by military patronage. The governor stressed the paramount importance of "keeping public sentiment right in New Jersey, and of doing nothing to cause a revulsion of the noble and patriotic spirit, which now prevails throughout the state." To have such a governor at such a time, one who did so much, so well, so fast, was to both Olden's and the state's credit. Most New Jerseyans, both Democrats and Republicans, praised Olden's vigorous leadership and solid achievements.[28]

**B**y mid-1861 some conservatives, including some who had supported the war earlier, began to question whether the North should make peace or war. Following similar efforts in neighboring states, peace supporters in New Jersey held their first known meetings in Newark on June 12 and 19. They petitioned Congress to end the fighting and to authorize a national convention, which in turn could reach a permanent settlement with the South. At one conclave opponents left it to organize a protest meeting outside. They pointed out that the peacemakers ignored the previous failure of the Washington peace convention to reach a successful formula. Moreover, neither northern nor southern officials wanted another such meeting. The South had fired the first shot; if the rebels had wanted peace, they would not have started war. Cries for peace, charged the prowar *Morristown Banner*, sought to lure northerners "under the banner of peace in order to lead them blindfolded" into the hands of the enemy. Thus the Democratic ranks began to divide between minority peacemakers, who urged peace for the sake of the Union, and majority war supporters, who urged war for the sake of the Union. The two sides agreed on their ultimate objective but differed on the all-important means.[29]

Opposition to the war continued to issue from the offices of the *Newark Journal.* Characterizing the war as unwinnable, the *Journal's* firebrand editor Fuller demanded that the war stop and peace negotiations start. His apocalyptic editorials described the conflict as a conspiratorial "war of invasion and aggression by the North upon the South." War opponents denounced Lincoln's "reign of despotism and tyranny" in which "Abe the First" rode roughshod over the people's constitutional rights and liberties in conducting "Lincoln's war."[30]

Naar of the *Trenton American* also expressed skepticism about what he regarded as Lincoln's coercive policy, but his editorial approach differed markedly from Fuller's abusive tone and confrontational style. Accordingly, the *Newark Mercury* charged that Naar attempted to "accomplish insidiously what it dare not do openly." After a decisive show of federal force in Maryland in the spring of 1861 to keep that state in the Union, to protect federal troops after some Baltimoreans attacked them, and to guard the strategic railroad line to Washington, other opponents joined the unrealistic criticism of Lincoln's tactics. They condemned his orders imposing army occupation of Maryland, objected to the violation of the rights of the states, and protested the restriction of the civil liberties of rebel sympathizers.[31]

The *Mercury* observed that the inflammatory *Journal* grew "continually more unpatriotic and treasonable," even if it had not sunk quite so low as New York City's antiwar newspapers. Republicans dismissed this nascent peace sentiment as hypocrisy wedded to disloyalty. In their opinion, its supporters covered their sympathy toward secession with a thin veneer of patriotism. By insinuating that the purpose of the war included freeing the slaves and imposing equality between the races or by stigmatizing Lincoln's administration as a military despotism, such Democrats aided the enemy by trying to undermine war morale. According to the Republicans, the peace party intimated that peace would follow if only Lincoln said the word, yet responsible people realized that peace would come only if southerners ended their rebellion. As the Republican *Camden Press* declared, "Any offer of compromise with traitors in arms is treason and nothing less." The Democratic *Morristown Banner* also objected to any negotiations, asking "Are we only to have peace by sacrificing the Union and surrendering the Constitution?"[32]

On July 21, 1861, the armies of the North and the South joined battle at Bull Run in Manassas, Virginia. In this first major engagement of the war, the Confederates defeated the Union army. Retreat turned into a rout as northern troops panicked. On hearing the shocking news of the debacle, many New Jerseyans despaired; defeat jolted them to reality. One Elizabeth man spoke for many: "*I fear we have a long and bloody war before us.*" Ryerson predicted a conflict that "will try the courage, fortitude, and patience of our people to the very utmost."[33]

Yet defeat taught prowar New Jerseyans an invaluable lesson: playing at war by employing sunshine patriots, "mere holiday soldiers," and "imbecile generals" had to stop. Raw recruits needed rigorous training and discipline. The troops required more competent, more reliable junior officers with steadier nerves, and the army needed more capable generals to coordinate Union forces and devise a bolder, craftier strategy to outwit and overwhelm the enemy. The home front had to back up the battlefront. The people needed to make greater sacrifices with more work and more unity, less talk and less criticism. The North needed to tap its abundant but unused resources.[34]

Bull Run also spawned defeatism. It emboldened war opponents to raise more doubts, stir more dissension, and sow more disaffection on the home front. The *Newark Journal* predicted that both sides would bleed to death in a fruitless fratricidal war until, in the end, the "North is destined to sure defeat." The *Journal* recommended that the North immediately call an armistice and pursue peace through diplomatic channels. In the interim, war opponents vowed not to pay federal taxes in support of Lincoln's war.[35]

On July 27 peace advocates held a meeting at Alloway in Salem County. A handbill described the meeting as opposition to this "unnecessary war." Rumors circulated that known secessionists from Delaware would appear as featured speakers, but only John R. Sickler, a Gloucester County physician, turned up to attack Lincoln's policies. A proposed resolution recommended peaceful separation, because force alone could not hold the Union together. Protesters in the audience, however, denounced the resolution, derided the speaker, and finally silenced him by throwing rotten eggs and stones.[36]

Led by a Bergen contingent, Breckinridge men organized another meeting on July 30 in Schraalenburgh (Dumont). Writer Thomas Dunn English of Hackensack denounced Lincoln's despotism and predicted the election of an anti-administration Congress that would impeach him. Earlier in the meeting, the leaders had approved formal resolutions that covered much the same ground as in Alloway. The peace supporters pledged conditional loyalty to the Union, dependent on the proper behavior of government officials, and condemned Lincoln and his administration for numerous incursions on individual liberties in the guise of military necessity.[37]

More occurred at this meeting than some Democratic newspapers reported. The audience interrupted and heckled the antiwar speakers. When the peace men finished, prowar Democrats demanded time to speak. The organizers of the meeting refused. Faced with an angry audience ready to riot, the managers abruptly adjourned the meeting but kept control of the platform in order to prevent opponents from speaking. Undeterred, the war supporters walked to a nearby field, where they wheeled a wagon into place as a makeshift platform. Samuel A. Jones, an Englewood physician, called for a vigorous prosecution of the war as the only way to save the Union. The crowd loudly applauded his remarks and approved the prowar resolutions. Thus war supporters turned a peace conclave into a war rally in the heart of Bergen County.[38]

Peace supporters scheduled still another meeting for August 29 in Middletown, in staunchly Democratic Monmouth, but supporters of the war distributed a broadside referring to peace men as subversives "rearing their reptile heads." Treason was treason, whether it came from a speaker's mouth in the North or from a cannon's barrel in the South: "Those who advocate peace, before Rebellion is put down, are Traitors!" The broadside called on Union sympathizers to assemble and protest the peace meeting. In response, the peace organizers nailed a notice on the tavern door, canceling their meeting.[39]

The Union men, undeceived, assembled anyway in force at the meeting site. Then the peace men arrived in a caravan. At first each side mistook the other as reinforcements, and cheered wildly. The war men, however, soon discovered their mistake and took over the location. They organized a meeting of their own, selected a prominent local Democratic leader, George C. Murray, to preside, and adopted resolutions supporting the war.

When the war rally ended, the peace group decided to hold its meeting elsewhere. As featured speaker English entered his carriage to leave, the prowar crowd surrounded the carriage and demanded that he pledge support to the Union cause. When he refused, the menacing crowd rocked the carriage and tried to turn it over. A federal marshal arrived just in time to save English from being lynched. The marshal dragged him into a nearby inn and hid him in the attic. English, trying to explain his position to the marshal, reversed his stand and declared that he supported the war. Later he slipped out the back door. The war men recognized him at once, and he hastily retreated inside. When the crowd broke into the inn, English hid in a closet, narrowly escaping the mob.[40]

These generally abortive conclaves followed a pattern similar to that of meetings organized in New York, Pennsylvania, and Connecticut. In fact, a peace meeting in neighboring Rockland County, New York, had paved the way for the meeting in Dumont, where the keynote speaker hailed from Rockland. New Jersey's peace supporters held most of their meetings in Democratic strongholds in the northeastern corner of the state: in Newark, in rural Middletown on Raritan Bay near New York City, and in rural Dumont in northeastern Bergen County, close to both the Hudson River and Rockland. The meeting in the southwestern part of the state took place in rural Alloway, located in southern Salem and near the slave state of Delaware. Most meetings, then, except for the Newark gathering, were held in comparatively isolated areas. Located mainly on the geographical periphery of the state, the views expressed in these meetings were on the political periphery as well.

Blacks in Salem constituted the highest proportion of the total population of any county in the state, 12 percent, a lightning rod to fearful white racists. The black share of Bergen's population was the second highest in the state, 8 percent. Monmouth's share, 7 percent, ranked fifth highest. Given the fact that the statewide average was slightly less than 4 percent, racial concerns likely strengthened antiwar appeal in the three counties.[41]

The peace meetings provoked widespread indignation and bipartisan condemnation by local newspapers. The Republican *Woodbury Constitution* claimed disbelief that the Alloway "resolutions speak the sentiments of the Democratic party of New Jersey. They will repudiate them, as very many of the leading prominent men who adorn the party, have done." Similarly, the Democratic *Salem Sunbeam* exhorted that the Democracy must not be "chained to the chariot wheels of secession and sedition." A reporter of the Republican *Paterson Guardian* believed that organizer English had been "repudiated thoroughly by the Democrats of Bergen County."[42]

The *Freehold Democrat* disparaged the projected meeting in Middletown because "everything that tends to embarrass the Government, only protracts the war." Even so, the newspaper condemned the unlawful, riotous tactics of the war supporters who prevented the peace meeting: "*The mob* is far more dangerous in New Jersey than traitorous assemblies." The *Camden Democrat*, however, contended that New Jerseyans should not allow people to talk of peace when an armed rebellion threatened "our existence as a nation." The *Camden Press* noted the hypocrisy of the peace men: they were sticklers for any infraction of the law or violation of liberty in the North, but blind to rebellion against the Constitution and national authority by the South. At this stage of the war, then, peace overtures found little favor, as even antiwar editor Fuller of the *Newark Journal* had conceded earlier. The *Princeton Standard* dismissed the peace meetings as "too absurd to amount to anything of importance." Clearly these scattered peace meetings in 1861 did not represent a cause finding fertile ground in New Jersey. One Warren County observer likened the peace men attending their meetings to an animal coming out of its hiding place on a warm spring day, only to find a hostile reception and to scurry back into its hole.[43]

Throughout 1861, and especially during the fall, for every peace meeting held, war supporters organized innumerable nonpartisan meetings and Union party conventions across the state. The biggest demonstrations occurred in Newark and Trenton. War sympathizers also held meetings at several Bergen County sites, including Ho-Ho-Kus, Fort Lee, and Englewood. At the Englewood meeting, a former state senator, Hackensack Democrat

Thomas H. Herring, expressed the unionist consensus of New Jerseyans: the only way to permanently settle the national problem was to prosecute the war vigorously. The *Mercury* summed up the prevailing view: "He who today talks 'Compromise' is a Coward; and he who talks 'Peace' is a Traitor."[44]

The ferocious criticism leveled against the peace press also illustrated the unpopularity of the peace faction in the state in 1861. It revealed impatience, even intolerance toward dissent. Following the steps taken against pro-southern newspapers in New York and elsewhere, New Jerseyans pressured city governments to repudiate journals regarded as subversive, to withdraw financial support, and even to suppress them. Providing a patriotic covering fire and urging an end to politics as usual, Republican politicians and editors in particular tried to stop the municipal subsidies of certain Democratic newspapers. Of the fifteen daily newspapers published in New Jersey's five largest cities (Newark, Jersey City, Trenton, Paterson, and New Brunswick), three dailies had associations with the peace movement and came under attack for spreading treasonable sentiments. Two lost invaluable city patronage during August.

Republicans first seized the initiative in Trenton, where they dominated the common council. On August 6 the council decided, on a strictly partisan vote, to stop all city printing in Naar's *Trenton American*. Simultaneously, Republican and Democratic newspapers attacked Naar's editorial position. In late August, Naar's beleaguered journal suspended daily publication for forty-three days, only to resume publication on October 7.[45]

On August 19, in Paterson, city authorities in a bipartisan move voted to ban municipal printing or advertising in the *Paterson Register*. The *Paterson Guardian* remarked that "no man or paper can stand against the current of patriotism now rushing like a torrent for the National defense." Seeing where the *Register*'s interests lay, editor Andrew Mead quickly moderated its editorial tone.[46]

The next action occurred in Newark on September 13, when the Democratic majority on the city council rebuked the editors of the *Newark Journal*. Although the council decided not to discontinue city printing in the *Journal*, Newark's only Democratic newspaper, as the Republicans proposed, the Democratic councilmen distanced themselves from the paper by declaring that publication of city notices in the *Journal* did not mean an endorsement of its editorial views. Clearly the prowar Democrats wished to dissociate themselves from the politically embarrassing peace minority.[47]

During 1861 eight of the eighty-six weekly newspapers in the state represented the antiwar faction. At the start of the war the peace weeklies were John Simerson's *Belvidere Journal*, Adam Bellis's *Flemington Democrat*, William Abel's *Hackettstown Gazette*, Nathan Harper's *Mount Holly Herald*, Albert R. Speer's *New Brunswick Times*, Charles J. Wilson's *Plainfield Gazette*, and Josephus Shann's *Rahway Democrat*. Later in the year C. Chauncey Burr's and Eben

Winton's *Hackensack Democrat* joined them; in 1862 Orson C. Cone's *Somerville Messenger* did so. These organs represented about 10 percent of the state's total number of weeklies—within the normal proportion of dissident views represented in a healthy political society.[48]

Federal authorities, concerned about sedition in New Jersey and having taken similar actions in New York and elsewhere, decided to move against these "editorial tools of the Rebellion." On September 25, 1861, a federal grand jury issued a statement naming the *Newark Journal*, the *Plainfield Gazette*, the *New Brunswick Times*, the *Hackettstown Gazette*, the *Belvidere Journal*, and the *Flemington Democrat* as treasonable in tone and unrepresentative of the "sentiments of any considerable portion of the people of New Jersey." The statement urged New Jerseyans not to patronize these newspapers. Noting their recent change of tone, however, the jury did not hand down an indictment.[49]

In rebuttal, the peace journals denied any disloyalty and declared their opposition to secession. They interpreted as vindication the lack of an indictment or, in some cases, omission of a particular newspaper from the list. The editors vowed to continue to exercise their right to criticize governmental policy. Yet some of the peace papers evidently took the warning seriously enough to mute their stridency, at least temporarily.[50]

Although peace proponents constituted only a small, though vocal, minority in New Jersey during the first year of the war, they caused a hysterical overreaction. The *Somerville News* advised every citizen to "watch the speech and acts of his neighbors, so as, upon discovering of treasonable sympathies, to bring them under the scorpion lash of an indignant patriotism." Journals called on loyal men to fall into line: southern sympathizers should be ostracized or driven away. The *News* went even further: such traitors "will keep their filthy mouths shut," it declared, or will be thrown into prison. Wild rumors of southern spies and conspiracies in New Jersey spread. At one extreme, some ardent, impatient war supporters complained that while the government and the people strained every nerve to preserve the Union, Lincoln's government undermined them by treating northern traitors too leniently. The *Mercury*, occupying a middle position, sensibly drew a line between dissent and obstruction of the war effort. At the other extreme, some virulent antiwar critics, disregarding the emergency of civil war, rigidly rejected any interference with free expression; such interference would jeopardize liberty and invite dictatorship. As a result, assorted threats and isolated assaults against both war protesters and war supporters proliferated across the state.[51]

During this uproar the federal government sometimes tried to suppress the peace press by curtailing distribution. Such an action against New York City's antiwar *News* embroiled James Wall in one controversy. A Burlington lawyer and politician, Wall believed untrammeled free expression to be essential to liberty and so regarded a free press as an absolute right. He ignored the competing interests, pressing concerns, and existing power of government to cope with sedition and restrict the press when it imperiled national security. In late August this fiery opponent of the war wrote a stinging letter to Montgomery Blair, in which he condemned the postmaster general's seizure of copies of the *News*. In response, federal authorities arrested Wall in September and imprisoned him at Fort Lafayette in New York Bay for nearly two weeks, until he swore allegiance. Upon his release, he returned to his hometown in triumph as a martyr. Republican newspapers attributed Wall's arrest to his alleged activity in encouraging Maryland to secede, but Wall denied any involvement.[52]

Lincoln's administration, which generally tolerated hostile newspapers despite extreme provocation, stumbled in this case by arresting Wall without specific charges and without giving him an opportunity to defend himself. The prowar *Freehold Democrat* claimed that federal officials deliberately kept Wall in confinement just long enough to allow the news of his fate to become well known in New Jersey. At the same time the Republican press in the state described Wall as a prominent Democrat in order to embarrass the state party.[53]

The momentary excitement over the affair encouraged the peace faction to play up the incident. The distasteful experience recharged the irrepressible Wall's political batteries; he lashed out at military despotism and arbitrary power. The sympathetic *Belvidere Journal* dubbed his prison the "Lincoln Bastille." Federal forbearance was preferable to the imprisonment of this voluble, impulsive individual, and far more politic. Moreover, New Jersey was not Maryland, where disloyalty and disorder had required emergency federal attention and decisive army action in the spring.[54]

By September, with the situation in Maryland under control, the allegation that Wall promoted secession was no longer important. Wall, then, was not a public menace but merely a local nuisance. His imprisonment rested on shaky grounds that might undermine the war effort to a minor extent in some circles in the state. Still, his imprisonment set an example; as the *Trenton Patriot* pointed out, the "frowning walls of Fort Lafayette also cast its shadows upon their cowardly fears and sealed up their treacherous utterances."[55]

In the course of the war federal authorities arrested and jailed several other New Jerseyans who made treasonable statements or discouraged military service. Daniel Cory, one minor antiwar activist of Warren in Somerset County, spent thirty-six days in jail in 1862. His antiwar neighbors in November 1863 elected him to the assembly and the following year reelected him. Later in the war, federal officials arrested a few antiwar editors. Reporting an incendiary speech of Cory, the Republican *New Brunswick Fredonian* put the whole matter in perspective with this acid remark: "It is to be hoped the government will survive the effects of his speech."[56]

For the most part those who encountered trouble with federal authorities were not politically prominent individuals. Sometimes they made a bold anti-war statement to the wrong person at the wrong time. Sheer stubbornness also played a role: federal officials imprisoned a Salem physician, Edward S. Sharp, for refusing to take a loyalty oath. He remained in jail for five long months because he inexplicably continued to refuse. He was finally released without taking the oath.[57]

Some obscure individuals underwent arbitrary arrest and imprisonment. Many individuals arrested were jailed for a short time and then released without trial. The thirty-seven known New Jerseyans who were arrested and tried in federal court hailed from both country towns and large cities. Their usual offense was opposition to military recruitment, evidenced by disrupting enlistment meetings, attacking recruiting officers, resisting military service, encouraging desertion, or aiding deserters.

After the introduction of conscription, such incidents increased during 1863 and 1864, and trials became more frequent. When a draft resister physically assaulted an enrolling officer, the federal prosecutor came into court with a virtually open-and-shut case and achieved a high conviction rate. A typical case involved only one or two individuals in an isolated incident. (The nine Holmdel farmers who hurled stones at an enrolling officer in June 1864 were an exception.) When persons extended help to deserters, however, little evidence could be obtained to sustain the charges; thus the federal officials secured few convictions. Punishment of convicted offenders hardly approached the draconian. Jail sentences were extremely rare. Instead, there was usually a stiff fine. Federal officials evidently wished to set a good example and to discourage resistance to the draft.

In contrast to other lower northern states, including Indiana and Illinois, and the border slave states which experienced serious problems of dissent and disaffection, these problems were not widespread in New Jersey. Federal officials did not mount a brutal campaign to ban political dissidents or impose a reign of terror on Jerseyans. Only Wall, Cory, and a number of harmless individuals ran afoul of the law. Despite wartime provocations and a few overreacting officials, robust, even raucous Jersey politics continued in an atmosphere of diverse opinion. To be sure, the punishment did not always match the offense. Army officers and federal officials sometimes made mistakes when they bypassed the regular court proceedings of formal charges and trials with cross-examination, or when they worked in secret without public accountability, official review, or legal appeal. The unfortunate few persons languishing in jail cells could hardly take comfort from the fact that their plight was the exception, not the rule, however. Yet for most New Jerseyans their civil liberties were not limited as they sometimes were elsewhere. Ironically, the very freedom that existed in Jersey made it appear more antiwar than it was in contrast to a state such as Maryland, where dissent and disaffection were greater in fact but were suppressed.[58]

S upport for the war by New Jerseyans in 1861 showed itself in the state's delegation to Congress during its summer session when its four Democrats generally supported war measures. Many other leaders of the New Jersey Democracy also stood loyally behind the war effort, including Moses Bigelow, Theodore Runyon, Ryerson, Peter Vroom, and Benjamin Williamson. Democratic congressmen from New Jersey and other northern states, however, favored exploring every avenue to reach a possible accommodation with the South.[59]

Just as northerners were unprepared militarily to fight this war, they were uncertain what to do politically. Thus the proper role of political parties and the specific role of the loyal opposition during an unprecedented civil war became one of the leading questions in the fall campaign. Some individuals, hoping to avoid the bitter partisan divisions that had occurred in the Mexican War and the War of 1812, proposed that neither party make nominations for some or all offices but form common tickets instead. Others went further and suggested the abolition of political parties because partisanship undermined unity: politics as usual should end until the war ended. Many Democrats greeted this proposal uneasily.

Proposals for the general abandonment of party were unrealistic. Party government, after all, continued in Washington. There was neither time nor inclination to form a government of national unity and to share power. Republicans, who had never before controlled the executive branch, would not relinquish hard-won control and patronage, although Lincoln did appoint former Democrats as generals and cabinet secretaries in order to broaden support for the war. Democrats, for their part, desired no connection with the Republicans' radicalism. Because the parties had disagreed over national policy before the war, it was natural that they continued to disagree. Members of each party also distrusted the other's integrity and loyalty. The death of Douglas, fifty-four days after the war began, dealt the final blow. Without Douglas to act as leader of the prowar Democrats and to serve as the major spokesman of the responsible, loyal opposition, the rudderless Democracy drifted.

Differences also split the parties internally. Republican ranks in New Jersey consisted of three amorphous groups. Radical Republicans formed a tiny left wing; they wished to transform the war for the Union into a war for emancipation of the slaves. The conservative Republicans, who formed the right wing, defended the status quo and opposed the radicals' emancipationist zeal. Moderates disagreed with both the impatient idealists and the timid conservatives. Members of this group, including Lincoln and many Republicans in the state, were ready and willing to adjust policy as war developments warranted and as public opinion shifted. They realized that the timing of change was as important as change itself.

New Jersey Democrats held different notions of their wartime role. Some so-called war Democrats enlisted in the Republican party for the duration and became full-fledged Republicans. Others, styling themselves Union Democrats, cooperated with Lincoln's administration and supported its war effort as nominally independent Democrats.[60]

Most Democrats in the state, however, remained regular party members and aligned with one of the two major factions in their party. Prowar Democrats formed the majority and strongly opposed secession. In some fashion and at various times, they supported the war effort to reunite the Union. Yet they often opposed major Republican measures, notably confiscation of rebel property and emancipation of the slaves. Peace Democrats wanted peace at any price and sought negotiations with the South to end hostilities. They regarded peace as the only way to secure future reunion, but occasionally they concluded reluctantly that northerners must accept temporary or permanent division of the Union. The peace Democrats opposed both Lincoln's prosecution of the war and his imposition of restrictions on traditional liberties. Thus the war faction of the Democrats was pro-Union yet anti-administration; the peace faction was both antiwar and anti-administration. The peace Democrats ranged from passive southern sympathizers to active obstructionists of the war effort.

Bipartisanship found few advocates, for good reason. The existence of a political opposition furnished Republican politicians in the states with incentives to remain loyal to Lincoln's administration. In addition, an opposition party could expose incompetence and check the potential abuse of power by the party in control. Without an opposition party, dissatisfied persons would have lacked an acceptable means to propose an alternative policy. Also, without two political parties, people with grievances would have lacked proper channels to allow them to let off steam. Parties kept both dissent and choices within limits. Paradoxically, an opposition party, operating within bounds, helped rather than hampered the war effort in the long run. Political competition, the lifeblood of democracy, continued even while civil war raged.[61]

In local contests in New Jersey during the fall of 1861, candidates were left to fend for themselves without help from the state party organization. Because the parties were balanced fairly evenly in the state, Republicans attempted to convert Democrats with an ostensibly nonpartisan plea for a single party of patriots. Preserving the Union, they declared, meant "no party work, for this is no time to talk of party or party issues, of being a Democrat or a Republican—our country is above and beyond party, and party requirements—our glorious Union is worth more than all parties that ever existed, and the only issue now before the people is that of Union or Disunion." Party nominations, they claimed, hurt the war effort, distracted and divided the North, and encouraged rebels to redouble their efforts and prolong the war. The Republicans crafted a message cleverly designed to attract voters who distrusted both parties and all politicians. The people, the *Hightstown Gazette* declared, wanted a Union movement now; only greedy old party hacks and corrupt cliques expected politics as usual and demanded the spoils of office. Proponents advocated formation of loyal leagues to canvass neighborhoods and spread the message.[62]

The Democrats looked askance at this gratuitous Republican scheme to disband the only party that defended law and order and stood as a safe haven against abolitionism, which they regarded as a growing scourge in the Republican party. They also resented what they viewed as a double standard, whereby Republicans pleaded for bipartisan cooperation while branding Democrats as secessionists and denying them federal patronage. Democrats complained that fusion would promote only Republican interests. The *Camden Democrat* pointed out that Republicans promoted a Union party in Democratic urban and rural strongholds, but in Republican bastions Republicans did not call for an end to parties. They wished to change the Republican party to the Union party in places where it needed more votes, but not to change the party name in safe districts. Dismissing this Republican call for bipartisanship as self-serving, New Jersey Democrats retained their regular party organization and straight Democratic tickets.[63]

The first test of the hoped-for Republican Union movement came in the Newark city election on October 8, 1861. All the Democratic factions, including Breckinridge's and Douglas's supporters, reunited behind a straight party ticket, adopted a strongly antisecessionist platform, and renominated prowar mayor Bigelow as the Democratic Union candidate. The Republicans, joined by a sprinkling of Democrats (estimated at 14 percent of the convention delegates), nominated prowar Democrat Charles L. C. Gifford as their People's Union nominee.

Newark Republican journalist Daniel Porter reported that Republicans intended to seize control by sweeping the Democrats out of the common council. It was immaterial to Republicans whether they did their job with a "whisk broom or a scrubbing brush. So they chose the scrubbing brush." The housecleaning campaign, however, deteriorated quickly into a mudslinging contest as each party wildly charged its mayoral opponent with disloyalty to the Union. Bigelow trounced his younger, less experienced opponent and doubled his majority, while Democrats increased their number of aldermen. The Democrats now dominated Newark so strongly that they could control Essex and elect the county sheriff.[64]

The Republicans meanwhile equated their defeat with rejection of their Union strategy. Evidently fusion bred confusion and even demoralization.

Many Republicans refused to vote. Another Newark Republican journalist, however, John Y. Foster, did not mourn the defeat; as he stated, "it will put an end forever to the Union fusion policy."[65]

The Democrats harbored no more doubts about maintaining their party organization intact. The *Newark Journal* crowed that the "no Party humbug, it appears, has played out." It added that "the Democracy, for a dead party, appears to be wonderfully alive." The *New York Herald* summed up the Newark election: "Long before the election the Democrats placed themselves squarely upon the Union platform . . . so that the few secessionist sympathizers in the North cannot get a grain of consolation out of this Democratic success."[66]

In the campaign for the legislature that followed, Democrats throughout the state seized the initiative by making their own Democratic Union nominations, usually bolstered with unionist resolutions and with an invitation to Republicans to join their patriotic cause. Republicans deplored such partisan nominations. The *Mercury* mourned the hope "for this era of good feeling in New Jersey," in which the unhealthy fogs and mists of party would have been swept away by the fresh breezes of patriotism.[67]

As Democrats had observed, where Republicans considered themselves weak, they made a nonpartisan appeal. They nominated some unionist Democrats in Democratic cities, and often formed Union tickets in North Jersey. In secure places such as South Jersey, they variously nominated Republican Union or Republican slates. Despite variations in party names, party lines were drawn even more firmly than before.[68]

Both parties supported the war and radiated patriotism. Still, keen party competition and deep distrust of the other party surfaced quickly. Each side tried to exploit fears and deliberately misrepresented the position of the other. Presenting the alternatives as either Republican patriot or Democratic traitor, Republicans portrayed all state Democrats as either disloyal Breckinridgers or camp followers of the peace party. Republicans charged Democrats would transform the legislature into a juggernaut that would gut war measures.[69]

Democrats labeled every state Republican a false patriot or a subversive sectionalist. In contrast, Democrats noted, in "nearly all the Legislative Districts where 'Regular Democrats' were elected, resolutions favorable to the prosecution of the war and the support of the government were adopted." The Republicans retorted about these Democrats, who, in the words of the *Mercury*, "all at once burst into a torrent of loyal professions." Their sudden conversion did not convince Republicans: "The Administration is identified with the Government. The assailant of the former, whether open or covert, is the enemy of the latter. Away, then, with the cant of being in favor of the Union and the Government, but opposed to the Cabinet or to the President!" At the very least, the *Paterson Guardian* observed, it was frequently difficult to tell prowar Democrats from antiwar Democrats. The Democrats responded that they supported the national government in maintaining the Union, but, they added, this "does not involve any approval whatever of the peculiar partisan views and platform of the party which for the time being may administer the Government."[70]

The abolition of slavery arose as a minor issue. Emancipation as a political and military expedient of the war divided the Republicans. Radical Republicans favored it on both idealistic and practical grounds; they declared that slavery was not only morally repugnant but also the cause of the war and the source of southern strength. Thus only an end to slavery could assure a speedy close to the war. Moderate Republicans opposed freedom for the slaves, arguing that it would prolong the war by undermining unionist support in the vitally important border slave states and by strengthening southern resolve.[71]

The possibility of emancipation united all factions of state Democrats, who regarded it as unwise, unconstitutional, and inconsistent with the goal of reuniting the nation. The *Jersey City Standard* insisted that Lincoln's sole concern must remain "whether we are Confederate or United States." Both Democrats and Republicans agreed that only a small minority in the North actually favored emancipation. Everyone regarded their numbers within the state as negligible. The "people of New Jersey are not abolitionists," stressed the *Mount Holly Herald*.[72]

Yet if the war dragged on long enough, northerners would eventually accept the restriction of slavery as a war measure. Then, Brownson predicted, slavery would receive its death blow, "Nobody has engaged in the war with the intention of putting an immediate end to slavery: All who have responded to the call of the President and buckled on their armor, have done so to vindicate the Constitution, to enforce the prevailing laws, and to preserve the Union. But if the Rebels prove themselves able to protract the struggle and to gain some victories, if . . . the passions of the non-Slaveholding States become roused and embittered, slavery must go, and the war will be in effect a war of liberation." Disagreeing, Democrats made it clear, in the words of the *Trenton American*, that "if this is to be an abolition war, abolitionists [meaning Republicans] will have to fight it" alone.[73]

The issue of emancipation figured prominently only in the contest for the assembly in Ocean County, where radical Republicans pushed through an endorsement of emancipation in the platform at the party's county convention. Partly in retaliation, Republican Ephraim P. Emson became the Democratic candidate. Emson supported the war but also had grown frustrated with the Republican incumbent for failing to back a town boundary change. Running against the incumbent, opposing emancipation and accusing his opponent of not supporting railroad construction, Emson won.[74]

The lightness of the vote across the state reflected voters' apathy during the campaign. Some citizens had gone off to fight the war, and their absence affected small Republican towns most of all. A few commentators speculated that some Republicans had become disenchanted with their own fusion movement, which had nominated unionist Democrats in Democratic districts. Other observers accused Democratic candidates of seducing a few Republicans by their unionist professions. Whatever the reason, a slightly greater proportion of Republicans than of Democrats actually changed parties. Conceivably, some unionist Democrats voted Republican because of the Republicans' appeal to patriotism.[75]

The overall result in New Jersey was a draw. The precarious balance between the parties continued; Democrats barely retained control of the legislature. Although they won their greatest percentage of the assembly vote in ten years, they gained only a single seat each in both the assembly and the senate. Both sides expressed pleasure with the result.[76]

In the seven senate races the Republicans won three safe counties (rural Burlington and Cape May in South Jersey and urban Passaic in North Jersey), while the Democrats carried three safe North Jersey counties (urban Hudson along with rural Hunterdon and Sussex). The only change in party control occurred in more competitive Middlesex; there the Camden and Amboy Railroad reportedly had supported an old-line Democrat, who won out over a regular Republican. Thus the Democrats would control the senate nominally, by only one vote.

Republicans nevertheless solidified their ranks in the senate and strengthened their support for the war when a party regular replaced defector Norcross. Despite Wall's problems with the administration, the Republican nominee carried his county. Theodore F. Randolph, the new Democratic senator from Hudson, had made a strong record in the assembly by supporting the war effort. He replaced Wescott, who had voted against the war loan and then resigned. Overall the war party now included all the Republicans and several Democratic recruits, and so retained control of the senate.[77]

The assembly races also resulted in a virtual tie. Although most assembly elections were quiet, some heated contests in certain districts generated intense interest when the issue turned on war or peace. In clear-cut contests between prowar and antiwar candidates, the war party emerged victorious. In Bergen two Hackensack Democrats fought for the seat in the first district. Independent, unionist Democratic candidate Thomas Ward defeated incumbent Abraham Carlock, a prominent war opponent. In Hudson, unionist Democrat Josiah Conley of Harrison won over regular Democrat Hugh Mooney of Union. In Union County voters rejected Israel O. Maxwell of New Providence, who was regarded as the leader of the peace Democrats, and instead elected independent, unionist Democratic candidate John J. High of Rahway. Similarly, in the third district of Monmouth voters preferred unionist Democrat George Murray of Middletown to his peace challenger, William

S. Hornor of Matawan. In Mercer, Republican George W. Johnston of Lawrence defeated Breckinridge Democrat Henry D. Johnson of Princeton. In Trenton the Union fusionist candidate, independent Democrat John G. Stevens, won over Democrat William S. Yard, whose voting record raised serious questions about his reliability in furthering the war effort. None of the strongest peace assemblymen who served in 1861 returned in 1862.[78]

Elsewhere the prowar forces failed to capitalize on the issue and organize their forces. Some peace men exploited the void and declared themselves eleventh-hour converts to the Union cause. Some succeeded in convincing the voters. In Warren, for example, two Democratic candidates, David Smith of Oxford and William W. Strader of Washington, defeated token opposition candidates. In addition, John R. Post of Franklin in Bergen and Nelson H. Drake of Flanders in Morris returned to the assembly. Nevertheless, the war party held a majority in the assembly; possibly six unionist independents held the balance of power. Republican newspapers lauded the election of many outstanding regular war Democrats, who were regarded as Union men and reliable supporters of the war effort. One Republican newspaper commented that "in both houses there will be a steady majority of Union men."[79]

Although the Republican strategy of a nonpartisan fusion—partisan patriotism, in fact—did not eliminate Democratic competition, the effort paid off in keeping control of the legislature in the hands of war supporters. Still, Democrats had beaten the Republicans at their own Union game. Observers contended that the peace Democracy in fact had lost ground.

Election of the prowar but bipartisan legislature, however, did not materially strengthen the state's Republican party. Moreover, bipartisan agreement on restoring the Union did not assure agreement on the method for achieving that objective. Nevertheless, the election returns showed that New Jerseyans still strongly supported suppression of the rebellion and a vigorous prosecution of the war. Despite the debacle at Bull Run, the 1861 election in New Jersey witnessed no shift in the war tide.

# 7 New Jerseyans Go to War

One of every ten New Jerseyans marched off to war. A profile of New Jersey's servicemen provides clues to the state's nature and character. The motives, experiences, and attitudes of the common soldier, who was a microcosm of the people of the state, shed light on the state's war effort and its politics. The observations of servicemen retold in person or by letter influenced public opinion and the state's commitment to the war. These accounts show whether Jersey's troops were similar to those of other northern states. Their experience also enhances an understanding of the war as a whole. An analysis of Jersey military men, moreover, provides a biting commentary on the notion of New Jersey as a copperhead state. The often harsh treatment of Jersey's soldiers by servicemen from other states pungently conveyed the virulence of New Jersey's copperhead reputation. The return of Jersey's soldiers and sailors after the war forged their sense of identity as veterans with a common interest that stamped postwar politics. On the home front as well, wartime concerns, activities, and dislocations affected civilians socially, economically, and politically.

Wartime experiences, then, tested and shaped the general attitudes and the political views of participants, both servicemen and civilians. Contrary to the view that there were two different spheres, the battlefront and the home front, in New Jersey's schizoid conduct of the war—with loyal Jersey servicemen fighting bravely for the Union cause while disloyal, reactionary Jerseyans held sway at home and sabotaged the war effort—this dichotomy does not correspond to the actual wartime experience. The state's solid record on the home front in fact buttresses the state's creditable record in battle. Both underscore the state's bedrock unionism and patriotic commitment. Thus, in a real sense, the boundaries between the battlefront, the home front, and the political front were artificial demarcations. It was, after all, their interrelationship that provides an understanding of how the war was waged and won.

The North was largely unprepared for war. State militias, including New Jersey's, functioned mainly as social clubs. The small regular army was thinly scattered across the frontier. Lincoln's call in April for seventy-five thousand three-month volunteers to suppress the rebellion put the burden of responsibility on the states to raise a volunteer force that would provide the backbone of the Union army. The northern governors did this by forming thousand-man infantry and artillery regiments and twelve-hundred-man cavalry regiments. Each was designated by a number and a state name. Thus a huge volunteer army was rapidly created, virtually from scratch. Inevitably, however, inefficiencies crept into military mobilization as the war continued and widened.

In the course of the war New Jersey's military recruitment passed through different stages, which paralleled the experiences and problems of other northern states. In 1861, carried on a tidal wave of enthusiasm, more than ten thousand volunteers enlisted. This first response was so overwhelming that New Jersey authorities turned away many eager patriots in the early days. Neighboring states with more aggressive recruiting programs grabbed these men.

In 1862, however, the supply of volunteers slowed to a trickle. The Union army had achieved few important gains in the East. This fact, combined with an improvement in the economy and better prospects for employment, made military service less attractive. The federal government attempted to offset this decline in volunteers by offering shorter periods of enlistment than the current three-year term.

By 1863 a fuller understanding of the realities and dangers of soldiering chilled the ardor of many able-bodied men of military age. In addition, as the war dragged on, critics denounced government officials for mismanaging the war, greedy businessmen for war profiteering, and craven politicians for using the war to seize the spoils. One member of the Twenty-sixth Regiment, a staunch Democrat, expressed his disenchantment: "I am disgusted with this war. It is a bloody money making concern—kept up by politicians for the purpose of filling their pockets. If the North was only half as united as the South, we would have whipped the rebels long ago. But as it is, we can never whip the rebels." To cynics, the war had become a giant swindle in which incompetent generals wasted soldiers as cannon fodder. Realists, however, saw the difficulty of the struggle. Ira S. Dodd of the same unit spoke for most New Jersey troops when he found that the "day for illusions was passing; the grim character of the struggle was becoming too evident."[1]

As defeats, casualties, and dissatisfaction mounted, authorities began to rely on financial inducements to attract volunteers to fill depleted ranks and meet rising enlistment quotas. Localities raised money to pay for bounties. In addition, federal law provided for commutation and substitution in lieu of military service. Individuals thus formed clubs to hire substitutes or to put up commutation fees. With only a limited number of men willing to serve for a price and with the onset of competitive bidding, the cost of avoiding army duty climbed steeply. By the latter part of the war, New Jersey, like other northern states, was enlisting virtually all comers—resident and nonresident, native-born and immigrant, white and black, qualified and unqualified. Brokers dealing in substitutes snatched up gullible immigrants as they arrived in New Jersey's cities.

In the process, inequities, abuses, and cheating became rampant, as in other states. Many men collected their bounties and deserted at the first opportunity, only to enlist again and collect another bounty. Many were too old, too young, too unhealthy, or otherwise unfit for soldiering. One man in the Seventh Regiment considered most mercenaries who enlisted "for the sake of gain" to possess "no principle and less patriotism." Enough stalwart veterans reenlisted to supply fit troops and experienced leaders, however.[2]

In the face of the need for more recruits, the responsibility for raising volunteers necessarily shifted from state to federal control. Federal authorities supervised this effort increasingly, and in 1862 Congress authorized drafts of able-bodied men in the states. New Jersey, however, filled its quota by securing volunteers, except in the town of Warren in Somerset County, where the quota was not met and so a draft was held.

In 1863 Washington assumed complete control of conscription in all states, and federal officials took direct charge. Because quotas were unfilled, the army's Provost-Marshal General held a statewide draft starting in May and June 1864; drafts continued into 1865. The draftees were selected by local lotteries in which men were blindfolded and drew cards. While only 951 Jerseymen actually were inducted into service, the threat of conscription convinced many more to enlist. With commutation and substitution existing as alternatives to being drafted, many men regarded both as acceptable because compulsory military service had no precedent. In result, 4,196 New Jerseyans avoided military service by each paying three hundred dollars; 5,454 hired substitutes.[3]

Approximately 74,300 New Jersey men served in the war, although estimates vary. By the end of 1861 New Jersey had formed fourteen infantry regiments (including four ninety-day militia regiments), one cavalry regiment, and two artillery batteries. In the following year, sixteen additional infantry regiments joined the service. During 1863 one cavalry regiment, three infantry regiments, three artillery batteries, and a regiment for the Pennsylvania emergency to help repel Confederate invaders were added to the forces. In 1864 the state raised one cavalry regiment, three infantry regiments, and one company for the Maryland emergency to help stop another rebel invasion. New units in 1865 consisted of one infantry regiment, which brought New Jersey's total contribution to thirty-five regiments of infantry (including the force for the Pennsylvania emergency), three regiments of cavalry, and five batteries of light artillery. In addition, roughly eight thousand New Jerseyans served in the navy and the marines; another thousand belonged to the regular army during the war years. Almost three thousand blacks, both Jersey residents and southerners, served in units organized by other states or in the United States Colored Troops, but New Jersey authorities did not form a black unit.[4]

New Jersey's volunteers joined the army for a variety of reasons ranging from the idealistic to the practical, and sometimes combining the two. One private, Alfred Bellard of the Fifth Regiment, spoke for many enlistees when he declared that when the rebels fired on Fort Sumter his patriotic indignation "rose to a boiling pitch." A New Brunswick volunteer vowed to "shoot some of the rascals who have defied the laws and insulted the flag of our Government." Journalist J. Madison Drake attributed his enlistment to the "defense of the Constitution and the maintenance of the Union." To recruit J. Condit Baldwin, editor of the *Hackensack Journal*, the choice was clear and compelling. In a farewell editorial he promised to "bear arms in a contest between law and anarchy, between right and wrong, between the wisest and best government ever formed and a band of traitors who seek to subvert and destroy it as a meek offering to the Juggernaut of Slavery."[5]

In 1864 another volunteer still affirmed that the "cause is right" and vowed that the Union army will not surrender "*never No Never.*" A member of New Jersey's Sixth Regiment wrote, "If I get killed I know that I shall die in a glorious cause, an honorable cause. I have firmly made up my mind never to see that grand old flag trail in the dust as long as I can raise my gun." A soldier in the Twenty-second Regiment agreed and declared he would reenlist if necessary: "I would rather come right back after my nine months rather than see the North give in to the South. I would rather fight ten years than see the South victorious. . . . I say we are into it now—fight it out." Officer James Rusling in the Fifth Regiment pledged to restore "one Union, and one People, one Flag, and one Freedom."[6]

Adventure, freedom, or status lured others. Recruitment rallies stirred impulsive young men who at the start of the war viewed it as an exciting game. They rushed to enlist before they lost the opportunity to escape the tyranny of the plow, the back-breaking work of the factory, or the monotonous routine of clerking. A lieutenant in the Twenty-first Regiment declared he wanted to "see the fun." One high-spirited volunteer considered himself honored to participate in an event "worth a dozen lifetimes of ordinary existence." A soldier's uniform supposedly made a man a hero in the eyes of many women and enhanced courtship possibilities. In a letter home, one cavalryman pointed out that two lieutenants in his company "are pre-eminent on the score of *good looks* and soldier-like bearing. (Let the ladies of your county make a note of this, as they are all single men.)" One enthusiastic Cumberland County man remarked: "The popular phrase among the boys is, 'Who wouldn't be a soldier?'"[7]

Local pride also induced many men to volunteer. Dodd recalled that Newarkers vied with people in the countryside to sign up the most volunteers. Rival villages also competed with each other to collect the most recruits in the shortest time. Ethnic pride similarly spurred immigrant groups: Irish and especially Germans enlisted in the same units, such as the artillery batteries and the Third Cavalry. In 1864 one wounded man, who dubbed himself "one of the fighting sons of ERIN," explained, "I have fought and bled . . . for my adopted country."[8]

Peer pressure and conformity also played an important role. Fellow members of clubs, colleges, labor unions, and other organizations enlisted together. Friends followed friends to join; going to war together lessened the fear of the unknown. When men volunteered at great personal sacrifice, their hesitant able-bodied neighbors also enlisted because they were too embarrassed to stay home and feared being branded cowards.

Self-betterment played an important part as well. With wages low and jobs scarce at the start of the war, many men were induced to enlist by the opportunity to receive a bounty and earn regular pay while securing other benefits. The average workingman's monthly wage came to about twelve dollars; in view of that, one soldier declared, "I am fighting for neither the laws or the 'niggers,' but for 13.00 per month and board and clothes." The ambitious wanted to make a mark for themselves, earn a promotion, possibly win fame and glory. Later in the war, facing the prospect of a draft, some civilians preferred to volunteer, collect bonuses, choose their outfit, and avoid the stigma of being a conscript.[9]

Volunteers first enrolled at recruiting stations scattered throughout the state in villages, towns, and city wards. These local offices forwarded the men in groups to larger rendezvous centers, where the recruits were organized into new regiments. Draftees and substitutes followed a slightly different course; these men assembled at a special draft rendezvous camp in Trenton. Generally they were assigned as individual replacements in units already at the front.

Draftees and volunteers alike passed through one of the induction centers spread across the state. Not all of these camps were in use at the same time, and a few had more than one name at different periods. They included Camps Cadwallader and Stratton in Beverly; Camp Burlington; Camps Fair Oaks and Kearny in Flemington; Camp Vredenburgh in Freehold; a camp each in Hoboken and in Jersey City; Camp Frelinghuysen in Newark; Camps Bayard, Delaware, Halsted, Olden, Parker, and Perrine in Trenton; and Camp Stockton in Woodbury. There, for several weeks at the most, officers tried to whip enlisted men into shape by turning civilians into soldiers.

The daily routine began with early rising, followed by incessant drilling throughout the day, and ended with a smart dress parade in the evening for the benefit of visitors, especially girlfriends. Bellard described the main business of camp as initiating troops into the mysteries of "keeping our heels on a line. Toes out at an angle of 45 degrees. Belly in. Chest out and such other positions as tend to make a full fledged veteran out of a raw recruit." Troops were trained in operating weapons and maneuvering in battle.

Upon receiving his orders, the commanding officer formed his regiment. Members received uniforms and weapons and were mustered into active federal service. To effusive send-offs and women kissing volunteers good-bye, soldiers usually boarded trains bound for Washington and then marched to the front in Virginia. There five to seven regiments assembled to form a brigade. As a morale booster, the War Department sometimes tried to build brigades of regiments all from the same state. New Jersey was fortunate to have two such brigades.[10]

At the start soldiers expected a holiday excursion filled with excitement and a hint of danger. They soon learned otherwise. A man in the Second Infantry told armchair soldiers back home, "Shoulder your musket, join us in our vicissitudes and hardships for a while, and the *romance* of a volunteer's life will fade like a fog before the sun, while the disagreeable reality will stare you in the face with ten-fold sternness." Dodd summed up his first impressions: "It was a rude beginning of real life." A member of the Twelfth Regiment, William P. Haines, observed, "The hustling, busy life of a soldier was a great change from that of a quiet citizen; the whole life so different, the diet such a change, the hard-tack such a contrast to the nice hot rolls and homemade bread of our mothers; the discipline necessarily so strict, no more running out at nights or visiting our sweethearts and relations whenever we took the notion, and staying out as late as we wish. Now we must get a pass, subject to good conduct, and be back at camp in time for evening roll-call. The oath of enlistment is so binding—complete surrender of your own will and mind." A private in the Third Infantry concluded glumly, "A soldier's life is not very inviting."[11]

Conditions depended on terrain, season, weather, outpost, operations, and the stage of the war, but the weather governed all. New Jerseyans shivered through winter wind, snow, and ice, and came to disbelieve in the sunny South. Requests for furloughs reached their height during this season. The spring thaw brought fog, rain, and the ever-present mud, up to a foot or more deep. Mud restricted operations, made marching slow and treacherous, and turned daily existence into a miserable experience. Surveying Virginia's landscape, one Jerseyman described the place Camp Mud: "Mud at the present time has an undisputed title; it reigns supreme, holding us in obedience to its will; we walk in mud, eat in mud, sleep in mud, and drink muddy water." Across the Potomac in Maryland, Rusling agreed wholeheartedly. The endless drizzles turned the countryside into "mud! Maryland mud! Mud everywhere! Mud black! Mud yellow! Mud splashy! Mud unfathomable!" Roads became "a bottomless stretch of mud through which men and horses wade and struggle and wallow, as though Satan himself were beneath and devilishly bent on dragging everybody and everything down deep into its horrible abyss." In summer the troops wilted in the humid heat, while country roads and trails became suffocatingly dusty.[12]

The monotonous lives of New Jersey soldiers were marked by grinding routine, endless drudgery, interminable roll calls, maddening drum calls, and unceasing close-order drill, as well as standing guard, washing dishes, excessive strictness, and seemingly pointless inspections. An infantryman in the Fifteenth Regiment observed about army life: "We 'fall in line' for almost everything we get. It's 'fall in line' for your rations, 'fall in line' for your money, and 'fall in line' for your letters. Yesterday we 'fell in line' to be vaccinated. . . . Our boys said this was the last thing they thought of 'fallin in' for." One man in the Ninth Regiment remarked, "How dull it seems."

The troops lived on rations of salt pork, beans, bitter coffee, and a saltless, crackerlike bread called hardtack. Soldiers joked that even a musket ball could not penetrate their stale biscuits. One soldier reported to his father that the army wished to "develop the muscles of the jaw to enable them to bite off the ends of cartridges. The plan I think is a good one." Troops rarely changed their clothes, and sometimes lived in filthy, disease-infested small tents or log huts. Some infantrymen in the Fifteenth Regiment filled up the cracks in a log house they built with "Virginia mud, which is a very peculiar kind of mud, and just now there is plenty of it. It sticks like molasses candy, and answers the place of mortar very well, besides being already mixed." Insects, especially mosquitoes, tormented men. One Morristown volunteer declared: "Talk about your Jersey mosquitoes!" Compared to the southern variety, Jersey mosquitoes, he stated, "ain't nowhere."[13]

Troops found their endurance and tempers tested by long, aimless marches at double-quick time; they carried heavy loads over rough terrain, without adequate rations and without engaging the enemy. Trentonian Washington A. Roebling found the uncertainty about his unit's point of destination the "only charm there is about a march." Many men fell victim to sunstroke or hypothermia. Frenetic activity punctuated long periods of inactivity. Idleness, discomfort, and discontent fed on each other. One trooper remarked, "We are all getting tired here doing nothing." Another soldier expressed his utter frustration: "Time hangs so heavy on my hands, sometimes, that I have to take a *waddle*, (not a run), out into the mud to drive off the blues."[14]

Soldiers improvised to meet everyday needs under difficult conditions. One militiaman said that the ground of his tent "serves at once for bed, sofa, chair, table, writing-desk, and corner-cupboard." A man in the Fourteenth Regiment searched for a soft place on the ground to lie and found "a *soft* stone for a pillow." Another soldier noted, "I am seated on the top of an old camp pail, my writing desk is a knapsack, and my inkstand a tin apartment in a cartridge box."[15]

Living in close quarters tested relationships. Dodd's company consisted mainly of neighbors with familiar faces or of like-minded people from the same section of the state. Yet he remarked that it was one thing to meet a man every day on the road or even at work; it was quite another to be compelled to bunk with him, sleep under the same blanket, and take breakfast out of the same camp kettle. Dodd commented, "We learned our own hitherto-unsuspected faults, we discovered the good qualities of even our most faulty comrades, we saw human nature at close range." Men shared prolonged hunger, thirst, fatigue, and exhaustion. Above all, they faced common danger, which forged a powerful bond of comradeship. Roebling explained why he rejected a higher-rank commission in another outfit: he had been with his "present comrades so long that I want to stick to them to the end of the war." Another soldier described his companion: "Us two boys go together, sleep together, eat together, and expect to fight together; and if either of us falls, we will revenge one another, whichever of us lives."[16]

Enlisted men also had to adjust to military discipline and to that special breed known as officers. As Haines put it, "Obey your officers, right or wrong; in cheerful silence hold your tongue; no arguing or back talk; obey every order without asking the reason why, even though the officer as a civilian may have been your inferior in education, judgment, or social position; he may be passionate, tyrannical, or overbearing; no matter, he is there to command, you to obey." Still, volunteer enlisted men did not consider themselves members of the regular army, and acted accordingly. During the early part of the war, enlisted men elected their company officers. This practice often softened relations, but sometimes soured them when officers did not associate with enlisted men or did not turn out as anticipated.

Civilians at heart and strong individualists, most volunteers disliked military discipline, hated regimentation, distrusted authority, resented martinets, and remained skeptical of officers. Enlisted men were comfortable with the unkempt appearance of their volunteer outfits and relished slack discipline. Haines observed, "Though you may often find little ways to vex and make it warm for such an officer, be careful not to carry things too far, or the guardhouse, buck and gag or ball and chain will eventually be your portion." Bellard got into trouble with a sergeant by not complying with an "order soon enough to suit his lordship," and they began to shout and shove each other. Expressing the prevailing view, Dodd declared that "we believed in our cause, in the war, and in final victory; but we were not soldiers for the love of it. The end of fighting and *home* was the goal." A soldier in the Thirty-fifth Regiment dreamed of an oyster supper in Jersey City and the "feed we would have in Jersey 'when this cruel war is over.'"[17]

Yet New Jersey soldiers also realized that their outfit formed part of a larger whole. "A man is but a cog in the wheels of a remorseless machine, and he must move with it," as Dodd put it. Even the sometimes rebellious Bellard conceded that "orders were orders and had to be obeyed." Although the troops reluctantly recognized the need for discipline and for officers to enforce it, they also were aware that officers' competence varied. Thus, enlisted men obeyed, but did not follow blindly.[18]

Soldiers expected a higher-ranked man to prove himself. A good officer pushed for top fighting efficiency but still allowed his troops some room for individualism. In referring to a lieutenant, one trooper in the Third Infantry noted a "feeling of fraternity, mingled with confidence and trust, and we know he is capable of his position." Soldiers expected officers not only to lead them, but also to attend to their needs. A member of the Thirty-fifth Regiment said that troops "will do anything, undergo anything, suffer anything, accomplish anything, if they are only fed and clothed." Enlisted men respected officers who shared their work and dangers, exhibited comradeship, showed physical courage, demonstrated leadership, inspired them, led them into battle. An infantryman in the Third Regiment declared, when the "men have unbounded confidence" in such an officer, they were willing to follow him "to the end."[19]

Officers who behaved as cowards, hotheads, and frequently drunkards were subject to enlisted men's contempt and insubordination. The ranks petitioned for the removal of unworthy officers, who often resigned or were reassigned by the army to noncombat duties. By trial and error the unfit were weeded out as the unit underwent brutal testing. Experience began to produce competence.[20]

When entering battle, officers appealed to the enlisted men's pride—individual, unit, and state—to rouse them to action. On one occasion a general rode up to the Third Infantry before combat and said, "Now my boys you go down to battle. You are Jerseymen. . . . Jersey is a little state, but a big one. Three cheers for New Jersey."[21]

Spoiling for a fight, many eager, enthusiastic troops shouted and cheered when they first marched proudly into battle. A Cumberland man in the Third Infantry described his first battle: "When our brigade went on the field I thought it one of the grandest sights I ever saw." To "see artillery, cavalry, and infantry drawn up in line on rolling land," with the bright steel rifle barrels and bayonets glistening in the morning's sun, "is a very nice thing to look at."[22]

But the "scene was soon to change," as this same infantryman reported, for "to go down in a woods filled with men pouring out a perfect hail storm of bullets is looking at the other side of the picture." Bellard observed that while "marching over this field I experienced for the first time a sensation of fear. I got so sick at the stomach that I thought I should have to fall out of the ranks to relieve myself." With bullets flying thick and fast, the infantryman in the Third Regiment saw men "began to fall on each side of me, but steadily onward we moved in the face of the foe." Worrying whether the next bullet would be his, a member of the Tenth Regiment "looked around at my comrades and wondered whose time it would be to fall or get wounded." A member of the Twenty-eighth Regiment described that scene: "Shells and other missiles were hissing their deafening sounds in our ears, and the poor fellows fell each instant about us. The dead, dying, and wounded were scattered on every side." He saw that "our men were slaughtered—yes, that is the only word that will fully express the facts: literally mowed down by the shower of bullets, shot, and shell."[23]

Brigadier General Robert McAllister, in the trenches near Petersburg, feared the worst for his men and warned superiors not to send his troops into a death trap, but to no avail. Receiving orders to attack, he described how the "rebels poured down upon us lead and iron by musketry and cannon that cut our men down. . . . We had to advance a long distance up a cleared plain. Our ranks melted away." When the smoke cleared after the battle of Spotsylvania, Robert Love of the Tenth Regiment saw a scene "horrible beyond description; the bodies of the mangled victims, some Union but mostly Rebel, covered the ground as far as the eye could see." A "heavy rain had washed the blood from the unfortunate victims of this terrible slaughter, causing every depression in the ground to have the appearance of being filled with pools of blood."[24]

For some troops the pounding pace of combat brought intoxicating excitement with the rush of adrenalin as the killer's instinct took over. One soldier confessed: "When we see the enemy, the tiger gets into us, we forget our tiredness, and only think of the blood of the rebels." But little glory and much gore were the result. After experiencing the fury of battle with its noise and brutality, the sting of defeat, the shame of retreat, the pain of wounds, or the shock of screaming, dying comrades, many troops had "seen enough" and had become "very sick of it." Revulsed at the sight and worn out by the experience, most men grew weary of the carnage, wary of danger, and especially impatient with incompetent leaders.[25]

Through such experience, too, troops became hardened, battlewise veterans. Now used to the carnage, one man in the Seventh Regiment declared: "Dead men are no longer a source of antipathy to me. I could lie down by the side of them and sleep now, provided decomposition had not taken place." Soldiers vowed to see the war through, and win. After one battle, a member of the Sixth Regiment remarked, "The worst is not yet. But our soldiers cannot and do not think of giving up." Knowing they would have to fight again when they "entered the hell of deadly battle," the soldiers concentrated on not growing careless and acting foolishly. They understood that they could not panic. Each man had to pull his own weight and not disgrace himself before his comrades. When their lives depended on split-second decisions, they learned to rely on each other by operating as a team in a squad, company, or regiment. Such teamwork not only strengthened individual morale, the unit's cohesiveness, and overall effectiveness in combat, but also increased chances of survival.[26]

The soldiers also learned the futility of ineffective tactics and useless sacrifice. Mounting a Napoleonic offense with a frontal assault in close formation against a midcentury defense of improved rifles and cannon with greater firepower was frequently suicidal. A man in the Twelfth Regiment at Gettysburg stood on Cemetery Ridge and saw the rebels make their famous charge on the second day. "On they came like fiends, closing up their ranks as the death dealing grape [shot] and canister mowed them down like ripened wheat before the keen blade of the scythe." Describing a similar senseless onslaught of southern troops, one New Jersey trooper said the "way the enemy were cut up was sickening." They "moved up, regiment after regiment, only to be cut down by hundreds." He concluded, "I saw some fearful sights, such as I never wish to see again." Recognizing the cost of such attacks, some experienced officers began to change tactics by opening up ranks and employing skirmish lines when attacking. Veteran troops learned to take cover, dig trenches, and build fortifications. Generals sometimes came to rely on laying siege in a battle of attrition. In addition, commanders conducted total war against the civilian economy and private property in order to destroy the enemy's means and will to fight.[27]

Soldiers frequently sought diversion and escape from army life and monotony. Amusements were simple and crude: the troops gossiped, sang, laughed, swore, read, wrote letters to people at home to maintain close ties, smoked, gambled, played pranks and games, had snowball fights, and drank. A great wave of excitement went through quarters when the liquor dealer arrived. One soldier in the Fourteenth Regiment looked around the camp and declared: "It was lager here, lager there, and lager everywhere." An enlisted man enviously described the living quarters of the Seventh Regiment: "They have everything they want. I was in several of their tents; there was plenty of brandy bottles, cigar boxes, and everything that fast young men could desire." Noting the fast conversion to alcohol, a member of the Seventh Regiment observed, "Many a youth who had not tasted its poison when enlisted, now imbibes it with all the avidity of an 'old toper.'"[28]

In enemy country, Union soldiers made southerners pay the price of treason by wantonly damaging houses, by stealing money, jewels, and watches as war booty. They took rail fences for campfires. Sometimes existing on scanty rations, they scouted for daily fare. As one soldier in the Third Regiment wrote of his comrades, "They get nothing to eat, only what they forage." The troops, under orders not to use precious ammunition, engaged in wholesale butchery. A member of the Thirty-fifth Regiment in Alabama described "how the chickens did suffer and the pigs squeal; considering the death they had to die, they took it pretty cool. I have honestly heard a pig squeal after receiving about twenty or thirty bayonets through him."[29]

Off duty, rowdy troops sometimes drank themselves into reckless blowouts that could erupt into barroom brawls. Young, footloose servicemen, deprived of social and sexual companionship with women, flocked to prostitutes. Although the troops relished the sexual pleasure and the psychological release, they most prudishly kept such encounters out of their diaries and letters. Religion, too, found its place in camp; many soldiers carried their own copy of the Bible. Regimental chaplains did their best to counter temptation, and outfits experienced more than one revivalist movement.[30]

The staggering number of casualties caused nerve-racking anxiety not only on the battlefield but also on the home front. The endless waiting to learn about the toll of killed and wounded at a particular battle intensified the strain of separation. One Parsippany wife wrote simply to her husband, "I feel very sad and lonesome. I would like to see you very much." Roebling remarked in 1864 to his sweetheart that the "rebs are making raids from Canada in all directions. How I would like to come to New York and make a raid on my Emy."[31]

Ellen McAllister took pride in New Jersey's troops, who she said "behaved like soldiers," but she cautioned her husband not to make himself a target by riding his horse in battle or raising his hand in leading his men. Revealing her own inner conflict between pride and fear, she confessed, "Do not be angry, but I hope you will miss the fighting. I am afraid you might be killed or wounded; at the same time I would have you a man." Mirroring the ebb and flow of battle, she remarked, "My spirits go up and down as our victory and defeat attend us. I think the South will begin to think one southerner is not so good as six northerners."[32]

The views of New Jersey's troops about the South reflected prevailing views back home. The soldiers' attitudes varied over time, were formed by diverse experiences, and were influenced by different personalities. Many New Jerseyans, both soldiers and civilians, looked down on the South as a poor, backward place. A Hightstown woman characterized the region as filled with "dilapidated and uninhabited dwellings, and barren and desolate country." McAllister found Burkeville Junction, Virginia, a "very forlorn country, uninteresting, with nothing to relieve the eye or mind. Rolling hills and hollows are badly cultivated, scarcely a green field is to be seen. Old lands are growing up with pines. Fences are bad; buildings are miserable, dilapidated, and few and far between." Rusling wrote, "Do you wonder, then, that our gallant Jersey Blues persistently declare, 'that sich a country haint worth fighting for!' Why should it be? For over a century slavery has existed here, and even a blind man can't help seeing that."[33]

Troops frequently viewed southern civilians with contempt and suspicion.

Many New Jersey soldiers considered southerners slow, lazy, rough, ignorant, and stupid. Unlike southern men, who had little to say, a former Camden editor found that North Carolina white women in 1864 vented their feelings: "They are conquered but not subdued." Sharing a similar experience in Virginia, Roebling commented that the "women here are very secesh, and I was saluted for the first time with the title of Northern Vandal when I was paying a quarter for a very small pie." In one extraordinary incident Roebling encountered a Confederate woman on the battlefield operating a cannon, and remarked that "she was very independent and saucy, as most Southern ladies are."[34]

Some soldiers encountered trouble. Seven unsuspecting infantrymen belonging to the First Infantry gladly ate some hot mince pie offered to them by a friendly, elderly Virginian woman. Shortly after eating the pie, however, they became very sick. Doctors saved them only by pumping their stomachs: the kindly old lady had baked a nearly lethal dose of arsenic into the pie.[35]

A New Jersey surgeon serving aboard a navy steamer off Vicksburg reported about a navy captain, who was carrying on a love affair with a Mississippi belle. "Utterly overcome" by her "winning ways," he ordered the return of her slaves, who had fled from her plantation to the Union ships. The Jersey doctor in 1862 remarked: "Now there are none of us that are abolitionists, but the slaves came to us and claimed our protection." The doctor later discovered that the woman, after claiming to have "missed her niggers," flogged them all night, had them tied while they were bleeding, then set bloodhounds on them.[36]

In other instances southern civilians, especially in the upper South, befriended Yankee troops. One infantryman in the Second Regiment reported from Beltsville, Maryland, that "all the Southern people are not so bad as they are represented to be. You can find plenty of Union men here and they want to hang onto the Stars and Stripes." Yet another soldier in the same unit, reflecting the wider view of New Jersey servicemen, found Virginians shared an overriding loyalty to their state and concluded: "I admire their spunk, but pity their ignorance." Bellard similarly wrote off southerners as a "deluded and misguided people."[37]

Like most northerners, New Jersey's white troops on the whole remained prejudiced against blacks. Although staunch Democratic soldiers expressed such views more openly, most of the white troops agreed. Sometimes, however, experience forced them to reconsider the stereotypes. Firsthand observation of the poor treatment received by slaves, as well as help and military intelligence furnished by blacks, revised some opinions. The black soldiers' fighting qualities earned respect. Nevertheless, most Jersey soldiers stayed indifferent, if not hostile, to blacks in general and to contrabands (runaway slaves who entered Union lines and became freedmen) in particular; troops blamed them for the war and for their military service. Yet even so hardened a man as McAllister, who revealed indifference and a racial blind spot, showed appreciation for a group of some enthusiastic contrabands who flocked to the "'land of liberty.'" Although he was not certain whether the freedmen would show themselves worthy of their freedom, he did not dismiss the opportunity; rather he welcomed it.[38]

Attitudes toward rebel soldiers varied from amicability to implacable hatred. When they had guard duty within hearing distance, Yankee and Confederate sentries conversed as fellow Americans and fellow soldiers, despite a ban on communication. Opposing troops sometimes fraternized by going swimming, playing cards, and singing. New Jerseyans bartered coffee or clothes for southern tobacco; the soldiers traded caps and uniform buttons. One infantryman in the Third Regiment found that "our boys were getting somewhat friendly with the rebels." He related that "one of the boys gave them an envelope with the picture of a traitor on the gallows and with the inscription of 'Death to traitors' underneath. They were quite merry over it, as though that would never be the case."[39]

When first serving, New Jersey men respected Confederates as tough opponents. The Jersey soldiers also respected Confederate generals. As Roebling observed, "Uncle Robert Lee isn't licked yet by a long shot and if we are not mighty careful he will beat us yet." In discussing the rebels' defense of Petersburg in 1864, Roebling lamented that "old men with silver locks lay dead in the trenches side by side with mere boys of 13 or 14; it almost makes one sorry to have to fight against people who show such devotion for their homes and their country."[40]

Yet when their comrades died and when Confederates resorted to tricks and traps, even showing Union or white flags to disguise attacks, many embittered New Jersey soldiers began to despise them. One infantryman in the Third Regiment described the change. "Our men now begin to realize that we are not here on a pleasure excursion, but have an enemy to meet that does not scruple to kill an opponent under the most cowardly circumstances, such as shooting pickets single and alone, while they (the rebels) are in ambush in squads of twenty." An officer of the First Infantry described the rebels as "nasty, dirty, insignificant, pusillanimous villains." One incident particularly angered McAllister. Under a flag of truce, Union forces brought wounded and dead rebels on wagons to the Confederate line, but the "hardhearted" rebel "villains refused to receive them and they had to return. *What a blot on Southern history*! But this will tell in our future battles."[41]

When New Jersey troops experienced treachery and witnessed atrocities, they vented their horror and rage. Adversaries then became bitter enemies. In December 1864, when McAllister received a report about the fate of seven of his men, he went to the spot to see for himself and found a "sad sight . . . from appearances they had been stripped of all their clothing, and, when in the act of kneeling in a circle, they were shot in the head—

murdered in cold blood by the would-be 'Chivalry of the South.'" This point-less murder, he declared, "holds up to light the true character of those who are pushing the rebellion to the destruction of our glorious Union. Need I now tell you why our boys burnt buildings?" On another occasion rebels cut off one Yankee's head. In still another instance a soldier in the Seventh Regiment reported: "Some of the rebels treated our wounded with humanity, but others, especially the Louisiana Tigers, run bayonets through the dead and dying, and mutilated the bodies in a horrid manner."[42]

After discovering this, many New Jersey troops grew to hate rebel soldiers. Confederate soldiers, to be sure, had no monopoly on dirty tricks; incidents occurred on both sides. Jersey troopers, however, remembered the rebels' deeds and swore vengeance.

The combat record of New Jersey's servicemen was impressive and brought credit to the state. Those who gave their lives so that the Union would live included indomitable Captain John E. Beam of the Second Battery of Light Artillery, who died at Malvern Hill. The bold, dashing, but vain General Philip Kearny was shot at Chantilly, just as his fame as an infantry commander gained national attention. Having survived two gunshot wounds, George Bayard at age twenty-seven was the youngest brigadier general in the Union army. He was hit by a shell at Fredericksburg and died shortly afterward. A rebel sharpshooter picked off courageous Colonel Henry O. Ryerson at the Wilderness. The confident and beloved leader Colonel Abraham Zabriskie was shot through the throat at Drewry's Bluff. The able General Charles G. Harker, who had managed several narrow escapes before, fell at Kennesaw Mountain. Coolheaded, quick-witted Colonel Hugh H. Janeway, having earlier been wounded eleven times, was shot through the head at Amelia Springs and died just four days before the end of the war. Many others died bravely. Among those who survived was the courageous but headstrong and erratic cavalry commander Hugh Judson Kilpatrick. Other well-known survivors included two brevet major generals, Gershom Mott and Alfred T. A. Torbert, and five brevet brigadier generals, Robert McAllister, George W. Mindil, William S. Truex, E. Burd Grubb, and Ezra A. Carman. Fortunately, several incompetent commanders, including George W. McLean from First Bull Run and Joseph W. Revere from Chancellorsville, had been weeded out long before.[43]

Twenty-five young Jerseymen, both officers and enlisted men, earned the army's Medal of Honor. Their audacious exploits became local legends. Among them were Drake, one of the first to enter the Confederate works at New Bern, who stayed in the line all day and night. Later he escaped as a prisoner of war and finally reached Union lines. Charles F. Hopkins, although twice wounded in the attempt, rescued a fallen commander at Gaines' Mill. William J. Sewell, severely wounded at Chancellorsville, nonetheless galloped to the front line, shouting, "'Jerseymen at least will follow me.'" Rallying them around his colors, he led them into battle for several hours, and they took many prisoners. Amos J. Cummings rescued part of a field battery from an exposed position at Salem Church. John J. Toffey, although ill and excused from duty, commanded a company fighting out of a rebel ambush at Missionary Ridge, was cut down by a ball in the hip, and never walked again. Edmund English seized the colors during an ordered retreat, rallied the men, and drove the enemy back at the Wilderness. John P. Beech, under fierce fire and with all members of the artillery battery out of action, loaded cannon and stopped a rebel charge at Spotsylvania. William Magee, only fifteen years old, led troops at Stones River against stiff enemy resistance, captured two artillery guns, rounded up rebel horses, and routed a rebel regiment. Looking back on such exploits and pondering how each hero mastered both his own fears and enemy challenges, Rusling remarked, "So much depends on the right man, at the right place, at the right time."[44]

New Jersey's soldiers took an active part in most major campaigns in the eastern theater of operations, mainly in Virginia, and also in many minor engagements. In the last half of the war New Jersey units participated in several western campaigns as well. Although different outfits at various times protected the capital, guarded railroad and telegraph lines, cleared woods, constructed forts, built, widened, or planked roads, reconstructed sabotaged railroads, destroyed rebel railroads, enforced the draft, and quelled riots, most units saw combat. Some played major supporting roles in battle. Throughout the war New Jersey's sailors saw duty on Union ships patrolling southern coastal waters and blockading rebel ports. Black New Jerseyans performed valiantly in both the navy and the army.

Some of the New Jersey soldiers' outstanding deeds and costly battles deserve mention. During the winter of 1862 the sharpshooters of the Ninth Regiment took part in amphibious operations along the North Carolina coast to establish Union beachheads, and seized Roanoke Island and New Bern. In the spring of 1862 New Jersey's two infantry brigades were battered in some of the thickest of the fighting in the Peninsula campaign. In a furious battle at Williamsburg, a regimental band struck up a patriotic tune that roused the troops and bolstered their morale. Reinforcements arrived just in time to avert retreat. Sixty-nine men of the Sixth Regiment were killed and wounded; other units also sustained heavy casualties.

At Gaines' Mill, New Jersey troops, along with those from other states, lost their nerve when they were outnumbered and outmaneuvered, and were overwhelmed by the Confederate charge. The battle represented the worst single day in the war for New Jersey's infantrymen: thirty-five men died there in the Third, forty-five in the Fourth, and twenty-one in the First; total brigade casualties reached 1,072. (Other bloody battles were Gettysburg with 634 total casualties, including those killed, wounded, captured, and missing;

Williamsburg with 526; Second Bull Run with 339; and Chancellorsville and Spotsylvania.)

During the rest of 1862, state units also suffered heavy casualties in battles at Antietam and Fredericksburg. In the Antietam campaign in particular, New Jersey troops distinguished themselves on September 14, when the First Brigade under Torbert, along with two other brigades, chased the enemy up the mountainside and drove them off the steep summit of Crampton's Gap, Maryland.

In 1863, New Jersey soldiers at the battle of Chancellorsville took terrible casualties, especially in the Twelfth Regiment. In this campaign, New Jerseyans performed well at Salem Church on May 3, but the brave Fifteenth Regiment lost heavily. Jerseymen also participated in the pivotal battle of Gettysburg.

During the spring campaign in 1864 New Jerseyans made assaults in the face of murderous rebel fire that resulted in enormous casualties at the battles of the Wilderness, Spotsylvania, and Cold Harbor. The Fifteenth Regiment sustained seventy-five deaths at Spotsylvania. On July 9 the outnumbered Fourteenth Regiment, at a high cost, valiantly fought a delaying action at Monocacy Bridge in Maryland. Thus they cost the Confederates a day of advancing on Washington and allowed the Federals to reinforce the capital and save it. During September and October 1864, New Jersey's Third Cavalry and First Brigade helped clear the Confederates out of the Shenandoah Valley. Also during 1864, some state units, including the Thirteenth, the Thirty-fifth, and the battle-worn Thirty-third, fought under General William T. Sherman from Chattanooga to Atlanta, then marched to the sea, and in 1865 pushed northward through the Carolinas.

In 1864 and 1865 most of New Jersey's troops took part in General Ulysses S. Grant's siege of Petersburg. In the spring of 1865 New Jerseyans, including the Fourteenth and Thirty-ninth Infantry and the First Cavalry, joined in the pursuit of the rebels toward Appomattox Court House. Of the three hundred Union regiments that bore the brunt of the fighting in the war, New Jersey contributed twelve: the First Cavalry and the First, Third, Fourth, Fifth, Sixth, Seventh, Eighth, Eleventh, Twelfth, Fourteenth, and Fifteenth Infantry. Of the forty-five Union regiments that lost more than 200 men in battle, the Fifteenth New Jersey ranked twelfth highest, with 240 (20 percent) killed.[45]

New Jersey's death toll was high; estimates ranged between 5,754 and 6,300. The higher figure represented nearly one percent of the state's total population. More soldiers died from infections than from shot, shells, and bullets; 419 New Jerseyans died in rebel prisons. The state's percentage of total deaths ranked higher than those of the Pacific coast states, Maryland, and Rhode Island, but below those of Pennsylvania and New York.[46]

Although the desertion rate among New Jersey servicemen was extremely high for a northern state (only New Hampshire, Connecticut, and Kansas outstripped New Jersey), most of New Jersey's troops stayed with their outfits. Their perseverance carried them through many brutal campaigns. The overall quality of the state's troops was so high, their views were so similar to those of other northern soldiers, and the support for the Union army by both the state government and the people was so strong as to cast serious doubt on the notion that widespread sympathy for the Confederate cause existed among New Jerseyans. Jersey soldiers earned a reputation as resourceful, tenacious, tough fighters. Like most northern troops, the state's units fought bravely in most engagements and often suffered heavily. New Jersey's battle-worthy servicemen performed well, sometimes magnificently, as at Crampton's Pass and in the Shenandoah Valley; occasionally they fought unimpressively when surrounded or poorly led, as at Gaines' Mill; on the whole they fought creditably.

Enduring the discomfort of camp, the hardship of the march, the horrors of battle, New Jersey's servicemen brought honor to their state and to themselves. One sergeant in the Ninth Regiment observed, "General Burnside called us Jersey muscrats, when he seen us in the mud and up to our necks, but the rebels call us the bloody ninth. They say we can swim and fight." After another battle and while under a flag of truce, Confederates asked New Jersey artillerymen "what Battery that Black Battery was. We told them it was a Jersey battery. They said they expected as much as Jersey as a general rule gave them a lot of trouble." Confirming this estimate in still another engagement, a surgeon in the Sixth Regiment reported that rebel soldiers were frequently heard to say: "'*Only break the lines of the Jerseymen, and we've got 'em.*'" A Camden man aptly described the state's troops as having the "*grit* of the true Jersey Blue."[47]

I n the course of the war, home defense ranked low as a federal priority. Federal officials were naturally preoccupied with winning the war and protecting the national capital. Much to the dismay of many northerners, security of the northern states was not an important concern. Responsibility for defending the Jersey shore rested with national authorities, who commanded army forts and naval vessels; state maritime brigades assisted the coast guard in securing the coastline. When war broke out, officials focused their attention on the defense of southwestern New Jersey. In April 1861 Olden, concerned about the potential threat from Confederate naval raiders on vulnerable Delaware Bay, ordered the reopening of a telegraph line connecting Cape May to Camden, so authorities could be notified of any invasion from the sea. He also pressured the navy to patrol the bay and protect commercial vessels from rebel privateers.

In 1862 Olden, legislators, and New Jersey's congressmen, joined by Pennsylvania and Delaware officials, lobbied for construction of additional forts and for the return of a gunboat to coastal waters. During the war the federal government built new forts mounted with large guns. These included installations in Delaware and near Philadelphia, and another (completed shortly after the war) at Fort Mott on Finn's Point in Pennsville.

Fort Delaware, on Delaware's marshy Pea Patch Island, a mile from the state's shore and opposite Harrisonville, New Jersey, guarded the Delaware River channel to Wilmington, Philadelphia, and Camden. This large fort, completed in 1859, became a source of anxiety when hostilities broke out. If slave-owning Delaware seceded and if the fort fell into enemy hands, it would cut access both to the sea and to the Delaware and Chesapeake Canal. The fort was manned quickly by northern troops, who reinforced it with cannon. (Fort Delaware later became an overcrowded, disease-infested camp for captured Confederate soldiers.)

Many New Jerseyans showed little concern for vulnerable Raritan Bay and New York Bay in the first half of the war. As late as 1863, only one fort—Sandy Hook—commanded entrance to New York's main ship channel through the Lower Bay. After four years of construction this fort remained unarmed, unmanned, uncompleted. In fact, this strategic site loomed as a potential threat: a small invading force could easily seize Sandy Hook, seal the harbor, and hold New York City and its Jersey neighbors hostage for a time, or a Confederate raider could lie in wait near the main channel and destroy vessels at will. If Britain or France declared war, their ironclad vessels could attack the city itself.

To protect the Upper Bay, the government manned half a dozen federal forts and mounted them with heavy cannon, particularly at the Narrows. Yet with limited funds federal forces concentrated on furnishing men and supplies for the major battlefronts and on blockade duty. Expensive defense projects along the North Atlantic coast had low priority because officials in Washington considered attacks unlikely and because the war would presumably be over by the time the forts were built. As a result, the Mid-Atlantic states were largely left to care for themselves.

Security-conscious New Jerseyans during the early part of the war worried about naval attacks on the coast (which were unlikely), but often failed to consider the more probable Confederate army expeditions mounted from neighboring states. The Confederate invasion of Maryland in September 1862 ended this maritime preoccupation for some time. With the enemy within striking distance, Olden ordered county militia to fill empty ranks and to begin training so that home guard units could defend the state. Similar and more pressing emergencies recurred in 1863 and 1864. In response, state authorities in 1864 formed and armed a small active militia. The state still remained unprepared to repel Confederate invaders on short notice, however. Because so many able-bodied men had enlisted in federal service, few remained to serve in the active militia. Moreover, the training of the militia went much too slowly.

The naval threat to shipping returned with a vengeance in August 1864, when a rebel raider off Long Island attacked unarmed commercial vessels. Despite the efforts of the wartime governors, state and federal authorities still neglected the mundane duty of home defense on both land and sea.[48]

The war profoundly influenced not just servicemen, but also civilians, whose lives, outlooks, and values were altered in some fashion. New Jerseyans on the home front took their civilian responsibilities seriously. At first the war spurred both patriotic fervor and humanitarian endeavors. New Jersey women volunteered their services to help the war effort. Like women elsewhere in the North, they sewed quilts, knitted mittens, rolled bandages, and bottled preserves. They collected food, clothing, sheets, and blankets, then shipped the supplies to the troops. They pledged to do without frivolous fashions and imported luxuries. They joined local groups to support the efforts of the Sanitary Commission to care for the sick and relieve hardship. They helped the Christian Commission to meet the troops' spiritual needs by sending pocket Bibles. Both women and men raised money for medical supplies for the wounded and relief of their families. They held church bazaars as well as local and regional fairs; major fairs took place in 1864 in New York City and Philadelphia. At the latter fair, New Jerseyans presented Lincoln with a cane made from the wood of the triumphal arch erected to honor Washington as he entered Trenton in April 1789. They exhibited and offered for sale two donations: a draft of one of Lincoln's proclamations, and the flag of John Paul Jones's ship.

State and local governments assisted soldiers' families by paying a small allowance, but, as in other states, haphazard arrangements, bureaucratic bungling, political infighting, and inadequate funds hampered the effort. Civilians founded hospitals for wounded soldiers in New Jersey, for which the government later assumed responsibility. Some plucky women, notably Cornelia Hancock of Salem, nursed soldiers in army field hospitals. Working at Gettysburg after the battle and commenting on the usefulness of the Sanitary Commission, Hancock observed, "Uncle Sam is very rich, but very slow, and if it was not for the Sanitary, much suffering would ensue."[49]

New Jersey's economy suffered in the early 1860s because of the loss of southern markets and raw materials and, even more important, because of a business slump in the North triggered by political crisis and economic uncertainty. Poor business and gloomy prospects damaged the economies of Newark and some other cities. Reduced sales of locomotives, machinery, metals, vehicles, leather goods, clothing, jewelry, and luggage sharply cut the state's production, triggered layoffs, and ruined about 150 firms. To relieve unemployment, Newark's leaders went to Washington to plead for military orders, and the city government put the unemployed to work paving streets. Congressmen pressed federal officials to establish an armory in the state, to move the Naval Academy to Perth Amboy, and to construct vessels in several local shipyards. Factory owners scrambled to "get a good fat contract." In the fall of 1861, when federal orders started coming in, a number of factories began to hum again. In 1862 only sixty-five firms went bankrupt.

Farmers also suffered in 1861, but eventually they profited through supplying the fast-growing metropolitan and military markets. They slaughtered cows and pigs, produced dairy products, and raised crops of grains, potatoes, vegetables, and fruit. The farmers soon encountered difficulty in obtaining hired hands, however, for many of them had left the countryside to join the army or work in factories. Western grain producers gained such a wartime competitive edge that New Jersey farmers in the postwar years were forced to take up truck farming. During the first year and a half of the war business as a whole did not improve. Yet conditions varied; some towns, notably Trenton, which had more diversified, more balanced economies, remained relatively unscathed.

By the end of 1862, war production had taken up the slack and made cities prosperous. Business revived with federal purchases of guns and parts, iron cable for army bridges, military equipment, and woolen uniforms. Iron foundries in Trenton, Newark, Jersey City, and Paterson began to flourish, as did locomotive works in Paterson, rubber factories in New Brunswick, clothing mills in Paterson and Newark, and mining in North Jersey. In June 1863 a Newark editor stated, "We can get along even without the southern trade." The war boom enabled entrepreneurs to build new factories or expand existing ones and to earn handsome, often spectacular profits. Ironmasters invented new techniques for manufacturing steel gun barrels and rails. Mass production of ready-made clothes expanded. At the end of the war a Trenton politician commented, "This war has left us at the North far more prosperous than when it commenced." In 1860, 4,173 factories existed in New Jersey; ten years later this number had increased to 6,636.

Because so many skilled workers were joining the army, unskilled or semi-skilled workers took their places in factories and on farms. Yet the real wages of many persons in the labor force lagged behind consumer prices, which almost doubled. Immigrants furnished cheap labor and thus kept wages from rising as fast as prices. Women and children toiled in factories for meager pay, overlong hours, and in poor conditions, but at least they had jobs, which they desperately needed. Skilled as well as unskilled male workers did much better, but did not retain their purchasing power. Workers protested inadequate wages or poor working conditions and struck various industries during the war with some success.

Although some manufacturing specialties, such as woolens, silk, and glass, expanded greatly, others, notably cotton textiles, contracted. The number of manufacturing firms grew impressively, but the percentage of increase in the value of the state's industrial production declined drastically. The number of industrial workers in New Jersey increased only slightly, while the proportion of factory workers in the state's work force remained the same. Thus the war produced both big winners and conspicuous losers.[50]

Northerners on the home front experienced changes, even if daily life went on as usual. War quickened the pace of life. "What a fever is to the individual, a state of war is to the nation," observed the *Jersey City Advocate.* "The wheels of society fly with increased velocity. Everything moves faster." The *Flemington Republican* noted that the "shock of war, while it threatens destruction, often seems to give new life and vigor to the nation, and to awake the slumbering energies of the people."

Many people, however, found that vulgarity and a decline in standards of behavior accompanied war. People condemned a wartime society infected with greed and with war profiteers who flaunted their wealth. Trenton lawyer Edward W. Scudder observed, "We live in a constant state of unrest, and all is feverish excitement. The great disturbance of the country is evident on all sides. Even our servants are more provoking and troublesome. Society is gayer and more dissipated. On every side we see speculation and gambling, fraud, and impurity that are shocking."

Peter Vroom criticized the changes wrought by war in a letter to an American overseas. "You will not find things here as they were when you left. Under ordinary circumstances, four years make a great change, but situated as we have been, the change is much more remarkable. It is seen and felt in our public, social, and private relations—in the views and feelings of the community at large, in the customs and manners of society, and in the general relaxation of those high moral principles, which once bound us together as a people. All this is the effect of war." Swearing, brawling, and drunkenness had become endemic, noted various observers. Activities that previously had existed underground now flourished openly. The bordellos of Pink Row, lining Merchant Street in Newark, enjoyed a brisk business, as did their counterparts elsewhere in the state.

War forced other changes that broke the crust of custom, at least temporarily. With men absent on military service, occupations previously restricted to men now opened up to women. Women became clerks and often took men's jobs as farm and factory hands. Although economic necessity brought new opportunities, it hardly brought equality: women received lower wages than their male co-workers. Moreover, women, now often the sole support of their families, did not always find desperately needed jobs because of the war's early disruption of the economy.

The *Trenton Monitor* generally approved of the "enlargement of women's sphere of usefulness." The *Newark Advertiser* agreed in principle but cautioned against women's changing their essential nature, "being unsexed" as workers and becoming unladylike, offering undue competition to remaining male workers, or "running too violently counter to prevalent customs, usages, or prejudices." Even so, women's greater visibility during the war brought ideas for greater change. After the war some advocates of women's rights recalled their wartime contributions and asserted that women deserved rights and the franchise just as much as blacks. The war had accelerated change.[51]

# 8 Partisanship in Wartime, 1862

During the first three months of 1862, the legislature by various actions confirmed unionist sentiment in the state. Charles Haight, a Freehold Democrat whose unconditional unionism even Republicans extolled, predictably won election as speaker of the assembly. As president, the senate chose the independent war Democrat Joseph Crowell, an outspoken and dedicated unionist. When the senate earlier had become deadlocked, Crowell broke the impasse by casting the sole Democratic vote for himself. Regular Democrats resented Crowell's independence; peace Democrats distrusted his uncompromising views on waging total war. Crowell apportioned senate assignments in bipartisan fashion with each senator heading one standing committee. A coalition of Republicans and prowar Democrats commanded the strategic joint committee on federal relations. Thus unionists consolidated control of both chambers.[1]

Unionists also made a concerted effort to control distribution of state patronage. With Crowell holding the balance of power, prowar editor Morris Hamilton of the *Camden Democrat* defeated antiwar editor Albert Speer of the *New Brunswick Times* for the post of secretary of the senate. In a struggle over which newspapers would receive lucrative printing work, the unionist forces again prevailed. They ended all patronage for David Naar, the antiwar editor of the *Trenton American*, and gave it instead to John H. Lyon, the prowar editor of the *Jersey City Standard*. As the *Newark Advertiser* observed, "Union feeling evidently pervades, and predominates over all."[2] Despite this trend, the war faction suffered a minor if disquieting setback. The Democrats, bound by their decision in party caucus to support all their nominees in the joint meeting of the legislature, elected county judges that included four peace men.[3]

The war at large went well for the North during February 1862. The Union army seized coastal fortifications in North Carolina, penetrated river entrances to Tennessee, and made major advances in the border states. Elated, the legislature approved without dissent a series of patriotic resolutions praising these triumphs. Even the harshest critics of the war, including the *Newark Journal*, joined in. Many New Jerseyans expected the war to be over by summer. The more wary *Newark Mercury*, however, cautioned: "Danger lies in this overweening confidence." The hard work had just begun, the newspaper later observed: "It is not a sudden, spasmodic burst of patriotism that will save us; it is the stern and fixed determination on the part of the whole people to win."[4]

On March 27, in the final days of its session, the legislature unanimously approved a series of resolutions that thanked New Jersey's volunteers for defending "our glorious Union from the assaults of wicked and rebellious people." The legislature praised Lincoln's efforts to preserve the Union, maintain the Constitution, defend the flag, and suppress rebellion. Most important, the legislature in a bipartisan vote overwhelmingly approved a tax package that raised a half-million dollars to help fund the two million dollars of war expenditures authorized in 1861. Again the war party in the legislature had succeeded in keeping New Jersey firmly on the Union track.[5]

The legislature's war factions also handled deftly a potential embarrassment in the person of rabidly antiwar James Wall. Frustrated in his attempts to seek redress from federal authorities for his two-week imprisonment in September 1861, Wall in January 1862 attempted to exploit this incident. Anointed by the *Newark Journal* as "the distinguished political martyr," Wall requested the legislature to instruct New Jersey's congressmen to demand that the secretary of war explain the reasons for his incarceration. The Democratic majority of the assembly conceded that Wall's detention without trial or examination had violated his rights, but it coolly reminded Wall to seek redress in federal court, which held sole jurisdiction in the matter.[6]

Also in March of 1862, the legislature reshaped the congressional districts in the northern part of the state. Rapid population growth in Newark and Jersey City had swelled the number of inhabitants in the fifth district. Despite wild rumors of extravagant schemes to gerrymander every district, Republicans found the new division fairer than anticipated but nonetheless unhelpful to them. Although the legislature kept the first and second districts intact, it transferred marginally Democratic Union County from the fifth district to the strongly Democratic third district. In addition, the legislature transferred Essex County, except for the city of Newark, from the fifth to the fourth district. Thus the legislature neutralized Republican voters in suburban Essex by making them a minority in a Democratic district. The fifth district seat was made more Democratic by being restricted to the party's strongholds of Newark and Hudson County.[7]

The spring municipal elections demonstrated that unionist sentiment in the legislature did not result in Republican strength at the polls. Although local matters dominated these contests, politicians also addressed national concerns. On the Democratic side, the *Jersey City Standard* urged all voters who opposed radicalism and the "proposed equality of the negro race" to rally behind local Democratic candidates. On the Republican side, partisans voiced patriotic themes. The *Paterson Guardian* demanded that "no rebel sympathizer be elected to any office in this city."[8]

The returns indicated that the Democrats carried or gained in many towns, notably Paterson, Morristown, Jersey City, Elizabeth, New Brunswick, Somerville, and Trenton. Democrats showed themselves more united and more successful than in the previous year. Republicans' efforts to attract supporters by building a unionist coalition failed. In addition, New Jersey soldiers outside the state could not vote. The *Camden Democrat* remarked that the results "augur well for the fall election." Dejected, the *Camden Press* described the Republican craft as empty and drifting. Republican John Foster confessed privately that the "prospect for the fall campaign in the State looks dark."[9]

Meanwhile most of New Jersey's congressmen backed various war measures considered between December 1861 and July 1862. Of the state's four Democrats, Senator John Thomson and Representatives George Cobb and William Steele, along with their three Republican colleagues, favored the war effort. Early on, even Newark's cranky Nehemiah Perry supported some measures to finance the war.[10]

Representative Clement L. Vallandigham of Ohio, the leader of the antiwar forces, attempted in May 1862 to fill the vacuum in the Democratic party left by the death of Douglas. Opposing Republican policies, Vallandigham defended the right and the necessity of the opposition in a democracy to criticize the party in power. He maintained that the defeat of the Confederate army was the only legitimate objective of the war. Republicans, Vallandigham believed, overstepped this purpose with vengeful plans to violate southern rights, emancipate their slaves, and abolish their state governments. Both state and individual rights could not be tampered with, even in wartime.

Vallandigham originally called for compromise with the South. After the stunning military defeat of the Union army at Fredericksburg in December 1862, he went much further, calling for an unconditional armistice and insisting that the fighting must stop, regardless of any preconditions or subsequent negotiation. Vallandigham furnished a voice and a vision for northern war opponents: "*Maintain the Constitution As It Is, and to Restore the Union As It Was.*"[11]

Among members of the state's congressional delegation, only Perry, who by late spring had joined the extremist ranks of the antiwar Democrats, signed Vallandigham's address. Enemies of the war naturally endorsed it at a time when they were further emboldened by military setbacks during the spring and summer of 1862. Conjuring up the specter of an impoverished North and a desolated South, the *Newark Journal* contended that the war's costs and losses made it senseless. The *Hackensack Democrat* agreed. Both newspapers demanded an immediate armistice to restore peace even at the price of dissolving the Union. Several influential Democratic newspapers, however, attacked the *Journal's* open opposition to the war. Even the conservative

*Somerville Messenger* criticized the *Journal* as damaging the state Democracy with "its ultra articles and useless clamor." The prowar *Newton Herald* went further: the "*Journal* in pursuing this course stands alone in New Jersey, and we can but believe, entirely misrepresents the sentiments of the Democratic masses of Newark."[12]

State Democrats who supported the war decried Vallandigham's extremism. The *Morristown Banner* denounced his desire to "purchase peace from a rebellion, by conceding amendments to the Constitution, is to invite, reward, and encourage treason." "A compromise," predicted Jacob Vanatta, "would only scab over the sore, leaving the morbid virus festering beneath and sure to break out again." The *Somerville Messenger* argued that the "government cannot now fall back, nor should it. To talk of compromise is equally futile— the leaders of the Southern Confederacy would laugh such a proposition to scorn."[13]

Republicans castigated Vallandigham's address as tantamount to a declaration of war against a government that was trying to rescue the Union and the Constitution, for which he professed such loyalty and love. Even while pleading for a "Union as it was," Vallandigham acknowledged that southern secession had divided it permanently. Questioning his vague slogan, "Constitution as it is," Republicans wondered whether Vallandigham worried more about the imagined destruction of the Constitution than about the impending dissolution of the Union. The *Newark Advertiser* asked, "Is the Constitution 'as it is' so defective an instrument that robbery may be shielded, treason protected, rebellion apologized for, and the Union broken into fragments" without recourse or remedy, without any act of self-preservation?[14]

More than any other issue, the question of emancipating the slaves separated the parties. New Jersey's Democratic congressmen generally opposed emancipation during the 1862 session. They regarded abolition as unconstitutional because it deprived slaveholders of their property without their consent and represented massive federal interference in state matters. In early March, however, when Congress endorsed freeing the slaves in the border states by paying the slave owners, Thomson and Cobb supported the measure. State Democrats denounced their apostasy.[15]

Republicans countered that the slave owners, by rebelling against the Union and repudiating their constitutional responsibilities, had forfeited their rights, including protection of their property. As the radical *Elizabeth Unionist* declared, "What we could not do, treason has now made constitutional. Traitors have no rights." Thus the army had the duty to confiscate enemy property and to liberate the slaves. Emancipation would shorten the conflict by depriving the rebels of slave labor. Freedom for the slaves also would attract sympathy and support abroad for the Union cause. Abolition would discourage possible recognition and aid for the Confederacy by Britain and France.[16]

Without the destruction of slavery there appeared to be no prospect of lasting peace because slavery would continue to poison national politics and life. "'*The Union As It Was*'—Who does not see that is impossible?" asked the *Toms River Emblem*. To attempt to restore the Union with slavery still present and with slaveholders "still intolerant, haughty, imperious, domineering, *is to be beaten in the contest.*" The *Unionist* concluded, "Policy, humanity, necessity demand emancipation."[17]

Republicans Orestes Brownson and Charles Hodge urged abolition as a means to an end rather than as an end in itself. Even some Douglas Democrats, notably Martin Ryerson, agreed that the time for liberating the slaves had finally arrived. But Catholic bishop James R. Bayley, along with others, feared that such a step would divide public opinion in New Jersey. A supporter of the war, Bayley worried that the "abolition party in Congress by striving to make the present war, a war against Slavery, are breaking up the unity of the North."[18]

The state's Republican congressmen consisted of moderates, who, like the conservatives, distrusted the radical Republicans' incessant demands to hasten emancipation. Partly reflecting their constituents' opinion, these moderates preferred gradual emancipation with the slave owners' consent. The moderates further desired that abolition reflect the will of the majority, and wanted state authorities to oversee it. Such an approach harmonized with legal requirements, historical precedent, and their desire to avoid social convulsion and racial conflict. These Republicans preferred evolution to revolution.

The moderates nonetheless considered change necessary to preserve order and came to view emancipation as a needed war measure. In April 1862 Representatives John Nixon and John Stratton, along with Senator John Ten Eyck, voted with fellow Republicans to enact immediate, involuntary emancipation in the District of Columbia, with only partial compensation to slave owners. In June, Congress prohibited slavery in all the federal territories. In July, in the boldest move of all, Congress approved the Second Confiscation Act, which for the first time provided for immediate, uncompensated emancipation. This measure permitted confiscation of all property of rebels, authorized freedom for all the slaves of rebels within the Union lines, and granted the president sweeping authority to take action. Every New Jersey Republican congressman voted for the act.[19]

"We are in a war, a real war," announced the *Unionist*. The time had arrived for the Union to stop fighting with one hand behind its back for fear of angering people in the border slave states, and to begin doing as much damage to the rebels as rebels inflicted on northerners. A frontal assault on slavery had begun.[20]

New Jersey's Democrats believed that these measures went too far. Still, they had no illusions that liberation ever would be undone where it had occurred. Blacks celebrating in Newark regarded confiscation as only the prelude to general emancipation. As thousands of slaves flocked toward northern troops, slavery crumbled away before the Union lines. "The tread of the Northern soldier practically makes the soil free," exclaimed one Newarker, "The fact is that where our army goes, the reign of Slavery ceases."[21]

As general emancipation became more likely, New Jerseyans worried about a possible mass exodus of former slaves from the South to the North. The prospect of a stampede of blacks to New Jersey had worried some whites in the past, especially in 1860, as it had elsewhere in the lower northern states that bordered slaveholding states. By 1862 concern had mounted. White residents of South Jersey, especially Camden County, feared a huge influx of freedmen. According to some reports, fugitive slaves already had arrived in the county from Philadelphia, which white New Jerseyans regarded as a magnet for southern blacks.[22]

Although the matter was mentioned in Congress, it became more pressing in the legislature, where some Democrats sought to exploit racial fears. Some members proposed that freed Negroes be barred from entering New Jersey, just as they had been barred from some western states. Democrats blamed Republicans for emancipation and warned that New Jerseyans would suffer because of this Republican scheme to elevate blacks at the expense of whites. Democrats predicted that black laborers would take away whites' jobs by working for lower wages. The presence of blacks would constitute a public nuisance and a tax burden; these reputedly footloose people would fill the jails and poorhouses. Blacks would endanger the property, prosperity, even the physical safety of whites. As the finishing touch to this apocalyptic scenario, Democrats asserted that race riots would erupt. Amalgamation would occur. Eager black males would crawl into bed with the wives and daughters of white men. Unless the legislature imposed a ban on black immigration, Democrats argued, New Jersey's whites would become pauperized and Africanized.[23]

In response, the Republicans denounced exclusionary legislation as patently unconstitutional and unnecessary. They claimed that Democrats wildly exaggerated the potential problem and were exploiting it for political effect. These demagogues, they said, ignored the fact that southern Negroes preferred to stay in the more congenial South, with its sunnier climate. The South was their home and provided them with work on its farms. Yet an influx of a limited number of blacks, they maintained, might relieve the shortage of servants in the state. Republicans also warned that hysterical talk could trigger race riots and cause the murder of innocent people. During debate one Passaic Republican assemblyman suggested sarcastically that because most of the commotion centered on Camden, the state should purchase the county and colonize all the state's Negroes there. This proposal cut discussion short.

After pondering the matter, the joint committee on federal relations, packed with moderates and war supporters, made no recommendation to prohibit immigration of blacks into the state.[24]

I n spring, attention turned to November, when voters would elect a governor, legislators, and congressmen. The Republicans, considering themselves at a disadvantage, decided to gain a few steps on the Democrats by holding their state convention in the summer rather than the fall. They announced their convention with a broad nonpartisan appeal, inviting all friends of the Union to support the party of the Union.

During the campaign the party continued to employ a variety of names in an attempt to blur party lines and circumvent partisan issues. Terms included Republican Union, Union Republican, Union War, Loyal Men, Administration, Administration Union, Union Administration, and Friends of the National Administration. Only in safely Republican South Jersey did party members refer to themselves frequently as Republicans. In contrast, the Democrats generally continued to call themselves Democrats but sometimes used the names Democratic Union or Union Democratic.

Despite the changes of names, both party organizations remained intact, relying on their core of loyal supporters while attempting to broaden their appeal. In addition, the Democrats tried to attract supporters among conservative and moderate Republicans. The Republicans, hoping to lure prowar Democrats, nominated some Douglas Democrats, featured them as campaign speakers, and subsidized Democrat Charles W. Jay's *Trenton Patriot*.[25]

The Republicans weighed possible choices for governor. Attempts to create a bipartisan coalition failed when talk of nominating Crowell came to nothing. Then in August it was reported that some prominent Republicans had tried to establish a unionist coalition by choosing a Democrat to head the ticket. As before, this strategy encountered stiff Republican opposition; it collapsed when Daniel Haines, a Douglas Democrat and former governor, refused to run as the candidate. Without a fusion nominee, no bipartisan unionist coalition could be formed.

Meanwhile William Newell suggested Marcus Ward as the nominee. Before the war, Newarker Ward had increased the family fortune as a successful businessman. An active philanthropist with a touch of the reformer, he remained more a realist than an idealist. Although he had held no elective office, he had strongly supported the Republican party from its inception and worked hard for its presidential candidates. Ward was flattered by suggestions that he run for governor, although he did nothing publicly to advance his candidacy.

Party members considered Ward's Republicanism to be as firm as his patriotism. His wealth could help fund a campaign. More important, his work on behalf of New Jersey's soldiers and their families had earned him respect and gratitude. He attempted to furnish Jersey troops in the field with items from home and assisted wounded veterans by furnishing medical supplies, improving sanitary conditions, and establishing a fine military hospital in Newark. An innovator credited with devising the first system in the North for collecting, advancing, and forwarding the pay of soldiers in the field to their families at home, Ward employed clerks at his own expense to administer the system and operate a veterans' office.

Republicans hoped the popular allure of Ward's patriotic, philanthropic record would compensate for his political inexperience. By late July his nomination seemed assured. When the Republican convention assembled in Trenton on August 21, the delegates selected Ward by acclamation. As for the platform, it lauded the efforts of Lincoln to crush the rebellion, but the platform made no reference to confiscation of rebels' slaves.[26]

The Democrats approached the campaign with caution and once again debated their proper role in wartime. Vanatta forcefully reminded his fellow Democrats that their foremost duty was to ensure the stability of the government by winning the war and restoring the Union. He disagreed with the view that the Democrats should just obstruct for the sake of opposing and offer no constructive alternative. Vanatta even criticized some antiwar newspapers for ignoring the reality of war and the necessity of using extraordinary remedies to handle extraordinary situations.[27]

Significantly, only war supporters sought the Democratic nomination for governor. The antiwar faction feared that state voters would reject a candidate of their own stripe in the general election, and divided over several candidates that war Democrats might accept. All of the Democrats understood that internal dissension would guarantee defeat.

One major contender, Newark mayor and war supporter Moses Bigelow, sought the nomination so eagerly that he reportedly welcomed the support of war opponents. His nomination, however, was challenged by the equally ambitious Newarker Theodore Runyon, another staunch supporter of the war who had served briefly at the battlefront. During primary meetings in Newark, supporters of each contender became so hostile when they were defeated that they walked out of meetings and started fistfights. This struggle left their home base of North Jersey so deeply divided that neither candidate appeared likely to secure the nomination.[28]

Attention thus focused on Joel Parker, from strongly Democratic Monmouth, as a consensus candidate. Douglas Democrats, reportedly including such major leaders as Ryerson and Vanatta, strongly backed Parker as one of their own, but other Douglas men favored Runyon. Skeptical Republican observers doubted that any Douglas man could beat the reputedly more adept managers of the antiwar faction.[29]

The Democrats assembled in Trenton on September 4. The first ballot produced an exciting race between Bigelow and Parker. Although Bigelow increased his total on the next two ballots, Parker pulled ahead by picking up additional southern and northwestern support. The decisive turn came after the fourth ballot, when the large delegations from Essex and Hudson, previously divided between supporters of Bigelow and Runyon, changed to Parker. With loud approval, the delegates made his nomination unanimous. Parker accepted the nomination in person and delivered a stirring address, which the delegates frequently interrupted with thunderous applause. The nomination unified the fractious party and broadened the ticket's appeal to independents and disaffected Republicans.[30]

Parker had many of the same characteristics as Olden. Dignified, amiable, unaffected, both men possessed sound judgment, common sense, firm patriotism, and political prudence. Both preferred conciliation and consensus to confrontation or domination. Both navigated between contending factions and tacked to the prevailing wind while maintaining course. Both were popular and respected.

The similarities ended there, however. At sixty-three Olden looked old, thin, and weary. Parker, with flashing black eyes and black hair, looked rotund and vigorous at forty-six. In personality, too, Parker, a buoyant extrovert, contrasted with the quiet Olden. He was as direct and as forceful a speaker as Olden, but did not shun the stump as readily as the older man. A successful lawyer who had served with aplomb as Monmouth prosecutor for five years, Parker had polished his speaking style in court. Having acquired his father's taste for politics, the nominee as a youth gained firsthand experience working in the state government. Later, during five years as an assemblyman, the highly ambitious Parker earned recognition for intelligence and diligence, and he advanced quickly to influential positions of leadership. He promoted tax and suffrage reform, which the Democratic party made winning issues. Active during the 1850s in reorganizing and reinvigorating the local militia, he was appointed one of its generals. Parker in the meantime canvassed the state extensively in various campaigns and became known as one of the state's best stump speakers.

Unlike Olden, who played the role of the nonpartisan politician in public while practicing his highly effective brand of personal politics behind the scenes, Parker relished public attention. An unabashed partisan, he stood with his party come what may. As a strict constructionist he wished to restrict the national and the state governments to their respective constitutional spheres. As a moderate Democrat Parker opposed both the sectionalism that had propelled the nation toward disintegration and what he regarded as the dangerous centralism that concentrated power in Washington. Parker abhorred extremism in any form, whether southern separatism or northern abolitionism.

Parker steadfastly backed Douglas in 1860 but adjusted quickly to joining the coalition of the anti-Lincoln forces and became one of the victorious presidential electors. A committed supporter of the war, Parker recalled accurately in 1876, "When war was declared I was for the Union, first, last, and all the time."[31]

According to both Republican and most Democratic newspapers, a war supporter had won the party's nomination. With Parker's victory, reported the Republican *Newark Advertiser*, the "Union supporting wing of the party has signally triumphed over the anti-war branch." The Republican *Princeton Standard* similarly characterized Parker's selection as a "triumph of the War and Douglas element over the antiwar and Breckinridge element of the party, to the credit of the State." Some Republicans speculated that the antiwar men backed him only to prevent the defection of the Douglas men to Ward; the *Trenton Patriot* labeled Parker's nomination a "concession to the loyal sentiment of the State, extorted under fear of a defeat at the ballot box."[32]

Although some Republicans distrusted any Democratic candidate because they feared the antiwar men would strongly influence or even control the nominee, those Republicans who personally knew Parker did not worry. They reassured people that whichever party won the election, the governorship would remain in safe hands. Regardless of the outcome, the state's war effort would continue unhindered. Nevertheless, Parker's nomination generally discouraged Republican politicians because they assessed it, correctly, as the strongest choice the Democrats could have made.[33]

After much closed-door wrangling, the resolutions committee reported a platform that the Democrats largely considered sensible and the Republicans regarded as duplicitous. With its call for the speedy "suppression of the rebellion by all Constitutional means" and its commendation of state volunteers for emulating the heroism of the "old 'Jersey Blues,'" the major resolution especially pleased the war supporters. The platform refrained from criticizing higher war taxes or troop recruitment quotas, and it did not charge Republicans with sole responsibility for the war. The platform also pleased the war opponents, however, because it construed presidential war powers narrowly and denounced Lincoln for his flagrant abuse of executive power. Various resolutions condemned the federal government for making arrests without due process of law, infringing on freedom of speech and press, wasting money, causing corruption, and emancipating the slaves. According to this platform, Lincoln had done nothing right in his attempts to defend the Union. Some Republicans regarded the Democratic platform as less objectionable than its counterpart in Pennsylvania, and saw it as close to New York's.[34]

Republicans pointed out that the Democratic rallying cry, "'Constitution as it is, and the restoration of the Union as it was,'" tried, in the words of the *Newark Advertiser*, to please "both those who advocate and those who oppose the Government policy." The *Newton Register* lashed out at the artful dodging of the Democrats, who devised equivocal phrases and split constitutional hairs to retain the support of "'conditional' Unionists." The *Camden Press* expressed the Republican consensus: Democrats had nominated a creditable candidate to stand on a discreditable platform.[35]

Many years later Parker himself admitted that this contradictory platform arose from the need to please both those who wished to fight the war to the finish and those who yearned for immediate peace. Parker devised a campaign strategy that straddled the platform. Avoiding specifics, he told fellow Democrats that he wholeheartedly backed the effort to "conquer the rebellion." He declared secession a political heresy that violated the Constitution and subverted the government. As the candidate of the loyal opposition, however, Parker criticized what he termed the rampant corruption and gross mismanagement in Lincoln's administration. He also opposed any infringement of the laws or violation of the people's rights for any reason by federal authorities; the army's arbitrary arrests of northern citizens had to stop.[36]

In early September Parker told Democratic delegates that his views were already well known, but he promised to elaborate on them during the campaign. Once nominated, however, this war supporter stopped attending both war rallies and campaign meetings. He became uncharacteristically quiet. When he broke his campaign silence in Wall on October 18, he attributed his absence from the canvass to an unspecified illness. He simultaneously endorsed the war for the Union and enshrined the Constitution. Concerning emancipation, he said almost nothing; he only vaguely deplored the spirit of abolition. Noting this lack of commitment, Republican Frederick T. Frelinghuysen, the state attorney general, observed that if Parker promised to sacrifice slavery to save the Union, peace supporters would not vote for him. If he promised to save slavery even if the Union perished, war supporters would not vote for him. As Frelinghuysen concluded, "therefore, he chose to be silent."[37]

Republicans used Parker's silence as an opening wedge. The *Trenton Gazette* remarked that the Democratic candidate in the campaign had "preserved the most complete silence." Perhaps this uncharacteristic silence reflected a change in his position. His newfound support among the most notorious antiwar men in the state certainly lent credence to a change, insinuated the Republicans. The *Gazette* deduced "but one interpretation of General Parker's failure to comply with his promise to further declare himself to the people. He has, we fear, surrendered himself to the Breckinridge politicians." Other Republican newspapers also believed he had capitulated to the peace men; otherwise he would not have received their support. The *Freehold Herald* observed, "If it be true that birds of a feather flock together, we think that if Joel sits in the Gubernatorial nest, he will hatch a nasty, loathsome little monster of Secession in the State of New Jersey." The *Somerville Whig*, however, advanced a less sinister interpretation of the peace faction's support: they had no one else to support and preferred any sort of Democrat to a Republican.[38]

Both candidates for governor were so honest and capable, so widely respected, that party loyalists supported their nominees, while most partisan opponents refused to question their personal or professional qualifications. Without a shred of evidence, a few Republicans depicted Parker as a lukewarm unionist, while some Democrats described Ward as a captive of the radicals. Partisan rhetoric aside, each candidate served as a powerful patriotic symbol, either as the militia general or as the friend of the soldier.[39]

Neither candidate waged an active public campaign. Parker spoke only three times; Ward evidently not at all. Both, however, toured county fairs from Cumberland to Sussex, meeting voters and mobilizing supporters. In a peculiar twist of fate that tested the adage that politics made strange bedfellows, a Newton hotel manager put the two candidates not only in the same room but in the same bed at the same time.[40]

Behind the scenes, however, each candidate devised his own strategy and managed his own campaign. Parker reached out to the peace wing; that wing, after all, had in one sense lost the nomination, and some of its members had shown marked coolness at the start of the campaign. To assuage Wall, Parker made it a point to denounce arbitrary arrests. Parker asked another war opponent, Rodman Price, for campaign suggestions. To both men, he stressed the importance of a unified party to achieve victory for the Democrats. Parker's broad appeal as champion of both the Union and liberty, along with his jovial personality, endeared him to fellow Democrats.[41]

Ward's quieter manner suited the more staid style of many Republicans. Ward preferred to stay out of the limelight and to continue helping soldiers, but his silence served a purpose. In contrast to the Democratic campaign, which tried to draw party lines tightly and to emphasize partisan issues, Ward assumed a nonpartisan posture. His cautious approach also revealed Republicans' fears about campaigning openly as Republicans. Instead they attempted to organize a bipartisan statewide coalition of the friends of Lincoln's administration in order to sustain the government in this supreme crisis. Ward, however, interceded in federal patronage matters behind the scenes to help advance his party's canvass.

Unfortunately for Ward's campaign, he was so sure of victory that he overplayed his nonpartisan role. By failing to appear personally at the Republican convention or to wage a more energetic campaign, the overconfident Ward and the state Republican central committee were inefficient in mobilizing their frequently apathetic supporters across the state. Although Republicans formed patriotic societies supporting the Union cause and their candidates, Republicans held too many rallies, frequently with poor turnouts, rather than concentrating on fewer, better-attended meetings. Altruistic as ever, Ward worked unstintingly in helping soldiers at the front who could not participate in the election. Observing Ward's attention to those who could not vote instead of those who could, Newark Republican Isaac P. Trimble reported that Ward "could not see the danger"; he "couldn't see it at all and I couldn't bear to tell him." Some New Jersey veterans did not even make the right connection between the candidate and the soldier's friend. Trimble, coming from Ward's veterans' office, met an Irishman who asked, "'Kin you tell me where Marcus L. keeps his Ward?'"[42]

The races for Congress varied greatly. South Jersey's incumbent Nixon declined to run, so first district convention Republicans nominated Camden iron manufacturer John F. Starr in his place. Both Starr and the delegates pledged strong support for the Union cause. After a protracted fight among many contenders, Democrats nominated as a compromise candidate the popular, influential Cumberland senator, Nathaniel Stratton. Stratton dubbed himself a Union Democrat and campaigned as such in this uphill contest.[43]

In the second district, Republicans replaced moderate incumbent John Stratton with the more radical Ocean senator, William F. Brown. Democrats nominated a strong unionist candidate, George Middleton, a former assemblyman, an Allentown tanner, and a Quaker. At the outset of the campaign many expected that the second district might remain Republican, but Democratic prospects brightened because of Brown's aloof personality and his record as an inactive, absentee senator. His ineffective campaign style contrasted with Middleton's polished performance. And a Democratic nominee who belonged to the Quakers provided just the right touch.[44]

In contrast to these campaigns, the contests elsewhere exhibited more spirit and posed more clear-cut choices. Republicans fielded distinguished individuals to oppose entrenched incumbents. At the Democratic convention in the third district, no one opposed Steele for renomination. Steele as a congressman strongly opposed arbitrary arrests and emancipation. He participated fruitfully in a bipartisan investigation of federal war contracts in order to eliminate waste and corruption, but some Republicans accused him, inaccurately, of leaning quietly toward peace.[45]

The Republicans picked Brownson, who had not sought the nomination. He harbored serious doubts about his ability to wage an effective campaign or, if elected, to serve as an active member of Congress. A renowned intellectual, earnest reformer, ardent Catholic, and a state resident for only four years, Brownson was an unusual choice for Republicans in the Democratic third district. A former Democrat and now a radical Republican, Brownson criticized Lincoln for his sluggish pace in waging war and for not pushing immediate emancipation.

Counting on the support of Catholic voters, Brownson ran hard for Congress, stumping the entire district. Democrats ridiculed his candidacy as preposterous and denounced him as an abolitionist troublemaker and a New

York carpetbagger. The *Trenton American* dismissed him as a "religious whirligig and political windmill."[46]

In the fifth district incumbent Perry, who had become an antiwar stalwart in Congress but a hard worker for his constituents, won the usual renomination after serving his first term. At the Democratic district convention Perry received the support of the delegates from his home city of Newark, but most Hudson delegates opposed him. Dissatisfaction with Perry's nomination grew so great among some Hudson Democrats, however, that they nominated the Republican candidate on an independent Democratic ticket.

In various speeches, Perry opposed all unconstitutional actions of Lincoln's administration, but in response to public opinion in his district he urged war to the hilt to end the rebellion. The district convention's platform endorsed the state party platform and condemned secession, emancipation, and violations of individual rights.[47]

Perry was a potentially vulnerable candidate even in a safely Democratic district; the Republicans quickly juxtaposed his pretense of patriotism with his antiwar voting record in Congress. They countered with a formidable, if reluctant, political newcomer, Joseph P. Bradley. A political moderate and a prominent Newark attorney, Bradley's major client was the Camden and Amboy Railroad.[48]

To this point the congressional campaign held no surprises. Moderates with unionist inclinations faced off once again downstate. In safe North Jersey districts Democratic incumbents voiced only unionist sentiments; their Republican opponents did not have a chance. In the fourth district, however, the campaign took an unexpected turn. The generally popular incumbent Cobb, independently wealthy, politically independent, the strongest supporter of the war effort among the state's Democratic members of Congress, and the ablest of all the state's congressmen in the last decade, incurred the wrath of some reactionaries in his district. He had supported compensated emancipation in the border states and failed to vote against abolition of slavery in the District of Columbia. The district's antiwar minority laid a trap; they opposed Cobb's nomination clandestinely so as not to alarm his complacent supporters. The Republicans likewise regarded Cobb as so unassailable that they seriously considered the possibility of not contesting his reelection. Caught completely off guard, some of Cobb's overconfident delegates did not even attend their party's district convention.

When the convention met, the opponents of the war seized the initiative. First the chairman of the resolutions committee, Andrew J. Rogers, a young Newton lawyer and an incendiary opponent of Lincoln's administration, presented the convention's platform. A strongly worded plank condemned Lincoln's recent efforts to advance emancipation as inexpedient and unconstitutional. The delegates immediately accepted the platform. Next the convention approved a resolution requiring its nominee to endorse this platform. For whatever reason, perhaps a fit of absentmindedness, Cobb's forces on the floor agreed to this resolution. Then the convention adjourned for a long lunch. During the recess the resolutions committee met with Cobb and asked him whether he could run on the convention's platform. Insulted, Cobb refused, saying that he was the only candidate for Congress in the state required to endorse the platform of the district convention, and specifically its denunciation of Lincoln's maneuvers toward emancipation.

When the convention resumed, Rogers reported to the delegates that Cobb would not endorse the platform and asked the convention to rescind its previous resolutions. Price angrily denounced Cobb for his rejection of the convention's work. Others, however, praised his courage in objecting to the platform before his nomination rather than ignoring or repudiating it after he received the nomination. Finally, after two hours of stormy debate, the convention decided not to change its platform. In effect it denied Cobb renomination.

The bold surprise tactics of the war opponents had disarmed the war supporters and left them in disarray. Various candidates dropped out; in the end, only war opponents consented to run for the nomination. The delegates chose resolutions chairman Rogers as their candidate. The platform had been set up to dump Cobb and make Rogers heir apparent. In his acceptance speech Rogers admitted he had written the entire platform and so naturally supported it. Rogers also professed to favor vigorous prosecution of the war by all constitutional means, but he opposed emancipation and illegal arrests.

The news infuriated leading unconditional unionists in the Democratic camp and drove some of them, including Ryerson, from the party. Both Democrats and Republicans expressed outrage at the replacement of such a fair, capable, respected, popular member of Congress by such an unfit, intemperate candidate. Republicans found in Rogers's speeches the thinnest veneer of patriotism, which could not cover the fact that he had never aided the war effort, but rather had worked daily to paralyze the government and make it an easy prey to its enemies. Republicans interpreted Cobb's treatment as an unmistakable warning of the trickery and the insidious influence of the antiwar Bergen clique that had pulled off this coup. The sleight of hand stunned many residents in the fourth district, the sturdy bastion of independent farmers and Douglas Democrats.[49]

Recognizing that their district figured as the major battleground in the state campaign for Congress, Republicans tried unsuccessfully to persuade Cobb to accept their nomination. They hoped that many incensed war Democrats would reelect the popular Cobb. The Republicans also considered other war Democrats, but nothing came of it. When the bipartisan Union convention assembled in Morristown, with such leading war Democrats as Ryerson and assemblyman Thomas N. McCarter participating, the delegates nominated Newton lawyer John Linn, an inactive Republican, to head the Union ticket.[50]

A sharp contest thus ensued. Linn, an eloquent speaker, championed the Union cause in high-minded fashion and warned that those who obstructed the war effort only prolonged the struggle. Rogers, however, a slick stump speaker as well as a pothouse populist, emphasized his self-made wealth and his affinity for the poor man. He appealed to the credulous and swayed crowds with emotional and racist appeals. One observer commented that Rogers pandered to the meanest prejudices, pitting the poor against the rich. No matter which side they took, everyone ranked this campaign as the most interesting, most heated, most important race for Congress in the state, and probably the closest as well.[51]

In legislative contests, more competition developed in the races for the assembly than for the senate because most of the seven senatorial contests occurred in Republican-dominated counties. Hotly fought senatorial campaigns occurred in Morris and Mercer, however. The Republicans expected to gain senate seats in Cumberland and Burlington, and possibly in Morris. Except for uncertain downstate counties, Democrats also exuded confidence because they had swept the elections held in Newark and in Pennsylvania, Ohio, and Indiana during October. Analysts speculated that apathetic Newark Republicans had let their contest go by default, so that the Republican ticket did not receive full Republican support, while the Irish and the Germans voted Democratic to defend their right to drink whiskey and beer. As Republican senator James M. Quinby of Essex observed, the Germans sided with the Republicans on national issues involving principle, "but in all local matters, they will go for the locals; the rum and lager beer interest outweighs everything else with them and they know the Democracy can be depended upon on these questions."[52]

The issues of the campaign also gave the Democrats an edge. After a year and a half of war the outcome remained stubbornly inconclusive. The burden of taxes, the magnitude of the national debt, the rising prices, the unending calls for additional recruits, and the mounting casualties began to test the people's resolve.

When the rivers of Virginia ran red with the blood of soldiers and when New Jersey's newspapers printed long lists of Jerseymen killed or wounded in the latest battle, the horrors of war sank in. The funerals—whether an elaborate cortege winding through the hushed streets of a city or a simple ceremony mourning a man in a quiet country church—were poignant reminders of the cost of war. A Hunterdon man reported that the local funeral of a fallen soldier "shows us what rebellion is."[53]

Worse, the dramatic military victories of the first four months of 1862 did not continue. The Union campaign on Virginia's James Peninsula during the spring and early summer, as well as the second battle of Bull Run in late August, went disastrously for the North. When the southern army escaped across the Potomac, the maddeningly indecisive outcome of the battle of Antietam in mid-September discouraged northerners. Although the Yankees repelled the Confederate invasion of Maryland and saved Washington from capture, such achievements did not erase the stunning Union defeats of the spring and the summer. The Union army in Virginia seemed always on the defensive, perpetually stalemated.

From the strongest war supporters to the staunchest opponents of the war, New Jerseyans criticized army operations openly, sometimes bitterly. By fall most Jerseyans had grown disillusioned with generals who failed to command, squandered resources, missed opportunities, and seldom won.

Although this sentiment generally took neither anti-Union nor pro-Confederate form, New Jersey Democrats exploited discouragement with the war's progress and asked the voters to elect Democrats to the Capitol and the State House. Defeatism and pacifism, however, were minor themes, voiced only by avowed war opponents, especially when the Federals lost a battle. Most Democrats promised not to stop the war but to turn it around and win it. War supporter Edward Scudder, the Democratic senatorial candidate in Mercer, urged prosecution of the war with greater energy, efficiency, and responsibility. The *Jersey City Standard* called for a return of the Democrats to power. After eighteen months under the Republicans in Washington the country suffered from a bungled war. Commenting on the inconclusive outcome of the war so far, a Sparta man declared, "I'm no Administration man, for they are too slow in settling up our affairs."[54]

Both parties agreed that the war had bogged down but disagreed as to where the fault lay. New Jersey Republicans blamed General George McClellan, commander of the Army of the Potomac, for his failure both to capture Richmond in the Peninsula campaign and to cut off the retreat of the Confederate army after Antietam. Critics considered lethargic McClellan a pen-and-ink man; he expended nine-tenths of his energy getting ready to begin. McClellan, they concluded, undertook war without the will to win, with neither daring nor ferocity to take necessary risks. "He has no snap in him," declared one Jerseyman.[55]

State Democrats defended McClellan, a Democrat unhappy with Lincoln's military direction and drift toward emancipation. If Lincoln, the radical Republicans, and the abolitionists had not sabotaged McClellan, they argued, he would have succeeded. Lincoln and his other generals, not McClellan, had mismanaged the war. Given a free hand and the necessary reinforcements, McClellan would win the war rapidly. In addition, the Democrats asserted that as long as a Republican administration waged war, all Republicans remained responsible for it. Both parties, then, found convenient scapegoats.[56]

The most ominous development in middle and late 1862 was New Jerseyans' growing recognition that the North might lose the war. A Blairstown man observed in late July that "things look to me darker than ever, just now. I have never felt any doubts about the result of this war until recently." In mid-September the *Elizabeth Unionist* asserted that "at no time since the breaking out of the rebellion has our cause appeared as gloomy as it does now." At the start of November Foster expressed his forebodings in a letter. The "war still drags wearily along—incapacity, delay in every field—discontent, despair in every heart." The "President is weak—Generals are timid—politicians rule, botching, ruining all they touch." Foster concluded, "Emphatically, the nation is in peril. The most hopeful begin to contemplate a failure as possible."[57]

Emancipation also figured as an important campaign issue. Pressure built on Lincoln to issue a stern proclamation. As the *Unionist* remarked, Lincoln "knows that amputation is the remedy, but yet is afraid the patient will bleed to death." Then, after Union troops had snatched a defensive victory at Antietam, Lincoln decided the right time had arrived. On September 22 he issued his Preliminary Emancipation Proclamation: beginning in 1863, all slaves in rebel territory or those who could reach the Union lines would be free.[58]

Most New Jersey Republicans accepted Lincoln's declaration, so long expected yet so long delayed, with varying degrees of enthusiasm. The decision naturally pleased radicals, who thought Lincoln finally had taken a step in the right direction. They found fault, however, with Lincoln's tardiness and failure to order immediate emancipation.

Lincoln's decree left moderate Republican politicians both reassured and unsettled. They supported it, but anxiously, and defended it as the logical, indeed inevitable extension of the Second Confiscation Act. They rejoiced that presidential decision and determination finally had replaced vacillation and indecision. Yet the moderate *Newark Advertiser* was unsure whether history would regard this proclamation as a mighty landmark or would mock it as an empty pronouncement inaugurating a fruitless experiment. Some stunned conservative Republicans, who earlier had opposed extension of slavery, refused to endorse wholesale abolition. The *Newton Register*, however, regarded Lincoln's edict as one of transcendent importance. The *Unionist* went further, declaring, "It is the greatest event in our history." In the words of the *Trenton Gazette*, Lincoln's proclamation of emancipation combined necessity with a "great act of justice."[59]

Some Democrats reacted with alarm to Lincoln's announcement. They believed it would divide northerners, harden the rebels' resolve, and prolong the war. Other Democrats dismissed the decree as ineffective and irrelevant: Lincoln, they mocked, might as well have issued a proclamation to the Mormons to cast off their extra wives before the first of January, or to every drinking man to become a teetotaler on or before that day. Moreover, his paper manifesto had no power of enforcement: slaves would remain slaves wherever they still had rebel masters. The *Jersey City Standard* asserted that the "good which emancipation will produce is not demonstrable, but the evil it will entail is palpable."[60]

Lincoln's proclamation marked a new stage in the war and drew new battle lines between the parties. His announcement dramatized and defined the issue as well as redefined Republicanism. The president now had committed the Republicans to his policy of emancipation, while the great majority of Democrats stood diametrically opposed to emancipation as a war measure. The voters, contended the *Paterson Register*, had felt that Lincoln "was heart and soul for the Union and nothing but the Union; they do not believe so now." A Westfield man believed that the war for the Union had become a "war for the negro" to overthrow slavery. Emancipation, feared Democratic war hawk Runyon, would drive away some of the Democratic war supporters.[61]

State Republican politicians nervously assessed the effect of the proclamation on the campaign. Already on the defensive because of the inconclusive conduct of the war, they worried that Lincoln's announcement would weaken them further by eroding both Democratic and Republican support. The congressional district conventions, most of which met after Lincoln had issued his declaration, used their platforms to respond. Three Democratic district conventions in North Jersey explicitly condemned Lincoln's proclamation. Softer Democratic platforms downstate merely endorsed the party's state platform, which had denounced all emancipation measures before Lincoln made his announcement. Following the cue of the Republican state convention, which also had met before Lincoln's declaration, Republican district conventions did not explicitly endorse emancipation or the subsequent proclamation. Cautious Republicans offered implicit, general support of Lincoln's war measures but little more. The Republican convention in the third district, however, especially supported Lincoln's policies and came closest to an outright endorsement of his proclamation. Some prominent Republicans, notably Bradley, explicitly endorsed Lincoln's proclamation, as did most Republican newspapers and the party supporters at several local Republican meetings. Nonetheless, avoidance prevailed in the platforms of their conventions. Republican delegates clearly regarded the proclamation, coming in the middle of a difficult campaign, as an additional liability for Republicans in the state.[62]

Looking back after the election, the *Trenton Gazette* commented that Republican campaigners failed to show the "justice and expediency" of Lincoln's policy until too late in the campaign. This "want of bold adherence to, and advocacy by, the Republican press and orators" in the *Gazette*'s view crippled the Republican campaign. Taking advantage of the Republicans' silence, the

Democrats meanwhile hammered home their opposition to Lincoln's proclamation, and, concluded the *Gazette*, "by false statements and unwarranted inferences turned the current of popular sentiment against it."[63]

Racist whites, both Democratic and Republican, worried about the possibility that emancipation would unleash an enormous influx of free blacks into New Jersey. The Democratic *Belvidere Journal* argued that the "present contest is a contest between the white and black races for supremacy. President Lincoln and the Abolitionists have made it so. The white race is represented by the Democratic party—the black race by the Abolition Republican party." The newspaper hammered home the message by focusing on the congressional candidates: "Steele is for the white men and their rights. Brownson is for degrading the white man and giving negroes imaginary rights. Steele would make the negroes work and support themselves. Brownson is for making white men work to support negroes."[64]

Democrats also stressed the campaign issue of trampled rights; party candidates and platforms routinely denounced arrogant officials, arbitrary arrests, and unconstitutional laws. The inalienable rights and the delegated powers of the Constitution had to be upheld in both peacetime and wartime in order to maintain both the Union and liberty.[65]

These attacks threw Republicans still further on the defensive. Bradley countered by minimizing these matters in comparison to the one great issue of saving the Union; without a country, the Constitution meant nothing. James Scovel, running for the assembly, questioned what one would do if a burglar entered one's home and held a knife to the throat of one's child. The father would not first ask the intruder whether he entered through the window or by a trap door, but would attack him. The people, announced the *Unionist*, were not fooled by "masked hypocrisy and treason that have been cloaked under the false clamor of infringing Constitutional rights." According to the *Unionist*, the "real traitor and enemy of the Constitution" was the person "who will not use means at his disposal to save the country." The *Camden Press* warned voters against Democrats who prated about the violations of their rights by Republicans but who uttered not a word of rebuke to the rebels: "Beware of those wolves in sheep's clothing."[66]

Republican speakers and editors in the campaign stressed that the cause of saving the Union dwarfed any divisive partisan issues. They portrayed Lincoln as president of the whole nation, not merely the leader of a political party. The speakers both saluted New Jersey's soldiers in their gallant defense of the Republic and sent a political message. The *Salem Standard* observed, "Our brethren of the cartridge box in Virginia must be sustained by the ballot box at home." To back the war effort, the State House had to remain in safe hands. New Jersey, warned Horace Congar, must avoid the curse of having "some quibbling traitor in the Executive position," who would sabotage the effort. The Republicans predicted that the Democrats would clog the wheels of state governments and would cripple their efforts by withholding appropriations, preventing recruitment, and refusing supplies. With the army deprived of men and materiel, the war would falter.[67]

The Republicans made loyalty the overriding issue and identified themselves with the Republic and its defense. They asserted that as the party of the government, only they could save the Union. One banner at the Republican state convention epitomized the Republican campaign message: "We know no Party but our Country." Party stalwart Cortlandt Parker declared, "Republicanism is Unionism . . . Unionism is Republicanism."[68]

In stark contrast, Republicans identified Democrats with disloyalty and treason. Although this charge generally was inaccurate and unfair, many Republicans considered it valid and voiced it frequently. In late October they began to label all antiwar Democrats copperheads, a term derived from the copperhead snake, which not only is highly venomous but also conceals itself until it strikes at its victim without warning. The *Somerville News* conceded that although not all Democrats were disloyal, just being a Democrat raised a "*suspicion* in our mind." Republicans, notably the editor of the *Newark Mercury*, drew an important distinction between those Democratic party leaders and editors who sympathized with rebels, "whose hands are at the nation's throat," and the party's rank and file, who remained largely true to the Union cause.[69]

According to the Republicans, the Democracy harbored covert subversives, secret rebel sympathizers, and noisy copperheads. During the election campaign the *Trenton Patriot* found that the disloyal assumed a "flimsy disguise of loyalty." Yet most of the time they systematically undercut the war effort by opposing the war measures of the administration, offering peace feelers to the rebels, and putting partisanship ahead of patriotism. The *Mercury* saw no way of "opposing, thwarting, weakening the Administration, and at the same time saving the country."[70]

Democrats retaliated by defending their loyalty to the country and attacking Republicans for "their flimsy disguise of Unionism." Democrats ridiculed the pious Republican proposal to abolish all parties except their own while downplaying or discarding the name of their own party. The *Morristown Banner* mocked the Republicans' supposed willingness to abandon their party stands: "No abolitionism—no black republicanism—no nigger—no nothing, but the country. Who believes this stale trick?" Democrats vigorously justified their wartime role as the loyal opposition. Vanatta told fellow Democrats, "You can no more have fire without heat than a free government without parties." Vanatta and other Democrats cautioned that "our opponents should be closely watched, and their errors and wrongs properly exposed."[71]

Democrats also asked, "Loyalty to what?" They sharply distinguished opposition to the administration from disloyalty to the government. They argued that an administration did not constitute a government any more than a watchmaker constituted a watch. The president and his officials temporarily ran an administration; the permanent government was the whole machine, including the bureaucrats and the laws. Loyalty to the country and the Constitution prevailed over loyalty to a regime or a party. In fact, the Democratic *Newton Herald* asserted, "Democracy is synonymous with loyalty—a true Democrat is a true patriot."[72]

The Republicans countered that the Democrats' differentiation between the government and the administration was a distinction without a difference; there was no possible way to support the government while opposing the administration. If Democrats rejected virtually everything the government did in trying to win the war, they stood guilty of sabotaging the war effort. Brownson pointed out that while Lincoln served his term of office, as a practical matter the "Administration is the Government, and to labor to embarrass it, or to thwart it in its efforts to conduct the war to a successful issue, is to labor to defeat the Government, and therefore the country itself."[73]

An ill-advised speech by James Courter at the Democratic Newark convention in early October added credence to Republicans' charges of Democrats' disloyalty. During an impromptu stump speech Courter denounced the accursed crew of abolitionists. He even proposed scuttling the ship of state to drown the crew. Republicans quickly capitalized on his incendiary remark as proof of disloyalty; the issue dogged Democrats for the rest of the campaign.[74]

During the campaign, politicians raised the question of giving the franchise to servicemen on duty outside the state. During the fall other states had considered doing so. Such consideration seemed unlikely for New Jersey, whose legislature did not meet until 1863. Republicans favored soldiers' voting; even one Democratic newspaper supported the idea. Without servicemen's votes, the Republicans expected that the Democrats probably would carry the state. The Democrats disputed this point, claiming that most Jersey soldiers were Democrats. One man in the Fifteenth Regiment retorted that politicians might debate whether most soldiers were Democratic or Republican, "but the true political complexion of the army is, they Know Nothing but the Union." Viewing matters in this way, most soldiers favored the Republicans. Their support of Ward was especially strong because he did so much for them. As one of them stated, "Mr. Ward is the best friend the soldier ever had in New Jersey."[75]

As the campaign reached a climax, each party presented apocalyptic visions depicting what victory by its opponents would bring. According to the *Patriot*, the Democrats would "detach New Jersey from her Union moorings and float her into the black, unfathomed sea of secession." A Jersey soldier agreed that the Republicans "must succeed or the Union is lost." Another soldier said he wished the election results would help to "overthrow this accursed, hell-born rebellion," and hoped that "while we fight the enemy here, our friends will fight the enemy at the election, by electing true Union men instead of Secesh Sympathizers." The *New Brunswick Fredonian* summed up the Republican case succinctly: "All who prefer freedom to slavery, true Democracy to slavish aristocracy, the Union to disunion, honor to dishonor . . . will vote for Mr. Ward." But "every man who prefers the preservation of slavery to the preservation of the Union; every man who has more sympathy for rebels than for loyal men . . . will vote for General Parker."[76]

The Democrats played variations on Parker's theme that New Jerseyans must save the country by defeating fanaticism and subversion, south and north. A district convention in Union County, for example, considered it the duty of every true Democrat to "put down Northern *abolitionism* at the ballot box, and the Southern *secessionism* at the point of the bayonet. There will be no peace until both factions are subdued." The *Somerville Messenger* appealed to those voters who "love the Union more than the negro" to rally behind the Democratic Union party. The *Trenton American* agreed: "That is the issue—the *negro* against the *white* man."[77]

Election Day—November 4, 1862—dawned bright and sunny. Despite the excitement of the campaign, voting was orderly and unmarred by disturbances. Northerners soon learned that an anti-Republican tide had swept across the North. Democrats won a majority of congressmen in the lower North, gained a total of thirty-four seats, and cut the Republican majority in half. (In congressional elections during 1863, however, Republicans did well in the upper North and in the border slave states, and so retained a narrow working majority in the House of Representatives.) If all the congressional elections had taken place in November 1862, Lincoln probably would have lost control of the House. He barely avoided the catastrophe of a divided government, in which the Democrats could have seriously impeded the war effort.

Lincoln took the bad news philosophically, regarding the election as a serious but temporary setback. He knew he had a country to save and a war to win. He had to find the right general in a hurry and proceeded to fire McClellan. Lincoln realized he no longer could afford to neglect the weakened Republican parties in the lower North. He would have to do everything possible to help them, including furloughing servicemen to vote at home and recruiting federal war contractors to persuade workers to vote Republican. Now that the election was over, however, it was too late to rescue New Jersey.[78]

The Democrats made great gains in state races, capturing both the governorship and the legislature in New Jersey and retaining both in Rhode Island.

In New York, Democrat Horatio Seymour became governor. In addition, Democrats won control of the state houses in Delaware, Indiana, and Illinois, and secured a majority of the joint ballot in Pennsylvania.

In numerous celebrations New Jerseyans shouted themselves hoarse for Parker. They had elected him by an astounding margin of 14,597, the largest majority yet for a gubernatorial candidate. Parker won 56.8 percent of the popular vote, the highest percentage of any Democratic statewide ticket in the North in 1862. He carried fourteen counties, losing only seven downstate. Although in half of the counties the race between Parker and Ward was relatively close, Parker built his total in urban Essex and Hudson, as well as in the rural strongholds of Bergen, Hunterdon, Monmouth, Morris, Somerset, Sussex, and Warren.[79] Given the Democratic landslide, the Republicans' claim that the soldier vote would have made a difference in the outcome appears groundless.[80]

In elections for the legislature, Democrats defeated three Republican senatorial candidates by slim majorities in Atlantic, Mercer, and Burlington, and gained ten assemblymen. With decisive control of the legislature, the Democrats would choose the next federal senator. In congressional races the Democrats won four of the five seats; they gained one seat in the second district with Middleton, a staunch war backer. In the fourth district, however, the election of noisy peace man Rogers entailed the loss of a seat occupied previously by a war champion. Even so, war supporters maintained a three-to-two majority of the state's delegation.

The election hardly represented a political revolution, if that meant a copperhead victory, but the New Jersey Democrats reached the height of their strength during the war. Since the mid-1850s the Democrats and the Opposition had roughly balanced each other. Elections had become intensely competitive. Then the Democrats' performance improved gradually after 1858, reaching its highest level in 1862 with a decisive Democratic victory. In that year the Republican percentages of the gubernatorial, congressional, and legislative votes cast were lowest in such elections since the Republicans' inception as a party. Although Democratic leaders had expected victory, the Democratic majorities far exceeded their most confident predictions. One Democratic newspaper scarcely exaggerated when its headline announced, "*Hills on Hills and Alps on Alps of Democratic Success.*"[81]

A great wave of popular disenchantment with a mismanaged war and with the military stalemate crested on Election Day and submerged the Republicans in New Jersey. Foster stated that "hundreds of mild Republicans voted to *rebuke* the Administration." In this vein the *Mercury* contended that many voters grew "indignant at the delays and inaction of the Army; wearied by the indecision and inertia of the Executive." The northerners' patience had been worn thin by the disastrous Peninsula campaign and the defeat at Second Bull Run. The "war movements have been failures," observed Congar, "and no administration can bear the burden of an unsuccessful contest." Voters, declared the *Somerville News*, were "dissatisfied with the imbecile manner in which the war has been carried on."[82]

The election, then, became Lincoln's midterm crisis. One prominent Democrat remarked later that the election was a vote of no confidence in Lincoln's leadership, for the people "do not believe in the war *as conducted by the administration.*" The *Mercury* observed that "to impute the success of the Democratic ticket to any other cause is folly." Clearly, too, Lincoln's Emancipation Proclamation and the black influx issue hurt the Republican campaign. The Democratic victory in New Jersey can be explained by popular protest against the slow progress of the war, not by agreement with the copperheads. As a soldier put it, Jersey voters did not reject Republicans because voters "thought the Administration wrong in its efforts to suppress rebellion, but because it was not right enough."[83]

The magnetic pull of personalities and parties also played a role. "Against you," Congar told Ward, "the Democrats nominated a strong candidate for Governor. He was an out and out Douglas man, and yet the traitorous Breckinridge men supported him in their hatred of Republicanism. We had nothing against him and a dominant party for him." Parker's unionist credentials, his personal popularity, and the united support by his party's rank and file added up to formidable advantages. The Republicans had made a good choice in Ward, but they could have done better by nominating a likeminded Democrat. The Democrats' selection of Parker proved a masterstroke.[84]

Ecstatic Democrats interpreted the election returns according to their persuasion. The minority peace men, represented by the *Newark Journal*, gloated, "Uncle Abraham will hear the thunder at the White House and make a note of the fact that the Jersey blues are aroused in defense of their own rights and liberties." The *Journal* proclaimed that the people had forced Lincoln's reign of terror to end, although only war opponents had concerned primarily themselves with this issue.[85]

Most Democrats regarded the election result as a rebuke to Republican radicalism, a "denunciation of the policy of the Administration in converting the war into an Abolition crusade," in the words of the prowar *Camden Democrat*. Democratic newspapers asked Lincoln to withdraw his proclamation of emancipation. Despite its pacifistic penchant, the *Journal* conceded that the triumphant Democrats remained pledged to a "vigorous prosecution of the war to put down the rebellion." Most New Jerseyans, including most Democrats, still backed the war.[86]

As for the future, Republican attitudes ranged from the philosophical to the pessimistic. Ira M. Harrison, a Newark businessman, observed optimistically: "I suppose you will regard the recent Democratic triumphs in our elections as foreboding evil. I do not. They have gone before the people and declared for a vigorous prosecution of the War." Others were unnerved by the election. One Monmouth man confessed, "I have never felt so completely disheartened." As consolation for Republican leaders, the election ended the awkward difficulty of sharing power and responsibility with the Democrats in the State House. Without a Republican governor, Republicans in the future could run negative campaigns against the incumbent Democrats.[87]

Observers in both parties wondered how the Democratic party—now "almost overgrown"—would conduct itself. Many people asked themselves whether an unopposed Democratic party in the State House would continue its role of loyal opposition to Lincoln's administration. Celebrating victory in Newark two weeks after the election, the Democrats revealed their differences by giving either nationalist or state rightist toasts. Observers, too, wondered what political driftwood was carried on the high tide to the State House. Even Democrats worried whether Democratic leaders could control the new recruits, the eager opportunists, and the rash copperheads in the new legislature. Speaking for the Republicans, Quinby predicted, "We are likely to have a rather disagreeable time of it, then, this winter with a strong majority in both houses against us."[88]

# 9 The Perils of Power: Democratic Factionalism in Early 1863

On January 1, 1863, Lincoln declared free all slaves in enemy territory. At a meeting in Jersey City, seventy-five blacks and five whites honored the Emancipation Proclamation. Black religious leader Henry Highland Garnet described it as "the most able, manly and important document ever penned by man," and encouraged Negroes to volunteer for the army and fight for their freedom. Garnet asked whites to consider the black man's fighting ability over the color of his skin. He assured them that black soldiers wished to stand not ahead or behind white soldiers, but beside them as equals.

Participants in the meeting cheered Lincoln. Then one individual proposed three cheers for the state government of New Jersey, but several persons objected: blacks found New Jersey a hard place in which to thrive because whites blocked entrance to the voting booth and the neighborhood school. In a compromise, Garnet urged the group to praise emancipation and pray for its opponents.[1]

Although the Emancipation Proclamation united blacks, it divided whites and exacerbated differences within as well as between the political parties in New Jersey. Antiwar editors denounced the declaration as wrong in both principle and law. The *Trenton American* called it the "most stupendous act of folly and usurpation" ever perpetrated by an American president. In the editor's opinion, Lincoln had changed the war's purpose from preservation of the Union to revolution in the cause of emancipation. If emancipation supposedly was so noble, he asked sarcastically, why did it not apply to the loyal slave states remaining in the Union?[2]

The *Newark Journal* expected that the proclamation would turn the North against Lincoln. His folly soon would leave him powerless and thus unable to "curse the country" any longer. Similarly, the *Somerville Messenger* observed mockingly that with this absurd tyranny "Lincoln has certainly out-Lincolned Lincoln." Because he had violated the rights of property and assumed powers never granted a president under the pretext of military necessity, "there is no use of a Constitution and no limit to the powers of our Autocrat." After all, "if he can trample with impunity upon one section of the Constitution, he can trample upon all the rest."[3]

Prowar Democrats also strongly opposed Lincoln's policy, but for more pragmatic reasons. The *Camden Democrat* contended that Lincoln had signed the proclamation only to placate the abolitionists. Moreover, it struck them as fruitless because Lincoln merely had "freed all the slaves *not in his possession.*" The Democrats dismissed the declaration as an empty gesture because it freed no slaves except on paper. At the same time, they believed, the edict would stiffen southern resolve. Facing the fact that emancipation would result if they lost the war, southerners would redouble their resolve to fight and thus would make restoration of the Union impossible.[4]

Some Republican newspapers supported Lincoln's proclamation unreservedly. The *Camden Press* considered the decree Lincoln's most important state paper because it wiped out that curse—slavery—"repugnant to every feeling of humanity." The Union League's Trenton chapter likened Lincoln's emancipation policy to the "club of Hercules destroying the Hydra-headed serpent of Rebellion." For every traitor killed, a loyal freeman would take his place. Now the Union army, instead of protecting slavery by hunting runaways, could wage total war against the South.[5]

Other Republican journals gave only qualified approval. According to the more radical *Paterson Guardian,* Lincoln's delay in making the proclamation had diminished its potency. "We fear it is too late, yet hail it as something." The newspaper grudgingly conceded that the "*effect* of this proclamation will tend to the good of humanity." The moderate *Princeton Standard* believed that a white backlash against abolition had spent itself in Republican defeats in 1862, and hoped the decree would now hasten the end of the rebellion. The often moderate Republican *Newark Advertiser* again expressed ambivalence: it hailed emancipation as "the most momentous event of our history—if not of modern times," but cautioned about its unknown consequences.[6]

New Jersey troops also disagreed about emancipation. Many men disapproved; they did not sympathize with blacks and did not wish to battle for the freedom of blacks. One Newton man serving in the Twenty-seventh Regiment complained in a Democratic newspaper that "we are fighting for the Negro and the Negro only—no Union or Constitution about it." Another trooper observed that "when we enlisted it was done under the impulse of the moment. Fort Sumter had been attacked; our glorious old flag had been fired upon and insulted by a people who should have been first to protect it; Washington, our Capital, was in danger. We, looking only to the present, rushed to our country's call to support the *laws* and *Constitution.* But is that what we are fighting for now? No sir."[7]

Some soldiers, however, viewed Lincoln's action differently. Impassioned James Rusling in the Fifth Regiment earlier had characterized slavery as "this 'sum of all villainies'—this sin against God and crime against humanity." He then asked: "Why should we longer permit it to brutalize and barbarize four millions of our citizens, who not only love the Union but are panting and eager to speak and to fight for it. . . . why longer hesitate to strike with a rod of iron this hoary wrong that seeks to erect a despotism over the grave of

Liberty?" One Paterson trooper declared he was "fighting for freedom. Every day makes me gather more hatred toward the South when I see the poor black people coming over here at the risk of their lives to gain their freedom, with their backs all lacerated with scars—It will make any man with common sense to cry out against the South." A man in the Fifteenth Regiment, however, asserted, "We are not fighting for the negro—we are battling for the stability of free institutions—for the supremacy of the laws." A member of the Twelfth Regiment enlarged on this view: "We have heard men say that this is a war for the purpose of destroying the institution of slavery. So it is; that peculiar institution is the foundation of the rebellion, and in order to defeat the enemies of our government in open revolt, it is compulsory to destroy their power, no matter what influence is brought to bear upon them." Whether as an end in itself or as a means to an end, some New Jersey troops accepted abolition.[8]

No measured responses came from the copperheads, a minority of New Jersey Democrats that opposed both emancipation and war. Pointing out that politics is not merely numbers but intensity, Englishman Edmund Burke in 1792 had compared the political roles of the inert majority and of a determined minority. Burke observed that minority activists, "more expedite, awakened, active, vigorous and courageous, who make amends for what they want in weight by their superabundance of velocity, will create an acting power of the greatest possible strength."[9]

This characterization described New Jersey's copperheads. Bold, apocalyptic reactionaries, voicing polarized positions, they advanced their cause by any means they could. They compensated for their lack of supporters by single-minded drive. Although the state's copperheads did not reflect dominant opinion, their spokesmen received enormous publicity through the use of shrewd timing, sensationalistic style, and aggressive tactics.

Copperhead editors wrote fiery editorials. Sometimes their trenchant criticism hit home, but often their windy editorials reflected rigid, ritualistic posturing. Their rhetoric mixed stale, heavy-handed declamations with ponderous, repetitive tirades. Enjoying the martyrdom of a besieged political minority, these iconoclastic, demagogic editors frequently preached not so much to persuade and convert as to pander to the true believers.

Caught up in their own rhetoric with its webs of constitutional theory, the copperheads frequently ignored practical politics. War supporters denounced copperhead editors as a nuisance and even a menace. The Republican *Newton Register* condemned them as "peddlers of sedition." The prowar Democratic *Jersey City Standard*, although highly critical of Lincoln's policies, castigated the copperheads for incorrectly charging Lincoln's administration with repression of opponents and suppression of democracy.[10]

Many copperhead editors in New Jersey had no previous connections with the state. None of the editors of the leading antiwar dailies was a native New

Jerseyan. David Naar of the *Trenton American* had migrated from the West Indies. Andrew Mead of the *Paterson Register* hailed from Connecticut; Edward Fuller of the *Newark Journal*, from New Hampshire. Eben Winton of the *Hackensack Democrat* had immigrated from England. The *Democrat*'s first owner, editorial firebrand C. Chauncey Burr, came from New York. He founded a journal which he appropriately named *The Old Guard*.[11]

Copperhead politicians drew recruits heavily, although not exclusively, from the ranks of New Jerseyans who had supported Buchanan and his policies in the 1850s and Breckinridge in 1860. Espousing what they called pure Democracy, they championed untrammeled individual and state rights in time of war. Their leaders included James Wall, Rodman Price, Nehemiah Perry, and Andrew Rogers. In the legislature two Bergen politicians led the copperheads: Senator Daniel Holsman, once a Philadelphian, and Assemblyman Thomas Dunn English, a former New Yorker who had lived in Virginia. Despite their scant political credentials, these intense, impatient copperheads demonstrated ability as speakers and writers. As self-appointed crusaders, they relished debate and controversy. They loved to launch a thunderbolt and eagerly awaited the results.[12]

During the war years copperhead legislators dominated the delegations from Bergen and Warren. In addition, copperheads held most of the Union and Hunterdon seats. These latter three counties formed part of the third congressional district. A majority of the copperheads were elected in the Democratic landslide of 1862. As a result, in the 1863 legislative session, the copperhead assemblymen hailed from twelve counties, mainly rural areas and mostly Democratic strongholds in North Jersey. Those copperhead assemblymen monopolized the entire delegation from Bergen, Warren, Union, and Salem, and accounted for two-thirds of the delegation from Hunterdon and Monmouth.[13]

Many people considered Bergen County the state's copperhead center. Nonetheless, Union men from Bergen remained active throughout the war, and some of its leaders joined forces with other unionists in various statewide movements. In fact, in November 1861 the county's voters in the first district elected a Democratic war supporter and rejected a prominent war opponent. After 1861, however, only copperheads represented Bergen in the legislature.

Why did Bergen show this political penchant? Some observers have linked the county's supposed copperhead sympathies to its large number of Dutch descendants, with their reputed conservatism and significant representation as leaders of the copperhead faction. Yet many major figures, both in the county's Republican party and in the unionist faction of the Democracy, also had Dutch surnames. The war and the war effort divided many Dutch Americans, as well as other Americans. (In the Middle West many Dutch favored the Union and voted Republican during the war.) Moreover, English surnames appeared among the county's copperhead leaders as well. In any case it is difficult to distinguish Dutch residents with Anglicized surnames from residents with British and German backgrounds.[14]

Dutch language, customs, and influences, moreover, had declined through assimilation, intermarriage, and an influx of new residents. New Jersey's ethnic diversity and cosmopolitan influences, radiating from nearby Paterson and Newark, disrupted folkways even among the close-knit, inward-looking, apolitical Dutch American farmers in sparsely populated Bergen. In addition, recent immigration of Dutch to the state, especially to Passaic and Bergen, created sharp cultural and religious differences between the old Dutch settlers and the Dutch newcomers. Thus it is risky to identify specific traits with one particular ethnic group; this process ignores complexity, change, individual characteristics, and historical developments. Nevertheless, differences between the native-born and the foreign-born, or between one ethnic or religious group and another, existed and presented challenges for inhabitants and politicians alike.[15]

Some people have claimed a link between copperheads and the Dutch Reformers. The Dutch Reformed Church had the fourth largest membership in the state. During the four decades before the Civil War, explosive religious schisms had racked the church and had left it fragmented. One small conservative splinter sect, the True Reformed Dutch Church, which was concentrated in Bergen and Passaic, took no official position on the war (or on any public question, for that matter). Most of its members evidently held conservative social and political views and probably opposed abolitionists and Republicans. Larger wings of the Reformed Church emphatically supported the war. In 1864 the small Christian Reformed Church, which maintained some congregations in Passaic, even refused communion to copperhead members. Most important, the largest and most mainline group, the Reformed Dutch Church, adopted resolutions in strong support of the war and Lincoln's leadership. Indeed, by 1864 it eagerly anticipated the end of slavery.

For the great majority of Reformed Church parishioners, membership could not be equated with political conservatism. It is suggestive that although more members of the Reformed Church resided in Somerset County than elsewhere, fewer copperhead activities occurred there than in Bergen County. In the populous northeastern counties, where the Reformed Church maintained most of its congregations, no discernible connection between the church and the copperheads can be found.[16]

Possibly Bergen served as the stalking horse for antiwar New York politicians from nearby Rockland and Westchester counties as well as New York City. Certain copperhead leaders in Bergen had close ties to many of New York's leading copperheads. In particular, a number of articulate county residents held common political views and happened to live in or around

Hackensack. Gradually people identified Bergen County with this particular clique of publicists and politicians. Most important, entrenched party factions that had backed Vallandigham during the war expressed the most recent manifestation of political extremism. Except in Lodi, the Democratic party monopolized power in the county between 1862 and 1864 without the usual checks and restraints of two-party competition.

Widespread disloyalty did not manifest itself in Bergen during the Civil War, however, and reactionary rhetoric did not lead to revolutionary action. No significant movement formed to resist recruitment, encourage desertion, or engage in sedition. Despite wild rumors and isolated incidents, the county saw no mob violence, race riots, espionage networks, sabotage, or guerrilla skirmishes. Instead the people of Bergen did their patriotic duty, as did other New Jerseyans. The county, according to one report, filled its quota of recruits for army duty. Indeed, rural central New Jersey, which formed the third congressional district, posed more recruitment problems for federal officials than Bergen did.[17]

The activity of two demagogues who lived in Bergen during the war helped to shape the popular view of the county and to make it conspicuous, even notorious. Burr and English—who had stirred up so much animosity at public meetings throughout the state that riots nearly broke out, and who escaped only narrowly with their lives—incorrectly came to symbolize the county in the minds of many people. Copperheads outside New Jersey lionized both men as spokesmen for the Jersey Democracy and extravagantly praised the county and the state for their association with them. Republicans, however, within and outside the state, excoriated both of these two extremist copperheads and the county's residents as a whole. As the *Newark Mercury* observed sarcastically, "It should be remembered by those who regard New Jersey as out of the United States that Bergen is out of the world." The *Jersey City Chronicle* referred to "our Egyptian county of Bergen." In fact, the county resembled Warren, where most wartime legislators and some other individuals also expressed copperhead sentiments. Yet the stereotype of a copperhead-infested Bergen endured.[18]

Emboldened both by the war's poor progress and by the attention they received, copperheads pressured the legislature to pass antiwar measures. In a speech delivered at a March meeting in Trenton, Naar declared, "We are not now fighting for the Constitution and Union, but for the freedom of the negro. We are cutting each other's throats for the sake of a few worthless negroes." Naar deplored the fact that after two years of war the North had little to show for the millions of dollars spent and the thousands of lives lost. Yet at the same time he boasted about the fighting prowess of New Jersey's troops and suggested that they could be employed to prevent the federal government from oppressing New Jerseyans. Warning Lincoln not to ignore their wishes, Naar added that Jersey boys "charge as though the enemy were a field of cornstalks. There is no give in in the New Jersey regiments, and there will be no give in in those who are left at home."[19]

English, speaking bluntly at a January meeting in Fort Lee, warned that if Lincoln did not respond to the popular demand to change his policy, Democrats must turn their cannon on the federal government. Burr, in a speech delivered in Philadelphia in February, branded Lincoln a greater traitor than Jefferson Davis; Davis merely contested territory, while Lincoln assaulted the Constitution. Vallandigham, in an address at Newark in mid-February, denounced Lincoln's unnecessary war to loud applause, but his plan to coax the rebels back into the Union found few sympathizers. One Newark Republican commented that Vallandigham's speech "here has done good, brought our people together and made them mad—and frightened some of the Democrats."[20]

Meanwhile the Union's military situation deteriorated. The bloody defeat at Fredericksburg in December 1862 shattered northern morale. People complained about inflation, taxes, mounting debt, and additional calls for troops. Although the Republicans did not question the purposes of the war, they, too, bemoaned its bungled execution. Radical Orestes Brownson hoped Lincoln would resign. Journalist John Foster condemned Lincoln's indecisiveness and the inaction of his generals. He contended that only military victories could restore public confidence.[21]

Democratic politicians exploited the growing discontent. Then, in February, Lincoln's government arrested several Democratic journalists outside the state on charges of sedition. In early March, Congress imposed national conscription with federal supervision, and authorized suspension of the writ of habeas corpus at Lincoln's discretion. On both measures, New Jersey's congressmen divided along party lines. Such measures infuriated the Democrats, especially the copperheads. To them it provided proof that the Republicans refused to recognize the meaning of the autumn elections. In the face of widespread discontent, Lincoln had not budged an inch after all. He had not shifted his policy or changed his cabinet. In fact, the Democrats asserted, radical Republicans steadily gained influence in his administration. Bowing to their demands, Lincoln had embraced emancipation and fired McClellan. "Fanaticism reigns supreme at Washington," railed the copperhead *New Brunswick Times*.[22]

The copperheads decided to force a showdown. Because the ballot box had failed to represent the voice of the people, the *Times* threatened, "they will speak in another and a more emphatic way." Somehow Lincoln's "senseless war" had to end. Earlier, New Jerseyans commonly had branded such talk unpatriotic. Now, war supporter Foster observed, "treason is talked as loudly on every street corner, North, as it ever was at the Confederate capital." Jetur Riggs now considered it safe to utter antiwar views: "It has been till quite recently somewhat dangerous to avow them openly. But the time has now come in my judgment when true patriotism demands action to be taken to stop this Suicidal War."[23]

The midwar crisis that began in 1862 gained momentum in early 1863. The legislatures of Pennsylvania, Indiana, and Illinois elected feisty Democrats to the United States Senate to challenge Lincoln's war measures. In spring election campaigns the Democrats, especially those who opposed the war, maneuvered for advantage. Connecticut Democrats endorsed an antiwar platform. Both there and in New Hampshire, Democrats nominated antiwar candidates for governor. In the fall, Democrats in Pennsylvania and Ohio followed suit. Some northerners worried that Republican defeat endangered popular support for the war. "This political battle, quite as much as any other," warned the Republican *New York Times*, "will decide the fate of the Union."[24]

The reaction also struck New Jersey. Democrats eagerly anticipated dominating both the executive and the legislative branches of the state government for the first time in six years. Bipartisan observers envisioned Democratic majorities too large to be controlled by party leaders. Democratic war supporters in particular feared that copperheads would undermine the state's war effort. As Cumberland County Democrat Lucius Q. C. Elmer advised, "We have radical Democrats, as well as radical Republicans, and both are dangerous. If we can only have patience and wait, I do not fear the result, but I do fear any precipitate action. A 'masterly inactivity' is in my opinion the true policy of the Democrats, just now." According to this strategy, the legislature should confine itself strictly to state business and should let the Republicans in Washington mismanage national affairs until the Democrats came to the rescue in the presidential election of 1864.[25]

Republicans also worried about the havoc copperheads might wreak in the legislature. In his final annual message, Olden opposed any change that would weaken the national government's ability to put down rebellion. "We want peace," he declared, "but not until those in arms against the Government are overcome." The *Mercury* praised this position. "If ever such words were needed, it is now, when desperate men are striving . . . to plunge the country into the vortex of anarchy, and to sell us, bound hand and foot, into the hands of our enemies."[26]

On Inauguration Day, January 20, 1863, numerous country wagons, decorated with colorful bunting and packed with eager visitors, rattled into Trenton. Sixteen militia units, in close formation and short of breath, paraded. Immense crowds formed to cheer the new governor. Spectators crowded the State House and the grounds, while invited guests jammed the senate chamber. Instead of delivering his address in the chamber, as was customary, Parker walked to the rear of the building and delivered his address from the south portico to the large crowd below.[27]

Laying to rest both unfounded fears and exaggerated hopes, Parker's speech contained nothing new. Parker reassured both peace advocates and war supporters. He appealed to state pride and goodwill by complimenting Olden on leaving the state treasury in sound condition. Parker also proposed revitalizing the state militia in order to defend the state from invasion. He endorsed prompt payment of New Jersey's servicemen and better care for the wounded.

Parker devoted most of his address to national affairs. He reiterated his support for efforts to suppress rebellion and secure reunion. Parker repudiated the theory that a state could secede from a perpetual Union, and found no grievances to justify revolution. Yet even while he was cold to the Confederates and their sympathizers, he defended both the lawful rights of the states and the unfettered liberties of the people. This point struck him as especially compelling in time of war, when popular passions ran high and federal power tended to encroach on law and liberties. Parker criticized Lincoln for his exaggerated interpretation of the war power when, by presidential fiat, he ordered arbitrary arrests and imposed emancipation. Emancipation, Parker feared, would only prolong the war. He hoped the matter would be postponed until after the war, when the people in the states could emancipate voluntarily and gradually without federal compulsion. As a member of the loyal opposition, he urged Lincoln to return to a constitutional conduct of the war.

In the meantime, Parker asked citizens not to violate the law, as did the rebels, the radicals, and federal officials. He cautioned them to exercise self-restraint and to tolerate the opinions of others. Such statements were neither novel nor unexpected. Parker, however, suggested by indirection that negotiation might play a role: "We should not be afraid of peace—an honorable and permanent peace—whether it come by the exercise of power, or by the exercise of conciliation." This ambivalent remark stood at variance with Parker's unqualified support of the war. Yet he did not endorse negotiations; instead he merely left the door open a crack.[28]

People of every shade of opinion found something pleasing in Parker's deft address. The Democrats agreed with Parker's stringent criticism of Lincoln's policy. War supporters in the Democratic camp, such as the *Jersey City Standard*, praised Parker for his promise that New Jersey would not array itself against the federal government. Parker's speech struck many observers as remarkably similar to the inaugural address of New York's Horatio Seymour. Both governors protested the purported unlawful assumption of power by Lincoln's government but pledged support to Lincoln's administration in waging war. In a swipe at the Republicans, the *Trenton American* found Parker's speech "loyal—if not according to the abolition standard of loyalty—at least so to those who make fidelity to the Constitution the test of loyalty."[29]

On the whole, the antiwar faction liked Parker's speech. Only the *Newark*

*Journal* had a mild word of criticism: the governor did not "fully represent the rapidly growing peace sentiments of the people" because the peace movement had not yet assumed tangible form. The copperheads evidently hoped for a political honeymoon with Parker.[30]

Republicans, especially moderates, congratulated Parker for maintaining his unionist resolve in the face of copperhead pressure, but they nevertheless mixed sharp criticism with their compliments. Parker, the Republicans observed, attempted to sit on two stools at once. War supporters had expected more resolve from him. A testy *New York Times* correspondent considered Parker too soft on the rebels to "command the respect of loyal men." A *Mercury* reporter, however, sensed too little sting and not enough poison in his "mean, narrow, carping partisanship" to satisfy the peace hunters. The censorious *New York Tribune* regarded the speech as "decidedly opposed to the Administration, and as artfully in favor of the Rebels as the warmest Secessionist could desire." Most New Jersey Republicans did not share this view, but they worried about whether Parker would give in to future copperhead pressure.[31]

The legislature convened in mid-January. The Democrats elected Anthony Reckless of Shrewsbury as president of the senate and James T. Crowell of Perth Amboy as assembly speaker. Both men exercised considerable power, because they made the appointments to committees. Neither had sided previously with the antiwar faction; both had supported full funding for the war in 1861. Upon taking the chair, Reckless delivered a careful message with a decidedly unionist theme. In contrast, Crowell failed to mention the Union cause. Instead he critiqued federal policy with an apocalyptic vision: "Now when clouds and darkness overshadow our land—when war and confusion hold high carnival in our midst, when the rights of the citizen and the State may be placed in jeopardy at any hour," the legislature should take care to guard the interests of the state against the presumed federal menace.[32]

Distribution of patronage also underscored the differences between the senate and the assembly. Senate Democrats selected two prowar editors for the major posts: Morris Hamilton as secretary and Louis Vogt of the *Morristown Banner* as printer. In contrast, the assembly gave assorted jobs and printing plums to some of the most outspoken copperhead editors in the state. Even to prowar assembly Democrats, support of party publications was paramount.[33]

During the first three months of 1863, copperheads across the North agitated for an immediate end to the war. They demanded that their legislatures adopt resolutions favoring an unilateral armistice and direct negotiations with the rebels. Democrats in the Delaware legislature called for a cease-fire. In Indiana and Illinois the Democrats, who dominated both legislatures, struggled with Republican governors. In Illinois, the lower chamber of the legislature actually approved antiwar resolutions. When Republican legislators walked out, however, the Republican governor temporarily suspended the session for lack of a quorum. In Indiana, Republicans tried to prevent passage of similar resolutions and to block legislative interference with the militia. The Republicans finally withdrew from the legislature, forcing it to adjourn indefinitely and leaving the Republican governor to operate the state government for two years without appropriations. In Pennsylvania, the Democrats in the lower chamber endorsed resolutions calling for a peace conference. The antiwar feeling threatened to tear the North apart.[34]

Antiwar sentiment found favor in New Jersey as well. Copperheads demanded approval of antiwar resolutions, a buildup of the state militia as a counterweight to the federal government, election of a copperhead to the United States Senate, and exclusion of emancipated slaves from the state. Reports circulated during December that copperhead legislators had concocted plans to call for an armistice and peace negotiations with the South.[35]

As soon as the state senate organized on January 13, the first day of the session, Holsman opened fire. He offered a sweeping series of resolutions condemning Republican war measures. Lincoln's violations of liberty, Holsman maintained, had turned everything in the North topsy-turvy: "Legislation is now called proclamation, servility is called loyalty, free thought is called disloyalty, free speech is treason, abolishing slavery is a military necessity, changing generals is a political necessity, a war for liberty shows the folly of habeas corpus, and an emancipation war [is] one which enslaves the people. The President's power in war is unlimited except to make peace; the most capricious usurpation is the most constitutional interpolation; Presidential caprice is political truth; cracking jokes is the essence of statecraft."[36]

Holsman in particular demanded that the legislature endorse the declaration of an immediate, unilateral armistice for six months. During the third month elected delegates from all the states, both loyal and rebel, could attend a peace conference to hammer out an agreement. Without submitting these important resolutions to a party caucus, Holsman struck boldly on his own. He breached the defenses by his surprise attack.[37]

Stunned by Holsman's sudden onslaught, no colleague, Democrat or Republican, objected immediately. Some doubtless lacked the courage to speak up. Others probably kept quiet because patronage considerations were uppermost in their minds. Still others bided their time. The Republicans probably hoped the Democrats would embarrass themselves.

Protest came within days. Both Republicans and Democrats vigorously denounced Holsman's attempt to push his resolutions through the senate before opponents had time to organize. Regular Democrats, including Hamilton in his newspaper, took Holsman to task for not taking party leaders into his confidence beforehand. Opponents censured Holsman's sudden shift from the previous year's Democratic platform, which pledged unswerving unionist loyalty. Peace men of Holsman's stripe, prowar Democrats declared, did not speak for most Democrats in the state. As to the copperheads' claim that the recent state election constituted a mandate for abandoning the war, independent Democratic senator Joseph Crowell retorted, "I deny the assertion. The Democracy went into the late canvass as a *War Party, in favor of a more vigorous prosecution of the contest.*" Drawing on numerous quotations from various Democratic platforms and speeches in the recent campaign, Crowell cogently demonstrated that the election result did not represent a condemnation of the war.[38]

Especially unpalatable were Holsman's call for a unilateral armistice and his insistence on peace negotiations without first setting conditions. The South had started the war, the prowar Democratic *Newton Herald* pointed out, so it retained sole responsibility for requesting an armistice. Among copperhead newspapers, only the *Hackensack Democrat* and the *Hackettstown Gazette* endorsed Holsman's resolutions explicitly. A Trenton Republican remarked that most New Jersey Democrats remained unready to "bow the knee to red-handed rebellion, and beg pardon for daring to take up the sword in defense of the Union."[39]

Among the Republicans, Holsman's proposal invited ridicule. They found it absurd to suppose that Lincoln would act at the request of a Democratic legislature and would tolerate a state government's meddling in federal matters. Republicans were astonished by the notion that Lincoln would virtually acknowledge the independence of the Confederacy by conferring with its representatives. Alarmed Republicans declared that peace by barter with "beggars for peace" would carry the terrible price of humiliating surrender. The *Newton Register* warned, "It won't do to cry Peace, when there is no Peace." It added, "It won't do to expose the throat of this great nation to be cut by Jeff Davis."[40]

Peace, if it meant anything at all, had to be won, not made. Permanent peace, in the words of the *Somerville News*, required suppression of "this Rebellion, as rebellion." The *Lambertville Beacon* agreed: "If we can conquer the rebellion, there is no necessity for compromise on our part; if the rebels cannot be conquered, there is no necessity for them to compromise with us." Moreover, because American government was rooted in the "right of the majority to govern," to compromise with a minority in rebellion would only encourage a future minority to refuse acceptance of the majority's decision. Accordingly, the Republicans introduced their own resolutions defending Lincoln's administration and backing its war effort.[41]

Democratic war hawks meanwhile mounted a skilled counterattack. Against the wishes of leading copperheads, a bipartisan coalition of war supporters maneuvered to create a joint committee on federal relations. The proponents wished to use the committee to either reshape or kill Holsman's resolutions. In a major test vote in the assembly on January 21, 1863, twenty copperheads opposed formation of the committee, but the legislature approved the plan. All three of the senate members appointed to the committee supported the war. Except for English, appointees from the assembly did not include any avowed copperhead. The war supporters claimed victory.[42]

Representing the Parker Democrats, Senator Theodore Randolph on February 4 presented a series of resolutions to replace Holsman's. Randolph's more specific, more limited version actually presented a more powerful critique of supposedly illegal federal war measures. He singled out the dismemberment of Virginia by the creation of West Virginia, military interference with the civil government in places far from the battlefront, arbitrary arrests, and the Emancipation Proclamation. Unlike some copperheads, however, he did not urge resistance to paying federal taxes for emancipating slaves or encourage defiance of the federal conscription law. Unlike Holsman, Randolph denounced neither the appointment of military governors nor infringement of a free press, nor did he assert or imply state sovereignty.[43]

In effect, Randolph's proposals called on Lincoln to execute a midcourse correction by ending alleged excesses. If Lincoln failed to do so, the Democrats had useful issues in store for future campaigns. They had expressed displeasure with Lincoln's prosecution of the war and had exploited public uneasiness with his policies.

As for the central copperhead demand for a unilateral cease-fire, war supporter Randolph dismissed an armistice or negotiations as futile and unnecessary. The rebels already had scorned peace feelers.

Randolph's and Holsman's positions on this pivotal matter represented the fundamental difference between the two Democratic factions. In a letter to Wall, Holsman accused Randolph of promoting his alternative out of fear of losing influence to Holsman in the senate. Holsman understood that the "fight will be upon the armistice."[44]

Even Randolph's more moderate resolutions found no favor with the Republicans, who complained that Randolph denounced them but not the rebels. As in other states at this time, his Democratic manifesto criticized war measures but did not condemn the insurrection that made them necessary. Republicans pointed out that Randolph did not offer a single constructive suggestion for a more effective prosecution of the war. The *Mercury*'s Trenton reporter observed, "Any fool can complain. Shame on those who insist upon tearing open afresh the gaping wounds the Republic has received." An editorial in the *Mercury* advised Democratic legislators to stop putting down the rebellion by mere resolutions; paper pellets inflicted no damage. In any event, approval of such resolutions by other northern legislatures had no chance from the outset because Republicans controlled most of those legislatures. More important, the earlier spate of resolutions favoring peace in many legislatures in the secession winter of 1861 had not prevented war. The recent flurry on the part of a few legislatures did not make peace any more likely in the winter of 1863.[45]

On February 11, after a month of controversy, the Democratic caucus discussed the conflicting approaches. Randolph, along with Lyman A. Chandler, Robert Hamilton, Edward Scudder, and Jacob Vanatta, led the hawks. John Y. Dater, English, and Holsman represented war opponents. The debate grew acrimonious as the meeting dragged on toward midnight. Finally the caucus voted by a margin of two-thirds to endorse the majority report of the joint committee on federal relations, thus repudiating the copperheads' position. The majority report accepted all of Randolph's original resolutions except the last, which scoffed at negotiations with the rebels. To placate some peace men and to secure their future support on this and other pending matters, the majority report tacked on a futile, even farcical, recommendation that Lincoln consider dispatching emissaries to the Confederate capital. They could investigate the possibilities of peace, provided that Lincoln judged this arrangement "consistent with the honor and dignity of the national government." The resolution, then, did not bypass federal authority but left the matter up to Lincoln; the majority knew he could be relied on to do nothing.[46]

The copperheads stormed out of the caucus meeting. Thus the dividing line between party regulars and party mavericks turned on whether the North should declare an immediate armistice. The Parkerites would have nothing to do with it; the copperheads made it their principal demand. Legislators faced a choice between Randolph's resolutions, which protested Lincoln's policies, and Holsman's resolutions, which endorsed peace on any terms. By preferring Randolph's resolutions, most Democrats in the legislature emphatically rejected ending the war, repudiating the Union cause, or surrendering to the rebels. By spurning the peace resolutions advanced by the copperheads, the Democratic members demonstrated how little most of them sympathized with the copperhead cause.[47]

After the Democratic caucus, a long, spirited debate on the resolutions took place in both chambers of the legislature. This exchange covered no new ground and changed few votes; passage appeared to be a foregone conclusion. The debate, however, underscored again the profound differences between the Democracy's peace and war wings. The senate on February 26 and the assembly on March 17 accepted Randolph's revised resolutions by straight party votes. Only independent Democrat James Scovel, a unionist, voted against the pending proposal. In the end, believing half a loaf to be better than none, Holsman, English, and their copperhead followers supported Randolph's version. Some Democratic legislators reportedly congratulated themselves by "imagining Old Abe nearly scared out of his boots." Having scuttled unacceptable copperhead demands and thus limited the damage, Parker quietly signed the joint resolution on March 24.[48]

Though stripped of unilateral initiatives and of a call for an armistice, both the interim and the final resolutions embarrassed a great many New Jerseyans and distorted the state's reputation in the eyes of Republicans inside and outside the state. Republican newspapers pictured copperheads running rampant across the state. The indignant *New York Tribune*, displaying both ignorance and arrogance, discovered that the "infamous" resolutions approved by the "infamous" legislature had historical roots: "Now, as in the Revolution, New Jersey is earning a reputation for being the chosen home of Tories and Traitors." A newspaper in Washington carried the blazing headline: "*Treason in the New Jersey Legislature.*" Newsboys cried the same words on every street corner in that city. In this atmosphere a Washington correspondent reported to his Jersey readers that the "Copperhead Democracy of your State Legislature, and their abettors throughout the State, seem to have very little conception of the evil they are inflicting upon the loyal name of the 'Jersey Blues.'" Incorrectly characterizing the legislature as under copperhead control, the *New York Times* dubbed New Jersey a "peace State," at the same time contemptuously dismissing New Jersey's action as inconsequential in view of the state's insignificant size and population.[49]

Some New Jerseyans were taunted as traitors and cowards on the streets of New York City and Philadelphia. Congress, angered by the resolutions, refused to appropriate funds for an ordnance factory in Weehawken. Republican journals once again ridiculed New Jersey as a reactionary backwater. Abolitionists also libeled New Jerseyans' loyalty and integrity. Overnight the state became the talk, even the scandal, of the North. On the opposite side, the reactionaries, for the same wrong reasons, praised New Jersey. A Democratic newspaper declared, "A war for the Union and the supremacy of the Constitution is all New Jersey can support. She protests solemnly against a war waged for the freeing of the slaves." This copperhead reputation unjustifiably gained wider credence. Yet one former New Jerseyan remained skeptical: "I am far from believing that any large portion of the people of New Jersey or of any state in the North are disloyal to the country."[50]

Surely New Jerseyans had to shoulder part of the blame for their notoriety. Both sides had indulged in name-calling and hyperbole. Jersey Republicans had indiscriminately accused all state Democrats of treason. Upon approval of the resolutions, the *Mercury* carried the title: "New Jersey Debased." The *Advertiser* ran a story under the headline "New Jersey's Dishonor." Some New Jerseyans conveniently blamed the trouble on outsiders. Recalling the colonial quip, one Newark Republican assemblyman likened New Jersey to a barrel tapped at both ends by copperheads from Philadelphia and New York City, who made all the patriotic cider of New Jersey run out. Whatever the cause, many found the state marching out of step with fellow northerners. A Republican physician from Gloucester remarked that the "majority in our Legislature have made themselves the Laughing Stock of all Loyal people."[51]

Democratic war supporters were appalled. A week after approval of Randolph's resolutions, they hastily decided to repair the reputation of both the state and its Democratic party. On March 24 Randolph introduced another series of resolutions designed to correct the false impression that New Jersey lacked patriotism and might even resist federal authority by force. In these resolutions, Randolph characterized the people of the state as loyal and law-abiding. New Jerseyans, he said, looked only to the courts to redress grievances and to the ballot box to solve problems. An amendment added that the state pledged its support to the effort of the federal government in maintaining the Union.

The Republicans reacted to these resolutions with ambivalence. Although quick to praise Parker's patriotism, they expressed wariness about this latest Democratic move. One of Randolph's resolutions stated that no political extremists existed in the state, although, as Republicans knew well, the copperhead members of the Democratic party continued their attack. Republicans viewed these resolutions as a Democratic attempt to save face and would have nothing to do with them. On March 25 both chambers of the legislature approved Randolph's latest resolutions, but the damage to the state's reputation had been done.[52]

Despite the unwarranted abuse heaped on New Jersey as a copperhead state, approval of Randolph's first set of resolutions as revised by the Democratic party caucus marked not the triumph of the copperheads but their defeat at the hands of the Parker Democrats. As one prowar Democratic legislator remarked, the copperheads "have kicked so high that they have broken their damned necks." The resolutions, moreover, did not mean what many people in heated overreaction asserted they meant. The resolutions did not call for or threaten resistance to the war effort by the people and the state government. Without a demand for an armistice they did not, strictly speaking, constitute peace resolutions. The resolutions did not incorporate a schedule for negotiations, provide for direct participation by state representatives, or spell out specific terms. These resolutions left the initiative for negotiation to an unsympathetic president.[53]

Randolph's resolutions of March 17, 1863, were far less significant than the vigorous prowar resolutions adopted by the legislature on May 8, 1861, March 27, 1862, and March 25, 1863. These resolutions reflect New Jersey's true record, as do the state's annual appropriations to support the war, the dominant unionist sentiment of most New Jerseyans, and the state's substantial military contribution. Then, too, unique circumstances enabled New Jersey to become the only free state to pass such resolutions. Only the prorogation of the Illinois legislature and the adjournment of the Indiana legislature prevented passage of resolutions stronger than Randolph's. In fact, the Delaware legislature went much farther than New Jersey's: it approved a resolution calling for an armistice and passed a law banning arbitrary arrests and election enforcement by the army.

New Jersey's resolutions expressed the deep misgivings of regular Democrats in the state about what they regarded as Lincoln's precipitous policies, clumsy methods, and inconclusive results. This unease was expressed widely by Democrats elsewhere in the North. Thus the resolutions served to relieve the emotions and frustrations of many members of the loyal opposition but were largely symbolic and irrelevant. Randolph's resolutions of March 17, the *New York Times* noted, represented a "mixture of scolding with whining." They amounted to an empty and ultimately meaningless gesture. Words and protests, moreover, could not alter the course of the war or, for that matter, change New Jersey's wartime role.[54]

A more direct and more dangerous maneuver, attempted simultaneously but unsuccessfully by midwestern copperheads, sought to put the state militia on a war footing. Even war supporters, including Parker, realized that New Jersey's militia needed strengthening in case the state had to defend itself in an emergency. The copperheads, however, had an entirely different plan, at which they had hinted earlier. They envisioned the state militia as a force to resist the federal government. As the *Newark Journal* reasoned, Lincoln's government undermined state government by centralizing power in Washington. Thus, the state would redress the balance by building up local power and making various northern states into armed camps to stop Lincoln's revolutionary assault on the rights of the people and the sovereignty of the states.[55]

English, dubbed "the *Virginian* representative of New Jersey," seized the initiative on March 5. After a copperhead rally in Trenton, during which several speakers demanded that federal tyranny be met with physical opposition, English submitted a bill to transform the militia into a huge state force and to appropriate several million dollars to fund the buildup. In fact he proposed to spend as much money on the project as the state already had spent on fighting the rebels. Predictably, the copperheads applauded. Some spoke of open defiance of federal authority and resistance to the recent acts of Congress. Copperheads in the legislature, however, defended the bill as a temporary, purely defensive measure to counter foreign or rebel invaders.[56]

War supporters were not deceived. Parker objected strenuously because the bill undermined executive authority over the military. Opponents of the bill noted the potential for insurrection implicit in the creation of such a large state force. Moreover, such a force invited collision with federal forces if New Jersey rejected federal authority. The *Newton Register* bluntly warned that this copperhead scheme amounted to an overt act of treason.[57]

The *Paterson Guardian* pointed to the inconsistencies in the copperhead argument. When the Union army needed ten thousand men from the state, copperheads groaned over the blood shed in a cruel war, but when English proposed to form an unneeded state force of forty thousand men, they applauded the effort to arm New Jersey to the hilt. Indeed, they became positively bloodthirsty for a fight with the Federals. While screaming against federal taxes and debts, they proposed to run up huge bills for the defense of the state when no foe, foreign or domestic, menaced it. The copperheads attacked Lincoln as a dictator, but favored granting carte blanche to state authorities to turn New Jersey into an armed camp. No copperhead could call himself a pacifist any longer, the *Guardian* concluded. A reporter later observed that the copperheads stood only for peace with the rebels; with everyone else, they prepared for war.[58]

If New Jersey really had been a copperhead state in popular sympathy, and if its government had been controlled by the copperheads, the legislature would have approved English's bill quickly and would have put it into effect energetically. Because the copperheads did not control the legislature, the Parkerites applied pressure to English to drop his madcap proposal. He did so, for it never had a chance of approval.

One of New Jersey's seats in the United States Senate had fallen vacant when John Thomson died on September 12, 1862. On November 22, after the general election and before the legislature began its next session, Olden made an interim appointment to fill the few weeks remaining in Thomson's term. He chose lawyer Richard Field, his neighbor and fellow Republican, to serve in the final session of the Thirty-seventh Congress, which would convene at the start of December.

The Republicans applauded this selection, but the Democrats denounced it. In the recent campaign Field had gone out of his way to attack the Democrats for obstructing the war effort. He had indiscriminately labeled every Democratic leader and newspaper editor in New Jersey a traitor. Field praised Lincoln's emancipation policy in such extravagant terms that he gave no quarter to Democrats. Describing the ship of state tossing on the waves of the worst storm, he urged jettisoning the mast of the Constitution in order to save the ship.[59]

On learning of Field's appointment, editor Hamilton described Field as a "cold-blooded aristocrat, a black-hearted abolitionist, a wily demagogue, and a reckless fanatic." In addition, the timing of the appointment infuriated the Democrats. On the heels of a crushing defeat of the Republicans, Olden had the effrontery to appoint this bellicose "Republican of the *Strictest Sect.*"[60]

Field knew he was serving as a lame duck during the last session of Congress. As a short-timer and a political loner, he decided to make the most of his office and worked hard to secure a federal appointment. Rubbing salt in New Jersey Democrats' wounds in speeches delivered on December 9, 1862, and January 7, 1863, he defended Lincoln's temporary suspension of the right of habeas corpus when military necessity required it. Just as the war party had found its scapegoat in James Courter three months before, when he vowed to sink the ship of state in order to drown the abolitionist crew aboard, so now the peace party pounced on Field for his advice to cast off the mast of the Constitution.[61]

Clearly Field, as an effective advocate and an unflinching unionist, was whisking away various constitutional cobwebs painstakingly spun by the copperheads. Yet Field, an intelligent man, must have known that his frank comments and uncompromising position would stir up a hornet's nest. His abrasive remarks on the campaign stump and his bulldog combativeness on the Senate floor enraged Democrats across the state, who felt he had abused their party, dishonored the Senate by his partisanship, and misrepresented the state by his extreme views. The *Somerville Messenger* declared he had done more to disgrace New Jersey in a few days than any previous senator from the state had managed to do in a full term of six years. The *Morristown Jerseyman* scarcely exaggerated when it dubbed Field the "best abused man in the State."[62]

Although Field caused an uproar in Democratic circles, he gained an instant reputation as a radical and won the respect of Republican colleagues in the Senate. He also found an avid listener in Lincoln. Plainly the president was pleased with such unqualified support just a month after the discouraging elections and from such an unlikely place as New Jersey. When Field vacated his seat on January 14, 1863, Lincoln appointed him judge of the federal district court for New Jersey, a lifelong position. In response, the Trenton reporter of the *New York Times* observed, "Justice, at all events, will be done, and done, too, by the clear light of unswerving fealty to the Government." In selecting Field, however, Lincoln ignored the unanimous bipartisan recommendation of the state's congressional delegation to name to the bench outgoing Republican representative John Nixon. Reaction to Field's appointment ran predictably along partisan lines: Republicans voiced jubilation; Democrats were shocked. Thus Field's short, stormy term of fifty-one days in the Senate succeeded sensationally. Few senators had accomplished so much for themselves in such a short time.[63]

Field so rankled the Democrats that they worked to replace him speedily when the legislature convened in mid-January. The *Mount Holly Herald* sounded the call, declaring that the "importance of ousting Mr. Field next Tuesday from the United States Senate will be quickly perceived by reading his speech in the Senate on the Seventh." The newspaper continued, "How many days, how many hours, are the people of New Jersey to be misrepresented by such a Senator?" The leading contender was Douglas Democrat William Cook of Bordentown, chief engineer of the Camden and Amboy Railroad and the most popular presidential elector in 1860.[64]

Wall had not figured as a serious possibility until Field's appointment cata-

pulted that archcopperhead into the limelight. After Field delivered his startling speeches in the Senate, Wall became the leading candidate of incensed
Democrats bent on retaliation against the insults to their party. Ironically,
Field antagonized so many Democrats that they willingly supported Wall's
unlikely candidacy, thus undermining the election of a Douglas Democrat
and staunch unionist.[65]

For some people, Wall's arbitrary arrest in September 1861 enhanced his
appeal. As the victim of Lincoln's heavy hand, he provided a fitting rebuke
to Field; selecting Wall would signal the Democrats' protest against arbitrary
arrests. His presence in the Senate would be an embarrassing reminder for
Lincoln and the Republicans. Moreover, poetic justice called for the replacement of a radical-sounding Republican with a reactionary Democrat.

Still, it remained unclear whether Wall could muster enough backing, even
for the interim term. One Jersey City Democrat believed that Wall commanded little support in most of northeastern New Jersey, where "he is considered too rash and imprudent." Some Democrats objected to Wall's bluster
and titanic temper. Wall also lacked political experience and a distinguished
record. He had never been a member of the legislature. He had served only
as mayor of Burlington, and had lost two races for Congress.[66]

Both Republicans and prowar Democrats detested Wall's copperhead views.
During 1863 he not only opposed the war, but also regarded reunion as impossible. On January 19 Wall announced: "I am a peace man, and have been
from the first, because I never could understand how war, with all its horrors and atrocities, could restore the Union. I never believed that blood, nor
do I now, could ever cement the broken fragments of this Union together."
On March 17 he predicted that "there would be no peace, except on the
basis of separation" with formal recognition of the Confederacy. On July 4
he observed, "When you talk to me about a war for the Union, you state a
contradiction in terms." War, he contended, never restored goodwill or reunited warring peoples. Coercion could never take the place of consent and
conciliation; force struck him as a poor substitute for free men exercising
the franchise. Stating his priority, Wall declared on June 30, 1864, "I will always put Liberty before Union."[67]

Rigidly doctrinaire, Wall regarded the Republican enemy as a monolithic
power. He feared that the Republicans had the strength and the will to tear
down the pillars of the Constitution and to overwhelm all opposition. He
opposed supporting any aspect of the Republican war effort because such
support undercut the antiwar position and did nothing either to stop the
war or to end Republican rule. Cooperation with the Republicans only encouraged abuses and solidified their power. "It seems to me," he stated, "to
be the supremest nonsense that the Democratic party can cry out for a
vigorous prosecution of the war, and yet expect to beat the party *that is*

*vigorously prosecuting it and controlling the sinews at the same time.*" Democrats must not support the war by embracing, in effect, the main features of Lincoln's policy while protesting "against the means employed." In his view, only peace could restore the Union. Indeed, he declared myopically in 1864, "Peace is Union. Peace unbroken would have saved it, peace restored will, I hope, at some time reconstruct it."[68]

An even more important consideration entered into the calculations of Democratic legislators in selecting Wall. All of the candidates and their supporters knew they could get rid of a rival most effectively by selecting him for the very short term of six weeks, thus making room for their favorite as successor to serve for the much longer term of six years. Politicians expected that if a Douglas man was chosen for the interim term, that branch of the party would accept someone outside their wing to receive the senatorship for the full term. Parker, a Douglas man, had received the nomination for governor; therefore it struck some politicians as a fair trade-off to allow someone not associated with this wing to secure the senatorship in the new Congress. Thanks to Olden and Field, however, the pendulum was swinging from selection of a war man to selection of a war opponent even for the rest of the term. Interest in Wall for the short term increased steadily, but Wall resisted. He regarded such a position as a barren, even demeaning prize, suggesting lack of trust in his ability to serve in Washington more than six weeks.[69]

On January 13, 1863, the Democrats in the legislature caucused. The voting reflected the deep-seated division of the party between the war wing and the peace wing. On the first ballot Cook received twenty-four votes and Wall nineteen. On the second ballot Cook's lead narrowed, twenty-five to twenty-two. Charles Skelton ran a poor third with six votes on each ballot. Moderate copperhead Charles Sitgreaves of Warren County received six votes on the first ballot, but only two on the second. On the third and final ballot, various Democrats shifted to Wall to make him the winner.

Wall defeated Cook by six votes, or 54 percent, over all opponents. He garnered his total of thirty votes when five of Skelton's men, two backers of Sitgreaves, and one of Cook's supporters changed over. Clearly, Cook's leaders had managed their forces badly. Cook, in fact, was so confident of election that he did not bother to go to the State House to press his claims. Observers speculated that his absence may have cost him the election; his connection with the unpopular Camden and Amboy Railroad did not help his candidacy. In addition, during the struggle for the senatorship, Naar brought considerable personal influence to bear on Skelton's delegates and others in persuading them to switch to Wall.

In contrast to Cook, Wall personally went to the State House to prevent his election for the short term, but his presence had the opposite effect.

Some members of the legislature, believing that his frail health was the result of his federal imprisonment, supported him out of personal sympathy, not political proclivity.

In a joint meeting the next day, January 14, the Democratic legislators ratified their decision in party caucus and supported Wall as their candidate. The Republicans put Field forward in a symbolic gesture. In the voting, fifty-three Democrats backed Wall, twenty-three Republicans supported Field, two Camden Republicans backed William Newell, and independent Democrat Joseph Crowell stayed with Cook. Senator Scudder and Assemblyman William P. McMichael, both Democrats and war supporters, absented themselves deliberately in order to avoid voting for Wall. According to some Trenton reporters, many Democrats swallowed the bitter pill of their caucus nominee with wry faces and smothered voices. Some Democrats were downright ashamed, but they voted for Wall either out of party loyalty or for fear of refusing to support their party's choice. Thus the "most implacable anti-administration, anti-war, anti-Union man in the state," and recently a United States prisoner for two weeks, became United States senator for six.[70]

Daniel Porter summed up the meaning of the election: "Jim Wall was elected for the short term to spite the Republicans, and to get him out of the way." Wall consented reluctantly to the election. He did so with assurance of support for his reelection from friends and in the hope that the short term might serve as a stepping-stone to the long term. Meanwhile, Burlington residents could boast of their county as the home of both federal senators. The Democrats in the legislature had brushed aside both regional balance and common sense.[71]

Copperhead newspapers exulted in the choice of Wall as the savior of the North. In an unintentional pun, they saw pacifist "handwriting on the wall" and read the doom of Republicanism. The *New York World* declared that the "'whirligig of time' has rarely brought about so complete and satisfactory a revenge" for Wall's arrest by Lincoln's officials. Some prowar Democratic journals candidly considered Wall an unlikely choice but welcomed any Democrat over a Republican. Several prowar Democratic editors, however, remained silent out of embarrassment.[72]

Some Republican newspapers indulged in overreaction. Republicans grieved that the treasonable copperheads had taken over first the state Democracy, then the state government, and finally the state itself. The *Trenton Gazette* mourned the ascendancy of the peace Democrats in the legislature, where they would "control the party." Wall's election, declared the breathless reporter of the *New York Tribune*, represented the "greatest crime against the intelligence and loyalty of a State that history can furnish." Republicans noted that six months before, many influential Newark Democrats had killed the suggestion of Wall as the keynote speaker at the city's Fourth of July ceremonies; now the very same Democrats lionized him. Contrasting the prowar posture of Democratic candidates in the gubernatorial election with the selection of an antiwar senator, the *Freehold Herald* proclaimed, "How these proceedings comport with the specious promises made by the Democrats of being in favor of a vigorous prosecution of the war, we leave to a swindled people to judge." Not succumbing to overreaction, the *Toms River Emblem* rejected the charge of a disloyal state when it asked whether anyone really imagined that "New Jersey has gone off into the mundane regions of Secesh?"[73]

Republicans hoped that Wall's election would benefit them. As one candid partisan put it, the "worse selection they make, the better for us." Wall's selection by the Democrats, predicted the *Camden Press*, "will open the eyes of those who were duped into voting for *loyal* Democrats, merely because they professed loyalty." The newspaper predicted that given a chance, voters would punish the Democrats for bringing the loyalty of the state into question. Lincoln purportedly joked that New Jersey's legislature, in electing a senator, drove him to the *wall*, so he appointed a district judge and took to the *field*.[74]

Wall's term as U.S. senator proved brief and insignificant. Other copperheads also served in that body during the war; none ever jeopardized Republican control and legislation. During his tenure Wall comported himself with unexpected restraint. Impressed, perhaps even awed by his surroundings, he began to sound and look like a senator, even when (with fitting revenge) he rebutted Field's argument on arbitrary arrests. Wishing to serve as senator for a full term, Wall intended to make a good impression on Democratic legislators in Trenton. His election also showed that the right to dissent remained intact, and even was rewarded, while civil war raged. The expressed will of a slim majority of Democrats in caucus prevailed, even though Wall's views differed from those of most people, including most Democrats, in the state. Wall's election, however, did not obstruct even slightly the war effort in New Jersey, which went forward without interruption while federal power increased steadily at the expense of the states.[75]

Wall's election, then, revealed rich ironies. By arresting and imprisoning Wall, Lincoln's administration made a hero and a martyr of a most unlikely candidate. Left alone, Wall would have faded into obscurity. In addition, the copperheads' animosity toward Field helped in his selection as federal judge in the most important presidential appointment for the state during the war. If some of these copperhead dissidents later had to face Field presiding in court, to their disadvantage, they could blame themselves in part. As a result of these events, the legislature had elected an antiwar man from a prowar state. New Jerseyans simply had to endure James Wall's brief misrepresentation of their state.

Between Wall's election in mid-January and the slated election of a U.S. senator for a full term in late February, eight contenders scrambled for support. The leading candidates threw lavish parties and lobbied legislators.

Former governors Peter Vroom and Price, along with legislators Vanatta and Randolph, and outgoing representative George Cobb, joined the leading hopefuls, Wall, Benjamin Williamson, and William Wright. Although Wright had served as U.S. senator in the 1850s, he still lacked a single qualification except his wealth. Wright had made a fortune in the leather business; in a day of bribe givers and bribe takers, he showed no bashfulness in pursuing his political ambition. Wall counted on the copperheads' support, while Wright relied on the size of his wallet to gain readmission to the U.S. Senate. Observers believed that Senator Wall had little chance, so the race narrowed to a contest between Williamson and Wright—"brains against money"—with Wright running on the inside track.[76]

The Democratic caucus wrestled with the matter on the evening of February 25. The exciting, increasingly bitter contest continued until midnight, with twenty-three ballots cast. Wall received only nine votes at the start of the balloting; thereafter his support declined steadily. His stalwart supporters included hard-core copperheads English and David H. Wyckoff of Monmouth, along with Simeon R. Huselton of Hunterdon. Various candidates divided the ranks of the war supporters. Vanatta peaked with nineteen votes, far more than were cast for his competitors Williamson and Randolph. On every ballot the combined opposition outnumbered Wall and generally outvoted Wright. On the final ballot, however, Wright won by a margin of four votes (54 percent) over all opponents. Money, according to various accounts, triumphed in the end. Porter reported that Wright "bled freely, as usual." The *Trenton Gazette* observed, "Nothing but his wealth enabled him to be again elected." The *New York Tribune* aptly characterized Wright as holding his tongue in public while letting a flow of greenbacks speak for him. In describing the contest between Wright and Wall, the *Tribune*'s reporter stated, "Fort Bullion took Fort Lafayette."[77]

On the following day, February 26, the Democrats formally elected Wright in a joint meeting of the legislature. The copperheads reluctantly went along with the party's choice; the Republicans supported Newell. Two Democratic legislators, prowar Crowell and pro-Wall Huselton, failed to vote. Corruption, not copperhead support, secured Wright's election.[78]

To Republicans, Wright represented the lesser of two evils. In the words of the *Belvidere Intelligencer*, "If the money of Billy Wright had the effect to defeat Jim Wall's Jeff Davisism, it did much good. We would, any time, rather trust a fool than a secessionist." Similarly, the *Mercury* observed, "We are at least spared from the disgrace of having a graduate of a government prison standing as our representative in the Senate" for the next six years. Moreover, because people regarded Wright as both a personal and a political cipher, he could not do any serious harm in the Senate or obstruct the war effort. After all, he had neglected his senatorial duties in the past because of absenteeism, inattentiveness, and physical frailty. The *Newton Register* concluded: compared to the other leading candidates, Wright was simply incapable of "doing as much mischief."[79]

Yet Wright's selection was mischievous enough. Observers questioned the desirability of continuing to nominate senators in party caucus by secret ballot. In addition to the defective process, there was the lamentable result. Many able politicians in the state, including several prowar Democrats, could have represented New Jersey and its Democratic party more creditably. In view of the availability of such candidates as Vroom, Vanatta, Randolph, and Cobb, the election of Wright marked a disturbing, even disgraceful, development that marred the state's wartime record. For the rest of the war, the ailing Wright surpassed his previous record of incompetence. Measured against the challenges of the times, Wright and Wall left a record as two of the worst senators to represent the state in Washington. Even so, New Jersey hardly monopolized corruption or folly among the wartime legislatures of the North.[80]

To add confusion to ineffectiveness, Wright's stance on the major issues of the war remained unknown. He might hold copperhead convictions or he might, like his predecessor Thomson, support the war effort earnestly while remaining a staunchly conservative Democrat. Earlier a fiery Lecomptonite and a loyal Breckinridger, Wright had been a strong advocate of compromise during the secession crisis. During the war he became perhaps the quietest Democrat in the state. The *Mercury* pointed out that Wright, once principal owner of the *Newark Journal*, continued to help keep it afloat financially. "For venomous opposition to the war," declared the *Mercury*, the *Journal* had "no equal in the State. If this is a key to Mr. Wright's own sentiments, we gain nothing by the change of Senators, save that the new one will lack the power to make his views known to Congress or the country." The *Trenton Gazette* similarly observed that "Mr. Wright has said nothing, so far as we are aware, to show whether he is with the radicals [copperheads] or moderates of the Democracy; whether he is for peace at any cost or for an efficient prosecution of the war." Because the *Journal* supported Wright's quest for the senatorship, however, the *Gazette* supposed he would vote with the copperheads in Congress.[81]

Given Wright's present silence and previous ineffectuality, the *Mercury* predicted that Wright, if really a copperhead, would behave as a defanged one. Even so, prowar Democratic journals politely applauded his selection, although the *Newton Herald* confessed that it had other preferences. Significantly, the hard-core copperheads had strongly preferred Wall or other candidates and showed their displeasure with Wright's victory.[82]

In light of what Wall and Wright both supposedly represented—control of the legislature by the copperheads—their elections revealed a momentary tempest in the Trenton teapot. Wall probably would not have been selected, except for an unanticipated chain of events. Olden's troublesome appointment of Field, Field's troubled tenure, Cook's troubling absence from the State House, and Wright's successful strategy and hefty wallet played a role in filling two terms. New Jersey's legislature thus sent a crusty copperhead to serve temporarily and a Rip Van Winkle to doze through the war. New Jersey's Democrats had inflicted on the United States Senate a minor nuisance for six weeks and a total nonentity for four years.[83]

After settling the senatorial question, the legislature addressed a plan to ban nonresident blacks from New Jersey. A similar proposal had failed in 1862. Copperhead assemblyman John B. Perry of Jersey City introduced a bill to prohibit freed slaves from staying in the state. War supporter Vanatta, however, stole Perry's thunder by having his bill sidetracked in committee. Vanatta substituted for consideration a tougher measure to "kick the nigger out," as the *Hackettstown Gazette* described it. Instead of flogging free blacks, as was done in Delaware, apprenticing them, as mandated in Illinois, or fining them, as Perry's bill required, Vanatta proposed deporting the state's black nonresidents to countries where slavery did not exist.[84]

The measure sailed through the assembly on March 18, receiving support almost exclusively from North Jersey Democrats. Most South Jersey Democrats abstained, while assembly Republicans solidly opposed the measure. Three-fourths of the copperheads voted for the measure, which complemented their plans to sabotage emancipation. By restricting the interstate movement of freed blacks and banning liberated slaves from New Jersey, the copperheads hoped to undercut federal authority and to nullify presidential emancipation by independent state action.[85]

Republicans and Quakers regarded the measure as racist, unjust, and impractical. The *Mercury* called the bill "infamous"; the *Guardian* described it as an "atrocity." Republicans stressed the incongruity between federal support for emancipation and state restriction of that effort. Opponents of the measure also ridiculed it as patently unnecessary: blacks were as likely to overrun New Jersey from the South as were Indians to attack the state from the West. The *Camden Press* quipped that because this and other cowardly proposals of the copperheads had disgraced the state, New Jersey's reputation would improve markedly if all the state's copperheads left and an equal number of freed blacks replaced them.[86]

Perry tried to exploit the race issue, but the motives of both Vanatta and the senate leaders are less clear. Vanatta evidently wished to appease the copperheads, who were upset about the defeat of Holsman's peace resolutions and Wall's failure to secure the full term. Vanatta may have sought copperhead support for other Democratic measures, or perhaps he simply wished to advance his career. Some reports even suggested that Vanatta deliberately presented a bill unacceptable to the senate, knowing that no time remained for extensive amendment. If this was the case, he outfoxed the copperheads.[87]

In the more moderate senate, where Republicans remained far more influential, the Democrats greeted Vanatta's bill with uneasiness. Opposition from Jersey shore residents, warning of the resulting shortage of temporary black workers who provided summer help at shore resorts, evidently influenced senators. Critics also questioned the enormous expense of deportation. Others doubted the constitutionality of the bill and feared lawsuits or a collision with the national government. The proposal actually might backfire and help Republicans win elections in South Jersey. The bill finally lost because of approaching adjournment as well as doubts and fears among senate leaders.[88]

Meanwhile the legislature continued, usually by unanimous votes, to pay the state's share of the war effort. It authorized an additional war loan of one million dollars, bringing the wartime total to three million, and increased taxes as well. The legislature also broadened family benefits to militia members, attempted to strengthen state defense forces, and passed thirty-one acts to legalize the efforts of local communities that had raised money for war volunteers. Supporting such measures and speaking on the governor's behalf, Randolph declared that Parker wholeheartedly backed the national government and the federal Constitution. As a rebuke to the copperheads, Randolph and Parker dissociated themselves from any effort to seek remedies outside the law or politics. Both the war loan and Randolph's speech moved the *Advertiser* to remark that Randolph had knocked "into a cocked hat all the air castles of the copper-heads."[89]

Members of the legislature, along with those of Pennsylvania and New York, again pondered the question of allowing servicemen to vote. Few questioned its justification, but the proposal encountered objections because of the potential for fraud and the possibility of army officers' influencing enlisted men. Legislators also expressed doubts because there existed no constitutional provision that explicitly authorized voting outside the state. In addition, partisan self-interest influenced most Democratic legislators. They feared that troops would vote Republican in retaliation for the recent actions of the legislature. In the end the Democratic senators choked the bill to death by submitting numerous amendments just before adjournment, and so avoided a public showdown with a recorded vote.[90]

In 1863 many New Jersey soldiers repudiated New Jersey copperheads. A man in the Fifteenth Regiment declared that the "Copperheads are well named. They do not deserve the name of men." They, after all, were "playing into the hands of the rebels by their talk and actions." One ordnance officer described the copperheads who undermined the war effort as "false to liberty, false to humanity, false to their country." Another indignant man in the Fifteenth Regiment expressed "our abhorrence of that class called copperheads. We want sympathy from home; we want to *know* that we are fighting for an unconditional surrender of traitors and their abettors." Troops wanted no one in the rear, as one lieutenant in the Eleventh Regiment put it, "stabbing us in the back."[91]

Soldiers also condemned copperheads for giving the state a bad name. One writer contrasted the state's fighting men, who added luster to the state's name, with those treacherous politicians at home who "caused the very name of New Jersey to stink in the nostrils of patriotism." Some soldiers, however, recognized that the copperheads were only a minority in the state. As the officers of the Eleventh Regiment declared, "those few" copperheads "do not represent the people of New Jersey." A member of the Twelfth Regiment similarly observed, "I firmly believe that the great majority of the people of New Jersey are in favor of a vigorous prosecution of the war."[92]

When copperheads condemned Lincoln's war policies and then Wall became senator, New Jersey's soldiers fulminated. A lieutenant in the Ninth Regiment upbraided "those cowardly wretches, who stay at home crying 'Peace!' He concluded, "Language fails me in expressing my hate and disgust for these vile, sneaking, croaking copperhead traitors." An enlisted man in the Fifteenth Regiment declared, "I for one am ashamed of New Jersey. Its representatives in Congress and Legislature have disgraced their supporters in the field." Another soldier in the Fourteenth Regiment remarked, "We are sent here to put down the rebellion, while our leading men at home are crying '*Let the Secession reptile go in Peace.*'"[93]

Many New Jerseyans in the army found it dastardly that legislators approved resolutions striking a blow at the Union cause or that some Newarkers welcomed Vallandigham with open arms. In rebuke, several regiments, huddling around a campfire or standing at attention, adopted counterresolutions denouncing the copperheads and asked various newspapers in the state to publish their views. An officer in the Second Infantry, a Democrat, observed that Jersey troops, previously respected for their sturdy patriotism and steady discipline, now were "looked down upon as coming from a disloyal State" and were obliged to "endure the scoff of their companions in arms." Jersey Blues vowed to punish those who had sullied the state's reputation by voting them out at the earliest opportunity.[94]

The legislature adjourned in late March. The Republicans wished it good riddance and fired cannon in celebration. Yet in fact the legislature had repudiated extremism. Noisy but not numerous, irritating but not powerful, the copperheads indeed stirred up controversy and alarm during the early months of 1863. In the end, however, they did not accomplish any objectives of lasting importance. Legislators rejected Holsman's armistice resolutions, English's militia proposal, the black exclusion bill, and a six-year U.S. Senate term for Wall.

The actual record of this most Democratic of the state's wartime legislatures struck observers as fundamentally moderate, as even Republicans conceded in retrospect. The *Advertiser* stated that if the legislature had accomplished little good, it also had caused little harm. The *Mount Holly Mirror* conceded that the session's record had "turned out better than was expected." The 1863 legislature did nothing to obstruct the war effort or resist federal authority. On the contrary, it authorized a new state loan of one million dollars, passed numerous acts to help local governments raise money for volunteers for the war, and affirmed its support of the Union cause. The executive branch meanwhile promoted the recruitment of troops with energy and determination.[95]

New Jersey also avoided conflicts between the various branches of its state government, such as occurred in Delaware, Indiana, Illinois, and elsewhere. Unlike Indiana's experience, the New Jersey legislature never refused to appropriate funds for the executive branch. In contrast to legislators in both Indiana and Illinois, New Jersey's legislature did not try to tamper with the governor's control of the militia. Moreover, when the war went badly, New Jersey's Democracy did not nominate an antiwar man for its gubernatorial candidate in 1862, as occurred in New Hampshire, Connecticut, Pennsylvania, and Ohio during 1863. In accepting Randolph's resolutions in the middle of February, Democratic legislators acted less extremely than did Connecticut Democrats in the same month, when they opposed the war and demanded a cease-fire.

Some commentators have characterized New Jersey as a copperhead state under copperhead control during 1863, and support this claim with Wall's election and the adoption of Randolph's early resolutions. The legislative session, however, did not witness a statewide eruption of strong copperhead feeling, supposedly long simmering beneath the surface. The legislature's election of a copperhead to serve for six weeks in the United States Senate did not indicate the legislature's approval of the copperhead agenda. Few New Jerseyans sympathized with the copperheads, embraced peace at any price, espoused the Confederate cause, or wished to enlist in the Confederate army. Wall's election was a fluke; it resulted from unique circumstances at variance with the performance of the legislature and the actions of New Jerseyans. Governors Olden and Parker, moreover, both staunch supporters of the war, controlled the machinery of the state government throughout the war and backed the war effort unfailingly.

Wall's brief sojourn in Washington and a few partisan, fault-finding resolutions approved by the legislature during one of the low points of the war constituted minor incidents, not major developments. Gritty unionism meanwhile prevailed in the state. The Republican *Camden Press* remarked correctly, "New Jersey is at heart as sound as ever." Although the copperheads huffed and puffed mightily, the State House in Trenton and the Capitol in Washington did not fall down. Few New Jerseyans turned their backs on their sons on the battlefront, who continued to fight as valiantly as before.[96]

# 10 War Crises in 1863

**A** fter the legislative session of 1863 ended, town elections took place during March in South Jersey and during April in North Jersey. The elections turned on local issues and individual personalities. The Democrats generally made sizable gains, except in Camden. In most parts of the state they swept many towns, including Paterson, Jersey City, Elizabeth, and Trenton. One reporter figured that the Democrats won majorities in sixteen counties, the Republicans in five. The Republicans, seeking a quick return to power, found the results disappointing.[1]

In a bid for a political comeback and in an effort to combat supposed disloyal influences, Republicans and some independent war Democrats, mainly of the Douglas stripe, organized local chapters of the Loyal National League. They intended to turn back disaffection and defeatism, to counter the suspected secret societies of the copperheads, and to destroy the often imaginary conspiracies of disloyalists. They distributed pamphlets, tried to persuade the undecided, and mobilized voters to go to the polls. For the war cause they sold federal bonds and recruited volunteers for the army. For the welfare of soldiers and their families, they raised money for relief and found jobs for disabled veterans. Their organizations required a loyalty oath and provided fraternal rituals, which increased popular appeal. Although the League was originally formed in 1862, new chapters proliferated during the early part of 1863.[2]

Democrats criticized this new political organization. They complained it persecuted Democrats and caught the unwary by pretending nonpartisan patriotism. The *Somerville Messenger* advised townspeople who loved their country to stay away from its meetings. Meanwhile the Democrats formed rival groups.[3]

During the spring Loyal Leaguers held statewide meetings in Trenton. Republican newspapers, with their usual "Union party" appeal, urged the people, not the politicians, to take part. Editorials castigated legislators who had protested war measures and advocated peace proposals. In a keynote speech at one of these meetings, Frederick Frelinghuysen denounced the legislature's preliminary resolutions as neither representing the sentiments of most New Jerseyans and Democrats nor expressing the views of Parker. Admittedly, people out of state had criticized New Jerseyans for these resolutions, but Frelinghuysen, taking into consideration the truly loyal feelings of most New Jerseyans and the fine combat record of Jersey troops, rejected all charges against the state, to the loud applause from the audience. To preserve the Union, he urged people to support the Lincoln administration because it alone represented the government. In a similar vein the *Camden Press* remarked on how many Democrats pledged to support the government, yet worked to cripple the administration "just as if the one could be sustained without the other. If we are to have a government, those whose duty it is to administer that government must be supported until the expiration of their term of office or else we shall have anarchy."[4]

James Scovel also spoke in defense of the state. New Jersey, he said, had no need to apologize when the state had sent more than thirty thousand men to the front, where they fought long and well. Those northern opponents of Lincoln's administration who talked incessantly about maintaining the Union must understand that it was necessary to "put down the rebellion as it is, and we will have 'the Union as it was.'" John Foster, who spoke next, castigated the copperheads for sapping the moral authority of the government and sowing sedition: "We must teach the copperheads that they will not be permitted to hiss in the face of loyal men." Those who sympathized with treason must be treated as traitors. Later the delegates endorsed a resolution denouncing any capitulation to those who took up arms against the government of the Union. They supported peace secured only by the unconditional surrender of the insurgents.[5]

In addition to rallying popular support, the delegates created a network of coordinating county committees, which in turn would organize groups in various towns. Thus Union supporters and Republican managers established a statewide grass roots organization. By 1864, 150 groups with 15,000 members existed.[6]

New Jersey Democrats were furnished with a strong rejoinder by the army's arrest of Vallandigham in early May for his political pronouncements, and by his subsequent conviction, imprisonment, and deportation to the Confederacy. Many Democrats were enraged by this assault on free speech, and they organized meetings to protest the incident. At some meetings fistfights erupted between war men and peace men or between soldiers and civilians. Peace advocates no longer viewed Lincoln as a potential tyrant, but as an actual dictator who used the army to get rid of his leading critic. Chauncey Burr railed against this act of rank despotism, which made a villain of Lincoln and a patriot of Vallandigham.[7]

The *Newton Herald* urged people to protest Vallandigham's arrest and trial, "not for Vallandigham, but for our common liberty and freedom." The arrest of Vallandigham widened the rift between war supporters and peace advocates in the Democratic camp. Although both groups declared Vallandigham innocent of treason, the war faction rejected his pacifist message. At a Somerville meeting on July 2, elder statesman Peter Vroom remained decidedly cool about Vallandigham. Vroom and other prowar leaders advised fellow Democrats to obey federal law until a particular law was either repealed by Congress or declared void by a court.[8]

Prowar Democratic newspapers revealed differences of tone in judging Vallandigham and his supporters. The hostile *Jersey City Standard* dismissed Vallandigham as a noisy demagogue lacking both political skill and a solid record of accomplishment. After first stirring up people to hatred and violent solutions, observed the newspaper, this disunionist agitator invariably ended his speeches with a contradictory pitch for peaceful, legal remedies. Left to his own devices he would have burnt himself out, but, the newspaper argued, a bungling general and a blundering president made him a martyr.[9]

The prowar *Freehold Democrat*, however, saw the peace movement in the best possible light. It contended that both peace and war Democrats should oppose Republican attempts to suppress dissent. "We regard the opposition that has been shown towards the War as unwise and impolitic. We have not regarded it, however, as *unpatriotic*." Vallandigham as the leader of that faction "has never supported the war; he has denounced it; he has advocated peace. We have differed from him. But Mr. Vallandigham *has never advocated peace upon the basis of separation*."[10]

New Jersey Republicans unanimously denounced Vallandigham as a subversive troublemaker. One soldier in the Ninth Regiment referred to him as "*Villain-dam-him*." Some Republicans defended the army's proceedings: toleration of diverse opinion might be laudable, but acceptance of treason had no place. Although some Republicans conceded that the army's handling of the affair raised questions, they all agreed on one point: the distinction drawn by the *Freehold Democrat*—that Vallandigham had not sought separation of the states of the Union—amounted to a distinction without a difference. The fact remained that an armistice would result in dissolution of the Union.[11]

Republicans also pounced on the contradictory arguments of the Democrats, who accused Lincoln's administration of timidity and vacillation, then denounced it as tyrannical and despotic. It was puzzling how such incompetent weaklings could install a dictatorship to trample on the rights of the people. Then another disastrous Union defeat at Chancellorsville in early May, following on the heels of the furor over Vallandigham, threw Republicans further on the defensive.[12]

Parker and other prominent prowar Democrats kept their distance from Vallandigham's supporters. Parker defended free expression and denounced Vallandigham's arrest and trial as arbitrary and illegal. He saw no compelling reason to subject Vallandigham, a civilian living in peaceful, loyal Ohio, to a summary proceeding of a secret military court. Parker defended Vallandigham's right to trial by a jury of peers in an open civil court. He carefully avoided comment on Vallandigham's views, however, and did not attend even one protest meeting.

Parker warned that defense of the principle of free expression must not be broadened to include actions that crippled the war effort. In a veiled but stern warning to the copperheads, he declared, "Let no one seek to bend this question to serve mere personal or partisan ends" during this "crisis of the nation's life." The Republicans applauded Parker's moderate tone and patriotic message, and compared it favorably to the more inflammatory appeal of Horatio Seymour, Parker's Democratic counterpart in New York. In addition, Parker dismissed James Wall's hysterical suggestion to call out the state militia to defend the state from imminent attack by Lincoln's lackeys in the army. Rebuffed, Wall lashed out: "Parker is not a vertebrate animal." The issues raised by Vallandigham's treatment created yet more tension in the marriage of convenience between the peace and the war factions of the New Jersey Democracy.[13]

In mid-June, shortly after this unsettling affair, Confederate troops under Lee invaded southern Pennsylvania. Rebel soldiers soon stood on the banks of the Susquehanna River, less than sixty miles from the Delaware River and only twenty-four hours away by forced march. New Jerseyans feared that the rebels might swing east and invade New Jersey, with their cavalry fording the Delaware at Lambertville or their infantry marching across the railroad bridges at Trenton or Phillipsburg.

Parker telegraphed Lincoln to say that the "people of New Jersey are apprehensive that the invasion of the enemy may extend to her soil." Prominent New Jerseyans besieged Parker with requests to arm the state. The *Freehold Democrat* considered Lee's invasion the worst crisis in the war.[14]

With federal forces stationed on the Virginia front and guarding both Washington and Baltimore as well, the army at the outset did not wish to spare troops to defend Pennsylvania. Alarmed Pennsylvanian officials quickly turned to other northern states for help.

Parker, keeping in close touch with Pennsylvania's governor, responded decisively and firmly. He asked for New Jersey volunteers to enlist in the militia to go to the aid of Pennsylvania; 677 men responded. In addition, two returning infantry regiments awaiting discharge from federal service volunteered to serve there. New Jerseyans knew their first line of defense stood along the banks of the Susquehanna; people understood that Pennsylvania's battle was also New Jersey's. Republican journals, both inside and outside the state, complimented Parker for his promptness in coming to the rescue.[15]

Recognition of danger brought even extreme peace Democrats to their senses. The *Newark Journal* urged citizens to volunteer and repel the invading army. The prowar *Jersey City Standard* exhorted people to forget petty squabbles and partisan animosities: "Let us prove to the world, now, when the hour seems dark and the portents threatening, that New Jersey is loyal to the Union to her very heart's core."[16]

On the Fourth of July, boys set off firecrackers in the streets in honor of the national birthday. Adults, however, worrying about the huge armies converging on Gettysburg and the great battle probably raging there, did not celebrate as usual. They waited and prayed. Holiday festivities often divided along party lines; instead of attending patriotic community gatherings organized by their municipalities, many New Jerseyans in several cities attended separate partisan meetings. At a Democratic meeting in Newark, Wall delivered his usual discourse on ancient history to show the necessity of pursuing peace in the present.

At a Union League conclave in Newark, someone interrupted speaker Joseph Bradley to relay the news of a great Union victory at Gettysburg. The crowd was breathlessly silent for a moment, then burst into cheers. The band started to play "Yankee Doodle." Soon bells rang in churches and schoolhouses across the state. The *Newark Advertiser* exulted, the *"Nation Is Saved!"* Both Democratic and Republican editors rejoiced that General George G. Meade's forces had dealt the Confederates a stunning blow. The rebels, citizens agreed, fought better when defending their soil than when carrying on a war of invasion.[17]

The next day brought news that Vicksburg, the Gibraltar of the West, had fallen, splitting the Confederacy in two. Union forces now controlled all of the strategic Mississippi River. The war had taken a decisive turn in the North's favor. New Jerseyans now expected quick suppression of the rebellion.[18]

The twin victories encouraged a false euphoria during early July. The breakthroughs weakened but failed to destroy Confederate forces. The Yankees failed to capture the enemy army after their triumph at Gettysburg, thus missing another chance to end the war. The war and the preparations for federal conscription ground steadily on, and soon dashed the popular but unrealistic hopes of avoiding a draft.[19]

As the government sought more soldiers, the draft and the recruitment of blacks into the army became raging issues. Many Republicans strongly supported conscription and found ample constitutional authority. To maintain the Union, Republicans argued, the government must fight; to fight, it must have men. If men did not join the army voluntarily, the government would have to draft them.

Because able-bodied white men were lacking, Republicans concluded that Negroes should fight for both their country and their freedom. If New Jersey's black soldiers and sailors could shoot foreign foes in the American Revolution and the War of 1812, reasoned the *Camden Press,* they could "shoot a traitor!" The *Toms River Emblem* regarded it as fitting that *"The Oppressed Are The Appointed Ones To Put To Confusion The Oppressor."* Black enlistments, moreover, would reduce the need to draft white men. Federal official Anthony Q. Keasbey, writing to someone outside the country, referred to a family member who enlisted as a white officer in a black regiment: "He chooses the Colored Regiment as the best path to military distinction. This shows a revolution in public sentiment which may surprise you."[20]

This was hardly the prevailing attitude, however. Democrats and even a few Republicans objected to putting arms in the hands of blacks and treating them as virtual equals in the army. Blacks, as an inferior race, must occupy an inferior position, they reasoned. To elevate them would antagonize white troops and undermine morale. One New Jersey soldier found preposterous the idea of a white man marching shoulder to shoulder with a "*thick lipped, woolly headed, 'sharp shinned'* nigger to the cannon's mouth, battling with men of his own blood to elevate the negro equal to himself!!" The *Paterson Register* exclaimed, "White men can do their own fighting." Orestes Brownson agreed: "This, after all, is the white man's country—is to be the white man's country—and white men should defend it and fight its battles."[21]

Despite the pull of patriotism, many men of military age worried about the draft. Fear mounted when they heard of the terrible battle casualties at Gettysburg and Vicksburg. People also criticized the unpopular conscription law, regarding it as unfair because the wealthy could easily avoid the draft by paying three hundred dollars or finding a substitute to enlist for three years. They concluded, incorrectly, that poor men's blood and rich men's money fought the war.[22]

Critics questioned conscription on many grounds, viewing it as unconstitutional, unjust, or unnecessary. Democrats railed against the draft for abducting whites from the state in order to free blacks, who would compete for jobs with whites. Other, individualistic Americans objected to the policy of compulsory military service because it smacked of European militarism, would undercut traditional reliance on voluntary enlistments, and would create a national army at the expense of state militias.[23]

Dissatisfaction with the draft had showed itself in June 1863, when draft officers prepared for conscription. In certain Newark wards, where some intensely antiwar Irish working-class people lived, officers attempted to list the names of potential draftees. They encountered women who threw stones and refused to give the requested information. Officials returned in force, however, and finished the job without serious resistance. A few isolated incidents also occurred in Sussex County, but such protests were neither widespread nor dangerous.[24]

Making incendiary appeals, war opponents urged massive disobedience to the draft. Some New Jerseyans read the warning in the *New York Herald* that resistance to the government in the North would inevitably result in civil disturbance: "They are playing with fire over a mine of explosive combustibles."[25]

In mid-July, the mine exploded as the war reached another low point, not on some distant battlefield, but in a combined race, class, and draft riot on the nearby island of Manhattan. With its militia away on emergency duty in Pennsylvania, the lottery drawings named the first of the draftees. Mobs, consisting chiefly of Irish workers, rampaged through the streets on the East Side for four days, terrorizing city inhabitants. Symbols of authority and wealth became prime targets for looting and destruction. Rioters wrecked draft offices, an armory, the homes and offices of Republican officials and editors. Mobs ransacked luxury hotels and elegant stores. Ruffians stopped men in the streets, robbing them of money, watches, or jewelry. Crowds attacked beleaguered policemen, firefighters, and soldiers. Mobs brutally kicked the wounded or dying defenders of the city. During the disorder two New Jerseyans reportedly perished.

Blacks, scapegoats of the frustrations of striking white workers as well as objects of their prejudice and their competitors for jobs, became the main victims. Many whites bitterly resented having to serve involuntarily in the army in order to liberate blacks. Savage mobs vented their fury, burning a black orphanage and a church, hanging blacks from trees and lampposts, setting them on fire, and bashing black babies' heads on fire hydrants.

Finally, on the fourth day, after great destruction of property and loss of life, policemen and reinforced troops with rifles and cannons mowed down the rioters, dispersed them, and restored order. Community leaders calmed people both with promises to suspend the draft and with calls for peace.[26]

By way of contrast, New Jersey, a state with an exaggerated reputation as a hotbed of antiwar sentiment, suffered only minor disturbances. In the evening on July 13 a crowd in Newark booed prominent Republicans and cheered famous Democrats. A few beatings occurred. Rioters hurled paving stones at the windows of two buildings housing Republican newspapers. Smashing a glass door, the mob tried to destroy the *Mercury*'s offices upstairs, but police and employees on a darkened stairway blocked their entry. The mob next went to the home of the *Mercury*'s publisher, who also supervised the draft in the district, and battered his house with bricks. He and his family, warned in advance, had fled. City officials arrived just in time to save his house; they pleaded for calm and asked the crowd to leave. A heavy rain helped cool tempers and thinned the crowd, which finally scattered. The next night, fearing a repeat performance, defenders, augmented by returned soldiers, camped in the barricaded *Mercury*'s offices, but trouble never materialized.

Elsewhere in the state antidraft demonstrations took place without violence. Crowds in Bloomfield, Orange, Jersey City, and Princeton marched through the streets, hooting and howling. In Morristown and Hackensack protesters demanded to see copies of the draft enrollment. New Jersey, then, witnessed nothing like the violence that rocked other states. In contrast to New York City's disorder, in which more than one hundred persons died, New Jersey's draft disturbances caused no fatalities. Property damage in Manhattan ran into the millions of dollars; in Newark it amounted to fifty dollars. Compared to Manhattan's tidal wave, New Jerseyans witnessed a slight ripple. Unlike the draft resistance that resulted in incidents and riots in other states of the North, including Vermont, Massachusetts, Connecticut, New York, Pennsylvania, Ohio, Indiana, Illinois, Wisconsin, Minnesota, and Iowa, protests in New Jersey were mild affairs.[27]

During this crisis each party in New Jersey blamed the other for causing the riots. According to the Democrats, the rioters' lawlessness found precedent in the abolitionists' disregard of federal laws when they rescued fugitive slaves in the name of higher law and individual conscience. Republicans, with their presidential edicts, arbitrary arrests, and congressional measures, now trampled individuals' constitutional rights under the cover of military necessity and national loyalty. By their defiance of law, Republicans encouraged defiance in the people. The disturbances, declared the *Belvidere Journal*, grew logically from the teachings of the Republican party. Democrats saw poetic justice done when Republican newspapers became victims of the mob, because Republican editors earlier in the war had fomented mob violence and intimidation or had condoned both against Democratic papers.[28]

The *Newark Journal* again offered its simple solution to the unrest: stop the war and eliminate the need for the draft. War Democrats, however, distinguished popular dissatisfaction with unfair provisions of the draft law from general opposition to the war or support of the Confederate cause.[29]

The Republicans viewed the riot as the bitter fruit of the copperheads' inflammatory speeches and editorials. The *Salem Standard* found the copperheads supreme hypocrites, piously crying peace while "they covertly hound on the ignorant and depraved to scenes of violence and blood." The copperheads showed solicitude for constitutional rights, yet "hounded on the mob to the invasion of the most sacred and inviolable rights of peaceable, order-loving, law-abiding citizens." They invoked liberty while indulging in license. But good would come of all this, confidently predicted the *Woodbury Constitution*, because the "base purposes of the Copperheads are now better understood by many persons who could not before be made to see."[30]

For Republicans the federal show of force in suppressing the Manhattan rioters set a healthy example for future troublemakers. Clearly the Union could not suppress rebellion in the South if it ran rampant in the North. As the *Princeton Standard* put it, "mob rule is anarchy—not democracy." One Elizabeth man singled out the Irish for the "fiendish unreasoning cruelty they have exhibited to the unoffending blacks." Irish workers, however, had no monopoly on racial prejudice, and many Irish Americans fought the rioters in Manhattan and the rebels at the front. Each party had its convenient scapegoat.[31]

The destruction and the barbarity of the New York City rioters shocked New Jerseyans and caused revulsion against all forms of civil disobedience and mob violence. The *Princeton Standard* observed that New Yorkers had given the nation an ugly picture of a free people. Most Jersey residents strongly wished local and state authorities to maintain order.[32]

In addition to public opinion, a number of actions helped to defuse a potentially explosive situation in New Jersey. City officials and prominent prowar Democrats quieted Newarkers with an appeal for order and the promise to have the draft suspended; as an extra precaution they augmented the police force. Potential rioters realized that Lincoln intended to crush resistance whatever the cost, as the army had done in New York City.

On July 15 Parker issued a stern proclamation declaring that a clear choice existed between order and anarchy: violence never restored rights or remedied wrongs. He advised New Jerseyans to avoid heated discussions and assembling in large crowds, to refrain from acts of violence, and to maintain trust in law and elections. In response to Parker's plea, Lincoln agreed to delay the draft in the state until the spring of 1864. Parker, in return, offered to make a concerted effort to secure enough volunteers to fill the state's quota. Lincoln accepted Parker's wish to raise the state's quota in his own way for the time being, as was done elsewhere.[33]

The delay of the draft allowed time for tempers to cool and for volunteers to enlist. Fear of the draft pressured many more men to enlist and galvanized counties and towns to raise higher bounties to lure volunteers. The state reached two-thirds of its quota, not a trifling achievement in comparison with many other states. Meanwhile, federal enrolling officials unobtrusively continued their task. In any case, enforcement of the draft would not begin until enough federal troops became available to put down any resistance. When the draft started, it proceeded in an orderly and quiet fashion. Federal authority, local governance, the war effort, and the state's reputation all benefited.[34]

Lincoln and Parker thus combined forces to avert major trouble in the state. Democrat Parker, however, had his disagreements with Lincoln in their private communications. Several of these were more rhetorical than real, such as Parker's suggestion that Lincoln employ McClellan in the Gettysburg campaign. Parker also showed peevishness at times in military recruitment and use of the state militia. When Parker differed with Lincoln, however, he did so respectfully and cautiously, not wishing to undermine the president in his conduct of the war.

Unlike Seymour's performance, Parker's was steadier and sounder. Although both governors supported the war, Seymour conferred with copperheads and injudiciously attended their rallies, even making compromising statements that he would regret later. He also indirectly exploited the unpopularity of the draft for partisan purposes. In contrast, Parker persistently backed the war effort. His restraining influence largely succeeded: slowly but surely he outmaneuvered and discredited the copperheads. Parker's record showed him to be a governor as firm, loyal, and effective as Olden. As the Republican *Trenton Gazette* put it a year later, "New Jersey has a real democratic Governor, instead of a copperhead demagogue."[35]

The arrival of autumn shifted attention to the off-year contests: eight senate seats, all sixty assembly seats, and the Newark mayoralty. Yet without the prospect of a statewide election, neither party organization exerted itself.

The campaign retained a local flavor, although national issues intruded powerfully. With the forthcoming presidential election uppermost in their minds, some Democrats lobbied for a conclave of party leaders to launch the campaign a year in advance, an idea that leaders rejected. Several Republican observers, believing their party had a chance to win, also deplored the lack of a determined, systematic effort. One commentator despaired of the prospects of the Republican senatorial candidate in Essex, where everybody was too "busy, no time, no money, no work, and without these he has no chance."[36]

The campaign struck observers as unusually quiet. In Newark the mayoral election ignited the explosive question of whether the city government should support Catholic schools as well as public schools. The Democrats and their mayoral candidate, Theodore Runyon, although thrown on the defensive, defeated the Republicans with almost 55 percent of the vote, but Runyon won by a substantially smaller margin. Republicans increased their number of aldermen and regained their self-confidence.[37]

Although the North had greatly strengthened its military position in the war, the Democrats still made Lincoln's war leadership an issue. Both the peace and war factions repeated their criticism of assumed war powers and questionable war measures. They found fresh ammunition in mid-September, when Lincoln, convinced that the public safety required it, everywhere suspended the writ of habeas corpus in cases involving prisoners, spies, traitors, servicemen, draftees, and deserters. The Democrats immediately pronounced the writ dead. In addition, Democrats condemned the army's interference with elections, opposed emancipation and recruitment of black soldiers, and continued to grumble about the draft. War supporters vaguely promised peace under the Democrats, who would not press for emancipation but would win the war rapidly. Peace Democrats, often in muted fashion, opposed further prosecution of the war.

Wary of attempts by the Republican party to deceive by changing its name from Republican to Union, the Democratic *Belvidere Journal* observed, "'Union Party,' Indeed! Union of Black Republicans and Abolitionists." What mattered most, especially to the copperheads, was their rigid notion that, in Wall's words, "the Constitution is the Union." In their minds, destruction of the former automatically included subversion of the latter. In contrast, the Republican *Salem Standard* contended that preservation of the Union stood paramount: "Lose it, and all is lost."[38]

Racist appeals continued. The *Trenton American* announced that Democrats stood "opposed to having the negro slaves of the South placed upon an equality with the white freemen of the North." A Warren County man claimed the Republicans plotted to "free the nigger and enslave us." Only a Democratic victory, he declared, could prevent the exploitation of whites on behalf of blacks.[39]

New Jersey Republicans believed the tide was starting to turn in their favor. Union military victories at Gettysburg and Vicksburg had strengthened the Republican cause throughout the North. Unionist election victories in Pennsylvania and Ohio during October, when the electorate decisively rejected copperhead gubernatorial candidates, further boosted Jersey Republican morale.

Encouraged Republican candidates launched their attack. As usual, they dismissed all Democratic candidates as copperheads. The *Rahway Register* viewed adherents of the "Demon-ocracy" as clad entirely in copper. Republicans pointed to the Democratic legislators who had proposed peace resolutions, espoused a black exclusion law, elected Wall senator, and prevented soldiers from voting. Beating the war drum furiously, Republicans asked voters to choose patriotism by voting Republican. The *Woodbury Constitution* asked voters to support its county senatorial candidate as an unconditional Unionist: a "Union man without an *if* or a *but*," a man who "makes no distinction between the Administration and the Government," who supports a "vigorous prosecution of the war, as the best and only means of obtaining peace—permanent peace." A soldier from Paterson summed up the party view: "Loyal is that loyal does."[40]

Federal assistance in New Jersey's elections was limited, however. When Lincoln's government allowed servicemen to return home so they could vote, and tried in various ways to influence the outcome of important elections in the North, some Jersey Republicans pleaded for similar federal help. Scovel, a senatorial candidate, asked Lincoln to send available New Jerseyan troops home. He also requested postponement of the draft until after Election Day. Lincoln complied with that request, as he did in other states, but New Jersey did not figure prominently in Republican national strategy. The state was holding only off-year elections, in contrast to significant contests for governors and entire legislatures in the more populous states of the North. Lincoln channeled federal assistance to the states with the highest stakes: he had learned from the previous year. In 1863 he showed determination not to let another northern state go Democratic by default.[41]

Despite military and political success elsewhere, Republican gains in New Jersey did not decisively tip the scales in their favor. The election results did not change the relative positions of the parties in the legislature. Yet the small shifts suggested the potential for greater change in the future. Slightly more Republicans than Democrats remained loyal to their party in 1863; almost one-eighth of those Democrats who had voted in 1862 stayed home a year later. Turnout in the elections for the assembly declined by six percentage points, and Republicans made minor gains because of Democratic abstention. The Democratic vote for assemblymen declined by three percentage points. Moreover, in seventeen counties that featured contested senatorial or county officer races, the Democrats' share of the vote cast fell sharply, from 54.8 percent in the 1862 gubernatorial election to 51.8 percent in 1863. Although the Democratic popular majority was about 10,700 statewide, Republicans made striking gains, reducing the previous Democratic majority by about one-third.[42]

In senate contests, Unionists in South Jersey won easily in Republican Gloucester and narrowly (by 51 percent) in Camden and Salem. War supporters especially cheered Scovel's victory. This fearless war champion relished the limelight and continued to play his colorful, if controversial, role in state politics. The Democrats spared no effort to defeat him on both political and personal grounds; thus a Republican victory was even sweeter, especially because Scovel, a strong supporter of Douglas in 1860, was a former Democrat. The Democrats swept their northern strongholds of Warren, Somerset, and Union. Republicans did not even bother to contest the election in Monmouth. No party lost a senate seat except in Essex, where Democratic candidate John G. Trusdell defeated his Republican opponent by 51 percent. Senate Democrats had fourteen seats and their Republican counterparts seven.

In a few spirited assembly races, Republicans won four seats: two in Newark and one each in Jersey City and the southern part of Salem, all by 51 percent except for Salem (54). In an upset, however, Atlantic Democrats captured a Republican seat in a tight race, leaving assembly Republicans with a net gain of only three seats. Although several Republicans secured election by marginal votes, notably in Mercer, a striking number of Democratic assemblymen won by the thinnest of majorities in seven districts. The Democrats in the assembly thus held forty seats and the Republicans increased their total to twenty.[43]

Republicans in the assembly had hoped to take a giant stride, but in fact they took only a small if key first step. More important, the Republicans found themselves in position to score a possible comeback in the legislature in 1864. Indeed, if the Republicans had taken more seriously the elections in those marginal districts where they lost by a very few votes they would have gained more seats. In addition, the Republican comeback was limited because the war Democrats had defeated major copperhead initiatives in the legislature. Thus, at least to some extent, they had undermined the Republicans' ability to exploit the vulnerable parts of the Democratic legislative record. Nevertheless, various observers believed that the Democratic campaign was hurt, not helped, by Wall's election and by the antiwar Democrats' flirting with peace negotiations.

In the wake of the election, editors commented on politics, Jersey style. New Jersey's legislature remained Democratic while Republicans made gains elsewhere in the North, notably in New York, where voters elected a strongly Republican legislature. Democrats took solace in New Jersey and Indiana as Democratic oases in the Republican desert. A note of self-righteous exaggeration crept into the Democrats' praise of New Jersey, however. The copperhead *Newark Journal* declared that the "State of New Jersey alone in its political integrity . . . stands out before the world as the Switzerland of America, faithful among the faithless to the true constitutional principles and landmarks." Only in New Jersey, according to the *Trenton American*, had Democrats "succeeded in saving the State from the dominion of abolitionism." The *Journal* went further, asserting that the election result was a verdict by New Jerseyans against the war.[44]

Hawkish Democratic editors disputed this bizarre view that the state Democracy had campaigned on a peace plank and that voters had repudiated the war. Even milder antiwar newspapers, such as the *Trenton American* and the *New Brunswick Times*, agreed that the battle had not turned on the issues of war and peace. On the contrary, they found that Democrats had achieved victory only by playing down such differences during the campaign. Prowar Democratic papers interpreted the election result as a popular verdict in favor of a more concerted prosecution of the war under Democratic auspices.[45]

In the eyes of Republican stalwarts outside the state, New Jersey still marched out of step. *Harper's Weekly* viewed the elections as a vote of confidence in Lincoln's administration and its war effort in every northern state— "except New Jersey, which does not count." Such sneers were unfounded. The Republican *Somerville Unionist* dismissed as wrong and unjust the charges against New Jersey as a copperhead constituency and a disloyal state. New Jerseyans had done nothing for which to apologize. Most New Jerseyans, not confusing politics with patriotism, stayed loyal to the Union while remaining nominally Democratic. Yet the state to some extent now appeared to be a political anomaly in the North. Despite a marked decline in Democratic statewide strength, Republicans in New Jersey did not achieve a corresponding resurgence, as occurred elsewhere. Jersey Republicans suffered a number of major disadvantages. Their party was not as strong as it was elsewhere. As a result of ineffective leadership and inadequate organization, they had not conducted their recent campaign well. In addition, they were hurt by the lack of the servicemen's vote. Republicans desperately needed them, but Democrats prevented their voting.[46]

Republicans decried Democrats' complaints that in other states several thousand soldiers arrived home to vote on election day. "*Are volunteers not citizens?*" asked the *Paterson Press*. The *Mount Holly Mirror* condemned the hypocrisy of every Democratic legislature that "denies the right of the soldier to vote, and attacks the Executive for sending him home to do so." The *Absecon Republican* quipped, "Say the Democrats, 'None but Democrats go to war.' Say the Democrats further, 'Soldiers are sent home to vote the Republican ticket.'" Democrats had good reason to fear soldiers who exercised the franchise, because so many voted Republican and helped to swell Union party majorities in many states.[47]

As for the copperheads, their representation in the legislature remained almost the same as before. In the senate, prowar forces in fact lost influence through the election of two copperheads to represent the two Democratic strongholds of Union and Somerset. In the assembly, no known copperhead incumbent who ran for reelection lost his seat. Of twenty assemblymen identified as copperheads in the previous legislature, thirteen returned to Trenton. An additional seven did not run for reelection, and three copperheads won election for the first time.

In major contests, well-known copperheads did well. Bergen's two assemblymen actually gained ground at the polls. Thomas Dunn English, the most visible copperhead and the faction's leader in the assembly, won a fierce contest in the first district by exactly the same majority as in the previous election, despite a decrease in the total vote. John Dater in the second district increased his majority substantially. Because the copperheads held their own in legislative contests, it seemed inexplicable that many copperheads were discouraged in the last two months of 1863.

Two years of frustrating, bloody combat had blunted the patriotic, prowar enthusiasm shared by New Jerseyans during the early months of the war. Thus the rejection of copperheads in the 1861 legislative election did not repeat itself in 1863. Copperheads did not make major inroads into the legislative districts of prowar Democrats or Republicans, however. Instead the copperheads maintained their position, usually under favorable circumstances. In 1863 three-fourths of the copperheads ran in safe districts without viable competition. In four marginal districts the copperheads won election, but only narrowly.[48]

Voters knew they were voting Democratic, but generally remained unaware of the candidate's precise position. Copperheads usually did not campaign as such in 1862 and 1863. Indeed, only rarely did a vote in the legislature help identify copperheads, and many voters remained ignorant of these developments. Also, to achieve victory by fostering unity, virtually all Democrats, both war supporters and war opponents, tried to blur factional differences during the campaign. Thus most Democrats voted Democratic out of party loyalty, expressing dissatisfaction with Republican actions and paying little attention to a particular Democratic candidate's factional proclivity.

In late November, the Union army won significant victories at Lookout Mountain and Missionary Ridge in Tennessee. When Union forces threatened Atlanta and the rest of Georgia with attack, the copperheads' proposals became irrelevant. Referring to the state election, the Republican *Mount Holly Mirror* commented that the "power of Copperheadism in New Jersey was broken on the Third instant, and so seriously damaged, that it is no longer to be feared."[49]

Clearly the announcement of the copperheads' demise was premature.

Even if the election had not damaged the copperheads' limited power, the tactical draw and the psychological reaction to it by both copperheads and their opponents hinted at the erosion of copperhead influence. Both developments mattered more than the number of seats won in safe districts. The copperheads retained their minority position in the short run; the reaction to the election signaled their weakness in the long run. Union victories had changed the political situation and the atmosphere in the State House. The copperheads recognized that they were more vulnerable now than at any time since 1861. Their increasing isolation became clear in their postelection behavior. Their sharp decline became evident in showdown votes during the legislative session of 1864. Thus, by the end of 1863 the tide had begun to turn.

Although the Democrats in general were happy with the outcome in the state, they became discouraged with the overall result in the North. A Jersey City Democrat grumbled at Lincoln's phenomenal success in influencing so many northerners to "believe anything, do anything, say anything, or think anything this wonderful administration directs them to." War Democrats blamed Democratic defeats in other northern states on the peace faction, which nominated extremist candidates and ran on unpopular copperhead platforms. The Democrats recognized that to win in New Jersey, they had had to mute further their differences about the central issue of war or peace.[50]

New Jersey copperheads retorted that no man could be a Democrat and still back the war and support Lincoln's policies. "A white black bird is as easily found," remarked the *Newark Journal*. No "bastard patriot" or "abolition renegade" deserved the label "Democrat." A week after the election, the peace men broke openly with the Democratic war hawks. For the first time the *Newark Journal* called Parker's support of the war effort a mistake. No Democrat, declared the *Journal*, should go to war or induce others to bear arms. No local Democratic government should offer bounties to raise volunteers. "This wretched war" justified neither one more man nor one more dollar. Parker, suggested the *Journal*, knew that "every soldier sent from this State is an additional weapon in the hands of the Abolitionists." The newspaper urged every peace man to reject any compromise with war supporters, to oppose any "trimming of principles for the sake of expediency for office." Democrats must stop seeking success by disguising their opposition to the war. The *Journal* added that Parker's unstinting support of the war effort undermined the integrity of the state's executive branch and the independence of the state; this suggested that he did not represent the popular views of Democrats at all.[51]

In reply, prowar Democrats denounced the antiwar faction for misrepresenting state Democrats to New Jersey voters and troops, and dismissed them as having "little or no influence in this State." According to the *Jersey City Standard*, "They could not have played more completely into the hands of the abolitionists than they have done and are now doing when they wag their lawless tongues." By discouraging volunteering and withholding bounties to volunteers, they encouraged what they opposed—the odious draft. As to the conduct of the war, the newspaper minced no words: "It matters nothing that in our opinion the administration misconceives the object of the war and shamefully misconducts it. It matters not that on almost every conceivable point of public policy the administration is dangerously and we fear criminally wrong. Our duty is still plain to prosecute the war for the Union, and to stand faithfully by the brave soldiers who do our fighting." No matter how badly mismanaged, declared the *Standard*, the conflict was "a righteous war." Copperheads saw only what they wished to see: "no good in the administration" and "no evil in the common foe," the Confederacy.[52]

Prowar Democrats wished voters to do everything in their power to replace Lincoln's administration with a Democratic one, which could manage affairs better. To accomplish this, Democrats should devise a "policy to win by instead of to lose by." To follow the peace faction's destructive policy would so weaken the Union army that it would become easy prey for the rebels, who would kill its troops, including New Jerseyans. This situation would encourage a Confederate invasion of the North and New Jersey. The *Camden Democrat* queried the copperheads on their preference: did they wish to surrender to the rebel army, wait aimlessly for a draft call, declare war on the federal government and thus commit political suicide?[53]

As prowar Democrats recognized that outright opposition to the war diminished their party's chances, antiwar Democrats grew increasingly restless and impatient. Now that the campaign was over, Bergen's copperheads abandoned any pretense of trying to work with Parker. A copperhead club in Franklin, Rodman Price's hometown, issued a resolution that suggested equal culpability on the part of Parker and Lincoln for supposed wartime violation of rights and liberties.

At a celebration meeting held on November 24 in Paramus, copperheads aired their views in numerous toasts. One man yearned for the good old days before cowardice and treachery had demoralized the Democratic party. Another declared that supporters of the war should go to fight and that opponents of the war should stay at home and enjoy peace. Still another described a war Democrat as a "white man's face on the body of a negro."[54]

The chief speakers at the meeting included three copperhead leaders—Daniel Holsman, Price, and Burr. Burr denounced prowar Democrats as lunatics for backing a war whose purposes they opposed. He declared that "every Jerseyman in favor of this war is a foe to his own State." Because Parker had encouraged mobilization and had allowed federal authority to encroach on state authority, Burr asserted that the "State of New Jersey has ceased to exist; it is only a military district." He believed that secession, although unfortunate, was only a minor crime; it reduced the nation's territory but left the remaining states intact. Lincoln, however, with dagger drawn, eagerly stabbed liberty to death as he annihilated rights, subverted states, and imposed a dictatorship. Burr dismissed the rebel as a mere runaway and pronounced Lincoln the real enemy of the Union.[55]

Most New Jerseyans, both Republican and Democratic, greeted the Paramus festival with amazement and indignation. The *Jersey City Chronicle* wondered what copperheads had to celebrate, given the recent unionist triumphs both on the battlefront and at the ballot box. The *Newark Mercury* stated that the degradation to which the copperheads subjected New Jersey had reached a new low with the Paramus meeting. Many Bergen Democrats repudiated the Paramus meeting. "The smallest possible minority of the Democracy in the State" share such views, declared the *Newton Herald*. Of the state's newspapers, the *Herald* counted only the *Newark Journal* in favor of the message of the meeting, which placed it "alone in all New Jersey."[56]

The first half of 1863 marked a nadir in the war for the Union. Some northerners and New Jerseyans plainly lost their nerve. As the year progressed, however, the rebels experienced significant setbacks. Both the resourceful Union army and the resilient northern people regained their morale.

In Washington, the dome of the Capitol, with symbolic significance, neared completion, supported by structural iron beams made in a Trenton factory. Earlier in the war a New Jersey soldier had looked at the dome and remarked: "True, its dome is not yet completed; neither is the Republic finished." On December 2, 1863, the builders hoisted to the dome the final section of the Statue of Freedom. A man raised the national flag, and guns representing all the states of the Union fired a salute. Northerners were on the verge of both saving the Union and transforming it.[57]

In New Jersey, as elsewhere in the North, even though the copperheads attracted attention and gained notoriety, they failed to transform a lack of confidence in the Republicans' management of the war into a vote of no confidence in the war itself. As the copperheads in early 1863 shifted from general faultfinding with the conduct of the war to advocacy of a cease-fire to end the war, they began to lose their credibility. When New Jersey copperhead legislators Holsman and English suddenly introduced an armistice resolution in the legislature, most New Jerseyans regarded it as foolish and overwhelmingly chose reunion by war over disunion by peace. Moreover, the copperheads' support of expensive, unnecessary programs, such as deportation of blacks and a gigantic buildup of the state militia, earned no credibility among New Jerseyans.

Many New Jerseyans started to question not only the copperheads' cause but also their political style. Their impatience, melodramatic exaggeration, and obstructionist tactics undercut their political effectiveness in the legislature. The copperheads, as Newark businessman Silas Merchant observed, had become "emboldened by ill success of the Federal troops," and "struck out boldly and became blatant in their treason and were ahead of public sentiment." He concluded that the "copperhead portion of the Democrats are now by our national successes left out in the cold."[58]

The revulsion against the copperheads and their peace cause began in March, when a Gloucester physician noticed "a wholesome reaction beginning in the North." He remarked, "These selfish leaders will ultimately become as odious as the Tories of the Revolution." The prowar Democratic *New York Herald* asserted that "thinking Democrats are beginning to find out that copperheadism is not popular." Speaking for state Democrats, the hawkish *Jersey City Standard* in late November contended that the result of the copperhead offensive with all its extremist excesses during 1863 had "put us on a miserable *defensive*, when we should have been triumphantly on the *offensive*." War supporters saw the wisdom of leaving the copperheads alone, giving them just enough rope to hang themselves. The physician found that people now were "influenced by but one absorbing idea—that the Rebellion *Must* be put down, let it cost, in men and money, what it may. The public faith is strong in our Ultimate Success."[59]

# 11 Preelection Skirmishing in Early 1864

I n his annual message on January 13, Governor Joel Parker gave
the state Democratic keynote address, opening the presidential campaign at the same time. He condemned secession but
criticized Lincoln's war policies and abuses of power. Faulting Republicans
for confusing dissent with disloyalty, Parker termed emancipation unconstitutional and unwise. The year before, he had attempted to placate the copperheads, but now, after their attacks, he gave them a tongue-lashing. Parker
warned that peace, however desirable, could come only by prosecuting the
war until the Confederates surrendered. No longer did he balance his rhetorical position between the war Democrats and the peace Democrats; circumstances and opinion had changed. Now he identified openly with the
war wing of the Democracy.[1]

Reaction to Parker's address varied according to party and faction. Misrepresenting the meaning of the address, the Republican *New York Times*
printed the headline "*New Jersey versus the United States.*" The *Somerville Unionist*, although less malicious, nevertheless complained that Parker suggested
no constructive alternative either to Lincoln's war measures or to the copperheads' peace proposals. The Republicans disagreed with Parker on federal policies, yet thanked him magnanimously for his unwavering support of
the North's military effort. The *Camden Journal* declared: "There has not been
a day since the inauguration of Governor Parker that he has not devoted his
entire energies and official position to aid the Government in putting down
the Rebellion. He has no sympathy with copperheads, or anyone else who
endeavors to bring the fair name and character of our State into disrepute."
Predictably, Democratic war supporters applauded Parker's address, while
antiwar Democrats criticized it. The copperhead *Newark Journal* doubted
whether perpetual civil war was preferable to disunion, temporary or permanent.[2]

During the legislative session the copperheads marked time and cursed
their isolation and impotence. Once again the prowar Democrats generally
rejected the proposals of the peace men. An incident in the assembly revealed the copperheads' bitterness. Thomas Dunn English refused huffily
when chosen to call on Parker and notify him that the members of the assembly had completed their organization. Reportedly he huffed, "No, I am
not one of Joel Parker's boot-blacks; I would go to take a rope to hang him,
with pleasure. That is the only purpose for which I would call on him." The
decline of the copperheads, which had begun with their decisive losses during

the legislative session of 1863, accelerated in 1864 as their defeatist passivity replaced frenetic activity.[3]

Battles over leadership and patronage revealed the political complexion of the legislature. The Democrats chose officials with no strong ties to the copperheads. The senate bypassed copperhead Daniel Holsman as its presiding officer in favor of Amos Robins of Woodbridge, a respected party stalwart. Although in the past Robins had aligned himself occasionally with copperhead ultras, his acceptance speech and his support of war measures did not reflect copperhead views. The senators rejected several prominent copperhead candidates for secretary, gave the public printing work to war supporter Louis Vogt, unanimously backed various prowar actions and resolutions, and killed a few irresponsible proposals from the assembly. The senate unanimously refused to confirm the appointment of David Naar, whom the governor, as a sop to the copperheads, had nominated as one of the six riparian commissioners. With the help of six Democrats, the senate also rejected James Wall and instead selected two Republican commissioners. Indeed the senate as a whole eschewed copperhead connections.[4]

Similarly, the assembly, with a somewhat larger proportion of copperheads, passed over copperhead leader English for speaker and selected war hawk Joseph N. Taylor of Paterson. When Taylor died in early April, the assembly unanimously chose as his replacement Robert Hamilton of Newton, another war hawk. The peace men, however, remained Democrats in good standing. Parker Democrats in the chamber wished strongly to maintain party unity as much as possible, and so gave copperhead editors many public printing contracts. Despite the usual heated conflict in party caucus over patronage between various factions, localities, and interests, Democrats presented a united front for their party's nominations.[5]

Once again the legislature backed the war effort. The senate unanimously authorized an additional war loan of one million dollars and approved higher taxes. The assembly passed the war loan with only two Hunterdon copperheads, David Banghart and David Boss, voting against it. The legislature legalized local and county war bounty bonds and, after some partisan sparring over wording, thanked the soldiers for their patriotic enlistment for the duration of the war. Legislators also endorsed medical support of the troops, ordered official flags for the state's regiments, and authorized a study of the needs of disabled veterans. The legislature sidetracked English's second attempt to strengthen the militia on his terms and named mainly war hawks to direct a study of state defense. War opponents experienced one major setback after another.[6]

Seizing the initiative as the presidential election loomed closer, Republicans demanded voting for soldiers as a matter of both self-interest and simple justice. Republican activists wrote editorials, held rallies, and mounted a massive petition drive. Petitions from every county, signed by more than thirty-seven thousand citizens and soldiers, poured into the legislature. The Republicans argued that if a man risked his life to defend his country, he deserved the ballot. As a soldier, moreover, he had not forfeited his rights as a citizen.[7]

Specifically, the Republicans maintained that soldiers did not lose their legal residence and voter qualification just because they served outside the state. No provision of the state constitution expressly prohibited either absentee voting or proxy voting. Other states devised various methods that allowed soldiers to vote. If, as the Democrats boasted, most New Jersey troops favored their party, then Democratic legislators had no reason to oppose enfranchisement. Yet, as the Republicans pointed out, Democratic newspapers and politicians failed to champion soldier voting precisely because they feared the troops would not vote for Democrats.[8]

Because of the high stakes and the Republican barrage, the atmosphere in the Democratic-controlled legislature became highly charged. Although the Republicans did not seriously expect Democrats to concede a major advantage, nonetheless they pressed for a showdown vote in order to embarrass the Democrats and create a damaging campaign issue. As the *Absecon Republican* stated, the "day is coming when this injustice will be remembered, and remembered with a vengeance."[9]

Ignoring the precedent whereby the state allowed absentee voting by servicemen during the War of 1812, prowar Democrats in the legislature found legal obstacles to justify their position. They contended that the state constitution required a voter to reside in his county for five months preceding an election. They argued further that the law required an eligible voter to cast a ballot personally in his county.

Hoping to defuse the issue, the Democrats approved a resolution requesting army authorities to grant leaves so New Jersey's servicemen could return home to vote. (Combat supposedly would stop in Virginia out of respect for elections held in New Jersey.) On March 9, in virtually a straight party vote, the assembly approved the resolution 39 to 9. On March 15 the senate similarly accepted the preamble, which declared absentee voting unconstitutional.[10]

The Democratic effort to ramrod this resolution through the legislature betrayed desperation. Yet the Democrats all along regarded the Republicans' enfranchisement effort as a cheap electioneering trick because the state constitution tied the legislature's hands. In the end, the New Jersey Democrats, along with Democratic legislatures in other states, rejected the option of soldiers voting in the field. As a result of such disfranchisement, the Republican *Trenton Monitor* was sufficiently discouraged to predict that the "Union men of New Jersey are to have a hard contest."[11]

After the legislature refused to enfranchise soldiers, one trooper observed acidly, "We are proud of the name of a Jersey soldier, and are always willing to acknowledge that we are of those honored 'Jersey Blues' who have done honor to the cause of liberty and right." Troops had brought no disgrace upon their native state, he declared, but its Democratic politicians had done so. The man denounced them for treating soldiers as "no more citizens of New Jersey, by refusing to grant us the right of suffrage." Thus "we of the 11th Regiment are still, as ever, the sons of New Jersey, but we have reason to deplore our parentage, and sometimes are tempted to disown our relation to our mother State."[12]

A member of the Fifteenth Regiment referred contemptuously to those politicians who enjoyed all the rights of citizens, yet voted in the legislature to deny soldiers the right to vote "when those rights are preserved to them by the soldiers, and by them alone." He continued, "I don't like to see men feign a care and love for the soldier by passing resolutions urging the commanding officers to let them *go home to vote* when they know the chances are all against their being thus sent." On this point, two men in the Sixth Regiment protested: "But we may vote if we come home. Ha! Ha! Ha! Suppose we did go home to vote, and all the other State troops did the same"; the rebels would take advantage of their absence to invade the North. The man in the Fifteenth New Jersey concluded, "I don't like to see wolves in sheep's clothing, much less Traitors acting under the garb of 'Union and Constitution.'"[13]

Another restriction on soldiers was promoted by English. He proposed to ban any soldier carrying arms near or at a polling place on election day. He claimed that army interference in elections that had occurred in the border states made such a bill necessary. English as well as other copperheads regarded individual soldiers as champions of a hateful war, which made them both personal and political enemies.[14]

Although editorials in a few antiwar newspapers supported English's bill, the Republicans blasted it. The *Camden Press* pointed out that the "copperhead vote in the army is not worth cultivating." The Trenton reporter of the *Newark Advertiser* dismissed it as another one of those "frantic efforts of Mr. English to do something *dashing* in opposition to the federal government." The correspondent asked, "Does this not look as if the 'peace' party were getting afraid of their own shadow? Surely there has never been in this State any interference in our elections by the soldiers." One Bergen resident observed that troops up to this point had worn their uniforms proudly as a badge of honor, but if English's bill became law, a volunteer's uniform would become a badge of dishonor, subjecting the wearer to restrictions imposed upon no other citizens.[15]

The showdown came on March 15, when the assembly killed the bill on a tie vote. The Republicans opposed the measure unanimously. Many Democratic war supporters had decided to back the bill in an attempt to create an election issue in the upcoming campaign, to embarrass the Republicans, and to take pot shots at Lincoln's handling of border state elections. Yet when the assembly voted, not all Democrats went along with this calculation of political expediency. Eight resisted the party and opposed the bill. Even the copperhead ranks broke: half of the eight who opposed this measure had voted as copperheads before; three defectors hailed from competitive districts. Overall, six of the eight Democratic dissidents represented close districts. The defectors evidently opposed the bill because it faced certain defeat in the senate, and they feared that their support for the bill would jeopardize their reelection. The failure of English's bill underscored the general decline of copperhead influence. It also suggested strongly that the tug-of-war between copperheads and Democratic hawks in the legislature was winding down rapidly.[16]

The legislature also considered several sensitive issues involving race relations. English introduced a bill banning intermarriage between whites and blacks. Some Democratic newspapers fed on racial fears by spreading the notion of Republicans as "nigger-worshippers" bent on imposing social equality for blacks. Most Republicans in fact opposed miscegenation and accused Democrats of practicing it in the slave states. To undercut the Democrats' race baiting, Republican assemblymen supported English's bill. Although the assembly approved it unanimously, the more moderate senate killed the measure outright on April 6 by repealing its enacting clause.[17]

Then, in the words of the Trenton reporter of the *Newark Advertiser*, "English broke out with another paroxysm of his chronic malady, the negrophobia." He proposed amendments to a pending bill to incorporate Trenton's board of education and sought to impose racial segregation on its public schools. The assembly's Republicans, however, along with many nonvoting Democrats, defeated this proposal and finally scrubbed the entire bill in late March.[18]

Meanwhile, some black Trentonians requested that an unreceptive legislature amend the constitution by enfranchising Negroes. In their petition they noted that thousands of black New Jerseyans currently were fighting for the Union and thus had earned the first right of citizenship.[19]

A pending bounty bill for Union County, which contained a provision prohibiting payment of bounties to black volunteers raised the subject of recruiting black troops. The *Trenton Gazette* exclaimed, "Are we then to think that the county of Union, after having enlisted these men under pretense of paying them bounties, is now trying to defraud them of money that is honestly due them?" Democratic senator Edward Scudder agreed and opposed the provision. Eliminating the racial exclusion, the senate passed the bill. Union's Democratic senator James Jenkins then introduced a more comprehensive bill forbidding payments to all black recruits in the state. The Republicans attacked it for its repudiation of government policy, federal law, and elemental fairness. In the face of concerted opposition, the sponsors of the bill abandoned it in mid-March.[20]

Meanwhile, black troops in pitched battles earned increasing recognition for their valor. Respect deepened in April in the wake of the news that rebels had bayoneted black prisoners and buried wounded blacks alive at Fort Pillow in Tennessee. This massacre angered many New Jerseyans; opposition to employing black soldiers declined after this incident.[21]

In July Parker, although still unhappy about arming Negroes, reluctantly accepted black recruits from outside the state to meet the state's quota. The Confederates undermined opposition further in the fall, when some rebels suggested turning slaves into soldiers. Although die-hard copperheads continued to oppose the use of black soldiers and criticized their military effectiveness, the legislature mandated in 1865 that servicemen's families should receive the same benefits regardless of race.[22]

Spring municipal elections largely emphasized local matters. Democrats railed as usual against fanaticism, referring to Republicans as "the Abolitionists." Republicans, following their usual unionist strategy, told voters they faced a choice between proud patriots and hissing copperheads. Voter participation declined. The Democrats retained power in the northern part of the state and in such cities as Jersey City, Trenton, Elizabeth, New Brunswick, and Hoboken. The Republicans, however, showed strength in South Jersey and made considerable gains in many contests elsewhere. They reduced Democratic majorities significantly, did well in Camden, Rahway, and Orange, and succeeded in recapturing Paterson. These results encouraged Republicans to redouble their effort in the fall campaign. Although the Democrats denied any concern, they did not exude great confidence.[23]

New Jersey's congressional delegation, like the state's politicians, remained deeply divided. The war hawks consisted of two Republicans, Senator John Ten Eyck and Representative John Starr, and two Democrats, George Middleton and William Steele. Two Democrats generally opposed various war measures: Andrew Rogers, a moderate peace man in his voting although a fiery orator, and Nehemiah Perry, frequently an extreme copperhead but a milder speaker than Rogers.[24]

Division, inactivity, indecision, and a high rate of absenteeism characterized the delegation's overall performance. Constituents and editors throughout the state, both Republicans and Democrats, complained about their poor quality. Horace Congar's excessively harsh description of Ten Eyck as "certainly a small specimen of a Public Man" might have been more applicable to the other members of the delegation. At a time when the state needed strong representation, it lacked it.[25]

The proposed constitutional amendment abolishing slavery became a test of strength between the parties in Congress. On April 8 the United States Senate approved the amendment in a partisan vote. Ten Eyck supported it;

ailing William Wright was among the absentees. On June 15 the House failed to reach the required two-thirds majority and so rejected the amendment. Starr supported it; Perry, Rogers, and Steele opposed it. Middleton was absent, probably on purpose, and drew criticism from fellow Democrats for failing to hew to the party line.

In important test votes for Ten Eyck, he voted against mandating the enfranchisement of Negroes in Montana Territory but supported the final bill that did so. He also opposed black suffrage in the District of Columbia. On reconstructing the rebel states, the New Jersey Democrats, usually joined by Ten Eyck, opposed radical initiatives, which in their view treated the South harshly.[26]

A different type of controversy swirled around the Camden and Amboy Railroad's monopoly of intercity traffic across central New Jersey. Congress considered ending this monopoly by federal fiat. With the state in the national spotlight, this issue challenged vested interests, cut across state and federal jurisdictions, divided Republican ranks in a presidential election year, and raised questions about the state's political position.

New Jersey's railroads had helped carry troops and supplies to the front line of defense in Virginia. The war brought the state's railroads new opportunities for profit, but also imposed unprecedented demands on its limited rail capacity. The prosperous, powerful Camden and Amboy Railroad played a pivotal role. Under federal pressure, the railroad completed a straightened and double track in 1864 and improved train connections. Yet as a monopoly defending its exclusive privileges and resorting to heavy-handed lobbying, the railroad denied the power of the federal government, even in the most pressing military emergencies, to send troops over any railroad line other than its own. The corporation reaped profits by overcharging riders while providing inadequate service on its overtaxed lines.

Reporting on rail service between New York City and Washington, a committee of Congress condemned it: a "more disagreeable, annoying, and unsatisfactory line of railroad, for the length and importance of it, is not to be found in the United States." A trip that should have taken seven to nine hours required twelve to fourteen. The New Jersey leg between New York and Philadelphia lasted four hours, at least an hour more than necessary. The overall route, described as "the most travelled and most vital thoroughfare in the Union," required a passenger to change trains three times. Congress discussed the problem during 1862 and 1863. It took no action, although various members reiterated that public safety and public interest required federal intervention.[27]

In 1863 the War Department bypassed the Camden and Amboy Railroad by using the adjacent Raritan and Delaware Bay Railroad to transport some servicemen and equipment. In retaliation, the Camden and Amboy sued to prevent the Raritan and Delaware from carrying military traffic between New York and Philadelphia. In early February 1864 a state court ruled in favor of the Camden and Amboy, requiring that both civilian and military interstate traffic between the two cities be hauled over its rails. To enforce the state's grant of a monopoly to the Camden and Amboy, the court banned all competition and ordered payment of damages.

Infuriated by this decision and by the actions of the Camden and Amboy, Republicans in the House of Representatives decided during the spring of 1864 to pit federal power against both state and corporate prerogative in the interest of cheaper, faster, safer service. They planned to authorize another rail line as a federal post route across central New Jersey, competing with the Camden and Amboy in direct violation of New Jersey's charter and its court's decision.

The Camden and Amboy mobilized its lobbyists and supporters to prevent or delay federal action. The railroad, however, had to counter the powerful patriotic appeal of military necessity, its own record of poor service, and the increasing unpopularity of corporate and state privileges. The ensuing fight raised thorny issues between the national interest and state rights, free enterprise and privileged monopoly, military necessity and the sanctity of corporate property, unimpeded interstate commerce and restricted intrastate transit, public convenience and customary usage, and violation of a contract and inviolability of a contract. Despite the serious issues involved, members of Congress enjoyed any respite. Roars of laughter greeted an anonymous congressman's assertion that no rail problem really existed because New Jersey's narrow width allowed for only one railroad track.[28]

A small but vocal minority of New Jerseyans favored the immediate end of the monopoly. A much larger bipartisan majority supported the monopoly's legal rights, although many people reaffirmed their opposition to any extension of existing privileges and expressed relief that the franchise would end in 1869. Despite serious misgivings about the monopoly, many Jerseyans resented what they regarded as cavalier disregard of a state charter by Congress.

In late March, Governor Parker and members of both parties in the legislature spoke out against the anticipated federal interference. Their protest sailed through the assembly without recorded dissent; in the senate only two members, George Horner and James Scovel, both downstate Republicans, opposed the resolution. All of the state's congressmen opposed ending the monopoly before the expiration date. The antimonopoly *Newton Register*, however, dismissed Parker's message and the legislature's resolutions as "only a harmless display of rhetorical indignation." New Jersey's railroad monopoly gained additional support from other members of Congress, especially those from southeastern Pennsylvania and from Delaware and Maryland, which monopolized and benefited from the interstate traffic on the main line between Philadelphia and Washington. In Maryland, for instance, the Baltimore and Ohio Railroad in effect imposed a tax on passengers, just as the Camden and Amboy did in New Jersey.[29]

Defenders of the railroad claimed that the federal government would overstep its bounds by discarding state legislation by a simple act of Congress. To regulate their internal affairs New Jerseyans needed to govern as they saw fit, tax as they deemed necessary, and authorize a railroad franchise as it suited them. They considered any meddling with the state's jurisdiction over intrastate transportation to be mischievous, and interference with the exclusive privileges of a state-authorized artery illegal. They contended that the plan to construct a new rail line to help military transportation would serve no purpose because the war would likely end before its completion. Moreover, competitive lines within New Jersey might weaken or even bankrupt one or both of the interstate railroads. Improving the existing line as quickly as possible was the best and least disruptive solution. In addition, if the army required the use of a railroad, ample federal authority could be found under the Railroad Act of January 30, 1862, which authorized all railroads as post routes and made them subject to army orders. C & A supporters clinched their case—at least for many New Jerseyans—by pointing out that the state's railroad monopoly furnished most of the state government's revenue.[30]

The antimonopolists contended that only federal intervention could break the railroad's stranglehold. Kentuckian George H. Yeaman expressed their sentiment in the House of Representatives: "Monopolies are odious; they are contrary to the spirit of our Government; they are contrary to the spirit of the age; they are ruinous to commerce . . . and they are an offense to that great *Democratic Idea* which is conquering the world in its ever-aggressive warfare on prerogative and its traditions." Yeaman also questioned the anomalous situation in which New Jersey's control of intercity traffic interfered with interstate commerce: "How can this State regulate the commercial intercourse of the two greatest cities on the continent, neither of which is in her borders? . . . how can Congress regulate it if New Jersey may say it shall only go on a particular route?" Yeaman argued that the power to regulate interstate commerce rested ultimately with Congress; thus the "monopoly fails when Congress so wills."

The *Philadelphia Dispatch* observed that New Jersey had built a great wall across its territory, leaving open a single gate and forcing all travelers to enter and leave by this gate alone. The *Newton Register* added similarly that New Jersey did not have the "power to clog and obstruct the greatest thoroughfare in the Union."

Scovel summed up the antimonopolist position: the state ought to own the railroad, not the railroad the state. The *Absecon Republican* claimed that the Camden and Amboy had won its case in court only because the monopoly controlled its judges. It declared: "All political power comes from the monopoly. Hence all office holders and office seekers willingly sell themselves to its service." Senator Charles Sumner spoke of a "vampire monopoly which, brooding over New Jersey, sucks the life-blood of the whole country."[31]

The antimonopolists, however, ignored the existence of eighteen other railroads in New Jersey, only half a dozen of which were tied to the Camden and Amboy. Other transportation monopolies behaved just as high-handedly and greedily when fighting off a competitor. In addition, the Camden and Amboy had to contend with rival railroads and cope with competing regional interests.

If self-interest prompted defense of the monopoly, opportunism also motivated the antimonopolists. Some received support and subsidy from railroad speculators in New York City and Philadelphia who wished to enrich themselves by breaking the monopoly. Under the pretext of military necessity and fair play, the representatives of the Raritan and Delaware Railroad, competitors of the Camden and Amboy, hoped to use the federal government to bypass the C & A for their own profit. They wished to transform their bad speculation with worthless stock into a lucrative investment. The motive of the antimonopolists, the *Toms River Emblem* observed, was the same one that had given birth to the Camden and Amboy's monopoly—namely profit. It was the source, declared the *Emblem*, "of their much boasted 'principle,' and it does not require a close observer to ascertain in this case that the '*interest*' far exceeds the '*principle*.'" If the Camden and Amboy monopoly had acted arrogantly, abused its privileges, brushed aside the public interest, lobbied recklessly, and profited greatly from its franchise, its opponents just as surely hoped to follow suit.[32]

On May 12, 1864, after extended, heated debate, the House approved a bill that would have ended the Camden and Amboy's railroad monopoly. Only one New Jerseyan, Middleton, opposed the bill; the rest of the delegation did not vote. The Senate, however, scuttled the bill; disagreement over committee jurisdiction and the press of emergency legislation contributed to inaction. During the lame duck session in early 1865 the Senate again considered such a bill several times, only to put it aside. Concerted opposition from the monopoly's strong lobby evidently contributed to defeat in both years. The waning of the war emergency and the need to act on more urgent matters also contributed to the defeat of the railroad bill. After the war, however, more rail competition developed in New Jersey.[33]

The debate over the railroad monopoly brought yet more abuse of New Jersey. The *New York Tribune* condemned New Jersey for becoming "The State of Camden and Amboy." The *New York Herald* stated that "the railroad is the State and the State the railroad." *Harper's Weekly* declared that "every citizen of New Jersey, in a matter which concerns the Camden and Amboy Railroad, is liable to suspicion until the State emancipates itself from its control." Observers pictured New Jersey as an isolated island of jealous power and privilege, a selfish state that put its narrow self-interest ahead of the national interest even in wartime. The *Princeton Standard* deplored New Jersey's concern for "the monopoly first—the Country afterwards." Several Jersey newspapers voiced the hope that the state would abandon its railroad policy, which was alienating other states and ruining New Jersey's reputation.[34]

Because some New Jerseyans defended their railroad monopoly as a matter of state rights, the state also suffered from guilt by association with southern defenders of state rights. Critics pointed out that both New Jersey and South Carolina used such discredited arguments to defend unacceptable practices. Sumner observed, "It is not unnatural that the doctrines of South Carolina on State rights should obtain a shelter in New Jersey. Like seeks like." As one reporter explained, the "excessive, mischievous and unconstitutional powers claimed for the State governments by the secessionists of the South have caused all Union men to look with suspicion and distrust upon every claim of 'State Rights.'"[35]

Critics also identified the absence of free enterprise in the Camden and Amboy's monopoly as akin to the absence of free labor in the South. Just as the nation was at the mercy of the South, the North now was at the mercy of New Jersey's rail monopoly. Once slavery and monopoly had held sway, but both now had to be abolished.

The *Newton Register* employed anti-slavery rhetoric in dismissing most members of New Jersey's legislature as slaves of a corrupt corporation: "Puppets— of soulless serfs, owned by them as absolutely as the blacks who toil for a Southern Planter." The *Princeton Standard* glibly observed that the New Jersey Democracy had "as completely sold itself to Camden and Amboy, as the national Democracy had sold itself to the slave power prior to the Rebellion." The *Trenton Monitor* declared, "Slavery is a monopoly, and monopoly is slavery. Both trample freedom under foot." Thus Republicans and antimonopolists called for emancipation of the slaves in the South and liberation of New Jerseyans from the monopoly. If Jersey molders of opinion on the antimonopoly side were so ready to castigate the state, it scarcely was a wonder that some outsiders took a dim view of New Jersey. The *Bordentown Register*, however, disputed the rhetoric of the antimonopolists: the "presumption that New Jersey advocates doctrines entertained by southern fire-eaters, relative to 'State rights' is as nonsensical as it is untrue."[36]

Some Republican opponents of the monopoly wildly accused it of sympathizing with the secession cause and jeopardizing the war effort. The *Monitor* referred cryptically to "monopoly power" and "monopoly treason." "By their machinations and money," it asserted boldly, the monopoly "held loyal New Jersey in the Copperhead traces." Going further, the newspaper derided the Joint Companies as the "Confederate Companies." The *Newton Register* added that only the monopoly prevented Republicans from winning the state. Republican congressmen from outside New Jersey, too, questioned New

Jerseyans' loyalty. Vermonter Frederick E. Woodbridge considered New Jersey's political condition "as bad as it can be." According to Pennsylvanian John M. Broomall, many believed that "New Jersey is in the habit of voting wrong." Indeed, he added, the state assumed a position as "near out of the Union" as possible. Thus the notion of a treasonable monopoly enlarged to embrace the idea of a treasonable state.[37]

While the entire episode divided New Jerseyans, the combination of anti-monopoly and anti-New Jersey sentiment united many northerners against both the Camden and Amboy Railroad and the state. The debate in Congress and in the country revealed that many northern politicians and editors regarded the state's railroad monopoly as a national nuisance. By creating and defending it, New Jersey in the eyes of many had fallen into national disfavor. The unpopular monopoly also served as a convenient scapegoat for intensely partisan Republicans from outside the state who wished to punish New Jerseyans for voting Democratic. (In defense of the state an editorial in the Republican *Trenton Gazette* pointed out that even though the worst bottlenecks on the railroad route between New York and Washington occurred south of New Jersey, there nevertheless "seems to be a peculiar spite at New Jersey" because only it "is singled out for punishment.") New Jersey's Republicans hoped the railroad controversy during 1864 would not figure as a partisan issue within the state. Some state Republicans, however, conceded that the ongoing dispute between the Republican national government and the Democratic state government could hardly help the Republican cause in the upcoming elections when Republicans in Washington openly condemned, even threatened, New Jersey.

If they accomplished nothing else in the short run, the antimonopolists helped popularize the view of New Jersey as a dishonest, disloyal state. The *Trenton Monitor* argued that the railroad monopoly had oppressed New Jerseyans for too long, had "dictated your laws, caused courts to tremble, corrupted your legislators, and absolutely made you a stench in the nostrils of all your sister States." As antimonopoly sentiment grew outside New Jersey, the myth gained ascendancy. The *New York Herald* titled an editorial "New Jersey in Rebellion." The wartime frenzy and sheer repetition added credibility to the denunciations of New Jerseyans as promonopoly and therefore pro-southern. Credulity reinforced this viewpoint. Although the rhetoric did not match the record, New Jersey fell into disrepute, even disgrace.[38]

# 12 The Wounds of War: The Presidential Election of 1864

**N**othing is more unpredictable than war or more uncertain than an election held during war. Looking to Election Day in November, the Republican *Trenton Monitor* remarked that the "next election is the decision of the fate of the nation. Upon its result depends the restoration or the destruction of the Union." The Democratic *Paterson Register* agreed that the "nation's life hangs in the scale." Impartial observers considered this presidential election the most important in the nation's history. Republicans predicted that a reelected Lincoln would win the war in his second term and reunify the nation. Silas Merchant contended that Lincoln's victory "would do more to discourage the Southern people than a defeat of their armies on the battle field. For it would say to them in language too plain to be misunderstood that the heart of the northern people were with Lincoln in this matter, and there would be no use in contending against."[1]

The Democrats saw an opportunity to win power by promising a quick end to the war. Also, the election could serve as a useful safety valve because the disaffected now had a national forum in which to voice grievances, both real and imagined.[2]

Yet war supporters were troubled by conducting a presidential campaign during wartime. A wartime election would severely test the nation's capacity and maturity to govern. A divisive campaign might, in Martin Ryerson's words, jeopardize "all our efforts, sacrifices, and successes." The Republicans could well lose the election and then the "cause of the Union is defeated; the Nation is destroyed; anarchy is begun." A few alarmed New Jersey Republicans went so far as to oppose an election. One Hoboken man even suggested that "an able dictatorship for two years might prove beneficial."[3]

Democrats, especially copperheads, feared Lincoln would commandeer the army to steal the election. The Democrats vowed that blood would flow in the streets if Republicans attempted a forced plebiscite. As the copperhead *Hackensack Democrat* warned, "We must be prepared to enforce a Constitutional ballot, if need be, by Constitutional bullets." Even the hawkish *Camden Democrat* threatened that Democrats "have made up their minds to have a free election or a free fight." Democratic politicians advised voters to keep arms at the ready. A Perth Amboy resident predicted that "no efforts will be left untried by his desperate crew to avert defeat. They have the sword, the purse, and power."[4]

Lincoln handled the upcoming election in the same way as he prosecuted the war. He methodically went about the business of winning renomination by exploiting to the fullest his position as leader of the party and dispenser of federal patronage. Even with no major challenger for the nomination, Lincoln still left nothing to chance. He prevailed upon Republican office-holders to back him. Further, he set an early date for the national party convention to deprive any opponent of the chance to mount a serious challenge. During the spring Lincoln remained popular with many unconditional unionists, who still appreciated his prudence and perseverance, his tactical resiliency and strategic single-mindedness. A Hightstown man declared, "Abraham has friends here, friends to him because he is true to his country and dares to deal justly by the negro and *justly* to the red-handed traitors."[5]

Some New Jersey editors had endorsed Lincoln's candidacy in the spring of 1863. By early 1864 Lincoln's federal officeholders and most Republican editors in the state supported his renomination. Soon most Republican legislators, as well as several chapters of the Union League, declared their preference for Lincoln. One Trenton reporter for the *New Brunswick Fredonian* noted, "It is not easy to meet a man who professes to be a Union man who is not also a Lincoln man." The *Trenton Monitor* dismissed his replacement as the "height of madness and folly." The *Princeton Standard* agreed: "To change our Leader in front of the enemy at this time, without necessity, and take an untried man would, we think, be an egregious blunder." The Republican state convention, held in mid-May, virtually endorsed Lincoln's renomination. Across the North, state party organizations joined his column.[6]

Although Lincoln's renomination was virtually assured, some radical Republicans called for a bolder leader. Orestes Brownson complained, "I do wish we could have a *man* for our candidate." Reflecting the idealist's impatient view of politics, Brownson found Lincoln an adroit politician but a poor statesman, a crafty tactician but a deficient strategist. Lincoln, he believed, "never had that mental culture, never acquired that breadth of view" indispensable to a man in his position. As a result, Lincoln simply sought power for its own sake and merely remained "a politician—nothing more, nothing less." Thus he had "floated with the current, or been borne along by it, without any fixed principles or well-defined policy of his own." Worst of all, according to Brownson, Lincoln possessed "no greatness of soul, no moral grandeur, no lofty or heroic aspirations." Brownson pronounced Lincoln a miserable failure.[7]

During the spring restive Republicans pressured party politicians to postpone the national convention from June 7 to early fall when they might have a better chance to dump Lincoln and find a candidate to rescue the party from defeat. Some German-American radicals in the state, notably in Hoboken and Newark, agreed and wanted another candidate.[8]

Just before the Republican convention assembled, some radical dissidents took action. On May 31 in Cleveland they nominated John Fremont on an independent ticket. The movement actually benefited Lincoln by drawing off some of the radical visionaries, thus enhancing Lincoln's reputation for moderation. Few New Jersey Republicans followed Fremont; Republicans in the state agreed that the Pathfinder had strayed. They scoffed at his coterie of malcontents, who were taken seriously only as spoilers who might throw the election to the Democrats.[9]

Energized by this unexpected competition, the confident National Union party assembled in Baltimore. On June 8 the delegates, including all the New Jerseyans, nominated Lincoln on the first ballot. In accepting the nomination Lincoln introduced his major campaign theme, the danger of changing horses while crossing a raging stream. The Republicans selected for vice president a Tennessee war supporter, Andrew Johnson, to secure the support of war Democrats, strengthen the party's campaign in the border states, and polish the organization's image as a national party. The platform pledged to end rebellion by winning the war and to abolish slavery by amending the Constitution. Most Republicans praised their candidates as strong and their platform as both bold and sound. As the *Millville Republican* remarked, "We can deliver no more crushing blow to this atrocious rebellion than to re-elect Mr. Lincoln."[10]

Republican malcontents, however, continued to grumble. By August some people talked of convening another Republican convention to replace Lincoln. Others suggested another independent ticket to improve on Fremont. Still other restive Republicans reluctantly accepted the fact that the party was stuck with Lincoln.[11]

The Democrats were pleased with Lincoln's renomination. The *Newark Journal* regarded his selection as a "veritable ten-strike for the Democracy." Democrats dismissed the president for having broken his oath, the law, and numerous pledges. He was the "Father of all Iniquity," as the *Hackensack Democrat* declared. "Continuance of that dangerous man in power will be the death knell of the Union." One Middlesex copperhead termed Lincoln a thief, robber, and murderer. Democrats regarded him as a fifth-rate country lawyer. In the words of the *Somerville Messenger*, he was a "Presidential pygmy."[12]

Lincoln's personal style also came under fire: the *Hackensack Democrat* described him as a "backwoods buffoon," while James Wall dubbed him a "foul-mouthed gorilla." John Stockton called him a "grinning monkey," whose incessant joking mocked the tragedy and miseries of war. One Democrat yearned for a "decent, respectable and dignified President." The *Belvidere Journal* denounced the forthright Republican platform as composed equally of "buncombe and the negro."[13]

Hoping that opposition to Lincoln would swell, the Democrats in late June postponed their national convention from early July to the end of August. Should the Union army suffer another crushing defeat and Grant's campaign fail against Petersburg, Democrats could exploit war weariness. Antiwar men worked feverishly to advance their agenda. They maneuvered to have the national convention run a peace candidate on a peace platform. If the Democratic party were to go "for peace by professing to go for war," in the words of Wall, dishonor and defeat would follow.[14]

The Democrats met in Chicago and on August 31 nominated for president the dashing George McClellan. As a famous general, Yankee patriot, rigid conservative, dedicated Democrat, and bold critic of Lincoln's measures, McClellan could attract voters as well as uniting the party's war and peace factions. Politicians also counted on the most popular commander of the Army of the Potomac to gain the servicemen's votes. His lack of a partisan record made him an ideal candidate. To assure geographical and factional balance, Democrats picked for vice president the Ohio congressman and peace advocate George H. Pendleton. Thus both sides achieved their goals: the war party nominated McClellan and the peace men selected Pendleton.[15]

McClellan, who lived in West Orange for long periods of time, appealed strongly to New Jersey's Democrats. Out of state pride and personal conviction they dubbed him "the New Jersey Exile," a victim of the imbecility and despotism they saw prevailing in Washington. They blamed Lincoln and the Republicans for slandering the martyred McClellan, sabotaging his command, and then removing him. The general had the enthusiastic support of both the prowar and antiwar wings. His candidacy unified the state party, disposed of its factional problems, and probably assured victory for the ticket in New Jersey. At their state convention on May 18, Democrats had cheered enthusiastically for him.[16]

Some prominent copperhead hard-liners, notably the *Newark Journal*, earlier had opposed McClellan because he supported continuing the war. The peace men, however, neither controlled this state convention nor wrote the innocuous, evasive platitudes in its platform, which failed to call for an armistice. Possibly in retaliation, the antiwar forces blocked a maneuver to have New Jersey's delegation at Chicago vote as a unit (presumably for McClellan). In the end, however, the entire state delegation in Chicago, including copperhead loner Daniel Holsman, voted for McClellan.[17]

Republicans disputed McClellan's credentials as a New Jerseyan and an inactive general who yet remained on the army's payroll. The *Mount Holly Mirror* dismissed him as a "military squatter" trying to use his position in the army as a stepping-stone to the presidency. They criticized his overcautious, unsuccessful record as commander. Fooled at Yorktown, absent at Williamsburg, surprised at Seven Pines, outflanked at Gaines' Mills, scared at Malvern Hill, tardy at Second Bull Run, he crowned his ineptitude by failing to cut off the rebel retreat after Antietam. The newspapers portrayed McClellan as a strategist of inaction, a voice of whining irresolution, and a symbol of defeatism. The *Morristown Jerseyman* regarded his unbridled public pronouncements as tantamount to insubordination: the "only fault he has ever found with the Administration is that it has not conducted the war on *his plan*."[18]

Moreover, McClellan's political inexperience disqualified him for the presidency. Republicans accused him of riding the wave of pacifism as a purported unionist. As the *Trenton Gazette* put it, "McClellan is neither a traitor nor a disunionist. He is simply the candidate of such." The Republicans predicted that the copperheads would easily use this figurehead for their purposes. The *Gazette* contended, "Political necessity will compel the candidate to ignore his better nature, and become the agent of traitors without being in sympathy with them." The *Paterson Press* argued that if impatient radical critics objected to Lincoln's caution in politics as he waited for public opinion to catch up, McClellan personified inertia in comparison. Yet the *Gazette* predicted that McClellan "will be saved from disgrace by defeat."[19]

New Jersey Democrats greeted McClellan's nomination with great enthusiasm. The Democrats attempted to turn his inexperience to advantage. They contended that McClellan's stern, soldierly traits qualified him for public service; they lauded his integrity, leadership, and administrative ability. As the *Jersey City Standard* maintained, a "good soldier is a man of comprehensive mind and can scarcely fail of being a wise statesman." The nation's best presidents, Washington and Jackson, had been generals. The country now needed a military man who would replace incompetent civilians and instead appoint "men who *understand war*."[20]

Long on hope and short on specifics, Democrats predicted that the statesman McClellan would magically transform the political situation by undercutting southern secessionists and northern abolitionists while reinvigorating unionists everywhere. His conciliatory posture would "bring back each wandering star to its proper place in the galaxy of our Union." The *Salem Sunbeam* dubbed him the "man for the crisis." According to the *Camden Democrat*, "any change in the Administration must be for the better—it can't possibly be worse than it is." The *Freehold Democrat* agreed that the "only hope left for rescuing our country from its peril is in a change of leaders and a change of policy."[21]

Preoccupied with securing the nomination, McClellan's war hawks failed to build a platform on which McClellan could stand. McClellan's forces lost control of the subcommittee that drafted the platform. Fearing that the conclave might turn into another Charleston convention, with a massive walkout of delegates, the prowar men refused to offer a fight in the resolutions committee or on the convention floor. They quickly endorsed the peace men's platform in a voice vote with only four dissents. Having secured their nominee, McClellan's supporters went along with any platform. The peace men, now concerned exclusively with the platform, were prepared to accept any nominee.[22]

In its final formulation, the Democratic platform specifically declared its attachment to the Union but did not spell out national responsibilities to maintain it. One plank commended servicemen for their sacrifices but did not suggest that they fought for a just and necessary cause. The platform did not condemn those responsible for the rebellion, but criticized the Republican measures designed to suppress it. Pronouncing the war a failure, the Democrats requested an immediate, unconditional armistice. They proposed a restoration of the Union through negotiations at a peace conference.[23]

Pledged to an armistice with a war man as its nominee, the Democracy acknowledged its contradictory position as half peace and half war. Democrats, one Hightstown Republican observed, had "good digestion and can take most anything," including McClellan's swallowing the equivalent of Holsman's resolution that New Jersey Democrats had rejected earlier.[24]

In analyzing the peace plank, the Republicans considered three possibilities: recognition of southern independence, reunion on southern terms, or reinvigoration of the rebel war effort. First, a cease-fire could lead to ultimate recognition of the Confederacy. If the North eased its military pressure on the South, the North surrendered its most powerful inducement to the South to give up its objective of independence. The result would be the creation of an independent and hostile southern nation. An interval of peace would prove merely a prelude to future war even fiercer than the present one. The *Trenton Monitor* argued that if slavery remained rooted in the southern part of America, the arrogance and violence of slavery would ensure another war, just "as it caused this war."[25]

The prowar Democratic *Morristown Banner* also opposed an armistice: "Withdraw our soldiers from the field, and what would be the consequence? The independence of the Southern Confederacy would become upon the instant a fixed fact." The Republican *Hoboken Standard* asked, "What have we been fighting for for the last four years, if it was not to perpetuate our glorious Union?" The *Flemington Republican* remarked, "Our best negotiators for the present are Sherman's marches and Grant's death grip."[26]

Republicans predicted that Confederate leaders would never abandon their rebellion until the North destroyed the rebel armies. The *Camden Press* reiterated that peace could come only "when the spirit of rebellion has been completely destroyed, and by war alone can this spirit be destroyed." The *Jersey City Times* demanded only "peace through victory." The *Mount Holly Mirror* would have a "national grave sooner than national suicide! Surrender, never!" Preferring an honorable war to a dishonorable peace, Republicans rejected a cease-fire.[27]

A second possible outcome allowed reunion on terms favorable to the South. A political settlement would create a merely nominal Union, in fact a loose confederation of powerful, quasi-independent states along the lines of the discredited Articles of Confederation. With such an arrangement, the Republicans expected the Democrats, including southern extremists, to regain national control. Merchant and others predicted that the "South will demand and obtain their own terms which will probably be the assumption of their war debt by the United States, the reestablishment of Slavery with the broadest State rights," the expansion of slavery, and the emasculation of federal authority. The *Princeton Standard* warned voters that they had to choose a "peace by subduing the Rebellion or by yielding to and conciliating traitors." One placard at a Paterson rally summed up the Republican position: "Compromise, the meanest word in the English language." Even if northern participants at a peace conference agreed to such unfavorable conditions, Republicans pointed out that changes in the federal Constitution required approval by the president, Congress, and state authorities.[28]

Third and most likely the stalemate between the North and the South would continue. Neither side was willing to sacrifice interests deemed important enough to fight for; hence negotiations were doomed. Yet neither side was able to land the decisive blow, so the protracted struggle would go on. Thus the war supporters worried that a temporary, fruitless truce would prove a disastrous military and psychological setback for the Union. If the northern blockade were lifted and the rebel army had the opportunity to secure fresh recruits and replenish supplies, the Confederate army would recover its will and its strength. With southern resistance rejuvenated, combat would intensify, casualties would increase, and the war would last longer.

In the Republicans' view, the Democratic peace platform amounted to a rescue of the beleaguered rebels in the nick of time. The *Millville Republican* dismissed the platform as an outrageous hoax to fool credulous people. A ticket with a war head and a body of peace betrayed the Democrats' desperation and undercut their credibility.[29]

Although McClellan was not completely naive in politics, as Republicans charged, he mixed a dash of expediency with a heavier dose of amateurishness. During 1863 he tried to ingratiate himself with the copperheads. He stumbled rightward by endorsing the Democratic candidate for governor in Pennsylvania, a peace man, and by never denouncing publicly the antidraft riots in New York City. During 1864, as the Democratic front-runner, he continued clumsy and unprepared, stayed above the fray, and failed to send his campaign manager to the national convention. He ignored the importance of the platform and allowed the peace Democrats to take control of it by default.[30]

During the campaign McClellan exhibited his characteristic egotism and his distaste for politicians. His political isolation made him "equally unsuccessful as a political leader and as a military commander." The prospect of McClellan leading the nation in waging a civil war struck many as a dangerous gamble. To place power into new and inexperienced hands struck observers as an act of historic irresponsibility. Fearing a return to power of the Democrats whom he distrusted, Charles Hodge observed, "I regard General McClellan as a first rate captain in a very bad ship and with a horridly bad crew, and I have no notion of going to sea with him." The *Plainfield Union* expressed the Republican consensus: "If General McClellan was and is the strongest Union war Democrat in the Union, he is not strong enough to control the men who framed a Peace Platform for the gallant Democratic party if he should be elected. Peace men made that platform, and peace men controlled the convention."[31]

"Battles control ballots," observed Anthony Keasbey during the presidential campaign. Both parties held Lincoln, as commander in chief, accountable for the conduct of the war. The *Morristown Jerseyman* maintained that the "success or failure of the military operations now going forward must of necessity exercise a large influence." Democrats agreed with a vengeance. The *Paterson Register* remarked that Lincoln lacked either the will to win the war or the skill to negotiate its end. As the *Jersey City Standard* put it, Lincoln "*is incapable of making either war or peace.*" A Republican journalist conceded that success at the polls "depends entirely on success in the field." Lincoln could win reelection only if the Yankees "strike telling and effective blows—blows which must result in something decisive. If not, then Goodbye to the Republic."[32]

The smashing setbacks dealt the rebels in July of 1863 came to a halt in the first half of 1864. In the early spring, Federal campaigns unraveled in Mississippi and in Louisiana. Then, in May and early June, Grant's grand offensive in eastern Virginia stalled after he lost three of the fiercest and costliest engagements of the war. In the terrifying Battle of the Wilderness, savage fighting raged in the tangled brush. Combat became confused as generals lost contact with their units, while squads lost their way. Troops on both sides shot their own men. Soldiers fired point-blank at the enemy. With fires blazing in the dry woods, screaming, crippled troops burned to death. Describing the battle, one New Jersey soldier declared, "I never saw such fighting in my life—one complete roar of musketry all the time." He went on: "I wish you could have seen the woods after we had fought over it so much there wasn't a tree the thickness of your finger pinky, but what was all cut to pieces with balls, and the dead and wounded was laying thick. It was an awful sight."[33]

At vicious Spotsylvania, in a thick fog during a cold downpour, men crowded into small pockets locked in hand-to-hand fighting with bayonets and rifle butts. The Federal attackers burst through southern defenses, but the rebels counterattacked and regained lost ground. At murderous Cold Harbor the Confederates, firing from trenches with muskets and cannon, mowed down exposed Yankees who were attempting a senseless frontal assault. Grant's worst defeat ranked as one of the bloodiest and most reckless days of the war for the Yankees.

In just one month the bloodbath in Virginia cost Grant more than fifty thousand men. Lee lost roughly half that number but could afford even less to lose them. This campaign exceeded all the rest in sheer desperation and fierce determination.

Despite these crushing setbacks, in the middle of June Grant laid siege to the strategic stronghold of Petersburg. The town defended Richmond, the rebel capital, and linked it by rail with the rest of the Confederacy. In early July, Union forces under Sherman besieged Atlanta, another rebel stronghold and the key to the Southeast. Defenders resolved to hold both citadels until beaten or starved out. "Bull-dog Grant never lets go his hold" on the rebels, stated the *Paterson Press* admiringly.[34]

The Confederates, however, repelled one Yankee assault after another. Still Grant and Sherman maintained unrelenting pressure. As the *Bordentown Register* observed, Grant "gives and takes, gives and takes." But his army in Virginia, mired in the mud, went nowhere. One New Jersey soldier at the front, Washington Roebling, viewed the stalemate pessimistically: "Our matters here are at a deadlock; unless the rebs commit some great error they will hold us in check until kingdom come; neither of our two commanding Generals seem to be smart enough to do anything beyond mediocrity. We are all getting thoroughly tired and disgusted; these two armies remind me very much of two schoolboys trying to stare each other out of countenance."[35]

In July the Confederates once again invaded Maryland, cut its major telegraph and railroad lines, and threatened Baltimore and Washington. People panicked until the rebels pulled back to Virginia.

In August the *Tallahassee*, a rebel raider, preyed on commercial ships sixty miles off the Jersey shore: approaching unarmed vessels, the swift steamer suddenly hauled down its American flag and raised the Confederate colors. In this way the raider seized thirty-five merchant ships and fishing smacks. Confederates used a pilot boat to board vessels, take prisoners, then burn or scuttle the captured ships. Without a swift navy ship available to handle the emergency, no Yankees pursued the raider. Such bold, impudent raids, on both land and sea, shocked northerners and prompted bitter criticism of the military for bungling the war in the South and mishandling defense in the Northeast.[36]

With victory nowhere in sight, the Democrats shook their heads at what they regarded as the senseless killing or wounding of half a million men. Even the Democratic war supporters became pessimistic. The *Jersey City*

*Standard* decried Lincoln's mismanagement. With sieges at both Petersburg and Atlanta stalled, disillusioned northerners dismissed Grant as a colossal failure and Sherman as a miserable fizzle. Grant had pledged to fight it out if it took all summer. With summer soon to end and Grant no closer to Richmond, the *Camden Democrat* remarked, "We hope he will not close his 'summer' campaign by an 'unconditional surrender' in the wrong way." The newspaper accused Republican politicians and generals of losing the war and sacrificing Union troops to "partisan ambition, military jealousy, and reckless fanaticism." Amid gloom and defeatism, another crisis of confidence pervaded the North.[37]

Republicans in New Jersey expressed the prevailing pessimism. At the beginning of July, one Jersey City lawyer regarded both victory and reunion as increasingly improbable. If the war continued a few more years, he predicted, the North would reach its limits of manpower, resources, and stamina. A Trenton Democrat earlier had asked, "When is this to end? Can we conquer?" In early September, a Republican newspaperman observed that the "masses of the people are tired of the war, tired of the apparently slow progress we are making, and consider that a change of administrations could not possibly make things any worse. The unthinking masses now, as they always did, go with the current, and they believe that could the Democrats obtain the power, there would be peace, though they don't know nor care exactly how it is to be effected." Although worried, most Republican newspapers denied that the military situation had grown desperate. They pointed to the military gains and the number of southern states captured, and counseled patience. A Newarker remarked, "I have seen these depressions before and I have seen them dissipated like chaff before the tempest."[38]

Lincoln remained adamant that the war must continue until both rebellion and slavery ceased: unconditional peace could only follow unconditional surrender. During the summer he tried to convince northerners that attempts at peace negotiations by various third parties had ended in failure because southerners would recognize only northern acceptance of their independence. By demonstrating the futility of such negotiation, the Republicans dismissed Democratic agitation for peace. The election, then, became a referendum on both the purpose and the prosecution of the war.

Without military victories, Republican prospects throughout the lower North continued to decline and war supporters recognized this. Ryerson advised Lincoln that "unless we speedily have great military successes" so decisive as to convince the people that the war would end soon, his reelection looked "quite doubtful." In late July, John Stratton bemoaned recent developments: "The late disgraceful raid into Maryland, the siege of the Capital, the call for five hundred thousand more men, and the seeming slowness of Grant's movements have tended greatly to dispirit the people." On August 18, editor Horace Greeley decided that "Lincoln is already beaten. He cannot be elected." The impulsive Greeley and other impatient Republicans maneuvered to change horses in the presidential contest. They toyed with the idea of Grant replacing Lincoln on the ticket. On August 23, even Lincoln himself predicted privately that he would lose the election.[39]

Suddenly, during August, Union forces seized and held the offensive. Pounding away at pivotal rebel positions, Yankees achieved one smashing victory after another. Between August 5 and 23, in the largest naval operation of the war, Admiral David G. Farragut's fleet seized control of Mobile Bay, bottled up the most important enemy port left on the Gulf coast, and thus tightened further the naval blockade of the Confederacy.

On September 2, in the most decisive military victory of the year, the army under Sherman captured Atlanta, split the Southeast, and shattered rebel morale. As the *Jersey City Standard* observed, "Even those who called General Sherman 'crazy' must at least acknowledge 'there is method in his madness.'" The *Paterson Press* declared that the rebels had never received a more staggering blow than the one dealt them by Sherman. General Philip H. Sheridan followed these successes with more victories in September, most notably at Winchester; by mid-October he had swept the Confederates from Virginia's strategic Shenandoah Valley. Except for Petersburg, the war was almost won. Officer James Rusling exclaimed, "Atlanta has fallen; and victory at Atlanta means success everywhere!" He predicted McClellan's defeat in November.[40]

These breakthroughs electrified the North. New Jerseyans rejoiced; in honor of the victory in Atlanta, Parker ordered the firing of cannon. Church bells rang out across the state. People now expected that Grant's forces, poised before Petersburg, would soon seize Richmond. Springing their traps on the rebels, Farragut at Mobile, Sherman at Atlanta, and Sheridan at Winchester had done their own electioneering and might rescue Lincoln from defeat.[41]

Jubilant Republicans now attacked the Democrats' peace offering to the South. The Democrats had called the war a fiasco, but Atlanta discredited them. The *Newark Advertiser* observed, "What a commentary is this upon the timid, time-serving resolutions of the Chicago Convention, which declared this war for the Union to be a failure! How quickly and effectively have our heroic soldiers rebuked the insult and disproved the charge!" The newspaper added scornfully, "Our heroic soldiers at Atlanta have just proved by their own forcible logic, the falsehood of the Chicago declaration that the war for our National defense is a failure! At the same time they are showing how surely *they* will secure a lasting peace on Union terms without regard to the suicidal demand of the Convention for a suspension of hostilities." The *Newton Register* argued that to "give the rebels a truce, at this time, would be an act of folly and madness." "To falter now just as success is within our grasp," declared the *Camden Press*, "would indeed be a shameful disgrace."[42]

Peace candidate Pendleton received a scolding along these lines. The *Millville Republican* pointed out that McClellan several times had requested food and clothing for his army, but his running mate Pendleton voted in Congress against feeding and clothing that army. One Republican described Pendleton as a loose spoke in the wheel, which stopped it from running. What if chief executive McClellan died? What would happen to the prosecution of the war if Pendleton became president? The *Trenton Gazette* concluded that the "fall of Atlanta was not only a ruinous blow to the rebellion, but to the Chicago candidates." The Republicans closed ranks behind Lincoln. Even Fremont admitted, in effect, that he had lost the way. On September 17 he testily withdrew as a candidate.[43]

Antiwar Democrats viewed the military victories differently. The *Trenton American* contended that the recent triumphs made it all the more imperative to change administrations. Only the Democrats could take advantage of the changed military situation by undertaking comprehensive negotiations with the southerners. The *Newark Journal* denied that the victories meant the war would end soon: the southerners would hold out for a long time. The *Journal* warned voters "that a vote for Lincoln is a vote for four years more of war."[44]

Some war supporters in the Democratic camp deftly rejected the party's peace platform. Jacob Vanatta repudiated it by likening it to a platform on a railroad car: very convenient and necessary to use in stepping aboard, "*but very dangerous to stand on.*" McClellan recognized the antiwar platform and Pendleton's nomination as major liabilities. Then the victory at Atlanta left his campaign adrift. Members of the party's war and peace wings meanwhile bombarded him with requests to follow their advice in drafting his acceptance letter. McClellan understood the necessity of the Union, the justice of the war, and the suppression of the rebellion. He rejected outright the pacifists' call for an armistice and realized after Atlanta that he would lose pivotal New York and Pennsylvania if he failed to renounce an armistice. By both conviction and calculation, he dissociated himself from the peace plank and the peace faction. Therefore, in his acceptance letter on September 8, he agreed to run but repudiated the platform. McClellan demanded reunion as the indispensable condition of permanent peace. Although he rejected the view of the war as a failure, he did not insist that southerners surrender unconditionally by emancipating the slaves, as Lincoln required.[45]

McClellan's letter delighted and reassured prowar Democrats. An Orange neighbor told McClellan that his letter had just "dropped a two hundred pound shell in Abraham's Camp." They praised him for his lack of evasion, as well as for his unqualified pledge to preserve the Union. Many war supporters regarded the peace plank as a stupendous blunder: the *Jersey City Standard* observed, "What shame and confusion must come to those who, for political purposes, have insisted upon General McClellan's willingness to have peace upon a basis of disunion!"[46]

Reactions from war opponents varied, but most of them backed McClellan. Both the *Newark Journal* and the *Trenton American* criticized those copperheads who denounced McClellan for renouncing the party's platform. Preferring their own way, the disgruntled copperheads pronounced the platform the soul of the party and the candidate the body; neither could exist without the other. New Jersey's war opponents, however, recognized that peace initiatives could follow only a Democratic victory; opposition to Lincoln constituted a sufficient platform.

Nevertheless some members of the peace faction justified support for McClellan by feebly deemphasizing or ignoring the differences between his letter and the party's platform. The *Newark Journal* suggested that McClellan lacked the authority to change the platform and remained bound by it. The *Trenton American*, however, considered McClellan's letter a side issue and ridiculed the peace plank as simplistic. It asked, "Would they wish him to say that when elected President of the United States, he will proclaim a peace upon any terms, disband the army and navy of the United States, and leave it to the Confederate authorities to make the terms to which the United States shall submit?" Such a course might be appropriate only if the North lost the war.[47]

The *Hackensack Democrat* accepted McClellan's candidacy despite his letter, for the copperheads had no alternative. The irreconcilables, notably Chauncey Burr, steadfastly disapproved of McClellan's substituting a platform of his own creation, but infinitely preferred it, and him, to another Lincoln administration. Most New Jersey copperheads predicted that McClellan as president would restore common sense and sane policy to federal governance.[48]

New Jersey Democrats held their electoral convention in Trenton on October 6, and endorsed both the national platform and McClellan's acceptance letter as the price of party harmony. In addition, they saluted the servicemen for their devotion to duty and thus struck a more patriotic note than the national platform. In more partisan fashion, the Democrats condemned equality for blacks.[49]

Parker at Freehold in late August gave a pep talk and made points that pleased all factions. He promised that Republican abuses would cease when McClellan became president. Parker flattered New Jersey Democrats by comparing the state to a rock in midocean that beat back the "waves of fanaticism" which surged around it. The unifying speech pleased both peace and prowar Democrats; the Republicans dismissed it.[50]

The Republican responses to McClellan's footwork varied. The *Newark Advertiser* interpreted his acceptance letter as a rebuke to the platform. Nevertheless, Republicans questioned how McClellan could ride both the peace and the war horse when they did not travel the same road. Unionists found McClellan's attempt to reconcile the contradictory demands of his party's war and the peace wings another demonstration of deception by the Democrats, who cried peace and declared war in the same breath. The *Paterson Press* viewed McClellan's political maneuver as altogether in keeping with his military actions: "General Timidity" remained a master at the art of falling back from a dangerous position in the field.[51]

Some Lincoln supporters, however, remained worried. Because "McClellan's acceptance is artful and jesuitical," Ryerson predicted that McClellan would attract conservative and moderate Republicans who were tired of the war. McClellan's shrewd, carefully worded appeal to all loyal Democrats would prove successful because the Democrats could not afford a feud during the campaign.[52]

Looking back on the startling changes in military and political fortunes, Keasbey assessed the shift in public opinion. He found the Republican cause hopeless at the end of August, when Lincoln's supporters gave "full play to that thoughtless and desperate desire for change that besets weak minds in adversity." Keasbey observed, "We were ready to crumble to pieces and surrender without a struggle. I verily believe that two weeks ago one third of our Republicans would have voted for McClellan on any decent platform."

Keasbey breathed more freely, however, after he read the Chicago platform: "I knew that the soul of the people would revolt against it." As he saw immediately, "Weak knees stiffened up. Hopeful words were heard at the street-corners—a visible change was taking place and grew swiftly on till Saturday morning, when the lightning flash that said to us 'Atlanta is ours and fairly won!' seemed to thrill every nerve and loosen every tongue." Keasbey never had seen so great a change in sentiment in so short a time: the Democrats, who plotted to "swindle the Country into a change of Administration," suddenly saw their elaborate plans come apart.[53]

The congressional races varied according to district composition, the contenders' personalities, and the keenness of the competition. In the Republican first district, zealous Republican incumbent John Starr easily brushed aside a challenge for the nomination from restless James Scovel, who single-mindedly championed the antimonopoly cause. Starr went on to compete against a political featherweight, Isaac Dickinson, a Woodstown lawyer.

In the second district the Republicans hoped to mount a strong challenge to the Democratic incumbent in a competitive district, but Republican chances appeared jeopardized when promonopolists and antimonopolists fought bitterly for the Republican nomination. The Republicans ended this brawl when they nominated a compromise candidate, the popular William Newell. Thus Democratic representative George Middleton faced a strong challenger. One reporter described Middleton in exaggerated terms as an "anti-slavery Quaker, elected to Congress by pro-slavery Democrats in a Republican District." Sensing danger, Middleton frequently dodged important votes, but remained too hawkish to suit peace men and too partisan to satisfy independent Republicans. He secured renomination despite the opposition of most delegates from his home county.

The Republicans had no chance to win in the third district, a Democratic bastion. Conservative Democratic newcomer Charles Sitgreaves, a Phillipsburg lawyer, competed with Charles Scranton, a Warren County businessman. In the fourth district dissatisfied Democrats, including copperheads, considered their congressman not enough of a hard-liner and tried to defeat his renomination. But Andrew Rogers—whom Republicans nicknamed "Jumping Jack" and dubbed a "gassy, gabby, ranting, canting, two-faced" politician—fought hard and secured renomination. Because prominent politicians were refusing invitations to run, the Republicans nominated a person completely unlike Rogers—Theodore Little, a Morristown lawyer without political experience.

Republicans in the fifth district nominated Edward B. Wakeman, a Hudson attorney. Using singularly poor judgment, the Democrats passed over able senator Theodore Randolph and picked a conservative, the ailing Edwin Wright, described by Ryerson as "now almost a drunken vagabond."[54]

The campaign for the assembly reflected the new atmosphere after the victory at Atlanta. Ten copperheads, including Thomas Dunn English, chose not to run again. Except for two districts in Hudson, all of those who quit politics hailed from safe constituencies and so had nothing to fear from Republican opponents; evidently they decided to leave politics because of the changed situation. In a major fight for the Democratic nomination in Union in the second district, Democrats at their convention overwhelmingly rejected copperhead Noah Woodruff, leaving only eight identified copperheads in search of reelection.

Spirited races in swing districts, where former competitors faced off, once again turned into grudge matches. In the swing counties of Burlington, Middlesex, and Passaic both parties conducted vicious campaigns; the senate races in the one-party counties were dull in comparison. Politicians knew that much hinged on control of the legislature.[55]

The issues in the campaign struck New Jerseyans as few, plain, and simple, yet momentous. The most sharply defined issue naturally concerned the war. Each party promised that its candidate would continue the war until the Union was restored.[56]

Democrats in their congressional conventions in the first, second, and third districts followed the evasive platform of the state convention. All three endorsed both the national platform and McClellan's nomination, but did so in different ways. The first district's resolutions contradictorily endorsed both the Chicago platform and McClellan's letter of acceptance. The second district made no mention of the platform, McClellan, or his letter, but merely supported the action of the national convention and its nominations. Delegates in the third district supported both the national platform and McClellan but ignored his letter. The convention in the fourth district, meeting in the middle of August before the Chicago convention, vaguely pledged support for both the Union and the Constitution, but rejected the endorsement of an immediate armistice proposed by one delegate. Democrats in the fifth district avoided the problem by presenting no platform.

Nervous Democratic congressional candidates talked both war and peace in acceptance speeches. Dickinson tortuously equated the Chicago platform with McClellan's acceptance letter. He supported a speedy peace but only on reunionist terms. Middleton stressed national reconciliation. Sitgreaves denounced Lincoln's despotism, but (like Middleton) did not take a stand on the war. Rogers opposed Lincoln's misrule and viewed the war as an abolitionist crusade to destroy liberty and the Union, but he did not call for an armistice. He supported war to maintain the Union, yet pushed for compromise to achieve peace and reunion. Wright had nothing to say. The Democrats' division and equivocation contrasted sharply with Republican unity on the war.[57]

Democrats condemned Lincoln for dictating to the people of the southern states that they could not return to the Union until they abolished slavery. Lincoln's unilateral condition not only violated the law but also prolonged the war by driving southern whites to fight abolition to the last man in the last trench. As the *Hackettstown Gazette* observed, a "war for the Union may be a short one; a war to destroy slavery will certainly be a long one." Democrats contended that Lincoln's policy divided previously united northerners. The *Newton Herald* considered Lincoln's emancipation policy a "millstone around the neck of the Union cause." In the early years of the war, the *Bordentown Register* conceded, Lincoln had made the Union paramount over emancipation, but the newspaper asked, "Which is paramount now?" The *Jersey City Standard* advised voters on Election Day, "If you want Union, vote for McClellan. If you want Abolition, vote for Lincoln."[58]

Republicans countered that copperheads preferred dissolution of the Union to abolition of slavery. Republican editorials justified emancipation because only the overthrow of slavery would end secession. The *Salem Standard* argued that "Rebellion and Slavery are synonymous. So long as Rebellion is able to raise its head in the South, Slavery is alive; the one will live as long as the other, and both will expire together." The *Elizabeth Journal* justified abolition "not so much out of sympathy for the negro, as it is from a firm resolve that another rebellion shall not arise."[59]

Occasionally a more idealistic note crept into the discussion. The *Absecon Republican* looked forward to a free republic "where the rights of all, whether high or low, rich or poor, white or black, shall be respected and secure." Yet no Republican congressional district platform mentioned slavery, let alone emancipation. The silence reflected lack of confidence, even fear, about openly championing this controversial subject.[60]

Some Republicans mixed their support of Lincoln's leadership with criticism. A confidential letter from Keasbey referred to Lincoln's recent pronouncements as "imprudent." Keasbey charged that Lincoln had guaranteed the failure of negotiations with the South by his insistence that slavery must end before any discussions could take place. The moderate *Newark Advertiser* considered Lincoln's messages to the South ill-timed, ill-advised, and wholly unauthorized, and hinted that campaign pressures had caused even this adroit politician to stumble at times. Yet the newspaper criticized Democratic overemphasis on Lincoln's comments. No doubts entered the minds of New Jersey's blacks, however. In a meeting at Trenton in September, they strongly backed all efforts to rid the nation of both slavery and prejudice. The blacks praised Lincoln for "leading our people out of the land of bondage into the land of liberty." In a resounding resolution, they declared, "We go for Abraham Lincoln—*first, last,* and all the time."[61]

The Democrats reinforced their campaign argument by resorting to their usual racist appeal. As the *Hoboken Democrat* put it, whites died pointlessly for the welfare and equality of "three million idle, shiftless, thriftless negroes."[62]

Republicans ridiculed Democrats' predictions of an impending racial apocalypse. A few Republican newspapers even condemned racial prejudice and saw the oppressed blacks in a more favorable light. At one party conclave a Somerset Republican politician told voters that blacks remained indomitable despite all the hardship and cruelty they had long experienced.[63]

Republicans occasionally indulged in racist remarks to counter those of the Democrats. At a New Brunswick rally a newspaperman said that Democrats "call us the nigger party, yet when I look over this audience it seems as if we were a white man's party. They say if we are kept in power the niggers will be exalted above the whites; but I am not afraid of any nigger getting ahead of me." In the next breath he declared, "One star differeth from another in magnitude and so it is with men, and in many cases I think the nigger would compare favorably with those who want to oppress him." To further combat Democratic charges, Republicans sometimes went out of their way to oppose suffrage for blacks, a matter that did not interest many whites at the time.[64]

Economic concerns paled in comparison to the great issues of the war. Nevertheless, the Democrats again stressed the heavy costs of war and the gross mismanagement of the economy. They painted a picture of reckless spending, widespread waste, and unrestrained corruption. They pointed to staggering debts and chronic shortages as the bitter fruits of war. Democrats blamed Republicans for the hundredfold increase in taxes and for the devaluation of the dollar to fifty cents. Democratic newspapers told voters to reelect Lincoln if they wished to continue to pay thirty cents a pound for sugar when they used to pay seven, sixteen dollars a ton for coal instead of five, fifteen dollars a barrel for flour instead of seven.[65]

Although they conceded that such problems existed, the Republicans pointed to the increase in jobs, the rise in wages, and the general prosperity. The standard of living, moreover, would be reduced if the South left the Union permanently. If the South returned on its terms and the North assumed the Confederate debt, their taxes would double. Republicans blamed current war expenses and the cost of living on southerners for starting the rebellion and on Democrats for allowing it to happen.[66]

The Democrats again condemned conscription. At first they had jeered at Lincoln's delay in replenishing the army as a sign of cowardly concern for his reelection. When he ordered a draft call, however, they denounced "Lincoln's lottery," because it discouraged volunteering and fell disproportionately on men who could not afford to hire substitutes. In one inflammatory appeal, the *New Brunswick Times* warned that a vote for Lincoln meant perpetual war, unending drafts, and the horrifying prospect of sending still more northerners to "Southern slaughter pens." The *Rahway Democrat* asserted, the "appetite for blood of the vampires at Washington is never to be satiated."[67]

Republicans readily admitted that northerners "have lost heavily." Republicans, however, pointed to a bright, peaceful future, yet they reminded voters that a determined effort still was required to bring the war to a speedy end. The fact remained that many New Jerseyans dreaded conscription; this fear undercut the Republican campaign.[68]

Democrats repeated their attack on Lincoln's disregard of the Constitution, which they likened to a man disobeying the Bible purportedly to save his soul. Republican violations of free speech and due process would come to an end only when Democrats regained power.[69]

In rebuttal the Republicans strongly defended federal emergency actions to secure reunion. They attacked the Democrats for emphasizing rights at the expense of responsibilities. The Republicans also attempted to neutralize the issue of arbitrary arrests by reminding voters that McClellan had personally ordered the arrest of disloyal members of Maryland's legislature.[70]

As for freedom of the press, the copperheads represented the strongest evidence of this unfettered liberty. Had censorship prevailed, the copperheads' dissent would have been stifled. Freedom of expression became a minor issue during July and August, when federal officials arrested three copperhead editors: Orson Cone of the *Somerville Messenger*, Eben Winton of the *Hackensack Democrat*, and Edward Fuller of the *Newark Journal*. Federal authorities, however, indicted only the outspoken Fuller for advocating resistance to the draft.

Unlike Wall in 1861, Fuller received much more cautious treatment. Federal authorities never imprisoned him, tried him in strict accordance with the letter of the law, and thus denied him the rewards of martyrdom. The Republicans defended his arrest. The Democrats condemned his prosecution as an effort to muzzle the press.[71]

To overcome a statewide Democratic majority, the Republicans required maximum harmony and unity. They had neither at the outset, when antimonopolists insisted on raising the railroad question and thus threatened to create divisions in Republican ranks. The state Republican convention held in mid-May exploded in acrimony. In quarreling over whether to support or condemn the Camden and Amboy's monopoly, some delegates almost came to blows. A committee then rejected the antimonopoly position, which a few Republican newspapers previously had demanded. In an aside to the antimonopolists, the convention approved a resolution that condemned any side issues that would divide the party. Then the exasperated delegates from South Jersey rejected antimonopolist Scovel as a delegate to the national convention. Furious, Scovel took the matter to the convention floor and accused the railroad lobby of stabbing him in the back. He appealed to the delegates, especially those from North Jersey, for their support for the disputed seat, and won.

Scovel's bullying tactics angered many South Jersey delegates, who in turn became infuriated with their North Jersey counterparts for overturning the original selection. Scovel's victory was ironic in view of his wild charge that the railroad power controlled the delegates. Some observers asserted that his offensive was the first battle in a larger campaign by the antimonopolists to seize control of the state Republican party. But did Scovel really win on antimonopolistic grounds? Evidently not; most of the delegates were not swept off their feet by his powerful oratory. Under ordinary circumstances the convention delegates probably would not have bypassed their South Jersey colleagues to name Scovel. Cool political calculation carried the day, however. For the sake of the campaign and Scovel's continued usefulness in the senate, the time seemed unpropitious to reject him, with his credentials as a Douglas Democrat, to represent the state party at the national convention. As delegate John Blair confessed candidly about Scovel, "He is in the State Senate, and can do us much good, as well as hurt, and it was not policy to drop him."

Thus Scovel's confrontational style and exaggerated claims prevailed when he brought the railroad issue to center stage, but at a high price. One Camden Democratic editor earlier had dismissed Scovel as a "hifalutin, spread-eagle, star-spangled-banner, addle-brained nincompoop." A Camden Republican publisher contended that his insatiable ambition led to self-advertisement and shifting positions. The *Woodbury Constitution* condemned his raising of the railroad question because the subject had not been pending before the convention. After watching Scovel single-handedly derail the Republican convention for a while, many ardent Republicans left the convention, disgusted.

Scovel and his antimonopoly supporters insisted that they championed Lincoln and the Union cause above all. In fact, Scovel was more interested in having his own way than in having a Republican party at all. He used his influence to divide and weaken the party, damaging Lincoln's reelection chances by sowing disharmony among Republicans. In addition, the *Trenton Gazette* observed that the editor of the antimonopolist *Trenton Monitor* "has warred with more zeal against a railroad company than he has against the rebellion." This opposition, stated the *Gazette*, would result in "discord, division, and defeat." The *Gazette* further declared its support for any congressional nominee named by the Republicans—"no matter what his opinions are on the Railroad Question. This is a Union—and not a railroad—paper, and stands by Union candidates. The *Monitor*, on the contrary, is a railroad paper, and stands by railroad candidates only." In warning about the self-inflicted wounds of disunity, the *Gazette* advised Republicans to focus on essentials. When the "life of a Nation is at stake," the newspaper concluded, the party should not "quarrel over railroad and other local issues." The *Trenton Monitor* nevertheless retorted that the "people of New Jersey have been sold to the Monopoly too often and too long, to desire to be again bound in its chains. They must break them now."

As campaign activity intensified in the fall, antimonopolists floated rumors that the railroad monopoly intended to extend its privileges; the faction also condemned candidates of both parties as tools of the monopoly and vowed to defeat these railroad lobbyists. When Republicans met on September 22 to name their presidential electors, the irrepressible Scovel again brought the monopoly issue to the convention floor and rocked the delegates by demanding that an antimonopoly plank be added to the state party platform. One delegate shouted that if Scovel insisted on talking about railroads, he wished to discuss steamboats. The derisive laughter revealed the sentiment of the delegates, and they killed Scovel's proposal. Republican editorials again denounced Scovel's course as mischievous folly. Meanwhile the Camden and Amboy Railroad looked everywhere for potential votes to defeat the pending proposal in Congress.[72]

The question of voting by soldiers arose again. Sensing a winning issue while championing a principle, the Republicans condemned the refusal of Democratic legislators to uphold soldiers' right to vote. Their opposition showed that the Democrats feared soldiers would not vote for McClellan.[73]

Democrats in fact did fear how soldiers were likely to vote. To counter this bad impression, Democratic politicians featured veterans as speakers at some rallies and sometimes nominated veterans as candidates. Parker, hoping to shift responsibility to the Republicans, asked Lincoln to let state troops return for the election. Lincoln in turn left the matter up to the war department or to respective unit commanders.[74]

Although New Jersey soldiers could not vote, they did not lack political opinions. Everywhere at the front they talked politics. Republican newspapers reported informal polls favoring Lincoln; Democratic journals published stories of McClellan winning. Hardened by combat, many troops saw politics in a new light. Many Jersey Democrats in the field evidently converted to the Union party, but certainly not all did so. One member of the Ninth Regiment regarded the election as deciding whether the "White Man is to be first—the Nigger last." Republicans in the army meanwhile strengthened their political loyalties.[75]

Soldiers scorned pseudopatriots. They derided Democratic sophistry and castigated Democratic peace advocates as cowardly and treasonable. Reflecting the general contempt for the copperheads, one infantry sergeant ridiculed talk of peaceful compromise because his experience had taught him that the "South will never return to the Union until they are forced to." The Democratic plank demanding an armistice infuriated soldiers who had been fighting so hard for so long to save the Union. A chaplain observed that however much the troops still liked McClellan, "they cannot swallow the '*Chicago Platform.*'" Most of the soldiers regarded the platform and Pendleton as deadweights that McClellan could not shake off and thus wanted nothing to do with him.[76]

Rebel reactions also influenced New Jersey servicemen. One trooper in the Eighth Regiment, a former Democrat, while on picket duty asked one of the Confederate soldiers nearby what regiment he belonged to. The rebel answered, "The Chicago Convention," and explained that most southerners favored McClellan's election in the hope that he would leave the South alone. An officer in the Twelfth Regiment similarly observed: "I firmly believe the rebels only hope now is in the coming election. Last evening I had a long talk with the rebels on the picket line. They entertained great hopes of McClellan getting elected. They said he was going to have peace right away if he did. They think he will let them do as they please. After awhile they cheered for McClellan and we cheered for Old Abe, and both parties went to firing again." Such encounters probably moved many undecided Jersey soldiers to favor Lincoln. Reacting to Confederate troops shouting their support of McClellan at Federal soldiers in the trenches before Petersburg, a Hudson-City man commented, "Mac has few friends here, and every rebel cheer makes their number less." Another soldier in the Fifth Regiment summed up the election choices as "*Live or die*, Sink or Swim. Abraham Lincoln or Jefferson Davis." A hospitalized soldier hoped New Jerseyans would show people outside the state that a "Jersey Blue, a name the rebels fear, is the name of a Union loving people."[77]

Both parties worked hard and resourcefully during the campaign. Parties recruited workers to get out the vote and even to pay nonresidents to vote in swing districts. Republicans employed their Union Leagues and the Young Men's Lincoln Clubs and had the active participation of federal employees. Democrats formed competing McClellan Clubs and Democratic Associations. Campaign rallies in the cities attracted immense throngs, and in the countryside meetings were held in town halls and schoolhouses.

Republicans pressed federal authorities to fire non-Republican employees and hire fellow partisans. They appealed for postponement of the latest draft to reduce anti-Republican feeling. Compared with previous political campaigns, this was the best wartime campaign conducted by state Republicans, with thorough canvassing and unprecedented efforts.

Nevertheless certain weaknesses remained. Although the Republicans cultivated the ground in rural Democratic bastions, they neglected the job in Hunterdon, Somerset, and Monmouth. In addition, they needed to organize earlier and work harder in Democratic cities to get out Republican voters, counter fraudulent naturalization, and prevent illegal voting. Moreover, able Horace Congar did not return to manage the campaign and act as party spokesman because of his wife's illness.

Once again the Republicans promoted themselves as the Union party. The Democrats followed suit, calling their party the Democratic Union party. Each side set out to discredit the other's sloganeering and unionist credentials. Objecting to the confusion between partisanship and patriotism, the *Trenton American* complained that the "old cry is again to be inaugurated, Abraham Lincoln is the administration, the administration is the government. Everyone who opens his mouth to say that Lincoln is not the greatest, wisest, ablest, purest, firmest President and General that ever existed is a Copperhead and consequently a traitor." The *Hackettstown Gazette* observed that Republicans professed that they were the "Union men"; indeed they claimed to be the "*only* 'Union men.'"[78]

The *Newark Journal* dismissed the Republicans as the "political party which sails under false Union colors." The *Hackettstown Gazette* asked, "What can be hoped for from a party which plays the hypocrite and the bully—a party which talks 'Union,' and practices disunion?" The *Flemington Democrat* railed against Republicans who always stood ready to assume any name that promised to conceal their purposes: "They will appear as a 'People's Party' today, a 'Union Party' tomorrow, the 'Opposition' of everything the day after, and so on, until they have exhausted the stock of political designations; and yet they remain as they were, a horde of Union hating, Negro loving, office buying, bigoted and proscriptive outsiders, who have not the manly courage to meet the Democracy in a square, stand-up fight." The *Somerville Messenger* pointed out that the "bleaching bones at Fredericksburg and Shiloh belong to Democrats as well as Republicans; the blood that sprinkles the grass on the James or trickles in the bay of Mobile comes from the hearts of one party as well as the other."[79]

The Republicans retorted that in contrast to Democrats, who complained instead of governing, their aptly named Union party backed the administration to save the Union. The *Absecon Republican* added that Republicans had shown unwavering devotion to the "Union, and to the support of the Government, without which the Union is nothing." The *Salem Standard* similarly argued that to "sustain the Administration is to weaken the rebellion, and to weaken the Administration is to strengthen the rebellion."[80]

Although Republicans in the war years had used the Union banner and had reached out to former Democrats to seek their support, they now pursued this strategy far more vigorously than before and enjoyed surprising success in recruiting prominent Democrats. Major Democratic politicians from Sussex, Morris, and Bergen, frequently former Douglas supporters, rejected the Democratic ticket, backed Lincoln, and became full-fledged Republicans. Ryerson and George Cobb took the lead, joined by Joseph Crowell, Ashbel Green, Thomas Herring, Thomas McCarter, and Edward Moore. Most of these prominent recruits played major roles in the Republican campaign. Their defection infuriated the Democrats: the *Newton Herald* charged that Ryerson had so disgraced himself that people distrusted and despised him. Cobb's unexpected last-minute defection stunned Democrats across the state.[81]

As the contest neared its close, the political role of churches and clergymen became a heated issue. Democrats attacked preachers who turned pulpits into political rostrums. One Sussex man observed that the "preachers of today are preachers of blood and thunder; they are howling for the blood of every Southern man."[82]

The Republicans happily defended the right of ministers as community leaders to take an active interest in politics. Newark Baptist minister and avowed Republican Henry Fish was one of the political activists. Convinced that Lincoln's reelection would be the major turning point of the war, he wrote in his diary, "I cannot be silent." In his congregation, he commented, "most of my people go with me," but some disagreed and became inveterate enemies.[83]

The Republicans particularly commended the Congregationalists, Baptists, Methodists, and Presbyterians, as well as Rutgers College and the Seminary of the Reformed Church, for supporting Lincoln and his anti-slavery policies. The Republicans also praised Episcopalians, Catholics, and members of the Reformed Church for repudiating some conservatives in their ranks.[84]

Politicians in both parties attempted to broaden their base by appealing to various ethnic groups, notably Irish, German, and Dutch voters. The Democrats characterized the Republicans as nativists, and selected Dutch candidates in Hudson. They also encouraged German meetings and tried to set the Irish against the blacks. The Republicans responded by championing Irish independence and claiming that British aristocrats backed McClellan.

The Republicans chose a German to run as a presidential elector and German candidates for sheriff and the assembly. They selected Dutch candidates for the assembly in Hudson, Passaic, and Somerset. In Lodi the party distributed pamphlets in English, German, and Dutch. Pointing to the ethnocentric penchant of all ethnic groups, one observer declared that the Dutch hated to vote against anyone with a "Van" in his name.[85]

Sometimes, however, the nomination of an ethnic backfired. The Democrats' selection of an Irish Catholic as candidate for Essex sheriff caused a nativist backlash. This development spurred Republicans to wage an unusually active and ultimately successful campaign in Essex. Republicans exploited antiforeign feeling in South Jersey as well: the *Woodbury Constitution* praised the Republican candidate for the assembly in the second district of Gloucester as "not an Irishman. He is a Jerseyman."[86]

In city wards the Republicans faced their toughest challenge in trying to recruit immigrants, who were cultivated by the Democrats. One Republican newspaper reported that more than eight hundred Irish Catholics in Hudson alone became voters just before the election, and it regarded virtually all of them as Democrats. Many immigrants also became voters at the last minute in Newark and Orange.[87]

Because the Democrats selected their presidential nominee at the end of the summer, the campaign was unusually short and exceptionally fierce. The two-party competition sharpened party differences and simplified choices for the voters. The Democrats assumed the position of a populist conservative party holding the political center against purported political extremism on each flank. "We, the conservatives of the country," according to the *Hackettstown Gazette*, fought both the "Southern spirit of rebellion against the Union" and the "Northern spirit of rebellion against the Constitution." The Democrats promised that McClellan, armed with miracle cures for the nation's ills, would instantly restore the nation to its former health and sanity. Although Democrats promised comprehensive change, stated the *Jersey City Standard*, they rallied their forces to "resist all unnatural and monstrous change."[88]

The Republicans assumed a popular progressive posture and championed constructive reform, depicting the Democrats as representing subversive, even satanic forces. Republicans especially warned voters against change for its own sake, an especially risky step while fighting an unfinished war.[89]

By early November newspaper editorials were producing a torrent of scare stories, wild charges, incendiary denunciations, and apocalyptical exaggerations. Democratic papers of all factions became hysterical. The *Hackensack Democrat* denounced Lincoln's diabolical conspiracy as the work of a gang of "monsters and barbarians" and predicted that if Republicans remained in power the southern people would "be totally exterminated, half the men in the North" killed, the nation bankrupted, and the war continued for "*thirty years.*" According to the *Rahway Democrat*, victory for Lincoln meant a "Union which can never be restored, a debt that never can be paid, and more misery than the world ever saw." The *Morristown Banner* accused Lincoln's administration of having "fastened itself on the vitals of the country, shedding its heart's blood like water; robbing it of its last dollar." Exploiting battlefield casualties, Democrats in parades carried pictures of bones in coffins and weeping widows. The *Paterson Register* framed the choice for voters as "Lincoln and Despotism—McClellan and Freedom. The black man or the white man. A Union of hearts and hands, or a Union held together by bayonets."[90]

Condemning these distortions, the *Trenton Monitor* lashed out at the Democratic party: "It is ready to let the country fall if only the Administration which it hates may fall with it. It will oppose every endeavor of the Government, though the Government alone can preserve the nation. It will not sustain the Administration in the war, though its failure is the destruction of the country." The *Trenton Gazette* declared, "It is an issue between Union and Disunion; between Freedom and Slavery; between Democracy and Aristocracy."[91]

As the campaign grew increasingly ugly, both sides resorted to venomous name calling. Republicans called Democrats cowards, copperheads, and traitors. Democrats denounced Republicans as warmongers, radicals, revolutionaries, and blacks. Joking about McClellan's nickname, Little Mac, Republicans belittled him as a little soldier and a pygmy statesman, and promised to lay out cold "Little Mac-erals" after the election. One Piscataway Republican dismissed McClellan as the "Great Unready." The Democrats repeated their epithets against Lincoln.[92]

Overheated rhetoric sometimes kindled violence. In Trenton, when a railroad locomotive accidentally struck a wagon in a Democratic procession and injured several women, infuriated male participants picked up clubs, chased the signalman to his home, smashed down the front door, and beat him to death in front of his pleading wife and children. His death drove his wife insane. Republicans condemned the mob and called for a murder trial; Democrats blamed the signalman for indicating that the track was clear. At rallies across the state opponents tried to drown out speakers, disrupted meetings, tore down posters, ripped banners, stole flags, smashed windows, set fires, threw eggs, hurled bricks, attacked people, fired pistols, and in one case killed a child. Despite their loud protests against Lincoln's invasion of civil liberties, rowdy Democrats in particular resorted repeatedly to interference with the rights of their political opponents.[93]

The elections held in mid-October in three major states influenced the outcome in New Jersey. Republicans scored smashing victories in Indiana and Ohio, but only carried Pennsylvania with the soldier vote. In Newark's municipal election Republicans gained three aldermen, but Democrats received almost the same percentage of the vote as in the previous year, with about the same turnout. Because of the narrow win in Pennsylvania and the mixed results in Newark, the October elections carried unmistakable warnings to New Jersey Republicans. As Ryerson observed, "I pray there may not be a false confidence among our friends; that feeling damaged us in Pennsylvania."[94]

On November 8, a foggy, rainy day, a huge number of New Jersey voters streamed to the polls in generally quiet, orderly fashion. Democrats in the fifth ward of Jersey City, however, reportedly drove Republican challengers from the polls, assaulted one of them, and stripped off his clothes. For three hours only Democrats, including some New Yorkers, voted, while Democrats prevented Republicans from doing so. Democrats in the sixth ward used similar methods to reduce the Republican vote. One observer estimated that at least one thousand fraudulent votes were cast in Jersey City. Disturbances and irregularities reportedly occurred as well in Morristown, Newark, and South Amboy. As to choices, Brownson explained, "After the disloyal resolutions of Chicago I had no alternative" but to vote for Lincoln.[95]

Lincoln won every state except Kentucky, Delaware, and New Jersey. Although he secured only 55 percent of the North's popular vote, he received 91 percent of the electoral vote. The election turned on the populous states of the lower North, where the vote was closest and the Democrats strongest. Lincoln carried most of the Mid-Atlantic states by the narrowest of margins, winning Pennsylvania by 52 percent, Connecticut by 51 percent, and New York by 50 percent. With political preferences in these states matched almost evenly, Lincoln's supporters barely edged out McClellan's. In New Jersey, McClellan won by only 7,301 votes, almost 53 percent. (Parker's popular majority in 1862, almost 57 percent, had been virtually double in the raw vote.) Lincoln carried all the southern counties, while McClellan won all the more populous central and northern counties except Essex and Passaic. McClellan carried most of the large towns.

In comparison to 1860, Lincoln lost ground in every Mid-Atlantic state, but his share of the popular vote declined less in New Jersey than elsewhere in the region. Nevertheless, he picked up every Mid-Atlantic electoral vote but New Jersey's. Roughly 3 percent of Lincoln's 1860 Jersey supporters shifted to the Democrats; virtually no Democrats changed over to Lincoln. Abstainers in 1860 generally did not vote in 1864 either. Of the relatively few who did so, two backed McClellan for every previous abstainer who voted for Lincoln.[96]

New Jersey Republicans greeted the national victory gleefully. The *Toms River Wave* proclaimed "*No Compromise with Traitors!*" It declared, "*Copperheads Squelched! Snakes Selling at a Discount.*" Scovel congratulated Lincoln: "George Washington made the Republic. Abraham Lincoln will save it." A Bloomfield man remarked, "I think the election of Lincoln is equal to the greatest battle fought during the war. I think it will prove disastrous to them now they know just what they have to do. . . . I think we have just passed through the crisis of the war." For Republicans the decisive electoral vote freed the nation's arm to deliver the death blow to the rebellion. The *Jersey City Times* predicted that the war's "end is very near." As for McClellan's victory in the state, Jersey Republicans vowed to retake the state in 1865.[97]

New Jersey Democrats found solace in their state victory. The *New Brunswick Times* exclaimed, "New Jersey all Right. She Still Adheres to the Union and the Constitution." "New Jersey," remarked the *Newark Journal*, "is still within the pale of the Constitutional Union, if there still exists any such institution." "New Jersey almost solitary and alone has done her duty nobly," declared the *Morristown Banner*. Depending on their position, the Democrats blamed their national defeat either on their war wing or on the peace faction. Five months later, bitter Fuller asserted that "McClellanism was simply a subterfuge and a sham" to demoralize or convert the party. The *Hackensack Democrat* argued that the "War Platform of the Democracy has not succeeded, and hereafter must be abandoned if we desire victory." Repudiating this view, the *Patersonian* stated that "we want no more copperhead sentiment. . . . *We must conquer a Peace.*" This newspaper, which regarded peace sentiment as highly unpopular, concluded that the Democratic party "cannot afford to carry the deadweight further."[98]

Democrats accused Republicans of exploiting federal power and patronage. Although keenly disappointed, many Democrats accepted the result with quiet resignation, given the electoral landslide. The *Patersonian* declared, "We bow to the will of that majority." McClellan, who had expected to win, deplored the result for the sake of the nation, but did not despair of the Republic; he conceded that the "people have decided with their eyes wide open."[99]

Free elections during war proved risky but indispensable. The Democratic *Jersey City Standard* observed, "Our people, having let off their superfluous steam through this *safety valve*, have resumed their occupations with calm acquiescence." The Republican *Trenton Gazette* contended that the election demonstrated the "fitness of the people for self-government." Lincoln agreed: two nights after the election, he told supporters in Washington that government had to reconcile order with liberty. At one extreme, government could overreact in preserving order and so could act too strongly, thus endangering the liberties of the people. At the other extreme, however, government could act too weakly; thus it would not "be strong enough to maintain its existence in great emergencies." Lincoln believed that the recent election had emphatically "demonstrated that a people's Government can sustain a national election in the midst of a great civil war."[100]

In the course of the campaign Republicans in New Jersey had received federal help and had created an efficient state organization. They conducted a vigorous campaign, despite some handicaps. The usually censorious *New York Tribune* called the state's Union canvass "spirited and judicious." The often critical *New York Times* agreed. Yet downstate Republicans complained bitterly that their North Jersey counterparts had not campaigned hard enough and that the proximity of wily Democratic politicians and editors in New York City had influenced North Jersey voters unduly. No evidence supports either claim, however. The usual charge that the Camden and Amboy Railroad had bought the election for the Democrats also made no sense. The railroad monopoly in fact contributed to both parties, and its influential officials supported both parties and all wings.[101]

Yet the war burden hurt New Jersey Republicans. As one Newarker observed about the desperate need for hands to operate farms, the "draft did us much damage in the agricultural districts." In addition, McClellan's personal magnetism as a military man and his stirring appeal as a Jersey resident influenced some voters in a close race. Parker's stump speeches also helped the Democratic campaign. Pivotal new voters in Hudson and in North Jersey cities—legal and illegal—counted powerfully. Above all, New Jersey servicemen could not cast absentee ballots. As a result, the Republicans could not carry the state. One lieutenant in the Twelfth Regiment believed that the "soldier's vote would have changed Jersey's vote."[102]

In congressional races across the North, Democrats lost half of their seats. Republicans gained enough votes in the House to secure the more than two-thirds majority required to introduce constitutional amendments. The election, the *Flemington Republican* declared, "decided that the Nation shall live and Slavery shall die."[103]

In New Jersey, Newell in the second district won narrowly, by slightly under 52 percent, and so regained the seat lost in 1862. Elsewhere the dominant party and every incumbent running for reelection retained their districts. Democrats in the fourth and fifth districts of North Jersey did so with 54 percent of the vote. Wakeman almost carried Newark, but Democratic voters in Hudson overwhelmingly outnumbered Republican supporters.

Even with the imminent departure of copperhead Nehemiah Perry, the election of Sitgreaves and the reelection of Rogers guaranteed that the state's congressional delegation still would include reactionaries in Democratic ranks. Although peace Democrats still were well represented in the congressional delegation because of party hegemony or incumbency, their role in Congress as members of a minority within a minority party declined further because the Democratic party as a whole was weaker as a result of the congressional elections.[104]

As for the legislature, the outcome of the six state senate races did not alter Democratic control of the upper chamber, but the Republicans picked up a seat in Burlington. The parties' strongholds were Cape May for the Republicans and Hunterdon and Sussex for the Democrats. In close contests, the Democrats kept Middlesex with 54 percent of the vote; the Republicans barely retained Passaic with 50 percent. Democrats outnumbered Republicans by five seats.

In the assembly, Republicans gained ten seats and tied Democrats for control of the body. Although they lost one district in Jersey City, Republicans won two new seats each in Burlington, Camden, and Passaic and gained a single seat each in Atlantic, Essex, Middlesex, Salem, and Union. Resourceful Republicans won nineteen, or three-fourths, of the competitive districts. The number of districts won by Democrats without opposition decreased dramatically, from ten in 1863 to just two in 1864. In consistently contested assembly districts, Republicans won almost 45 percent of the vote in 1862, 48 percent in 1863, and 49 percent in 1864. Not quite winning absolute control of the legislature, the Republicans lacked five indispensable seats in the assembly to gain a majority on a joint ballot and elect a federal senator. Their comeback had almost succeeded.

Of the assembly copperheads who stood for reelection, most hailed from safe districts and hence faced no serious challengers. Of the four in competitive districts, Republicans defeated two, Chalkley Albertson in Camden's third district and Simon Hanthorn in Atlantic. The *Camden Press* observed that the "most signal victory is the defeat of Albertson. . . . he could not stand up against the popular indignation his course had awakened among the people." Only twelve copperheads were left in the assembly; their power continued to erode, but they still were capable of making mischief on occasion in the future. With English gone, no well-known copperhead remained. As a symbol of the change, Crowell won the seat in the second district of Union formerly occupied by a die-hard copperhead.[105]

Proponents of the view that New Jersey was a copperhead state could point out that political conditions in the state worsened for the Republicans between Lincoln's first election and his second. Clearly they did so because of the costs of war. Lincoln's percentage of New Jersey's popular vote declined in 1864; in that year he received a mere 47 percent, compared with 55 percent nationwide. In 1864 Lincoln received no Jersey electoral votes, as compared with four in 1860. Indeed New Jersey was the only free state carried by McClellan; to some this result was sufficient proof that New Jersey was not merely unique or even wayward, but downright coppery in its politics.

Several compelling considerations have been overlooked in reaching this facile conclusion. First, just as in 1860, when advocates of Douglas opposed both Lincoln and southern secessionists, a great many of McClellan's supporters in 1864 were not copperheads but Parkerites. They backed the war and military recruitment; so did McClellan, with his pledge to secure reunion as the condition of peace.

Second, New Jersey Republicans gained one congressional seat. Indeed, they increased their overall share of the vote by four percentage points over 1862. They improved their performance over 1862 in every congressional district. Although the voters' loyalties froze between 1862 and 1864, previous abstainers who voted in 1864 voted for Republican congressional candidates by a margin of roughly five to three.

Third, in contests for the assembly, the Republicans made a net gain of ten seats and became deadlocked with the Democrats for control. Republicans won nearly 49 percent of the vote, compared with 45 percent in 1863.

Fourth, the influence of the copperheads in the legislature continued to erode during 1864 and 1865.

Fifth, in the sixteen northern states in which Republicans battled Democrats in 1863, Republicans won 56.6 percent of the total vote, compared to 55.4 percent of the total won by Lincoln in 1864. Lincoln's share of the vote was smaller, even though he had the benefit of soldiers' voting in more states in 1864 than in 1863. In New Jersey, however, Republicans went against this trend: the Republican share of votes cast in contested assembly districts in 1863 amounted to 47.8 percent of the total votes cast. In contrast, in 1864 Lincoln won 48.5 percent of the vote and Republican assemblymen achieved 49.4 percent in the same districts. The 1864 election in New Jersey thus reflected a shift in public sentiment toward the Republican party, even though McClellan won the state.

McClellan's military and Jerseyan credentials, strong Irish-Catholic support, and the New Jersey soldiers' inability to vote by absentee ballot clinched the contest for the Democrats. New Jersey, then, was neither a coppery anomaly nor a copperhead state, but rather a Mid-Atlantic state becoming increasingly Republican. The tide had turned but not yet crested.[106]

Before the election both Democratic and Republican observers from outside the state predicted that New Jersey was likely to go Democratic. McClellan's Jersey victory surprised few politicians. His narrow win and the Democrats' precarious edge in the new legislature, however, were a major surprise. The recent election in the state indicated a "great improvement" in Republican fortunes, as Marcus Ward observed. Ward suggested that accusations against the state were altogether unfounded. New Jerseyans were not led by a bunch of copperheads, as many northerners had supposed. As Ward put it, New Jersey "should not be counted against the government, but for it."[107]

Attacks on the state and on its wartime role decreased after the election. Recognition of reality—unionism in Democratic ranks and a Republican resurgence in the state—increased. New Jersey, after all, was soundly patriotic.

# 13 Northern Triumph and National Tragedy

The election results indeed hastened the downfall of the rebellion. Southern soldiers, facing a deteriorating situation at the front, realized that no call for an armistice would come from the North. They sensed that the Confederacy was doomed, and many troops surrendered or deserted. A New Jersey officer reported from Virginia that the "mass of the southern people are for peace on any terms while some of their leading men are for war to the bitter end. I think we can accommodate them either way. They know to their cost that we are not backward in fighting. They know also that they can have peace—unconditional peace—at any time. Ten rebels came in our lines last night. They state that things and time are getting desperate over there."[1]

In mid-November 1864 Sherman ordered his troops to burn parts of Atlanta. After they had done so, they advanced steadily across Georgia and the Carolinas. Crippling the Confederate war effort, Sherman's army cut off indispensable supplies for Lee's army in Virginia by wrecking railroads. To shatter southern morale, his army devastated the civilian economy. In quick succession triumphant Yankees smashed pockets of resistance. They took Savannah on December 21, occupied Columbia and Charleston in mid-February of 1865, captured the port of Wilmington in late February, and seized Goldsboro on March 21. Reacting to some of these victories, the Jersey officer observed, "We are in great hopes of the war coming to a close very soon."[2]

Except for some die-hard copperheads, New Jerseyans back home recognized the end of the Confederacy. The imminent demise brought both rejoicing and reflection. A wounded veteran from Trenton remarked, "What a great amount of misery and suffering this war has entailed on the American People." Peter Vroom looked back on the effect "of civil war, the worst of all wars, because the most embittered and enduring," and observed that the "war seems to have changed the whole tone and current of feeling. Three years ago the report of a battle filled people with terror. All mourned the dead and sympathized with the living. Now we read of battles and carnage and desolation, with almost as little concern, as if they had taken place in India or Turkey."[3]

Recurrent rumors of Confederate capitulation swept New Jersey. A Hightstown woman voiced her anxiety about her husband, who was still serving in the army: "If we only could say the Victory is won and the war is done." Hearing the news that Columbia had fallen, Marcus Ward predicted that the rebellion and slavery along with it "will, I think, soon be over." The *Camden Press* announced that the "rebellion is in its last throes. Exhausted in men and means, it is waging a hopeless war."[4]

The fall of Charleston, the birthplace of the rebellion, where the first blood of the war was shed, stirred people in Perth Amboy to celebrate. One abolitionist schoolteacher observed, "Flags from windows, from all poles, from tops of houses, from masts of ships wave in glad welcome."[5]

When Lincoln took the presidential oath for the second time on March 4, he made no explicit appeal to southerners to rejoin the Union. Some impatient Democrats criticized his omission. The *Absecon Republican* countered, "The South will respect our power when they feel it, and will respect nothing else." New Jerseyans looked forward to the day when the Union army would throw the knockout punch.[6]

Expounding on national affairs in his annual message, Parker pleased neither copperheads nor Republicans. Incensed copperheads objected to his use of Republican code words, such as loyal and rebel, for their implied support of the war. The *Newark Journal* attacked Governor Parker's inconsistency: he supported Yankee soldiers in killing rebels, but rejected the freeing of slaves by Union troops. The copperheads were pleased, however, by Parker's call for the victorious North to act magnanimously toward the defeated South and by his critique of Republican actions. Republicans criticized Parker for finding fault once again with Lincoln's war policy. They charged Parker with trying to please both antiwar Democrats and prowar Democrats. The Republican *Paterson Press* observed that Parker's patriotic actions helping the war effort did not square with his partisan rhetoric. The *Press* stressed that what really counted was what Parker did, not what he said, for his bark was worse than his bite.[7]

Politicians wrestled with the immediate challenge of organizing the legislature. Although Democrats enjoyed a decisive majority in the senate, other considerations intruded. If Parker were elected to succeed John Ten Eyck in the United States Senate, the president of the state senate automatically would become acting governor. With this possibility in mind, the senators again ruled out copperhead Daniel Holsman and selected Edward Scudder, a staunch war supporter and moderate Democrat, a man completely acceptable to Republicans. In his inaugural remarks Scudder pledged allegiance to federal laws and the Constitution.[8]

Formidable difficulties arose in organizing the assembly, which had equal numbers of Republican and Democratic members. The tug-of-war began at the start of the January 10 session when the vote for speaker resulted in a tie. Without a leader and frequently without a quorum, the assembly could not transact business. As each party maneuvered desperately for mastery, the deadlock continued. The Republicans believed they had been cheated of control by the fraudulent election of two Hudson Democrats.

Then, on January 14, a Sussex Democratic assemblyman died, leaving the Democrats in the minority until a successor could be elected. A special election to fill the vacancy could not take place until the assembly authorized it. Authorization, in turn, could not occur until the assembly organized and elected a speaker, and until the speaker signed the order.

The Republicans, now the majority party, insisted on a Republican speaker. The Democrats refused, contending that a quorum required for conducting business must count the dead member. The Republicans disagreed but offered patronage to entice Democrats to accept Republican organization.

After many acrimonious sessions and much fruitless negotiation, the assemblymen reached a compromise in which the parties divided the patronage equally and ratified the agreement on January 26. The two parties jointly organized the lower house and unanimously elected Joseph Crowell, a former independent Democrat who had become a Republican, as speaker. Crowell had earned a reputation as an articulate, fearless legislator and as one of the most formidable opponents of the copperheads in the state. Thus, with both the speakership and the clerkship in their hands, New Jersey Republicans prevailed at long last.[9]

Why did the Democrats drop their strong objections to Crowell? The Republicans would have agreed earlier to a Democratic clerk, but they were infuriated by the Democrats' insistence on deciding which Republican would be speaker, as well as by their delaying tactics. The Republicans rejected the Democrats' demand to abandon Crowell as speaker, then succeeded in bullying and bribing the Democrats. During the tense negotiations, Democratic legislators began to take seriously the Republicans' threats to adjourn the assembly for a year. This would prevent election of a federal senator, paralyze the state government, delay patronage, and block payment of legislators' salaries and daily living expenses. Demoralized Democratic legislators lost their nerve in the face of the Republicans, who bargained from a position of strength and outmaneuvered their opponents. As a compromise, both parties and their factions received a share of the public printing. When selecting a new state treasurer, however, Republicans did not insist on a mutually acceptable candidate. As a result, the position went to David Naar, party war-horse and moderate copperhead, who had lost his lucrative public printing work. Still, the election of Crowell as speaker overrode all other appointments. The Democrats could not disguise their stunned reaction to this defeat.[10]

As 1865 opened, rumors abounded as to who might seek the seat in the United States Senate. Parker figured in the speculation as one of the leading candidates of the moderate Democrats. His chances were not improved, however, by his wooing of the copperheads. According to the shrewd Trenton correspondent of the *New Brunswick Fredonian*, his "motive is too apparent and the execution too weak to strengthen his cause."[11]

Reporters also mentioned McClellan as a contender, but virtually all of the Democratic politicians ruled him out. As a resident he had run for president as a state favorite, but not as a native son. He was not enough of a New Jerseyan to run for senator. The *Patersonian* argued that the state ought to be represented in the Senate by "Jerseymen in every sense of the word."[12]

With McClellan away in Europe, interest in his candidacy soon flagged, especially when rivals jockeyed for the senatorship. Commentators mentioned John Stockton, the eldest son of Robert Stockton. The younger Stockton was an able attorney, an excellent speaker, an upright individual, and a war supporter; his personal charm, public experience, and moderate position attracted widespread support. In addition, his father led the Joint Companies, which could influence some legislators.[13]

The copperheads adamantly opposed Parker. They also objected strenuously to McClellan and Stockton. They called for a true-hearted Democrat, namely James Wall. In a public letter, Chauncey Burr bluntly rejected anyone else as a counterfeit Democrat. For the Senate seat he preferred no senator at all, or even a detested Republican, to an "unsound Democrat," a "pliant inanity" who backed the evil war. He advised, "Let us send the right man or send none at all."[14]

Recognizing that the moderate Democrats had enough votes in the party caucus to prevail and that all persons attending the joint caucus would have to abide by its decision, nine copperhead hard-liners declined to go into the Democratic caucus in February and March until the moderates withdrew their candidates. The moderates refused to do so. The timing of this copperhead maneuver took an ironic twist: while Yankee troops battered rebel forces during the winter, the oblivious and wildly ideological New Jersey copperheads obstructed the right of the majority to rule and threatened rebellion if the minority did not get its own way. Though they were few in number, the position of these irreconcilables was vital because no Democrat could be elected without their support, given the number of Republican legislators. Thus the copperheads remained strong enough to block Parker and prevent the choice of another man. Realizing this, moderate Democrats applied immense pressure to the dissidents. Even copperhead newspapers condemned the nine for their disloyalty to the party; their stubbornness might result in the election of a Republican. These copperheads continued to hold out, while denying rumors of an alliance with Republicans to defeat any prowar Democrat.[15]

Republican legislators meanwhile considered whether they should prevent a joint meeting and thus delay the election of a senator for a year, at which time they might gain control of the legislature. They reached no consensus. In early February the Republicans decided to participate in a joint meeting after reaching agreement with the Democrats on how to distribute state patronage in various counties. Moreover, they hoped they might win, given the division among the Democrats. Without dissent, the joint Republican caucus backed Ten Eyck for another term.[16]

At a joint meeting of the legislature on February 15, with the Democrats in control, the legislators adopted a resolution requiring a majority of all members, forty-one votes, to elect a senator. In effect this rule both prevented the Republicans from electing a senator and kept copperheads from throwing the election away. Because of the Democrats' divisions, this rule also bought time for Stockton's supporters to acquire support from the copperheads. By the end of February the Democratic caucus favored Stockton, but the copperheads still refused to support him. Stockton's supporters worked feverishly to suppress mutiny before the legislative session ended. Reports circulated that the heavy-handed Wall, perennial candidate for a full term in the Senate, lobbied so hard for support that he succeeded in converting one senatorial ally into an opponent.[17]

Another joint meeting was held on March 15, with all legislators in attendance. At that time the Democrats rescinded the requirement of an absolute majority and substituted a rule requiring only a plurality. This extraordinary new rule passed by a single vote. Burlington Republican senator George M. Wright, reportedly both an employee and an investor in the Stockton family's Joint Companies, provided the vote that made it possible to hold an election. Thus he helped ensure the defeat of fellow Burlington Republican Ten Eyck and the election of a Democrat.

In the vote for U.S. senator, virtually all of the Democrats supported Stockton. His backers included six previous dissidents, who reportedly came into line after receiving various inducements from the Joint Companies. Three copperhead state senators—Joshua Doughty, James Jenkins, and Henry R. Kennedy—still refused to back Stockton. Each cast a ballot for an individual of his choice. All of the Republicans backed Ten Eyck except the independent-minded, iconoclastic James Scovel, who purportedly rejected Ten Eyck as an ally of the monopoly and voted instead for Frederick Frelinghuysen. Stockton was elected with only forty votes, a mere plurality; forty-one legislators cast ballots for other candidates, including thirty-seven for Ten Eyck. Because of the Republicans' ignorance at the outset about the number of Democratic dissidents, coupled with their confusion about the meaning of the rule change and the abrupt adjournment of the joint meeting, Stockton's shrewd managers were able to outwit the Republicans.[18]

The Republicans immediately disputed the legality of Stockton's election, while the Democrats defended it. In victory, Democrats became magnanimous toward their copperhead dissidents. The Republicans denounced their own defectors as traitors; some party members even called for their resignations. The Republicans condemned Wright for his vote supporting the change in the rules, and read him out of the party. They also lashed out at Scovel for his idiosyncratic action. The *Trenton Gazette*, noting that Scovel had failed to attend the Republican caucus, quipped that he "belongs to a party of which he is the only member. He is a law unto himself." The Republicans consoled themselves with the thought that the Democrats could have selected an infinitely worse man but instead had made a respectable choice.[19]

Stockton's election clearly represented a shift from the party's old guard to the young Democracy. Nevertheless, the circumstances of the election raised questions about its validity, aroused suspicions of bribery in securing last-minute conversions, left Republicans with nagging regrets about lost opportunities, and enraged Wall and his copperhead crew of bitter-enders.

Most northern Democrats conceded that slavery would be dead when the war ended. Even so, they stubbornly refused to sign the death certificate. They balked at legalizing emancipation by approving the proposed Thirteenth Amendment to the federal Constitution. On January 31, 1865, every Republican in the House of Representatives, including John Starr, supported the amendment. Most Democrats opposed it, including William Steele and Nehemiah Perry. Yet deft lobbying and resourceful patronage by Lincoln's men paid off, as did the powerful persuasion of loyal border state Democrats. Sixteen Democrats, mainly lame ducks, were reconciled to adoption of the amendment and supported it; none were from New Jersey.[20]

Eight Democrats absented themselves from the voting, thus enabling the measure to receive the two-thirds majority required to begin the process of amending the Constitution. Among the eight absentees were two New Jersey congressmen, George Middleton and Andrew Rogers. Middleton's absence plainly reflected his anti-slavery views, his lame duck status, and his tendency to avoid tough votes. But the reportedly ill Rogers, a noisy copperhead with a cautious voting record, had indicated during the debate that he strongly opposed ratification. His failure to oppose the amendment provoked especially harsh comment. The *Newton Register* characterized him as a shrewd politician whose deliberate absence safeguarded his political future; his supposed illness served as a convenient excuse to avoid a politically damaging vote and fit his voting pattern.[21]

Rumors of a possible deal between the Camden and Amboy's lobbyists and various politicians in Washington and Trenton circulated in early 1865. According to one report, the United States Senate would kill the antimonopoly railroad bill in exchange for approval of the Thirteenth Amendment by the House of Representatives. The railroad's men could induce New Jersey's Democratic congressmen not to vote on the amendment and thus enable it to pass. Other reports suggested an even more tenuous proposal: if no antimonopoly measure passed Congress, the monopoly's lobbyists in Trenton could influence enough Democratic legislators to vote for ratification of the Thirteenth Amendment as well as throwing the election of a federal senator into the hands of the Republicans.[22]

The rumors (if true) could explain Rogers's failure to vote on the amendment. It might indicate his cooperation with the monopoly, but the evidence is inconclusive. His reasons also may have been solely political. His stance clearly represented an exception in New Jersey's congressional delegation, whose voting on the Thirteenth Amendment did not appear to reflect the influence of railroad lobbyists. The voting in the legislature on both the amendment and the senatorship refutes the likelihood of such a deal: the Democrats opposed both ratification of the amendment and selection of a Republican for senator.

The Camden and Amboy Railroad's support of Stockton's senatorial candidacy showed clearly that the rumored trade-off between Washington and Trenton had no foundation in fact. Either no such deals were ever made or, if they were made, the powerbrokers were unable to deliver. Perhaps some railroad lobbyists convinced various New Jersey Republicans that a deal existed, or perhaps those Jersey Republicans simply deluded themselves into thinking such a trade-off had been arranged. Acting on that unfounded conviction, they pressured Republicans in Washington to induce the United States Senate to sidetrack the railroad bill, in the giddy expectation that ratification of the Thirteenth Amendment and election of a Republican senator would sail magically through the legislature with Democratic help.[23]

In any event, when Congress sent the proposed Thirteenth Amendment to the state legislatures for action, the *Paterson Press* declared, "The greatest victory of the war has been gained in the peaceful halls of Congress." The *New Brunswick Fredonian* had observed earlier that the "war which Slavery inaugurated to preserve and strengthen the institution has killed it." On the public square in Morristown people fired guns, rang bells, and raised flags in celebration of the congressional action. The Democratic *Newark Journal* took a different view, describing the projected amendment as "another nail driven in the coffin of the Union." The *Paterson Register* also considered passage "another bar to the making of peace between the North and the South." The *Journal* lashed out at those Democratic congressmen who either had supported the amendment or had dodged the vote on a measure "so obnoxious to all conservative people and in glaring defiance of the spirit of the Constitution."[24]

Members of the legislature engaged in an exhaustive debate on the amendment. No Republican questioned the legality or necessity of abolishing slavery by constitutional amendment. The Republicans affirmed the people's right to change their government. Representing the people in Congress, the Republicans possessed ample power to take national action. They also maintained that the states had never enjoyed exclusive jurisdiction over slavery, but rather had shared it with the federal government. Congress had regulated slavery at various times and places. If a conflict arose between national and state powers, Nathan S. Abbott stated, "I admit, Mr. Speaker, that States have rights which ought to be respected, but the Federal Government—the government of all the States—has rights which take precedence," in a war to maintain the nation's existence. Republicans also defended the amendment as the only constitutional way to make national abolition permanent in peacetime.[25]

Justifying immediate emancipation, some Republicans took the high ground of legal equality. They welcomed the eradication of a great evil. "What is morally wrong cannot be politically right," declared Philander C. Brink.[26]

Most Republicans preferred safer, practical grounds. Destroying slavery, the root of the rebellion, would "repay" northerners for sacrificing and suffering through four years of fire and blood, remarked Thomas B. Peddie. Eradicating slavery would ensure lasting peace by eliminating "this demon of discord," declared Robert Moore. Otherwise, James H. Nixon argued, Americans would remain a "divided people, with different institutions, different interests, and different aims. The Union restored with slavery, will be a union only in name." In addition, Republicans pointed to the record of brave black soldiers in the Union army, who had earned emancipation for their race. The Republicans contended that slavery had been abolished in fact and now must be ended by law; if slavery was dead, why not bury it?[27]

The Democrats rejected ratification on several grounds, but only two copperheads defended slavery. Although generally not advocates of slavery, most Democrats disagreed with the method and the timing of abolition. As conservatives they trembled at suddenly turning loose millions of ignorant, impoverished slaves. Emancipation, they asserted, would upend southern society and bring disaster to both races. As capitalists they feared the confiscation of private property without compensation. As Democrats they regarded the amendment as an intensely partisan measure.

As localists who viewed national powers narrowly and state rights broadly, the Democrats insisted that the institution of slavery came under the exclusive control of the states. They contended that no amendment prohibiting slavery in the states could be adopted legally and that no such change could be made without the consent of all the slave states. The Democrats regarded the pending measure not as an amendment of the Constitution but as an alteration: approval would end federalism. State institutions would be destroyed, state boundaries obliterated, states reduced to provinces, and citizens treated as mere subjects. As racists, Democrats opposed federal efforts to advance blacks, although only a few copperheads explicitly denied the principle of racial equality. Finally, as proponents of reconciliation, Democrats saw abolition as a roadblock to reunion. Leon Abbett declared that the North should not "punish the South; we would endeavor to heal old wounds by kindness and a spirit of conciliation."[28]

Not all New Jersey Democrats argued against the amendment. Some, sensing the growing popularity of the amendment, viewed Democratic intransigence as a political liability. The *Patersonian* advocated acquiescence: "Slavery is dead. Shall the Democracy longer be chained to its carcass?" Jacob Vanatta exhorted Democrats to cut loose from the past by endorsing ratification. He asserted that the federal power previously used to govern slavery could now be employed to abolish it. Was a free people competent only to rivet human chains but utterly powerless to knock them off? Most Democrats disagreed, however. As the *Trenton American* contended, "Expediency is a poor substitute for principle." The newspaper warned that "three-fourths of the States have the right to amend the Constitution, not to destroy it." [29]

Differences among Democrats in the legislature reflected breaches in party ranks statewide. Some Democratic senators rejected party efforts to bottle up the amendment in committee. In fact persistent rumors circulated that some Democratic senators favored ratification. In the assembly on February 28, the Democratic majority on the judiciary committee called for voters to pass judgment on the amendment before the legislature acted. When the proposal came to a vote, it was rejected by eight Democratic assemblymen, half of them copperheads, along with the Republicans. For opposite reasons, the two groups favored immediate action. Some observers viewed bipartisan ratification of the amendment as a strong possibility.

Prima donna Scovel, with only the Camden and Amboy Railroad on his mind, dashed chances of approval with a bitter partisan speech that infuriated potential Democratic allies and put them in an awkward position if they voted for ratification. Scovel charged that railroad lobbyists had influenced moderate senators to ratify the Thirteenth Amendment in the New Jersey senate as part of a deal to derail antimonopoly railroad legislation in the United States Senate.

As the legislators heatedly debated the amendment, partisan feeling intensified. Democratic editors warned their party members in the legislature of the dangers of dissension. Such pressure and persuasion drew the party lines more clearly. Worrying about the upcoming gubernatorial election, moderate Democrats probably calculated that division on the amendment would enrage conservatives, who might refuse to campaign or vote in the fall, and thus would cause Democratic defeat. Having prevailed over the conservatives on so many measures, the moderates now needed to placate them; thus most of the prowar faction decided to oppose the amendment. They made up in inflexibility what many lacked in true conviction. When the assembly met on March 1, it rejected the amendment by a tie vote. All of the Republicans supported the amendment; the Democrats opposed it solidly. The senate, also voting along straight party lines, defeated the amendment on March 16. According to reports, Theodore Randolph and Scudder would have voted in favor if their votes would have secured ratification. [30]

The Democrats gleefully praised their party's unity and integrity. The *Hoboken Democrat* exulted, "New Jersey knows her rights, and will maintain them." Republicans inside and outside the state denounced the Democrats' action. By rejecting the amendment the legislature merely repeated what most Democratic legislators did in other states; New Jersey simply behaved as a Democratic northern state. The rejection by New Jerseyans, moreover, did not seem then to imperil the amendment: the Republicans considered ratification by the remaining legislatures to be assured.[31]

More important, New Jersey Democratic obstructionism played into Republican hands by providing a ready-made campaign issue for the upcoming gubernatorial contest. The *Jersey City Times* jeered that the Democrats lacked the common sense to avoid suicide. The *Princeton Standard* told New Jerseyans not to bow their heads in shame. By prolonging agitation of the slave question, the Democrats had provided the Republicans with the means to defeat them and to restore the good reputation of the state. The Republicans hoped that the Democrats, by not burying slavery in March, would be digging their own political graves in November.[32]

With the arrival of spring, Grant began a new offensive. Ending the stalemate at Petersburg, his forces drove several wedges through the weakened enemy line on April 2. On the next day, launching a fierce assault on the rebel citadel, Grant's army seized the city, whose mayor surrendered it to the commander of the Fortieth New Jersey. Expecting the worst and fearing encirclement, Confederate troops and officials had abandoned both Petersburg and Richmond the night before and fled westward.[33]

The New Jersey troops wildly cheered the capture of the Confederate capital. A soldier eagerly anticipated an end to the "terrible roar of artillery, the rattle of musketry, or the sharp crack of the skirmisher's rifle."[34]

On the home front, the news spread by telegraph and word of mouth. The *Absecon Republican* exclaimed, "*Richmond Is Ours*," and added, "*Victory To Grant!*" Writing to her husband in the Union navy, a Hightstown woman observed the neighbors lighting up their homes at night and beating drums. Yet she considered this demonstration premature: there had been many disappointments before, when victory seemed assured, so she did not join in celebrating. "I think the people are rejoicing too much, too soon. I shall wait until the news is peace and then I can illuminate and rejoice with them." Hearing an approaching parade, she ran outside her house to see it pass. Returning, she wrote, "It looked beautiful but they did not cheer me. I had not lit up but I am just as loyal as if it was lit up. Not a bit of copperhead blood in my veins." A relative declared that the "glorious news of the few days past is enough to intoxicate any Loyal heart, and turn every Copperhead into a patriot."[35]

Thomas T. Kinney, publisher of the *Newark Advertiser*, regarded the fall of Richmond as a foregone conclusion, but "it nevertheless caught us with a sudden surprise and the people everywhere were thrown into a delirium of joy." In Newark, Kinney and others saw flags flying everywhere; bunting on every building fluttered in the breeze. The air was filled with the sound of gongs pounding, drums beating, bells ringing, steam whistles blowing, cannons firing, fireworks exploding. People crowded meetings to hear stirring speeches and sing songs. Some celebrated with whiskey. Kinney observed, "People of all professions and trades let off their enthusiasm with 'a perfect looseness,' regardless of dignity or decorum."[36]

The end came quickly. The rebel retreat turned into disaster when the Federals, who had chased them for almost a hundred miles, cut off their main escape route. On April 9 vastly superior Yankee forces virtually surrounded Lee's crippled, shriveled army. Exhausted and demoralized, the troops had run out of rations and stopped to search for food. Desperate for clothing, they had even stripped dead Union soldiers of their uniforms. Lee preferred humiliating capitulation to pointless annihilation, and met with Grant on the same day at Appomattox Court House. He agreed to surrender his forces in Virginia. Commanders of other Confederate armies followed suit. The war was over.[37]

New Jersey troops near Appomattox soon heard the news from General Meade. Riding up to men in the Twelfth Regiment, Meade announced, "Boys your work is done, Lee has surrendered and you can go home." The troops responded by throwing their hats in the air or placing their caps on their bayonets, raising their rifles, yelling, and firing cannons. James Rusling exclaimed, "Why, it is almost too good to be true! We have been very jolly here. Nothing but cannon flying, flags firing, and people hurrahing! I have made a mistake there, about the '*flying* and *firing*,' but you know what I mean, so where's the difference?" A member of the Twelfth Regiment recounted how, with a lump in his throat, "I sat down on a pile of rails, saying nothing, trying to comprehend the fact and all it included. 'The war over.' I had lived to see the Union arms triumph. The Union was saved. The many weary marches, the many hard fought battles, the colds of winter, the heats of summer had not been braved in vain." One man in the Fourteenth Regiment praised the downfall of the rebellion: "Amid the ruins lie buried all its vain glory, its false pride, its vaunted strength." A member of the Thirty-third Regiment stated that the "traitorous South" had been taught a painful "lesson of obedience to law."[38]

When Lee surrendered to Grant, a Trenton reporter pronounced "the rebellion crushed." The result vindicated democracy and repudiated treason. "Freedom is not a mockery, Liberty is not a myth, and Progress is real!" he concluded. New Jerseyans resumed celebrating; some quickly worked themselves up to a fine pitch of alcoholic patriotism. On a more sober note, a Montclair resident commented that "great victories are always expensively attained. While a nation rejoices, individuals weep. Thus has it ever been. War is cruel business."[39]

"*We are all patriots* now," exclaimed one Republican, but in fact many intense partisans, both Democratic and Republican legislators, preferred to spar and squabble with each other. As the war of the rebellion neared its end, Democrats obtusely refused to call the rebellion unjustifiable. In a partisan gesture they struck out the name of Lincoln in a vote of thanks to the troops. As Democrat Abbett, explained, Lincoln had nothing to do with achieving victory; in fact he had been an impediment to the war effort, and the war would have ended long ago without him in Washington. Republicans were avenged nine months later, when the legislature approved their brand of patriotic resolutions.[40]

Everyone looked forward to peace, but the road to reunion was rocky. People disagreed profoundly about how to treat the southerners. Many New Jersey Republicans feared that Lincoln might pardon the Confederate leaders. Denouncing those who insisted on a fraternal embrace with traitors, the *Paterson Press* demanded the death sentence for rebel leaders. In the opinion of one serviceman, those who had caused the death of hundreds of thousands of men on the bloody battlefields and had starved northern troops in southern prisons should be tried as murderers and then hanged. The *Jersey City Times*, too, opposed general amnesty for rebel officials and generals. At the very least, it argued, they should not vote or hold office. Martin Ryerson advised, "I do hope the President will not follow the advice of Greeley in pardoning Davis and Company, the prime movers, the guilty wretches. The blood of our slain kindred cries aloud against them, and the horrible sufferings of our prisoners demand their condign punishment."[41]

Other Republicans wished to punish the rebel leaders but not all southerners. If peace was to be firm and lasting, it had to be generous and merciful. Speaking for many Democrats, the *Paterson Register* appealed for understanding and statesmanship. Vengeance and vindictiveness could not reunite Americans and reunify the nation. The *Register* wished the vanquished southerners to be treated magnanimously as estranged, erring brothers, as fellow countrymen again. The *Paterson Guardian* asserted, "If the war is over, bury the hatchet, guillotine, rope and all. If the war is ended, end it."[42]

Five days after the surrender, rejoicing turned into sorrow. A medical student at Georgetown College, James Knox, who had served in New Jersey's Twenty-first Regiment, described what he saw. Attending a play at Ford's Theater in Washington and sitting in the second row of the orchestra just beneath the presidential box, he heard a muffled pistol shot. He saw a man jump from the presidential box to the stage and hurt himself. Limping across the stage, the man shouted, "The South is avenged." Fearing the worst, Knox and another man sprang instantly to the stage and pursued this man, who ran out of the theater, jumped on his horse, and rode off. Many people in the audience considered the entire episode part of the play. Then Mrs. Lincoln started to scream. Someone shouted that Lincoln was shot. The audience now knew the awful truth: they had just witnessed the assassination of their president. Men cursed in rage and pounded chairs in frustration. Women wept.[43]

Taking advantage of the densely crowded theater and the lax security, a deranged Maryland actor and rabid secessionist, who lacked the courage to fight in the Confederate army, had cravenly fired a bullet into the back of Lincoln's head. Playgoers in the presidential box saw parts of Lincoln's brain oozing out. People carried him to a nearby house. Doctors found his condition hopeless; the only signs of life were labored breathing and spasmodic attempts to lift one arm. Lincoln died the next morning, April 15, and Andrew Johnson became president. Knox said in horror, "May I never see another such night." Witnessing the "saddest tragedy" in American history, he likened the nation to a ship without a rudder. "Outwardly are we quiet, but in each heart what terror, misgiving, and despair." Trying to control his fury, Knox declared, "Let no man ever speak to me again of Southern Chivalry or talk in sympathy with traitors."[44]

Like the rest of the North, New Jerseyans went into mourning after Lincoln's assassination. Infuriated Jersey troops talked wildly of destroying the entire South in revenge. Throughout the state men, women, and children wept openly. People tore down red, white, and blue blunting and draped public buildings and homes in black. They lowered flags to half mast and placed a black ribbon above the stars and stripes. Church pulpits displayed pictures of Lincoln, arranged in the folds of the national flag. Citizens wore black bands on their left arms. Baptist minister Henry Fish found Newarkers "overwhelmed with sorrow and indignation and surprise."[45]

At Parker's suggestion, New Jerseyans scheduled funeral services in churches and public places on April 19, the day of the state funeral in Washington. Trains across the state stopped running during the time of the funeral. Newark's mayor suspended business for the day. At sunrise Newarkers fired cannons. At noon weeping worshippers assembled for various church services. At 2 P.M. a procession began to move through the main streets, marching slowly and silently. Veterans, both the wounded and the fit, police, and a military guard marched in front of a hearse escorted by honorary pallbearers. Officials and civic groups followed. Bands played dirges. Paraders decorated horses with flags and draped wagons in black. One wagon carried a temple of liberty with an empty chair inside. "The tolling of the bells, the booming of the minute guns, the steady tramp of the mourning multitude, the melancholy flapping of the muffled flags, the somber appearance of the buildings, and the sad faces of the immense and quiet throngs which filled the streets" made a profound impression, reported a local newspaperman. The procession ended in Military Park, where Frelinghuysen praised the slain leader. After the speech the crowd sang the national anthem and "Rally Round the Flag."[46]

Not everyone mourned. To show his contempt, one Cape May farmer draped his hog pen in black on the day of Lincoln's funeral services. Both a Hunterdon man and a Bridgeton resident vowed to light up their homes in celebration. A Piscataway woman said the news was too good to be true. Some die-hards in Princeton rejoiced openly when they heard of Lincoln's death. A Perth Amboy man declared that his murder served him right. These rare but brazen expressions of hatred enraged the majority. One Hunterdon man knocked down his copperhead neighbor. A Piscataway proprietor threw a customer out of his store for "his traitorous talk." An Episcopal congregation in Belvidere fired its minister for refusing to pray for Lincoln's family.[47]

The assassination further enraged New Jerseyans against the South; they denounced it as a land of daggers and duels. A Caldwell Presbyterian minister echoed Knox's reaction when he declared, "Let no man speak of Southern chivalry as a high-toned manhood," given "its meanness and depravity." Most Jerseyans demanded revenge for the blood shed in the war and in Ford's Theater. The *Camden Press* stated that Lee, Davis, and hundreds of other Confederate leaders "deserve to die the death of traitors." A Paterson Presbyterian minister told parishioners that the murder had stifled the "last feeling of pity towards the guilty agents of treason and rebellion." New Jerseyans believed that Lincoln had died a martyr to the nation's cause. The minister stressed that the nation had just been "baptized in the blood of their President." He said, "As long as Jefferson Davis lives, this nation will feel that the death of Abraham Lincoln is unavenged. Die he must."[48]

Frelinghuysen and other speakers saw Lincoln's death as one of the products of slavery and rebellion. As a Bayonne Reformed minister argued, slavery prompted rebellion; the rebellion prompted the assassination. Even if no connection existed between the rebel leaders and the assassin, the defiant, lawless spirit of rebellion tied them together. Other speakers found the source of the assassination in the copperheads' belief that Lincoln was a tyrant. Lincoln was murdered not only by an assassin's bullet but also by fanaticism and the frenzied denial of rebel defeat. One speaker likened the assassin to a dying scorpion that lashes out in a final display of its venomous power. An Elizabeth woman remarked on the irony in Lincoln's murder: "How sad that one so kind to his enemies should be slain by them." Her brother in the army agreed: "They killed their best friend."[49]

Democratic newspapers and even copperhead organs ceased their torrent of criticism and abuse. The incendiary *Newark Journal* confessed to a "higher appreciation of the man than we had ever before held." Renouncing the vilification of Lincoln as a power-mad dictator and a fanatical revolutionary, the *Journal* now characterized him as a populist democrat and political moderate. The *Newton Herald* conceded, "We, who have differed in most points with the political policy of Mr. Lincoln, can hardly be expected to eulogize that policy now; but we will not do him the injustice to presume that he was not sincere in the belief that he was right." Lincoln's political faults, moreover, remained the faults of his party, which he served as spokesman and chief. The bitterly antiwar *The Old Guard* agreed with the prowar *Jersey City Standard* that Lincoln's assassination was the supreme national calamity: "No greater evil could possibly have befallen the country."[50]

At dawn on April 24 the funeral train, consisting of nine cars, entered New Jersey on the way to the burial in Illinois. When the slow-moving train, with its glass-windowed second-to-last car carrying the president's remains, came to a stop at Trenton, military units presented arms and a band played a dirge. Trenton and other towns along the route tolled bells and fired salutes. At every railroad station and in open fields immense crowds, orderly and hushed, lined the tracks for miles on both sides. As the train passed slowly, people stood erect and silent. Men lifted their hats as a mark of respect; women removed their bonnets. Schoolchildren held patriotic signs. Black citizens sobbed and shuddered. At Newark, those aboard the train saw a sea of humanity whose stillness and "simple unanimity" in grief struck them with its poignancy.[51]

These spontaneous demonstrations along the entire route revealed the strong hold that Lincoln still held on New Jerseyans' hearts. "Such mourning we have never known!" announced a Hackettstown resident. At 10 A.M. the funeral train reached Jersey City, where the depot clock marked 7:22, the hour of his death. A sign adorning the clock read, "The Nation's heart was struck April 15th, 1865." Veterans lifted Lincoln's coffin on their shoulders and carried it to a plain glass hearse. Parker followed. Six gray horses pulled the hearse aboard a waiting ferryboat. Over the gates of the ferry appeared the inscription, "*George Washington The Father, Abraham Lincoln The Saviour of Our Country.*" During the passage across the Hudson River to Manhattan, German choirs sang dirges. New Jerseyans had given their farewell.[52]

Mourning ceased in Washington at the end of May, when Meade's and Sherman's armies on separate days paraded triumphantly down Pennsylvania Avenue from the Capitol to the White House. About two hundred thousand spectators watched about two hundred thousand troops pass. The sweating, thirsty, swearing troops walked twenty abreast. The spectators were awed by their numbers, their muscle, and their martial élan, especially by Sherman's men with their dirty uniforms, broad-brimmed hats, and large physiques.[53]

New Jersey's units marched proudly in both parades. A reporter of the

*Newark Advertiser* described the "gallant veterans from New Jersey, whose thinned ranks, bronzed faces, and tattered battle-flags attested the hardships they had endured in the nation's service." The New Jerseyans in the reviewing stands "looked upon their representatives with mingled pride and sorrow—pride at the achievements of the ever-brave 'Jersey Blues,' sorrow at the absence of many daring leaders, who now filled honored graves." The war was over but its experience had seared the memory of Americans for all time.[54]

# 14 The Fruits of Victory: The State Election of 1865

With peace at hand, demobilization proceeded. First in a trickle, then in a flood, well over fifteen thousand New Jerseyans came home. Eager to return to their families and friends, and anxious to gain a head start in the "race for place in civil life," the servicemen soon became frustrated and angry with the slow pace of discharges. A few units, however, made up part of the occupation forces in the South.[1]

Some New Jersey troops suffered from the state's unfounded reputation as a copperhead state and encountered discriminatory treatment. Writing on behalf of several soldiers, one Jerseyman saw troops from other states leaving daily for home, but, he observed, "Jersey seems to be left out in the cold entirely. We are snubbed on every side." When enlisted men asked officers about their release from the army, "their reply is that Jersey does not belong to the Union and that we will have to take the oath of allegiance before we can be discharged. All this is very aggravating to the men." Another New Jersey soldier found that an order for demobilization of one army corps did not include any plan to discharge Jersey regiments. He asked, "Why are we thus excluded? Have we not fought as faithfully as any other state troops?" This soldier contended that New Jersey troops were singled out and made to suffer for the actions of a few Jersey copperheads. He protested and remarked that the "soldiers of New Jersey are true to the Union and to New Jersey, and we pledge ourselves on next November to wipe out the foul stain that has been cast upon our state." Complaining bitterly about this treatment, Jersey troops sought help in leaving the army as fast as possible. They criticized Parker for not intervening and hastening their return.[2]

Expecting a hero's welcome or at least a fitting reception, early arrivals reached the state unannounced. Nobody was on hand with food and drink to greet the tired, hungry, thirsty men at the Trenton railroad station. No officials saluted; no bells rang. The troops swore at state officials, and at New Jersey copperheads in particular.

Quickly taking heed, the politicians rushed into action. Regiments returning later received magnificent bipartisan receptions. Bands played, residents served dinner, and officials praised the contributions and bravery of the troops. In many communities the locally raised units paraded proudly, and the inhabitants held elaborate celebrations in their honor. Civilians tried to find jobs for veterans and to give them preference in hiring.[3]

While most of New Jersey's troops waited to return home, state politics intruded. The Jersey Republicans seized the opportunity. Their activity was spurred by genuine concern for the welfare of the state's soldiers, combined with confidence in most soldiers' political support. A regimental chaplain asked Marcus Ward to visit the troops again in Virginia. Ward made repeated visits to the men in their camps and hospitals, and tried to expedite their return home. As the chaplain put it, Ward's efforts would prove "good in the State this fall." The state Union League also devised a plan to welcome the returning troops, to sign them up as members at no charge, and to secure "their influence in the coming election." In the meantime, soldiers still in service received political pamphlets.[4]

The troops immensely appreciated Ward's tireless efforts on their behalf. One trooper remarked, "We want to get home to vote, too; we have been denied that long enough; we are determined Mr. Ward shall be Governor." One cavalryman, who wanted an early release, told Ward he was the "*only friend that every Jersey soldier knows and trusts.*" Besides, he added, "the great party of freedom needs our votes this fall, 'help us and we will help you.'"[5]

A new era—the reconstruction of the country—began as New Jersey held its first postwar political campaign. Yet the fall gubernatorial contest turned mostly on the old topics. Wartime emotions still shaped issues and strongly influenced the electorate. To the dismay of nervous Democrats, national rather than state concerns continued to dominate. Nevertheless the Democrats' political priests repeated the party catechism, chanted their litanies, and clung to their idols. Now that the war was over, however, observers questioned whether the old-time religion could still rally all the faithful. The parties stood evenly divided, and the Republicans saw a rare opportunity to seize power. Local elections in the spring and summer resulted in a virtual standoff in the major towns. Although Republicans made stunning gains in New Brunswick and Morristown, no one regarded those gains as barometers.[6]

The hopeful Republicans held their convention on July 20 at Trenton. Neither of the two leading candidates, Ward and Alexander G. Cattell, represented long-standing party factions with decided views. Rather, their candidacies reflected rival ambitions. Cattell of Camden County, a wealthy Philadelphia banker and grain dealer, worked assiduously to become a kingpin in state politics. Facing no serious competitors downstate, he pledged to fund his campaign and created an efficient organization. He acquired some support upstate because of misgivings about Ward, whom some politicians regarded as a loser.[7]

Just before voting began at the convention, the delegates welcomed two returning regiments. The veterans cheered spontaneously for Ward. A local conclave of New Jersey officers on the same day backed Ward for the nomination and sent a delegation to the convention expressing their support. The colorful but controversial cavalryman Hugh Judson Kilpatrick provided the most interesting development with a surprising candidacy just before the balloting began. His stirring speech electrified the delegates and started a stampede for his nomination. Support for Kilpatrick threatened to derail the candidacies of both Cattell and Ward.

The Democrats claimed that Ward's friends had engineered Kilpatrick's candidacy, and they accused Kilpatrick's managers of arranging a diversion to defeat Cattell. In fact, the war Democrats promoted Kilpatrick, himself a former Democrat, as a compromise choice to unite the party and to appeal to independent-minded Democrats. Kilpatrick and the other candidates' managers, however, rejected the call for his nomination by acclamation and insisted on voting without delay. Incontrovertibly, Kilpatrick's candidacy prevented Cattell from obtaining a majority on the first ballot and succeeded on later ballots in luring away Cattell's North Jerseyan supporters.

Finally, after a struggle lasting nearly three hours in a noisy, overcrowded, suffocating hall, enough delegates changed over to nominate Ward on the fourth ballot. Overcoming their doubts, the delegates backed Ward because the returned servicemen expected his nomination and because the Republicans desperately needed their support to win the governorship. Moreover, some delegates distrusted Kilpatrick's erratic judgment and considered Cattell more a Philadelphian than a New Jerseyan.[8]

All the unsuccessful contenders, including Cattell, had pledged in speeches at the convention to support Ward. All except Cattell began to work enthusiastically for the nominee. Cattell held out for several weeks, doing little more than attending party rallies. By September Ward had grown concerned about the lack of Republican activity in South Jersey. His inner circle began to work hard to enlist Cattell, who wished intensely to become federal senator. As Anthony Keasbey observed, the "Senatorship is a vital matter in connection with the governorship." Subsequently Cattell received firm pledges of support for his senatorial bid if the Republicans won the legislature and if the Republican-controlled United States Senate ousted John Stockton. After these assurances were given, Cattell and his people worked energetically on Ward's behalf.[9]

On August 30 the Democrats assembled in Trenton to select their nominee. When the first ballot began not a single antiwar Democrat remained in the contest. By the fourth ballot, with the weaker candidates winnowed out, two generals wrestled for the nomination. Gershom Mott of Lamberton, who had served ably throughout the war, rallied mostly South Jerseyans to his side. Genial Theodore Runyon, Newark's mayor and militia commander, received support mainly from North Jerseyans. Runyon commanded the First Militia Brigade in Virginia at the start of the war, but, unlike Mott, he did not serve for the duration or experience combat. As the *Philadelphia Bulletin* stated mockingly, the delegates considered Runyon the "nearest approach to a civilian with a military title they could find." Nevertheless Runyon's credentials as a full-fledged Democrat and as leader of the state's largest city, together with energetic canvassing by his supporters, gave him the advantage. The Democrats, trying to accommodate to partisan pressures while keeping the veterans in mind to neutralize Ward's appeal, nominated Runyon.[10]

Despite Mott's military record, the Democrats worried about his lack of political experience and doubted his Democratic credentials. The Republicans greeted Mott's defeat with relief: as a war hero wounded several times and as one of New Jersey's most distinguished officers, he probably would have divided the soldier vote. Fearing Mott's possible candidacy, the Republicans earlier had offered him inducements to join the Republican cause, but his asking price—an army promotion—was impossible, and his negotiations with the Democrats aroused suspicion. Having failed in their attempt, the Republicans behind the scenes pressed the War Department to keep him in the army and to release their own generals quickly. The Republicans regarded pseudosoldier Runyon as the weakest possible nominee, barring the selection of a conspicuous copperhead. They concluded that the Democrats had blundered by spurning Mott.[11]

Both party platforms struck observers as wordy; the Democratic platform seemed especially windy. Both avoided controversy. The Democrats said nothing about the proposed amendment abolishing slavery. The Republicans dodged the question of Negro suffrage. Both parties pledged support of Andrew Johnson's southern policy, which still was not fully defined. The Republicans called for stiff requirements to secure lasting peace and reestablish enduring loyalty. The Democrats, eager to restore the old Union, contended that the southern states had forfeited none of their rights.

Each platform emphasized the war and its results. The Republicans praised the victory and dismissed all war critics as blind partisans. The Democrats condemned both abolitionists and secessionists for causing the war, while continuing to find fault with the conduct and the great costs of the war; they ignored its manifestly positive results. They praised the white soldiers' valor while deliberately ignoring the black soldiers' contributions. The Democrats as usual reaffirmed constitutional liberties, defended state rights, and opposed Negro suffrage. The negative message of the New Jersey Democrats resembled the platform adopted a few days earlier by their Pennsylvania counterparts.[12]

The Democratic platform received severe criticism from Republicans and even met a cool reception from a few Democratic newspapers outside the state. The *Paterson Press* ridiculed it for the lack of a single positive idea. As the opposition party, the Democracy opposed everything the federal government had done or was doing. The Republicans repudiated the Democrats' charge that the army had tried to install a dictatorship. On the contrary, the Republicans pointed out, the army had been disbanded immediately after the war. The military had not challenged civilian control. The Republicans underscored the reactionary character of the platform, which stood in sharp contrast to the more progressive stance assumed subsequently by the New York Democrats: their platform acknowledged the end of slavery. The *New Brunswick Fredonian* remarked, "New Jersey Democracy, like the Bourbons, have forgotten nothing, nor learned anything during the past four years, but cling to the dead issues of the past." The *New York Herald* found the platform astonishing in its political senility and irrelevancy. The *Chicago Republican* observed mockingly that if the Jersey Democrats "succeed with such a platform, the state ought to be cut off from the rest of the Union," towed out to sea, and left to sink. Clearly the Democrats would have helped their campaign if they had substituted their more constructive wartime platform of 1862 for this backward postwar pronouncement.[13]

The Republicans repeated their wartime tactics of identifying the prowar majority of New Jersey Democrats with the copperhead minority. They intentionally misread criticism as obstruction and deliberately confused speech with action. The Republicans purposefully ignored the Democratic legislature's full funding of military recruitment and Parker's persistent efforts in raising troops. They also tried to discredit some prowar Democrats as sunshine patriots who praised the war and the army in victory, but during the war had exploited discontent with military defeat or stalemate. These politicians, Republicans charged, resorted to extremist positions and wholesale condemnation of Lincoln's war measures, especially when an election loomed. The Republicans depicted Runyon as such a wartime politician.

By the fall of 1865 Democrats found themselves in a trap of their own making, unable to easily repudiate their careless remarks and partisan posturing during the war. The national Democratic platform of 1864 struck a raw nerve, with its characterization of the war as a failure and its call for an armistice. People could not forget or forgive such stands, nor could Democrats deny them, a mere fourteen months later. Now that peace was secured, such wartime positions struck many people as unpatriotic and mischievous. In addition, the Democrats' denunciation of federal despotism during the war now sounded stale, even cranky. Harsh wartime criticism of Lincoln seemed especially bad, now that the martyred leader lay buried in Illinois. Thus the Republicans selectively dredged up "atrocious speeches," "abominable resolutions," and "outrageous articles" to successfully smear Democrats. Although the charges against many Democratic war supporters were intellectually dishonest and historically inaccurate, the Republican campaign caught the public's imagination, tapped emotions, and appealed especially to the young and ardent. Moreover, the Republican charges appeared credible after voters read the Democratic platform.[14]

Republican speakers launched their offensive with conviction and confidence. Republican editors denounced "the copperhead party." Capitalizing on the joy of victory in the war, Republicans displayed flags and signs bearing the names of northern generals on the walls and stages at party rallies. Party newspapers called up old recruits and appealed for new ones to "rally round the Union flag; join the party of the Union." Distinguishing genuine from imitation Democracy by differentiating between Thomas Jefferson and Jefferson Davis, Republicans urged prowar Democrats and returning veterans to march under the Union banner to victory in the great parade, to be held on November 5.[15]

Republican campaigners hit Runyon hard and kept pounding him. Runyon in fact had supported Douglas before the war and had run as one of his presidential electors. When war broke out he backed the Union and the war effort wholeheartedly. He served in the army for three months. The Democrats deliberately exaggerated his brief service. The Republicans dismissed him as a "holiday general." Referring to his noncombatant role at First Bull Run, Republicans joked about militia General "*Run(y)on.*" Partisans on both sides made a great fuss over little. Closer to the mark, Republicans pointed out Runyon's inexhaustible capacity for self-promotion.[16]

Runyon had returned from the war in triumph and practiced law. Serving as Newark mayor in 1864 and 1865, this loyal Democrat strove to keep the Democratic coalition intact by retaining both war supporters and peace men. Energetically and enthusiastically he stumped the state to promote party candidates during the war. Like most fellow partisans, he appealed to Democrats' prejudices for electioneering purposes. This tactic, combined with a penchant for impassioned oratory and melodramatic overstatement, impelled him to make injudicious comments, which embroiled him in controversy. By taking his statements out of context, Republicans easily portrayed him as unpatriotic, even subversive, with his apparent opposition to the draft, his defamation of Lincoln, and his denunciation of federal troops. The ready defense of Runyon by prominent copperheads did not enhance his credibility as an unswerving war supporter. The Republicans succeeded in damaging him by using his own words because Runyon had delivered so many inflammatory speeches.[17]

Speaking for the besieged Democrats, Morris Hamilton defended their loyalty. They had met their wartime responsibilities and had laid down their lives defending the country. The *Trenton American* denounced the "insulting epithets" of the Republicans who labeled Democrats as "'rebels,' 'traitors,' 'slavemongers.'" Some Republicans even went so far as to "declare that every Democrat ought to be cast into prison or be hung." The Democratic believers in law and liberty remained unintimidated.[18]

Nothing that the Democrats said, however, could free them from the wartime albatross. Although copperheads had not dominated the state Democracy or controlled Governor Parker, Runyon suffered from guilt by association. The copperheads' existence in the state haunted the Democratic campaign. The copperheads' position left the New Jersey Democracy in the untenable position of purportedly favoring not only the wrong cause but also the defeated side. Worse, mainstream Democrats could not repudiate the copperheads because they desperately needed every voter they could find. Also, whether or not the prowar Democrats liked or agreed with the copperheads, the Democracy ultimately had to assume responsibility for all party members.

New Jersey veterans, united by strong camaraderie and pride, constituted a new, important interest group. Politicians of both parties regarded their votes as the balance of power in the election. Refusal to let soldiers vote figured as yet another damaging campaign issue; Democratic legislators again had rejected soldiers' voting rights in March. The Republican platform denounced this. Who but the Democrats, asked one Elizabeth Republican, made Jerseymen "fit to be soldiers, fit to fight, fit to die, fit to be starved in Andersonville, but unfit to vote?" When the Democrats tried to explain away their opposition with legalistic excuses, Republicans denounced their hypocrisy. The Democrats, Martin Ryerson observed, "remind one of the anaconda that slavers all over its victim before swallowing it: for they are now slavering all over these same soldiers, whom they despise, that they may swallow their votes." In one Republican newspaper an artist sketched a copperhead about to stab a soldier in the back as he marched off to war; when the soldier returned, the copperhead hid his dagger behind his back and smiled in welcome.[19]

The Democrats tried to place Ward in a bad light. The *Trenton American* said scornfully that he got involved in military business without ever "having smelled gunpowder." Democrats wildly accused Ward of helping soldiers in order to help himself, charging for his services, and discriminating against known Democratic troops. Such charges backfired when the Republicans countered persuasively that Ward had given freely of his own time and money, indeed sacrificing his own ease and comfort to help soldiers. Not surprisingly, the Republicans enjoyed much greater success than the Democrats in recruiting soldiers. Having shot at southern disunionists, they vowed to vote against those whom they considered northern disunionists.[20]

Andrew Rogers summarized the Democratic side when he denounced Republicans for trying to "slander us." He reminded fellow Democrats, "We are the only Union party in this land," because only the Democracy stood true to the Union and the Constitution. The *Paterson Press* summed up the Republican case: "We have the disloyal record of the Democratic party, with which to blast and wither them; we have their malignant hostility to President Lincoln to lash them with; we have the aid and comfort they have practically given to treason, to scathe them with; we have their refusal to the soldiers of their right to vote, to confound and annihilate them with, and we have the men whose rights they thus insolently denied, *citizens now, to help us do it.*" On such issues the Democrats had left themselves defenseless.[21]

For the Republicans, the question of the ratification of the Thirteenth Amendment provided a "potent engine of success" with which to unite their ranks. The Republicans asserted that national ratification of the freedom amendment now depended on New Jersey's approval, and only Republican control of the legislature could accomplish this. As the *Newark Advertiser* urged voters, "Upon the people of this State, therefore, rests the grave and vast responsibility of deciding this whole question of the future policy of the nation as to slavery." By their previous rejection of the amendment, Republicans contended, the Democrats had positioned themselves as the enemies of liberty. Ward shrewdly urged Republicans to ask Runyon publicly whether he favored the amendment. If he expressed opposition, observed Ward, "he is lost." If he declared that he favored it, his party would dump him or reactionaries would defect.[22]

The Democrats replied weakly that the amendment was irrelevant. With slavery dead, the *Morristown Banner* pronounced the amendment the "least important issue" in the canvass. Emancipation would be soon legal when the southern legislatures ratified the amendment, long before New Jersey's legislature had another chance to act on it. The Democrats hoped that ratification by the South would help to reconcile southerners, reunify the divided nation, and assure the permanence of emancipation. Thus the Democrats deliberately downplayed the amendment and tried to avoid discussing it. Several of their candidates, when questioned, refused to respond.[23]

Trying desperately to assume the offense, the Democrats charged that New Jersey Republicans dodged the question of race. Democrats resorted to their usual scare tactics and told voters that the real issue was the "'nigger' question." The *Belvidere Journal* proclaimed, "Disguise it as you will, *negro suffrage, negro equality, negro citizenship* is the main issue." The Democrats predicted that Republicans in power would impose social equality, reducing whites to the level of backward blacks. White children would have to attend the same schools as blacks. In contrast, Democrats described Runyon as the "*White Man's Nominee for Governor*"; Runyon, too, resorted to this appeal.[24]

Most Republicans disavowed any attempt to mandate equality between races and denied that it figured as a practical issue to New Jerseyans. The Republicans charged that the Democrats agitated the Negro question to divert attention from their damaging wartime record. As the *Trenton Gazette* observed, "Democrats, instead of blacking the negro, you had better be active in whitewashing your record!" The *Absecon Republican* pointed out the fundamental contradiction in Democratic thinking. Democrats pronounced blacks inferior but assumed that if given an even chance, they would become the equal of whites; so whites tried to prevent equal opportunity. Yet if blacks were naturally inferior, there was no need to create barriers against them. The newspaper concluded, "If God made the negro inferior to the whites, man can't make him equal, and all the ranting about 'negro equality' is insufferable nonsense and stupidity." The *Salem Standard* met the issue head on: "But you say you have prejudices against the Blacks. So had we, but we have overcome them. . . . Can there be a more unworthy prejudice than that against a fellow man because of the color of his skin or hair?"[25]

Democrats, including Runyon, put most of their campaign ammunition into the Negro suffrage issue. Straining credulity, Democrats predicted that the devilishly clever Republican Congress somehow would stretch the enforcement clause of the Thirteenth Amendment to impose enfranchisement as well as emancipation. The *Newark Journal* warned that the "man who votes for the Constitutional Amendment votes for negro suffrage, not only at the South, but here in New Jersey." Once given the ballot, Democrats continued, blacks would pervert voting, corrupt politics, trample democracy, wreck local governance, debase society, and hence ruin the state.[26]

The Democrats accused New Jersey Republicans of plotting with the help of the black voters to seize control of the state. The *Trenton American* predicted, "Give the Republicans the power in New Jersey, and see how soon they will. . . . 'give the negroes the right to vote, because it would give the power to the Republican party.' It is their object and aim." Editorials reminded voters that white control was at stake and that only Democrats could defeat black suffrage. The *Belvidere Journal* called on voters to support the view that "this is a *White Man's Government, To Be Administered By White Men, and For The Benefit of White Men.*"[27]

Republicans denied that Negro suffrage formed part of their agenda. The subject had nothing to do with legalizing emancipation and was irrelevant in the campaign. They declared it a matter of little consequence, given that the number of black New Jerseyans was small compared with the number living in the South. The *Newark Advertiser* dismissed the Democratic assault, pointing out that Democratic spokesmen continued to labor with "insane zeal to demolish an imaginary foe." Day after day, declared the *Advertiser*, the Democrats "fulminate against a doctrine which nobody advocates." The Republicans also recognized that many New Jerseyans opposed voting by blacks. To achieve victory in November and to prevent party disunity, Republican delegates at their state convention rejected a black suffrage plank in their platform, despite protests from a few radicals.[28]

Although Republicans refused to endorse black suffrage, the party showed markedly greater tolerance of blacks than it had in the 1850s. Racial prejudice still affected Republicans, but influenced them far less than it did the Democrats. The Republicans instead discussed the Negroes' relative lack of formal education and civic experience. Many Republicans regarded literacy as the proper test of fitness to vote for all Americans. On the whole, Republicans remained publicly cautious, quiet, even evasive about the question, and concentrated on the Democrats' liabilities.[29]

A few New Jerseyans nevertheless openly championed the enfranchisement of Negroes. Blacks, for their part, organized an equal rights league to restore black suffrage, which had existed in the state before 1807. At their convention in mid-July, only days before the Republicans met, they lobbied for the right to vote. The delegates insisted that they were entitled to this right as loyal, law-abiding citizens and had earned it as volunteer soldiers. One Republican suggested that enfranchisement would serve as a fitting monument to the martyred Lincoln. Alluding to New York's election of a Republican governor, he pointed out that "it was the 'colored vote' that saved the State from the rule of Mr. Seymour." The *Hoboken Standard* contended that to win New Jersey, the state's Republicans needed black voters to offset Irish voters. Some radical Republican newspapers favored enfranchisement, but once the campaign began they became close-mouthed on the matter.[30]

New Jersey's unfounded reputation as a disloyal state became a campaign issue. The Republicans harped on the embarrassments that had tarnished the state's image. One Somerset Republican bemoaned in a speech "what our real reputation is! It can't be denied that we hold a very unenviable position. It can't be denied that we are the scoff and jeer of all the Free States in the Union." Frederick Frelinghuysen charged that "New Jersey has been under an odious rule too long." In a similar vein the *Paterson Press* called for an end to Democratic control that had made New Jersey's "name a hissing and a by-word among the loyal states."[31]

The Republicans vowed to rebuild shaken confidence in New Jersey, to repair its reputation, and to end its political isolation. One minister preached on the need for a "political revolution in New Jersey." Union party members urged New Jerseyans angered by insults and derision to vote for change and to show that New Jersey was all right. The *Princeton Standard* called on voters to "wipe out the disgrace" and "redeem the honor and good name of New Jersey." In short, the Republicans promised to rescue the state from the copperheads and to bring New Jersey into line with all the other free states. Otherwise, the *Jersey City Times* predicted, the state would remain the national outcast: "Jersey will always be called 'foreign territory,' and witty allusions to our 'being admitted into the Union,' will always be made so long as we are saddled with this Rip Van Winkle Democracy." Thus the Republicans tapped into patriotism and state pride. As James Scovel put it, "We *have New Jersey to save*, that is the issue in this campaign. Shall New Jersey side with rebellion or stand in happy accord with the Union?" Such appeals found an audience.[32]

The Democrats responded defensively to the undeserved abuse. They contended that New Jersey remained the only northern state that had kept faith with the founding fathers. The *Camden Democrat* castigated Republicans who "tell us that 'New Jersey stands alone in her infamy—clinging to the barbarisms of a past age.' For '*infamy*' read *glory*, and for '*barbarism*' read *conservative principles*, and then the *honor* which attaches to the position of New Jersey during the last four years of perilous trial." Democrats lashed out at those who maligned Parker's performance and smeared the state. If these critics did not like New Jersey, they should leave it at once. Parker himself decried the Republicans' misrepresentation of the state's role in the war for the Union. "They charge us with disloyalty and sympathy with the rebels; call us traitors; stigmatize us as the left wing of Lee's army," he lamented. The *Trenton American* urged voters to stay with the Democracy rather than "consent to place in power over you men who stigmatize you as 'traitors,' and who defame your State as 'disloyal,' because you have refused to bend the knee at the footstool of tyranny."[33]

In contests for the legislature, the Republicans worked with skill and diligence. Building on their previous gains in 1864 and trying to lure Democratic defectors, Republicans ensured that strong nominations were made in the places they had to win. Atlantic, Mercer, and Morris counties figured as the major battlegrounds for control of the senate. The influential George Cobb finally consented to run as the senatorial candidate in Morris. Observers regarded this nomination as masterful.[34]

Everyone viewed the October 10 election for mayor of Newark as a straw vote for November. Many people saw the election as a vote of confidence in outgoing Mayor Runyon. The Republicans selected as their candidate the popular Thomas Peddie, manufacturer and legislator. They recruited veterans' support by nominating a colonel for auditor and exploited discontent and division in Democratic ranks. The Republicans captured the city by 55 percent and the mayoralty for the first time in nine years. The number of Democratic defections and the size of the Republican majority amazed everyone. The discouraged Democrats doubted that Runyon could win anywhere if the Democrats failed to win his hometown.[35]

Emboldened Republicans spared no effort. They started several campaign newspapers. Ward pursued federal patronage because he knew that "we must have the hearty cooperation of the Government—we have no patronage in this State to offer to our workers. The Government can aid us by giving us some appointments—and they must." State Republicans also requested national speakers, especially the "big guns," and recruited several army officers to be keynote speakers at rallies. The most popular debates pitted Kilpatrick against Andrew Rogers, and Ryerson against Chauncey Burr. The crowds attending these debates became excited and enthusiastic, and they heckled speakers.[36]

During the campaign, Republicans attempted to win over swing voters. The Republicans assessed both their state and federal officeholders. Union party leaders even threatened the Camden and Amboy Railroad with congressional antimonopoly legislation if it bankrolled the Democrats. The ministers' influence counted mightily; many clergymen supported Ward, other Republican candidates, and the emancipation amendment on moral grounds.[37]

The Republicans' management of the campaign did not go altogether smoothly, however. A shortage of money plagued party efforts. When New Jersey Republicans opened an office in New York City while keeping the state committee headquarters in Trenton, the unclear division of work and responsibility resulted in confusion and conflict. Ward's operatives became upset with the inefficiency of the state committee. People working for the committee felt neglected and bypassed. Even so, the Republican campaign went forward. Horace Congar in Washington in effect served as campaign manager and supreme strategist. Ward, in contrast to his 1862 inactivity, worked resourcefully behind the scenes, carefully monitoring the campaign and focusing shrewdly on the trouble spots. Although he did not stump the state, he attended a few county fairs and party rallies. The *Newton Register* aptly characterized him as a man of deeds, not words. Ward strongly preferred that able party spokesmen present the Republicans' case, expose the Democrats' vulnerability, and press a relentless attack.[38]

The Democrats assumed that Runyon's magnetic popularity and their previous successes would suffice. Weakened by overconfidence, they neglected organization and mobilization. Their campaign began late and never gained momentum. They held fewer rallies than the Republicans and started fewer campaign newspapers. Responding defensively to the Republicans' charges, the Democrats denounced the slanderous charges of the "Black Snakes." Disconcerted by the Republicans' unprecedented activity, they did not counterattack as usual. Although party leaders of the war wing made speeches on behalf of Runyon, both Democratic participants in the two major series of debates—Rogers and Burr—came from copperhead ranks. A few Democratic war supporters deplored the use of copperheads as party spokesmen. The Democrats remained entrenched in the executive branch of the state government, but a lack of money plagued their canvass.[39]

Signs that the campaign was faltering began to emerge in September. A month later the decisive defeat in the Newark election augured disastrous reversals. Some Democrats and even a few of their newspapers warned publicly of danger. The reversal in Newark spurred many Democratic candidates to redouble their efforts, but some Democratic leaders and their workers became resigned to defeat and did little or nothing. Even a few New York Democrats viewed some New Jersey Democratic positions as a serious liability. In mid-September the Republican *Trenton Gazette* observed dismissively that the Democrats were "short of money, short of speakers, short of principles, and will find themselves short of voters in November."[40]

The overheated rhetoric and the partisan misrepresentation sometimes exceeded the recent presidential campaign in virulence. Although the canvass did not reach the physical violence that marred the campaign in 1864, minor violence did erupt. The *Philadelphia Press* did not exaggerate in its characterization of the New Jersey contest: "There never was a canvass more bitterly conducted."[41]

On November 7 New Jerseyans went to the polls in the heaviest turnout since 1860. By a narrow but still decisive margin of 2,789, or 51 percent, they elected Ward. He swept Republican strongholds in South Jersey, greatly increased the Republican majorities in Essex and Passaic, captured highly competitive Mercer, Middlesex, and Morris, all of which Lincoln had failed to carry in 1864, and made deep inroads in other Democratic bastions across North Jersey. Runyon retained most of the Democratic counties that McClellan had carried but Runyon's margins of victory were remarkably slim, except in Sussex, where fraudulent voting by Democrats might have occurred. Unimpressive in Bergen, Monmouth, and Somerset, he barely carried Union; in pivotal Hudson the Democratic vote plummeted.

Ward won because he did well with three groups of voters. First, he picked up more than 5 percent of those who had voted Democratic in 1864. Second, he also picked up more than 5 percent of the previous abstainers, while Runyon acquired virtually none. Third, he secured solid support from returning soldiers. As a Boonton politician reported, the "'Boys in Blue' were out in full force here and carried everything by storm at our polls. They voted in companies, *cheering* loudly for [Ward] as they approached the ballot box." During the fall one veteran had told him, "Can't keep me a mile from the ballot box." Another vowed that no Democrat could buy his vote, after one had tried to do so. Still another asserted that he would "rather lose my right arm than not vote for Ward." The veterans remembered their friends.[42]

The Republicans, dealing the state Democracy another blow, seized control of both chambers of the legislature and secured a majority on joint ballot. Republicans gained three senate seats in Atlantic, Mercer, and Morris by slim majorities. Although they narrowly lost one assembly seat in Burlington, they picked up seven seats altogether in Essex, Hudson, Mercer, Middlesex, and Passaic. The Republicans made a net gain of six seats in highly competitive districts, but won every seat by a narrow vote, usually by a very small majority.

The number of copperhead assemblymen shrank from twelve to four. All of the four who returned to the State House hailed from safe districts, one in Newark and the rest in rural Bergen, Hunterdon, and Warren. The *Newark Patriot* congratulated New Jerseyans on delivering the death blow to the copperheads, whom the newspaper described as "traitorous in the hour of danger . . . despised in the hour of triumph."[43]

Now that New Jersey finally had broken loose from the Democrats' grip, the Republicans celebrated. The *New York Tribune* declared, "*Let the Eagle Scream.*" The state no longer was a political outcast, and the *Newark Advertiser* rejoiced: "Thus New Jersey redeems her fair fame; thus she sustains the administration, and refutes the foul slander of her sympathy with the rebellion, which those who misrepresented her in the State and national councils have ignobly encouraged." A New Jerseyan expressed his feelings to Ward, saying, "The State has honored herself by your election." Two Jersey City Republicans exclaimed that no longer could the state be called "this 'Rip Van Winkle' State, this State of 'Camden and Amboy,' this '*Copperhead State of New Jersey!*" In the words of the *Paterson Press*, every New Jersey man now felt that a "reproach has been removed that he bore a share of by reason of his nativity: That now he can avow himself a Jersey Blue without shame."[44]

Stunned Democrats tried to find meaning in their worst statewide defeat in seventeen years. Referring to the *Tribune*'s rejoicing in the national eagle's screaming, Chauncey Burr in *The Old Guard* retorted, "Yes, that is right—the eagle ought to *scream* as if cut through the heart with a *knife!*" Samuel Bayard believed that "Runyon had no personal popularity" and regarded the entire campaign as "miserably mismanaged," a view shared by many members of both parties.[45]

The war wing, disavowing a standstill policy and accepting inevitable change to attract voters, conceded that the Democratic party's opposition to the Thirteenth Amendment was one major reason for the debacle. As the *Jersey City Standard* commented, it proved "useless to attempt to stem the current of popular opinion"; the newspaper went on to say that "with a different policy we believe the result might have been different." The *Hoboken Democrat* regarded opposition to the amendment as a "suicidal policy." Bayard contended that the Democracy had become "too much tainted with sympathy for the South."[46]

Democrats also lost votes by clinging to positions laid to rest by the war. The *Hoboken Democrat* characterized Democratic candidates as having "allowed themselves to go into the struggle with weapons old and almost obsolete, to contest about old issues, some of which have been settled by the result of war." The *New York Herald* found the roots of the defeat in the "folly of the Democratic managers in adhering to the dead issues of the past, and in ignoring or fighting the living and controlling issues of the present."[47]

Republicans, too, believed the Democrats had deserved defeat; yet they conceded that they could have won the election with the appropriate platform and the right candidate. Had they nominated Mott or Theodore Randolph, pointed out the *Newton Register*, they might have succeeded. The *New York Post* argued that victory might have been possible if the Democrats had "boldly turned their backs upon their past record, and varnished over their close ambition with a semblance of patriotic zeal."[48]

Ultraconservative Democrats remained defiant; they would rather be right than successful. They considered the setback merely the result of poor tactics, and no reflection on the soundness of the party's policy. They claimed that in the face of rampant demagoguery and prevailing extremism, nothing could have been done to avert defeat. These unyielding Democratic ideologues prided themselves on not sacrificing their old-fashioned party principles to expediency. The *Newark Journal* asserted that if any defect in policy existed in the recent Democratic campaign, it was the failure of the state platform to oppose the Thirteenth Amendment outright instead of evading the matter. The *Journal* hoped the Democrats would indoctrinate loyal partisans more fully in the party line, but, above all, remain faithful to the party's position. The *Hackensack Democrat* boasted that Democratic "principles are unchangeable as truth itself." As the *Newton Herald* proclaimed, Democrats "had rather be beaten on the principles involved than to have carried the State by truckling to a false sentiment."[49]

During the campaign Democratic politicians unnecessarily defended indefensible positions. It was strange, perhaps even unconsciously suicidal, that Democrats adopted a platform that sneered at a war won by Yankee and New Jersey troops just three months before. The compromising statements made by their prowar candidate in the heat of wartime campaigns did nothing to enhance the party's postwar image. Democrats could blame only themselves for their vulnerability. Out of touch with reality, adhering to positions out of step with events, and sounding out of tune with public opinion, the backward-looking Democrats had grown out of date. Their brand of ritualistic conservatism and their crew of candidates were not merely bankrupt but irrelevant.

O n December 18, 1865, upon ratification by twenty-seven states, the Thirteenth Amendment became part of the Constitution. Twenty-two days later New Jersey's legislature convened and reconsidered the amendment. Parker, a realist, acknowledged abolition in fact as well as in law. In a refreshing departure he virtually recommended ratification in his message. Noting Parker's changed position, the *Trenton Gazette* mocked his rationalization as well as his strained version of events: that New Jersey helped to lessen sectional bitterness by postponing ratification until the southern states had ratified voluntarily. The *Gazette* quipped, "Of course such were the benevolent ideas of our Democratic friends last winter!" The newspaper remarked that Parker "evidently thinks New Jersey contributed to the adoption of the constitutional amendment by refusing to ratify it."[50]

Ward strongly recommended ratification in his inaugural message. Some Democrats, however, clung to their earlier rejection of the amendment, contending that any attempt now to reverse action on the already approved amendment was unnecessary and without legal effect. The Republicans, insisting on a new vote, believed that the honor of the state and their own reformist credentials were at stake.[51]

On the following day, January 17, 1866, the Republican assembly approved the amendment. A half-dozen Democrats supported ratification; a greater number dodged the vote. Only a minority of the assembly Democrats ventured to oppose it. On January 23 the senate followed suit, with two Democratic senators supporting the measure.[52]

Although New Jersey's approval of the amendment was a month late and hence only symbolic, the vote and the absences of Democratic legislators conveyed how strongly the tide had turned and why so many Democrats refused to swim against it. Two Trenton firemen who had served in the Union army in the South and had caught an eagle there gave the new governor some eagle's plumes trimmed with red, white, and blue ribbons. Fittingly, Ward used one plume as a pen to sign the joint resolution ratifying the Thirteenth Amendment. The editor of the *Gazette* exclaimed, "New Jersey is right at last."[53]

When John Stockton took his seat in the United States Senate, Republican legislators contested the validity of his election because of his failure to secure an absolute majority. Nothing came of this protest. In 1866, however, the question suddenly assumed pressing national importance when political warfare broke out between President Johnson and the Republican Congress. Realizing that they needed to expel one Democratic senator in order to override presidential vetoes, Republican senators conveniently found Stockton's election irregular and ousted him on March 27.

Although New Jersey Republicans were delighted to fill the vacancy with a Republican, they failed to make a choice for almost half a year. By holding the balance of power in the state senate, Scovel single-handedly obstructed action until eventually he relented under intense pressure. Finally the legislature, which had been called into special session by Ward, elected Cattell on September 18, 1866. Forty-four days later William Wright died. On November 10 Ward appointed formidable Frelinghuysen as interim senator. On January 23, 1867, the legislature elected him senator. In less than two months New Jersey Republicans replaced both Democratic senators and at last achieved both power and patronage.[54]

# Conclusion

Charles Hodge spoke for his fellow New Jerseyans when he said the war had "settled the fact that we are a nation, and not a confederacy of nations." Even while Jerseyans calculated the cost of the war—the lives lost, the suffering borne, the scars left—they took pride in the fruits of victory. In concert with other northerners they had repudiated secession, reunited the nation, rejuvenated American nationality, revitalized the Constitution, freed the slaves, and reinvigorated democracy. "War," concluded the *Jersey City Advocate*, "is a great revolutionist."[1]

Between 1854 and 1865, state politics pivoted increasingly on national questions. New Jersey's politics were first influenced, then dominated by the expansion of slavery, by the power of the South, by southern rebellion, by northern resistance to rebellion, and by the very existence of slavery. In the war years, both parties' fortunes fluctuated with the vicissitudes of the battlefield and the skill of the politicians. New Jersey's parties were nearly balanced. In Congress the Democrats retained a majority of the state's delegation. Republican governor Olden served twenty-one months in office during the war; Democratic governor Parker performed wartime duty for twenty-nine months. Although the Democrats won the governorship in 1862 and the legislature in 1863 and 1864, the highly competitive parties shared legislative control in 1862 and 1865. Republicans in Trenton sometimes found themselves in the opposition; yet because Republicans were in power in Washington, Jersey Republicans suffered from the liabilities of national incumbency when the war went badly.

This situation, coupled with mounting opposition to emancipation, fear of the draft, and resentment of other war measures, weakened the Republican party in the state. The party also was hurt by the loss of Republicans who volunteered for military service and by the influx of 100,000 people from outside the state during the war. After losing elections, often by frustratingly narrow margins and after fumbling opportunities, dispirited Republicans remarked repeatedly that they could have done better. This loser's whine became a recurring refrain and a defensive rationalization, not only during the war but before and after. Buoyed by northern success in the war, however, energized Republicans seized the initiative in the fall of 1864; in November 1865 they succeeded in wresting power from the Democrats.[2]

In contrast, New Jersey Democrats had the best of all possible situations. Sometimes holding power in Trenton, yet without power in Washington, they could and did blame everything that went wrong on Lincoln and the Republicans. Their faultfinding, however, did not correspond to the actions they usually took. With few exceptions the Parker Democrats, the moderates who dominated the party and controlled the legislature, showed responsibility and restraint in exercising power. They revealed flinty nationalism and iron determination in mobilizing New Jersey to help win the war for the Union. Although a few progressive Democrats wished to embrace various wartime Republican reforms, the Democracy as a party did not. During the war most Democrats feared jeopardizing party unity on national policies by offending hard-liners. So the Democrats did what an opposition party normally did: it opposed. After the war centrist Democrats accepted or acquiesced in various reform measures, notably the amendments to the federal Constitution, but they did so only after the fact, when the reform in question had gone into effect nationally and had become politically less controversial in New Jersey. If Republicans often lacked tactical nerve, Democrats frequently lacked strategic imagination.

Partisan differences can be somewhat misleading, however. Sharp differences on certain issues sometimes emerged within parties. By the end of 1864 New Jersey Republicans had come to accept emancipation, but the postwar question of suffrage for blacks became a controversial and divisive issue. Deeper divisions plagued the Democracy throughout the era; disagreements arose between Douglasites and Buchananites, war supporters and peace advocates, pragmatic moderates and doctrinaire reactionaries.

During the war it became increasingly evident in New Jersey that minorities, notably the copperheads, abused their rights far more than did any majority. Their vitriolic style, aggressive agenda, irresponsible positions, and blind obstructionism gave trouble to Parker and war supporters, Democrats and Republicans alike, especially in the assembly during 1863. Copperheads were noisy nuisances who achieved nothing of fundamental importance. Their peace resolutions were not adopted by the legislature in 1863. Their favorite projects throughout the war came to nothing. By circumstance and luck, copperhead James Wall became senator for an unexpired term, but his tenure lasted only six weeks; he failed to win the prize of serving for six years.

The copperheads were highly publicized and brought notoriety, even infamy, not only to themselves but also to New Jersey as a whole. At the end of 1863 the Republican *Somerville Unionist* took note of this, observing, "A great deal of senseless, unjust, and ignorant criticism is fulminated against New Jersey" as a "Copperhead State." Such charges, previously made in "jesting derision," now were believed by many northerners because, as the *Unionist* put it, "lies well reiterated have all the pungency of the truth. Now this business must be stopped." The charges did not stop, however. The copperhead minority succeeded in giving the state a bad name.[3]

In fact, much was made of little. New Jersey's war experience needs to be seen in a broader context. This experience was neither exceptional nor unique, but was typical of states in the lower North, especially in the Mid-

Atlantic region. War weariness and discontent with Republican war measures ran strong in other northern states, and the copperheads tried to exploit both. Intensely competitive politics in the Mid-Atlantic states exacerbated the tensions built up during a long and bloody war, resulting in a fierce, bitter variety of politics.

In addition, New Jersey generally followed the political trends. The movement of voters toward the Democrats in 1862 and then toward the Republicans in both 1863 and 1865 mirrored results throughout the North. In fact New Jersey's voters moved slightly toward the Republicans in 1864, while northern voters as a whole actually moved slightly toward the Democrats. Only in 1861, when Republicans nationwide fared slightly better than in 1860, did the Democratic gains in New Jersey show a deviation from the national trend. Even in that year, New Jersey's voters defeated many conspicuous copperheads running for the legislature.

Like their counterparts in New York, New Jersey voters elected a Democratic governor in 1862. In the same year other free states, notably Indiana and Illinois, elected Democratic legislatures. Jersey Democrats, however, never went to the extreme of nominating a copperhead as their gubernatorial candidate, as happened in New Hampshire, Connecticut, Pennsylvania, and Ohio. Democrats adopted antiwar resolutions in Delaware's legislature and in the lower legislative chambers of both Pennsylvania and Illinois, but no such resolutions were approved by New Jersey's legislature. New Jerseyans, moreover, did not resort to violence, as did New Yorkers, Indianans, and other northerners in 1862 and 1863, when federal officials were killed or wounded and when troops were sent in to restore order and enforce federal law. A Rahway resident grasped the issue of the state's wartime reputation when he observed that "some states, like individuals whom we all know, get a higher and some a lower estimate of their worth than they are justly entitled to." Actually, he contended, New Jersey "occupies a position equal to that of many of her sisters who assume airs of superiority."[4]

Englishman Thomas Fuller wrote in 1642 that fame develops like a mushroom and grows without having any root. New Jersey's reputation for cultivating copperheads similarly lacks roots in reality. The depiction of New Jersey as a copperhead state misrepresents the political position of most New Jerseyans and the public actions of its governors and most legislators during the war. The great majority of New Jerseyans united to counter the common danger and to promote a common defense. President Lincoln and Governor Olden called New Jerseyans to arms in support of the Union; New Jerseyans answered the call. Federal and state officials, including Governor Parker, encouraged additional enlistments; the enlistments grew. Lincoln, Olden, and Parker asked state legislators to pay for recruiting and equipping troops by state appropriation; the legislators complied. When Washington imposed conscription it permitted bounties as a respectable, patriotic alternative; bounties swelled. In considering the state's record, the *Freehold Herald* concluded, "New Jersey does not deserve the slurs that have been cast upon her." *The Jersey City Times* echoed this view when it observed of the copperheads, "These men have given New Jersey a bad name both at home and abroad, which her people do not deserve." Indeed the state's reputation aptly fits what one anonymous nineteenth-century observer defined as fame: "That singular mixture of undeserved praise and equally undeserved abuse."[5]

Throughout the war New Jersey did not teeter between loyalty and disloyalty. Rather, Republicans and Democrats engaged in a fierce tug-of-war for control. Although both parties remained unionist in their loyalties, they disagreed about the purposes, powers, and policies of Lincoln's government. Instead of playing the wrong role in the right war, New Jersey played the right role in a cause worth fighting for. Charles Olden and Joel Parker, excellent governors of a patriotic state, worked tirelessly to promote the Union cause. Their record shows that the governance of New Jersey remained as consistent, as creditable, and as substantial as the state's combat record. Just as Jerseymen at the front were tested in battle, New Jerseyans on the home front faced challenges as the war became a test of endurance.

New Jersey's war supporters who served as able leaders and major contributors to the war effort included George Middleton, Theodore Randolph, John Thomson, and Jacob Vanatta among the regular Democrats; George Cobb, Joseph Crowell, and Martin Ryerson among the war Democrats; and Horace Congar, William Dayton, Thomas Dudley, Richard Field, Frederick Frelinghuysen, John Ten Eyck, and Marcus Ward among the Republicans. Their role and their record mattered infinitely more than the strident minority led by C. Chauncey Burr, Thomas Dunn English, Edward Fuller, Daniel Holsman, Nehemiah Perry, Rodman Price, Andrew Rogers, and James Wall. If the reverse were true—if copperheads had dominated state politics and controlled the state government—then the state government would have done little or nothing for the war effort, would have refused state funding of military recruitment, would have rejected conscription, and would not have sent seventy-four thousand troops to the battlefront. New Jersey would have hamstrung Lincoln's governance, defied national authority, resisted federal law, tried to rebel against the North, and attempted to secede from the Union. None of this happened.

Despite the facts, New Jersey's image as a copperhead state flourished. The copperhead myth took hold in people's minds, both inside and outside the state. New Jerseyans were hurt, humiliated, ashamed of their state's reputation. This distorted view, a caricature of the state's role in the Civil War, contributed to a growing inferiority complex among many New Jerseyans. Yet in fighting the war on both the home front and the battlefront, most New Jerseyans had no cause for shame and in fact a great deal in which to take pride. To be sure, some individuals acted foolishly and contemptibly, but most people did what was expected of them, and a few played heroic roles.

On the whole, New Jerseyans left an admirable record, indeed an outstanding record in comparison to that of several leaders and many residents of New York City. Moreover, during the war New Jerseyans neither politically nor socially resembled those inhabitants of the border slave states who shared an affinity for the South and its values. New Jersey's wartime actions were not ambivalent at all. Nor did Jerseyans just exhibit bravery on the battlefront and behave disgracefully on the home front. Like other northerners, New Jerseyans played their part by doing their duty; they persevered and ultimately prevailed over adversity in America's worst war. New Jerseyans stood true to the nation, the Constitution, their state, their history, their traditions, and themselves. New Jerseyans had shown their true colors—true blue, Jersey blue.[6]

# Statistical Appendix

*Lex Renda\**

**Table 1  New Jersey's Voting Patterns in Principal Elections, 1854–1865 (as percentages of the votes cast)**

| Year | D | R | OP | A | T | U | DD |
|------|------|------|------|------|-----|----|-----|
| 1854 C | 43.1 | 8.7 | 43.2 | | 5.0 | | |
| 1856 P | 47.2 | 28.5 | | 24.3 | | | |
| 1856 G | 48.7 | | 51.3 | | | | |
| 1856 C | 47.8 | 12.5 | 31.6 | 8.1 | | | |
| 1858 C | 43.6 | 8.8 | 43.7 | 3.9 | | | |
| 1859 G | 49.2 | | 50.8 | | | | |
| 1860 P | 49.2 | 47.9 | | | | .5 | 2.4 |
| 1860 C | 50.6 | 49.4 | | | | | |
| 1862 G | 56.8 | 43.2 | | | | | |
| 1862 C | 56.2 | 43.8 | | | | | |
| 1864 P | 52.8 | 47.2 | | | | | |
| 1864 C | 52.3 | 47.7 | | | | | |
| 1865 G | 48.9 | 51.1 | | | | | |

Note: For further details on the years 1852 to 1865, see table 2.
Key: P (Presidential), G (Gubernatorial), C (Congressional), D (Democrat), R (Anti-Nebraska Democrat in 1854, Republican afterward), OP (Opposition), A (American), T (Temperance), U (Straight Bell), DD (Straight Douglas)

*Professor Renda's preparation of eight tables, including ecological regression estimates of electoral behavior in New Jersey's congressional districts between 1852 and 1864 and his explanation of the statistical methodology, can be found in the book manuscript deposited in the Rutgers University Library.

**Table 2 Turnout and Voting Patterns in Principal New Jersey Elections, 1852–1865 (as percentages of the potential electorate)**

| Year | Turnout | Democrat | Principal Opponent[a] | Principal 3rd Party | Other | Abstain |
|------|---------|----------|-----------------------|---------------------|-------|---------|
| 1852 P | 74.1 | 39.1 | 34.0[b] | 0.7[c] | 0.3[d] | 25.9 |
| 1852 C | 73.7 | 39.1 | 33.7[b] | 0.9[c] | | 26.3 |
| 1853 G | 62.4 | 32.8 | 29.6[e] | | | 37.6 |
| 1854 C | 65.6 | 28.2 | 35.1[f] | 3.3[g] | | 34.4 |
| 1856 P | 77.5 | 36.6 | 22.1 | 18.8[c] | | 22.5 |
| 1856 G | 77.3 | 37.6 | 39.7[f] | | | 22.7 |
| 1856 C | 76.9 | 36.7 | 34.0[h] | 6.2[c] | | 23.1 |
| 1858 C | 68.8 | 30.3 | 36.1[h] | 2.7[c] | | 31.2 |
| 1859 G | 73.2 | 36.0 | 37.2[f] | | | 26.8 |
| 1860 P | 81.9 | 40.3[i] | 39.2 | 2.0[j] | 0.4[k] | 18.1 |
| 1860 C | 82.1 | 41.5[i] | 40.6 | | | 17.9 |
| 1862 G | 69.9 | 39.7 | 30.2 | | | 30.1 |
| 1862 C | 69.5 | 39.1 | 30.4 | | | 30.5 |
| 1864 P | 80.2 | 42.4 | 37.8 | | | 19.8 |
| 1864 C | 80.6 | 42.1 | 38.5 | | | 19.4 |
| 1865 G | 80.9 | 39.6 | 41.3 | | | 19.3 |

Notes: (a) Republican, unless otherwise indicated; (b) Whig; (c) Native American or American; (d) Free Soil; (e) the Whig candidate had both Native American and Temperance endorsements; (f) Opposition; (g) Temperance; (h) Republican/Opposition; (i) Fusion Democratic/Constitutional Union; (j) straight Douglas Democrat; (k) straight Constitutional Union. The Opposition party refers, in 1854, to Whigs, Whig-Americans, and anti-Nebraska Democrats; in 1856, to Republican-Americans; and in 1858, to Republican-Americans or anti-Lecompton Democrats.

Key: P (Presidential), G (Gubernatorial), C (Congressional)

Table 3 Ecological Regression Estimates of New Jersey Voters' Behavior, 1852–1865

| Elect. Pair/ Office | Opposition | | | | Democrat | | | | Abstain | | | |
|---|---|---|---|---|---|---|---|---|---|---|---|---|
| | OP | D | A | Oᵃ | OP | D | A | Oᵃ | OP | D | A | Oᵃ |
| 1852P–1854 C | 80 | 0 | 20 | | 26 | 68 | 6 | | 6 | 8 | 86 | |
| 1853G–1854 C | 93 | 0 | 7 | | 23 | 77 | 0 | | 7 | 7 | 86 | |
| 1852P–1856 C | 96 | 0 | 4 | | 9 | 91 | 0 | | 20 | 12 | 68 | |
| 1854C–1856 C | 84 | 16 | 0 | | 4 | 96 | 0 | | 20 | 14 | 66 | |
| 1856P–1856 Cᵇ | 100 | 0 | 0 | | 0 | 100 | 0 | | 4 | 0 | 96 | |
| 1853G–1856 G | 96 | 0 | 4 | | 7 | 93 | 0 | | 23 | 19 | 58 | |
| 1854C–1856 G | 84 | 16 | 0 | | 4 | 96 | 0 | | 20 | 14 | 66 | |
| 1856C–1856 G | 97 | 3 | 0 | | 0 | 97 | 3 | | 0 | 4 | 96 | |
| 1856P–1856 Gᵇ | 100 | 0 | 0 | | 0 | 97 | 3 | | 0 | 4 | 96 | |
| 1852P–1856 P | 48 | 0 | 4 | 48 | 13 | 87 | 0 | 0 | 7 | 15 | 68 | 10 |
| 1854C–1858 C | 90 | 10 | 0 | | 13 | 83 | 4 | | 13 | 13 | 74 | |
| 1856C–1858 C | 89 | 3 | 8 | | 16 | 75 | 9 | | 0 | 9 | 91 | |
| 1856G–1858 C | 88 | 3 | 9 | | 18 | 73 | 9 | | 3 | 9 | 88 | |
| 1856P–1858 Cᶜ | 95 | 0 | 5 | | 13 | 75 | 13 | | 0 | 9 | 91 | |
| 1858C–1859 G | 76 | 18 | 6 | | 15 | 85 | 0 | | 10 | 10 | 80 | |

continued

Table 3 Ecological Regression Estimates of New Jersey Voters' Behavior, 1852–1865 (continued)

| Elect. Pair/ Office | Opposition | | | | Democrat | | | | Abstain | | | |
|---|---|---|---|---|---|---|---|---|---|---|---|---|
| | OP | D | A | Oᵃ | OP | D | A | Oᵃ | OP | D | A | Oᵃ |
| 1856G–1859 G | 91 | 3 | 6 | | 10 | 84 | 6 | | 6 | 16 | 78 | |
| 1858C–1860 C | 79 | 21 | 0 | | 12 | 88 | 0 | | 20 | 22 | 58 | |
| 1859G–1860 C | 91 | 9 | 0 | | 6 | 94 | 0 | | 14 | 17 | 69 | |
| 1860P–1860 Cᵈ | 97 | 3 | 0 | | 3 | 95 | 3 | | 4 | 4 | 92 | |
| 1856P–1860 Pᵉ | 100 | 0 | 0 | 0 | 7 | 83 | 3 | 7 | 11 | 29 | 61 | 0 |
| 1858C–1860 P | 79 | 9 | 6 | 6 | 12 | 88 | 0 | 0 | 17 | 27 | 56 | 0 |
| 1859G–1860 P | 91 | 6 | 3 | 0 | 6 | 88 | 0 | 6 | 11 | 20 | 69 | 0 |
| 1860S–1861 S | 64 | 14 | 22 | | 8 | 66 | 26 | | 0 | 0 | 100 | |
| 1861S–1862 S | 80 | 16 | 4 | | 7 | 85 | 7 | | 13 | 13 | 75 | |
| 1858C–1862 C | 65 | 19 | 16 | | 4 | 96 | 0 | | 11 | 16 | 73 | |
| 1860C–1862 C | 77 | 9 | 14 | | 0 | 86 | 14 | | 0 | 3 | 97 | |
| 1860P–1862 Cᶠ | 76 | 9 | 15 | | 3 | 89 | 8 | | 0 | 0 | 100 | |
| 1862G–1862 C | 96 | 4 | 0 | | 3 | 94 | 3 | | 0 | 0 | 100 | |
| 1859G–1862 G | 78 | 3 | 19 | | 0 | 97 | 3 | | 8 | 15 | 77 | |
| 1860C–1862 G | 77 | 6 | 17 | | 0 | 89 | 11 | | 0 | 7 | 93 | |
| 1860P–1862 Gᶠ | 79 | 6 | 15 | | 0 | 92 | 8 | | 0 | 3 | 97 | |

| | | | | | | | | | |
|---|---|---|---|---|---|---|---|---|---|
| 1862S–1863 S | 96 | 4 | 0 | 0 | 88 | 12 | 5 | 0 | 95 |
| 1860C–1864 C | 94 | 6 | 0 | 0 | 88 | 12 | 6 | 15 | 79 |
| 1862C–1864 C | 100 | 0 | 0 | 0 | 100 | 0 | 17 | 10 | 73 |
| 1862G–1864 C | 100 | 0 | 0 | 0 | 100 | 0 | 17 | 10 | 73 |
| 1864P–1864 C | 97 | 0 | 3 | 3 | 97 | 0 | 0 | 3 | 97 |
| 1860P–1864 P[f] | 97 | 3 | 0 | 0 | 94 | 6 | 6 | 12 | 82 |
| 1862C–1864 P | 100 | 0 | 0 | 0 | 100 | 0 | 17 | 10 | 73 |
| 1862G–1864 P | 100 | 0 | 0 | 0 | 100 | 0 | 17 | 10 | 73 |
| 1862G–1865 G | 100 | 0 | 0 | 3 | 97 | 0 | 23 | 7 | 70 |
| 1864C–1865 G | 100 | 0 | 0 | 6 | 94 | 0 | 6 | 0 | 94 |
| 1864P–1865 G | 100 | 0 | 0 | 6 | 94 | 0 | 6 | 0 | 94 |

Notes: (a) Americans in 1856, Straight Douglas party in 1860; (b) of Fillmore Americans, 94% voted for Opposition gubernatorial and congressional candidates, 6% voted Democratic; (c) of Fillmore Americans, 88% voted for the Opposition, 6% voted Democratic, and 6% abstained; (d) virtually 100% of straight Douglas voters supported the Opposition Democratic congressional ticket; (e) of Fillmore Americans, 80% voted Republican, 13% supported the Fusion Democratic ticket, and 7% abstained; (f) when the 1860 presidential election is the first of an election pair, all non-Republicans are combined into a single party.

Key: P (Presidential), G (Gubernatorial), C (Congressional), S (Assembly), OP (Principal anti-Democratic Opponent), D (Democrat), A (Abstain), O (Other).

# Notes

For brevity, I have greatly compressed the notes. In Special Collections at Rutgers University Library in New Brunswick, the interested reader can find a more complete book manuscript with fuller citations, an amplified bibliographical note, a bibliography, a statistical appendix, and an uncut index.

A few procedures require explanation. Emphasis has not been added to quotations. Unless otherwise indicated, the recipient of a letter is the person whose papers bear his name; Mary R. Murrin's *New Jersey Historical Manuscripts: A Guide to Collections in the State* (1987) is the standard reference tool and lists other published guides as well. The titles of printed material were standardized; places of publication and publishers were omitted; Donald A. Sinclair's *The Civil War and New Jersey: A Bibliography* (1968) lists the printed sources and furnishes bibliographical information. Daily editions of newspapers were used unless indicated otherwise; titles were standardized; their variations appear in the *Directory of New Jersey Newspapers, 1765–1970* compiled by William C. Wright and Paul A. Stellhorn (1977). When a particular year is eliminated in certain chapters in the notes, omission includes the date of publication of all published works, and the legislative session. All census citations refer to the federal census unless otherwise indicated.

## Abbreviations

| | |
|---|---|
| AGR | N.J. Adjutant General, *Record of Officers and Men of New Jersey in the Civil War*, 2 vols. (1876) |
| APP | Statistical Appendix by Lex Renda |
| DR | Ira S. Dodd, *The Song of the Rappahannock: Sketches of the Civil War* (1898) |
| FR | John Y. Foster, *New Jersey and the Rebellion* (1868) |
| HL | Huntington Library |
| HSP | Historical Society of Pennsylvania |
| KP | Charles M. Knapp, *New Jersey Politics during the Period of the Civil War and Reconstruction* (1924) |
| LC | Library of Congress |
| MB | David Herbert Donald, ed., *Gone for a Soldier: The Civil War Memoirs of Private Alfred Bellard* (1975) |
| MR | Edward McPherson, *Political History of the United States During the Rebellion* (1882) |
| NA | National Archives |
| NJHS | New Jersey Historical Society |
| NJSA | New Jersey State Archives |
| NYHS | New York Historical Society |
| NYT | *New York Times* |

NYTR      *New York Tribune*

OR       *War of the Rebellion: Official Records of the Union and Confederate Armies,* 128 vols. (1880–1901)

PE       Svend Petersen, *Statistical History of American Presidential Elections* (1963)

PU       Princeton University Library

RU       Rutgers University Library

SR       Hermann K. Platt, ed., *Charles Perrin Smith: New Jersey Political Reminiscences, 1828–1882* (1965)

UC       University of Chicago Library

USAMHI    U.S. Army Miltary History Institute

*Introduction*

1. Lincoln Steffens, "New Jersey: A Traitor State," *McClure's Magazine* 24 (April 1905): 649–664.

2. Francis B. Lee, *New Jersey,* 4 vols. (1902), IV, 64–72; cf. KP, 1–38.

3. William S. Myers, *The Story of New Jersey,* 5 vols. (1945), I: 222–223; William C. Wright, "Secession and Copperheadism in New Jersey during the American Civil War" (M.A. diss., University of Delaware, 1965), 1–46; John T. Cunningham's *New Jersey: America's Main Road* (1976), 172–177; Thomas Fleming, *New Jersey: A Bicentennial History* (1977), 115–118. Two studies accepted this view in various ways: Philip C. Davis, "The Persistence of Partisan Alignment: Issues, Leaders, and Votes in New Jersey, 1840–1860" (Ph.D. diss., Washington University, 1978), 378; and Maurice Tandler, "The Political Front in Civil War New Jersey," *Proceedings of the New Jersey Historical Society* 83 (October 1965): 223–233.

4. *Jersey City Standard,* January 28, October 9, 1860; *Newark Mercury,* February 7, 1860; *Newark Advertiser,* April 8, 1862; *Paterson Guardian,* March 19, 1862; *Camden Democrat,* February 1, 1862; *Trenton American,* April 20, 1861.

5. *Globe,* 36th Cong., 1st sess., appendix, 295; *Camden Democrat,* December 10, 1859; *Newark Journal,* October 27, 1860; *Newark Advertiser,* February 10, 1859.

6. *Freehold Democrat,* October 11, 1860.

7. NYT, January 1, 1863; *Annual Report of State Geologist for 1871,* 24.

8. *Newark Mercury,* January 5, 1860, July 2, 1856.

9. NYTR, May 2, 1861.

10. 1860 Census, *Population,* 312–313; 1840 Census, *Enumeration,* 475; *Negro Population, 1790–1915* (1918), 51.

11. Ward to Nicholas Longworth, February 11, 1861, Marcus L. Ward MSS, NJHS; V. Wales, July 21, 1856, Nathaniel P. Banks MSS, LC; *Trenton American,* September 17, 1860; PE, 144, 25–32; NYTR, March 21, 1854.

12. C. Henry, April 19–May 20, 1854, Charles Sumner MSS, Harvard University Library.

13. *Newark Advertiser,* May 10, 1854; NYTR, March 21, 1854.

14. Speech, Samuel J. Bayard MSS, PU.

15. *Negro Population,* 51; Raymond M. Ralph, "The Urbanization of Newark, New Jersey, 1830–1860" (Ph.D. diss., New York University, 1978), 182–189.

16. *Memorial of the American Colonization Society* (1867), 190; 1870 Census, *Population,* 5.

17. Cf. KP, iii–iv, 24.

18. John P. Roche, "The Founding Fathers: A Reform Caucus in Action," *American Political Science Review* 55 (December 1961): 799–816.

19. Monroe Work, *The Negro Yearbook* (1931), 293. On November 8, 1870, an election riot between whites and blacks occurred in Newton, Camden County.

20. Cornelius Vermeule, appendix, 4, in Rollin D. Salisbury, *Physical Geography of New Jersey* (1898); 1860 Census, *Population*, 319.

21. *Morristown Banner*, April 3, 1862.

22. Vermeule, appendix, 3–4, 135.

23. George Washington Doane, *The Goodly Heritage of Jerseymen* (1848), 8–9.

24. NYTR, March 25, 1858; Wheaton J. Lane, *From Indian Trail to Iron Horse: A History of Transportation in New Jersey, 1620–1860* (1939), 258–319.

25. William E. Sackett, *Modern Battles of Trenton, Being a History of New Jersey's Politics and Legislation from the Year 1868 to the Year 1894* (1895), 1–17; Lane, *Transportation*, 323–370.

26. Sackett, *Battles*, 18.

27. Lane, *Transportation*, 361–362.

28. Ellis R. Meeker, *New Jersey* (1906), 148; Davis, "Alignment," 33; 1860 Census, *Population*, 320–321.

29. Meeker, *Jersey*, 148.

30. *Trenton Gazette*, September 14, 1864.

31. 1940 Census, *Population*, I, 21; 1870 Census, *Industry*, 86–393; Davis, "Alignment," 43–48.

32. Vermeule, appendix, 152–158; 1860 Census, *Population*, 312–318; 1940 Census, *Population*, I, 21; Davis, "Alignment," 10–19.

33. 1860 Census, *Population*, xxix–xxxi, 318; Vermeule, appendix, 153; Davis, "Alignment," 20–27.

34. 1860 Census, *Population*, 319; Doane, *Heritage*, 15.

35. Davis, "Alignment," 7–37.

36. Richard P. McCormick, *The History of Voting in New Jersey, 1664–1911* (1953), 86–158.

37. Lucius Q. C. Elmer, *The Constitution and Government of the Province and State of New Jersey* (1872), 240; McCormick, "An Historical Overview," in Richard Lehne and Alan Rosenthal, eds., *Politics in New Jersey* (1979), 1–28.

38. Duane Lockard, *The New Jersey Governor* (1964), 62–67; Ralph, "Newark," 37–38, 251–293.

39. *Camden Democrat*, February 1, 1862; Charles Mackay, *Life and Liberty in America* (1859), 112; Doane, *Heritage*, 8–10, 20, cf. 11–19; Jacob W. Miller, *The Iron State—Its Natural Position and Wealth* (1854), 6; *Belvidere Intelligencer*, September 20, 1861.

40. *Trenton Gazette*, April 19, 1862; *Bridgeton Pioneer*, July 19, 1862.

41. *Hackensack Journal*, October 30, 1858; *Flemington Republican*, August 31, 1859; NYT, February 12, 1993; *Newark Mercury*, June 26, 1858, January 5, 1860; Miller, *State*, 6–7.

## Chapter 1. Change and Continuity

*Note:* Unless indicated otherwise, the year for citations in this chapter for notes 1–23 is 1854; 24–73, 1856.

1. *Newark Mercury*, January 7–26; NYT, January 3–12.

2. George Vail, February 20, Rodman M. Price MSS, RU.

3. *Trenton American*, February 1.

4. *Newark Mercury*, April 20–May 26. Not all German Americans held radical views; older immigrants, especially Catholics and Lutherans, constituted the majority and

remained Democratic. In Newark, however, German Protestants far outnumbered German Catholics.

5. *Trenton Gazette*, April 15–July 10.

6. *Globe*, 33rd Cong., 1st sess., appendix, 190; *Trenton Gazette*, January 24.

7. *Newark Mercury*, January 30; *Newark Advertiser*, June 6.

8. *Globe*, 33rd Cong., 1st sess., appendix, 190; *Newton Herald*, February 18.

9. *Woodbury Constitution*, May 30; *Newton Herald*, February 25; *Newton Register*, February 18.

10. *Newton Register*, June 17.

11. *Trenton Gazette*, June 10; *Trenton American*, June 12; Price, June 9, Stephen A. Douglas MSS, UC.

12. *Newark Mercury*, September 15–October 13; *Newark Advertiser*, October 17–21; *Trenton American*, April 15, September 25–29, October 9–12.

13. *Newarker Zeitung* in *Newark Mercury*, June 12–19.

14. *N.J. Laws*, 387–390; Lane, *Transportation*, 356–411.

15. Opposition congressional victors were divided equally between anti-Nebraska Whigs and Know-Nothings. Major anti-Democratic candidates received 52 percent of the votes cast; Democratic candidates obtained only 43 percent. The opposition to Pierce's administration won by a landslide in the first and second districts and by 54 percent in the third and fifth districts. Only pro-Nebraska Vail survived, squeaking through by a mere 465 votes (51.6 percent) in the strongly Democratic fourth district. The opposition won five of the seven contested senate seats, gained control of the assembly, and secured a majority of the legislature on a joint ballot of both chambers. All these developments brought about the political revolution of 1854.

The rout of Democrats in the assembly was reflected in the Democratic share of the vote cast, the percentage of seats gained, and the proportion of districts won—their worst record in the 1850s. The election results showed that many New Jerseyans did not vote. The state turnout, 65.6 percent of the estimated eligible electorate, was the lowest of any federal election held between 1852 and 1860. Indeed, the Democratic turnout, 28.2 percent, was the lowest for any election in that period. APP.

16. *Mount Holly Herald*, November 16; *Trenton American*, October 26; *Newark Mercury*, November 11; *Trenton Gazette*, June 19–November 10.

17. *Newark Mercury*, October 31; *Hightstown Record*, November 24; NYTR, April 10, 1856.

18. *Camden Jerseyman*, *Salem Standard*, November 15; *Hightstown Record*, November 24.

19. *Newark Advertiser*, November 8. An examination of the state's voting patterns underscores the difference between the old parties and the new coalitions. The Kansas-Nebraska Act failed to bring back to the polls most of the Whigs who had dropped out in 1853. On the contrary, even more voters deserted the Whigs. The refusal of such Whigs to join this new coalition in 1854 suggests their recognition of a decisive shift in the membership, direction, and leadership of opposition forces.

20. APP; *Newark Mercury*, October 31.

21. *Newark American*, May 14, 1859; *Trenton Gazette*, August 16; NYT, February 22, 1856; *Jersey City Standard*, May 31, 1860.

22. Letterbook, January–February, 1855, Charles D. Deshler MSS, RU; *Newark Mercury*, June 8, 1855.

23. *Newark Advertiser*, September 6; NYTR, September 8.

24. NYT, February 22–26, September 18–19.

25. *Trenton American*, June 23; Robert Stockton, August 8, Millard Fillmore MSS, Library, State University of New York at Oswego; *Newark Advertiser*, February 7, May 29–June 11.

26. John Haskes, August 15, Henry Lafetra, August 5, Fillmore MSS.

27. NYT, June 30–July 21; *Mount Holly Mirror*, July 17; C. Hodge to Hugh Hodge, July 8, Charles Hodge MSS, PU.

28. I. Breed, November 2, Fillmore MSS.

29. *Newark Advertiser*, July 9–16, September 8.

30. APP; Cynthia Kierner, "The Know Nothing Interlude" (graduate paper; University of Virginia, 1983), 29–47.

31. *Trenton Gazette*, August 16, 1854; *New Brunswick Semi-Weekly Fredonian*, June 13, 1884; *Newark Mercury*, April 10, May 29; Hornblower, March 22, Sumner MSS.

32. NYT, June 19–20.

33. Morgan to Russell Sage, June 28, letterbook, Edwin D. Morgan MSS, New York State Library; Thurlow Weed, November 12, Simon Cameron MSS, LC.

34. Z. Pangborn, June 25, Banks MSS; Dayton, June 30, Morgan to Dayton, August 8, letterbook, Morgan MSS; Dayton, July 12, Israel Washburn MSS, LC; Dayton to Morgan, August 15, Gideon Welles MSS, LC.

35. NYTR, June 19–20.

36. *Newark Advertiser*, July 16.

37. *Flemington Democrat*, July 2; essay, Neilson Family MSS, RU.

38. *Trenton Gazette*, April 5; NYT, June 5–7.

39. A. Clark to brother, October 26, Addison S. Clark MSS, RU; Vroom to Phineas B. Kennedy, August 5, Peter D. Vroom MSS, Columbia University Library; *Trenton American*, August 19.

40. *Morristown Jerseyman*, June 12; *Newark Advertiser*, October 28.

41. Thomas Gordon, June 11, Sumner MSS; *Newark Mercury*, July 2; *Morristown Banner*, June 25.

42. *Morristown Jerseyman*, June 26.

43. Henry C. Fish, *The Voice of Our Brother's Blood*, 7.

44. *Newton Register*, July 5.

45. *Mount Holly Herald*, July 10; *Belvidere Journal*, June 21; *New Brunswick News*, August 23; *Trenton American*, June 26.

46. *Newark Mercury*, July 17; *Trenton American*, June 16.

47. NYTR, July 15; *Newark Mercury*, April 15.

48. Ephraim Marsh, *The Presidency*, 3.

49. J. Franklin, June 19, Isaiah D. Clawson MSS, PU; *Newark Mercury*, June 18.

50. *Newark Mercury*, July 17.

51. *Newark Advertiser*, September 25.

52. *Newark Mercury*, October 16–18.

53. Ibid., October 3–31.

54. Ibid., June 5.

55. *Flemington Democrat*, June 25; *Hightstown Record*, June 13; *Trenton American*, June 6.

56. *Trenton American*, September 15.

57. Ibid., August 7.

58. *Newark Mercury*, September 17, October 20–29; Joseph Pancoast, January 16, 1857, Clawson MSS.

59. *Newton Herald*, November 1; Deshler, October 27, Fillmore MSS.

60. Deshler, October 27, Joseph F. Randolph, September 1, October 2–29, November 3, Fillmore MSS; Dudley, August 1, Henry C. Carey MSS, HSP.

61. *Trenton Gazette*, August 5–29, September 2–22, October 29.

62. Dayton, October 28, Jacob W. Miller MSS, Macculloch Hall.

63. James Parker Diary, November 4, Parker Family MSS, NJHS. The Democratic share of the state's eligible electorate declined from 39 percent for Pierce in 1852 to

37 percent for Buchanan in 1856. Democratic gains from previous abstainers more than compensated for the one-eighth of the Democratic voters who went for Fremont. Fremont ran ahead of Fillmore in the central and northern parts of the state, except for Bergen, Middlesex, and Monmouth. Fillmore generally swept South Jersey. APP.

64. New Jersey, with 29 percent, had the second-lowest percentage of popular support of Fremont in the North (behind California's but closest to third-ranked Pennsylvania's 33 percent). PE, 35.

65. In congressional contests the Democratic statewide share of the potential electorate increased dramatically from 28 percent in 1854 to 38 percent in 1856; about 16 percent of the Opposition electorate in 1854 voted Democratic in 1856. Voters returning to the Democratic party probably represented two-thirds to three-fourths of all Democrats who had changed over to the Opposition in 1854. Overall the Opposition's share of the popular vote amounted to 52 percent.

The first district reelected Clawson. Incumbent Robbins won in the second district, but by only 52 percent. The Democrats captured the third and the fourth districts with 52 percent and 53 percent. In the fifth district the failure of the Americans and the Republicans to unite on a single candidate resulted in a Democratic victory. In the gubernatorial contest virtually none of the Republicans who supported Fremont voted Democratic for governor, but an estimated 6 percent of Fillmore's supporters did so. Among the supporters of Democratic gubernatorial candidate Price in 1853, only 7 percent changed to Newell in 1856, whereas 23 percent of Price's voters had voted for the Opposition in 1854. APP.

66. *Newark Mercury*, November 19; *Newton Register*, November 15.

67. *Philadelphia Press*, October 5, 1860; NYTR, August 24, 1859.

68. APP.

69. *Trenton Gazette*, January 21, 1860.

70. *Belvidere Journal*, November 8; *Flemington Democrat*, November 12; *Somerville Messenger*, November 13.

71. *Newark Advertiser*, November 13; Potts, November 14, Samuel B. How MSS, RU; Wall, April 20, 1857, Peter D. Vroom MSS, RU.

## Chapter 2. Precarious Balance

*Note:* Unless indicated otherwise, the year for citations in this chapter for notes 5–24 is 1858; 25–41, 1859; 42–53, 1860.

1. *Newark Advertiser*, December 16, 1856; SR, 88–94; *Trenton American*, August 19, 1858.

2. *Trenton American*, March 9, 1857; *Newark Advertiser*, March 17, 1857.

3. *Newark Mercury*, November 6, 1857, February 4, 1858; *Trenton American*, November 5, 13, 1857, May 24, 1859; *Newark Advertiser*, October 18, 1859; APP.

4. NYT, December 9, 1857, February 3, 1858; *Newark Advertiser*, December 9, 1858; *Camden Jerseyman*, December 9–23, 1857.

5. Robert Adrain, February 3, James Buchanan MSS, HSP; Price to Henry Phillips, February 24, Dreer Autographs, HSP; Thomson, February 28, George Sykes MSS, RU; *Newark Mercury*, January 14.

6. *Assembly Minutes*, 269–273; *Newark Mercury*, January 13–28, February 10–March 23; Edward Moore, February 27, Douglas MSS, UC.

7. *Newark Mercury*, February 5.

8. Garnett Adrain to George Butler, February 10, George Bancroft MSS, Massachusetts Historical Society; *Newton Herald*, December 12, 1857.

9. *Newark Advertiser*, March 9.

10. *Morristown Jerseyman*, May 1; *Newark Mercury*, August 27.

11. Jacob Freese, May 28, Thomas H. Dudley MSS, HL; *Trenton Gazette,* June 2–26.

12. *Trenton American,* August 31; *Newark Journal,* October 7.

13. *Newark Journal,* September 24; *Newark Mercury,* February 20, May 5–15, August 13.

14. *Newark Mercury,* June 26–28, September 9–10, October 21; *Trenton American,* October 8.

15. *Newark Advertiser,* August 21; *Trenton American,* September 15, June 26, October 5; *Newton Herald,* October 16; *Newark Mercury,* August 20.

16. *Somerville Messenger* in *Trenton American,* March 26; *Newark Mercury,* August 21, September 17, October 1–15.

17. Kennedy, November 10, Peter D. Vroom MSS, NJHS; *New Brunswick News* in *Trenton American,* April 14; Vroom to A. Smalley, October 14, Vroom MSS, RU.

18. Charles Vail to Robert Hunt, October 21, John I. Blair MSS, NJHS; *Salem Standard,* October 13.

19. *Newark Mercury,* September 17.

20. NYTR, November 5; *Trenton Gazette,* October 12.

21. Ryerson, November 19, Douglas MSS, UC. In the congressional elections, about 16 percent of the state's Democratic voters of 1856 and roughly 13 percent of those who voted Democratic in 1854 defected to the Opposition in 1858, but their numbers hardly approximated the one-fourth who defected between 1852 and 1854. Also, one-tenth of the Opposition in 1854 changed over to the Democrats in 1858. Because only 3 percent of the Opposition of 1856 voted Democratic in 1858, this figure suggests that most of those who strayed back to the Democracy in 1856 remained Democratic in 1858. Still, Democratic defections proved substantial enough to produce a political rout.

Democratic disaffection appeared greatest in the geographically opposite parts of the state: 31 percent of Democratic voters in South Jersey's first district and 25 percent in North Jersey's fourth and fifth districts went over to the Opposition. Democratic desertion seemed lowest in the central second and third districts. In 1858 the estimated statewide turnout of the potential electorate fell to 69 percent, the second lowest of any federal election held in the state between 1852 and 1860. Similarly, the estimated Democratic percentage of the eligible electorate in 1858 plummeted to 30 percent.

In combination, all anti-Lecompton congressional candidates won 56.4 percent of the votes cast. Major electoral changes occurred only in North Jersey, where Democratic congressional majorities in 1856 changed to anti-Lecompton Democratic majorities in 1858 in Sussex, Warren, and Morris. Bergen, Monmouth, and Hunterdon, however, remained Democratic bastions against the Opposition. In the most important development, seven of every eight voters who had been Fillmore Americans in 1856 voted the fusion ticket in 1858. APP.

22. *Newark Advertiser,* November 3; *Newark Mercury,* November 4–20; *Morristown Jerseyman,* November 6; *Flemington Republican,* November 10; *New York Herald,* November 4; Ryerson, November 19, Douglas MSS, UC.

23. NYT, November 5; *St. Louis Democrat* in *Woodbury Constitution,* November 16.

24. *Newark Journal,* November 3–8; *Newark Mercury,* March 31.

25. *New Brunswick Weekly Fredonian,* September 15; Ryerson, February 22, Douglas MSS, UC; Vanatta, December 5, 1858, January 7, Andrew B. Cobb MSS, Morristown Public Library; NYT, March 26; Joseph Randolph, April 9, John J. Crittenden MSS, LC; *Newark American,* July 23.

26. *Newark Mercury,* August 25; *Philadelphia Press,* August 26.

27. *Paterson Guardian,* August 29; *Jersey City Standard,* August 31.

28. Ryerson, August 24, Douglas MSS, UC.

29. *Newark Mercury*, September 8, January 18, 1860; *Jersey City Standard*, March 13, 1861.

30. NYTR, *New York Herald*, September 8.

31. *New Brunswick Times*, September 15; *Trenton American*, October 5–11; *Belvidere Journal*, October 7; *Somerville Messenger*, October 6; *Flemington Democrat*, October 26.

32. *Newark American*, June 18–July 23.

33. *Newark Journal*, September 8.

34. *Jersey City Standard*, September 8–27, October 14, November 10–12; Bishop to Peter Clark, October 27, Clark MSS.

35. *Newark Mercury*, October 20; *Newark Journal*, October 18–19; *Freehold Democrat*, October 27.

36. *Newark Journal*, October 19; *Paterson Register*, October 25; *New Brunswick Times*, November 3; *Trenton American*, October 20–November 7; Thomson, November 1, Buchanan MSS.

37. *Newark Advertiser*, October 24–28; *Newark Mercury*, October 20–26; *Flemington Republican*, November 2; *Princeton Standard*, October 26; *Paterson Guardian*, October 27; *Newark American*, November 26.

38. *Newark Mercury*, November 10. Olden won by merely 50.76 percent of the vote cast, in comparison with Newell's 51.29 percent in 1856 and the Opposition's congressional average of 52.3 percent in 1858. Newell had won by a majority of 2,557. With a smaller proportion of the electorate actually voting but with an increase of almost fifteen thousand voters, Olden's majority appeared shaky. Wright failed in his attempt to regain the full Democratic vote of 1856 by recruiting from anti-Lecompton ranks in such previous strongholds as rural Sussex and Warren. The Democrats succeeded, however, in increasing the Democratic city vote in Hudson and Essex, especially among immigrants naturalized at the last minute. This tactic helped to narrowly capture Newark, the state's largest city.

The defection of the Jones-Stockton Americans in South Jersey reduced the Opposition vote there. Roughly 50 percent of Jones's supporters voted for Wright; only 29 percent supported Olden. Newell did better in South Jersey in 1856 than did Olden in 1859, notably in Camden, Gloucester, and Cape May, but not in Atlantic. In that county, new German and Yankee settlers apparently accounted for the shift toward the Opposition.

Outside South Jersey, Olden generally fared better than Newell. Olden's personal strength in central Jersey, along with the support of anti-Lecompton Democratic voters in that area and in northwestern Jersey, proved decisive. In one interesting development, the majorities in many strong Democratic counties decreased; yet the vote for the Democracy frequently increased in Opposition counties. In the most telling paradox of all, the most significant Democratic increases occurred in opposite parts of the state, but for different reasons: in the southwest because of Jones's Americans and in the northeast because of the immigrants, the enemies of the nativists. APP.

39. Thomson, November 22, Buchanan MSS; *New Brunswick Times*, *Newark Advertiser*, November 17.

40. *Newark Mercury*, November 12–December 2; *Newark Journal*, December 3; *Trenton Gazette*, December 3; *Newton Register*, November 18; *Newark Advertiser*, December 3.

41. *Newark Journal*, December 3; *Camden Democrat*, December 10.

42. Undated newspaper clipping, Raritan-Eagleswood MSS, NJHS; *New Brunswick Fredonian*, March 17–27; Caroline Leighton, March 29, Thomas Wentworth Higginson–John Brown MSS, Boston Public Library.

43. Pennington, January 6, Ward MSS; *Newark Mercury*, January 5; *Trenton Gazette*, January 18.

44. *Newark Mercury*, December 22–28, 1859; *Trenton Gazette*, December 21–30, 1859.

45. *Senate Journal*, 665–736; *Assembly Minutes*, 1020; cf. KP, 21.

46. *Newark Mercury*, January 25.

47. *Princeton Standard*, December 14, 1859; *Newark American*, November 26, 1859.

48. *Newark Journal*, December 10–27, 1859; Wall, December 19, 1859, Lewis S. Coryell MSS, HSP; Vroom to John Mann, December 14, 1859, Vroom MSS, NJHS.

49. *Jersey City Standard*, September 20.

50. *Newark Mercury*, March 26.

51. *Jersey City Standard*, November 10, 1859.

52. *Newark Mercury*, July 14, 1858, November 12, 1859; *Newark Advertiser*, December 17.

53. *Trenton Gazette*, February 27; Davis, "Alignment," 15–95, 222–233, 368–377.

## Chapter 3. Presidential Nominations of 1860

*Note*: Unless indicated otherwise, the year for citations in this chapter is 1860.

1. John Vroom, December 8, 1859, Vroom MSS, NJHS; *Globe*, 36 Cong., 1st sess., 650–655; NYT, February 2. Controlling the assembly, Democrats and dissident nativists elected a Democratic speaker. *Newark Advertiser*, January 11.

2. *Newark Mercury*, January 18–April 12; *Jersey City Standard*, January 23.

3. *Newark Mercury*, March 9–31; *Trenton American*, March 9; *Jersey City Standard*, March 10–14.

4. *Newark Mercury*, April 10–27; Pennington to A. Condit, April 27, William Pennington MSS, NJHS; Pennington, April 24–May 11, Ward MSS; James Sherman, March 23, Welles MSS; Congar, April 16, William H. Seward MSS, University of Rochester Library.

5. John Stratton, April 4, Account, Dudley MSS; SR, 221–225; Pennington, April 24, Ward MSS; Memorandum, Blair MSS; *Springfield Republican*, May 17; *Newark Mercury*, May 19–June 4; NYT, May 18–19.

6. *Newark Mercury*, May 19–24; *Flemington Republican*, May 25; *Newton Register*, May 25.

7. *Jersey City Standard*, May 24–28.

8. *Flemington Republican*, June 22; *Newark Mercury*, June 1.

9. *Freehold Democrat*, May 24; *Camden Democrat*, June 16; *Paterson Register*, May 28.

10. *Jersey City Standard*, *Newark Mercury*, May 11.

11. *Newark Mercury*, *Paterson Register*, May 12. Alabaman William Yancey led the fire-eaters.

12. *Newark Journal*, April 23.

13. Ryerson, January 6, August 25, 1859, Vanatta, January 9, George Halsted, June 4, Douglas MSS, UC; *Trenton American*, February 20; *Jersey City Standard*, March 26; *Newark Mercury*, May 12.

14. *Newark Mercury*, March 29; Pennington, January 6, Ward MSS.

15. NYT, April 24–May 3; *Newark Mercury*, May 15–26; B. Williamson to David Naar, May 2, Isaac H. and Benjamin Williamson MSS, NJHS.

16. *Newark Mercury*, May 5.

17. *Newton Herald*, May 12; *Paterson Register*, May 1.

18. *Newark Journal*, May 3; *Belvidere Journal*, May 11; *Morristown Banner*, June 7.

19. *Flemington Republican*, May 4; *Trenton Gazette*, May 4; *Princeton Standard*, May 9; *Newark Mercury*, May 9; Wall, June 15, Vroom MSS, NJHS.

20. *Newark Journal*, June 12; *Trenton American*, June 14; NYT, June 19–25.

21. *Newark Journal*, August 21; *Newton Herald*, June 30; *Somerville Messenger*, July 12.

22. *Trenton American*, June 28; Vanatta to William King, July 14, Canfield-Dickerson MSS, NJHS; *Morristown Banner* in *Newark Mercury*, July 9.

23. *Paterson Register,* June 25; *Camden Democrat,* June 30.
24. *Camden Democrat,* August 4; *Mount Holly Herald,* October 11.
25. *Newark Mercury,* July 6.
26. *Newark Journal,* July 2–August 25.
27. *Morristown Banner,* August 30; *Philadelphia Press,* October 31.
28. Douglas to Nathaniel Paschall, July 4, Fogg Autographs, Maine Historical Society; George Halsted, July 13, Scovel, December 10, Douglas MSS, UC.
29. *Trenton Gazette,* July 28; NYTR, June 30; *Newark Mercury,* July 9–24. In mid-July 1860, eight daily newspapers in the state endorsed Lincoln, two each supported Douglas and Breckinridge, and one favored Bell. Out of sixty-six weeklies, Lincoln received endorsements from twenty-five, Douglas from thirteen, Breckinridge from seven, and Bell from one. Twenty weeklies remained neutral. In comparison to 1856, Lincoln had twice as many editorial endorsements as Fremont; Douglas had one more endorsement than Buchanan. For the North in general, according to one estimate, Douglas was endorsed by 78 percent of those newspapers which supported Democratic candidates; Breckinridge received the remaining 22 percent of the endorsements.
30. Charles Stratton, July 25, Hallen Nutt MSS, HL; *Paterson Guardian,* July 13; *Newark Journal,* July 25–27.

## *Chapter 4. Party Paralysis and Unionist Consensus*

*Note:* Unless indicated otherwise, the year for citations in this chapter is 1860.
1. *Trenton American,* September 5–20; cf. KP, 35–185.
2. *Princeton Standard,* October 31.
3. *Princeton Press,* November 2.
4. *Morristown Banner,* August 30.
5. *Newark Journal,* August 25; *Morristown Banner,* September 20; *Newark Mercury,* August 24.
6. *Trenton American,* September 17.
7. Speech, Robert Voorhees MSS, RU.
8. *Newark Advertiser,* August 4.
9. *Jersey City Standard,* October 9–November 7; *Trenton American,* October 10.
10. *Trenton American,* September 8; *Newark Advertiser,* November 2; *Jersey City Standard,* September 6; *Freehold Democrat,* November 1.
11. *Trenton Gazette,* May 2–July 4; Speech, Voorhees MSS; *Flemington Republican,* November 2.
12. *Princeton Standard,* October 24.
13. *Newark Democrat,* November 3; *Newton Herald,* August 18; *Jersey City Standard,* November 2.
14. *Freehold Democrat,* November 1; *Newark Journal,* October 17; *Trenton American,* October 8.
15. *Newark Advertiser,* September 6.
16. *Newark Mercury,* October 18; *Flemington Democrat,* September 5; *Cape May City Wave,* November 1; *Jersey City Standard,* January 13.
17. Archibald Hodge, October 17, Hodge MSS.
18. *Newark Journal,* September 19.
19. *Newark Mercury,* September 17–October 19.
20. *Trenton Gazette,* March 9; *Morristown Jerseyman,* October 27; cf. KP 35–36.
21. *Newark Mercury,* August 25, September 21, October 11; *Camden Democrat,* September 29; *Trenton Gazette,* September 6; *Trenton American,* September 27; *Newark Advertiser,* September 15–October 5; *Morristown Banner,* October 18; *Newark Journal,* September 29–October 2.

22. *Paterson Guardian,* October 3–8; Pennington to unknown addressee, October 8, William Pennington MSS, RU.

23. *Paterson Guardian,* September 6; Jesse Clark, October 16, Dudley MSS; *Newark Mercury,* June 7–November 10.

24. *Trenton Gazette,* October 20; *Newark Mercury,* September 17–October 11; *Newark Journal,* September 17.

25. Joseph Randolph, September 8, Price to Randolph, September 14, R. M. Price MSS; *Newark Advertiser,* October 27; Daniel Dodd to Barker Gummere, October 27, Gummere, October 27, Dudley MSS; Scovel, December 10, Douglas MSS, UC; *Newark Democrat,* October 27; *Paterson Register,* September 18; *Newark Mercury,* November 6.

26. *Trenton American,* November 5; *Trenton Gazette,* April 23; *Hightstown Record,* November 2; Allen H. Brown Diary, November 6, Atlantic County Historical Society; Parker Diary, November 6; Stephen Vail Journal, November 6, Stephen Vail MSS, Historic Speedwell; APP.

27. PE, 37–38; *Paterson Guardian,* November 7.

28. NYTR, November 10; *Princeton Press,* November 9; *New Brunswick Fredonian,* November 7; Gummere, November 9, Dudley MSS; APP.

29. *Philadelphia Press,* November 15; PE, 38; APP.

30. *Belvidere Journal,* November 9; *New York Express* in *New York World,* November 9; *New York Day Book* in *Newark Advertiser,* November 10; *Paterson Guardian,* October 16.

31. *Trenton Gazette,* November 9; Miller, November 14, Seward MSS.

32. NYT, November 8–10; Marcus Kitchen, November 10, Ward MSS.

33. *Newark Mercury,* November 8–10; *Trenton American,* November 9.

34. *Trenton Gazette, Paterson Guardian,* November 15.

35. *Paterson Guardian, Newark Mercury,* November 15.

36. *Trenton Gazette,* November 15.

37. Ibid., November 9; NYTR, November 16–27; APP.

38. *Newark Mercury,* November 9.

39. APP.

40. PE, 37–38.

41. *New Brunswick Fredonian,* September 13.

42. *Newark Mercury,* December 15

43. *New York World,* November 9; *Newark Democrat,* November 7; *Newton Register,* November 9; *Paterson Guardian,* November 9.

44. *Newark Mercury,* September 21.

## Chapter 5. The Union in Peril

*Note:* Unless indicated otherwise, the year for citations in this chapter for notes 1–25 is 1860; 26–67, 1861.

1. *Flemington Republican,* November 9.

2. *Trenton American,* November 10.

3. MR, 2–12.

4. Samuel Eddy Diary, RU, February 9, 1861.

5. *Newark Advertiser,* December 19; *Trenton American,* January 19, 1861.

6. *Cape May City Wave,* November 15–29; *Trenton Gazette,* February 7; Ward to Longworth, February 11, Ward MSS.

7. *Newton Register,* December 28.

8. *Newton Herald,* November 24; *Camden Democrat,* November 17; *Somerville Messenger,* December 27; *Jersey City Standard,* January 7, 1861.

9. *Globe,* 36th Cong., 2d sess., 396.

10. John C. Rankin, *Our Danger and Duty* (1861), 7.

11. *Morristown Jerseyman, New Brunswick Fredonian*, November 24; *Newark Mercury*, November 12, February 9, 1861.

12. *Trenton American*, November 12.

13. *Trenton Gazette*, December 5; *Somerville Messenger*, December 20.

14. *Trenton Gazette*, December 5; *Newark Advertiser*, December 5; SR, 107; Pennington to Hornblower, December 8, Hornblower Family MSS, NJHS; Pennington to Albert Condit, December 25, Pennington MSS, NJHS; *Morristown Jerseyman*, December 22, February 16, 1861; *Paterson Guardian*, December 17.

15. E. Ford to H. Ford, November 24–December 20, April 17–May 20, 1861, Ford Family MSS, Morristown National Historical Park.

16. A. Hodge, November 8–23, December 7, C. Hodge to Hugh Hodge, April 28, 1861, Hodge MSS.

17. *Paterson Register*, December 10, cf. January 9, 1861; *Newark Journal*, December 19, April 4, 1861.

18. *Camden Democrat*, April 13, 1861.

19. *Hackettstown Gazette*, April 18, 1861; *Trenton Gazette*, September 21, 1861; cf. KP, 52–54; cf. SR, 102; cf. Wright, "Copperheadism," 47–93.

20. *Jersey City Standard*, January 10, April 6–18, 1861; *Princeton Standard*, April 12, 1861; *Newark Journal*, April 11, 1861; *Trenton American*, April 9–13, 1861; *Camden Democrat*, April 13, 1861.

21. *Newark Advertiser*, December 6; *Freehold Democrat*, December 27, January 31, 1861, cf. November 15; *Globe*, 36th Cong., 2d sess., 779; *Trenton Gazette*, December 31.

22. *Jersey City Standard*, November 12.

23. NYT, December 12.

24. *Paterson Guardian*, December 8; *Newark Mercury*, December 13; Field, December 15, Hodge MSS; *Camden Democrat*, January 5, 1861.

25. *Jersey City Standard*, December 14.

26. Ibid., January 10.

27. *Paterson Guardian, Freehold Democrat*, January 10.

28. *New Brunswick Times*, January 17–March 21; *Paterson Guardian*, January 10–March 16.

29. *Trenton American*, January 14–16.

30. *Trenton Gazette*, January 22–28.

31. *Senate Journal*, 94–104; *Assembly Minutes*, 170–200; *Newark Mercury*, January 26–31.

32. Dudley, December 22, 1860, John Sherman MSS, LC.

33. *Newark Mercury*, January 22–February 12; Ward to M. Webb, February 1, Ward MSS; *Camden Press*, January 23.

34. *Paterson Guardian*, January 23.

35. *Princeton Standard*, December 26, 1860; C. Hodge to Robert Dabney, January 29, Hodge MSS; *Newark Mercury*, January 28.

36. *Trenton American*, January 12.

37. *Newark Mercury*, January 18; *Paterson Guardian*, February 12; *Trenton Gazette*, January 26.

38. *Newark Mercury*, December 17, 1860; *Morristown Jerseyman*, January 5.

39. *New Brunswick Fredonian*, November 24, 1860.

40. Dudley to James Harvey, December 8, 1860, Dudley MSS; *Newark Mercury*, December 18, 1860, January 18; *Princeton Press*, December 14, 1860; *Princeton Standard*, November 28, 1860; *Paterson Guardian*, December 17, 1860; A. Van Fleet to Henry Race, February 11, Emley-Race MSS, Hunterdon County Historical Society.

41. Pennington to Hornblower, December 8, 1860, Hornblower MSS; Pennington to Condit, December 25, 1860, Pennington MSS, NJHS.

42. *Freehold Democrat,* January 10; *Paterson Register,* January 15; *Paterson Guardian,* January 18.

43. *Newark Mercury,* January 18; *Trenton American,* January 24; *Morristown Banner,* January 31.

44. *Paterson Register,* January 15–31.

45. *Morristown Jerseyman,* January 5; *Trenton Gazette,* February 7.

46. Dudley S. Gregory, December 17, 1860, Morgan MSS; *Freehold Democrat,* December 27, 1860.

47. MR, 52–90; *Newark Advertiser,* October 13, 1864.

48. *Globe,* 36th Cong., 2d sess., 779; *Newark Advertiser,* February 12; *Flemington Republican,* January 18.

49. *Princeton Standard, Newton Register,* March 8; *Trenton Gazette,* December 31, 1860; *Morristown Jerseyman,* April 13; Pennington, December 18, 1860, Ward MSS.

50. *Jersey City Standard,* December 22, 1860; *Newton Herald,* December 29, 1860, January 12–February 16.

51. Eddy Diary, February 2; *Newark Advertiser,* February 12.

52. *Newark Mercury,* December 3, 1860; *Camden Democrat,* December 15, 1860.

53. Dudley, December 19, 1860, Seward, March 11, Abraham Lincoln MSS, LC.

54. Olden, February 1, ibid.; Lincoln to Olden, February 6, Abraham Lincoln MSS, NJSA; *Newark Mercury, Newark Advertiser,* February 22; *Assembly Minutes,* 501–502; *Freehold Democrat,* February 28; Duane, February 21, Robert Anderson MSS, LC; *Morristown Jerseyman,* February 23; *Somerville Messenger,* February 28.

55. *Newark Mercury, Newark Journal, Paterson Register, Jersey City Standard,* March 5; *Bordentown Register,* March 8; *Freehold Democrat,* March 7; *Camden Democrat,* March 9; *Trenton American,* April 5.

56. *Paterson Guardian,* March 11; *Trenton Gazette,* March 14.

57. *Newark Mercury,* March 25–April 1; *Camden Press,* March 13–27.

58. *Trenton American,* March 14–April 5.

59. *Newark Mercury,* April 5–12.

60. *Trenton Gazette,* April 9.

61. *Freehold Herald,* April 4; *Paterson Guardian,* April 5; Eddy Diary, April 6; Vanatta to Frederick Canfield, April 12, Canfield-Dickerson MSS.

62. *Newark Mercury,* April 6; *Princeton Standard,* April 12; *Trenton Gazette,* April 8; NYTR, April 15.

63. *Trenton Gazette,* April 8; *Newark Mercury,* April 8–10; *Camden Press,* April 10.

64. *Newark Journal,* April 10; *Jersey City Standard,* April 12.

65. *Newark Mercury,* April 8; *Bordentown Register,* April 12.

66. *Newark Mercury,* April 13–15; *Trenton American,* April 15.

67. *New Brunswick Fredonian,* June 11, 1864.

## Chapter 6. The Politics of Patriotism

*Note:* Unless indicated otherwise, the year for citations in this chapter is 1861.

1. *Hackettstown Gazette,* April 25; Olden to Cameron, May 1, OR, ser. III, vol. 1, 143.

2. *Morristown Banner,* August 29; G. Bayard, April 13, Bayard MSS; *Egg Harbor Democrat* in *Camden Democrat,* September 7; *Jersey City Chronicle,* October 7, 1863.

3. M. Ward to Marcus Kitchen, April 15, Ward MSS; Stephen Vail Journal, April 20–25.

4. *Newark Advertiser,* April 23; NYT, April 17; *Toms River Emblem,* April 24.

5. Frederick Olmsted to Mary Olmsted, June 28, Frederick L. Olmsted MSS, LC.

6. Consistory Minutes, June 6, Paramus Classis Report, April 18, 1863, Old Paramus Reformed Church of Ridgewood.

7. Jacob Wandling to John Wandling, undated, Jacob C. Wandling MSS, RU; *Jersey City Times*, October 20, 1864.

8. *Trenton American*, April 16–July 8; *Jersey City Standard*, April 18–July 9; *Newark Journal*, April 17–July 8; *Newark Mercury*, April 19.

9. *Newark Advertiser*, April 13–September 23; Thomson, April 28, Buchanan MSS.

10. *Camden Democrat*, May 25; *Morristown Banner*, April 25; Oliver Halsted, April 20, Stephen A. Douglas MSS in Margaret Douglas's possession; Edwin Wright to Olden, April 27, OR, ser. III, vol. 1, 130; *New Brunswick Times*, April 18; *Somerville Messenger*, May 9.

11. Freese, May 4, Ward H. Lamon MSS, HL; *Mount Holly Herald* in *Belvidere Journal*, May 24; *Trenton Gazette*, April 19; *Morristown Banner*, August 1; *Brownson's Quarterly Review*, July, 398; *Methodist Quarterly Review*, April, 1864, 311.

12. *Morristown Banner*, May 2, July 10, 1862; *Jersey City Standard*, June 29; *Senate Journal*, 710; *Newark Mercury*, September 13, 1862.

13. *Jersey City Standard*, June 29; *Paterson Guardian*, June 1, 1863; *Newark Advertiser*, July 21, 1864.

14. Field, April 22, Dudley MSS; O. Halsted, April 20, Douglas MSS in M. Douglas's possession; *New Brunswick Weekly Fredonian*, May 23; Thomson, April 28, Buchanan MSS.

15. William Kite to Lydia Kite, October 31, Quaker Collection, Haverford College.

16. *Flemington Democrat*, April 17.

17. *Camden Democrat*, May 4.

18. *Morristown Jerseyman*, April 20; *Paterson Register*, April 13; *Newark Journal*, May 3; *Brownson's Quarterly Review*, July, 400; *Paterson Guardian*, May 18.

19. *Newark Mercury*, April 18–25; Field, April 22, Dudley MSS. Some contended that New Jersey's loyalty during the spring of 1861 was highly questionable. In contrast to Field's criticism that Olden had not done enough, they argued that he had come to the rescue single-handedly. Specifically they maintained that only Olden's sheer will and pivotal influence saved the state. Without Olden in the State House, New Jersey conceivably could have balked at suppressing the rebellion.

This exaggerated notion has as little merit as the erroneous characterization of New Jersey as the northernmost of the border states during the 1850s or the incorrect assumptions that the state favored secession and was ready to secede and join the South before the outbreak of war. In fact, during the early months of the war most New Jerseyans recognized that they had no choice but to oppose rebellion and support the government. Most were eager, even impatient, to stamp out secession. As the war fever reached its height, they talked of shouldering muskets and marching southward to teach the southerners a needed lesson. New Jerseyans volunteered readily to join the Union army. *Jersey City Standard*, April 25; cf. KP, 56; cf. SR, 102.

20. *Assembly Minutes*, 1106–1113; OR, ser. III, vol. 1, 766.

21. *Assembly Minutes*, 1103; *Senate Journal*, 652–710.

22. Ryerson, June 1, Seward MSS; *Newark Advertiser*, May 4; *Newark Mercury*, May 6; *Annual Cyclopedia of 1861*, 516–517; *Assembly Minutes*, 1150–1161.

23. *Senate Journal*, 691–697; *N.J. Laws*, 554–556.

24. Edwin Wright, May 7, Whitfield Johnson, May 4, Ward MSS; *Assembly Minutes*, 1143, 1169–1171, 1195–1196, 1207; *Trenton Gazette*, May 6–11.

25. The assemblymen who on the final vote opposed the war loan were Abraham Carlock, John Post, Nelson Drake, Nathan Horton, David Smith, Israel Maxwell, and James Arrowsmith. Carlock, Maxwell, and Arrowsmith also joined John Bennett and James Patterson to support Bennett's amendment to halve the number of state weapons. Joseph T. Crowell, *Speech at the Union Convention, Held at Scotch Plains*.

26. *Trenton Gazette*, May 14; *Jersey City Standard*, May 13.

27. *Trenton Gazette*, June 29, October 13, 1871; FR, 19–26.

28. *Jersey City Standard*, December 9, 1862; Olden, May 11, Lincoln MSS, LC.

29. *Newark Journal*, June 13–July 11; *Morristown Banner*, August 8.

30. *Newark Journal*, June 5–20; *Paterson Register*, July 16; *Belvidere Intelligencer*, September 6.

31. *Trenton American*, August 6–14; *Newark Mercury*, August 6.

32. *Newark Mercury*, July 1; *Camden Press*, August 21; *Morristown Banner*, July 18.

33. David Magie, July 27, John Maclean MSS, PU; Ryerson, August 24, Lamon MSS.

34. *Newark Mercury*, July 23.

35. *Newark Journal*, July 27.

36. *Woodbury Constitution*, August 6.

37. *Newark Journal*, August 1–2.

38. Knapp, 59–60, misunderstood what happened at the meeting by taking antiwar reports of the meeting at face value, gave it a symbolic importance, thus exaggerated the extent of antiwar feeling in Bergen and elsewhere. Yet the facts do not support this view. First, the *Newark Mercury* (August 1), the leading Republican newspaper in the state, did not become excited about the meeting, and devoted a mere two sentences to it. Second, two Republican newspapers told in detailed reports what really happened and noted the deep-seated division of sentiment. (*Paterson Guardian*, August 2–September 11; *Hackensack Journal*, August 3.) Third, the Democratic *New York World* (August 1) first sketched the actual story of the meeting and estimated that roughly half of the audience at the meeting were war supporters. Although Knapp cited this report, he ignored its meaning. Fourth, the antiwar *Newark Journal* (August 2) carried a misleading version of the peace meeting. The *Journal* described the gathering as "immense" and "enthusiastic," but in fact the meeting was neither large nor ardent for the peace cause. This article did not report the actual meeting in detail but printed only the formal resolutions of the peace advocates. Knapp quoted from the *Journal*'s headline and conveyed the same incorrect account of the meeting.

39. *Treason.*

40. *Trenton Gazette*, August 30.

41. *Paterson Guardian*, July 29–August 2; 1860 Census, *Population*, 314.

42. *Salem Sunbeam* in *Woodbury Constitution*, August 20; *Paterson Guardian*, August 2.

43. *Freehold Democrat*, September 5; *Camden Democrat*, September 7; *Camden Press*, September 11; *Newark Journal*, June 11; *Princeton Standard*, August 23; *Belvidere Intelligencer*, September 20.

44. *Paterson Guardian*, October 12; *Newark Mercury*, September 9.

45. *Trenton American*, August 8–24, October 7; *Trenton Gazette*, August 7–26.

46. *Paterson Guardian*, August 20–21.

47. *Newark Mercury*, September 14–20.

48. New Yorker James McNally, antiwar editor of the *Newton Herald*, left the newspaper in August 1861 and was replaced by Henry Kelsey, a war supporter. The *Hackensack Democrat* began publication in December. The *Somerville Messenger* under Alexander Donaldson supported the war, but it reversed its course when Cone became editor in November 1862. *New York Herald*, August 13; *Paterson Guardian*, August 22.

49. *Trenton Gazette*, August 21–September 26.

50. *Newark Journal*, September 27.

51. *Somerville News*, August 14, 1862; *Newark Mercury*, August 21.

52. *Newark Journal*, September 5; *Trenton Gazette*, September 12; OR, ser. 2, vol. 2, 771–778, vol. 7, 937, and ser. 1, vol. 39, pt. 2, 238.

53. *Freehold Democrat,* October 3.

54. *Belvidere Journal,* September 27.

55. *Trenton Patriot* in *Belvidere Intelligencer,* March 28, 1862; cf. KP, 63–74. Newspapers revealed that in August 1863 Wall had urged antiwar men in the Midwest to purchase imported rifles. *Paterson Press,* August 25, 1864.

56. OR, ser. 2, vol. 2, pt. 2, 801; *New Brunswick Weekly Fredonian,* January 21, 1864.

57. *Camden Democrat,* January 31, 1863.

58. Index to, and Case Files of, Investigations by Levi C. Turner and Lafayette C. Baker, 1861–1866, in Record Group 94, Records of the Office of the Adjutant General; Minutes and Criminal Case Files, Records of the United States District Court for the District of New Jersey, in Record Group 21, Records of the District Courts of the United States, NA.

59. MR, 195–196, 286–295, 357–361.

60. Prominent prowar Democrats who cooperated with or became Republicans included Daniel Barkalow, Charles Bartles, Crowell, James M. Hannah, Herring, Edward Moore, Potts, Ryerson, and Scovel. *Camden Democrat,* April 11, 1863.

61. *Newark Mercury,* July 31.

62. Ibid., September 2; *Hightstown Gazette,* August 22.

63. *Camden Democrat,* October 12.

64. Porter, September 26, Horace N. Congar MSS, NJHS.

65. Ibid., Foster, October 31.

66. *Newark Journal,* October 21; *New York Herald,* October 11.

67. *Newark Journal,* September 16; *Newark Mercury,* September 19.

68. *Trenton American,* October 8; *Morristown Jerseyman,* September 21.

69. *Trenton Gazette,* October 17–25; *Newark Mercury,* October 23.

70. *Trenton American,* November 12; *Newark Mercury,* October 23–24; *Paterson Guardian,* October 31; *Newton Herald,* October 12.

71. *Paterson Guardian,* October 9; *Newark Advertiser,* October 19.

72. *Jersey City Standard,* July 24; *Belvidere Journal,* May 24.

73. *Brownson's Quarterly Review,* July, 401; *Trenton American,* August 6.

74. Emson, November 7, John Gulick, February 16, 1862, James S. Yard MSS, Monmouth County Historical Association; *Freehold Democrat,* November 14.

75. *Newark Mercury,* October 21–November 11; APP.

76. Unionist Democrats accounted for one (and one half) percent of the total vote. APP.

77. *Trenton Gazette,* November 8.

78. *Paterson Guardian,* November 6–18. In a comparison between 1860 and 1861 in the assembly districts with competitive contests, party lines held fairly even; nearly two-thirds of both Republicans and Democrats remained loyal to their respective parties, and about one-quarter of each party's voters abstained. Roughly one of every seven Republicans and almost one-tenth of the Democrats changed parties. APP.

79. *Trenton Gazette,* January 13, 1862; *Newark Advertiser,* January 14, 1862.

## Chapter 7. New Jerseyans Go to War

1. FR, 16–19; Osborn to Louise Landau, March 16, 1863, Joseph B. Osborn MSS, LC; DR, 42.

2. *Morristown Jerseyman,* April 30, 1864.

3. *Annual Message,* (1863) 4–9; *Annual Report of the Adjutant General of the State of New Jersey, for the Years 1864 and 1865,* 889–912; *Rahway Register,* September 18, 1862.

4. OR, ser. 3, vol. 4, 1270, vol. 5, 662; AGR, 6–7, 1574; *Newark Journal,* August 13, 1864. The average of all estimates of New Jersey's servicemen comes to 77,795; if the

first estimate given below is excluded, the average is 74,292. However figured, New Jersey's recruitment record was not as good as claimed by the state's adjutant general, who counted 88,305 servicemen. Using federal definitions to meet the state's quota, William C. Wright, "New Jersey's Military Role in the Civil War Reconsidered," *New Jersey History* 92 (Winter 1974), 197–210, arrived at 78,817. William F. Fox, *Regimental Losses in the American Civil War* (1889), 533, used the federal estimate of 76,814. On the low side, Benjamin A. Gould, comp., *Investigations in the Military Statistics of American Soldiers* (1869), 24–25, took reenlistments into consideration and estimated 59,300 white soldiers. If figures for black soldiers and for all New Jersey sailors and marines are added, the total figure reaches 67,245.

In comparing New Jersey's recruitment record with those of other states, Fox, *Losses*, 536, 535, 15, found that if all men were included in the armed forces or who paid commutation, New Jersey's percentage would rank higher than New York's, but lower than that of Pennsylvania. If those who paid commutation were excluded and the total reduced to a three-year standard, recruitment as measured by the percentage of a state's able-bodied white males sent to the war would indicate that New Jersey had the poorest recruitment rate of any free state (excluding the worse records of the Pacific coast states), but a better record than the loyal border slave states. Draft evasion, however, burgeoned outside New Jersey.

5. MB, 3; *New Brunswick Fredonian,* April 26, 1861; *Elizabeth Journal,* June 11, 1861; *Hackensack Journal,* April 27, 1861.

6. *Absecon Republican,* September 24, 1864; Thomas Stratton, September 28, 1862, Charles W. Mount MSS, NJSA; John Ackerman to Stephen Ackerman, March 10, 1863, Civil War MSS, New Jersey Civil War Centennial Commission Records, NJSA; *Trenton Gazette,* October 19, 1861.

7. *New Brunswick Weekly Fredonian,* May 23, 1861; *Jersey City Standard,* November 22, 1862; Love to friend, December 27, 1864, John J. H. Love MSS, NJHS; *Newton Herald,* September 21, 1861; *Bridgeton Pioneer,* June 29, 1861.

8. DR, 43; *Jersey City Times,* October 20, 1864.

9. Aaron Crane, December 24, 1861, Louisa W. Cook MSS, RU.

10. MB, 4; *New Brunswick Weekly Fredonian,* May 30, 1861; *Paterson Guardian,* September 27, 1861.

11. *Newark Advertiser,* January 3, 1862; DR, 99; William P. Haines, *History of the Men of Co. F, 12th New Jersey Vols.* (1897), 263; *Woodbury Constitution,* July 2, 1861.

12. *Bridgeton Pioneer,* February 22, 1862; *Trenton Gazette,* February 10, 1862.

13. Dayton E. Flint to sisters, February 15, 1863, December 28, 1862, Civil War Miscellanous Collection, USAMHI; *Princeton Standard,* November 25, 1864; *Paterson Register,* May 25, 1861; *Paterson Guardian,* August 29, 1861.

14. Washington Roebling to Elvira Roebling, July 19, 1861, Roebling Family MSS, RU; *Newark Advertiser,* January 14, 1862; *Camden Press,* February 25, 1863.

15. *Camden Democrat,* June 22, 1861; *Trenton Gazette,* May 2, 1863; *Newark Mercury,* May 27, 1861.

16. DR, 100; W. Roebling to John Roebling, March 7, 1862, Roebling MSS; *Paterson Guardian,* August 28, 1861.

17. Haines, *History,* 263; MB, 112; DR, 129; *Jersey City Chronicle,* May 4, 1864; *Hackettstown Gazette,* March 30, 1865.

18. DR, 61; MB, 117.

19. *Bridgeton Pioneer,* June 22, 1861; *Newark Advertiser,* April 11, 1865; *Woodbury Constitution,* July 2, 1861.

20. *Mount Holly Mirror,* May 5, 1864.

21. *Bridgeton Pioneer,* July 19, 1862.

22. Ibid., July 19, 1862, June 29, 1861.

23. Ibid., July 19, 1862–June 6, 1863; MB, 80–81; *New Brunswick Fredonian*, December 29, 1862.

24. R. McAllister to Ellen McAllister, June 19, 1864, Robert McAllister MSS, RU; Robert Love, "A Boy Volunteer's War Record," 81, Gettysburg College Library.

25. *Flemington Democrat*, March 18, 1863; *Jersey City Standard*, December 29, 1862; John Mitchell, January 4, 1863, William F. Allen MSS, HSP; *Paterson Guardian*, December 25, 1862.

26. *Jersey City Courier*, June 26, 1862; Elwood Pullen, October 11, 1863, Mount MSS; DR, 105; MB, 141.

27. *Camden Gazette*, 1894, Operations Reports–Battle Accounts, Civil War Records, New Jersey Defense Department, NJSA; Crane, July 11, 1862, Cook, MSS; Roebling to Emily Warren, June 23, 1864, Roebling MSS.

28. *Freehold Herald*, April 23, 1863; John Donaldson Diary, May 28, 1861, Madison Township Historical Society; *Jersey City Standard*, May 31, 1862.

29. *Newton Register*, October 4, 1861; *Jersey City Chronicle*, May 4, 1864; *Newark Advertiser*, January 9, 1862.

30. *Trenton Monitor*, June 16, 1864; MB, 257.

31. Anna Van Fleet to William Van Fleet, May 8, 1864, Van Fleet Family MSS, Parsippany–Troy Hills Public Library; Roebling to Warren, November 5, 1864, Roebling MSS.

32. E. McAllister to R. McAllister, July 2–November 13, 1861, McAllister MSS.

33. Jennie Vaughn, September 28, 1864, Mount MSS; R. McAllister to E. McAllister, April 26, 1865, McAllister MSS; *Trenton Gazette*, February 10, 1862.

34. *Camden Press*, February 3, 1864; W. Roebling to Ferdinand Roebling, June 8, 1862, Roebling to Warren, June 7, 1864, Roebling MSS.

35. *Trenton American*, June 15, 1864.

36. Thomas Yard, June 26, 1862, Yard MSS.

37. *Jersey City Standard*, May 13, 1861; *Newark Advertiser*, November 7, 1861; MB, 42.

38. R. McAllister to E. McAllister, December 14, 1864–April 26, 1865, McAllister MSS.

39. *Newton Register*, October 4, 1861.

40. Roebling to Warren, May 15–July 7, 1864, Roebling MSS.

41. *Bridgeton Pioneer*, September 7, 1861; *Camden Press*, April 1, 1863; R. McAllister to E. McAllister, July 24, 1861, McAllister MSS.

42. R. McAllister to E. McAllister, December 11, 1864, McAllister MSS; *Paterson Register*, May 16, 1862; *Morristown Banner*, May 22, 1862.

43. *Trenton Weekly Times*, August 23–October 11, 1883; FR, 804–862.

44. *Camden Gazette*, 1894, NJSA; Meeker, *Jersey*, 38–40.

45. AGR, 8; *Elizabeth Journal*, June 14, 1864; FR, 75–666; OR, ser. 1, vol. 11, pt. 1, 450, pt. 2, 40; vol. 19, pt. 1, 375, 380; vol. 36, pt. 1, 144, 146.

46. Fox, *Losses*, 526–528; OR, ser. 3, vol. 5, 667–668; AGR, 8.

47. OR, ser. 3, vol. 5, 668–669; Stillwell to mother, March 20, 1862, Symmes H. Stillwell MSS, PU; William H. Clairville Memoir, December 18, 1862, RU; *Trenton Gazette*, May 21, 1862; *Camden Press*, April 1, 1863.

48. FR, 777.

49. Ibid., 784–793; Henrietta Jaquette, ed., *South after Gettysburg: Letters of Cornelia Hancock* (1937), 9.

50. NYT, January 1, 1863; Stephen Condict, July 24, 1861, Nehemiah Perry MSS, RU; Thomas Kinney to William Kinney, June 3, 1863, Kinney Family MSS, NJHS; C. P.

Smith, April 10, 1865, Dudley MSS; *Trenton Gazette*, September 14, 1864; Meeker, *Jersey*, 148; 1870 Census, *Industry*, 392–393.

51. *Jersey City Advocate*, February 23, 1864; *Flemington Republican*, July 29, 1864; Scudder, May 20, 1864, Vroom, December 1, 1864, William L. Dayton MSS, PU; *Trenton Monitor*, March 26, 1864; *Newark Advertiser*, December 28, 1861.

## Chapter 8. Partisanship in Wartime

*Note:* Unless indicated otherwise, the year for citations in this chapter is 1862.

1. *Trenton Gazette*, January 13–16.

2. *Newark Advertiser*, January 22.

3. *Senate Journal*, 336–343.

4. Ibid., 109–110; *Assembly Minutes*, 263–266, 696; *Newark Journal*, February 18–19; *Newark Mercury*, March 18–September 13.

5. *Assembly Minutes*, 673–716; *Senate Journal*, 284–309; cf. KP, 69.

6. *Newark Journal*, January 14; *Assembly Minutes*, 33, 327–330.

7. *Assembly Minutes*, 681–717; *Senate Journal*, 301.

8. *Jersey City Standard*, April 7; *Paterson Guardian*, April 14.

9. *Camden Democrat*, April 19; *Camden Press*, May 21; Foster, June 16, Congar MSS.

10. MR, 358–362.

11. *Newark Journal*, May 9.

12. Ibid., May 10–30; *Hackensack Democrat*, August 1; *Somerville Messenger* in *Plainfield Union*, August 5; *Newton Herald*, August 2.

13. *Morristown Banner*, June 5–July 10; *Plainfield Union*, August 5.

14. *Newark Advertiser*, September 26.

15. MR, 209–213.

16. *Elizabeth Unionist*, September 6.

17. *Toms River Emblem*, September 17; *Elizabeth Unionist*, May 31.

18. *Brownson's Quarterly Review*, January, 41–122; *Princeton Review*, January 1863, 152; Ryerson, January 27, Seward MSS; James R. Bayley Diary, December 16, 1861, Archdiocese of Newark Collection, Seton Hall University Archives.

19. MR, 196–288.

20. *Elizabeth Unionist*, May 31.

21. *Freehold Democrat*, May 22; *Newark Mercury*, June 19; Charles Waugh, May 28, Congar MSS.

22. *Senate Journal*, 34–116; *Assembly Minutes*, 62, 216–252, 313–395, 422–498, 542–599.

23. *Camden Democrat*, February 1.

24. *Newark Advertiser*, March 28–April 8.

25. *Newark Mercury*, July 14–15, August 22–October 14.

26. Ibid., August 9–30.

27. *Morristown Banner*, April 3.

28. *Paterson Guardian*, June 20–July 14; *Somerville Whig*, September 4; *Rahway Register*, September 4.

29. Jacob Weart, "Reminiscences of Governor Joel Parker," *New Jersey Law Journal* 23 (November 1900): 323–330.

30. *Newark Journal*, September 5.

31. Ibid., November 1; *New York Herald*, June 5, 1876.

32. *Newark Advertiser, Princeton Standard, Trenton Patriot*, September 5.

33. *Trenton Gazette, Morristown Jerseyman*, September 6.

34. *Newark Journal*, September 5.

35. *Newark Advertiser,* September 5; *Newton Register,* September 12; *Camden Press,* September 10.

36. Isaac T. Nichols, *Historic Days in Cumberland County, New Jersey, 1855–1865* (1907), 95; *Newark Journal,* November 1.

37. *Newark Journal,* September 5–November 1; *Newark Advertiser,* October 14.

38. *Trenton Gazette,* November 3; *Freehold Herald,* October 30; *Somerville Whig,* September 11.

39. *Rahway Register,* October 9; *Jersey City Standard,* October 31.

40. *Newark Mercury,* October 4.

41. Parker to Wall, September 11, Ford Family MSS; Parker, September 8, R. M. Price MSS.

42. Ward, September 22, Hiram Barney MSS, HL; SR, 138; *Newark Mercury,* October 6; Trimble, February 22, 1863, Congar MSS.

43. *Newark Mercury,* October 4; *Camden Democrat,* October 11.

44. *Trenton Gazette,* September 26; *Trenton American,* October 2.

45. *Somerville Messenger,* October 16; *Elizabeth Unionist,* September 20.

46. *Newark Advertiser,* October 11; Brownson, [October], Sumner MSS; *Trenton American,* November 10.

47. *Newark Journal,* September 18, October 10–November 1.

48. *Jersey City Standard,* October 13.

49. *Morristown Banner,* October 16; *Newton Register,* October 31.

50. *Newark Advertiser,* October 22.

51. Ibid., 18–30; *Paterson Guardian,* October 24.

52. *Newark Mercury,* October 2–24; Quinby, November 30, Congar MSS.

53. *Belvidere Intelligencer,* September 12.

54. *Trenton American,* October 13; *Jersey City Standard,* September 17; Whitfield Hurd to father, November 5, Vail MSS.

55. Benjamin Stainsby, July 9, Ward MSS.

56. *Paterson Register,* September 17.

57. Charles Vail to John Vail, July 28, Blair MSS; *Elizabeth Unionist,* September 13; Foster, November 1, Congar MSS.

58. *Elizabeth Unionist,* September 6; *Newark Advertiser,* September 23.

59. *Paterson Guardian, Newark Advertiser,* September 23; *Belvidere Journal,* October 31; *Newton Register,* September 26; *Elizabeth Unionist,* September 27; *Trenton Gazette,* October 8.

60. *Newark Journal,* September 23–24; *Jersey City Standard,* September 23.

61. *Paterson Register,* September 26; *Rahway Democrat,* October 16; *Newark Journal,* October 14.

62. *Princeton Standard,* September 26; Bradley to Louis Greiner, October 24, Joseph P. Bradley MSS, NJHS.

63. *Trenton Gazette,* November 10; *New Brunswick Fredonian,* November 20.

64. *Trenton American,* October 7; *Belvidere Journal,* October 17–31.

65. *Trenton American,* September 15–30.

66. *Newark Advertiser,* October 23; *Camden Press,* September 3–17; *Elizabeth Unionist,* September 13.

67. *Salem Standard,* August 13; Congar, August 16, Ward MSS.

68. *Newark Mercury,* March 25, June 4–August 22; *Newark Advertiser,* August 22.

69. *Newark Mercury,* July 22–October 28; *Somerville News,* February 19, 1863. The *Paterson Guardian,* June 1, 1863, broadly defined copperhead, in the popular usage of the day, as the antiwar faction of the Democratic party: "This party, the Peace or Copperhead party." Today several historians use the term copperhead to mean the

extreme wing of the peace faction. This study employs copperhead as used originally, to denote all Democrats who opposed the war.

70. *Trenton Patriot* in *Belvidere Intelligencer*, March 28; *Newark Mercury*, July 22.

71. *Newark Journal*, April 5; *Morristown Banner*, April 3–August 28.

72. *Newark Journal*, November 4; *Newton Herald*, July 26.

73. *Brownson's Quarterly Review*, April 1863, 191–192.

74. *Newark Journal*, October 3–6.

75. *Flemington Republican*, March 13, 1863; *Trenton Patriot*, October 3.

76. *Trenton Patriot* in *Camden Press*, October 15; John Ditmars, August 25, Ward MSS; *Trenton Gazette*, November 7; *New Brunswick Fredonian*, October 23–November 2.

77. *Newark Journal*, October 25; *Freehold Democrat*, *Somerville Messenger*, October 16; *Trenton American*, October 7.

78. *Newark Advertiser*, November 5–10.

79. Ibid., 3–26; APP. In comparison with the 1859 gubernatorial race, Republicans' strength was eroded in Burlington, Essex, Mercer, Middlesex, and Passaic. Nearly 6 percent of those who voted for Lincoln in 1860 (probably the conservatives) defected to Parker in 1862, while hardly any Democrats backed the Republicans. Roughly 9 percent of those who had voted Republican in the 1860 congressional elections defected in 1862.

In 1862 Democrats in the populous northern states, including New Jersey, increased their share of the popular vote by 5 percentage points over their share in 1860. Joel H. Silbey, *A Respectable Minority: The Democratic Party in the Civil War Era, 1860–1868* (1977), 22–70, 145.

80. Book 608, box 115, Civil War Military Records, NJSA; AGR.

81. *Jersey City Standard*, November 5.

82. Foster, November 10, Congar MSS; *Newark Mercury*, November 5; Congar, December 31, Ward MSS; *Somerville News*, November 13.

83. Thomas Pierson, September 5, 1863, Vroom MSS, NJHS; *Newark Mercury*, November 6; *Morristown Jerseyman*, November 22.

84. Congar, December 31, Ward MSS.

85. *Newark Journal*, November 5.

86. Ibid., 15; *Camden Democrat*, November 15. Knapp, *New Jersey Politics*, 74, maintained incorrectly that the issue of arbitrary arrests was the major cause of Republican defeat, yet Parker, who did not stress Wall's arrest, ran ahead of both copperhead congressmen, Rogers (58.4 percent to 56.1 percent), and Perry (61.3 percent to 58.6 percent).

87. Harrison, November 13, Congar MSS; Alfred Dayton, November 12, Dayton MSS.

88. *Elwood Democrat*, November 15; *Newark Journal*, November 20; Quinby, November 30, Congar MSS.

## Chapter 9. The Perils of Power

*Note:* Unless indicated otherwise, the year for citations in this chapter is 1863.

1. *Jersey City Standard*, January 13.

2. *Trenton American*, January 1–3.

3. *Newark Journal*, January 3; *Somerville Messenger*, January 8.

4. *Camden Democrat*, *Newton Herald*, January 10; *Freehold Democrat*, January 8.

5. *Camden Press*, January 7; Charles Hodge, Jr., December 22, Lincoln MSS, LC; *Newton Register*, January 9.

6. *Paterson Guardian*, *Princeton Standard*, *Newark Advertiser*, January 2.

7. *Newton Herald*, February 14; *Newark Journal*, January 9.

8. *Trenton Gazette*, February 25, 1862; *Paterson Guardian*, October 29, 1861; *Newton Register*, March 27; *Woodbury Constitution*, March 10.

9. *Hansard Parliamentary Debates*, 1st ser., vol. 29 (1817), col. 1390.

10. *Newark Journal*, April 24; *Newton Register*, March 13; *Jersey City Standard*, April 22.

11. *Paterson Guardian*, August 22, 1861.

12. *Newark Journal*, December 29, 1862; *Paterson Press*, December 28–29.

13. In 1863 those who supported the copperhead position constituted one-third of the assembly and 46 percent of all Democratic assemblymen. See note 42.

14. Cf. KP, 183–184, 59–61, 78–79, 100–103; Thomas Pierson, September 5, Vroom to Pierson, September 15, Vroom MSS, NJHS.

15. *Paterson Press*, June 14, 1864; *Jersey City Standard*, August 25, 1864.

16. 1860 Census, *Statistics*, 428; Henry Beets, *De Christelijk Gereformeerde Kerk in Noord Amerika* (1918), 168; Edward T. Corwin, *A Digest of Constitutional and Synodical Legislation of the Reformed Church in America* (1906), 402–407.

17. NYTR, July 29, 1864.

18. *Newark Mercury, Jersey City Chronicle*, November 28.

19. *Newark Journal*, March 5.

20. *Newton Register*, January 16; *Newark Advertiser*, February 10; *Newark Journal*, February 16; Trimble, February 22, Congar MSS.

21. Brownson, December 26, 1862, Sumner MSS; Foster, February 4, Congar MSS.

22. MR, 183–262; *New Brunswick Times*, January 1.

23. *New Brunswick Times*, January 1; *Belvidere Journal*, February 6; Foster, February 4, Congar MSS; Riggs to J. Wall, December 22, 1862, Garret D. Wall MSS, RU.

24. *Annual Cyclopedia of 1863*; NYT, February 2.

25. Elmer, January 7, Vroom MSS, NJHS.

26. *Annual Message*, 8–9; *Newark Mercury*, January 15.

27. NYT, January 21.

28. *Inaugural Address*, 16.

29. *Jersey City Standard*, January 20; *Trenton American*, January 21.

30. *Newark Journal*, January 21.

31. NYT, *Newark Mercury*, NYTR, January 21.

32. *Senate Journal*, 8; *Assembly Minutes*, 9.

33. *Assembly Minutes*, 309; *N.J. Laws*, 296.

34. NYT, January 22–March 1; *New York Herald*, February 16–March 30.

35. *Newark Mercury*, December 4–31, 1862; cf. KP, 78–79.

36. *Trenton American*, March 5.

37. *Senate Journal*, 10–11.

38. *Camden Democrat*, January 17; *Speech of Joseph T. Crowell, of Union County, in the Senate of New Jersey, January 22, 1863*, 2.

39. *Newton Herald*, January 24; *Hackensack Democrat*, January 30; *Hackettstown Gazette*, January 29; *New Brunswick Weekly Fredonian*, January 15.

40. *Newark Mercury*, February 13; *Newton Register*, February 6.

41. *Somerville News*, February 19; *Lambertville Beacon* in *Plainfield Union*, March 3; *Senate Journal*, 113–120.

42. *Senate Journal*, 16–27; *Assembly Minutes*, 30–33. The assemblymen who supported the copperhead position were Chalkley Albertson, Elijah Allen, David Banghart, William Bell, Joseph Cooper, Peter Crozer, Osborn Curtis, John Dater, English, John Freeman, Samuel Moore, John Perry, Samuel Pope, Adolph Schalk, David Smith, William Strader, Joseph Waddington, Joseph Wood, Noah Woodruff, and David H. Wyckoff.

43. *Senate Journal*, 70–72.

44. Holsman to Wall, [after January 22], Charles A. Philhower MSS, RU.

45. *Newark Mercury*, February 13–26.

46. *N.J. Laws*, 513.

47. *Newark Advertiser*, February 12–21; *New Brunswick Fredonian*, February 18; cf. KP, 79–90.

48. *Senate Journal*, 70–72, 157–193, 419; *Assembly Minutes*, 377–413; *N.J. Laws*, 510–515; *Paterson Guardian*, March 21.

49. NYTR, March 26; *Newark Advertiser*, February 25; NYT, March 20.

50. *Newton Register*, March 6; newspaper clipping, A. Ball Scrapbook, RU; Stephen Congar, April 10, Congar MSS; *New York Post*, March 25; *Camden Journal*, May 16.

51. *Newark Mercury, Newark Advertiser*, March 21; *Paterson Guardian*, March 20; Benjamin Howell to Joshua Howell, March 31, Howell Family MSS, Gloucester County Historical Society.

52. *Senate Journal*, 395–413; *Assembly Minutes*, 473; *Newark Advertiser*, March 25–26.

53. *Paterson Guardian*, March 13.

54. NYT, March 20.

55. *Newark Journal*, March 5; *Assembly Minutes*, 268, 357–444.

56. *Morristown Jerseyman*, February 7; *Hackensack Democrat*, March 20.

57. *Newton Register*, March 13.

58. *Paterson Guardian*, March 23; *New Brunswick Weekly Fredonian*, January 12, 1864.

59. *Newark Advertiser*, November 17–24, December 3, 1862.

60. *Camden Democrat*, November 29, 1862; John P. Stockton, November 25, 1862, Sumner MSS.

61. *Globe*, 37th Cong., 3d sess., 28–29, 216–220.

62. *Somerville Messenger*, January 22; *Morristown Jerseyman*, January 10.

63. NYT, January 16–25; *Newark Journal*, January 12.

64. *Mount Holly Herald*, January 10; *Newark Advertiser*, January 13.

65. Elmer, January 5, Vroom MSS, NJHS.

66. *Freehold Democrat*, January 1; J. Vroom, January 9–30, Vroom MSS, NJHS.

67. *Newark Journal*, January 21–July 6, July 11, 1864; *Mount Holly Herald*, March 28.

68. Wall to William Hurlbert, [1863] Samuel L. M. Barlow MSS, HL; *Oration of Hon. James W. Wall, at Keyport, New Jersey, on the 22d of February, 1864* (1864), 8.

69. *New Brunswick Weekly Fredonian*, January 15.

70. *Freehold Herald*, January 15; *New Brunswick Fredonian*, January 15–23; *Senate Journal*, 448–449.

71. Porter, February 25, Congar MSS.

72. *Newark Journal*, January 14; *New York World*, January 15; *Camden Democrat*, January 17.

73. *Trenton Gazette*, January 14; NYTR, January 16; *Freehold Herald*, January 15; *Toms River Emblem*, January 14.

74. *Newark Advertiser*, December 24, 1862; *Camden Press*, January 21; *Newark Journal*, January 21.

75. *Newark Advertiser*, February 27.

76. *Newton Register*, February 20.

77. Porter, February 25, Congar MSS; *Trenton Gazette*, NYTR, February 27–28.

78. *Senate Journal*, 449–450.

79. *Belvidere Intelligencer*, March 6; *Newark Mercury*, February 27; *Newton Register*, March 6.

80. *Trenton American*, September 24.

81. *Newark Mercury, Trenton Gazette*, February 27.

82. *Newark Mercury*, February 27; *Jersey City Standard*, February 28; *Newton Herald*, March 5; *Hackensack Democrat*, March 6.

83. Congar to wife, February 14, 1866, Congar MSS.

84. *Hackettstown Gazette*, March 12.

85. *Assembly Minutes*, 88–89, 363–380; *Senate Journal*, 403–418; *New Brunswick Fredonian*, January 29.

86. *Newark Mercury, Paterson Guardian*, March 26; *Camden Press*, January 28–March 18.

87. *Camden Democrat*, January 10–24, February 14; *Hackensack Democrat*, March 27; *Belvidere Intelligencer*, February 13.

88. *New Brunswick Weekly Fredonian*, April 23.

89. *Newark Advertiser*, March 24; *N.J. Laws*, 468–536; *Senate Journal*, 385–397; *Assembly Minutes*, 454–475.

90. *Newton Herald*, February 14; *Trenton American*, April 29; *Senate Journal*, 207–273, 342–373.

91. Jonathan P. Hutchinson to unknown addressee, [March], Norwich Civil War Round Table Collection, USAMHI: *Newark Mercury*, February 18; *Camden Press*, April 1; *Flemington Republican*, March 27; *Newton Register*, March 20.

92. *Newark Advertiser*, March 21; *Trenton Gazette*, April 24; *Woodbury Constitution*, March 3.

93. *Toms River Emblem*, December 10; Condit Yeomans to John Reiley, April 16, Blair MSS; *Freehold Herald*, February 26.

94. *Newark Advertiser*, March 9–19, April 15–16; *Newton Register*, March 27.

95. *Newark Advertiser*, March 26; *Mount Holly Mirror*, April 2.

96. *Camden Press*, February 18; cf. KP, 81–96.

## Chapter 10. War Crises in 1863

*Note:* Unless indicated otherwise, the year for citations in this chapter is 1863.

1. *Newark Journal*, April 16; *Elwood Democrat*, April 25.

2. *Newark Mercury*, February 24–April 2.

3. *Somerville Messenger*, March 26.

4. *Trenton Gazette*, April 17; *Camden Press*, June 10.

5. *Trenton Gazette*, April 17.

6. Ibid., June 11.

7. *Speech of C. Chauncey Burr Delivered at the Peace Convention, New York, June 3, 1863*; *Trenton American*, May 13–June 8.

8. *Newton Herald*, May 21; *Somerville Unionist*, July 9; P. Vroom to Garret Vroom, July 3, Vroom MSS, Columbia; *Freehold Democrat*, June 11.

9. *Jersey City Standard*, May 28.

10. *Freehold Democrat*, May 28.

11. *Toms River Emblem*, July 23; *Trenton Gazette*, June 2.

12. *Newark Mercury*, May 19.

13. Ibid., June 1; Wall, May 23, Manton Marble MSS, LC.

14. Parker, June 29, Lincoln to Parker, June 30, Lincoln MSS, LC; *Freehold Democrat*, June 18.

15. *Correspondence with the President, Heads of Departments and Others in Reference to Military Affairs, Accompanying the Governor's Message* (1865), 74–87; *Newark Mercury*, June 17–30.

16. *Newark Journal*, June 17; *Trenton American*, June 20; *Jersey City Standard*, June 17.

17. *Newark Advertiser*, July 6.

18. Ibid., 11.

19. *Newton Herald,* July 9.

20. Ibid., March 12; *Somerville Unionist,* March 5; *Camden Press,* June 24; *Toms River Emblem,* June 11; Keasbey, December 11, Congar MSS.

21. *Somerville Messenger,* January 22; *Paterson Register,* August 5, 1862; *Brownson's Quarterly Review,* July, 348.

22. *Hackensack Democrat,* March 20; *Newton Register,* April 13.

23. *Somerville Messenger,* March 12.

24. *Newark Journal,* June 13; *Newton Herald,* June 18.

25. *New York Herald,* March 13.

26. *Trenton Gazette,* July 16; *Absecon Democrat,* July 25.

27. *Newark Advertiser, Mercury, Journal,* July 14–17; *Newark Patriot,* September 18–19, 1865.

28. *Belvidere Journal,* July 17.

29. *Newark Journal,* July 13; *Camden Democrat,* July 18.

30. *Salem Standard,* July 22; *Woodbury Constitution,* July 21.

31. *Princeton Standard,* July 17; Magie, July 20, Maclean MSS.

32. *Princeton Standard,* July 17.

33. *Newark Advertiser,* July 15–29, January 13, 1864; Parker, July 15–21, Lincoln to Parker, July 20–25, Lincoln MSS, LC; *Correspondence,* 69–96.

34. Parker, November 4–5, Lincoln MSS, LC; OR, ser. 3, vol. 3, 496; cf. KP, 97.

35. NYT, October 24; *Trenton Gazette,* July 13, 1864.

36. Thomas Pierson, September 5–21, Vroom MSS, NJHS; Harrison, October 21, Congar MSS; *Paterson Press,* November 4.

37. *Newark Advertiser,* November 7.

38. *Belvidere Journal,* October 30; *Speeches for the Times by Honorable James W. Wall of New Jersey with a Sketch of his Personal and Political History* (1864), 54; *Salem Standard,* October 14.

39. *Trenton American,* October 20; *Hackettstown Gazette,* September 3.

40. *Trenton Gazette,* October 17; *Rahway Register,* September 3; *Woodbury Constitution,* October 27; *Paterson Press,* December 1.

41. Scovel, October 20–28, Lincoln MSS, LC.

42. Democrats won 44,468 votes in the seventeen counties, Republicans, 41,300; in 1862, Parker won 47,699 votes, Ward, 39,372. APP.

43. Ibid.

44. *Newark Journal,* November 16; *Trenton American,* November 9; *New York News,* November 10.

45. *Trenton American,* November 5; *New Brunswick Times,* November 12; *Jersey City Standard,* November 6; *Camden Democrat,* November 7.

46. *Harper's Weekly,* November 14; *Somerville Unionist,* November 19.

47. *Paterson Press,* November 12; *Mount Holly Mirror,* March 24, 1864; *Absecon Republican,* April 23, 1864.

48. Voters in two other safe districts elected copperhead newcomers. In Somerset's first district, Daniel Cory, imprisoned by Lincoln's administration in 1861, won easily. David Boss from the first district in Hunterdon also won. Copperheads emerged victorious from tough contests in four competitive districts. Joseph Cooper of Salem's first district and Chalkley Albertson of Camden's third district each won with 53 percent of the vote cast. In the first district of Morris, Henry Sanders won by only thirty–three votes (51 percent). In the closest race, in Union's second district, Noah Woodruff defeated war supporter Joseph Crowell by merely twenty–two votes (50 percent).

49. *Mount Holly Mirror,* November 12.

50. J. Vroom, November 14, Vroom MSS, NJHS; *Morristown Banner,* October 8.

51. *Newark Journal,* August 24, November 9–19.

52. *Jersey City Standard,* November 21–27, September 16.

53. Ibid., November 21; *Camden Democrat,* December 12.

54. *Paterson Press,* November 12; *Newark Journal,* November 25.

55. *Newark Journal,* November 30.

56. *Jersey City Chronicle, Newark Mercury,* November 28; *Newton Herald,* December 3.

57. *Trenton Gazette,* November 7, 1861; *Newark Advertiser,* December 4.

58. Merchant, August 26, Congar MSS.

59. B. Howell to J. Howell, March 24–31, Howell MSS; *New York Herald,* March 30; *Jersey City Standard,* November 21.

## Chapter 11. Preelection Skirmishing

*Note:* Unless indicated otherwise, the year for citations in this chapter is 1864.

1. *Newark Advertiser,* January 13.

2. NYT, January 17; *Somerville Unionist,* January 21; *Camden Weekly Journal,* June 11; *New Brunswick Weekly Fredonian,* January 21; *Jersey City Standard,* January 14; *Newark Journal,* January 14.

3. *Belvidere Intelligencer,* January 29.

4. *Senate Journal,* 10, 849–854; *New Brunswick Weekly Fredonian,* January 12; cf. KP, 105.

5. *Assembly Minutes,* 11–12, 725–726; *New Brunswick Weekly Fredonian,* December 4, 1863.

6. *Senate Journal,* 306–405, 808–819; *Assembly Minutes,* 229, 543; *N.J. Laws,* 730–843.

7. *Trenton Gazette,* January 29.

8. *New Brunswick Weekly Fredonian,* March 15.

9. *Absecon Republican,* April 16.

10. *Assembly Minutes,* 364–94, 470–473; *Senate Journal,* 479–480; cf. KP, 106–107.

11. *Trenton Monitor,* June 21.

12. *Flemington Republican,* April 8.

13. *Freehold Herald,* May 5; *Trenton Gazette,* July 14.

14. *Assembly Minutes,* 93.

15. *Newark Journal,* February 17; *Camden Press,* January 21; *Newark Advertiser,* February 5–18; *Paterson Press,* March 4.

16. *Assembly Minutes,* 463. The eight Democrats who opposed English's bill were Chalkley Albertson, Joshua Benson, Joseph Cooper, Abraham Duryee, James Lynch, Samuel Tatem, Michael Taylor, and Garret Van Reipen.

17. *Morristown Banner,* March 17; *Assembly Minutes,* 533; *Senate Journal,* 732; *Absecon Republican,* March 19.

18. *Newark Advertiser,* March 24; *Assembly Minutes,* 598–620.

19. *Senate Journal,* 568; *Trenton Gazette,* March 24.

20. *Senate Journal,* 245–282, 504; *Trenton Gazette,* February 20.

21. *Newark Monitor,* April 21–May 7.

22. *Trenton Gazette,* July 29; *Assembly Minutes,* 1865 sess., 191–193.

23. *Camden Democrat,* March 12–April 16.

24. MR, 299–300.

25. Congar, April 19, Dudley MSS.

26. MR, 240–318.

27. Congress, House, Committee on Roads and Canals, *Railroad Facilities,* 37th Cong., 2d sess., House Report 61, 1.

28. *Globe*, 38th Cong., 1st sess., 1166.

29. *Senate Journal*, 610–622; *Assembly Minutes*, 626–627; *Newton Register*, April 1; cf. KP, 107.

30. *Globe*, 38th Cong., 1st sess., 1237–1264, 2253–2262; *Camden Democrat*, February 27.

31. *Globe*, 38th Cong., 1st sess., 2257–2258, 2d sess., 792; *Philadelphia Dispatch* in *Trenton Monitor*, June 8; *Newton Register*, April 1; *Paterson Press*, March 10; *Absecon Republican*, January 21, 1865.

32. *Toms River Emblem*, March 24.

33. *Globe*, 38th Cong., 1st sess., 2264, 2d sess., 1394; cf. David Trask's view.

34. NYTR, February 9, 1854; *New York Herald*, November 14; *Harper's Weekly*, March 25, 1865; *Princeton Standard*, January 8.

35. *Globe*, 38th Cong., 2d sess., 793; *New Brunswick Weekly Fredonian*, March 15.

36. *Newton Register*, March 13, 1863; *Princeton Standard*, January 8; *Trenton Monitor*, March 26; *Bordentown Register*, February 25, 1865.

37. *Trenton Monitor*, April 4, February 16, 1865; *Newton Register*, April 15; *Globe*, 38th Cong., 1st sess., 1466, 1264.

38. *Trenton Gazette*, April 2; *Trenton Monitor*, July 11; *New York Herald*, March 26.

### Chapter 12. The Wounds of War

*Note*: Unless indicated otherwise, the year for citations in this chapter is 1864.

1. *Trenton Monitor*, September 1; *Paterson Register*, November 2; Merchant, August 28, Congar MSS.

2. *Paterson Register*, November 2.

3. Ryerson, October 20, 1863, Seward MSS; *Newark Advertiser*, August 13; Ed Pelz, June 10, Sumner MSS.

4. *Hackensack Democrat*, February 12; *Camden Democrat*, August 20; William Paterson, September 4, Cobb MSS.

5. E. Taylor, October 1, Mount MSS.

6. *New Brunswick Weekly Fredonian*, February 10; *Trenton Monitor*, February 29, May 13; *Princeton Standard*, May 6.

7. Brownson, March 18, Sumner MSS; *Brownson's Quarterly Review*, October, 422–428.

8. *Paterson Press*, April 20.

9. *Paterson Press*, June 1.

10. NYT, June 8–9; *Millville Republican*, June 18.

11. *Camden Press*, August 17.

12. *Newark Journal*, June 9; *Hackensack Democrat*, September 2–23; *Trenton Monitor*, July 21; *Somerville Messenger*, June 23.

13. *Hackensack Democrat*, July 29; *Toms River Emblem*, August 25; *Paterson Press*, September 17; *Newark Journal*, July 8; *Belvidere Journal*, June 10.

14. *Newark Journal*, June 23; Wall, May 5, Buchanan MSS.

15. NYT, September 1.

16. *Newark Journal*, March 30–May 19.

17. Ibid., July 1–September 1.

18. *Mount Holly Mirror*, October 20; *Trenton Gazette*, September 28; *Morristown Jerseyman*, August 27.

19. *Trenton Gazette*, *Paterson Press*, September 1.

20. *Newark Journal*, September 1; *Jersey City Standard*, March 14.

21. *Hackettstown Gazette*, October 13; *Salem Sunbeam*, August 12; *Camden Democrat*, September 3; *Freehold Democrat*, August 4.

22. NYT, August 30–31.
23. MR, 419–420.
24. Taylor, September 2, Mount MSS.
25. *Trenton Monitor*, September 2.
26. *Morristown Banner*, September 15; *Hoboken Standard*, September 3; *Flemington Republican*, September 2.
27. *Camden Press*, October 26; *Jersey City Times*, November 8; *Mount Holly Mirror*, October 27.
28. Merchant, September 2, Congar MSS; *Princeton Standard*, September 30; *Paterson Press*, October 28.
29. *Millville Republican*, September 10.
30. McClellan to Barlow, August 28, McClellan to William Prime, October 20, George B. McClellan MSS, LC.
31. *Princeton Standard*, September 16; C. Hodge to H. Hodge, September 16, Hodge MSS; *Plainfield Union*, October 11.
32. Keasbey, September 10, Porter, September 1, Congar MSS; *Morristown Jerseyman*, February 27; *Paterson Register*, August 1; *Jersey City Standard*, July 29.
33. Mitchell, May 20, Allen MSS.
34. NYT, May 6–June 25; *Paterson Press*, July 23.
35. *Bordentown Register*, June 24; Roebling to Warren, May 21, Roebling MSS.
36. NYT, July 6–September 29.
37. *Jersey City Standard*, September 16; *Camden Democrat*, July 23–August 27.
38. Abraham Zabriskie, July 4, Scudder, May 20, Dayton MSS; Porter, September 1, Harrison, September 3, Congar MSS; *Princeton Standard*, August 19.
39. Ryerson, April 18, Memorandum, August 23, Lincoln MSS, LC; John Stratton, July 22, Dayton MSS; Greeley to George Opdyke, August 18, John A. Stevens MSS, NYHS.
40. *Jersey City Standard*, September 3; *Paterson Press*, September 7; James F. Rusling, *Men and Things I Saw in Civil War Days* (1899), 333.
41. *Newark Advertiser*, September 1–22.
42. Ibid., September 3–5; *Newton Register*, September 9; *Camden Press*, September 14.
43. *Millville Republican*, November 5; M. Barnes, September 4, Ward MSS; *Trenton Gazette*, September 14; *Newark Advertiser*, September 22.
44. *Trenton American*, September 7; *Newark Journal*, September 14.
45. *Morristown Jerseyman*, September 10; *Newark Advertiser*, September 9; McClellan to Prime, August 10, McClellan MSS.
46. M. Vail to McClellan, September 11, McClellan MSS; *Jersey City Standard*, September 9.
47. *Newark Journal*, September 9–13; *Trenton American*, September 12.
48. *Hackensack Democrat*, September 16; *The Old Guard*, October.
49. *Trenton American*, October 7.
50. Ibid., August 23–24.
51. *Newark Advertiser*, September 9; *Paterson Press*, September 10.
52. Ryerson, September 10, Cameron MSS.
53. Keasbey, September 10, Congar MSS.
54. *Camden Press*, October 5; *Camden Democrat*, September 24; *Trenton Gazette*, October 1; *Mount Holly Mirror*, March 10; *Freehold Democrat*, October 6; *New Brunswick Fredonian*, September 29–October 5; *Flemington Democrat*, October 12; *Paterson Press*, September 29–October 6; *Morristown Banner*, August 18–25; *Morristown Jerseyman*, October 1; *Jersey City Times*, October 20; *Jersey City Standard*, October 17–18; Ryerson, October 22, Seward MSS.

55. Other copperhead assemblymen who did not run were David Banghart, William Bell, Joshua Benson, Osborn Curtis, John Dater, William Strader, Garret Van Reipen, David B. Wyckoff, and David H. Wyckoff. *Trenton Monitor*, November 8.

56. *Hackettstown Gazette*, October 13; *Elizabeth Journal*, November 1.

57. See note 54.

58. *Hackettstown Gazette*, October 20; *Newton Herald*, October 6; *Bordentown Register*, September 16; *Jersey City Standard*, November 8.

59. *Salem Standard*, May 11; *Elizabeth Journal*, February 23.

60. *Absecon Republican*, January 30.

61. Keasbey, September 10, Congar MSS; *Newark Advertiser*, August 8; *Trenton Gazette*, September 28.

62. *Hoboken Democrat*, July 30.

63. Speech, Voorhees MSS.

64. *New Brunswick Fredonian*, September 9.

65. *Jersey City Standard*, September 16; *Camden Democrat*, September 10.

66. *Jersey City Times*, October 7–November 7.

67. *Newark Journal*, June 24–September 26; *New Brunswick Times*, August 11; *Hackettstown Gazette*, July 28.

68. *Woodbury Constitution*, September 27.

69. *Hackettstown Gazette*, July 7.

70. *Woodbury Constitution*, October 25; *Trenton Gazette*, September 7.

71. At his trial, held on February 15, 1865, Fuller maintained his innocence, but admitted formal guilt and promised not to discourage drafting in future. Judge Field found Fuller guilty of violating the Conscription Act, but imposed only a token fine. The owners of the *Newark Journal*, however, felt the federal pressure keenly, and in April they forced Fuller to resign as editor. *Newark Journal*, July 19–August 11, February 16–April 15, 1865; *Hoboken Standard*, July 23.

72. *Jersey City Advocate*, May 13; Blair, May 24, Ward MSS; *Camden Democrat*, November 8, 1862; *Camden Press*, April 19; *Woodbury Constitution*, May 17; *Trenton Gazette*, June 21–July 9, August 13–30, September 23; *Trenton Monitor*, June 3.

73. *Woodbury Constitution*, May 3.

74. Parker, September 14, Lincoln MSS, LC; Parker, October 26, Abraham Lincoln MSS, NYHS.

75. *Newark Journal*, November 3.

76. Stillwell to mother, September 7, Stillwell MSS; Samuel Moore, September 9, Ward MSS.

77. *Belvidere Intelligencer*, September 16; Mitchell, October 28, Allen MSS; *Jersey City Times*, October 1, 20; Oden to wife, September 18, James T. Oden MSS, University of Virginia Library.

78. Newell, April 23, August 31, October 24, Lincoln MSS, LC; *Trenton American*, May 14; *Hackettstown Gazette*, October 20.

79. *Newark Journal*, January 4; *Hackettstown Gazette*, August 25; *Flemington Democrat*, May 11; *Somerville Messenger*, October 6.

80. *Absecon Republican*, October 29; *Salem Standard*, November 2.

81. *Newton Herald*, October 13.

82. *Newton Register*, November 4.

83. Henry C. Fish Journal, NJHS, October 9–November 8.

84. *Paterson Press*, October 1.

85. *Patersonian*, October 20.

86. Porter, November 11, Congar MSS; *Woodbury Constitution*, November 1.

87. *Jersey City Times*, November 9; *Morristown Banner*, November 17.

88. *Hackettstown Gazette*, November 3; *Jersey City Standard*, April 27.

89. *New Brunswick Fredonian*, October 26.

90. *Hackensack Democrat*, October 28; *Rahway Democrat*, November 3; *Morristown Banner*, November 3; *Paterson Register*, November 2.

91. *Trenton Monitor*, August 20; *Trenton Gazette*, October 5.

92. *New Brunswick Fredonian*, September 9–November 3; Abner S. Coriell Diary, RU, November 9; *Somerville Messenger*, September 29.

93. *Trenton Gazette*, November 7; *Trenton American*, November 5–7.

94. *Trenton Gazette*, October 21; Ryerson, October 22, Seward MSS; Porter, October 17, Congar MSS.

95. NYTR, November 9; *Trenton Gazette*, November 12; Brownson to Sumner, January 17, 1865, Orestes Brownson MSS, University of Notre Dame Archives.

96. PE, 40; APP.

97. *Toms River Wave*, November 10; Scovel, November 9, Lincoln MSS, LC; Elias Osborn, November 13, Osborn MSS; *Jersey City Times*, November 9.

98. *New Brunswick Times*, November 10; *Newark Journal*, November 9, April 15, 1865; *Morristown Banner*, November 17; *Hackensack Democrat*, November 18; *Patersonian*, November 23–December 3.

99. *Patersonian*, November 23; McClellan, November 10, Barlow MSS.

100. *Jersey City Standard*, November 11; *Trenton Gazette*, November 11; MR, 607.

101. NYTR, November 11; NYT, November 20.

102. Harrison, November 11, Congar MSS; Mitchell, November 13, Allen MSS. If one assumes Lincoln would have received 71 percent of the servicemen's vote, according to some straw votes, and estimates a total of 17,797 New Jersey servicemen in state units (not counting Jerseymen in other outfits to compensate for those not qualified to vote), Lincoln might have won the popular vote in New Jersey, but by only 174 votes.

103. *Flemington Republican*, November 25.

104. APP.

105. *Camden Press*, November 9. Copperhead assemblymen elected were Elijah Allen, David Anderson, David Boss, Abraham Coriell, Daniel Cory, Isaac Demarest, Philip Dougherty, James Goble, Charles Hoagland, Michael Taylor, John Van Vorst, and James Willever. APP.

106. APP. Excluded from analysis were three western and three border states.

107. Ward, November 21, Seward MSS.

*Chapter 13. Northern Triumph and National Tragedy*

*Note:* Unless indicated otherwise, the year for citations in this chapter is 1865.

1. Mitchell, February 17, Allen MSS.

2. Ibid., January 28.

3. Lewis H. Carty Diary, January 25, Civil War MSS, NJSA; Vroom, December 1, 1864, Dayton MSS.

4. Ann Mount, January 5, Mount MSS; Ward to Horatio Ward, February 18, Ward MSS; *Camden Press*, February 22.

5. Rebecca B. Spring Diary, February 23, Raritan–Eagleswood MSS.

6. *Absecon Republican*, March 11.

7. *Newark Journal*, *Trenton Gazette*, January 13; *Paterson Press*, January 25.

8. *Senate Journal*, 10–11.

9. *Assembly Minutes*, 11–36; *New Brunswick Fredonian*, January 12–25.

10. *New Brunswick Fredonian*, January 31; cf. KP, 142–143.

11. *New Brunswick Fredonian*, January 18–February 15.

12. *Patersonian*, December 10, 1864.

13. *Trenton Gazette*, February 27.

14. *Newark Journal*, January 9.

15. *New Brunswick Fredonian*, February 22; *New Brunswick Times*, February 28.

16. *Trenton Gazette*, February 4.

17. *Newark Journal*, February 17.

18. *Senate Journal*, 860–883; *New Brunswick Fredonian*, February 22–March 8, *Weekly Fredonian*, March 16–23.

19. *Trenton Gazette*, March 16; *Newark Advertiser*, March 16.

20. MR, 590.

21. *Newton Register*, February 17.

22. *Paterson Press*, February 20.

23. Cf. KP, 110–112.

24. *Paterson Press*, February 1; *New Brunswick Fredonian*, March 7, 1864; *Morristown Jerseyman*, February 11; *Newark Journal*, February 1; *Paterson Register*, February 1.

25. *Debates of the Eighty-Ninth General Assembly of the State of New Jersey on the Bill to Ratify an Amendment to the Constitution of the United States*, 91.

26. Ibid., 6.

27. Ibid., 85–86, 45, 60.

28. Ibid., 49, 23–103.

29. *Patersonian* in *Trenton Gazette*, February 22; *Newark Journal*, February 13; *Trenton American*, February 21.

30. *Assembly Minutes*, 372–392; *Senate Journal*, 61, 472; *New Brunswick Fredonian*, February 15–March 8.

31. *Hoboken Democrat*, March 18; *Paterson Press*, March 2–17.

32. *Jersey City Times*, March 6; *Princeton Standard*, March 3.

33. *Newark Advertiser*, April 1–4.

34. *Woodbury Constitution*, April 19.

35. *Absecon Republican*, April 8; A. Mount, April 4, Mary Mount, April 7, Mount MSS.

36. T. Kinney to W. Kinney, April 5, Kinney MSS; *Newark Journal*, April 4.

37. *Newark Advertiser*, April 5–10.

38. George A. Bowen Diary, April 9, Salem County Historical Society; Rusling, *Men*, 346; *Toms River Emblem*, May 25; *Newton Register*, May 12.

39. *Belvidere Intelligencer*, April 14; *Newark Advertiser*, April 12.

40. C. P. Smith, April 10, Dudley MSS; *Newark Journal*, April 5; *Assembly Minutes*, 509, 863; *Newark Advertiser*, January 25, 1866.

41. *Paterson Press*, April 5; *Woodbury Constitution*, April 19; *Jersey City Times*, April 11; Ryerson to Frederick Seward, April 13, Seward MSS.

42. *Trenton Gazette*, April 11; *Paterson Register*, April 6; *Paterson Guardian*, April 14.

43. James Knox to John Knox, April 15, Lincoln MSS, LC.

44. Ibid.; *Newark Journal*, April 15.

45. Fish Journal, April 15.

46. *Newark Advertiser*, April 20.

47. Josiah Baker Statement, April 25, Investigation File 3419, Turner-Baker Papers, RG 94, NA; C. Hodge to H. Hodge, April 15, Hodge MSS; Robert Seeley, April 18, Charles H. Seeley MSS, New York Public Library; Coriell Diary, April 15–27; *Belvidere Intelligencer*, April 21.

48. Isaac N. Sprague, *President's Lincoln's Death. A Discourse Delivered in the Presbyterian Church in Caldwell, N.J., on the Day of National Mourning*, 14; *Camden Press*, April 19; William H. Hornblower, *Sermon Occasioned by the Assassination of President Lincoln Delivered April 16, 1865, in First Presbyterian Church of Paterson, N.J.*, 6–15.

49. *Newark Advertiser*, April 20; Theodore W. Well[e]s, *Victory Turned to Mourning. A Memorial Sermon on the Occasion of the Assassination of Abraham Lincoln, Sixteenth President of the United States, April 14, 1865. Preached in the Reformed Dutch Church, Bayonne, N.J., Sabbath, April 23, 1865,* 18; Henrietta Price, April 19, E. Price to H. Price, April 22, Elias W. Price MSS, Southern Historical Collection, University of North Carolina Library; *Trenton Gazette,* May 1.

50. *Newark Journal,* April 15–17; *Newton Herald,* April 20; *The Old Guard,* May; *Jersey City Standard,* April 15.

51. *Newark Advertiser,* April 26; NYTR, April 25.

52. *Belvidere Intelligencer,* April 21; *Jersey City Standard,* April 24.

53. *Newark Advertiser,* May 24.

54. Ibid., May 25.

## Chapter 14. The Fruits of Victory

*Note:* Unless indicated otherwise, the year for citations in this chapter for notes 1–49 is 1865; 50–54, 1866.

1. W. Lambert to Jacob Stickle, June 8, Ward MSS.

2. Louis Powers, June 8, James Sherman, June 24, ibid.

3. *Trenton Gazette,* June 8–13.

4. Samuel Moore, May 16, Benjamin Morehouse, May 20, Ward MSS.

5. Ibid., David Flower, June 8, Lambert to Stickle, June 8.

6. *Newark Advertiser,* April 11–13.

7. Ibid., July 18; cf. KP, 150.

8. *Newark Advertiser,* July 21.

9. Keasbey, August 26, Ward, September 10, Gummere, August 16, September 4, October 20, Congar MSS.

10. *Philadelphia Bulletin* in *Newark Advertiser,* September 5, August 31.

11. C. P. Smith, July 27, Freese, September 8, Ward MSS.

12. *Jersey City Times,* October 13; *Freehold Democrat,* October 12.

13. *Paterson Press,* August 31; *New Brunswick Fredonian,* October 3; *New York Herald,* September 1; *Chicago Republican* in *Newark Patriot,* September 15.

14. *Newark Patriot,* September 28.

15. *Camden Press,* July 26; *Newton Register,* October 26.

16. *Newark Patriot,* September 20; *Belvidere Intelligencer,* September 1.

17. *Trenton Volunteer,* August 24.

18. *Newark Advertiser,* August 31; *Trenton American,* September 20.

19. *Assembly Minutes,* 472–474; *Newark Advertiser,* September 6; NYT, October 2; *Camden Press,* November 2.

20. *Trenton American,* July 21; *Newark Advertiser,* August 12–September 5.

21. *Freehold Democrat,* October 19; *Paterson Press,* July 21.

22. Merchant, September 16, Ward, September 4, Congar MSS; *Newark Advertiser,* September 28.

23. *Morristown Banner,* July 13.

24. *Newark Journal,* September 26; *Belvidere Journal,* October 27; *Newark Advertiser,* August 31.

25. *Trenton Gazette,* October 6; *Absecon Republican,* July 22; *Salem Standard,* November 8.

26. *Newark Journal,* October 30.

27. *Trenton American,* October 2; *Belvidere Journal,* October 27.

28. *Newark Advertiser,* October 30.

29. Ibid., July 19.

30. Ibid., May 16; Equal Rights League of the State of New Jersey, *Proceedings of the State Convention of Colored Men of the State of New Jersey held in the city of Trenton, N.J., July 13th and 14th, 1865*; *Hoboken Standard* in Hoboken *Democrat*, June 24.

31. Speech, Voorhees MSS; *Newark Advertiser*, September 2; *Paterson Press*, June 8.

32. Fish Journal, November 5; *Princeton Standard*, June 9; *Jersey City Times*, November 4; *Camden Press*, July 26.

33. *Camden Democrat*, August 5; *Freehold Democrat*, October 12; *Trenton American*, November 2.

34. *Jersey City Times*, November 6.

35. *Newark Advertiser*, October 4–11.

36. Ward, August 12, George Halsey, October 21, Congar MSS.

37. *Newark Advertiser*, October 9–November 7.

38. *Newton Register*, July 28; C. P. Smith, September 25–October 3, Congar MSS.

39. *Flemington Democrat*, October 25.

40. *Jersey City Standard*, September 22–25; *Trenton Gazette*, September 18.

41. *Newark Advertiser*, November 1; *Philadelphia Press*, November 3.

42. APP; John Hill, November 8, Ward MSS.

43. *Newark Patriot*, November 9.

44. NYTR, November 8; *Newark Advertiser*, November 8; William Bross, November 8, Ward MSS; William Lewis, Henry Greene, November 8, Andrew Johnson MSS, LC; *Paterson Press*, December 26.

45. *The Old Guard*, December, 572; S. Bayard to daughter, November 26, Bayard MSS.

46. *Jersey City Standard*, November 9; *Hoboken Democrat*, November 11; Bayard to daughter, November 26, Bayard MSS.

47. *Hoboken Democrat*, November 18; *New York Herald*, November 9.

48. *Newton Register*, November 9; *New York Post*, November 8.

49. *Newark Journal*, November 7–December 2; *Hackensack Democrat*, November 17; *Newton Herald*, November 9.

50. *Annual Message*, 25; *Trenton Gazette*, January 10.

51. *Trenton Gazette*, January 17–23.

52. *Assembly Minutes*, 39–45; *Senate Journal*, 52–53.

53. Letterbook, January 24, Ward MSS; *Trenton Gazette*, January 25.

54. *Newark Advertiser*, September 19, November 1–12, January 23, 1867.

*Conclusion*

1. *Princeton Review*, July 1865, 440; *Jersey City Advocate*, February 23, 1864.

2. 1865 N.J. Census, *Population*, 24.

3. *Somerville Unionist*, November 19, 1863.

4. *Jersey City Standard*, August 11, 1864.

5. Maximilian G. Walten, ed., *Thomas Fuller's The Holy State and the Profane State* (1938), 2: 215; *Freehold Herald*, March 10, 1864; *Jersey City Times*, December 28, 1864.

6. Elizabeth *Jersey Blue*, November 10, 1865.

# Bibliographical Note

Readers wishing to find references about national developments can consult three masterful one-volume accounts which contain extensive bibliographies: J. G. Randall and David Herbert Donald's *The Civil War and Reconstruction* (1969); James M. McPherson's *Battle Cry of Freedom: The Civil War Era* (1988); and McPherson's *Ordeal by Fire: The Civil War and Reconstruction* (1992). Two excellent analyses of New Jersey politics are Richard P. McCormick's *The History of Voting in New Jersey, 1664–1911* (1953) and "An Historical Overview," in Richard Lehne and Alan Rosenthal, eds., *Politics in New Jersey* (1979).

Although a rich literature on New Jersey exists, general histories are often misleading in their account of the state's political role in the Civil War. Understandably these authors cannot cover all the complex developments of wartime politics in their brief surveys of the state's entire history, especially when the monographic treatment of the period is inadequate. John Cunningham notes this dearth of studies on the Civil War era in a penetrating bibliographical essay, remarking that "this phase of state history has been almost completely overlooked by academic—and popular—historians." *New Jersey,* 313.

The only previous book-length study, Charles Knapp's work on New Jersey's wartime politics, was a pioneering effort for its time. The work, however, is thin in size, limited in depth, and unsound in interpretation. The book is seriously flawed because of hasty, insufficient research. Although Knapp implied extensive use of the New Jersey Historical Society's collection of wartime newspapers published in the state, he barely consulted this important collection or a representative variety of other state newspapers. Instead Knapp intermittently and uncritically used only four daily papers, two copperhead and two Republican, as his major sources. He did not undertake substantial manuscript research. As a result, he relied on deductive, broad statements rather than on explicit reasons and specific citations of evidence on which to base his conclusions. In addition, he lacked a firm sense of the developments in other northern states. Yet Knapp's faulty scholarship established or perpetuated many myths about New Jersey.

William Wright's dissertation on New Jersey's copperheads is a disappointingly thin treatment. By defining a secessionist so broadly as to lump together dissimilar, often incompatible political groups, Wright exaggerates the importance of reactionary extremists and underestimates the role of their opponents. Wright's analysis of wartime politics is skewed frequently by identification of the copperheads with all Democrats. By focusing only on the poison ivy and a few trees, Wright fails to see the forest.

In sharp contrast, Wright's fine article on New Jersey's military recruitment brings a fresh perspective and a sensible analysis to a neglected subject. In it he demolishes two persistent myths: that New Jersey supplied more men than required, and that the state never had a draft.

Few political reminiscences and biographies exist and still fewer proved valuable in this study. Hermann Platt's critical, careful, expert editing of Charles Perrin Smith's memoirs is useful, but it is often flawed (as editor Platt points out) by Smith's frequently unbalanced interpretation of the facts and by his tendency to exaggerate his personal role in shaping events. Cf. pp. 84, 102–110, 139–149, 221–225. This source is overrated; many primary sources furnished more detailed and reliable accounts of major events.

Manuscript sources vary in quantity, quality, chronological concentration, and subject matter. Unfortunately there are no official records of the governors for the period. In my original uncut notes, I cited 146 manuscript collections. The most useful collections for analyzing antebellum developments include the relatively few but invaluable letters of prominent New Jersey Democrats in the Stephen A. Douglas Papers at the University of Chicago Library and in the James Buchanan Papers at the Historical Society of Pennsylvania. Especially valuable records of the prewar Republicans are the Thomas H. Dudley Papers at the Huntington Library and the Isaiah D. Clawson Papers at the Princeton University Library. For wartime Republican politics, the major sources are the small but rich Horace N. Congar Papers and the larger, uneven, yet invaluable Marcus L. Ward Papers, both at the New Jersey Historical Society. In comparison, the various letters of Democrats are limited in both quantity and quality.

New Jersey's newspapers constituted an indispensable source, despite their brevity, limited coverage, repetitiveness, and partisanship. In the original uncut notes, I cited eighty New Jersey newspapers. By the midpoint of the war, nine daily English-language newspapers were published in the state.

Among the Republican journals, the moderately radical *Newark Mercury* published incisive editorials; it was arguably the best newspaper in the state when Congar ran it; it ceased publication at the end of 1863. The centrist *Newark Advertiser* often had decent news coverage and printed some penetrating editorials. On developments in the state capital, the *Trenton Gazette* and the *New Brunswick Fredonian* were especially useful. The *Paterson Guardian* sometimes was fruitful; midway in the war it became a Democratic journal. The often incisive *Paterson Press* began publication in September 1863 and filled a void left by the demise of the *Mercury*. A year later the pungent *Jersey City Times* added editorial weight to the Republican side.

The myopic but sometimes trenchant *Newark Journal*, along with the *Trenton American* and the *Paterson Register*, were copperhead papers, but each played unique variations on the major themes. Voicing the views of the state's Democratic majority, the invaluable *Jersey City Standard* expressed the prowar position of the Democrats.

As of early 1863, fifty-seven weeklies represented every county in the state and both major parties. The weeklies were informative, stimulating, and expressed all political viewpoints. The most fruitful weeklies were the Republican *Newton Register*, the *Camden Press*, the *Princeton Standard*, and the *Morristown Jerseyman*, as well as the Democratic *Camden Democrat*, the *Somerville Messenger*, the *Newton Herald*, the *Freehold Democrat*, and the *Morristown Banner*.

For guides to New Jersey sources, see page 339.

# Index

*About the Author*

William Gillette is Professor of History at Rutgers University. A Fulbright lecturer at the University of Salzburg and winner of the Landry and Chastain Prizes, he is the author of *The Right to Vote: Politics and the Passage of the Fifteenth Amendment; Retreat From Reconstruction, 1869–1879;* and eleven articles. Having attended Georgetown University as an undergraduate, he earned his M.A. at Columbia University and his Ph.D. at Princeton University.